July 1

But now, this is
the Lord says —
he who <u>created</u> you,
  O Jacob,
he who <u>formed</u> you,
  O Israel:
"Fear not, for I have
    redeemed you:
I have <u>called you</u> by name;
    <u>you are mine</u>.

                              Isaiah

                    love,
                    April

RICHARD FOSTER'S

TREASURY
OF
CHRISTIAN
DISCIPLINE

Celebration of Discipline

The Challenge of the Disciplined Life

Freedom of Simplicity

Celebration of Discipline

The Path to Spiritual Growth

REVISED EDITION

Richard J. Foster

To Carolynn
wife, counselor, companion, encourager

Contents

Acknowledgments

1978

Books are best written in community. I am deeply indebted to those whose lives have surrounded mine and have given substance to the ideas in this book. It was through the friendship and teaching of Dallas Willard that I first saw the meaning and necessity of the Spiritual Disciplines. For many years he has been my mentor in the Disciplines. His life is the embodiment of the principles in this book.

I owe much to Bess Bulgin, who carefully and prayerfully read each line of this book many times over. Her feel for rhythm has greatly enhanced its readability. Ken and Doris Boyce helped me more than they will ever know by their constant encouragement and enthusiasm. The help of Connie Varce, in typing, grammar, and optimism added a great deal. Mary Myton worked endlessly in typing both rough draft and the final manuscript. Stan Thornburg taught me about the Discipline of service with his words and his life. Rachel Hinshaw graciously offered her skills as a professional proofreader. My special thanks to Newberg Friends Church for releasing me to have time to write in the final weeks of this book, and especially to Ron Woodward, whose pastoral load of necessity increased as mine decreased.

My children, Joel and Nathan, were incredibly patient in allowing their daddy to cut short games and stories more than once. With the completion of this book comes the joy of once again lengthening those games and stories.

1988

It has been ten years since *Celebration of Discipline* was first published. I still find it true that books are best written in community; the only difference now is that the community to which I am indebted is vastly larger. Over the years numerous persons have written to encourage, challenge, correct, and stimulate my thinking. In addition, many have talked with me in person about their own strivings, learnings, and growings. All of these people and more have taught me much about the spiritual life and have contributed to this revision.

I especially want to thank my wife, Carolynn, who over the years has taught me more about walking with God than words can express. The dedication of this book to her has even more relevance now than it did ten years ago. Also, I want to express my appreciation to my administrative associate, Lynda Graybeal, who has worked tirelessly on the many details of this revision.

As I revise *Celebration*, I am struck profoundly by the weakness of words. At best they are broken and fragmented witnesses to God's truth. We do indeed see through a glass darkly. And yet I am struck even more profoundly by the fact that God can take something so inadequate, so imperfect, so foolish as words on paper and use them to transform lives. How this happens I do not know. It is a miracle of grace and points to the fact that, if there is anything in these pages that ministers life to you, it did not come from me. *Soli Deo Gloria!*

Richard J. Foster
Easter, 1988

Foreword

There are many books concerned with the inner life, but there are not many that combine real originality with intellectual integrity. Yet it is exactly this combination that Richard Foster has been able to produce. Steeped as he is in the devotional classics, the author has given us a careful study that may, itself, be valued for a long time. Though the present volume demonstrates indebtedness to the Classics, it is not a book about them; it represents, instead, genuinely original work.

What strikes us at once is the comprehensive character of the current undertaking. Many contemporary books deal with particular aspects of the inner life, but this one is different in that it deals with an astonishing variety of important topics, much of its freshness of treatment arising from its boldness. The author has undertaken to examine a wide spectrum of experience, from confession to simplicity to joy. Since the finished product is the outcome of wide reading and careful thinking, it is not the sort of book that can be dashed off quickly or cheaply.

The sources of insight are varied, the chief ones being the Holy Scriptures, and the recognized classics of devotion, but these are not the only fountains from which the author draws. The careful reader soon recognizes a large indebtedness to secular thinkers as well. In view of the fact that the author is himself a Quaker, it is not surprising that the contributions of the classic Quaker writers are prominent. These include the works of George Fox, John Woolman, Hannah Whitall Smith, Thomas Kelly, and many more. The purpose here is not sectarian but genuinely ecumenical, since important insights ought never to be limited to the group from which they arise. What we are given, accordingly, is an example of the catholicity of sharing.

The treatment of simplicity is especially valuable, partly because it is not simple. Indeed the ten "controlling principles" concerning simplicity, which are explained in Chapter 6, are themselves sufficient justification for the appearance of another book on the spiritual life. The ten principles enunciated, while rooted in ancient wisdom, are made astonishingly contemporary.

The author understands very well that the emphasis upon simplicity may itself become a snare. This is why he will not settle for anything so obvious as the adoption of a plain garb, though he can say tersely, "Hang the fashions. Buy only what you need." Here is a radical proposal which, if widely adopted, would be immensely liberating to people who are the victims of the advertisers, particularly those on television. A genuine cultural revolution would ensue if considerable numbers were to obey the trenchant command, "De-accumulate."

The greatest problems of our time are not technological, for these we handle fairly well. They are not even political or economic, because the difficulties in these areas, glaring as they may be, are largely derivative. The greatest problems are moral and spiritual, and unless we can make some progress in these realms, we may not even survive. This is how advanced cultures have declined in the past. It is for this reason that I welcome a really mature work on the cultivation of the life of the spirit.

D. Elton Trueblood

1. The Spiritual Disciplines: Door to Liberation

> I go through life as a transient on his way to eternity, made in the image of God but with that image debased, needing to be taught how to meditate, to worship, to think.
>
> —DONALD COGGAN

Superficiality is the curse of our age. The doctrine of instant satisfaction is a primary spiritual problem. The desperate need today is not for a greater number of intelligent people, or gifted people, but for deep people.

The classical Disciplines* of the spiritual life call us to move beyond surface living into the depths. They invite us to explore the inner caverns of the spiritual realm. They urge us to be the answer to a hollow world. John Woolman counsels, "It is good for thee to dwell deep, that thou mayest feel and understand the spirits of people."[1]

We must not be led to believe that the Disciplines are only for spiritual giants and hence beyond our reach, or only for contemplatives who devote all their time to prayer and meditation. Far from it. God intends the Disciplines of the spiritual life to be for ordinary human beings: people who have jobs, who care for children, who wash dishes and mow lawns. In fact, the Disciplines are best exercised in the midst of our relationships with our husband or wife, our brothers and sisters, our friends and neighbors.

---

*You may be wondering why the Disciplines described in this book are termed "classical." They are not classical merely because they are ancient, although they have been practiced by sincere people over the centuries. The Disciplines are classical because they are central to experiential Christianity. In one form or another all of the devotional masters have affirmed the necessity of the Disciplines.

Neither should we think of the Spiritual Disciplines as some dull drudgery aimed at exterminating laughter from the face of the earth. Joy is the keynote of all the Disciplines. The purpose of the Disciplines is liberation from the stifling slavery to self-interest and fear. When the inner spirit is liberated from all that weighs it down, it can hardly be described as dull drudgery. Singing, dancing, even shouting characterize the Disciplines of the spiritual life.

In one important sense, the Spiritual Disciplines are not hard.* We need not be well advanced in matters of theology to practice the Disciplines. Recent converts—for that matter people who have yet to turn their lives over to Jesus Christ—can and should practice them. The primary requirement is a longing after God. "As a hart longs for flowing streams, so longs my soul for thee, O God. My soul thirsts for God, for the Living God," writes the psalmist (Ps. 42:1, 2).

Beginners are welcome. I, too, am a beginner, even and *especially* after a number of years of practicing every Discipline discussed in this book. As Thomas Merton says, "We do not want to be beginners. But let us be convinced of the fact that we will never be anything else but beginners, all our life!"[2]

Psalm 42:7 reads "Deep calls to deep." Perhaps somewhere in the subterranean chambers of your life you have heard the call to deeper, fuller living. You have become weary of frothy experiences and shallow teaching. Every now and then you have caught glimpses, hints of something more than you have known. Inwardly you long to launch out into the deep.

Those who have heard the distant call deep within and who desire to explore the world of the Spiritual Disciplines are immediately faced with two difficulties. The first is philosophic. The materialistic base of our age has become so pervasive that it has given people grave doubts about their ability to reach beyond the physical world. Many first-rate scientists have passed beyond such doubts, knowing that we cannot be con-

---

*In another sense, they are hard indeed—that is a theme we will develop later.

fined to a space-time box. But the average person is influenced by popular science, which is a generation behind the times and is prejudiced against the nonmaterial world.

It is hard to overstate how saturated we are with the mentality of popular science. Meditation, for example, if allowed at all, is not thought of as an encounter between a person and God, but as psychological manipulation. Usually people will tolerate a brief dabbling in the "inward journey," but then it is time to get on with *real* business in the *real* world. We need the courage to move beyond the prejudice of our age and affirm with our best scientists that more than the material world exists. In intellectual honesty, we should be willing to study and explore the spiritual life with all the rigor and determination we would give to any field of research.

The second difficulty is a practical one. We simply do not know how to go about exploring the inward life. This has not always been true. In the first century and earlier, it was not necessary to give instruction on how to "do" the Disciplines of the spiritual life. The Bible called people to such Disciplines as fasting, prayer, worship, and celebration but gave almost no instruction about how to do them. The reason for this is easy to see. Those Disciplines were so frequently practiced and such a part of the general culture that the "how to" was common knowledge. Fasting, for example, was so common that no one had to ask what to eat before a fast, or how to break a fast, or how to avoid dizziness while fasting—everyone already knew.

This is not true of our generation. Today there is an abysmal ignorance of the most simple and practical aspects of nearly all the classic Spiritual Disciplines. Hence, any book written on the subject must provide practical instruction on precisely how we do the Disciplines. One word of caution, however, must be given at the outset: to know the mechanics does not mean that we are practicing the Disciplines. The Spiritual Disciplines are an inward and spiritual reality, and the inner attitude of the heart is far more crucial than the mechanics for coming into the reality of the spiritual life.

In our enthusiasm to practice the Disciplines, we may fail to practice discipline. The life that is pleasing to God is not a series of religious duties. We have only one thing to do, namely, to experience a life of relationship and intimacy with God, "the Father of lights with whom there is no variation or shadow due to change" (James 1:17).

The Slavery of Ingrained Habits

We are accustomed to thinking of sin as individual acts of disobedience to God. This is true enough as far as it goes, but Scripture goes much further.* In Romans the apostle Paul frequently refers to sin as a condition that plagues the human race (i.e., Rom. 3:9–18). Sin as a condition works its way out through the "bodily members," that is, the ingrained habits of the body (Rom. 7:5ff.). And there is no slavery that can compare to the slavery of ingrained habits of sin.

Isaiah 57:20 says, "The wicked are like the tossing sea; for it cannot rest, and its waters toss up mire and dirt." The sea does not need to do anything special to produce mire and dirt; that is the result of its natural motions. This is also true of us when we are under the condition of sin. The natural motions of our lives produce mire and dirt. Sin is part of the internal structure of our lives. No special effort is needed to produce it. No wonder we feel trapped.

Our ordinary method of dealing with ingrained sin is to launch a frontal attack. We rely on our willpower and determination. Whatever may be the issue for us—anger, fear, bitterness, gluttony, pride, lust, substance abuse—we determine never to do it again; we pray against it, fight against it, set our will against it. But the struggle is all in vain, and we find ourselves once again morally bankrupt or, worse yet, so proud of our external righteousness that "whitened sepulchers" is a mild

---

*Sin is such a complex matter that the Hebrew language has eight different words for it, and all eight are found in the Bible.

description of our condition. In his excellent little book entitled *Freedom from Sinful Thoughts* Heini Arnold writes, "We . . . want to make it quite clear that we cannot free and purify our own heart by exerting our own 'will.' "[3]

In Colossians Paul lists some of the outward forms that people use to control sin: "touch not, taste not, handle not." He then adds that these things "have indeed a show of wisdom in *will worship*" (Col. 2:20–23, KJV, [italics added]). "Will worship"—what a telling phrase, and how descriptive of so much of our lives! The moment we feel we can succeed and attain victory over sin by the strength of our will alone is the moment we are worshiping the will. Isn't it ironic that Paul looks at our most strenuous efforts in the spiritual walk and calls them idolatry, "will worship"?

Willpower will never succeed in dealing with the deeply ingrained habits of sin. Emmet Fox writes, "As soon as you resist mentally any undesirable or unwanted circumstance, you thereby endow it with more power—power which it will use against you, and you will have depleted your own resources to that exact extent."[4] Heini Arnold concludes, "As long as we think we can save ourselves by our own will power, we will only make the evil in us stronger than ever."[5] This same truth has been experienced by all the great writers of the devotional life from St. Augustine to St. Francis, from John Calvin to John Wesley, from Teresa of Ávila to Juliana of Norwich.

"Will worship" may produce an outward show of success for a time, but in the cracks and crevices of our lives our deep inner condition will eventually be revealed. Jesus describes this condition when he speaks of the external righteousness of the Pharisees. "Out of the abundance of the heart the mouth speaks. . . . I tell you, on the day of judgment men will render account for every *careless word* they utter" (Matt. 12:34–36, [italics added]). You see, by dint of will people can make a good showing for a time, but sooner or later there will come that unguarded moment when the "careless word" will slip out to reveal the true condition of the heart. If we are full of compassion, it will be revealed; if we are full of bitterness, that also will be revealed.

It is not that we plan to be this way. We have no intention of exploding with anger or of parading a sticky arrogance, but when we are with people, what we *are* comes out. Though we may try with all our might to hide these things, we are betrayed by our eyes, our tongue, our chin, our hands, our whole body language. Willpower has no defense against the careless word, the unguarded moment. The will has the same deficiency as the law—it can deal only with externals. It is incapable of bringing about the necessary transformation of the inner spirit.

The Spiritual Disciplines Open the Door

When we despair of gaining inner transformation through human powers of will and determination, we are open to a wonderful new realization: inner righteousness is a gift from God to be graciously received. The needed change within us is God's work, not ours. The demand is for an inside job, and only God can work from the inside. We cannot attain or earn this righteousness of the kingdom of God; it is a grace that is given.

In the book of Romans the apostle Paul goes to great lengths to show that righteousness is a gift of God.* He uses the term thirty-five times in this epistle and each time insists that righteousness is unattained and unattainable through human effort. One of the clearest statements is Romans 5:17, ". . . those who receive the abundance of grace and the *free gift of righteousness* [shall] reign in life through the one man Jesus Christ [italics added]." This teaching, of course, is found not only in Romans

---

*This includes both objective righteousness and subjective righteousness. In this book we are dealing with the issue of subjective righteousness (or sanctification if you prefer another theological term), but it is important to understand that both are gracious gifts from God. And, in fact, the Bible does not make the clear division between objective and subjective righteousness that theologians are accustomed to draw, simply because the biblical writers would find it ludicrous to talk of having one without the other.

but throughout Scripture and stands as one of the cornerstones of the Christian faith.

The moment we grasp this breathtaking insight we are in danger of an error in the opposite direction. We are tempted to believe there is nothing we can do. If all human strivings end in moral bankruptcy (and having tried it, we know it is so), and if righteousness is a gracious gift from God (as the Bible clearly states), then is it not logical to conclude that we must wait for God to come and transform us? Strangely enough, the answer is no. The analysis is correct—human striving *is* insufficient and righteousness *is* a gift from God— but the conclusion is faulty. Happily there is something we can do. We do not need to be hung on the horns of the dilemma of either human works or idleness. God has given us the Disciplines of the spiritual life as a means of receiving his grace. The Disciplines allow us to place ourselves before God so that he can transform us.

The apostle Paul says, "he who sows to his own flesh will from the flesh reap corruption; but he who sows to the Spirit will from the Spirit reap eternal life" (Gal. 6:8). Paul's analogy is instructive. A farmer is helpless to grow grain; all he can do is provide the right conditions for the growing of grain. He cultivates the ground, he plants the seed, he waters the plants, and then the natural forces of the earth take over and up comes the grain. This is the way it is with the Spiritual Disciplines— they are a way of sowing to the Spirit. The Disciplines are God's way of getting us into the ground; they put us where he can work within us and transform us. By themselves the Spiritual Disciplines can do nothing; they can only get us to the place where something can be done. They are God's means of grace. The inner righteousness we seek is not something that is poured on our heads. God has ordained the Disciplines of the spiritual life as the means by which we place ourselves where he can bless us.

In this regard it would be proper to speak of "the path of disciplined grace." It is "grace" because it is free; it is "disciplined" because there is something for us to do. In *The Cost of Discipleship* Dietrich Bonhoeffer makes it clear that grace is free, but it is not cheap. The grace of God is unearned and unearnable, but if we ever expect to grow in grace, we must pay the price of a consciously chosen course of action which involves both individual and group life. Spiritual growth is the purpose of the Disciplines.

It might be helpful to visualize what we have been discussing. Picture a long, narrow ridge with a sheer drop-off on either side. The chasm to the right is the way of moral bankruptcy through human strivings for righteousness. Historically this has been called the heresy of moralism. The chasm to the left is moral bankruptcy through the absence of human strivings. This has been called the heresy of antinomianism. On the ridge there is a path, the Disciplines of the spiritual life. This path leads to the inner transformation and healing for which we seek. We must never veer off to the right or the left, but stay on the path. The path is fraught with severe difficulties, but also with incredible joys. As we travel on this path, the blessing of God will come upon us and reconstruct us into the image of Jesus Christ. We must always remember that the path does not produce the change; it only places us where the change can occur. This is the path of disciplined grace.

There is a saying in moral theology that "virtue is easy." But the maxim is true only to the extent that God's gracious work has taken over our inner spirit and transformed the ingrained habit patterns of our lives. Until that is accomplished, virtue is hard, very hard indeed. We struggle to exhibit a loving and compassionate spirit, yet it is as if we are bringing something in from the outside. Then bubbling up from the inner depths is the one thing we did not want, a biting and bitter spirit. However, once we live and walk on the path of disciplined grace for a season, we will discover internal changes.

We do no more than receive a gift, yet we know the changes are real. We know they are real because we discover that the spirit of compassion we once found so hard to exhibit is now easy. In fact, to be full of bitterness would be the hard thing. Divine Love has slipped into our inner spirit and taken over our habit patterns. In the unguarded moments there is a spontaneous flow from the inner sanctuary of our lives of "love, joy, peace, patience, kindness, goodness, faithfulness, gentleness, self-control" (Gal. 5:22, 23). There is no longer the tiring need to hide our inner selves from others. We do not have to work hard at being good and kind; we *are* good and kind. To refrain from being good and kind would be the hard work because goodness and kindness are part of our nature. Just as the natural motions of our lives once produced mire and dirt, now they produce "righteousness and peace and joy in the Holy Spirit" (Rom. 14:17). Shakespeare observes that "The quality of mercy is not strained"—nor are any of the virtues once they have taken over the personality.

The Way of Death: Turning the Disciplines into Laws

The Spiritual Disciplines are intended for our good. They are meant to bring the abundance of God into our lives. It is possible, however, to turn them into another set of soul-killing laws. Law-bound Disciplines breathe death.

Jesus teaches that we must go beyond the righteousness of the scribes and the Pharisees (Matt. 5:20). Yet we need to see that their righteousness was no small thing. They were committed to following God in a way that many of us are not prepared to do. One factor, however, was always central to their righteousness: *externalism*. Their righteousness consisted in control over externals, often including the manipulation of others. The extent to which we have gone beyond the righteousness of the scribes and the Pharisees is seen in how much our lives demonstrate the internal work of God upon the heart. To be sure, this will have external results, but the work will be internal. It is easy in our zeal for the Spiritual Discplines to turn them into the external righteousness of the scribes and the Pharisees.

When the Disciplines degenerate into law, they are used to manipulate and control people. We take explicit commands and use them to imprison others. Such a deterioration of the Spiritual Disciplines results in pride and fear. Pride takes over because we come to believe that we are the right kind of people. Fear takes over because we dread losing control.

If we are to progress in the spiritual walk so that the Disciplines are a blessing and not a curse, we must come to the place in our lives where we can lay down the everlasting burden of always needing to manage others. This drive, more than any single thing, will lead us to turn the Spiritual Disciplines into laws. Once we have made a law, we have an "externalism" by which we judge who is measuring up and who is not. Without laws the Disciplines are primarily an internal work, and it is impossible to control an internal work. When we genuinely believe that inner transformation is God's work and not ours, we can put to rest our passion to set others straight.

We must beware of how quickly we can latch onto this word or that word and turn it into a law. The moment we do so we qualify for Jesus' stern pronouncement against the Pharisees: "They bind heavy burdens, hard to bear, and lay them on men's shoulders; but they themselves will not move them with their finger" (Matt. 23:4). In these matters we need the words of the apostle Paul embedded in our minds: "We deal not in the letter but in the Spirit. The letter of the Law leads to the death of the soul; the Spirit of God alone can give life to the soul" (2 Cor. 3:6, Phillips).

As we enter the inner world of the Spiritual Disciplines, there will always be the danger of turning them into laws. But we are not left to our own human devices. Jesus Christ has promised to be our ever-present Teacher and Guide. His voice is not hard to hear. His direction is not hard to understand. If we are beginning to calcify what should always remain alive and growing, he will tell us. We can trust his teaching. If we are wandering off toward some wrong idea or unprofitable practice, he will guide us back. If we are willing to listen to the Heavenly Monitor, we will receive the instruction we need.

Our world is hungry for genuinely changed people. Leo Tolstoy observes, "Everybody thinks of changing humanity and nobody thinks of changing himself."[6] Let us be among those who believe that the inner transformation of our lives is a goal worthy of our best effort.

I. THE INWARD DISCIPLINES

2. The Discipline of Meditation

> True contemplation is not a psychological trick but a theological grace.
>
> —THOMAS MERTON

In contemporary society our Adversary majors in three things: noise, hurry, and crowds. If he can keep us engaged in "muchness" and "manyness," he will rest satisfied. Psychiatrist Carl Jung once remarked, "Hurry is not *of* the Devil; it *is* the Devil."[1]

If we hope to move beyond the superficialities of our culture, including our religious culture, we must be willing to go down into the recreating silences, into the inner world of contemplation. In their writings all the masters of meditation beckon us to be pioneers in this frontier of the Spirit. Though it may sound strange to modern ears, we should without shame enroll as apprentices in the school of contemplative prayer.

Biblical Witness

The discipline of meditation was certainly familiar to the authors of Scripture. The Bible uses two different Hebrew words (הָגָה and שִׂיחַ) to convey the idea of meditation, and together they are used some fifty-eight times. These words have various meanings: listening to God's word, reflecting on God's works, rehearsing God's deeds, ruminating on God's law, and more. In each case there is stress upon changed behavior as a result of our encounter with the living God. Repentance and obedience are essential features in any biblical understanding of meditation. The psalmist exclaims, "Oh, how I love thy law! It is my meditation all the day. . . . I hold my feet from every evil way, in order to keep thy word. I do not turn aside from thy ordinances, for thou hast taught me" (Ps. 119:97, 101, 102). It is this continual focus upon obedience and faithfulness that most clearly distinguishes Christian meditation from its Eastern and secular counterparts.

Those who walked through the pages of the Bible knew the ways of meditation. "And Isaac went out to meditate in the field in the evening" (Gen. 24:63). "I think of thee upon my bed, and meditate on thee in the watches of the night" (Ps. 63:6). The Psalms virtually sing of the meditations of the people of God upon the law of God: "My eyes are awake before the watches of the night, that I may meditate upon thy promise" (Ps. 119:148). The psalm that introduces the entire Psalter calls all people to emulate the "blessed man" whose "delight is in the law of the LORD, and on his law he meditates day and night" (Ps. 1:2).

The old priest Eli knew how to listen to God and helped the young boy Samuel know the word of the Lord (1 Sam. 3:1–18). Elijah spent many a day and night in the wilderness learning to discern the "still small voice of Yahweh" (1 Kings 19:9–18). Isaiah saw the Lord "high and lifted up" and heard his voice saying, "Whom shall I send, and who will go for us?" (Isa. 6:1–8). Jeremiah discovered the word of God to be "a burning fire shut up in my bones" (Jer. 20:9). And on march the witnesses. These were people who were close to the heart of God. God spoke to them not because they had special abilities, but because they were willing to listen.

In the midst of an exceedingly busy ministry Jesus made a habit of withdrawing to "a lonely place apart" (Matt. 14:13).* He did this not just to be away from people, but so he could be with God. What did Jesus do time after time in those deserted hills? He sought out his heavenly Father; he listened to

*See also Matt. 4:1–11, Luke 6:12, Matt. 14:23, Mark 1:35, Mark 6:31, Luke 5:16, Matt. 17:1–9, and Matt. 26:36–46.

him, he communed with him. And he beckons us to do the same.

Hearing and Obeying

Christian meditation, very simply, is the ability to hear God's voice and obey his word. It is that simple. I wish I could make it more complicated for those who like things difficult. It involves no hidden mysteries, no secret mantras, no mental gymnastics, no esoteric flights into the cosmic consciousness. The truth of the matter is that the great God of the universe, the Creator of all things desires our fellowship. In the Garden of Eden Adam and Eve talked with God *and* God talked with them—they were in communion. Then came the Fall, and in an important sense there was a rupture of the sense of perpetual communion, for Adam and Eve hid from God. But God continued to reach out to his rebellious children, and in stories of such persons as Cain, Abel, Noah, and Abraham we see God speaking and acting, teaching and guiding.

Moses learned, albeit with many vacillations and detours, how to hear God's voice and obey his word. In fact, Scripture witnesses that God spoke to Moses "face to face, as a man speaks to his friend" (Exod. 33:11). There was a sense of intimate relationship, of communion. As a people, however, the Israelites were not prepared for such intimacy. Once they learned a little about God, they realized that being in his presence was risky business and told Moses so: "You speak to us, and we will hear; but let not God speak to us, lest we die." (Exod. 20:19). In this way they could maintain religious respectability without the attendant risks. This was the beginning of the great line of the prophets and the judges, Moses being the first. But it was a step away from the sense of immediacy, the sense of the cloud by day and the pillar of fire by night.

In the fullness of time Jesus came and taught the reality of the kingdom of God and demonstrated what life could be like in that kingdom. He established a living fellowship that would know him as Redeemer and King, listening to him in all things and obeying him at all times. In his intimate relationship with the Father, Jesus modeled for us the reality of that life of hearing and obeying. "The Son can do nothing of his own accord, but only what he sees the Father doing; for whatever he does, that the Son does likewise" (John 5:19). "I can do nothing on my own authority; as I hear, I judge" (John 5:30). "The words that I say to you I do not speak on my own authority; but the Father who dwells in me does his works" (John 14:10). When Jesus told his disciples to abide in him, they could understand what he meant for he was abiding in the Father. He declared that he was the good Shepherd and that his sheep know his voice (John 10:4). He told us that the Comforter would come, the Spirit of truth, who would guide us into all truth (John 16:13).

In his second volume Luke clearly implies that following his resurrection and the ascension Jesus continues "to do and teach" even if people cannot see him with the naked eye (Acts 1:1). Both Peter and Stephen point to Jesus as the fulfillment of the prophecy in Deuteronomy 18:15 of the prophet like Moses who is to speak and whom the people are to hear and obey (Acts 3:22, 7:37).* In the book of Acts we see the resurrected and reigning Christ, through the Holy Spirit, teaching and guiding his children: leading Philip to new unreached cultures (Acts 8), revealing his messiahship to Paul (Acts 9), teaching Peter about his Jewish nationalism (Acts 10), guiding the Church out of its cultural captivity (Acts 15). What we see over and over again is God's people learning to live on the basis of hearing God's voice and obeying his word.

This, in brief, forms the biblical foundation for meditation, and the wonderful news is that Jesus has not stopped acting and speaking. He is resurrected and at work in our world. He

---

*See also Deut. 18:15–18; Matt. 17:5; John 1:21, 4:19–25, 6:14, 7:37–40; Heb. 1:1–13, 3:7–8, 12:25.

is not idle, nor has he developed laryngitis. He is alive and among us as our Priest to forgive us, our Prophet to teach us, our King to rule us, our Shepherd to guide us.

All the saints throughout the ages have witnessed to this reality. How sad that contemporary Christians are so ignorant of the vast sea of literature on Christian meditation by faithful believers throughout the centuries! And their testimony to the joyful life of perpetual communion is amazingly uniform. From Catholic to Protestant, from Eastern Orthodox to Western Free Church we are urged to "live in his presence in uninterrupted fellowship."[2] The Russian mystic Theophan the Recluse says, "To pray is to descend with the mind into the heart, and there to stand before the face of the Lord, ever-present, all seeing, within you."[3] The Anglican divine Jeremy Taylor declares, "Meditation is the duty of all."[4] And in our day Lutheran martyr Dietrich Bonhoeffer, when asked why he meditated, replied, "Because I am a Christian."[5] The witness of Scripture and the witness of the devotional masters are so rich, so alive with the presence of God that we would be foolish to neglect such a gracious invitation to experience, in the words of Madame Guyon, "the depths of Jesus Christ."[6]

The Purpose of Meditation

In meditation we are growing into what Thomas à Kempis calls "a familiar friendship with Jesus."[7] We are sinking down into the light and life of Christ and becoming comfortable in that posture. The perpetual presence of the Lord (omnipresence, as we say) moves from a theological dogma into a radiant reality. "He walks with me and he talks with me" ceases to be pious jargon and instead becomes a straightforward description of daily life.

Please understand me: I am not speaking of some mushy, giddy, buddy-buddy relationship. All such sentimentality only betrays how little we know, how distant we are from the Lord high and lifted up who is revealed to us in Scripture. John tells us in his Apocalypse that when he saw the reigning Christ, he fell at his feet as though dead, and so should we (Rev. 1:17). No, I am speaking of a reality more akin to what the disciples felt in the upper room when they experienced both intense intimacy and awful reverence.

What happens in meditation is that we create the emotional and spiritual space which allows Christ to construct an inner sanctuary in the heart. The wonderful verse "I stand at the door and knock . . ." was originally penned for believers, not unbelievers (Rev. 3:20). We who have turned our lives over to Christ need to know how very much he longs to eat with us, to commune with us. He desires a perpetual Eucharistic feast in the inner sanctuary of the heart. Meditation opens the door and, although we are engaging in specific meditation exercises at specific times, the aim is to bring this living reality into all of life. It is a portable sanctuary that is brought into all we are and do.

Inward fellowship of this kind transforms the inner personality. We cannot burn the eternal flame of the inner sanctuary and remain the same, for the Divine Fire will consume everything that is impure. Our ever-present Teacher will always be leading us into "righteousness and peace and joy in the Holy Spirit" (Rom. 14:17). Everything that is foreign to his way we will have to let go. No, not "have to" but "want to," for our desires and aspirations will be more and more conformed to his way. Increasingly, everything within us will swing like a needle to the polestar of the Spirit.

Understandable Misconceptions

Whenever the Christian idea of meditation is taken seriously, there are those who assume it is synonymous with the concept of meditation centered in Eastern religions. In reality, the two ideas stand worlds apart. Eastern meditation is an attempt to empty the mind; Christian meditation is an attempt to fill the mind. The two ideas are quite different.

Eastern forms of meditation stress the need to become detached from the world. There is an emphasis upon losing personhood and individuality and merging with the Cosmic Mind. There is a longing to be freed from the burdens and pains of this life and to be released into the impersonality of Nirvana. Personal identity is lost and, in fact, personality is seen as the ultimate illusion. There is an escaping from the miserable wheel of existence. There is no God to be attached to or to hear from. Detachment is the final goal of Eastern religion.

Christian meditation goes far beyond the notion of detachment. There is need for detachment—a "sabbath of contemplation" as Peter of Celles, a Benedictine monk of the twelfth century, put it.[8] But there is a danger in thinking only in terms of detachment as Jesus indicates in his story of the man who had been emptied of evil but not filled with good. "When the unclean spirit has gone out of a man . . . he goes and brings seven other spirits more evil than himself, and they enter and dwell there; and the last state of that man becomes worse than the first" (Luke 11:24–26).[9]

No, detachment is not enough; we must go on to *attachment*. The detachment from the confusion all around us is in order to have a richer attachment to God. Christian meditation leads us to the inner wholeness necessary to give ourselves to God freely.

Another misconception about meditation is that it is too difficult, too complicated. Perhaps it is best left to the professional who has more time to explore the inner regions. Not at all. The acknowledged experts in this way never report that they were on a journey only for the privileged few, the spiritual giants. They would laugh at the very idea. They felt that what they were doing was a natural human activity—as natural, and as important, as breathing. They would tell us that we do not need any special gifts or psychic powers. Thomas Merton writes, "Meditation is really very simple and there is not much need of elaborate techniques to teach us how to go about it."[10]

A third misconception is to view contemplation as impractical and wholly out of touch with the twentieth century. There is a fear it will lead to the kind of person immortalized in Dostoevski's book *The Brothers Karamazov* in the ascetic Father Ferapont: a rigid, self-righteous person who, by sheer effort, delivers himself from the world and then calls down curses upon it. Many people believe that at its very best meditation leads to an unhealthy otherworldliness that keeps us immune to the suffering of humanity.

Such evaluations are far from the mark. In fact, meditation is the one thing that can sufficiently redirect our lives so that we can deal with human life successfully. Thomas Merton writes, "Meditation has no point and no reality unless it is firmly rooted in *life*."[11] Historically, no group has stressed the need to enter into the listening silences more than the Quakers, and the result has been a vital social impact far in excess of their numbers. William Penn notes, "True godliness does not turn men out of the world, but enables them to live better in it and excites their endeavors to mend it."[12]

Often meditation will yield insights that are deeply practical, almost mundane. Instruction will come on how to relate to your wife or husband, or how to deal with this sensitive problem or that business situation. It is wonderful when a particular meditation leads to ecstasy, but it is far more common to be given guidance in dealing with ordinary human problems. Meditation sends us into our ordinary world with greater perspective and balance.

Perhaps the most common misconception of all is to view meditation as a religious form of psychological manipulation. It may have value in dropping our blood pressure or in relieving tension. It may even provide us with meaningful insights by helping us get in touch with our subconscious mind. But the idea of actual contact and communion with the God of Abraham, Isaac, and Jacob sounds unscientific and faintly unreasonable. If you feel that we live in a purely physical universe, you will view meditation as a good way to obtain a consistent alpha brain-wave pattern. But if you believe that we live in a universe created by the infinite-personal God who delights in our communion with him, you will see meditation as communication between the Lover and the one beloved.

These two concepts of meditation are complete opposites. The one confines us to a totally human experience; the other catapults us into a divine-human encounter. The one talks about the exploration of the subconscious; the other speaks of "resting in him whom we have *found*, who loves us, who is near to us, who comes to us to draw us to himself."[13] Both may sound religious and even use religious jargon, but the former can ultimately find no place for spiritual reality.

How then do we come to believe in a world of the spirit? Is it by blind faith? Not at all. The inner reality of the spiritual world is available to all who are willing to search for it. Often I have discovered that those who so freely debunk the spiritual world have never taken ten minutes to investigate whether or not such a world really exists.

Let me suggest we take an experiential attitude toward spiritual realities. Like any other scientific endeavor, we form a hypothesis and experiment with it to see if it is true or not. If our first experiment fails, we do not despair or label the whole business fraudulent. We reexamine our procedure, perhaps adjust our hypothesis, and try again. We should at least have the honesty to persevere in this work to the same degree we would in any field of science. The fact that so many are unwilling to do so betrays not their intelligence but their prejudice.

Desiring the Living Voice of God

There are times when everything within us says yes to the words of Frederick W. Faber:

> Only to sit and think of God,
>   Oh what a joy it is!
> To think the thought, to breathe the Name
>   Earth has no higher bliss.[14]

But those who meditate know that the more frequent reaction is spiritual inertia, a coldness and lack of desire. Human beings seem to have a perpetual tendency to have somebody else talk to God for them. We are content to have the message second-hand. One of Israel's fatal mistakes was their insistence upon having a human king rather than resting in the theocratic rule of God over them. We can detect a note of sadness in the word of the Lord, "They have rejected me from being king over them" (1 Sam. 8:7). The history of religion is the story of an almost desperate scramble to have a king, a mediator, a priest, a pastor, a go-between. In this way we do not need to go to God ourselves. Such an approach saves us from the need to change, for to be in the presence of God is to change. We do not need to observe Western culture very closely to realize that it is captivated by the religion of the mediator.

That is why meditation is so threatening to us. It boldly calls us to enter into the living presence of God for ourselves. It tells us that God is speaking in the continuous present and wants to address us. Jesus and the New Testament writers clearly state that this is not just for the religious professionals—the priests—but for everyone. *All* who acknowledge Jesus Christ as Lord *are* the universal priesthood of God and as such can enter the Holy of Holies and converse with the living God.

To bring people to believe that *they* can hear God's voice seems so difficult. Members of the Church of the Saviour in Washington, D.C., have been experimenting in this area for some time. Their conclusion: "We think that we are twentieth- and twenty-first-century people; nonetheless, we have hints that one can receive directions as clear as those given Ananias, . . . 'Rise and go to the street called straight.' "[15] Why not? If God is alive and active in the affairs of human beings, why can't his voice be heard and obeyed today? It can be heard and is heard by all who will know him as present Teacher and Prophet.

How do we receive the desire to hear his voice? "This desire to turn is a gift of grace. Anyone who imagines he can simply begin meditating without praying for the desire and the grace to do so, will soon give up. But the desire to meditate, and the grace to begin meditating, should be taken as an implicit promise of further graces."[16] Seeking and receiving that "gift of grace" is the only thing that will keep us moving forward on the inward journey. And as Albert the Great says, "The contemplation of the saints is fired by the love of the one contemplated: that is, God."[17]

Sanctifying the Imagination

We can descend with the mind into the heart most easily through the imagination. In this regard the great Scottish preacher Alexander Whyte speaks of "the divine offices and the splendid services of the Christian imagination."[18] Perhaps some rare individuals experience God through abstract contemplation alone, but most of us need to be more deeply rooted in the senses. We must not despise this simpler, more humble route into God's presence. Jesus himself taught in this manner, making constant appeal to the imagination, and many of the devotional masters likewise encourage us in this way. St. Teresa of Ávila says, ". . . as I could not make reflection with my understanding I contrived to picture Christ within me."[19] Many of us can identify with her words, for we too have tried a merely cerebral approach and found it too abstract, too detached. Even more, the imagination helps to anchor our thoughts and center our attention. Francis de Sales notes that "by means of the imagination we confine our mind within the mystery on which we meditate, that it may not ramble to and fro, just as we shut up a bird in a cage or tie a hawk by his leash so that he may rest on the hand."[20]

Some have objected to using the imagination out of concern that it is untrustworthy and could even be used by the Evil One. There is good reason for concern, for the imagination, like all our faculties, has participated in the Fall. But just as we can believe that God can take our reason (fallen as it is) and sanctify it and use it for his good purposes, so we believe he can sanctify the imagination and use *it* for his good purposes. Of course, the imagination can be distorted by Satan, but then so can all our faculties. God created us with an imagination, and as Lord of his creation he can and does redeem it and use it for the work of the kingdom of God.

Another concern about the use of the imagination is the fear of human manipulation and even self-deception. After all, some have an "overactive imagination," as we say, and they can concoct all kinds of images of what they would like to see happen. Besides, doesn't the Bible warn against "the vain imaginations" of the wicked (Rom. 1:21)? The concern is legitimate. It is possible for all of this to be nothing more than vain human strivings. That is why it is so vitally important for us to be thrown in utter dependence upon God in these matters. We are seeking to think God's thoughts after him, to delight in his presence, to desire his truth and his way. And the more we live in this way, the more God utilizes our imagination for his good purposes. In fact, the common experience of those who walk with God is one of being *given* images of what can be. Often in praying for people I am given a picture of their condition, and when I share that picture with them, there will be a deep inner sigh, or they will begin weeping. Later they will ask, "How did you know?" Well, I didn't know, I just saw it.

To believe that God can sanctify and utilize the imagination is simply to take seriously the Christian idea of incarnation. God so accommodates, so enfleshes himself into our world that he uses the images we know and understand to teach us about the unseen world of which we know so little and which we find so difficult to understand.

Preparing to Meditate

It is impossible to learn how to meditate from a book. We learn to meditate by meditating. Simple suggestions at the right time, however, can make an immense difference. The practical hints and meditation exercises on the following pages are given in the hope that they may help in the actual practice of meditation. They are not laws nor are they intended to confine you.

Is there a proper *time* for meditation? When a certain proficiency has been attained in the interior life, it is possible to practice meditation at any time and under almost every circumstance. Brother Lawrence in the seventeenth century and Thomas Kelly in the twentieth both bear eloquent testimony to this fact. Having said that, however, we must see the importance for beginners and experts alike to give some part of each day to formal meditation.

Once we are convinced that we need to set aside specific times for contemplation, we must guard against the notion that to do certain religious acts at particular times means that we are finally meditating. This work involves all of life. It is a twenty-four-hour-a-day job. Contemplative prayer is a way of life. "Pray without ceasing," Paul exhorts (1 Thess. 5:17, KJV). With a touch of humor Peter of Celles notes that "he who snores in the night of vice cannot know the light of contemplation."[21]

We must come to see, therefore, how central our whole day is in preparing us for specific times of meditation. If we are constantly being swept off our feet with frantic activity, we will be unable to be attentive at the moment of inward silence. A mind that is harassed and fragmented by external affairs is hardly prepared for meditation. The church Fathers often spoke of *Otium Sanctum*, "holy leisure." It refers to a sense of balance in the life, an ability to be at peace through the activities of the day, an ability to rest and take time to enjoy beauty, an ability to pace ourselves. With our tendency to define people in terms of what they produce, we would do well to cultivate "holy leisure." And if we expect to succeed in the contemplative way, we must pursue "holy leisure" with a determination that is ruthless to our datebooks.

What about a *place* for meditation? This will be discussed under the Discipline of solitude so for now a few words will be sufficient. Find a place that is quiet and free from interruption. No telephone should be nearby. If it is possible to find some place that looks out onto a lovely landscape, so much the better. It is best to have one designated place rather than hunting for a different spot each day.

What about *posture*? In one sense posture makes no difference at all; you can pray anywhere, any time, and in any position. In another sense, however, posture is of utmost importance. The body, the mind, and the spirit are inseparable. Tension in the spirit is telegraphed in body language. I actually have witnessed people go through an entire worship service vigorously chewing gum without the slightest awareness of their deep inner tension. Not only does outward posture reflect the inward state, it can also help to nurture the inner attitude of prayer. If inwardly we are fraught with distractions and anxiety, a consciously chosen posture of peace and relaxation will have a tendency to calm our inner turmoil.

There is no "law" that prescribes a correct posture. The Bible contains everything from lying prostrate on the floor to standing with hands and head lifted toward the heavens. I think the best approach would be to find a position that is the most comfortable and the least distracting. The delightful fourteenth-century mystic, Richard Rolle, favored sitting, ". . . because I knew that I . . . longer lasted . . . than going, or standing or kneeling. For [in] sitting I am most at rest, and my heart most upward."[22] I quite agree, and find it best to sit in a straight chair, with my back correctly positioned in the chair and both feet flat on the floor. To slouch indicates inattention and to cross the legs restricts the circulation. Place the hands on the knees, palms up in a gesture of receptivity. Sometimes it is good to close the eyes to remove distractions and center the attention on Christ. At other times it is helpful to ponder a picture of the Lord or to look out at some lovely trees and plants for the same purpose. Regardless of how it is done, the aim is to center the attention of the body, the emotions, the mind, and the spirit upon "the glory of God in the face of Christ" (2 Cor. 4:6).

The Forms of Meditation

Christians throughout the centuries have spoken of a variety of ways of listening to God, of communing with the Creator of heaven and earth, of experiencing the eternal Lover of the world. The accumulated wisdom of their experience can be immensely helpful as we, like them, seek intimacy with God and faithfulness to God.

For all the devotional masters the *meditatio Scripturarum*, the meditation upon Scripture, is the central reference point by which all other forms of meditation are kept in proper perspective. Whereas the study of Scripture centers on exegesis, the meditation of Scripture centers on internalizing and personalizing the passage. The written Word becomes a living word addressed to you. This is not a time for technical studies, or analysis, or even the gathering of material to share with others. Set aside all tendencies toward arrogance and with a humble heart receive the word addressed to you. Often I find kneeling especially appropriate for this particular time. Dietrich Bonhoeffer says, ". . . just as you do not analyze the words of someone you love, but accept them as they are said to you, accept the Word of Scripture and ponder it in your heart, as Mary did. That is all. That is meditation."[23] When Bonhoeffer founded the seminary at Finkenwalde, a one-half hour silent meditation upon Scripture was practiced by everyone.

It is important to resist the temptation to pass over many passages superficially. Our rushing reflects our internal state and our internal state is what needs to be transformed. Bonhoeffer recommended spending a whole week on a single text! Therefore, my suggestion is that you take a single event, or a parable, or a few verses, or even a single word and allow it to take root in you. Seek to live the experience, remembering the encouragement of Ignatius of Loyola to apply all our senses to our task. Smell the sea. Hear the lap of water along the shore. See the crowd. Feel the sun on your head and the hunger in your stomach. Taste the salt in the air. Touch the hem of his garment. In this regard Alexander Whyte counsels us, ". . . the truly Christian imagination never lets Jesus Christ out of her sight. . . . You open your New Testament. . . . And, by your imagination, that moment you are one of Christ's disciples on the spot, and are at His feet."[24]

Suppose we want to meditate on Jesus' staggering statement, "My peace I give to you" (John 14:27). Our task is not so much to study the passage as it is to be initiated into the reality of which the passage speaks. We brood on the truth that he is now filling us with his peace. The heart, the mind, and the spirit are awakened to his inflowing peace. We sense all motions of fear stilled and overcome by "power and love and self-control" (2 Tim. 1:7). Rather than dissecting peace we are entering into it. We are enveloped, absorbed, gathered into his peace. And the wonderful thing about such an experience is that the self is quite forgotten. We are no longer worried about how we can make ourselves more at peace, for we are attending to the impartation of peace within our hearts. No longer do we laboriously think up ways to act peacefully, for acts of peace spring spontaneously from within.

Always remember that we enter the story not as passive observers, but as active participants. Also remember that Christ is truly with us to teach us, to heal us, to forgive us. Alexander Whyte declares, "with your imagination anointed with holy oil, you again open your New Testament. At one time, you are the publican: at another time, you are the prodigal . . . at another time, you are Mary Magdalene: at another time, Peter in the porch. . . . Till your whole New Testament is all over autobiographic of you."[25]

Another form of meditation is what the contemplatives of the Middle Ages called "re-collection," and what the Quakers have often called "centering down." It is a time to become still, to enter into the recreating silence, to allow the fragmentation of our minds to become centered.

The following is a brief exercise to aid you in "re-collection" that is simply called "palms down, palms up." Begin by placing your palms down as a symbolic indication of your desire to turn over any concerns you may have to God. Inwardly you may pray, "Lord, I give to you my anger toward John. I release my fear of my dentist appointment this morning. I surrender my anxiety over not having enough money to pay the bills this month. I release my frustration over trying to find a baby-sitter for tonight." Whatever it is that weighs on your mind or is a concern to you, just say, "palms down." Release it. You may even feel a certain sense of release in your hands. After several moments of surrender, turn your palms up as a symbol of your desire to receive from the Lord. Perhaps you will pray silently: "Lord, I would like to receive your divine love for John, your peace about the dentist appointment, your patience, your joy." Whatever you need, you say, "palms up." Having centered down, spend the remaining moments in complete silence. Do not ask for anything. Allow the Lord to commune with you, to love you. If impressions or directions come, fine; if not, fine.

A third kind of contemplative prayer is meditation upon the creation. Now, this is no infantile pantheism, but a majestic monotheism in which the great Creator of the universe shows us something of his glory through his creation. The heavens do indeed declare the glory of God and the firmament does show forth his handiwork (Ps. 19:1). Evelyn Underhill recommends, ". . . begin with that first form of contemplation which the old mystics sometimes called 'the discovery of God in his creatures.' "[26]

So give your attention to the created order. Look at the trees, really look at them. Take a flower and allow its beauty and symmetry to sink deep into your mind and heart. Listen to the birds—they are the messengers of God. Watch the little creatures that creep upon the earth. These are humble acts, to be sure, but sometimes God reaches us profoundly in these simple ways if we will quiet ourselves to listen.

There is a fourth form of meditation that is in some ways quite the opposite of the one just given. It is to meditate upon the events of our time and to seek to perceive their significance.

We have a spiritual obligation to penetrate the inner meaning of events, not to gain power but to gain prophetic perspective. Thomas Merton writes that the person ". . . who has meditated on the Passion of Christ but has not meditated on the extermination camps of Dachau and Auschwitz has not yet fully entered into the experience of Christianity in our time."[27]

This form of meditation is best accomplished with the Bible in one hand and the newspaper in the other! You must not, however, be controlled by the absurd political clichés and propaganda fed us today. Actually, newspapers are generally far too shallow and slanted to be of much help. We would do well to hold the events of our time before God and ask for prophetic insight to discern where these things lead. Further, we should ask for guidance for anything we personally should be doing to be salt and light in our decaying and dark world.

You must not be discouraged if in the beginning your meditations have little meaning to you. There is a progression in the spiritual life, and it is wise to have some experience with lesser peaks before trying to tackle the Mt. Everest of the soul. So be patient with yourself. Besides, you are learning a discipline for which you have received no training. Nor does our culture encourage you to develop these skills. You will be going against the tide, but take heart; your task is of immense worth.

There are many other aspects of the Discipline of meditation that could be profitably considered.* However, meditation is not a single act, nor can it be completed the way one completes the building of a chair. It is a way of life. You will be constantly learning and growing as you plumb the inner depths.

---

*Two topics that closely impinge upon meditation will be discussed under the Discipline of solitude: the creative use of silence and the concept developed by St. John of the Cross that he graphically calls "the dark night of the soul."

3. The Discipline of Prayer

I am the ground of thy beseeching; first, it is my will thou shalt have it; after, I make thee to will it; and after I make thee to beseech it and thou beseechest it. How should it then be that thou shouldst not have thy beseeching?

—JULIANA OF NORWICH

Prayer catapults us onto the frontier of the spiritual life. Of all the Spiritual Disciplines prayer is the most central because it ushers us into perpetual communion with the Father. Meditation introduces us to the inner life, fasting is an accompanying means, study transforms our minds, but it is the Discipline of prayer that brings us into the deepest and highest work of the human spirit. Real prayer is life creating and life changing. "Prayer—secret, fervent, believing prayer—lies at the root of all personal godliness,"[1] writes William Carey.

To pray is to change. Prayer is the central avenue God uses to transform us. If we are unwilling to change, we will abandon prayer as a noticeable characteristic of our lives. The closer we come to the heartbeat of God the more we see our need and the more we desire to be conformed to Christ. William Blake tells us that our task in life is to learn to bear God's "beams of love." How often we fashion cloaks of evasion—beam-proof shelters—in order to elude our Eternal Lover. But when we pray, God slowly and graciously reveals to us our evasive actions and sets us free from them.

"You ask and do not receive, because you ask wrongly, to spend it on your passions" (James 4:3). To ask "rightly" involves transformed passions. In prayer, real prayer, we begin to think God's thoughts after him: to desire the things he desires, to love the things he loves, to will the things he wills.

Progressively, we are taught to see things from his point of view.

All who have walked with God have viewed prayer as the main business of their lives. The words of the gospel of Mark, "And in the morning, a great while before day, he rose and went out to a lonely place, and there he prayed," stand as a commentary on the life-style of Jesus (Mark 1:35). David's desire for God broke the self-indulgent chains of sleep: "Early will I seek Thee" (Ps. 63:1, KJV). When the apostles were tempted to invest their energies in other important and necessary tasks, they determined to give themselves continually to prayer and the ministry of the word (Acts 6:4). Martin Luther declares, "I have so much business I cannot get on without spending three hours daily in prayer." He held it as a spiritual axiom that "He that has prayed well has studied well."[2] John Wesley says, "God does nothing but in answer to prayer,"[3] and backed up his conviction by devoting two hours daily to that sacred exercise. The most notable feature of David Brainerd's life was his praying. His Journal is permeated with accounts of prayer, fasting, and meditation. "I love to be alone in my cottage, where I can spend much time in prayer." "I set apart this day for secret fasting and prayer to God."[4]

For those explorers in the frontiers of faith, prayer was no little habit tacked onto the periphery of their lives; it *was* their lives. It was the most serious work of their most productive years. William Penn testified of George Fox that "Above all he excelled in prayer. . . . The most awful, living, reverend frame I ever felt or beheld, I must say was his in prayer."[5] Adoniram Judson sought to withdraw from business and company seven times a day in order to engage in the holy work of prayer. He began at dawn; then at nine, twelve, three, six, nine, and midnight he would give time to secret prayer. John Hyde of India made prayer such a dominant characteristic of his life that he was nicknamed "Praying Hyde." For these, and all those who have braved the depths of the interior life, to breathe was to pray.

Prayer is to the soul as breath to the body. It moves without reason and brings life to the heart.

Many of us, however, are discouraged rather than challenged by such examples. Those "giants of the faith" are so far beyond anything we have experienced that we are tempted to despair. But rather than flagellating ourselves for our obvious lack, we should remember that God always meets us where we are and slowly moves us along into deeper things. Occasional joggers do not suddenly enter an Olympic marathon. They prepare and train themselves over a period of time, and so should we. When such a progression is followed, we can expect to pray a year from now with greater authority and spiritual success than at present.

In our efforts to pray it is easy for us to be defeated right at the outset because we have been taught that everything in the universe is already set, and so things cannot be changed. And if things cannot be changed, why pray? We may gloomily feel this way, but the Bible does not teach that. The Bible pray-ers prayed as if their prayers could and would make an objective difference. The apostle Paul gladly announces that we are "co-laborers with God"; that is, we are working with God to determine the outcome of events (1 Cor. 3:9). It is Stoicism that demands a closed universe not the Bible.

Many people who emphasize acquiescence and resignation to the way things are as "the will of God" are actually closer to Epictetus than to Christ. Moses prayed boldly because he believed his prayers could change things, even God's mind. In fact, the Bible stresses so forcefully the openness of our universe that, in an anthropomorphism hard for modern ears, it speaks of God constantly changing his mind in accord with his unchanging love (see Exod. 32:14; Jon. 3:10).

This comes as a genuine liberation to many of us, but it also sets tremendous responsibility before us. We are working with God to determine the future! Certain things will happen in history if we pray rightly. We are to change the world by prayer. What more motivation do we need to learn this loftiest human exercise?

Prayer is such a vast and multifaceted subject that we instantly recognize the impossibility of even lightly touching on all its aspects in one chapter. There is a whole host of important philosophical questions. Why is prayer necessary? How does prayer work; that is, how can a finite human being enter into dialogue with the infinite Creator of the universe? How can an immaterial reality like prayer affect the material world? And many similar questions. There are also the many forms of prayers that have nurtured Christians throughout the centuries. There is discursive prayer, mental prayer, and centering prayer. There is the prayer of quiet, the prayer of relinquishment, and the prayer of guidance. And many more.

A myriad of genuinely good books have been written on prayer, one of the best being Andrew Murray's classic, *With Christ in the School of Prayer*. We would do well to read widely and experience deeply if we desire to know the ways of prayer. Since restriction often enhances clarity, this chapter will be confined to the prayer of intercession; that is, learning how to pray effectively for others. Modern men and women so desperately need the help that we can provide that our best energies should be devoted to this task.

Learning to Pray

Real prayer is something we learn. The disciples asked Jesus, "Lord, teach us to pray" (Luke 11:1). They had prayed all their lives, and yet something about the quality and quantity of Jesus' praying caused them to see how little they knew about prayer. If their praying was to make any difference on the human scene, there were some things they needed to learn.

It was liberating to me to understand that prayer involved a learning process. I was set free to question, to experiment, even to fail, for I knew I was learning. For years I had prayed for many things and with great intensity, but with only marginal success. But then I saw that I might possibly be doing some things wrong and could learn differently. I took the Gospels and cut out every reference to prayer and pasted them onto sheets of paper. When I could read Jesus' teaching on prayer at one sitting, I was shocked. Either the excuses and rationalizations for unanswered prayer I had been taught were wrong, or Jesus' words were wrong. I determined to learn to pray so that my experience conformed to the words of Jesus rather than try to make his words conform to my impoverished experience.

Perhaps the most astonishing characteristic of Jesus' praying is that when he prayed for others he *never* concluded by saying "If it be thy will." Nor did the apostles or prophets when they were praying for others. They obviously believed that they knew what the will of God was before they prayed the prayer of faith. They were so immersed in the milieu of the Holy Spirit that when they encountered a specific situation, they knew what should be done. Their praying was so positive that it often took the form of a direct, authoritative command: "Walk," "Be well," "Stand up." I saw that when praying for others there was evidently no room for indecisive, tentative, half-hoping, "If it be thy will" prayers.

There is, of course, a proper time and place to pray, "If it be thy will." First, in the prayer of guidance it is the great yearning of our hearts to know the will of God. "What is your will?" "What would please you?" "What would advance your kingdom upon the earth?" This is the kind of searching prayer that should permeate our entire life experience. And then in the prayer of relinquishment, we are committed to letting go of our will whenever it conflicts with the will and way of God. Obviously, our goal is to learn always to think God's thoughts after him, but we all have times when our human desires get in the way. At such times we must follow the lead of our Master who in the garden prayed, "Nevertheless not my will, but thine, be done" (Luke 22:42).

As I was learning I sought out persons who seemed to experience greater power and effectiveness in prayer than I and asked them to teach me everything they knew. In addition, I sought the wisdom and experience of past masters of prayer by securing and reading every good book I could find on the

subject. I began studying the pray-ers of the Old Testament—
Moses and Elijah and Hannah and Daniel—with new interest.

At the same time, I began praying for others with an expectation that a change should and would occur. I am so grateful
I did not wait until I was perfect or had everything straight
before praying for others, otherwise I would never have begun.
P. T. Forsythe says, "Prayer is to religion what original research
is to science."[6] I felt I was engaging in "original research" in
the school of the Spirit. It was thrilling beyond description.
Every seeming failure led to a new learning process. Christ was
my present Teacher so that progressively his word was being
confirmed in my experience; "If you abide in me, and my
words abide in you, ask whatever you will, and it shall be done
for you" (John 15:7).

To understand that the work of prayer involves a learning
process saves us from arrogantly dismissing it as false or un-
real. If we turn on our television set and it does not work, we
do not declare that there are no such things as electronic frequencies in the air or on the cable. We assume something is
wrong, something we can find and correct. We check the plug,
switch, circuitry until we discover what is blocking the flow of
this mysterious energy that transmits pictures. We know the
problem has been found and fixed by seeing whether or not
the TV works. It is the same with prayer. We can determine if
we are praying correctly if the requests come to pass. If not,
we look for the "block"; perhaps we are praying wrongly, perhaps something within us needs changing, perhaps there are
new principles of prayer to be learned, perhaps patience and
persistence are needed. We listen, make the necessary adjust-
ments, and try again. We can know that our prayers are being
answered as surely as we can know that the television set is
working.

One of the most critical aspects in learning to pray for others
is to get in contact with God so that his life and power can
flow through us into others. Often we assume we are in contact
when we are not. For example, dozens of radio and television

signals went through your room while you read these words, but you failed to pick them up because you were not tuned to the proper frequencies. Often people pray and pray with all the faith in the world, but nothing happens. Naturally, they were not tuned in to God. We begin praying for others by first quieting our fleshly activity and listening to the silent thunder of the Lord of hosts. Attuning ourselves to divine breathings is spiritual work, but without it our praying is vain repetition (Matt. 6:7). Listening to the Lord is the first thing, the second thing, and the third thing necessary for successful intercession. Søren Kierkegaard once observed: "A man prayed, and at first he thought that prayer was talking. But he became more and more quiet until in the end he realized that prayer is listening."[7]

Listening to God is the necessary prelude to intercession. The work of intercession, sometimes called the prayer of faith, presupposes that the prayer of guidance is perpetually ascending to the Father. We must hear, know, and obey the will of God before we pray it into the lives of others. The prayer of guidance constantly precedes and surrounds the prayer of faith.

The beginning point then in learning to pray for others is to listen for guidance. In the beginning it is wise to set aside Aunt Susie's arthritis for which you have been praying for twenty years. In physical matters we always tend to pray for the most difficult situations first: terminal cancer or multiple sclerosis. But when we listen, we will learn the importance of beginning with smaller things like colds or earaches. Success in the small corners of life gives us authority in the larger matters. If we are still, we will learn not only who God is, but how his power operates.

Sometimes we are afraid that we do not have enough faith to pray for this child or that marriage. Our fears should be put to rest, for the Bible tells us that great miracles are possible through faith the size of a tiny mustard seed. Usually, the courage actually to go and pray for a person is a sign of sufficient faith. Frequently our lack is not faith but compassion. It seems that genuine empathy between the pray-er and the pray-ee often makes the difference. We are told that Jesus was "moved with compassion" for people. Compassion was an evident feature of every healing in the New Testament. We do not pray for people as "things," but as "persons" whom we love. If we have God-given compassion and concern for others, our faith will grow and strengthen as we pray. In fact, if we genuinely love people, we desire for them far more than it is within our power to give, and that will cause us to pray.

The inner sense of compassion is one of the clearest indications from the Lord that *this* is a prayer project for you. In times of meditation there may come a rise in the heart, a compulsion to intercede, an assurance of rightness, a flow of the Spirit. This inner "yes" is the divine authorization for you to pray for the person or situation. If the idea is accompanied with a sense of dread, then probably you should set it aside. God will lead someone else to pray for the matter.

The Foothills of Prayer

We should never make prayer too complicated. We are prone to do so once we understand that prayer is something we must learn. It is also easy to yield to this temptation because the more complicated we make prayer, the more dependent people are upon us to learn how to do it. But Jesus taught us to come like children to a father. Openness, honesty, and trust mark the communication of children with their father. The reason God answers prayer is because his children ask. Further, there is an intimacy between parents and children that has room for both seriousness and laughter. Meister Eckhart notes that "The soul will bring forth Person if God laughs into her and she laughs back to him."[8]

Jesus taught us to pray for daily bread. Have you ever noticed that children ask for lunch in utter confidence that it will be provided. They have no need to stash away today's sandwiches for fear none will be available tomorrow. As far as they are concerned, there is an endless supply of sandwiches. Children do not find it difficult or complicated to talk to their parents, nor do they feel embarrassed to bring the simplest need to their attention. Neither should we hesitate to bring the simplest requests confidently to the Father.

Children also teach us the value of the imagination. As with meditation, the imagination is a powerful tool in the work of prayer. We may be reticent to pray with the imagination, feeling that it is slightly beneath us. Children have no such reticence. Neither did St. Teresa of Ávila: "This was my method of prayer; as I could not make reflections with my understanding, I contrived to picture Christ within me. . . . I did many simple things of this kind. . . . I believe my soul gained very much in this way, because I began to practice prayer without knowing what it was."[9] In the play *Saint Joan* by George Bernard Shaw, Joan of Arc insists that she hears voices that come from God. She is informed by skeptics that the voices come from her imagination. Unmoved, Joan replies, "I know, that is how God speaks to me."

Imagination often opens the door to faith. If God shows us a shattered marriage whole or a sick person well, it helps us to believe that it will be so. Children instantly understand these things and respond well to praying with the imagination. I was once called to a home to pray for a seriously ill baby girl. Her four-year-old brother was in the room, and so I told him I needed his help to pray for his baby sister. He was delighted, and so was I since I know that children can often pray with unusual effectiveness. He climbed up into the chair beside me. "Let's play a little game," I said. "Since we know that Jesus is always with us, let's imagine that he is sitting over in the chair across from us. He is waiting patiently for us to center our attention on him. When we see him, we start thinking more about his love than how sick Julie is. He smiles, gets up, and comes over to us. Then, let's both put our hands on Julie, and when we do, Jesus will put his hands on top of ours. We'll watch the light from Jesus flow into your little sister and make her well. Let's watch the healing power of Christ fight with bad germs until they are all gone. Okay?" Seriously, the little one nodded. Together, we prayed in this childlike way and then thanked the Lord that what we had prayed was the way it was going to be. Now, I do not know exactly what happened, nor how it was accomplished, but I do know that the next morning Julie was perfectly well.

Let me insert a word of caution at this point. We are not trying to conjure up something in our imagination that is not so. Nor are we trying to manipulate God and tell him what to do. Quite the opposite. We are asking God to tell us what to do. God is the ground of our beseeching, as Juliana of Norwich put it, and we are utterly dependent upon him. Our prayer is to be like a reflex action to God's prior initiative upon the heart. The ideas, the pictures, the words are of no avail unless they proceed from the Holy Spirit who, as you know, is interceding for us "with sighs too deep for words" (Rom. 8:26).

Children who experience problems in the classroom often respond readily to prayer. A friend of mine who teaches emotionally handicapped children decided God wanted him to pray for them. Of course, he did not tell the children what he was doing; he simply did it. When one of the children would crawl under his desk and assume a fetal position, my teacher friend would take the child in his arms and pray silently that the resurrected Christ would heal the hurt and self-hate within the boy. So as not to embarrass him, the teacher would walk around the room continuing his regular duties while he prayed. After a while the child would relax and was soon back at his desk. Sometimes my friend would ask the boy if he ever remembered what it felt like to win a race. If the boy said yes, he would encourage him to picture himself crossing the finish line with all his friends cheering him on and loving him. In that way the child was able to cooperate in the prayer project as well as reinforce his own self-acceptance. (Is it not ironic that people will be deeply concerned over the issue of prayer in the public schools but will seldom utilize the opportunity to pray for schoolchildren in this way, against which there can be no law!) By the end of the school year, every child but two was able to return to a regular classroom. Coincidence? Perhaps, but as Archbishop William Temple notes, the coincidences occur much more frequently when he prays.

God desires that marriages be healthy, whole, and permanent. You may know of marriages that are in deep trouble and need your help. Perhaps the husband is having an affair with some other woman. Ask God if this is a prayer task for you. If so, consider praying once a day for thirty days for this marriage. Picture the husband meeting the other woman and feeling dismayed and shocked that he had ever thought of getting involved with her. Watch the very thought of an illicit affair become distasteful to him. Imagine him walking into their home and seeing his wife and being overwhelmed with a sense of love for her. Envision them taking walks together and falling in love with each other as they did years ago. See them increasingly able to open up and talk and care. Ask God to build a large brick wall between the husband and the other woman. Construct a home for the husband and wife, not of brick and mortar, but of love and consideration. Fill it with the peace of Christ.

Your pastor and the services of worship need to be bathed in prayer. Paul prayed for his people; he asked his people to pray for him. Charles Spurgeon attributed his success to the prayers of his church. Frank Laubach told his audiences, "I am very sensitive and know whether you are praying for me. If one of you lets me down, I feel it. When you are praying for me, I feel a strange power. When *every* person in a congregation prays intensely while the pastor is preaching, a miracle happens."[10] Saturate the services of worship with your prayers. See the Lord high and lifted up filling the sanctuary with his presence.

We can pray for sexual deviations with genuine assurance that a real and lasting change can occur. Sex is like a river—it is a good and wonderful blessing when kept within its proper channel. A river that overflows its banks is a dangerous thing, and so are perverted sexual drives. What are the God-created banks for sex? One man with one woman in marriage for life. When praying for persons with sexual problems, it is a joy to picture a river that has overflowed its banks and invite the Lord to bring it back into its natural channel.

Your own children can and should be changed through your prayers. Pray for them in the daytime with their participation; pray for them at night when they are asleep. One delightful approach is to go into the bedroom and lightly place your hands on the sleeping child. Ask Christ to flow through your hands healing every emotional trauma and hurt feeling your child experienced that day. Fill him or her with the peace and joy of the Lord.

As a priest of Christ, you can perform a wonderful service by taking children into your arms and blessing them. In the Bible parents brought their children to Jesus not so he would play with them or even teach them, but so he would lay his hands on them and bless them (Mark 10:13–16). He has given you the ability to do the same. Blessed is the child who is blessed by adults who know how to bless!

"Flash Prayers" is an excellent idea developed by Frank Laubach in his many books on prayer. He purposed to learn how to live so that "to *see* anybody will be to pray! To *hear* anybody, as these children talking, that boy crying, may be to pray!"[11] Flashing hard and straight prayers at people is a great thrill and can bring interesting results. I have tried it, inwardly asking the joy of the Lord and a deeper awareness of his presence to rise up within every person I meet. Sometimes people reveal no response, but other times they turn and smile as if addressed. In a bus or plane we can invite Jesus to walk down the aisles, touching people on the shoulder and saying, "I love you. My greatest delight would be to forgive you and give you good things. You have beautiful qualities still in the bud that I would unfold if only you will say yes. I'd love to rule your life if you'll let me." Frank Laubach has suggested that if thousands of us would experiment with "swishing prayers" at everyone we meet and would share the results, we could learn a great deal about how to pray for others. We could change the whole atmosphere of a nation if thousands of us would constantly throw a cloak of prayer around everyone in our circle of nearness. "Units of prayer combined, like drops of water, make an ocean which defies resistance."[12]

We must learn to pray against evil. The old writers urged us to wage spiritual warfare against "the world, the flesh, and the devil." We must never forget that the enemy of our souls prowls about like a "roaring lion" seeking whom he may devour (1 Pet. 5:8). We in prayer fight against the principalities and powers. And we need to pray prayers of protection; surrounding ourselves with the life of Christ, covering ourselves with the blood of Christ, and sealing ourselves with the cross of Christ.

We must never wait until we *feel* like praying before we pray for others. Prayer is like any other work; we may not feel like working, but once we have been at it for a bit, we begin to feel like working. We may not feel like practicing the piano, but once we play for a while, we feel like doing it. In the same way, our prayer muscles need to be limbered up a bit and once the blood-flow of intercession begins, we will find that we feel like praying.

We need not worry that this work will take up too much of our time, for "It takes no time, but it occupies all our time."[13] It is not prayer in addition to work but prayer simultaneous with work. We precede, enfold, and follow all our work with prayer. Prayer and action become wedded. Thomas Kelly witnesses: "There is a way of ordering our mental life on more than one level at once. On one level we may be thinking, discussing, seeing, calculating, meeting all the demands of external affairs. But deep within, behind the scenes, at a profounder level, we may also be in prayer and adoration, song and worship, and a gentle receptiveness to divine breathings."[14]

We have so much to learn, so far to go. Certainly the yearning of our hearts is summed up by Archbishop Tait when he says, "I want a life of greater, deeper, truer prayer."[15]

4. The Discipline of Fasting

Some have exalted religious fasting beyond all Scripture and reason; and others have utterly disregarded it.

—JOHN WESLEY

In a culture where the landscape is dotted with shrines to the Golden Arches and an assortment of Pizza Temples, fasting seems out of place, out of step with the times. In fact, fasting has been in general disrepute both in and outside the Church for many years. For example, in my research I could not find a single book published on the subject of Christian fasting from 1861 to 1954, a period of nearly one hundred years. More recently a renewed interest in fasting has developed, but we have far to go to recover a biblical balance.

What would account for this almost total disregard of a subject so frequently mentioned in Scripture and so ardently practiced by Christians through the centuries? Two things. First, fasting has developed a bad reputation as a result of the excessive ascetic practices of the Middle Ages. With the decline of the inward reality of the Christian faith, an increasing tendency to stress the only thing left, the outward form, developed. And whenever there is a form devoid of spiritual power, law will take over because law always carries with it a sense of security and manipulative power. Hence, fasting was subjected to the most rigid regulations and practiced with extreme self-mortification and flagellation. Modern culture reacts strongly to these excesses and tends to confuse fasting with mortification.

Second, the constant propaganda fed us today convinces us that if we do not have three large meals each day, with several snacks in between, we are on the verge of starvation. This, coupled with the popular belief that it is a positive virtue to satisfy every human appetite, has made fasting seem obsolete. Anyone who seriously attempts to fast is bombarded with objections. "I understand that fasting is injurious to your health." "It will sap your strength so you can't work." "Won't it destroy healthy body tissue?" All of this, of course, is utter nonsense based upon prejudice. While the human body can survive only a short time without air or water, it can go for many days before starvation begins. Without needing to subscribe to the inflated claims of some groups, it is not an exaggeration to say that, when done correctly, fasting can have beneficial physical effects.

Scripture has so much to say about fasting that we would do well to look once again at this ancient Discipline. The list of biblical personages who fasted reads like a "Who's Who" of Scripture: Moses the lawgiver, David the king, Elijah the prophet, Esther the queen, Daniel the seer, Anna the prophetess, Paul the apostle, Jesus Christ the incarnate Son. Many of the great Christians throughout church history fasted and witnessed to its value; among them were Martin Luther, John Calvin, John Knox, John Wesley, Jonathan Edwards, David Brainerd, Charles Finney, and Pastor Hsi of China.

Fasting, of course, is not an exclusively Christian Discipline; all the major religions of the world recognize its merit. Zoroaster practiced fasting as did Confucius and the Yogis of India. Plato, Socrates, and Aristotle all fasted. Even Hippocrates, the father of modern medicine, believed in fasting. Now the fact that all these persons, in and out of Scripture, held fasting in high regard does not make it right or even desirable, but it should make us pause long enough to be willing to reevaluate the popular assumptions of our day concerning the Discipline of fasting.

Fasting in the Bible

Throughout Scripture fasting refers to abstaining from food for spiritual purposes. It stands in distinction to the hunger strike, the purpose of which is to gain political power or attract attention to a good cause. It is also distinct from health dieting which stresses abstinence from food for physical, not spiritual, purposes. Because of the secularization of modern society, "fasting" (if it is done at all) is usually motivated either by vanity or by the desire for power. That is not to say that these forms of "fasting" are wrong necessarily, but their objective is different from the fasting described in Scripture. Biblical fasting always centers on spiritual purposes.

In Scripture the normal means of fasting involves abstaining from all food, solid or liquid, but not from water. In the forty-day fast of Jesus, we are told that "he ate nothing" and that toward the end of the fast "he was hungry" and Satan tempted him to eat, indicating that the abstaining was from food but not from water (Luke 4:2). From a physical standpoint, this is what is usually involved in a fast.

Sometimes what could be considered a partial fast is described; that is, there is a restriction of diet but not total abstention. Although the normal fast seemed to be the custom of the prophet Daniel, there was a three-week period in which he declares, "I ate no delicacies, no meat or wine entered my mouth, nor did I anoint myself at all" (Dan. 10:3). We are not told the reason for this departure from his normal practice of fasting; perhaps his governmental tasks precluded it.

There are also several examples in Scripture of what has been called an "absolute fast," or abstaining from both food and water. It appears to be a desperate measure to meet a dire emergency. Upon learning that execution awaited herself and her people, Esther instructed Mordecai, "Go, gather all the Jews . . . and hold a fast on my behalf, and neither eat nor drink for three days, night or day. I and my maids will also fast as you do" (Esther 4:16). Paul engaged in a three-day absolute fast following his encounter with the living Christ (Acts 9:9). Since the human body cannot go without water much more than three days, both Moses and Elijah engaged in what must be considered supernatural absolute fasts of forty days

(Deut. 9:9; 1 Kings 19:8). It must be underscored that the absolute fast is the exception and should never be engaged in unless one has a very clear command from God, and then for no more than three days.

In most cases fasting is a private matter between the individual and God. There are, however, occasional times of corporate or public fasts. The only annual public fast required in the Mosaic law was on the day of atonement (Lev. 23:27). It was to be *the day* in the Jewish calendar when the people were to be in sorrow and affliction as atonement for their sins. (Gradually, other fast days were added until today there are over twenty!) Also, fasts were called in times of group or national emergency: "Blow the trumpet in Zion; sanctify a fast; call a solemn assembly; gather the people" (Joel 2:15). When Judah was invaded, King Jehoshaphat called the nation to fast (2 Chron. 20:1–4). In response to the preaching of Jonah, the entire city of Nineveh including the animals—involuntarily, no doubt—fasted. Before the trip back to Jerusalem, Ezra had the exiles fast and pray for safety while traveling on the bandit-infested road (Ezra 8:21–23).

The group fast can be a wonderful and powerful experience provided there is a prepared people who are of one mind in these matters. Serious problems in churches or other groups can be dealt with and relationships healed through unified group prayer and fasting. When a sufficient number of people rightly understand what is involved, national calls to prayer and fasting can also have beneficial results. The king of Britain called for a day of solemn prayer and fasting because of a threatened invasion by the French in 1756. On February 6 John Wesley recorded in his Journal, "The fast day was a glorious day, such as London has scarce seen since the Restoration. Every church in the city was more than full, and a solemn seriousness sat on every face. Surely God heareth prayer, and there will yet be a lengthening of our tranquillity." In a footnote he wrote, "Humility was turned into national rejoicing for the threatened invasion by the French was averted."[1]

Throughout history what could be called regular fasts also developed. By the time of Zechariah four regular fasts were held (Zech. 8:19). The boast of the Pharisee in Jesus' parable evidently described a common practice of the day, "I fast twice a week" (Luke 18:12).* The Didache prescribed two fast days a week: Wednesday and Friday. Regular fasting was made obligatory at the Second Council of Orleans in the sixth century. John Wesley sought to revive the teaching of the Didache and urged early Methodists to fast on Wednesdays and Fridays. He felt so strongly about this matter, in fact, that he refused to ordain anyone to the Methodist ministry who did not fast on those two days.

Regular or weekly fasting has had such a profound effect in the lives of some that they have sought to find a biblical command for it so that it may be urged upon all Christians. The search is in vain. There simply are no biblical laws that command regular fasting. Our freedom in the gospel, however, does not mean license; it means opportunity. Since there are no laws to bind us, we are free to fast on any day. Freedom for the apostle Paul meant that he was engaged in "fastings often" (2 Cor. 11:27, KJV). We should always bear in mind the apostolic counsel, "Do not use your freedom as an opportunity for the flesh" (Gal. 5:13).

There is a "discipline" that has gained a certain popularity today that is akin, but not identical, to fasting. It is called "watchings" and stems from Paul's use of the term in connection with his sufferings for Christ (2 Cor. 6:5, 11:27, KJV). It refers to abstaining from sleep in order to attend to prayer or other spiritual duties. There is no indication that this has any essential connection to fasting, otherwise we would be confined to very short fasts indeed! While "watchings" may have value and God at times may call us to go without sleep for specific needs, we must take care not to elevate things that

---

*A frequent practice of the Pharisees was to fast on Mondays and Thursdays because those were market days and so there would be bigger audiences to see and admire their piety.

have only the slightest biblical precedent into major obligations. Paul's warning should always be kept before us for, in any discussion of the Disciplines, we will discover many things that ". . . have indeed an appearance of wisdom in promoting rigor of devotion and self-abasement and severity to the body, but they are of no value in checking the indulgence of the flesh" (Col. 2:23).

Is Fasting a Commandment?

One issue that understandably concerns many people is whether or not Scripture makes fasting obligatory upon all Christians. Numerous attempts have been made to answer this question, resulting in a variety of conclusions. One of the finest defenses of an affirmative answer was penned in 1580 by Thomas Cartwright in a book, something of a classic in the field, entitled *The Holy Exercise of a True Fast*.

Although many passages of Scripture deal with this subject, two stand out in importance. The first is Jesus' startling teaching about fasting in the Sermon on the Mount.* Two factors bear directly on the issue at hand. His teaching on fasting is directly in the context of his teaching on giving and praying. It is as if there is an almost unconscious assumption that giving, praying, and fasting are all part of Christian devotion. We have no more reason to exclude fasting from the teaching than we do giving or praying. Second, Jesus states, "When you fast . . ." (Matt. 6:16). He seems to make the assumption that people will fast, and is giving instruction on how to do it properly. Martin Luther said, "It was not Christ's intention to reject or despise fasting . . . it was His intention to restore proper fasting."[2]

Having said this, however, we must realize that these words

---

*No attempt is made here to refute the heresy in Dispensationalism that the Sermon on the Mount applies to a future age rather than today. For a discussion of this issue, see "The Hermeneutics of Dispensationalism" by Daniel P. Fuller (doctoral thesis, Northwestern Baptist Seminary, Chicago).

of Jesus do not constitute a command. Jesus was giving instruction on the proper exercise of a common practice of his day. He did not speak a word about whether it was a right practice or if it should be continued. So, although Jesus does not say "If you fast," neither does he say "You *must* fast." His word is, very simply, "When you fast."

The second crucial statement of Jesus about fasting comes in response to a question by the disciples of John the Baptist. Perplexed over the fact that both they and the Pharisees fasted but Jesus' disciples did not, they asked "Why?" Jesus replied, "Can the wedding guests mourn as long as the bridegroom is with them? The days will come, when the bridegroom is taken away from them, and then they will fast" (Matt. 9:15). That is perhaps the most important statement in the New Testament on whether or not Christians should fast today.

In the coming of Jesus, a new day had dawned. The kingdom of God had come among them in present power. The Bridegroom was in their midst; it was a time for feasting, not fasting. There would, however, come a time for his disciples to fast although not in the legalism of the old order.

The most natural interpretation of the days when Jesus' disciples will fast is the present Church age, especially in light of its intricate connection with Jesus' statement on the new wineskins of the kingdom of God which follows immediately (Matt. 9:16, 17). Arthur Wallis argues that Jesus is referring to the present Church age rather than just the three-day period between his death and resurrection. He concludes his argument, "We are therefore compelled to refer the days of His absence to the period of this age, from the time He ascended to the Father until He shall return from heaven. This is evidently how His apostles understood Him, for it was not until after His ascension to the Father that we read of them fasting (Acts 13:2, 3). . . . It is this age of the Church to which our Master referred when He said, 'Then they will fast.' The time is now!"[3]

There is no way to escape the force of Jesus' words in this passage. He made it clear that he expected his disciples to fast after he was gone. Although the words are not couched in the form of a command, that is only a semantic technicality. It is clear from this passage that Christ both upheld the Discipline of fasting and anticipated that his followers would do it.

Perhaps it is best to avoid the term "command" since in the strictest sense Jesus did not command fasting. But it is obvious that he proceeded on the principle that the children of the kingdom of God would fast. For the person longing for a more intimate walk with God, these statements of Jesus are drawing words.

Where are the people today who will respond to the call of Christ? Have we become so accustomed to "cheap grace" that we instinctively shy away from more demanding calls to obedience? "Cheap grace is grace without discipleship, grace without the cross."[4] Why has the giving of money, for example, been unquestionably recognized as an element in Christian devotion and fasting so disputed? Certainly we have as much, if not more, evidence from the Bible for fasting as we have for giving. Perhaps in our affluent society fasting involves a far larger sacrifice than the giving of money.

The Purpose of Fasting

It is sobering to realize that the very first statement Jesus made about fasting dealt with the question of motive (Matt. 6:16–18). To use good things to our own ends is always the sign of false religion. How easy it is to take something like fasting and try to use it to get God to do what we want. At times there is such stress upon the blessings and benefits of fasting that we would be tempted to believe that with a little fast we could have the world, including God, eating out of our hands.

Fasting must forever center on God. It must be God-initiated and God-ordained. Like the prophetess Anna, we need to be "worshiping with fasting" (Luke 2:37). Every other purpose must be subservient to God. Like that apostolic band at Antioch, "fasting" and "worshiping the Lord" must be said in the same breath (Acts 13:2). Charles Spurgeon writes, "Our seasons of fasting and prayer at the Tabernacle have been high days indeed; never has Heaven's gate stood wider; never have our hearts been nearer the central Glory."[5]

God questioned the people in Zechariah's day, "When ye fasted . . . did ye at all fast unto me, even to me?" (Zech. 7:5, KJV). If our fasting is not unto God, we have failed. Physical benefits, success in prayer, the enduing with power, spiritual insights—these must never replace God as the center of our fasting. John Wesley declares, "First, let it [fasting] be done unto the Lord with our eye singly fixed on Him. Let our intention herein be this, and this alone, to glorify our Father which is in heaven. . . ."[6] That is the only way we will be saved from loving the blessing more than the Blesser.

Once the primary purpose of fasting is firmly fixed in our hearts, we are at liberty to understand that there are also secondary purposes in fasting. More than any other Discipline, fasting reveals the things that control us. This is a wonderful benefit to the true disciple who longs to be transformed into the image of Jesus Christ. We cover up what is inside us with food and other good things, but in fasting these things surface. If pride controls us, it will be revealed almost immediately. David writes, "I humbled my soul with fasting" (Ps. 69:10). Anger, bitterness, jealousy, strife, fear—if they are within us, they will surface during fasting. At first we will rationalize that our anger is due to our hunger; then we will realize that we are angry because the spirit of anger is within us. We can rejoice in this knowledge because we know that healing is available through the power of Christ.

Fasting reminds us that we are sustained "by every word that proceeds from the mouth of God" (Matt. 4:4). Food does not sustain us; God sustains us. In Christ, "All things hold together" (Col. 1:17). Therefore, in experiences of fasting we are not so much abstaining from food as we are feasting on the word of God. Fasting is feasting! When the disciples brought lunch to Jesus, assuming that he would be starving, he declared, "I have food to eat of which you do not know. . . . My food is to do the will of him who sent me, and to accomplish his work" (John 4:32, 34). This was not a clever metaphor, but a genuine reality. Jesus was, in fact, being nourished and sustained by the power of God. That is the reason for his counsel on fasting in Matthew 6. We are told not to act miserable when fasting because, in point of fact, we are not miserable. We are feeding on God and, just like the Israelites who were sustained in the wilderness by the miraculous manna from heaven, so we are sustained by the word of God.

Fasting helps us keep our balance in life. How easily we begin to allow nonessentials to take precedence in our lives. How quickly we crave things we do not need until we are enslaved by them. Paul writes, " 'All things are lawful for me,' but I will not be enslaved by anything" (1 Cor. 6:12). Our human cravings and desires are like rivers that tend to overflow their banks; fasting helps keep them in their proper channels. "I pommel my body and subdue it," says Paul (1 Cor. 9:27). Likewise, David writes, "I afflicted myself with fasting" (Ps. 35:13). This is not excessive asceticism; it is discipline and discipline brings freedom. In the fourth century Asterius said that fasting ensured that the stomach would not make the body boil like a kettle to the hindering of the soul.[7]

Numerous people have written on the many other values of fasting such as increased effectiveness in intercessory prayer, guidance in decisions, increased concentration, deliverance for those in bondage, physical well-being, revelations, and so on. In this, as in all matters, we can expect God to reward those who diligently seek him.

The Practice of Fasting

Contemporary men and women are largely ignorant of the practical aspects of fasting. Those who desire to fast need to acquaint themselves with this basic information.

As with all the Disciplines, a progression should be observed; it is wise to learn to walk well before we try to run. Begin with a partial fast of twenty-four hours' duration; many have found lunch to lunch to be the best time. This means that you would not eat two meals. Fresh fruit juices are excellent to drink during the fast. Attempt this once a week for several weeks. In the beginning you will be fascinated with the physical aspects of your experience, but the most important thing to monitor is the inner attitude of the heart. Outwardly you will be performing the regular duties of your day, but inwardly you will be in prayer and adoration, song, and worship. In a new way, cause every task of the day to be a sacred ministry to the Lord. However mundane your duties, for you they are a sacrament. Cultivate a "gentle receptiveness to divine breathings."[8] Break your fast with a light meal of fresh fruits and vegetables and a good deal of inner rejoicing.

After two or three weeks you are prepared to attempt a normal fast of twenty-four hours. Drink only water but use healthy amounts of it. Many feel distilled water is best. If the taste of water bothers you, add one teaspoon of lemon juice. You will probably feel some hunger pangs or discomfort before the time is up. That is not real hunger; your stomach has been trained through years of conditioning to give signals of hunger at certain hours. In many ways the stomach is like a spoiled child, and a spoiled child does not need indulgence, but needs discipline. Martin Luther says ". . . the flesh was wont to grumble dreadfully."[9] You must not give in to this "grumbling." Ignore the signals, or even tell your "spoiled child" to calm down, and in a brief time the hunger pangs will pass. If not, sip another glass of water and the stomach will be satisfied. You are to be the master of your stomach, not its slave. If family obligations permit it, devote the time you would normally use eating to meditation and prayer.

It should go without saying that you should follow Jesus' counsel to refrain from calling attention to what you are doing. The only ones who should know you are fasting are those who have to know. If you call attention to your fasting, people will be impressed and, as Jesus said, that will be your reward. You, however, are fasting for far greater and deeper rewards. The following was written by an individual who, as an experiment, had committed himself to fast once a week for two years. Notice the progression from the superficial aspects of fasting toward the deeper rewards.

"1. I felt it a great accomplishment to go a whole day without food. Congratulated myself on the fact that I found it so easy. . . .

2. Began to see that the above was hardly the goal of fasting. Was helped in this by beginning to feel hunger. . . .

3. Began to relate the food fast to other areas of my life where I was more compulsive. . . . I did not have to have a seat on the bus to be contented, or to be cool in the summer and warm when it was cold.

4. . . . Reflected more on Christ's suffering and the suffering of those who are hungry and have hungry babies. . . .

5. Six months after beginning the fast discipline, I began to see why a two-year period has been suggested. The experience changes along the way. Hunger on fast days became acute, and the temptation to eat stronger. For the first time I was using the day to find God's will for my life. Began to think about what it meant to *surrender* one's life.

6. I now know that prayer and fasting must be intricately bound together. There is no other way, and yet that way is not yet combined in me."[10]

After having achieved several fasts with a degree of spiritual success, move on to a thirty-six-hour fast: three meals. With that accomplished, it is time to seek the Lord as to whether he wants you to go on a longer fast. Three to seven days is a good time period and will probably have a substantial impact on the course of your life.

It is wise to know the process your body goes through in the course of a longer fast. The first three days are usually the most difficult in terms of physical discomfort and hunger pains. The body is beginning to rid itself of the toxins that have built up over years of poor eating habits, and it is not a comfortable process. This is the reason for the coating on the tongue and bad breath. Do not be disturbed by these symptoms; rather be grateful for the increased health and well-being that will result. You may experience headaches during this time, especially if you are an avid coffee or tea drinker. Those are mild withdrawal symptoms that will pass though they may be very unpleasant for a time.

By the fourth day the hunger pains are beginning to subside though you will have feelings of weakness and occasional dizziness. The dizziness is only temporary and caused by sudden changes in position. Move more slowly and you will have no difficulty. The weakness can come to the point where the simplest task takes great effort. Rest is the best remedy. Many find this the most difficult period of the fast.

By the sixth or seventh day you will begin to feel stronger and more alert. Hunger pains will continue to diminish until by the ninth or tenth day they are only a minor irritation. The body will have eliminated the bulk of toxins and you will feel good. Your sense of concentration will be sharpened and you will feel as if you could continue fasting indefinitely. Physically this is the most enjoyable part of the fast.

Anywhere between twenty-one and forty days or longer, depending on the individual, hunger pains will return. This is the first stage of starvation and the pains signal that the body has used up its reserves and is beginning to draw on the living tissue. The fast should be broken at this time.

The amount of weight lost during a fast varies greatly with the individual. In the beginning a loss of two pounds a day, decreasing to one pound a day as the fast progresses, is normal. During fasting you will feel the cold more simply because the body metabolism is not producing the usual amount of heat. If care is observed to keep warm, this is no difficulty. It should be obvious to all that there are some people who for physical reasons should not fast: diabetics, expectant mothers, heart patients, and others. If you have any question about your fitness to fast, seek medical advice.

Before commencing an extended fast, some are tempted to eat a good deal to "stock up." That is most unwise; in fact, slightly lighter than normal meals are best for the day or two before a fast. You would also be well advised to abstain from coffee or tea three days before beginning a longer fast. If the last meal in the stomach is fresh fruits and vegetables, you should have no difficulty with constipation.

An extended fast should be broken with fruit or vegetable juice, with small amounts taken at first. Remember that the stomach has shrunk considerably and the entire digestive system has gone into a kind of hibernation. By the second day you should be able to eat fruit and then milk or yogurt. Next you can eat fresh salads and cooked vegetables. Avoid all salad dressing, grease, and starch. Extreme care should be taken not to overeat. It is good during this time to consider future diet and eating habits to see if you need to be more disciplined and in control of your appetite.

Although the physical aspects of fasting intrigue us, we must never forget that the major work of scriptural fasting is in the realm of the spirit. What goes on spiritually is much more important than what is happening bodily. You will be engaging in spiritual warfare that will necessitate using all the weapons of Ephesians 6. One of the most critical periods spiritually is at the end of the fast when we have a natural tendency to relax. But I do not want to leave the impression that all fasting is a heavy spiritual struggle—I have not found it so. It is also ". . . righteousness and peace and joy in the Holy Spirit" (Rom. 14:17).

Fasting can bring breakthroughs in the spiritual realm that will never happen in any other way. It is a means of God's grace and blessing that should not be neglected any longer. Wesley declares, ". . . it was not merely by the light of reason . . . that the people of God have been, in all ages, directed to use fasting as a means: . . . but they have been . . . taught it of God Himself, by clear and open revelations of His Will. . . . Now, whatever reasons there were to quicken those of old, in the zealous and constant discharge of this duty, they are of equal force still to quicken us."[11]

Now is the time for all who hear the voice of Christ to obey it.

5. The Discipline of Study

He that studies only men, will get the body of knowledge without the soul; and he that studies only books, the soul without the body. He that to what he sees, adds observation, and to what he reads, reflection, is in the right road to knowledge, provided that in scrutinizing the hearts of others, he neglects not his own.

—CALEB COLTON

The purpose of the Spiritual Disciplines is the total transformation of the person. They aim at replacing old destructive habits of thought with new life-giving habits. Nowhere is this purpose more clearly seen than in the Discipline of study. The apostle Paul tells us that we are transformed through the renewal of the mind (Rom. 12:2). The mind is renewed by applying it to those things that will transform it. "Finally, brethren, whatever is true, whatever is honorable, whatever is just, whatever is pure, whatever is lovely, whatever is gracious, if there is any excellence, if there is anything worthy of praise, *think* about these things" (Phil. 4:8, [italics added]). The Discipline of study is the primary vehicle to bring us to "*think* about these things." Therefore, we should rejoice that we are not left to our own devices but have been given this means of God's grace for the changing of our inner spirit.

Many Christians remain in bondage to fears and anxieties simply because they do not avail themselves of the Discipline of study. They may be faithful in church attendance and earnest in fulfilling their religious duties, and still they are not changed. I am not here speaking only of those who are going through mere religious forms, but of those who are genuinely seeking to worship and obey Jesus Christ as Lord and Master. They may sing with gusto, pray in the Spirit, live as obediently as they know, even receive divine visions and revelations, and yet the tenor of their lives remains unchanged. Why? Because they have never taken up one of the central ways God uses to change us: study. Jesus made it unmistakably clear that the knowledge of the truth will set us free. "You will know the truth, and the truth will make you free" (John 8:32). Good feelings will not free us. Ecstatic experiences will not free us. Getting "high on Jesus" will not free us. Without a knowledge of the truth, we will not be free.

This principle is true in every area of human endeavor. It is true in biology and mathematics. It is true in marriages and other human relationships. But it is especially true in reference to the spiritual life. Many are hampered and confused in the spiritual walk by a simple ignorance of the truth. Worse yet, many have been brought into the most cruel bondage by false teaching. "You traverse sea and land to make a single proselyte, and when he becomes a proselyte, you make him twice as much a child of hell as yourselves" (Matt. 23:15).

Let us therefore apply ourselves to learning what constitutes the Spiritual Discipline of study, to identify its pitfalls, to practice it with joy, and to experience the liberation it brings.

What Is Study?

Study is a specific kind of experience in which through careful attention to reality the mind is enabled to move in a certain direction. Remember, the mind will always take on an order conforming to the order upon which it concentrates. Perhaps we observe a tree or read a book. We see it, feel it, understand it, draw conclusions from it. And as we do, our thought processes take on an order conforming to the order in the tree or book. When this is done with concentration, perception, and repetition, ingrained habits of thought are formed.

The Old Testament instructs the Israelites to write the Laws on gates and doorposts and bind them to their wrists so that "they shall be as frontlets between your eyes" (Deut. 11:18).

The purpose of this instruction is to direct the mind repeatedly and regularly toward certain modes of thought about God and human relationships. A rosary or a prayer wheel has the same objective. Of course, the New Testament replaces laws written on the doorposts with laws written on the heart and leads us to Jesus, our ever-present and inward Teacher.

We must once again emphasize that the ingrained habits of thought that are formed *will* conform to the order of the thing being studied. *What* we study determines the kind of habits that are formed, which is why Paul urges us to focus on things that are true, honorable, just, pure, lovely, and gracious.

The process that occurs in study should be distinguished from meditation. Meditation is devotional; study is analytical. Meditation will relish a word; study will explicate it. Although meditation and study often overlap, they constitute two distinct experiences. Study provides a certain objective framework within which meditation can successfully function.

In study there are two "books" to be studied: verbal and nonverbal. Books and lectures, therefore, constitute only half the field of study, perhaps less. The world of nature and, most important, the careful observation of events and actions are the primary nonverbal fields of study.

The principal task of study is a perception into the reality of a given situation, encounter, book, etc. We can go through a major crisis, for example, without any perception of the real nature of the tragic situation. But if we carefully observe and reflect upon what occurred, we can learn a great deal.

Four Steps

Study involves four steps. The first is repetition. Repetition regularly channels the mind in a specific direction, thus ingraining habits of thought. We may smile condescendingly at the old teaching method of recitation, but we must realize that sheer repetition without even understanding what is being repeated does affect the inner mind. Ingrained habits of thought can be formed by repetition alone, thus changing behavior. This is one reason why so many forms of spirituality emphasize the regular rehearsal of the deeds of God. This is also the central rationale behind psychocybernetics, which trains the individual to repeat certain affirmations regularly (for example, I love myself unconditionally). It is not even important that the person believe what he or she is repeating, only that it be repeated. The inner mind is thus trained and will eventually respond by modifying behavior to conform to the affirmation. This principle has, of course, been known for centuries but only recently has it received scientific confirmation.

This is why the issue of television programming is so important. With innumerable murders being portrayed each evening on prime time TV, the repetition alone trains the inner mind in destructive thought patterns.

Concentration is the second step in study. If, in addition to bringing the mind repeatedly to the subject matter, the person will concentrate on what is being studied, learning is vastly increased. Concentration centers the mind. It focuses the attention on what is being studied. The human mind has an incredible ability to concentrate. It constantly receives thousands of stimuli, each one of which is stored in its memory banks while it focuses on only a few. This natural ability of the brain is enhanced when, with singleness of purpose, we center our attention upon a desired object of study.

We live in a culture that does not value concentration. Distraction is the order of the day. Many will, for example, go through all the activities of the day and evening with the radio on. Some will read a book and watch TV at the same time. Most people find it virtually impossible to go through an entire day focusing on a single thing. We are the lesser for this dissipation of our energies.

When we not only repeatedly focus the mind in a particular direction, centering our attention on the subject, but understand what we are studying, we reach a new level. Comprehension then is the third step in the Discipline of study.

Jesus, as you remember, reminds us that it is not just the truth but the *knowledge* of the truth that sets us free (John 8:32). Comprehension focuses on the knowledge of the truth. All of us have had the experience of reading something over and over and then, all of sudden, we understand what it means. This "eureka" experience of understanding catapults us onto a new level of growth and freedom. It leads to insight and discernment. It provides the basis for a true perception of reality.

One further step is needed: reflection. Although comprehension defines what we are studying, reflection defines the *significance* of what we are studying. To reflect, to ruminate, on the events of our time leads us to the inner reality of those events. Reflection brings us to see things from God's perspective. In reflection we come to understand not only our subject matter, but ourselves. Jesus speaks often of ears that do not hear and eyes that do not see. When we ponder the meaning of what we study, we come to hear and see in a new way.

It soon becomes obvious that study demands humility. Study simply cannot happen until we are willing to be subject to the subject matter. We must submit to the system. We must come as student, not teacher. Not only is study directly dependent upon humility, but it is conducive to it. Arrogance and a teachable spirit are mutually exclusive.

All of us know persons who have taken some course of study or attained some academic degree who parade their information in an offensive manner. We should feel profound sorrow for such people. They do not understand the Spiritual Discipline of study. They have mistaken the accumulation of information for knowledge. They equate the spouting of words with wisdom. How tragic! The apostle John defines eternal life as the knowledge of God. "And this is eternal life, that they know thee the only true God, and Jesus Christ whom thou hast sent" (John 17:3). Even a touch of this experiential knowledge is sufficient to give us a profound sense of humility.

Now, having laid the basis, let us move on to consider the practical implementation of the Discipline of study.

Study of Books

When we consider study, we most naturally think of books or other writings. Though only half of the field, as I stated earlier, books are the most obvious and clearly important.

Unfortunately, many seem to think that studying a book is a simple task. No doubt this flippant attitude accounts for the poor reading habits of so many people. Studying a book is an extremely complex matter, especially for the novice. As with tennis or typing, when we are first learning it seems that there are a thousand details to master and we wonder how on earth we will keep everything in mind at the same time. Once we reach proficiency, however, the mechanics become second nature, and we are able to concentrate on our tennis game or the material to be typed.

The same is true with studying a book. Study is an exacting art involving a labyrinth of details. To convince people that they must *learn* to study is the major obstacle. Most people assume that because they know how to read words they know how to study. This limited grasp of the nature of study explains why so many people gain so little from reading books.

When we read a book, three intrinsic and three extrinsic rules govern our study.* The intrinsic rules may, in the beginning, necessitate three separate readings but in time can be done concurrently. The first reading involves *understanding* the book: what is the author saying? The second reading involves *interpreting* the book: what does the author mean? The third reading involves *evaluating* the book: is the author right or wrong? Most of us tend to do the third reading right away and often never do the first and second readings at all. We give a critical analysis of a book before we understand what it says. We judge a book to be right or wrong before we interpret its meaning. The wise writer of Ecclesiastes says that there is a time for every

---

*These matters are covered in detail in Mortimer J. Adler's *How to Read a Book* (New York: Simon & Schuster, 1940). I am indebted to him for these insights into the Discipline of study.

matter under heaven, and the time for critical analysis of a book comes *after* careful understanding and interpretation.

The intrinsic rules of study, however, are in themselves inadequate. To read successfully we need the extrinsic aids of *experience, other books,* and *live discussion.*

Experience is the only way we can interpret and relate to what we read. We read a book on tragedy with different eyes when we have walked through the valley of the shadow ourselves. Experience that has been understood and reflected upon informs and enlightens our study.

Other books can include dictionaries, commentaries, and other interpretative literature, but great books that precede or advance the issue being studied are more significant. Books often have meaning only when they are read in relation to other writings. People will find it exceedingly difficult to understand the New Testament books of Romans or Hebrews, for example, without a grounding in the literature of the Old Testament. It is nearly impossible to read *The Federalist Papers* without first having read the Articles of Confederation and the U.S. Constitution. The great writings that take up the central issues of life interact with one another. They cannot be read in isolation.

Live discussion refers to the ordinary interaction that occurs among human beings as they pursue a particular course of study. Often my students and I will read from Plato or St. Augustine and have only a fragmentary grasp of the meaning or significance of what we have read. But when we gather for discussion, debate, and Socratic dialogue insights emerge that would never have come without this exchange. We interact with the author, we interact with each other, and new creative ideas are born.

The first and most important book we are to study is the Bible. The psalmist asks, "How can a young man keep his way pure?" He then answers his own question, "By guarding it according to thy word," and adds, "I have laid up thy word in my heart, that I might not sin against thee" (Ps. 119:9, 11).

Probably the "word" that the psalmist refers to is the Torah, but Christians throughout the centuries have found this to be true in their study throughout Scripture. "All scripture is inspired by God and profitable for teaching, for reproof, for correction, and for training in righteousness, that the man of God may be complete, equipped for every good work" (2 Tim. 3:16, 17). Note that the central purpose is not doctrinal purity (though that is no doubt involved) but inner transformation. We come to the Scripture to be changed, not to amass information.

We must understand, however, that a vast difference exists between the study of Scripture and the devotional reading of Scripture. In the study of Scripture a high priority is placed upon interpretation: what it means. In the devotional reading of Scripture a high priority is placed upon application: what it means for me. All too often people rush to the application stage and bypass the interpretation stage: they want to know what it means for them before they know what it means! Also, we are not seeking spiritual ecstasy in study; in fact, ecstasy can be a hindrance. When we study a book of the Bible we are seeking to be controlled by the intent of the author. We are determined to hear what he is saying, not what we want him to say. We want life-transforming truth, not just good feelings. We are willing to pay the price of barren day after barren day until the meaning is clear. This process revolutionizes our lives.

The apostle Peter found some things in the epistles of "our beloved brother Paul" that were "hard to understand" (2 Pet. 3:15, 16). If Peter found it so, we will as well. We will need to work at it. Daily devotional reading is certainly commendable, but it is not study. Anyone who is after "a little word from God for today" is not interested in the Discipline of study.

The average adult Sunday School class is far too superficial and devotional to help us study the Bible. (There are exceptions and some churches offer serious courses in the Bible.) Perhaps you live close to a seminary or university where you can audit courses. If so, you are fortunate, especially if you find a teacher who dispenses *life* as well as information. If, however, that is not the case (and even if it is) you can do several things to begin studying the Bible.

Some of my most profitable experiences of study have come through structuring a private retreat of two to three days' duration. No doubt you will object that, given your schedule, you cannot possibly find that kind of time. I want you to know that it is no easier for me to set aside the time than for anyone else. I fight and struggle for every retreat, scheduling it into my datebook many weeks in advance. I have suggested this idea to many groups and found that professional people with busy schedules, laborers with rigid schedules, homemakers with multiple schedules, and others can, in fact, find time for a private study retreat. I have discovered that the most difficult problem is not finding time but convincing myself that this is important enough to set aside the time.

Scripture tells us that following the marvelous resurrection of Dorcas, Peter "tarried many days in Joppa with one Simon a tanner" (Acts 9:43, KJV). It was while tarrying in Joppa that the Holy Spirit got through to Peter (with visual aids no less) about his cultural and ethnic prejudices. What would have happened if, instead of tarrying, Peter had immediately struck out on a speaking tour to tell of the resurrection of Dorcas? Is it possible that he would have failed to come to that shattering insight from the Holy Spirit, "Truly I perceive that God shows no partiality, but in every nation any one who fears him and does what is right is acceptable to him" (Acts 10:34)? No one knows. But I do know this: God desires various "tarrying" places for all of us where he can teach us in special ways.

For many people, a weekend is a good time for such an experience. Others can arrange a block of time in the middle of the week. If only one day is possible, a Sunday is often excellent.

The best place is almost anywhere, as long as it is away from home. To leave the house or apartment not only sets us free from the telephone and domestic responsibilities, but it also sets our minds into a learning mode. Motels, as well as cabins, work well. Camping is less desirable since the tasks of living distract us more. Most retreat centers can accommodate private retreatants; Catholic centers in particular have a long tradition of encouraging private retreats and therefore have appropriate facilities.

Organized group retreats almost never take study seriously so you will probably need to structure the retreat yourself. Because you are alone you will need to discipline yourself and use your time carefully. If you are new at it you will not want to overdo and thus burn yourself out. With experience, however, you can put in ten to twelve hours of good study each day.

What should you study? That depends on what you need. I do not know your needs, but I know that one of the great needs among Christians today is simply the reading of large portions of Scripture. Much of our Bible reading is fragmentary and sporadic. I actually have known students who have taken Bible courses and never even read, as a whole, the book being studied. Consider taking a major book of the Bible, like Genesis or Jeremiah, and read it straight through. Notice the structure and flow of the book. Note areas of difficulty and return to them later. Jot down thoughts and impressions. Sometimes it is wise to combine the study of the Bible with the study of some great, devotional classic. Such retreat experiences can transform your life.

Another approach to the study of the Bible is to take a smaller book, like Ephesians or 1 John, and read it through each day for a month. More than any single effort this will put the structure of the book into your mind. Read it without trying to fit it into established categories. Expect to hear new things in new ways. Keep a journal of your findings. In the course of these studies you will obviously want to make use of the best secondary aids available.

In addition to studying the Bible, do not neglect the study of some of the experiential classics in Christian literature. Begin with *The Confessions of St. Augustine*. Next turn to *The Imitation of Christ* by Thomas à Kempis. Don't neglect *The Practice of the Presence of God* by Brother Lawrence. For an added pleasure read *The Little Flowers of St. Francis* by Brother Ugolino. Perhaps you might want something a bit heavier next like the *Pensées* of Blaise Pascal. Enjoy the *Table Talks* of Martin Luther before you wade into Calvin's *Institutes of the Christian Religion*. Consider reading the pacemaker of religious journal writing, *The Journal of George Fox*, or perhaps the better-known *Journal of John Wesley*. Read carefully William Law's *A Serious Call to a Devout and Holy Life*; its words carry a contemporary ring. From the twentieth century read *A Testament of Devotion* by Thomas Kelly, *The Cost of Discipleship* by Dietrich Bonhoeffer, and *Mere Christianity* by C. S. Lewis.

Obviously this is only a sampling. I completely passed over the *Revelations of Divine Love* by Juliana of Norwich, *Introduction to the Devout Life* by Francis de Sales, *The Journal of John Woolman*, and many other books. Nor should we forget the great body of literature by men and women from many walks of life. Many of these thinkers have unusual perception into the human predicament. Writers like Lao-tse of China and Zarathustra of Persia, Shakespeare and Milton, Cervantes and Dante, Tolstoy and Dostoevski, and, in our century, Dag Hammarskjöld.

One word of caution is in order. Do not be overwhelmed or discouraged by all the books you have not read. You will probably not read all those listed here and will undoubtedly read others not noted. These writings have been listed to help you see the excellent amount of literature at our disposal to guide us in the spiritual walk. Many others have traveled the same path and have left markers. Remember that the key to the Discipline of study is not reading many books, but experiencing what we do read.

Study of Nonverbal "Books"

We now come to the least recognized but perhaps the most important field of study: the observation of reality in things, events, and actions. The easiest place to begin is with nature. It is not difficult to see that the created order has many things to teach us.

Isaiah tells us that ". . . the mountains and the hills before you shall break forth into singing, and all the trees of the field shall clap their hands" (Isa. 55:12). The handiwork of the Creator can speak to us and teach us if we will listen. Martin Buber tells the story of the rabbi who went to a pond every day at dawn to learn "the song with which the frogs praise God."[1]

We begin the study of nature by paying attention. We *see* flowers or birds. We observe them carefully and prayerfully. André Gide describes the time when he observed a moth being reborn from its chrysalis during a classroom lecture. He was filled with wonder, awe, joy at this metamorphosis, this resurrection. Enthusiastically, he showed it to his professor who replied with a note of disapproval, "What! Didn't you know that a chrysalis is the envelope of a butterfly? Every butterfly you see has come out of a chrysalis. It's perfectly natural." Disillusioned, Gide wrote, "Yes, indeed, I knew my *natural* history as well, perhaps better than he. . . . But because it was natural, could he not see that it was marvelous? Poor creature! From that day, I took a dislike to him and a loathing to his lessons."[2] Who wouldn't! Gide's professor had only amassed information; he had not studied. And so the first step in the study of nature is reverent observation. A leaf can speak of order and variety, complexity and symmetry. Evelyn Underhill writes, "Gather yourself up, as the exercises of recollection have taught you to do. Then . . . stretch out by a distinct act of loving will towards one of the myriad manifestations of life that surround you. . . . As to the object of contemplation, it matters little. From Alp to insect, anything will do, provided that your attitude be right."[3]

The next step is to make friends with the flowers and the trees and the little creatures that creep upon the earth. Like the fabled Dr. Doolittle, talk with the animals. Of course, you can't really talk to each other . . . or can you? There is certainly a communication that goes beyond words, and often animals seem to respond to our friendship and compassion. I know this because I have experimented with it and so have some first-rate scientists, and we have found it to be true. Perhaps the stories of St. Francis taming the wolf of Gubbio and preaching to the birds are not so farfetched. Of this much we can be sure: if we love the creation, we will learn from it. In *The Brothers Karamazov* Dostoevski counsels, "Love all God's creation, the whole and every grain of sand in it. Love every leaf, every ray of God's light. Love the animals, love the plants, love everything. If you love everything, you will perceive the divine mystery in things. Once you perceive it, you will begin to comprehend it better every day."[4]

There are, of course, many other "books" beside nature that we should study. If we will observe the relationships that go on between human beings, we will receive a graduate-level education. Watch, for example, how much of our speech is aimed at justifying our actions. We find it almost impossible to act and allow the act to speak for itself. No, we must explain it, justify it, demonstrate the rightness of it. Why do we feel this compulsion to set the record straight? Because of pride and fear, because our reputations are at stake!

This compulsion is particularly easy to observe among salespeople, writers, ministers, professors—all those who earn their living by being good with words. If, however, we gradually make ourselves one of the principal subjects of study we will be delivered from a haughty spirit. In time we will be unable to pray like the Pharisee, "God, I thank thee that I am not like other men . . ." (Luke 18:11).

We should become attentive to the ordinary relationships we encounter throughout the day: at home, work, school. We notice the things that control people. Remember, we are not trying to condemn or judge anyone; we are only trying to learn. If we do find a judging spirit emerging within ourselves, we observe that and learn.

As I mentioned earlier, one of the principal objects of our study should be ourselves. We should learn the things that control *us*. We observe our inner feelings and mood swings. What controls our moods? Why do we like certain people and dislike others? What do these things teach us about ourselves?*

In doing all this we are not trying to be amateur psychologists or sociologists. Nor are we obsessed with excessive introspection. We study these matters with a spirit of humility, needing a large dose of grace. We want only to follow the dictum of Socrates: "Know thyself." And through the blessed Holy Spirit we are expecting Jesus to be our living and ever-present Teacher.

We would do well to study institutions and cultures and the forces that shape them. Also, we should ponder the events of our time, noting first, with a spirit of discernment, what things our culture lifts up as "great events." Let's look at the values of the culture—not what people say they are, but what they actually are.

Let's learn to ask questions. What are the assets and liabilities of a technological society? What has the fast-food industry done to the tradition of a family gathering for dinner? Why do we find it difficult in our culture to have time to develop relationships? Is Western individualism beneficial or destructive? What in our culture is in harmony with the gospel and what is at odds with it? One of the most important functions of Christian

---

*This counsel is for reasonably mature and well-adjusted individuals. It is not for mental depressives or others who are bowed low by the burdens of life. For them these exercises are too depressing and self-defeating. If you find your days too heavy for this kind of study, please do not attempt it. But there is hope and there is something you can do. See the chapters on confession and guidance.

prophets in our day is the ability to perceive the consequences of various forces in our culture and to make value judgments upon them.

Study produces joy. Like any novice, we will find it hard work in the beginning. But the greater our proficiency, the greater our joy. Alexander Pope says, "There is no study that is not capable of delighting us after a little application to it."[5] Study is well worth our most serious effort.

II. THE OUTWARD DISCIPLINES

6. The Discipline of Simplicity

> When we are truly in this interior simplicity our whole appearance is franker, more natural. This true simplicity . . . makes us conscious of a certain openness, gentleness, innocence, gaiety, and serenity, which is charming when we see it near to and continually, with pure eyes. O, how amiable this simplicity is! Who will give it to me? I leave all for this. It is the Pearl of the Gospel.
>
> —FRANÇOIS FÉNELON

Simplicity is freedom. Duplicity is bondage. Simplicity brings joy and balance. Duplicity brings anxiety and fear. The preacher of Ecclesiastes observes that "God made man simple; man's complex problems are of his own devising" (Eccles. 7:30, JB). Because many of us are experiencing the liberation God brings through simplicity we are once again singing an old Shaker hymn:

> 'Tis the gift to be simple,
>   'Tis the gift to be free,
> 'Tis the gift to come down where you ought to be,
>   And when we find ourselves in the place just right,
> 'Twill be in the valley of love and delight.
>
> When true simplicity is gained,
>   To bow and to bend we shan't be ashamed.
> To turn, turn will be our delight
>   'Till by turning, turning we come round right.

The Christian Discipline of simplicity is an *inward* reality that results in an *outward* life-style. Both the inward and the outward aspects of simplicity are essential. We deceive ourselves if we believe we can possess the inward reality without its having a profound effect on how we live. To attempt to arrange an outward life-style of simplicity without the inward reality leads to deadly legalism.

Simplicity begins in inward focus and unity. It means to live out of what Thomas Kelly calls "The Divine Center." Kierkegaard captured the nucleus of Christian simplicity well in the profound title of his book, *Purity of Heart Is to Will One Thing*.

Experiencing the inward reality liberates us outwardly. Speech becomes truthful and honest. The lust for status and position is gone because we no longer need status and position. We cease from showy extravagance not on the grounds of being unable to afford it, but on the grounds of principle. Our goods become available to others. We join the experience that Richard E. Byrd, after months alone in the barren Arctic, recorded in his journal, "I am learning . . . that a man can live profoundly without masses of things."[1]

Contemporary culture lacks both the inward reality and the outward life-style of simplicity. We must live in the modern world, and we are affected by its fractured and fragmented state. We are trapped in a maze of competing attachments. One moment we make decisions on the basis of sound reason and the next moment out of fear of what others will think of us. We have no unity or focus around which our lives are oriented. Because we lack a divine Center our need for security has led us into an insane attachment to things. We really must understand that the lust for affluence in contemporary society is psychotic. It is psychotic because it has completely lost touch with reality. We crave things we neither need nor enjoy. "We buy things we do not want to impress people we do not like."[2] Where planned obsolescence leaves off, psychological obsolescence takes over. We are made to feel ashamed to wear clothes or drive cars until they are worn out. The mass media have convinced us that to be out of step with fashion is to be out of step with reality. It is time we awaken to the fact that conformity to a sick society is to be sick. Until we see how unbalanced our culture has become at this point, we will not be able to deal with the mammon spirit within ourselves nor will we desire Christian simplicity.

This psychosis permeates even our mythology. The modern hero is the poor boy who purposefully becomes rich rather than the rich boy who voluntarily becomes poor. (We still find it hard to imagine that a girl could do either!) Covetousness we call ambition. Hoarding we call prudence. Greed we call industry.

Further, it is important to understand that the modern counterculture is hardly an improvement. It is a superficial change in life-style without dealing seriously with the root problems of a consumer society. Because the counterculture has always lacked a positive center it has inevitably degenerated into trivia. Arthur Gish states, "Much of the counter culture is a mirror of the worst features of the old sick society. The revolution is not free dope, free sex, and abortions on demand. . . . The pseudo-libertarian eroticism, elements of sadomasochism, and sexist advertisements in much of the underground press is part of the perversion of the old order and an expression of death."[3]

Courageously, we need to articulate new, more human ways to live. We should take exception to the modern psychosis that defines people by how much they can produce or what they earn. We should experiment with bold new alternatives to the present death-giving system. The Spiritual Discipline of simplicity is not a lost dream, but a recurrent vision throughout history. It can be recaptured today. It must be.

The Bible and Simplicity

Before attempting to forge a Christian view of simplicity it is necessary to destroy the prevailing notion that the Bible is ambiguous about economic issues. Often it is felt that our response to wealth is an individual matter. The Bible's teaching in this area is said to be strictly a matter of private interpretation. We try to believe that Jesus did not address himself to practical economic questions.

No serious reading of Scripture can substantiate such a view. The biblical injunctions against the exploitation of the poor and the accumulation of wealth are clear and straightforward. The Bible challenges nearly every economic value of contemporary society. For example, the Old Testament takes exception to the popular notion of an absolute right to private property. The earth belongs to God, says Scripture, and therefore cannot be held perpetually (Lev. 25:23). The Old Testament legislation of the year of Jubilee stipulated that all land was to revert back to its original owner. In fact, the Bible declares that wealth itself belongs to God, and one purpose of the year of Jubilee was to provide a regular redistribution of wealth. Such a radical view of economics flies in the face of nearly all contemporary belief and practice. Had Israel faithfully observed the Jubilee it would have dealt a death blow to the perennial problem of the rich becoming richer and the poor becoming poorer.

Constantly the Bible deals decisively with the inner spirit of slavery that an idolatrous attachment to wealth brings. "If riches increase, set not your heart on them," counsels the psalmist (Ps. 62:10). The tenth commandment is against covetousness, the inner lust to have, which leads to stealing and oppression. The wise sage understood that "He who trusts in his riches will wither" (Prov. 11:28).

Jesus declared war on the materialism of his day. (And I would suggest that he declares war on the materialism of our day as well.) The Aramaic term for wealth is "mammon" and Jesus condemns it as a rival God: "No servant can serve two masters; for either he will hate the one and love the other, or he will be devoted to the one and despise the other. You cannot serve God and mammon" (Luke 16:13). He speaks frequently and unambiguously to economic issues. He says, "Blessed are you poor, for yours is the kingdom of God" and "Woe to you that are rich, for you have received your consolation" (Luke 6:20, 24). He graphically depicts the difficulty of the wealthy entering the kingdom of God to be like a camel walking through the eye of a needle. With God, of course, all things are possible, but Jesus clearly understood the difficulty. He saw the grip that wealth can have on a person. He knew that "where your treasure is, there will your heart be also," which is precisely why he commanded his followers: "Do not lay up for yourselves treasures on earth" (Matt. 6:21, 19). He is not saying that the heart should or should not be where the treasure is. He is stating the plain fact that wherever you find the treasure, you *will* find the heart.

He exhorted the rich young ruler not just to have an inner attitude of detachment from his possessions, but literally to get rid of his possessions if he wanted the kingdom of God (Matt. 19:16–22). He says, "Take heed, and beware of all covetousness; for a man's life does not consist in the abundance of his possessions" (Luke 12:15). He counseled people who came seeking God, "Sell your possessions, and give alms; provide yourselves with purses that do not grow old, with a treasure in the heavens that does not fail . . ." (Luke 12:33). He told the parable of the rich farmer whose life centered in hoarding—we would call him prudent; Jesus called him a fool (Luke 12:16–21). He states that if we really want the kingdom of God we must, like a merchant in search of fine pearls, be willing to sell everything we have to get it (Matt. 13:45, 46). He calls all who would follow him to a joyful life of carefree unconcern for possessions: "Give to every one who begs from you; and of him who takes away your goods do not ask them again" (Luke 6:30).

Jesus speaks to the question of economics more than any other single social issue. If, in a comparatively simple society, our Lord lays such strong emphasis upon the spiritual dangers of wealth, how much more should we who live in a highly affluent culture take seriously the economic question.

The Epistles reflect the same concern. Paul says, "Those who desire to be rich fall into temptation, into a snare, into many senseless and hurtful desires that plunge men into ruin and destruction" (1 Tim. 6:9). A bishop is not to be a "lover of money" (1 Tim. 3:3). A deacon is not to be "greedy for gain" (1 Tim. 3:8). The writer to the Hebrews counsels, "Keep your life free from love of money, and be content with what you have; for he has said, 'I will never fail you nor forsake you' " (Heb. 13:5). James blames killings and wars on the lust for possessions: "You desire and do not have; so you kill. And you covet and cannot obtain; so you fight and wage war" (James 4:1, 2). Paul calls covetousness idolatry and commands stern discipline against anyone guilty of greed (Eph. 5:5; 1 Cor. 5:11). He lists greed alongside adultery and thievery and declares that those who live in such things will not inherit the kingdom of God. Paul counsels the wealthy not to trust in their wealth, but in God, and to share generously with others (1 Tim. 6:17–19).

Having said all this, I must hasten to add that God intends that we should have adequate material provision. There is misery today from a simple lack of provision just as there is misery when people try to make a life out of provision. Forced poverty is evil and should be renounced. Nor does the Bible condone an extreme asceticism. Scripture declares consistently and forcefully that the creation is good and to be enjoyed. Asceticism makes an unbiblical division between a good spiritual world and an evil material world and so finds salvation in paying as little attention as possible to the physical realm of existence.

Asceticism and simplicity are mutually incompatible. Occasional superficial similarities in practice must never obscure the radical difference between the two. Asceticism renounces possessions. Simplicity sets possessions in proper perspective. Asceticism finds no place for a "land flowing with milk and honey." Simplicity rejoices in this gracious provision from the hand of God. Asceticism finds contentment only when it is abased. Simplicity knows contentment in both abasement and abounding (Phil. 4:12).

Simplicity is the only thing that sufficiently reorients our lives so that possessions can be genuinely enjoyed without destroying us. Without simplicity we will either capitulate to the "mammon" spirit of this present evil age, or we will fall into an un-Christian legalistic asceticism. Both lead to idolatry. Both are spiritually lethal.

Descriptions of the abundant material provision God gives his people abound in Scripture. "For the Lord your God is bringing you into a good land . . . a land . . . in which you will lack nothing" (Deut. 8:7–9). Warnings about the danger of provisions that are not kept in proper perspective also abound. "Beware lest you say in your heart, 'My power and the might of my hand have gotten me this wealth' " (Deut. 8:17).

The Spiritual Discipline of simplicity provides the needed perspective. Simplicity sets us free to receive the provision of God as a gift that is not ours to keep and can be freely shared with others. Once we recognize that the Bible denounces the materialist and the ascetic with equal vigor, we are prepared to turn our attention to the framing of a Christian understanding of simplicity.

A Place to Stand

Archimedes once declared, "Give me a place to stand and I will move the earth." Such a focal point is important in every Discipline but is acutely so with simplicity. Of all the Disciplines simplicity is the most visible and therefore the most open to corruption. The majority of Christians have never seriously wrestled with the problem of simplicity, conveniently ignoring Jesus' many words on the subject. The reason is simple: this Discipline directly challenges our vested interests in an affluent life-style. But those who take the biblical teaching on simplicity seriously are faced with severe temptations toward legalism. In the earnest attempt to give concrete expression to Jesus' economic teaching, it is easy to mistake our particular expression of the teaching for the teaching itself. We wear this attire or buy that kind of house and canonize our choices as the simple life. This danger gives special importance to finding and clearly articulating an Archimedian focal point for simplicity.

We have such a focal point in the words of Jesus: "Therefore I tell you, do not be anxious about your life, what you shall eat or what you shall drink, nor about your body, what you shall put on. Is not life more than food, and the body more than clothing? Look at the birds of the air: they neither sow nor reap nor gather into barns, and yet your heavenly Father feeds them. Are you not of more value than they? And which of you by being anxious can add one cubit to his span of life? And why are you anxious about clothing? Consider the lilies of the field, how they grow; they neither toil nor spin; yet I tell you, even Solomon in all his glory was not arrayed like one of these. But if God so clothes the grass of the field, which today is alive and tomorrow is thrown into the oven, will he not much more clothe you, O men of little faith? Therefore do not be anxious, saying, 'What shall we eat?' or 'What shall we drink?' or 'What shall we wear?' For the Gentiles seek all these things; and your heavenly Father knows that you need them all. *But seek first his kingdom and his righteousness, and all these things shall be yours as well*" (Matt. 6:25–33, [italics added]).

The central point for the Discipline of simplicity is to seek the kingdom of God and the righteousness of his kingdom *first* and then everything necessary will come in its proper order. It is impossible to overestimate the importance of Jesus' insight at this point. Everything hinges upon maintaining the "first" thing as first. Nothing must come before the kingdom of God, including the desire for a simple life-style.

Simplicity itself becomes idolatry when it takes precedence over seeking the kingdom. In a particularly penetrating comment on this passage of Scripture, Søren Kierkegaard considers what sort of effort could be made to pursue the kingdom of God. Should a person get a suitable job in order to exert a virtuous influence? His answer: no, we must *first* seek God's kingdom. Then should we give away all our money to feed the poor? Again the answer: no, we must *first* seek God's kingdom.

Well, then perhaps we are to go out and preach this truth to the world that people are to seek first God's kingdom? Once again the answer is a resounding: no, we are *first* to seek the kingdom of God. Kierkegaard concludes, "Then in a certain sense it is nothing I shall do. Yes, certainly, in a certain sense it is nothing, become nothing before God, learn to keep silent; in this silence is the beginning, which is, *first* to seek God's Kingdom."[4]

Focus upon the kingdom produces the inward reality, and without the inward reality we will degenerate into legalistic trivia. Nothing else can be central. The desire to get out of the rat race cannot be central, the redistribution of the world's wealth cannot be central, the concern for ecology cannot be central. Seeking *first* God's kingdom and the righteousness, both personal and social, of that kingdom is the only thing that can be central in the Spiritual Discipline of simplicity.

The person who does not seek the kingdom first does not seek it at all. Worthy as all other concerns may be, the moment *they* become the focus of our efforts they become idolatry. To center on them will inevitably draw us into declaring that our particular activity *is* Christian simplicity. And, in fact, when the kingdom of God is genuinely placed first, ecological concerns, the poor, the equitable distribution of wealth, and many other things will be given their proper attention.

As Jesus made clear in our central passage, freedom from anxiety is one of the inward evidences of seeking first the kingdom of God. The inward reality of simplicity involves a life of joyful unconcern for possessions. Neither the greedy nor the miserly know this liberty. It has nothing to do with abundance of possessions or their lack. It is an inward spirit of trust. The sheer fact that a person is living without things is no guarantee that he or she is living in simplicity. Paul taught us that the love of money is the root of all evil, and I have discovered that often those who have it the least love it the most. It is possible for a person to be developing an outward life-style of simplicity and to be filled with anxiety. Conversely, wealth does not bring freedom from anxiety. Kierkegaard writes, ". . . riches and abundance come hypocritically clad in sheep's clothing pretending to be security against anxieties and they become then the object of anxiety . . . they secure a man against anxieties just about as well as the wolf which is put to tending the sheep secures them . . . against the wolf."[5]

Freedom from anxiety is characterized by three inner attitudes. If what we have we receive as a gift, and if what we have is to be cared for by God, and if what we have is available to others, then we will possess freedom from anxiety. *This is the inward reality of simplicity.* However, if what we have we believe we have gotten, and if what we have we believe we must hold onto, and if what we have is not available to others, then we will live in anxiety. Such persons will never know simplicity regardless of the outward contortions they may put themselves through in order to live "the simple life."

To receive what we have as a gift from God is the first inner attitude of simplicity. We work but we know that it is not our work that gives us what we have. We live by grace even when it comes to "daily bread." We are dependent upon God for the simplest elements of life: air, water, sun. What we have is not the result of our labor, but of the gracious care of God. When we are tempted to think that what we own is the result of our personal efforts, it takes only a little drought or a small accident to show us once again how utterly dependent we are for everything.

To know that it is God's business, and not ours, to care for what we have is the second inner attitude of simplicity. God is able to protect what we possess. We can trust him. Does that mean that we should never take the keys out of the car or lock the door? Of course not. But we know that the lock on the door is not what protects the house. It is only common sense to take normal precautions, but if we believe that precaution itself protects us and our goods, we will be riddled with anxiety. There simply is no such thing as "burglar proof" precaution. Obviously, these matters are not restricted to possessions but include such things as our reputation and our employment. Simplicity means the freedom to trust God for these (and all) things.

To have our goods available to others marks the third inner attitude of simplicity. If our goods are not available to the community when it is clearly right and good, then they are stolen goods. The reason we find such an idea so difficult is our fear of the future. We cling to our possessions rather than sharing them because we are anxious about tomorrow. But if we truly believe that God is who Jesus says he is, then we do not need to be afraid. When we come to see God as the almighty Creator *and* our loving Father, we can share because we know that he will care for us. If someone is in need, we are free to help them. Again, ordinary common sense will define the parameters of our sharing and save us from foolishness.

When we are seeking first the kingdom of God, these three attitudes will characterize our lives. Taken together they define what Jesus means by "do not be anxious." They comprise the inner reality of Christian simplicity. And we can be certain that when we live this way the "all these things" that are necessary to carry on human life adequately will be ours as well.

The Outward Expression of Simplicity

To describe simplicity only as an inner reality is to say something false. The inner reality is not a reality until there is an outward expression. To experience the liberating spirit of simplicity *will* affect how we live. As I have warned earlier, every attempt to give specific application to simplicity runs the risk of a deterioration into legalism. It is a risk, however, that we must take, for to refuse to discuss specifics would banish the Discipline to the theoretical. After all, the writers of Scripture constantly took that risk.* And so I follow their lead and suggest ten controlling principles for the outward expression of simplicity. They should never be viewed as laws but as only one attempt to flesh out the meaning of simplicity for today.

First, buy things for their usefulness rather than their status. Cars should be bought for their utility, not their prestige. Consider riding a bicycle. When you are considering an apartment, a condominium, or a house, thought should be given to livability rather than how much it will impress others. Don't have more living space than is reasonable. After all, who needs seven rooms for two people?

Consider your clothes. Most people have no need for more clothes. They buy more not because they need clothes, but because they want to keep up with the fashions. Hang the fashions! Buy what you need. Wear your clothes until they are worn out. Stop trying to impress people with your clothes and impress them with your life. If it is practical in your situation, learn the joy of making clothes. And for God's sake (and I mean that quite literally) have clothes that are practical rather than ornamental. John Wesley writes, "As . . . for apparel, I buy the most lasting and, in general, the plainest I can. I buy no furniture but what is necessary and cheap."[6]

Second, reject anything that is producing an addiction in you. Learn to distinguish between a real psychological need, like cheerful surroundings, and an addiction. Eliminate or cut down on the use of addictive, nonnutritional drinks: alcohol, coffee, tea, Coca-Cola, and so on. Chocolate has become a serious addiction for many people. If you have become addicted to television, by all means sell your set or give it away. Any of the media that you find you cannot do without, get rid of:

---

*It is sad to realize that often the attempt of Scripture to apply the principle of simplicity to a given culture has been universalized by succeeding generations and turned into soul-killing laws. Witness, for example, the laws against Christians braiding their hair or wearing rings because Peter had said to the people of his day. "Let not yours be the outward adorning with braiding of hair, decoration of gold, and wearing of robes" (1 Pet. 3:3).

radios, stereos, magazines, videos, newspapers, books. If money has a grip on your heart, give some away and feel the inner release. Simplicity is freedom, not slavery. Refuse to be a slave to anything but God.

Remember, an addiction, by its very nature, is something that is beyond your control. Resolves of the will alone are useless in defeating a true addiction. You cannot just decide to be free of it. But you can decide to open this corner of your life to the forgiving grace and healing power of God. You can decide to allow loving friends who know the ways of prayer to stand with you. You can decide to live simply one day at a time in quiet dependence upon God's intervention.

How do you discern an addiction? Very simply, you watch for undisciplined compulsions. A student friend told me about one morning when he went out to get his newspaper and found it missing. He panicked, wondering how he could possibly start the day without the newspaper. Then he noticed a morning paper in his neighbor's yard, and he began to plot how he could sneak over and steal it. Immediately he realized that he was dealing with a genuine addiction. He rushed inside and called the newspaper office to cancel his subscription. The receptionist, obviously filling out a form, asked courteously, "Why are you canceling your subscription to the newspaper?" My friend blurted out, "Because I'm addicted!" Undaunted, the receptionist replied, "Would you like to cancel your entire subscription or would you like to keep the Sunday edition?" to which he exclaimed, "No, I'm going cold turkey!" Now, obviously not everyone should cancel their subscription to the newspaper, but for this young man it was an important act.

Third, develop a habit of giving things away. If you find that you are becoming attached to some possession, consider giving it to someone who needs it. I still remember the Christmas I decided that rather than buying or even making an item, I would give away something that meant a lot to me. My motive was selfish: I wanted to know the liberation that comes from even this simple act of voluntary poverty. The gift was a ten-speed bike. As I went to the person's home to deliver the present, I remember singing with new meaning the worship chorus, "Freely, freely you have received; freely, freely give." When my son Nathan was six years old he heard of a classmate who needed a lunch pail and asked me if he could give him his own lunch pail. Hallelujah!

De-accumulate! Masses of things that are not needed complicate life. They must be sorted and stored and dusted and re-sorted and re-stored *ad nauseam*. Most of us could get rid of half our possessions without any serious sacrifice. We would do well to follow the counsel of Thoreau: "Simplify, simplify."

Fourth, refuse to be propagandized by the custodians of modern gadgetry. Timesaving devices almost never save time. Beware of the promise, "It will pay for itself in six months." Most gadgets are built to break down and wear out and so complicate our lives rather than enhance them. This problem is a plague in the toy industry. Children do not need to be entertained by dolls that cry, eat, wet, sweat, and spit. An old rag doll can be more enjoyable and more lasting. Often children find more joy in playing with old pots and pans than with the latest space set. Look for toys that are educational and durable. Make some yourself.

Usually gadgets are an unnecessary drain on the energy resources of the world. The United States has less than six percent of the world's population, but consumes about thirty-three percent of the world's energy. Air conditioners in the United States alone use the same amount of energy as does the entire country of China.[7] Environmental responsibility alone should keep us from buying the majority of the gadgets produced today.

Propagandists try to convince us that because the newest model of this or that has a new feature (trinket?), we must sell the old one and buy the new one. Sewing machines have new stitches, stereos have new buttons, cars have new designs. Such media dogma needs to be carefully scrutinized. Often "new" features seduce us into buying what we do not need.

Probably that refrigerator will serve us quite well for the rest of our lives even without the automatic ice maker and the fancy exterior.

Fifth, learn to enjoy things without owning them. Owning things is an obsession in our culture. If we own it, we feel we can control it; and if we can control it, we feel it will give us more pleasure. The idea is an illusion. Many things in life can be enjoyed without possessing or controlling them. Share things. Enjoy the beach without feeling you have to buy a piece of it. Enjoy public parks and libraries.

Sixth, develop a deeper appreciation for the creation. Get close to the earth. Walk whenever you can. Listen to the birds. Enjoy the texture of grass and leaves. Smell the flowers. Marvel in the rich colors everywhere. Simplicity means to discover once again that "the earth is the LORD'S and the fullness thereof" (Ps. 24:1).

Seventh, look with a healthy skepticism at all "buy now, pay later" schemes. They are a trap and only deepen your bondage. Both Old and New Testaments condemn usury for good reasons. ("Usury" in the Bible is not used in the modern sense of exorbitant interest; it referred to any kind of interest at all.) Charging interest was viewed as an unbrotherly exploitation of another's misfortune, hence a denial of community. Jesus denounced usury as a sign of the old life and admonished his disciples to "lend, expecting nothing in return" (Luke 6:35).

These words of Scripture should not be elevated into some kind of universal law obligatory upon all cultures at all times. But neither should they be thought of as totally irrelevant to modern society. Behind these biblical injunctions stand centuries of accumulated wisdom (and perhaps some bitter experiences!). Certainly prudence, as well as simplicity, demands that we use extreme caution before incurring debt.

Eighth, obey Jesus' instructions about plain, honest speech. "Let what you say be simply 'Yes' or 'No'; anything more than this comes from evil" (Matt. 5:37). If you consent to do a task, do it. Avoid flattery and half-truths. Make honesty and integrity the distinguishing characteristics of your speech. Reject jargon and abstract speculation whose purpose is to obscure and impress rather than to illuminate and inform.

Plain speech is difficult because we so seldom live out of the divine Center, so seldom respond only to heavenly promptings. Often fear of what others may think or a hundred other motives determine our "yes" or "no" rather than obedience to divine urgings. Then if a more attractive opportunity arises we quickly reverse our decision. But if our speech comes out of obedience to the divine Center, we will find no reason to turn our "yes" into "no" and our "no" into "yes." We will be living in simplicity of speech because our words will have only one Source. Søren Kierkegaard writes: "If thou art absolutely obedient to God, then there is no ambiguity in thee and . . . thou art mere simplicity before God. . . . One thing there is which all Satan's cunning and all the snares of temptation cannot take by surprise, and that is simplicity."[8]

Ninth, reject anything that breeds the oppression of others. Perhaps no person has more fully embodied this principle than the eighteenth-century Quaker tailor John Woolman. His famous *Journal* is redundant with tender references to his desire to live so as not to oppress others. "Here I was led into a close and laborious inquiry whether I . . . kept clear from all things which tended to stir up or were connected with wars; . . . my heart was deeply concerned that in [the] future I might in all things keep steadily to the pure truth, and live and walk in the plainness and simplicity of a sincere follower of Christ. . . . And here luxury and covetousness, with the numerous oppressions and other evils attending them, appeared very afflicting to me. . . ."[9] This is one of the most difficult and sensitive issues for us to face, but face it we must. Do we sip our coffee and eat our bananas at the expense of exploiting Latin American peasants? In a world of limited resources, does our lust for wealth mean the poverty of others? Should we buy products that are made by forcing people into dull assembly-line jobs? Do we enjoy hierarchical relationships in the company or factory that keep others under us? Do we oppress our children or spouse because we feel certain tasks are beneath us?

Often our oppression is tinged with racism, sexism, and nationalism. The color of the skin still affects one's position in the company. The sex of a job applicant still affects the salary. The national origin of a person still affects the way he or she is perceived. May God give us prophets today who, like John Woolman, will call us "from the desire of wealth" so that we may be able to "break the yoke of oppression."[10]

Tenth, shun anything that distracts you from seeking first the kingdom of God. It is so easy to lose focus in the pursuit of legitimate, even good things. Job, position, status, family, friends, security—these and many more can all too quickly become the center of attention. George Fox warns, ". . . there is the danger and the temptation to you, of drawing your minds into your business, and clogging them with it; so that ye can hardly do anything to the service of God . . . and your minds will go into the things, and not over the things. . . . And then, if the Lord God cross you, and stop you by sea and land, and take [your] goods and customs from you, that your minds should not be cumbered, then that mind that is cumbered, will fret, being out of the power of God."[11]

May God give you—and me—the courage, the wisdom, the strength always to hold the kingdom of God as the number-one priority of our lives. To do so is to live in simplicity.*

---

*For those looking for a fuller discussion of Christian simplicity see my book, *Freedom of Simplicity* (San Francisco: Harper & Row, 1981).

7. The Discipline of Solitude

Settle yourself in solitude and you will come upon Him in yourself.

—TERESA OF ÁVILA

Jesus calls us from loneliness to solitude. The fear of being left alone petrifies people. A new child in the neighborhood sobs to her mother, "No one ever plays with me." A college freshman yearns for his high school days when he was the center of attention: "Now, I'm a nobody." A business executive sits dejected in her office, powerful, yet alone. An old woman lies in a nursing home waiting to go "Home."

Our fear of being alone drives us to noise and crowds. We keep up a constant stream of words even if they are inane. We buy radios that strap to our wrists or fit over our ears so that, if no one else is around, at least we are not condemned to silence. T. S. Eliot analyzes our culture well when he writes, "Where shall the world be found, where will the word resound? Not here, there is not enough silence."[1]

But loneliness or clatter are not our only alternatives. We can cultivate an inner solitude and silence that sets us free from loneliness and fear. Loneliness is inner emptiness. Solitude is inner fulfillment.

Solitude is more a state of mind and heart than it is a place. There is a solitude of the heart that can be maintained at all times. Crowds, or the lack of them, have little to do with this inward attentiveness. It is quite possible to be a desert hermit and never experience solitude. But if we possess inward solitude we do not fear being alone, for we know that we are not alone. Neither do we fear being with others, for they do not control us. In the midst of noise and confusion we are settled into a deep inner silence. Whether alone or among people, we always carry with us a portable sanctuary of the heart.

Inward solitude has outward manifestations. There is the freedom to be alone, not in order to be away from people but in order to hear the divine Whisper better. Jesus lived in inward "heart solitude." He also frequently experienced outward solitude. He inaugurated his ministry by spending forty days alone in the desert (Matt. 4:1–11). Before he chose the twelve he spent the entire night alone in the desert hills (Luke 6:12). When he received the news of John the Baptist's death, he "withdrew from there in a boat to a lonely place apart" (Matt. 14:13). After the miraculous feeding of the five thousand Jesus "went up into the hills by himself . . ." (Matt. 14:23). Following a long night of work, "in the morning, a great while before day, he rose and went out to a lonely place . . ." (Mark 1:35). When the twelve returned from a preaching and healing mission, Jesus instructed them, "Come away by yourselves to a lonely place" (Mark 6:31). Following the healing of a leper Jesus "withdrew to the wilderness and prayed" (Luke 5:16). With three disciples he sought out the silence of a lonely mountain as the stage for the transfiguration (Matt. 17:1–9). As he prepared for his highest and most holy work, Jesus sought the solitude of the garden of Gethsemane (Matt. 26:36–46). I could go on, but perhaps this is sufficient to show that the seeking out of solitary places was a regular practice for Jesus. So it should be for us.

Dietrich Bonhoeffer in *Life Together* titled one of his chapters "The Day Together" and the following chapter "The Day Alone." Both are essential for spiritual success. He writes, "Let him who cannot be alone beware of community. . . . Let him who is not in community beware of being alone. . . . Each by itself has profound pitfalls and perils. One who wants fellowship without solitude plunges into the void of words and feelings, and one who seeks solitude without fellowship perishes in the abyss of vanity, self-infatuation, and despair."[2]

Therefore, we must seek out the recreating stillness of solitude if we want to be with others meaningfully. We must seek the fellowship and accountability of others if we want to be alone safely. We must cultivate both if we are to live in obedience.

Solitude and Silence

Without silence there is no solitude. Though silence sometimes involves the absence of speech, it always involves the act of listening. Simply to refrain from talking, without a heart listening to God, is not silence. "A day filled with noise and voices can be a day of silence, if the noises become for us the echo of the presence of God, if the voices are, for us, messages and solicitations of God. When we speak of ourselves and are filled with ourselves, we leave silence behind. When we repeat the intimate words of God that he has left within us, our silence remains intact."[3]

We must understand the connection between inner solitude and inner silence; they are inseparable. All the masters of the interior life speak of the two in the same breath. For example, *The Imitation of Christ*, which has been the unchallenged masterpiece of devotional literature for five hundred years, has a section titled "On the Love of Solitude and Silence." Dietrich Bonhoeffer makes the two an inseparable whole in *Life Together* as does Thomas Merton in *Thoughts in Solitude*. In fact, I wrestled for some time trying to decide whether to title this chapter the Discipline of solitude or the Discipline of silence, so closely connected are the two in the great devotional literature. Of necessity, therefore, we must come to understand and experience the transforming power of silence if we are to know solitude.

There is an old proverb to the effect that "all those who open their mouths, close their eyes!" The purpose of silence and solitude is to be able to see and hear. Control rather than no noise is the key to silence. James saw clearly that the person who could control his tongue is perfect (James 3:1–12). Under the Discipline of silence and solitude we learn when to speak and when to refrain from speaking. The person who views the Disciplines as laws will always turn silence into an absurdity: "I'll not speak for the next forty days!" This is always a severe temptation to any true disciple who wants to live under silence and solitude. Thomas à Kempis writes, "It is easier to be silent altogether than to speak with moderation."[4] The wise preacher of Ecclesiastes says that there is "a time to keep silence and a time to speak" (*Eccles. 3:7*). Control is the key.

James' analogies of the rudder and the bridle suggest to us that the tongue guides as well as controls. The tongue guides our course in many ways. If we tell a lie, we are led to telling more lies to cover up the first lie. Soon we are forced to behave in a certain way in order to give credence to the lie. No wonder James declares that "the tongue is a fire" (*James 3:6*).

The disciplined person is the person who can do what needs to be done when it needs to be done. The mark of a championship basketball team is a team that can score points when they are needed. Most of us can get the ball into the hoop eventually, but we can't do it when it is needed. Likewise, a person who is under the Discipline of silence is a person who can say what needs to be said when it needs to be said. "A word fitly spoken is like apples of gold in a setting of silver" (*Prov. 25:11*). If we are silent when we should speak, we are not living in the Discipline of silence. If we speak when we should be silent, we again miss the mark.

The Sacrifice of Fools

In Ecclesiastes we read, "To draw near to listen is better than to offer the sacrifice of fools" (*Eccles. 5:1*). The sacrifice of fools is humanly initiated religious talk. The preacher continues, "Be not rash with your mouth, nor let your heart be hasty to utter a word before God, for God is in heaven, and you upon earth; therefore let your words be few" (*Eccles. 5:2*).

When Jesus took Peter, James, and John up to the mountain and was transfigured before them, Moses and Elijah appeared and carried on a conversation with Jesus. The Greek text goes on to say, "And *answering*, Peter said to them . . . if you will I will make here three shelters . . ." (Matt. 17:4, [italics added]). That is so telling. No one was even speaking to Peter. He was offering the sacrifice of fools.

John Woolman's *Journal* contains a moving and tender account of learning control over the tongue. His words are so graphic that they are best quoted in full:

"I went to meetings in an awful frame of mind, and endeavored to be inwardly acquainted with the language of the true Shepherd. One day, being under a strong exercise of spirit, I stood up and said some words in a meeting; but not keeping close to the Divine opening, I said more than was required of me. Being soon sensible of my error, I was afflicted in mind some weeks, without any light or comfort, even to that degree that I could not take satisfaction in anything. I remembered God, and was troubled, and in the depth of my distress he had pity upon me, and sent the Comforter. I then felt forgiveness for my offence; my mind became calm and quiet, and I was truly thankful to my gracious Redeemer for his mercies. About six weeks after this, feeling the spring of Divine love opened, and a concern to speak, I said a few words in a meeting, in which I found peace. Being thus humbled and disciplined under the cross, my understanding became more strengthened to distinguish the pure spirit which inwardly moves upon the heart, and which taught me to wait in silence sometimes many weeks together, until I felt that rise which prepares the creature to stand like a trumpet, through which the Lord speaks to his flock."[5]

What a description of the learning process one goes through in the Discipline of silence! Of particular significance was Woolman's increased ability from this experience to "distinguish the pure spirit which inwardly moves upon the heart."

One reason we can hardly bear to remain silent is that it makes us feel so helpless. We are so accustomed to relying upon words to manage and control others. If we are silent, who will take control? God will take control, but we will never let him take control until we trust him. Silence is intimately related to trust.

The tongue is our most powerful weapon of manipulation. A frantic stream of words flows from us because we are in a constant process of adjusting our public image. We fear so deeply what we think other people see in us that we talk in order to straighten out their understanding. If I have done some wrong thing (or even some right thing that I think you may misunderstand) and discover that you know about it, I will be very tempted to help you understand my action! Silence is one of the deepest Disciplines of the Spirit simply because it puts the stopper on all self-justification.

One of the fruits of silence is the freedom to let God be our justifier. We don't need to straighten others out. There is a story of a medieval monk who was being unjustly accused of certain offenses. One day he looked out his window and saw a dog biting and tearing on a rug that had been hung out to dry. As he watched, the Lord spoke to him saying, "That is what is happening to your reputation. But if you will trust me, I will care for you—reputation and all." Perhaps more than anything else, silence brings us to believe that God can care for us—"reputation and all."

George Fox often speaks of "the spirit of bondage" and how the world lays in that spirit. Frequently he identifies the spirit of bondage with the spirit of subservience to other human beings. In his *Journal* he speaks of "bringing people off of men," away from that spirit of bondage to law through other human beings. And silence is one way of bringing us into this liberation.

The tongue is a thermometer; it gives us our spiritual temperature. It is also a thermostat; it regulates our spiritual temperature. Control of the tongue can mean everything. Have we been set free so that we can hold our tongue? Bonhoeffer writes, "Real silence, real stillness, really holding one's tongue comes only as the sober consequence of spiritual stillness."[6] St. Dominic is reported to have visited St. Francis, and throughout the entire meeting neither spoke a single word. Only when we learn to be truly silent are we able to speak the word that is needed *when* it is needed.

Catherine de Haeck Doherty writes, "All in me is silent and . . . I am immersed in the silence of God."[7] It is in solitude that we come to experience the "silence of God" and so receive the inner silence that is the craving of our hearts.

The Dark Night of the Soul

To take seriously the Discipline of solitude will mean that at some point or points along the pilgrimage we will enter what St. John of the Cross vividly describes as "the dark night of the soul." The "dark night" to which he calls us is not something bad or destructive. On the contrary, it is an experience to be welcomed much as a sick person might welcome a surgery that promises health and well-being. The purpose of the darkness is not to punish or to afflict us. It is to set us free. It is a divine appointment, a privileged opportunity to draw close to the divine Center. St. John calls it "sheer grace," adding:

> O guiding night!
>   O night more lovely than the dawn!
> O night that has united
>   The Lover with His beloved,
> Transforming the beloved in her Lover.[8]

What does the dark night of the soul involve? We may have a sense of dryness, aloneness, even lostness. Any overdependence on the emotional life is stripped away. The notion, often heard today, that such experiences should be avoided and that we always should live in peace and comfort, joy, and celebration only betrays the fact that much contemporary experience is surface slush. The dark night is one of the ways God brings us into a hush, a stillness so that he may work an inner transformation upon the soul.

How is this dark night expressed in daily life? When solitude is seriously pursued, there is usually a flush of initial success and then an inevitable letdown—and with it a desire to abandon the pursuit altogether. Feelings leave and there is the sense that we are not getting through to God. St. John of the Cross describes it this way, ". . . the darkness of the soul mentioned here . . . puts the sensory and spiritual appetites to sleep. . . . It binds the imagination and impedes it from doing any good discursive work. It makes the memory cease, the intellect become dark and unable to understand anything, and hence it causes the will also to become arid and constrained, and all the faculties empty and useless. And over all this hangs a dense and burdensome cloud which afflicts the soul and keeps it withdrawn from God."⁹

Twice in his poem *"Canciones del Alma"* St. John of the Cross uses the phrase, "My house being now all stilled."¹⁰ In this graphic line he indicates the importance of allowing all the physical, emotional, psychological, even spiritual senses to be silenced. Every distraction of the body, mind, and spirit must be put into a kind of suspended animation before this deep work of God upon the soul can occur. It is like an operation in which the anesthetic must take effect before the surgery can be performed. There comes inner silence, peace, stillness. During such a time Bible reading, sermons, intellectual debate— all fail to move or excite us.

When God lovingly draws us into a dark night of the soul, there is often a temptation to seek release from it and to blame everyone and everything for our inner dullness. The preacher is such a bore. The hymn singing is too weak. The worship service is so dull. We may begin to look around for another church or a new experience to give us "spiritual goose bumps." This is a serious mistake. Recognize the dark night for what it is. Be grateful that God is lovingly drawing you away from every distraction so that you can see him clearly. Rather than chafing and fighting, become still and wait.

I am not referring here to the dullness to spiritual things that comes as a result of sin or disobedience, but I am speaking of the person who is seeking hard after God and who harbors no known sin in his heart.

> Who among you fears the LORD
>   and obeys the voice of his servant,
> *who walks in darkness*
>   *and has no light,*
> yet trusts in the name of the LORD
>   and relies upon his God? (Isa. 50:10, [italics added])

The point of the biblical passage is that it is quite possible to fear, obey, trust, and rely upon the Lord and still "walk in darkness and have no light." We are living in obedience but we have entered a dark night of the soul.

St. John of the Cross indicates that during this experience there is a gracious protection from vices and a wonderful advance in the things of the kingdom of God. ". . . a person at the time of these darknesses . . . will see clearly how little the appetites and faculties are distracted with useless and harmful things and how secure he is from vainglory, from pride and presumption, from an empty and false joy, and from many other evils. By walking in darkness the soul . . . advances rapidly, because it thus gains the virtues."[11]

What should we do during such a time of inward darkness? First, disregard the advice of well-meaning friends to snap out of it. They do not understand what is occurring. Our age is so ignorant of such things that I recommend that you not even talk about these matters. Above all, do not try to explain or justify why you may be "out of sorts." God is your justifier; rest your case with him. If you can actually withdraw to a "desert place" for a season, do so. If not, go about your daily tasks. But whether in the "desert" or at home, hold in your heart a deep, inner, listening silence and there be still until the work of solitude is done.

Perhaps St. John of the Cross has been leading us into deeper waters than we care to go. Certainly he is talking about a realm that most of us see only "through a glass darkly." Yet we do not need to censure ourselves for our timidity to scale these snowy peaks of the soul. These matters are best approached cautiously. But perhaps he has stirred within us a drawing toward higher and deeper experiences, no matter how slight the tug. It is like opening the door of our lives ever so slightly to this realm. That is all God asks, and all he needs.

To conclude our journey into the dark night of the soul, let us ponder these powerful words of our spiritual mentor: "Oh, then, spiritual soul, when you see your appetites darkened, your inclinations dry and constrained, your faculties incapacitated for any interior exercise, do not be afflicted; think of this as a grace, since God is freeing you from yourself and taking from you your own activity."[12]

Steps into Solitude

The Spiritual Disciplines are things that we do. We must never lose sight of this fact. It is one thing to talk piously about "the solitude of the heart," but if that does not somehow work its way into our experience, then we have missed the point of the Disciplines. We are dealing with actions, not merely states of mind. It is not enough to say, "Well, I am most certainly in possession of inner solitude and silence; there is nothing that I need to do." All those who have come into the living silences have done certain things, have ordered their lives in a particular way so as to receive this "peace that passes all understanding." If we are to succeed, we must pass beyond the theoretical into life situations.

What are some steps into solitude? The first thing we can do is to take advantage of the "little solitudes" that fill our day. Consider the solitude of those early morning moments in bed before the family awakens. Think of the solitude of a morning cup of coffee before beginning the work of the day. There is the solitude of bumper-to-bumper traffic during the freeway rush hour. There can be little moments of rest and refreshment when we turn a corner and see a flower or a tree. Instead of vocal prayer before a meal consider inviting everyone to join into a few moments of gathered silence. Once while driving a carload of chattering children and adults, I exclaimed, "Let's play a game and see if everyone can be absolutely quiet until we reach the airport" (about five minutes away). It worked, blessedly so. Find new joy and meaning in the little walk from the subway to your apartment. Slip outside just before bed and taste the silent night.

These tiny snatches of time are often lost to us. What a pity! They can and should be redeemed. They are times for inner quiet, for reorienting our lives like a compass needle. They are little moments that help us to be genuinely present where we are.

What else can we do? We can find or develop a "quiet place" designed for silence and solitude. Homes are being built constantly. Why not insist that a little inner sanctuary be put into the plans, a small place where any family member could go to be alone and silent? What's to stop us? The money? We build elaborate playrooms and family rooms and think it well worth the expense. Those who already own a home could consider enclosing a little section of the garage or patio. Those who live in an apartment could be creative and find other ways to allow for solitude. I know of one family that has a special chair; whenever anyone sits in it he or she is saying, "Please don't bother me, I want to be alone."

Let's find places outside the home: a spot in a park, a church sanctuary that is kept unlocked, even a storage closet somewhere. A retreat center near us has built a lovely one-person cabin specifically for private meditation and solitude. It is called "The Quiet Place." Churches invest millions of dollars in buildings. How about constructing one place where an individual can come to be alone for several days? Catherine de Haeck Doherty has pioneered in developing "Poustinias" (a Russian word meaning "desert") in North America. These are places specifically designed for solitude and silence.*

In the chapter on study we considered the importance of observing ourselves to see how often our speech is a frantic attempt to explain and justify our actions. Having seen this in ourselves, let's experiment with doing deeds without any words of explanation whatever. We note our sense of fear that people will misunderstand why we have done what we have done. We seek to allow God to be our justifier.

Let's discipline ourselves so that our words are few and full. Let's become known as people who have something to say when we speak. Let's maintain plain speech: do what we say we will do. "It is better that you should not vow than that you should vow and not pay" (Eccles. 5:5). When our tongue is under our authority the words of Bonhoeffer become true of us: "Much that is unnecessary remains unsaid. But the essential and the helpful thing can be said in a few words."[13]

Go another step. Try to live one entire day without words at all. Do it not as a law, but as an experiment. Note your feelings of helplessness and excessive dependence upon words to communicate. Try to find new ways to relate to others that are not dependent upon words. Enjoy, savor the day. Learn from it.

Four times a year withdraw for three to four hours for the purpose of reorienting your life goals. This can easily be done in one evening. Stay late at your office or do it at home or find a quiet corner in a public library. Reevaluate your goals and objectives in life. What do you want to have accomplished one year from now? Ten years from now? Our tendency is to overestimate what we can accomplish in one year and underestimate what we can accomplish in ten years. Set realistic goals but be willing to dream, to stretch. (This book was a dream in my mind for several years before it became a reality.) In the

---

*The story of the development of these centers is described in her book, *Poustinia: Christian Spirituality of the East for Western Man* (Notre Dame, IN: Ave Maria Press, 1974).

quiet of those brief hours, listen to the thunder of God's silence. Keep a journal record of what comes to you.

Reorientation and goal setting do not need to be cold and calculating as some suppose. Goals are discovered, not made. God delights in showing us exciting new alternatives for the future. Perhaps as you enter into a listening silence the joyful impression to learn how to weave or how to make pottery emerges. Does that sound too earthy, too unspiritual a goal? God is intently interested in such matters. Are you? Maybe you will want to learn and experience more about the spiritual gifts of miracles, healing, and tongues. Or you may do as one of my friends: spend large periods of time experiencing the gift of helps, learning to be a servant. Perhaps this next year you would like to read all the writings of C. S. Lewis or D. Elton Trueblood. Maybe five years from now you would like to be qualified to work with handicapped children. Does choosing these goals sound like a sales manipulation game? Of course not. It is merely setting a direction for your life. You are going to go somewhere so how much better to have a direction that has been set by communion with the divine Center.

Under the Discipline of study we explored the idea of study retreats of two to three days' duration. Such experiences are heightened when they are combined with an inner immersion into the silence of God. Like Jesus, we must go away from people so that we can be truly present when we are with people. Take a retreat once a year with no other purpose in mind but solitude.

The fruit of solitude is increased sensitivity and compassion for others. There comes a new freedom to be with people. There is new attentiveness to their needs, new responsiveness to their hurts. Thomas Merton observes, "It is in deep solitude that I find the gentleness with which I can truly love my brothers. The more solitary I am the more affection I have for them. . . . Solitude and silence teach me to love my brothers for what they are, not for what they say."[14]

Don't you feel a tug, a yearning to sink down into the silence and solitude of God? Don't you long for something more? Doesn't every breath crave a deeper, fuller exposure to his Presence? It is the Discipline of solitude that will open the door. You are welcome to come in and "listen to God's speech in his wondrous, terrible, gentle, loving, all-embracing silence."[15]

8. The Discipline of Submission

A Christian is a perfectly free lord of all, subject to none. A Christian is a perfectly dutiful servant of all, subject to all.

—MARTIN LUTHER

Of all the Spiritual Disciplines none has been more abused than the Discipline of submission. Somehow the human species has an extraordinary knack for taking the best teaching and turning it to the worst ends. Nothing can put people into bondage like religion, and nothing in religion has done more to manipulate and destroy people than a deficient teaching on submission. Therefore, we must work our way through this Discipline with great care and discernment in order to ensure that we are the ministers of life, not death.

Every Discipline has its corresponding freedom. If I have schooled myself in the art of rhetoric, I am free to deliver a moving speech when the occasion requires it. Demosthenes was free to be an orator only because he had gone through the discipline of speaking above the ocean roar with pebbles in his mouth. The purpose of the Disciplines is freedom. Our aim is the freedom, not the Discipline. The moment we make the Discipline our central focus, we turn it into law and lose the corresponding freedom.

The Disciplines are for the purpose of realizing a greater good. In and of themselves they are of no value whatever. They have value only as a means of setting us before God so that he can give us the liberation we seek. The liberation is the end; the Disciplines are *merely* the means. They are not the answer; they only lead us to the Answer. We must clearly understand this limitation of the Disciplines if we are to avoid bondage.

Not only must we understand, but we need to underscore it to ourselves again and again so severe is our temptation to center on the Disciplines. Let us forever center on Christ and view the Spiritual Disciplines as a way of drawing us closer to his heart.

The Freedom in Submission

I said that every Discipline has its corresponding freedom. What freedom corresponds to submission? It is the ability to lay down the terrible burden of always needing to get our own way. The obsession to demand that things go the way we want them to go is one of the greatest bondages in human society today. People will spend weeks, months, even years in a perpetual stew because some little thing did not go as they wished. They will fuss and fume. They will get mad about it. They will act as if their very life hangs on the issue. They may even get an ulcer over it.

In the Discipline of submission we are released to drop the matter, to forget it. Frankly, most things in life are not nearly as important as we think they are. Our lives will not come to an end if this or that does not happen.

If you will watch these things, you will see, for example, that almost all church fights and splits occur because people do not have the freedom to give in to each other. We insist that a critical issue is at stake; we are fighting for a sacred principle. Perhaps this is the case. Usually it is not. Often we cannot stand to give in simply because it means that we will not get our own way. Only in submission are we enabled to bring this spirit to a place where it no longer controls us. Only submission can free us sufficiently to enable us to distinguish between genuine issues and stubborn self-will.

If we could only come to see that most things in life are not major issues, then we could hold them lightly. We discover that they are no "big deal." So often we say, "Well, I don't care," when what we really mean (and what we convey to others) is that we care a great deal. It is precisely here that silence fits in so well with all the other Disciplines. Usually the best way to handle most matters of submission is to say nothing. There is the need for an all-encompassing spirit of grace beyond any kind of language or action which sets others and ourselves free.

The biblical teaching on submission focuses primarily on the spirit with which we view other people. Scripture does not attempt to set forth a series of hierarchical relationships but to communicate to us an inner attitude of mutual subordination. Peter, for example, called upon the slaves of his day to live in submission to their masters (1 Pet. 2:18). The counsel seems unnecessary until we realize that it is quite possible for servants to obey their masters without living in a spirit of submission to them. Outwardly we can do what people ask and inwardly be in rebellion against them. This concern for a spirit of consideration toward others pervades the entire New Testament. The old covenant stipulated that we must not murder. Jesus, however, stressed that the real issue was the inner spirit of murder with which we view people. In the matter of submission the same is true; the real issue is the spirit of consideration and respect we have for each other.

In submission we are at last free to value other people. Their dreams and plans become important to us. We have entered into a new, wonderful, glorious freedom—the freedom to give up our own rights for the good of others. For the first time we can love people unconditionally. We have given up the right to demand that they return our love. No longer do we feel that we have to be treated in a certain way. We rejoice in their successes. We feel genuine sorrow in their failures. It is of little consequence that our plans are frustrated if their plans succeed. We discover that it is far better to serve our neighbor than to have our own way.

Do you know the liberation that comes from giving up your rights? It means you are set free from the seething anger and bitterness you feel when someone doesn't act toward you the way you think they should. It means that at last you are able to break that vicious law of commerce that says, "You scratch my back, I'll scratch your back; you bloody my nose, I'll bloody your nose." It means you are free to obey Jesus' command, "Love your enemies and pray for those who persecute you" *(Matt. 5:44)*. It means that for the first time you understand how it is possible to surrender the right to retaliate: "If any one strikes you on the right cheek, turn to him the other also" *(Matt. 5:39)*.

A Touchstone

You may have noticed that I have been approaching the matter of submission through the back door. I began by explaining what it does for us before defining what it is. This has been done for a purpose. Most of us have been exposed to such a mutilated form of biblical submission that either we have embraced the deformity or we have rejected the Discipline altogether. To do the former leads to self-hatred; to do the latter leads to self-glorification. Before we become hung on the horns of this dilemma, let's consider a third alternative.

The touchstone for the biblical understanding of submission is Jesus' astonishing statement, "If any man would come after me, let him deny himself and take up his cross and follow me" *(Mark 8:34)*. Almost instinctively we draw back from these words. We are much more comfortable with words like "self-fulfillment" and "self-actualization" than we are with the thought of "self-denial." (In reality, Jesus' teaching on self-denial is the only thing that will bring genuine self-fulfillment and self-actualization.) Self-denial conjures up in our minds all sorts of images of groveling and self-hatred. We imagine that it most certainly means the rejection of our individuality and will probably lead to various forms of self-mortification.

On the contrary, Jesus calls us to self-denial without self-hatred. Self-denial is simply a way of coming to understand that we do not have to have our own way. Our happiness is not dependent upon getting what we want.

Self-denial does not mean the loss of our identity as some suppose. Without our identity we could not even be subject to each other. Did Jesus lose his identity when he set his face toward Golgotha? Did Peter lose his identity when he responded to Jesus' cross-bearing command, "Follow me" *(John 21:19)*? Did Paul lose his identity when he committed himself to the One who had said, "I will show him how much he must suffer for the sake of my name" *(Acts 9:16)*? Of course not. We know that the opposite was true. They found their identity in the act of self-denial.

Self-denial is not the same thing as self-contempt. Self-contempt claims that we have no worth, and even if we do have worth, we should reject it. Self-denial declares that we are of infinite worth and shows us how to realize it. Self-contempt denies the goodness of the creation; self-denial affirms that it is indeed good. Jesus made the ability to love ourselves the prerequisite for our reaching out to others *(Matt. 22:39)*. Self-love and self-denial are not in conflict. More than once Jesus made it quite clear that self-denial is the only sure way to love ourselves. "He who finds his life will lose it, and he who loses his life for my sake will find it" *(Matt. 10:39)*.

Again, we must underscore that self-denial means the freedom to give way to others. It means to hold others' interests above our interests. In this way self-denial releases us from self-pity. When we live outside of self-denial, we demand that things go our way. When they do not, we revert to self-pity— "Poor me!" Outwardly we may submit but we do so in a spirit of martyrdom. This spirit of self-pity, of martyrdom, is a sure sign that the Discipline of submission has gone to seed. This is why self-denial is the foundation for submission; it saves us from self-indulgence.

Modern men and women find it extremely difficult to read the great devotional masters because they make such lavish use of the language of self-denial. It is hard for us to be open to the words of Thomas à Kempis, "To have no opinion of ourselves, and to think always well and highly of others, is great wisdom and perfection."[1] We struggle to listen to the words of Jesus, "If any man would come after me, let him deny himself and take up his cross and follow me" (Mark 8:34). Our difficulty is due primarily to the fact that we have failed to understand Jesus' teaching that the way to self-fulfillment is through self-denial. To save the life is to lose it; to lose it for Christ's sake is to save it (Mark 8:35). George Matheson set into the hymnody of the Church this wonderful paradox of fulfillment through self-denial:

> Make me a captive, Lord,
> And then I shall be free;
> Force me to render up my sword,
> And I shall conqueror be.
> I sink in life's alarms
> When by myself I stand;
> Imprison me within Thine arms,
> And strong shall be my hand.[2]

Perhaps the air has been sufficiently cleared so that we can look upon self-denial as the liberation that it really is. We must be convinced of this for, as has been stated, self-denial is the touchstone for the Discipline of submission.

Revolutionary Subordination as Taught by Jesus*

The most radical social teaching of Jesus was his total reversal of the contemporary notion of greatness. Leadership is found in becoming the servant of all. Power is discovered in submission. The foremost symbol of this radical servanthood is the cross. "He [Jesus] humbled himself and became obedient unto death, even death on a cross" (Phil. 2:8). But note this: Christ not only died a "cross-death," he lived a "cross-life." The way of the cross, the way of a suffering servant was essential to his

---

*I am indebted to John Howard Yoder for this term and for several of the ideas listed under it. His book, *The Politics of Jesus* (Grand Rapids, MI: Eerdmans, 1972), contains an excellent chapter on Revolutionary Subordination.

ministry. Jesus lived the cross-life in submission to all human beings. He was the servant of all. He flatly rejected the cultural givens of position and power when he said, "You are not to be called rabbi. . . . Neither be called masters . . ." (Matt. 23:8–10). Jesus shattered the customs of his day when he lived out the cross-life by taking women seriously and by being willing to meet with children. He lived the cross-life when he took a towel and washed the feet of his disciples. This Jesus who easily could have called down a legion of angels to his aid chose instead the cross-death of Calvary. Jesus' life was the cross-life of submission and service. Jesus' death was the cross-death of conquest by suffering.

It is impossible to overstate the revolutionary character of Jesus' life and teaching at this point. It did away with all the claims to privileged position and status. It called into being a whole new order of leadership. The cross-life of Jesus undermined all social orders based on power and self-interest.*

As I noted earlier, Jesus called his followers to live the cross-life. "If any man would come after me, let him deny himself and take up his cross and follow me" (Mark 8:34). He flatly told his disciples, "If any one would be first, he must be last of all and servant of all" (Mark 9:35). When Jesus immortalized the principle of the cross-life by washing the disciples' feet, he added, "I have given you an example, that you also should do as I have done to you" (John 13:15). The cross-life is the life of voluntary submission. The cross-life is the life of freely accepted servanthood.

---

*The Church today has failed to understand or, if it understands, has failed to obey the implications of the cross-life for human society. Guy Hershberger courageously explores some of these implications in his book, *The Way of the Cross in Human Relations* (Scottsdale, PA: Herald Press, 1958). He discusses how the way of servanthood should affect such issues as war, capitalism, trade unions, labor unions, materialism, employer-employee relations, race relations, and others. I am indebted to Hershberger for the term "cross-life."

Revolutionary Subordination as Taught in the Epistles

Jesus' example and call to follow the way of the cross in all human relationships form the basis for the teaching of the Epistles on submission. The apostle Paul grounds the imperative to the Church to "count others better than yourselves" in the submission and self-denial of the Lord for our salvation. "He . . . emptied himself, taking the form of a servant" (Phil. 2:4–7). The apostle Peter, in the middle of his instructions on submission, directly appeals to the example of Jesus as the reason for submission. "For to this you have been called, because Christ also suffered for you, leaving you an example, that you should follow in his steps. . . . When he was reviled, he did not revile in return; when he suffered, he did not threaten; but he trusted to him who judges justly" (1 Pet. 2:21–23). As a preface to the Ephesian *Haustafel** we read, "Be subject to one another *out of reverence for Christ*" (Eph. 5:21, [italics added]). The call for Christians to live the cross-life is rooted in the cross-life of Jesus himself.

The Discipline of submission has been terribly misconstrued and abused from failure to see this wider context. Submission is an ethical theme that runs the gamut of the New Testament. It is a posture obligatory upon *all* Christians: men as well as women, fathers as well as children, masters as well as slaves. We are commanded to live a life of submission because Jesus lived a life of submission, not because we are in a particular place or station in life. Self-denial is a posture fitting for all those who follow the crucified Lord. Everywhere in the *Haustafel* the one and only compelling reason for submission is the example of Jesus.

This singular rationale for submission is staggering when we compare it to other first-century writings. In them there was a

---

*A term coined by Martin Luther meaning literally "house-table," hence a table of rules for the Christian household. The *Haustafel* has come to be recognized as a particular literary form and can be found in Ephesians 5:21–6:9, Colossians 3:18–4:1, Titus 2:4–10, and 1 Peter 2:18–3:7.

constant appeal to submission because that was the way the gods had created things; it was one's station in life. Not a single New Testament writer appeals to submission on that basis. The teaching is revolutionary. They completely ignored all the contemporary customs of superordinate and subordinate and called everyone to "count others better than yourselves" (Phil. 2:3).

The Epistles first call to subordination those who, by virtue of the given culture, are already subordinate. "Wives, be subject to your husbands. . . . Children, obey your parents. . . . Slaves, obey in everything those who are your earthly masters . . ." (Col. 3:18–22 and parallels). The revolutionary thing about this teaching is that these people, to whom first-century culture afforded no choice at all, are addressed as free moral agents. Paul gave personal moral responsibility to those who had no legal or moral status in their culture. He made decision-makers of people who were forbidden to make decisions.

It is astonishing that Paul called them to subordination since they were already subordinate by virtue of their place in first-century culture. The only meaningful reason for such a command was the fact that by virtue of the gospel message they had come to see themselves as free from a subordinate status in society. The gospel had challenged all second-class citizenships, and they knew it. Paul urged voluntary subordination not because it was their station in life, but because it was "fitting in the Lord" (Col. 3:18).

This feature of addressing moral teaching to the cultural subordinates is also a radical contrast to the contemporary literature of the day. The Stoics, for example, addressed *only* the person on the top side of the social order, encouraging him to do a good job in the superordinate position he already saw as his place. But Paul spoke first to the people that his culture said should not even be addressed and called them to the cross-life of Jesus.

Next, the Epistles turned to the culturally dominant partner in the relationship and also called him to the cross-life of Jesus.

The imperative to subordination is reciprocal. "Husbands, love your wives. . . . Fathers, do not provoke your children. . . . Masters, treat your slaves justly and fairly . . ." (Col. 3:19–4:1 and parallels). Some most certainly will object that the command to the dominant partner does not use the language of submission. What we fail to see is how much submission those commands demanded of the dominant partner in his cultural setting. For a first-century husband, father, or master to obey Paul's injunction would make a dramatic difference in his behavior. The first-century wife, child, or slave would not need to change one whit to follow Paul's command. If anything, the sting of the teaching falls upon the dominant partner.[3]

Further, we need to see that these imperatives to husbands, fathers, and masters constitute another form of self-denial. They are just another set of words to convey the same truth, namely, that we can be set free from the need to have things our own way. If a husband loves his wife, he will live in consideration of her needs. He will be willing to give in to her. He will be free to regard her as more important than his own needs. He will be able to regard his children as more important than his own needs (Phil. 2:3).

In Ephesians Paul exhorts slaves to live in a spirit of joyful, voluntary, willing service to their earthly masters. Then he exhorts masters, "Do the same to them" (Eph. 6:9). Such a thought was incredible in first-century society. Slaves were chattel, not human beings. Yet Paul with divine authority counsels masters to give way to the needs of their slaves.

Perhaps the most perfect illustration of revolutionary subordination is found in Paul's tiny letter to Philemon. Onesimus, Philemon's runaway slave, had become a Christian. He was returning voluntarily to Philemon as part of what it meant for him to be a disciple of Christ. Paul urges Philemon to welcome Onesimus "no longer as a slave but more than a slave, as a beloved brother . . ." (Philem. 16). John Yoder remarks, "This amounts to Paul's instructing Philemon, in the kind of non-coercive instruction which is fitting for a Christian brother, . . .

, that Onesimus is to be set free."⁴ Onesimus was to be subordinate to Philemon by returning. Philemon was to be subordinate to Onesimus by setting him free. Both were to be mutually subordinate out of reverence for Christ (Eph. 5:21).

The Epistles did not consecrate the existing hierarchical social structure. By making the command to subordination universal they relativized and undercut it. They called for Christians to live as citizens of a new order, and the most fundamental feature of this new order is universal subordination.

The Limits of Submission

The limits of the Discipline of submission are at the points at which it becomes destructive. It then becomes a denial of the law of love as taught by Jesus and is an affront to genuine biblical submission (Matt. 5, 6, and 7 and especially 22:37–39).

Peter calls Christians to radical submission to the State when he writes, "Be subject for the Lord's sake to every human institution, whether it be the emperor as supreme, or to governors . . ." (1 Pet. 2:13, 14). Yet when the properly authorized government of his day commanded the infant Church to stop proclaiming Christ, it was Peter who answered, "Whether it is right in the sight of God to listen to you rather than to God, you must judge; for we cannot but speak of what we have seen and heard" (Acts 4:19, 20). Upon a similar occasion Peter stated simply, "We must obey God rather than men" (Acts 5:29).

Understanding the cross-life of Jesus, Paul says, "Let every person be subject to the governing authorities" (Rom. 13:1). When Paul, however, saw that the State was failing to fulfill its God-ordained function of providing justice for all, he called it to account and insisted that the wrong be righted (Acts 16:37).

Were these men in opposition to their own principle of self-denial and submission? No. They simply understood that submission reaches the end of its tether when it becomes destructive. In fact, they illustrated revolutionary subordination by meekly refusing a destructive command and being willing to suffer the consequences. The German thinker Johannes Hamel says that subordination includes "the possibility of a spirit-driven resistance, of an appropriate disavowal and a refusal ready to accept suffering at this or that particular point."[5]

Sometimes the limits of submission are easy to determine. A wife is asked to punish her child unreasonably. A child is asked to aid an adult in an unlawful practice. A citizen is asked to violate the dictates of Scripture and conscience for the sake of the State. In each case the disciple refuses, not arrogantly, but in a spirit of meekness and submission.

Often the limits of submission are extremely hard to define. What about the marriage partner who feels stifled and kept from personal fulfillment because of the spouse's professional career? Is this a legitimate form of self-denial or is it destructive? What about the teacher who unjustly grades a student? Does the student submit or resist? What about the employer who promotes his employees on the basis of favoritism and vested interests? What does the deprived employee do, especially if the raise is needed for the good of his or her family?

These are extremely complicated questions simply because human relationships are complicated. They are questions that do not yield to simplistic answers. There is no such thing as a law of submission that will cover every situation. We must become highly skeptical of all laws that purport to handle every circumstance. Casuistic ethics always fail.

It is not an evasion of the issue to say that in defining the limits of submission we are catapulted into a deep dependence upon the Holy Spirit. After all, if we had a book of rules to cover every circumstance in life, we would not need dependence. The Spirit is an accurate discerner of the thoughts and intents of the heart, both yours and mine. He will be to us a present Teacher and Prophet, instructing us in what to do in every situation.

The Acts of Submission

Submission and service function concurrently. Hence, much of the practical outflow of submission will come in the next chapter. There are, however, seven acts of submission that I would like to mention briefly.

The first act of submission is to the Triune God. At the beginning of the day we wait, in the words of the hymn writer, "yielded and still" before Father, Son, and Holy Spirit. The first words of our day form the prayer of Thomas à Kempis, "As thou wilt; what thou wilt; when thou wilt."[6] We yield our body, mind, and spirit for his purposes. Likewise, the day is lived in deeds of submission interspersed with constant ejaculations of inward surrender. As the first words of the morning are of submission, so are the last words of the night. We surrender our body, mind, and spirit into the hands of God to do with us as he pleases through the long darkness.

The second act of submission is to the Scripture. As we submit ourselves to the Word of God living (Jesus), so we submit ourselves to the Word of God written (Scripture). We yield ourselves first to hear the Word, second to receive the Word, and third to obey the Word. We look to the Spirit who inspired the Scriptures to interpret and apply them to our condition. The word of Scripture, animated by the Holy Spirit, lives with us throughout the day.

The third act of submission is to our family. The dictum for the household should be "Let each of you look not only to his own interests, but also to the interests of others" (Phil. 2:4). Freely and graciously the members of the family make allowance for each other. The primary deed of submission is a commitment to listen to the other family members. Its corollary is a willingness to share, which is itself a work of submission.

The fourth act of submission is to our neighbors and those we meet in the course of our daily lives. The life of simple goodness is lived before them. If they are in need, we help them. We perform small acts of kindness and ordinary neighborliness: sharing our food, baby-sitting their children, mowing their lawn, visiting over important and unimportant matters, sharing our tools. No task is too small, too trifling, for each one is an opportunity to live in submission.

The fifth act of submission is to the believing community, the body of Christ. If there are jobs to be done and tasks to be accomplished, we look at them closely to see if they are God's invitation to the cross-life. We cannot do everything, but we can do some things. Sometimes these are matters of an organizational nature, but most frequently they are spontaneous opportunities for little tasks of service. At times calls to serve the Church universal may come, and if the ministry is confirmed in our hearts, we can submit to it with assurance and reverence.

The sixth act of submission is to the broken and despised. In every culture there are the "widows and orphans"; that is, the helpless, the undefended (James 1:27). Our first responsibility is to be among them. Like St. Francis in the thirteenth century and Kagawa in the twentieth, we must discover ways to identify genuinely with the downtrodden, the rejected. There we must live the cross-life.

The seventh act of submission is to the world. We live in an interdependent, international community. We cannot live in isolation. Our environmental responsibility, or the lack of it, affects not only the people around the world but generations yet to be born. Starving peoples affect us. Our act of submission is a determination to live as a responsible member of an increasingly irresponsible world.

A Final Note

In our day there has arisen a special problem about submission as it relates to authority. The phenomenon that I am about to describe is something I have observed repeatedly. When people begin to move into the spiritual realm, they see that Jesus is teaching a concept of authority that runs completely counter to the thinking of the systems of this world. They come to perceive that authority does not reside in positions or degrees or titles or tenure or *any* outward symbol. The way of Christ is in another direction altogether—the way of spiritual authority. Spiritual authority is God-ordained and God-sustained. Human institutions may acknowledge this authority or they may not; it makes no difference. The person with spiritual authority may have an outward position of authority or may not; again, it makes no difference. Spiritual authority is marked by both compassion and power. Those who walk in the Spirit can identify it immediately. They know without question that submission is due the word that has been given in spiritual authority.

But, and here is the difficulty, what about people who are in "positions of authority" but who do not possess spiritual authority? Since Jesus made it clear that the position does not give the authority, should this person be obeyed? Can we not rather disregard all humanly ordained authority and only look for and submit to spiritual authority? These are the kinds of questions raised by persons who sincerely want to walk in the way of the Spirit. The questions are legitimate and deserve a careful answer.

The answer is not simple, but neither is it impossible. *Revolutionary subordination commands us to live in submission to human authority until it becomes destructive.** Both Peter and Paul called for obedience to the pagan State because they understood the great good that resulted from this human institution. I have found that human "authorities" often have a great deal of wisdom that we neglect only at our own peril.

To this I shall add another reason of my own why we should submit to persons in positions of authority who do not know spiritual authority. We should do so out of common courtesy and out of compassion for the person in that difficult predicament. I have a deep empathy for people in that plight for I have been there myself more than once. To be in a position of authority and to know that your roots are not deep enough into the divine life to command spiritual authority is a frustrating, almost desperate, quagmire. I know the frantic feeling

---

*See the section on "The Limits of Submission."

that makes a person strut and puff and devise clever gimmicks to manipulate people into obedience. Some may find it easy to laugh at these people and disregard their "authority." I do not. I weep for them because I know the inward pain and suffering that must be endured to live in such a contradiction.

Further, we may pray for such people that they will be filled with new power and authority. We may also become their friend and help in every way we can. If we will live out the cross-life before them, very soon we may discover that they are increasing in spiritual power, and so are we.

9. The Discipline of Service

Learn the lesson that, if you are to do the work of a prophet, what you need is not a scepter but a hoe.

—BERNARD OF CLAIRVAUX

As the cross is the sign of submission, so the towel is the sign of service. When Jesus gathered his disciples for the Last Supper they were having trouble deciding who was the greatest. This was no new issue for them. "And an argument arose among them as to which of them was the greatest" (Luke 9:46). Whenever there is trouble over who is the greatest, there is trouble over who is the least. That is the crux of the matter for us, isn't it? Most of us know we will never be the greatest; just don't let us be the least.

Gathered at the Passover feast, the disciples were keenly aware that someone needed to wash the others' feet. The problem was that the only people who washed feet were the least. So there they sat, feet caked with dirt. It was such a sore point that they were not even going to talk about it. No one wanted to be considered the least. Then Jesus took a towel and a basin and redefined greatness.

Having lived out servanthood before them, he called them to the way of service: "If I then, your Lord and Teacher, have washed your feet, you also ought to wash one another's feet. For I have given you an example, that you also should do as I have done to you" (John 13:14, 15). In some ways we would prefer to hear Jesus' call to deny father and mother, houses and land for the sake of the gospel than his word to wash feet. Radical self-denial gives the feel of adventure. If we forsake all, we even have the chance of glorious martyrdom. But in service we must experience the many little deaths of going beyond ourselves. Service banishes us to the mundane, the ordinary, the trivial.

In the Discipline of service there is also great liberty. Service enables us to say "no!" to the world's games of promotion and authority. It abolishes our need (and desire) for a "pecking order." That phrase is so telling, so revealing. How like chickens we are! In the chicken pen there is no peace until it is clear who is the greatest and who is the least and who is at which rung everywhere in between. A group of people cannot be together for very long until the "pecking order" is clearly established. We can see it so easily in such things as where people sit, how they walk in relation to each other, who always gives way when two people are talking at the same time, who stands back and who steps forward when a job needs to be done. (Depending on the job, it may be a sign of mastery or a sign of servitude.) These things are written across the face of human society.

The point is not that we are to do away with all sense of leadership or authority. Any sociologist would quickly demonstrate the impossibility of such a task. Even among Jesus and the disciples, leadership and authority are seen easily. The point is that Jesus completely redefined leadership and rearranged the lines of authority.

Jesus never taught that everyone had equal authority. In fact, he had a great deal to say about genuine spiritual authority and taught that many did not possess it. But the authority of which Jesus spoke is not the authority of a pecking order. We must clearly understand the radical nature of Jesus' teaching on this matter. He was not just reversing the "pecking order" as many suppose. He was abolishing it. The authority of which he spoke was not an authority to manipulate and control. It was an authority of function, not of status.

Jesus declares, "You know that the rulers of the Gentiles lord it over them, and their great men exercise authority over them. *It shall not be so among you* [italics added]." He totally and completely rejected the pecking-order systems of his day. How then was it to be among them? "Whoever would be great among you must be your servant . . . even as the Son of man came not to be served but to serve" (Matt. 20:25–28). Therefore the spiritual authority of Jesus is an authority not found in a position or a title, but in a towel.

Self-righteous Service Versus True Service

If true service is to be understood and practiced, it must be distinguished clearly from "self-righteous service."

Self-righteous service comes through human effort. It expends immense amounts of energy calculating and scheming how to render the service. Sociological charts and surveys are devised so we can "help those people." True service comes from a relationship with the divine Other deep inside. We serve out of whispered promptings, divine urgings. Energy is expended but it is not the frantic energy of the flesh. Thomas Kelly writes, "I find He never guides us into an intolerable scramble of panting feverishness."[1]

Self-righteous service is impressed with the "big deal." It is concerned to make impressive gains on ecclesiastical scoreboards. It enjoys serving, especially when the service is titanic. True service finds it almost impossible to distinguish the small from the large service. Where a difference is noted, the true servant is often drawn to the small service, not out of false modesty, but because he genuinely sees it as the more important task. He indiscriminately welcomes all opportunities to serve.

Self-righteous service requires external rewards. It needs to know that people see and appreciate the effort. It seeks human applause—with proper religious modesty of course. True service rests contented in hiddenness. It does not fear the lights and blare of attention, but it does not seek them either. Since it is living out of a new Center of reference, the divine nod of approval is completely sufficient.

Self-righteous service is highly concerned about results. It eagerly waits to see if the person served will reciprocate in kind. It becomes bitter when the results fall below expectations. True service is free of the need to calculate results. It delights only in the service. It can serve enemies as freely as friends.

Self-righteous service picks and chooses whom to serve. Sometimes the high and powerful are served because that will ensure a certain advantage. Sometimes the low and defenseless are served because that will ensure a humble image. True service is indiscriminate in its ministry. It has heard the command of Jesus to be the "servant of all" (Mark 9:35). Brother Francis of Assisi notes in a letter, "Being the servant of all, I am bound to serve all and to administer the balm-bearing words of my lord."[2]

Self-righteous service is affected by moods and whims. It can serve only when there is a "feeling" to serve ("moved by the Spirit" as we say). Ill health or inadequate sleep controls the desire to serve. True service ministers simply and faithfully because there is a need. It knows that the "feeling to serve" can often be a hindrance to true service. The service disciplines the feelings rather than allowing the feeling to control the service.

Self-righteous service is temporary. It functions only while the specific acts of service are being performed. Having served, it can rest easy. True service is a life-style. It acts from ingrained patterns of living. It springs spontaneously to meet human need.

Self-righteous service is insensitive. It insists on meeting the need even when to do so would be destructive. It demands the opportunity to help. True service can withhold the service as freely as perform it. It can listen with tenderness and patience before acting. It can serve by waiting in silence. "They also serve who only stand and wait."[3]

Self-righteous service fractures community. In the final analysis, once all the religious trappings are removed, it centers in the glorification of the individual. Therefore it puts others into its debt and becomes one of the most subtle and destructive forms of manipulation known. True service builds community.

It quietly and unpretentiously goes about caring for the needs of others. It draws, binds, heals, builds.

Service and Humility

More than any other single way, the grace of humility is worked into our lives through the Discipline of service. Humility, as we all know, is one of those virtues that is never gained by seeking it. The more we pursue it the more distant it becomes. To think we have it is sure evidence that we don't. Therefore, most of us assume there is nothing we can do to gain this prized Christian virtue, and so we do nothing.

But there *is* something we can do. We do not need to go through life faintly hoping that someday humility may fall upon our heads. Of all the classical Spiritual Disciplines, service is the most conducive to the growth of humility. When we set out on a consciously chosen course of action that accents the good of others and is, for the most part, a hidden work, a deep change occurs in our spirits.

Nothing *disciplines* the inordinate desires of the flesh like service, and nothing *transforms* the desires of the flesh like serving in hiddenness. The flesh whines against service but screams against hidden service. It strains and pulls for honor and recognition. It will devise subtle, religiously acceptable means to call attention to the service rendered. If we stoutly refuse to give in to this lust of the flesh, we crucify it. Every time we crucify the flesh, we crucify our pride and arrogance.

The apostle John writes, "For all that is in the world, the lust of the flesh and the lust of the eyes and the pride of life, is not of the Father but is of the world" (1 John 2:16). We fail to understand the force of this passage because of our tendency to relegate it all to sexual sin. The "lust of the flesh" refers to the failure to discipline the natural human passions. C. H. Dodd says that the "lust of the eyes" refers to "the tendency to be captivated by outward show." He defines the "pride of life" as "pretentious egoism."[4] In each case the same thing is seen: infatuation with natural human powers and abilities without any dependence upon God. That is the flesh in operation, and the flesh is the deadly enemy of humility.

The strictest daily discipline is necessary to hold these passions in check. The flesh must learn the painful lesson that it has no rights of its own. It is the work of hidden service that will accomplish this self-abasement.

William Law made a lasting impact upon eighteenth-century England with his book, *A Serious Call to a Devout and Holy Life.* In it Law urges that every day should be viewed as a day of humility. And how does he suggest that we do this? By learning to serve others. Law understood that it is the Discipline of service that brings humility into the life. If we want humility, he counsels us to ". . . condescend to all the weaknesses and infirmities of your fellow-creatures, cover their frailties, love their excellencies, encourage their virtues, relieve their wants, rejoice in their prosperities, compassionate their distress, receive their friendship, overlook their unkindness, forgive their malice, be a servant of servants, and condescend to do the lowest offices to the lowest of mankind."[5]

The result, then, of this daily discipline of the flesh will be the rise of the grace of humility. It will slip in upon us unawares. Though we do not sense its presence, we are aware of a fresh zest and exhilaration with living. We wonder at the new sense of confidence that marks our activities. Although the demands of life are as great as ever, we live in a new sense of unhurried peace. People whom we once only envied we now view with compassion, for we see not only their position but their pain. People whom we would have passed over before we now "see" and find to be delightful individuals. Somehow—we cannot exactly explain how—we feel a new spirit of identification with the outcasts, the "offscourings" of the earth (1 Cor. 4:13).

Even more than the transformation that is occurring within us, we are aware of a deeper love and joy in God. Our days are punctuated with spontaneous breathings of praise and adoration. Joyous hidden service to others is an acted prayer of thanksgiving. We seem to be directed by a new control Center—and so we are.

Yes . . . But

A natural and understandable hesitancy accompanies any serious discussion of service. The hesitancy is prudent since it is wise to count the cost before plunging headlong into any Discipline. We experience a fear that comes out something like this: "If I do that, people will take advantage of me; they will walk all over me."

Right here we must see the difference between choosing to serve and choosing to be a servant. When we choose to serve, we are still in charge. We decide whom we will serve and when we will serve. And if we are in charge, we will worry a great deal about anyone stepping on us, that is, taking charge over us.

But when we choose to be a servant, we give up the right to be in charge. There is great freedom in this. If we voluntarily choose to be taken advantage of, then we cannot be manipulated. When we choose to be a servant, we surrender the right to decide who and when we will serve. We become available and vulnerable.

Consider the perspective of a slave. A slave sees all of life from the viewpoint of slavery. He does not see himself as possessing the same rights as free men and women. Please understand me, when this slavery is involuntary it is cruel and dehumanizing.* When the slavery is freely chosen, however, everything is changed. Voluntary servitude is a great joy.

The imagery of slavery may be difficult for us, but it was not hard for the apostle Paul. He frequently boasted of his slavery to Christ, making lavish use of the first-century concept of the

---

*A good part of my doctoral study was on slavery in America. I am keenly aware of the horribly demonic nature of involuntary servitude.

"love slave" (that is, the slave who, out of love, has freely chosen to remain a slave). We do our best to soften Paul's language by translating the word "slave" as "servant." But whatever word we decide to use, let us be certain that we understand that Paul meant he had freely given up his rights.

Therefore, the fear that we will be taken advantage of and stepped on is justified. That is exactly what may happen. But who can hurt someone who has freely chosen to be stepped on? Thomas à Kempis instructs us to be "so subject . . . that all men may go over thee and tread upon thee as upon mire of the street."[6]

In *The Little Flowers of St. Francis* a delightful story is told about how Francis taught Brother Leo the meaning of perfect joy. As the two walked together in the rain and bitter cold, Francis reminded Leo of all the things that the world—including the religious world—believed would bring joy, adding each time "Perfect joy is not in that." Finally, in exasperation Brother Leo asked, "I beg you in God's name to tell me where perfect joy is," whereupon Francis began enumerating the most humiliating, self-abasing things he could imagine, adding each time "Oh, Brother Leo, write that perfect joy is there." To explain and conclude the matter he told Brother Leo, "Above all the graces and gifts of the Holy Spirit which Christ gives to His friends is that of conquering oneself and willingly enduring sufferings, insults, humiliations, and hardships for the love of Christ."[7]

We find those words hard to deal with today. (You must understand that I, too, struggle even to listen to the devotional masters on this point.) We fear that such an attitude will lead irrevocably down the path of excessive asceticism and self-mortification. In the Church we are only now emerging from a "worm theology" that terribly devalued human ability and potential. Does service lead back to that? No, certainly not. No doubt it is a danger we must always guard against. But we must also watch for the enemy in the opposite direction. As Bonhoeffer says, "If there is no element of asceticism in our lives, if we give free rein to the desires of the flesh . . . we shall find it hard to train for the service of Christ."[8]

Service in the Marketplace

Service is not a list of things that we do, though in it we discover things to do. It is not a code of ethics, but a way of living. To do specific acts of service is not the same thing as living in the Discipline of service. Just as there is more to the game of basketball than the rule book, there is more to service than specific acts of serving. It is one thing to *act* like a servant; it is quite another to *be* a servant. As in all the Disciplines, it is possible to master the mechanics of service without experiencing the Discipline.

To stress the inward nature of service, however, is not enough. Service to be service must take form and shape in the world in which we live. Therefore, we must seek to perceive what service looks like in the marketplace of our daily lives.

At the outset there is the service of hiddenness. Even public leaders can cultivate tasks of service that remain generally unknown. If all of our serving is before others, we will be shallow people indeed. Listen to the spiritual direction of Jeremy Taylor: "Love to be concealed, and little esteemed: be content to want [lack] praise, never be troubled when thou art slighted or undervalued. . . ."[9] Hiddenness is a rebuke to the flesh and can deal a fatal blow to pride.

At first thought it would seem that hidden service is only for the sake of the person served. Such is not the case. Hidden, anonymous ministries affect even people who know nothing of them. They sense a deeper love and compassion among people though they cannot account for the feeling. If a secret service is done on their behalf, they are inspired to deeper devotion, for they know that the well of service is far deeper than they can see. It is a ministry that can be engaged in frequently by all people. It sends ripples of joy and celebration through any community of people.

There is the service of small things. Like Dorcas, we find ways to make "coats and garments for the widows" (Acts 9:39). The following is a true story. During the frantic final throes of writing my doctoral dissertation I received a phone call from a friend. His wife had taken the car and he wondered if I could take him on a number of errands. Trapped, I consented, inwardly cursing my luck. As I ran out the door, I grabbed Bonhoeffer's *Life Together*, thinking that I might have an opportunity to read in it. Through each errand I inwardly fretted and fumed at the loss of precious time. Finally, at a supermarket, the final stop, I waved my friend on, saying I would wait in the car. I picked up my book, opened it to the marker, and read these words: "The second service that one should perform for another in a Christian community is that of active helpfulness. This means, initially, simple assistance in trifling, external matters. There is a multitude of these things wherever people live together. Nobody is too good for the meanest service. One who worries about the loss of time that such petty, outward acts of helpfulness entail is usually taking the importance of his own career too solemnly."[10]

Francis de Sales says that the great virtues and the small fidelities are like sugar and salt. Sugar may have a more exquisite taste, but its use is less frequent. Salt is found everywhere. The great virtues are a rare occurrence; the ministry of small things is a daily service. Large tasks require great sacrifice for a moment; small things require constant sacrifice. "The small occasions . . . return every moment. . . . If we want to be faithful to these small things, nature never has time to breathe, and we must die to all our inclinations. We should a hundred times rather make some great sacrifices to God, however violent and painful, on condition that we be freed with liberty to follow our tastes and habits in every little detail."[11]

In the realm of the spirit we soon discover that the real issues are found in the tiny, insignificant corners of life. Our infatuation with the "big deal" has blinded us to this fact. The service of small things will put us at odds with our sloth and idleness.

We will come to see small things as the central issues. Fénelon writes, "It is not elevation of the spirit to feel contempt for small things. It is, on the contrary, because of too narrow points of view that we consider as little what has such far reaching consequences."[12]

There is the service of guarding the reputation of others or, as Bernard of Clairvaux put it, the service of "Charity." How necessary this is if we are to be saved from backbiting and gossip. The apostle Paul taught us to "speak evil of no one" (Titus 3:2). We may clothe our backbiting in all the religious respectability we want, but it will remain a deadly poison. There is a discipline in holding one's tongue that works wonders within us.

Nor should we be a party to the slanderous talk of others. In one church I served we had a rule on the pastoral team that the members came to appreciate. We refused to allow any person in the congregation to speak disparagingly of one pastor to another pastor. Gently, but firmly, we would ask them to go directly to the offending pastor. Eventually, people understood that we simply would not allow them to talk to us about pastor so-and-so. This rule, held to by the entire team, had beneficial results.

Bernard warns us that the spiteful tongue "strikes a deadly blow at charity in all who hear him speak and, so far as it can, destroys root and branch, not only in the immediate hearers but also in all others to whom the slander, flying from lip to lip, is afterwards repeated."[13] Guarding the reputation of others is a deep and lasting service.

There is the service of being served. When Jesus began to wash the feet of those he loved, Peter refused. He would never let his Master stoop to such a menial service on his behalf. It sounds like a statement of humility; in reality it was an act of veiled pride. Jesus' service was an affront to Peter's concept of authority. If Peter had been the master, he would not have washed feet!

It is an act of submission and service to allow others to serve us. It recognizes their "kingdom authority" over us. We graciously receive the service rendered, never feeling we must repay it. Those who, out of pride, refuse to be served are failing to submit to the divinely appointed leadership in the kingdom of God.

There is the service of common courtesy. Such deeds of compassion have fallen on hard times in our day. But we must never despise the rituals of relationship that are in every culture. It is one of the few ways left in modern society to acknowledge the value of one another. We are "to be gentle, and to show perfect courtesy toward all men" (Titus 3:2).

Missionaries understand the value of courtesy. They would not dare to blunder into some village demanding to be heard without first going through the appropriate rituals of introduction and acquaintanceship. Yet we feel we can violate these rituals in our own culture and still be received and heard. And we wonder why no one will listen.

"But acts of courtesy are so meaningless, so hypocritical," we complain. That is a myth. They are extremely meaningful and not in the least hypocritical. Once we get over our egocentric arrogance about the fact that people don't really want to know how we are when they say "How are you?" we can see that it is just an American way of acknowledging our presence. We can wave and acknowledge their presence too without feeling the need to give a prognosis on our latest headache. Words of "thank you" and "yes, please," letters of appreciation and RSVP responses are all services of courtesy. The specific acts will vary from culture to culture, but the purpose is always the same: to acknowledge others and affirm their worth. The service of courtesy is sorely needed in our increasingly computerized and depersonalized society.

There is the service of hospitality. Peter urges us to "Practice hospitality ungrudgingly to one another" (1 Pet. 4:9). Paul does the same and even makes it one of the requirements for the office of bishop (1 Tim. 3:2; Titus 1:8). There is a desperate need today for Christians who will open their homes to one another.

The old idea of the guest house has been made obsolete by the proliferation of modern motels and restaurants, but we may seriously question whether the change is an advance. I have walked through the Spanish missions of California and marveled at the gracious and adequate provisions that were made for visitors. Perhaps it is the modern, shiny, depersonalized motels that should become obsolete.

I know of a couple who have sought to make the ministry of hospitality a priority in their lives. In any given month they may have as many as seventy people visit their home. It is a service to which they believe God has called them. Perhaps most of us cannot do that much, but we can do something. We can begin somewhere.

Sometimes we limit ourselves because we make hospitality too complicated. I remember an occasion where the hostess was scurrying around, attending to this and that, sincerely wanting to make everyone feel comfortable. My friend startled us all (and put everyone at ease) by saying, "Helen, I don't want any coffee. I don't want any tea. I don't want any cookies. I don't want a napkin. I just want to visit. Won't you sit down and talk with us!" Just a chance to be together and share—that is the stuff of hospitality.

There is the service of listening. "The first service that one owes to others in the fellowship consists in listening to them. Just as love to God begins with listening to His Word, so the beginning of love for the brethren is learning to listen to them."[14] We desperately need the help that can come through listening to one another. We do not need to be trained psychoanalysts to be trained listeners. The most important requirements are compassion and patience.

We do not have to have the correct answers to listen well. In fact, often the correct answers are a hindrance to listening, for we become more anxious to give the answer than to hear. An impatient half-listening is an affront to the person sharing.

To listen to others quiets and disciplines the mind to listen to God. It creates an inward working upon the heart that transforms the affections, even the priorities, of life. When we have grown dull in listening to God, we would do well to listen to others in silence and see if we do not hear God through them. "Anyone who thinks that his time is too valuable to spend keeping quiet will eventually have no time for God and his brother, but only for himself and for his own follies."[15]

There is the service of bearing the burdens of each other. "Bear one another's burdens, and so fulfill the law of Christ" (Gal. 6:2). The "law of Christ" is the law of love, the "royal law" as James calls it (James 2:8). Love is most perfectly fulfilled when we bear the hurts and sufferings of each other, weeping with those who weep. And especially when we are with those who are going through the valley of the shadow, weeping is far better than words.

If we care, we will learn to bear one another's sorrows. I say "learn" because this, too, is a discipline to be mastered. Most of us too easily assume that all we need to do is decide to bear the burdens of others and we can do it. Then we try it for a time, and soon the joy of life has left, and we are heavy with the sorrows of others. It does not need to be so. We can learn to uphold the burdens of others without being destroyed by them. Jesus, who bore the burdens of the whole world, could say, "My yoke is easy, and my burden is light" (Matt. 11:30). Can we learn to lift the sorrows and pains of others into the strong, tender arms of Jesus so that our burden is lighter? Of course we can. But it takes some practice so, rather than dashing out to bear the burdens of the whole world, let us begin more humbly. We can begin in some small corner somewhere and learn. Jesus will be our Teacher.

Finally, there is the service of sharing the word of Life with one another. The "Poustinias" that were established by Catherine de Haeck Doherty have a rule: those who go into the deserts of silence and solitude do so for others. They are to bring back any word they receive from God and share it with others. This is a gracious service to be rendered for no individual can hear all that God wants to say. We are dependent upon one another to receive the full counsel of God. The smallest member can bring us a word—we dare not despise the service.

It is, of course, a fearful thing to proclaim these words to each other. The *fact* that God speaks to us does not guarantee that we rightly understand the message. We often mix our word with God's word: "From the same mouth come blessing and cursing" (James 3:10). Such realities humble us and throw us in deep dependence upon God. But we must not draw back from this service for it is desperately needed today.

The risen Christ beckons us to the ministry of the towel. Such a ministry, flowing out of the inner recesses of the heart, is life and joy and peace. Perhaps you would like to begin by experimenting with a prayer that several of us use. Begin the day by praying, "Lord Jesus, as it would please you bring me someone today whom I can serve."

III. THE CORPORATE DISCIPLINES

10. The Discipline of Confession

The confession of evil works is the first beginning of good works.

—AUGUSTINE OF HIPPO

At the heart of God is the desire to give and to forgive. Because of this, he set into motion the entire redemptive process that culminated in the cross and was confirmed in the resurrection. The usual notion of what Jesus did on the cross runs something like this: people were so bad and so mean and God was so angry with them that he could not forgive them unless somebody big enough took the rap for the whole lot of them.

Nothing could be further from the truth. Love, not anger, brought Jesus to the cross. Golgotha came as a result of God's great desire to forgive, not his reluctance. Jesus knew that by his vicarious suffering he could actually absorb all the evil of humanity and so heal it, forgive it, redeem it.

This is why Jesus refused the customary painkiller when it was offered him. He wanted to be completely alert for this greatest work of redemption. In a deep and mysterious way he was preparing to take on the collective sin of the human race. Since Jesus lives in the eternal now, this work was not just for those around him, but he took in all the violence, all the fear, all the sin of all the past, all the present, and all the future. This was his highest and most holy work, the work that makes confession and the forgiveness of sins possible.

Some seem to think that when Jesus shouted "My God, my God, why hast thou forsaken me?" it was a moment of weakness (Mark 15:34). Not at all. *This was his moment of greatest triumph*. Jesus, who had walked in constant communion with the Father, now became so totally identified with humankind that he was the actual embodiment of sin. As Paul writes, "he made him to be sin who knew no sin" (2 Cor. 5:21). Jesus succeeded in taking into himself all the dark powers of this present evil age and defeated every one of them by the light of his presence. He accomplished such a total identification with the sin of the race that he experienced the abandonment of God. Only in that way could he redeem sin. It was indeed his moment of greatest triumph.

Having accomplished this greatest of all his works, Jesus then took refreshment. "It is finished," he announced. That is, this great work of redemption was completed. He could feel the last dregs of the misery of humankind flow through him and into the care of the Father. The last twinges of evil, hostility, anger, and fear drained out of him, and he was able to turn again into the light of God's presence. "It is finished." The task is complete. Soon after, he was free to give up his spirit to the Father.

> To shame our sins He blushed in blood;
> He closed His eyes to show us God;
> Let all the world fall down and know
> That none but God such love can show.
> —Bernard of Clairvaux

This redemptive process is a great mystery hidden in the heart of God. But I know that it is true. I know this not only because the Bible says it is true, but because I have seen its effects in the lives of many people, including myself. It is the ground upon which we can know that confession and forgiveness are realities that transform us. Without the cross the Discipline of confession would be only psychologically therapeutic. But it is so much more. It involves an objective change in our relationship with God and a subjective change in us. It is a means of healing and transforming the inner spirit.

"But I thought that Christ on the cross and redemption deals with salvation," you may say. It does. But salvation as the Bible speaks of it refers to far more than who comes to faith in Christ or who gets to heaven. The Bible views salvation as both an event and a process. To converted people Paul says, "Work out your own salvation with fear and trembling" (Phil. 2:12). In a sermon titled "The Repentance of Believers," John Wesley spoke of the necessity of Christians coming into more of the forgiving grace of God. The Discipline of confession helps the believer to grow into "mature manhood, to the measure of the stature of the fullness of Christ" (Eph. 4:13).

"But isn't confession a grace instead of a Discipline?" It is both. Unless God gives the grace, no genuine confession can be made. But it is also a Discipline because there are things we must do. It is a consciously chosen course of action that brings us under the shadow of the Almighty.

"How is it that confession is listed under the Corporate Disciplines? I thought this was a private matter between the individual and God." Again the answer is not "either/or," but "both/and." We are grateful for the biblical teaching, underscored in the Reformation, that "there is one mediator between God and men, the man Christ Jesus" (1 Tim. 2:5). We are also grateful for the biblical teaching, newly appreciated in our day, to "confess your sins to one another, and pray for one another . . ." (James 5:16). Both are found in Scripture and neither need exclude the other.

Confession is a difficult Discipline for us because we all too often view the believing community as a fellowship of saints before we see it as a fellowship of sinners. We feel that everyone else has advanced so far into holiness that we are isolated and alone in our sin. We cannot bear to reveal our failures and shortcomings to others. We imagine that we are the only ones who have not stepped onto the high road to heaven. Therefore, we hide ourselves from one another and live in veiled lies and hypocrisy.

But if we know that the people of God are first a fellowship of sinners, we are freed to hear the unconditional call of God's love and to confess our needs openly before our brothers and sisters. We know we are not alone in our sin. The fear and pride that cling to us like barnacles cling to others also. We are sinners together. In acts of mutual confession we release the power that heals. Our humanity is no longer denied, but transformed.

Authority to Forgive

The followers of Jesus Christ have been given the authority to receive the confession of sin and to forgive it in his name. "If you forgive the sins of any, they are forgiven; if you retain the sins of any, they are retained" (John 20:23). What a wonderful privilege! Why do we shy away from such a life-giving ministry? If we, not out of merit but sheer grace, have been given the authority to set others free, how dare we withhold this great gift! Dietrich Bonhoeffer writes, "Our brother . . . has been given to us to help us. He hears the confession of our sins in Christ's stead and he forgives our sins in Christ's name. He keeps the secret of our confession as God keeps it. When I go to my brother to confess, I am going to God."[1]

Such authority in no way threatens the value or efficacy of private confession. It is a wonderful truth that the individual can break through into new life in the cross without the aid of any human mediator. In the days of the Reformation that reality swept into the Church like a breath of fresh air. It became a trumpet call of liberation from the bondage and manipulation that had crept into the ecclesiastical confessional system. But we also need to remember that Luther himself believed in mutual, brotherly confession. In the Large Catechism he writes, "Therefore when I admonish you to confession I am admonishing you to be a Christian."[2] Nor should we forget that when the confessional system was first introduced into the Church it sparked a genuine revival of personal piety and holiness.

The person who has known forgiveness and release from persistent, nagging habits of sin through private confession should rejoice greatly in this evidence of God's mercy. But there are others for whom this has not happened. Let me describe what it is like. We have prayed, even begged, for forgiveness, and though we hope we have been forgiven, we sense no release. We doubt our forgiveness and despair at our confession. We fear that perhaps we have made confession only to ourselves and not to God. The haunting sorrows and hurts of the past have not been healed. We try to convince ourselves that God forgives only the sin; he does not heal the memory. But deep within our being we know there must be something more. People have told us to take our forgiveness by faith and not to call God a liar. Not wanting to call God a liar, we do our best to take it by faith. But because misery and bitterness remain in our lives, we again despair. Eventually we begin to believe either that forgiveness is only a ticket to heaven and not meant to affect our lives now, or that we are not worthy of the forgiving grace of God.

Those who in some small way identify with these words can rejoice. We have not exhausted our resources nor God's grace when we have tried private confession. In the Book of Common Prayer, following the call to self-examination and repentance, we read these encouraging words: "If there be any of you who by this means cannot quiet his own conscience herein but require further comfort or counsel, let him come to me or to some other minister of God's word, and open his grief. . . ."[3] God has given us our brothers and sisters to stand in Christ's stead and make God's presence and forgiveness real to us.

The Scripture teaches us that all believers are priests before God: "You are a chosen race, a royal priesthood" (1 Pet. 2:9). At the time of the Reformation this was called "the universal priesthood of all believers." One of the functions of the Old Testament priest was to bring the forgiveness of sins through the holy sacrifice. The book of Hebrews, of course, makes clear that Jesus Christ is the final and sufficient sacrifice. And Jesus has given to us his priesthood: the ministry of making that sacrifice real in the hearts and lives of other human beings. It is through the voice of our brothers and sisters that the word of forgiveness is heard and takes root in our lives. Bonhoeffer writes: "A man who confesses his sins in the presence of a brother knows that he is no longer alone with himself; he experiences the presence of God in the reality of the other person. As long as I am by myself in the confession of my sins everything remains in the dark, but in the presence of a brother the sin has to be brought into the light."[4]

The stylized form of this avenue of help has been called the Confessional or the sacrament of penance. Though many of us, myself included, would feel highly uncomfortable with that form of confession, it does have certain advantages. First, the formalized form of the printed confession does not allow for any excuses or extenuating circumstances. We must confess that we have sinned by our own fault, our own most grievous fault. Our sins cannot be called errors in judgment, nor is there any room to blame them on upbringing or family or mean neighbors. This is a Reality Therapy of the best sort since we are so prone to blame our sins on everybody and everything instead of taking personal responsibility for them.

A second advantage of the Confessional is that the word of forgiveness is expected and given in the absolution. The word of Scripture, or some similar word, is actually spoken out loud. "If we confess our sins, he is faithful and just, and will forgive our sins and cleanse us from all unrighteousness" (1 John 1:9). The penitent is then told in clear, authoritative words that he is totally forgiven and set free of his sin. The assurance of forgiveness is sealed in the Spirit when it is spoken by our brother or sister in the name of Christ.

There is a third advantage to the institutionalized Confessional, namely, penance. If penance is viewed as a way of earning forgiveness, it is dangerous indeed. But if it is seen as an opportunity to pause a moment to consider the seriousness of our sin, then it has genuine merit. Today we take our offenses to the love of God far too lightly. If we had only a tinge of the sense of revulsion that God feels toward sin, we would be moved to holier living. God pleads with us, "Oh, do not do this abominable thing that I hate!" (Jer. 44:4). The purpose of penance is to help us move into that deeper sense of the sinfulness of sin.

These things, of course, can be accomplished without a formalized Confessional. In fact, when we know what we are about, it is an enormous advance to see the ministry of confession as the common property of the people of God. How can this be done? Perhaps a living example will aid in making these concepts more concrete.

Diary of a Confession

Although I had read in the Bible about the ministry of confession in the Christian brotherhood, I had never experienced it until I was pastoring my first church. I did not take the difficult step of laying bare my inner life to another out of any deep burden or sense of sin. I did not feel there was anything wrong in the least—except one thing. I longed for more power to do the work of God. I felt inadequate to deal with many of the desperate needs that confronted me. There had to be more spiritual resources than I was experiencing (and I'd had all the Holy Spirit experiences you're supposed to have; you name them, I'd had them!). "Lord," I prayed, "is there more you want to bring into my life? I want to be conquered and ruled by you. If there is anything blocking the flow of your power, reveal it to me." He did. Not by an audible voice or even through any human voice, but simply by a growing impression that perhaps something in my past was impeding the flow of his life. So I devised a plan. I divided my life into three periods: childhood, adolescence, adulthood. On the first day I came before God in prayer and meditation, pencil and paper in hand. Inviting him to reveal to me anything during my childhood that needed either forgiveness or healing or both, I waited in absolute silence for some ten minutes. Anything about my childhood that surfaced to my conscious mind, I wrote down. I made no attempt to analyze the items or put any value judgment on them. My assurance was that God would reveal anything that needed his healing touch. Having finished, I put the pencil and paper down for the day. The next day I went through the same exercise for my adolescent years, and the third day for my adult years.

Paper in hand, I then went to a dear brother in Christ. I had made arrangements with him a week ahead so he understood the purpose of our meeting. Slowly, sometimes painfully, I read my sheet, adding only those comments necessary to make the sin clear. When I had finished, I began to return the paper to my briefcase. Wisely, my counselor/confessor gently stopped my hand and took the sheet of paper. Without a word he took a wastebasket, and, as I watched, he tore the paper into hundreds of tiny pieces and dropped them into it. That powerful, nonverbal expression of forgiveness was followed by a simple absolution. My sins, I knew, were as far away as the east is from the west.

Next, my friend, with the laying on of hands, prayed a prayer of healing for all the sorrows and hurts of the past. The power of that prayer lives with me today.

I cannot say I experienced any dramatic feelings. I did not. In fact, the entire experience was an act of sheer obedience with no compelling feelings in the least. But I am convinced that it set me free in ways I had not known before. It seemed that I was released to explore what were for me new and uncharted regions of the Spirit. Following that event, I began to move into several of the Disciplines described in this book that I had never experienced before. Was there a causal connection? I do not know, and frankly I do not care. It is enough to have obeyed the inner prompting from above.

There was one interesting sidelight. The exposure of my humanity evidently sparked a freedom in my counselor/friend, for, directly following his prayer for me, he was able to express a deep and troubling sin that he had been unable to confess until then. Freedom begets freedom.

Counsel in the Giving of a Confession

Not only is it true that "we love, because he first loved us," but we are enabled to make confession only and especially because he first loved us (1 John 4:19). The evidence of mercy and grace sparks a contrite heart and allows confession to flow. We are drawn to him as Hosea tells us, "with cords of compassion, with the bands of love" (Hos. 11:4). We come with hopeful hearts, for the One we are coming to waits for us like the father of the prodigal who saw his son when he was still a great way off and in compassion ran and embraced him and welcomed him back (Luke 15:20). His greatest delight is to forgive. He calls his light-filled creatures of heaven into celebration whenever one person makes confession.

What do we do? St. Alphonsus Liguori writes, "For a good confession three things are necessary: an examination of conscience, sorrow, and a determination to avoid sin."[5]

"An examination of conscience."* This is a time, as Douglas Steere writes, "where a soul comes under the gaze of God and where in His silent and loving Presence this soul is pierced to the quick and becomes conscious of the things that must be forgiven and put right before it can continue to love One whose care has been so constant."[6] We are inviting God to move upon the heart and show us areas that need his forgiving and healing touch.

In this experience of opening ourselves to the "gaze of God" we must be prepared to deal with definite sins. A generalized confession may save us from humiliation and shame, but it will not ignite inner healing. The people who came to Jesus came with obvious, specific sins, and they were forgiven for each one. It is far too easy to avoid our real guilt in a general confes-

---

*The ancient Christian idea of the examination of conscience as a preparation for confession is light years away from the modern secular idea of "let your conscience be your guide." The conscience by itself is depraved and culturally conditioned—a most unreliable guide in matters of ethics and belief.

sion. In our confession we bring concrete sins. By calling them concrete, however, I do not mean only outward sins. I mean definite sins, the sins of the heart—pride, avarice, anger, fear— as well as the sins of the flesh—sloth, gluttony, adultery, murder. We may use the method described earlier. Perhaps we will be drawn to the method Luther used in which he sought to examine himself on the basis of the Ten Commandments. We may be led to another approach altogether.

In our desire to be specific we must not, however, run to the opposite danger of being unduly concerned to rout out every last detail in our lives. With profound common sense Francis de Sales counsels, "Do not feel worried if you do not remember all your little peccadilloes in confession, for as you often fall imperceptibly, so you are often raised up imperceptibly."[7]

"Sorrow" is necessary to a good confession. Sorrow as it relates to confession is not primarily an emotion, though emotion may be involved. It is an abhorrence at having committed the sin, a deep regret at having offended the heart of the Father. Sorrow is an issue of the will before it is an issue of the emotions. In fact, being sorrowful in the emotions without a godly sorrow in the will destroys the confession.

Sorrow is a way of taking the confession seriously. It is the opposite of the priest, and undoubtedly the penitent, ridiculed by Chaucer in *The Canterbury Tales*:

> Full sweetly heard he confession,
> And pleasant was his absolution.[8]

"A determination to avoid sin" is the third essential for a good confession. In the Discipline of confession we ask God to give us a yearning for holy living, a hatred for unholy living. John Wesley once said: "Give me one hundred preachers who fear nothing but sin and desire nothing but God . . . such alone will shake the gates of hell and set up the kingdom of heaven on earth."[9] It is the *will* to be delivered from sin that we seek from God as we prepare to make confession. We must desire to be conquered and ruled by God, or if we do not desire it, to desire to desire it. Such a desire is a gracious gift from God. The seeking of this gift is one of the preliminaries for confessing to a brother or sister.

Does all this sound complicated? Do you fear you might miss one of the points and thus render everything ineffectual? It is usually much more complicated in the analysis than in the experience. Remember the heart of the Father; he is like a shepherd who will risk anything to find that one lost sheep. We do not have to make God willing to forgive. In fact, it is God who is working to make us willing to seek his forgiveness.

One further note on the preparation for confession; there must be a definite termination point in the self-examination process. Otherwise, we can easily fall into a permanent habit of self-condemnation. Confession begins in sorrow, but it ends in joy. There is celebration in the forgiveness of sins because it results in a genuinely changed life.

Then there is the practical matter of to whom we should go to confess. It is quite correct theologically to say that every Christian believer can receive the confession of another, but not every Christian believer will have sufficient empathy and understanding. Though it is unfortunate, it is a fact of life that some people seem unable to keep a confidence. Others are disqualified because they would be horrified at the revealing of certain sins. Still others, not understanding the nature and value of confession, would shrug it off with a "That's not so bad." Fortunately, many people do understand and would be delighted to minister in this way. These people are found by asking God to reveal them to us. They are also found by observing people to see who evidences a lively faith in God's power to forgive and exhibits the joy of the Lord in his or her heart. The key qualifications are spiritual maturity, wisdom, compassion, good common sense, the ability to keep a confidence, and a wholesome sense of humor. Many pastors—though by no means all—can serve in this way. Often ordinary folk who hold no office or title whatever are among the best at receiving a confession.

But what if there is an offense we could never bring ourselves to reveal? What if we lack the courage to open a particular corner of our lives? Then all we need to do is say to our brother or sister: "I need your help. There is a sin that I cannot bring myself to confess." Our confessor/friend will "then adopt an easy means of dragging from its den the wild beast that would devour you. All you will have to do is to answer Yes or No to his interrogations. And behold, both the temporal and the eternal hell have disappeared, the grace of God is recovered, and peace of conscience reigns supreme."[10]

Counsel in the Receiving of a Confession

Like any spiritual ministry there is a preparation involved in being able to hear rightly the confession of a brother or sister.

We begin by learning to live under the cross. Bonhoeffer writes, "Anybody who lives beneath the Cross and who has discerned in the Cross of Jesus the utter wickedness of all men and of his own heart will find there is no sin that can ever be alien to him. Anybody who has once been horrified by the dreadfulness of his own sin that nailed Jesus to the Cross will no longer be horrified by even the rankest sins of a brother."[11] This is the one thing that will save us from ever being offended in the confession of another. It forever delivers us from conveying any attitude of superiority. We know the deceptiveness of the human heart, and we know the grace and mercy of God's acceptance. Once we see the awfulness of sin we know that, regardless of what others have done, we ourselves are the chief of sinners.

Therefore, there is nothing that anyone can say that will disturb us. Nothing. By living under the cross we can hear the worst possible things from the best possible people without so much as batting an eyelash. If we live in that reality, we will convey that spirit to others. They know it is safe to come to us. They know we can receive anything they could possibly reveal. They know we will never condescend to them but, instead, understand.

When we live in this spirit, we do not need to tell others that we will keep privileged information privileged. They know we will never betray a confidence. We do not have to tell them. Nor will we ever be tempted to betray it, for we know the godly sorrow that has driven them to this difficult step.

By living under the cross we are delivered from the danger of spiritual domination. We have stood where our brother now stands and so the desire to use his confession against him is gone. Nor do we feel any need to control him or to straighten him out. All we feel is acceptance and understanding.

As we prepare for this sacred ministry it is wise that we regularly pray for an increase of the light of Christ within us so that, as we are with others, we will radiate his life and light into them. We want to learn how to live so that our very presence will speak of the love and forgiving grace of God. Also, we should pray for an increase of the gift of discernment. This is especially important when we minister to them following the confession. We need to be able to perceive the real healing needed in the deep, inner spirit.

It is important that when others are opening their griefs to us we discipline ourselves to be quiet. We will be tempted severely to relieve the tension of the situation by some offhanded comment. This is very distracting and even destructive to the sacredness of the moment. Neither should we try to pry out more details than are necessary. If we feel that out of embarrassment or fear they are holding something back, the best method is to wait silently and prayerfully.

On one occasion a woman was confessing her sorrow to me and to the Lord. When she finished I felt impressed to wait in silence. Presently, she began sharing a deep inward sin that she had never been able to tell anyone. Later she told me that as I waited, she looked at me and "saw" superimposed upon my eyes the eyes of Another who conveyed to her a love and acceptance that released her to unburden her heart. I had felt nothing nor did I "see" anything, but I do not doubt her experience for it did result in a wonderful inner healing.

That story illustrates another important factor in receiving a confession. It is often helpful by prayer to set the cross between yourself and the penitent. This protects them from receiving merely human emotion from you and protects you from receiving any harmful influences from them. Everything is filtered through the light of the cross. Your human compassion is heightened and enlivened by divine love. You are praying for them through the power of the cross.

It hardly needs to be said that as they share, you are praying for them. Inwardly and imperceptively (it would be unkind to make a display of your praying) you are sending prayers of love and forgiveness into them. Also, you are praying that they will share the "key" that will reveal any area needing the healing touch of Christ.

Finally, it is extremely important that you pray for the person and not just counsel with them. Before or during the prayer we should announce to them that the forgiveness that is in Jesus Christ is now real and effective for them. We can say this in words and tones of genuine authority for we have all of heaven behind the absolution (John 20:22, 23).*

The prayer is for the healing of the inner wounds that the sin has caused. It is best to accompany the prayer with the "laying on of hands" which is an elemental teaching of the Bible and is a means through which God communicates his life-giving power (Heb. 6:2). Invite God to flow into the deep inner mind and heal the sorrows of the past. Picture the healing. Thank him for it. Of this ministry of prayer Agnes Sanford

*In these words of Jesus we have not only the ministry of forgiving sins, but the ministry of retaining sins. "If you forgive the sins of any, they are forgiven; if you retain the sins of any, they are retained." The ministry of retaining sins is simply the refusal to try to bring people into something for which they are not ready. Sometimes peole are so anxious to get others into the kingdom that they will try to announce their forgiveness before they have sought it or even wanted it. Unfortunately, this malady is characteristic of a great deal of modern evangelism.

writes, "One makes a very deep rapport in this kind of prayer. One feels the feelings of the person for whom one prays; so much so that often the tears come from some deep center of compassion within the soul. Yet, if one weeps, it is not in grief but in joy, knowing that these tears are not one's own but are the tears of the compassionate heart of Christ brooding over this lost one, and the joy of Christ that at last He has been given a channel through which He can reach this person whom He loves."[12]

The Discipline of confession brings an end to pretense. God is calling into being a Church that can openly confess its frail humanity and know the forgiving and empowering graces of Christ. Honesty leads to confession, and confession leads to change. May God give grace to the Church once again to recover the Discipline of confession.

11. The Discipline of Worship

> To worship is to quicken the conscience by the holiness of
> God, to feed the mind with the truth of God, to purge the
> imagination by the beauty of God, to open the heart to the
> love of God, to devote the will to the purpose of God.
>
> —WILLIAM TEMPLE

To worship is to experience Reality, to touch Life. It is to know,
to feel, to experience the resurrected Christ in the midst of the
gathered community. It is a breaking into the Shekinah of God,
or better yet, being invaded by the Shekinah of God.*

God is actively seeking worshipers. Jesus declares, "The true
worshipers will worship the Father in spirit and truth, for such
the Father *seeks* to worship him" (John 4:23, [italics added]). It
is God who seeks, draws, persuades. Worship is the human
response to the divine initiative. In Genesis God walked in the
garden, seeking out Adam and Eve. In the crucifixion Jesus
drew men and women to himself (John 12:32). Scripture is re-
plete with examples of God's efforts to initiate, restore, and
maintain fellowship with his children. God is like the father of
the prodigal who upon seeing his son a long way off, rushed
to welcome him home.

Worship is our response to the overtures of love from the
heart of the Father. Its central reality is found "in spirit and
truth." It is kindled within us only when the Spirit of God
touches our human spirit. Forms and rituals do not produce
worship, nor does the disuse of forms and rituals. We can use
all the right techniques and methods, we can have the best
possible liturgy, but we have not worshiped the Lord until

---

*"Shekinah" means the glory or the radiance of God dwelling in the midst of
his people. It denotes the immediate Presence of God as opposed to a God
who is abstract or aloof.

Spirit touches spirit. The words of the chorus, "Set my spirit free that I may worship Thee," reveal the basis of worship. Until God touches and frees our spirit we cannot enter this realm. Singing, praying, praising all may lead to worship, but worship is more than any of them. Our spirit must be ignited by the divine fire.

As a result, we need not be overly concerned with the question of a correct form for worship. The issue of high liturgy or low liturgy, this form or that form is peripheral rather than central. We are encouraged in this perception when we realize that nowhere does the New Testament prescribe a particular form for worship. In fact, what we find is a freedom that is incredible for people with such deep roots in the synagogue liturgical system. They had the reality. When Spirit touches spirit the issue of forms is wholly secondary.

To say that forms are secondary is not to say that they are irrelevant. As long as we are finite human beings we must have forms. We must have "wineskins" that will embody our experience of worship. But the forms are not the worship; they only lead us into the worship. We are free in Christ to use whatever forms will enhance our worship, and if any form hinders us from experiencing the living Christ—too bad for the form.

The Object of Our Worship

Jesus answers for all time the question of whom we are to worship. "You shall worship the Lord your God and him only shall you serve" (Matt. 4:10). The one true God is the God of Abraham, Isaac, and Jacob; the God whom Jesus Christ revealed. God made clear his hatred for all idolatries by placing an incisive command at the start of the Decalogue. "You shall have no other gods before me" (Exod. 20:3). Nor does idolatry consist only in bowing before visible objects of adoration. A. W. Tozer says, "The essence of idolatry is the entertainment of thoughts about God that are unworthy of Him."[1] To think rightly about God is, in an important sense, to have everything right. To think wrongly about God is, in an important sense, to have everything wrong.

We desperately need to see who God is: to read about his self-disclosure to his ancient people Israel, to meditate on his attributes, to gaze upon the revelation of his nature in Jesus Christ. When we see the Lord of hosts "high and lifted up," ponder his infinite wisdom and knowledge, wonder at his unfathomable mercy and love, we cannot help but move into doxology.

> Glad thine attributes confess,
> Glorious all and numberless.[2]

To see who the Lord is brings us to confession. When Isaiah caught sight of the glory of God he cried, "Woe is me! For I am lost; for I am a man of unclean lips, and I dwell in the midst of a people of unclean lips; for my eyes have seen the King, the Lord of hosts!" (Isa. 6:5). The pervasive sinfulness of human beings becomes evident when contrasted with the radiant holiness of God. Our fickleness becomes apparent once we see God's faithfulness. To understand his grace is to understand our guilt.

We worship the Lord not only because of who he is, but also because of what he has done. Above all, the God of the Bible is the God who acts. His goodness, faithfulness, justice, mercy all can be seen in his dealings with his people. His gracious actions are not only etched into ancient history, but are engraved into our personal histories. As the apostle Paul says, the only reasonable response is worship (Rom. 12:1). We praise God for who he is, and thank him for what he has done.

The Priority of Worship

If the Lord is to be *Lord*, worship must have priority in our lives. The *first* commandment of Jesus is, "Love the Lord your God with all your heart, and with all your soul, and with all your mind, and with all your strength" (Mark 12:30). The divine priority is worship first, service second. Our lives are to be punctuated with praise, thanksgiving, and adoration. Service flows out of worship. Service as a substitute for worship is idolatry. Activity is the enemy of adoration.

The primary function of the Levitical priests was to "come near to me to minister to me" (Ezek. 44:15). For the Old Testament priesthood, ministry to God was to precede all other work. And that is no less true of the universal priesthood of the New Testament. One grave temptation we all face is to run around answering calls to service without ministering to the Lord himself.

Today God is calling his Church back to worship. This can be seen in high church circles where there is a renewed interest in intimacy with God. It can be seen in low church circles where there is a renewed interest in liturgy. It can be seen everywhere in between these two. It is as if God is saying, "I want the hearts of my people back!" And if we long to go where God is going and do what God is doing, we will move into deeper, more authentic worship.

Preparation for Worship

A striking feature of worship in the Bible is that people gathered in what we could only call a "holy expectancy." They believed they would actually hear the *Kol Yahweh*, the voice of God. When Moses went into the Tabernacle, he knew he was entering the presence of God. The same was true of the early Church. It was not surprising to them that the building in which they met shook with the power of God. It had happened before (Acts 2:2, 4:31). When some dropped dead and others were raised from the dead by the word of the Lord, the people knew that God was in their midst (Acts 5:1–11, 9:36–43, 20:7–10). As those early believers gathered they were keenly aware that the veil had been ripped in two, and, like Moses and Aaron, they were entering the Holy of Holies. No intermediaries were needed. They were coming into the awful, glorious, gracious presence of the living God. They gathered with anticipation, knowing that Christ was present among them and would teach them and touch them with his living power.

How do we cultivate this holy expectancy? It begins in us as we enter the Shekinah of the heart. While living out the demands of our day, we are filled with inward worship and adoration. We work and play and eat and sleep, yet we are listening, ever listening, to our Teacher. The writings of Frank Laubach are filled with this sense of living under the shadow of the Almighty. "Of all today's miracles the greatest is this: to know that I find Thee best when I work listening. . . . Thank Thee, too, that the habit of constant conversation grows easier each day. I really do believe *all* thought can be conversations with Thee."[3]

Brother Lawrence knew the same reality. Because he experienced the presence of God in the kitchen, he knew he would meet God in the Mass as well. He writes, "I cannot imagine how religious persons can live satisfied without the practice of the Presence of God."[4] Those who have once tasted the Shekinah of God in daily experience can never again live satisfied without "the practice of the presence of God."

Catching the vision from Brother Lawrence and Frank Laubach, I dedicated one whole year to learning how to live with a perpetual openness to Jesus as my present Teacher. I determined to learn his vocabulary: is he addressing me through those singing birds or that sad face? I sought to allow him to move through every action: my fingers while writing, my voice while speaking. My desire was to punctuate each minute with inward whisperings of adoration, praise, and thanksgiving. Often I failed for hours, even days at a time. But each time I came back and tried again. That year did many things for me, but it especially heightened my sense of expectancy in public worship. After all, he had graciously spoken to me in dozens of little ways throughout the week; he will certainly speak to me here as well. In addition, I found it increasingly easier to distinguish his voice from the blare of everyday life.

When more than one or two come into public worship with a holy expectancy, it can change the atmosphere of a room. People who enter harried and distracted are drawn quickly into a sense of the silent Presence. Hearts and minds are lifted upward. The air becomes charged with expectancy.

Here is a practical handle to put on this idea. Live throughout the week as an heir of the kingdom, listening for his voice, obeying his word. Since you have heard his voice throughout the week, you know that you will hear his voice as you gather for public worship. Enter the service ten minutes early. Lift your heart in adoration to the King of glory. Contemplate his majesty, glory, and tenderness as revealed in Jesus Christ. Picture the marvelous vision that Isaiah had of the Lord "high and lifted up" or the magnificent revelation that John had of Christ with eyes "like a flame of fire" and voice "like the sound of many waters" (Isa. 6; Rev. 1). Invite the real Presence to be manifest.

Next, lift into the light of Christ the pastor and other worship leaders. Picture the Shekinah of God's radiance surrounding them. Inwardly release them to speak the truth boldly in the power of the Lord.

When people begin to enter the room, glance around until you see someone who needs your intercessory work. Perhaps their shoulders are drooped, or they seem a bit sad. Lift them into the glorious, refreshing light of his Presence. See the burden tumbling from their shoulders as it did from Pilgrim's in Bunyan's allegory. Hold them as a special intention throughout the service. If only a few in any given congregation will do this, it will deepen the worship experience of all.

Another vital feature of the early Christian community was their sense of being "gathered" together in worship. First, they were gathered in the sense that they actually met as a group, and second, as they met, they were gathered into a unity of spirit that transcended their individualism.

In contrast to the religions of the East, the Christian faith has strongly emphasized corporate worship. Even under highly dangerous circumstances the early community was urged not to forsake the assembling of themselves together (Heb. 10:25). The Epistles speak frequently of the believing community as the "body of Christ." As human life is unthinkable without head, arms, and legs, so it was unthinkable for those Christians to live in isolation from one another. Martin Luther witnesses to the fact that "at home, in my own house, there is no warmth or vigor in me, but in the church when the multitude is gathered together, a fire is kindled in my heart and it breaks its way through."[5]

In addition, when the people of God meet together, there often comes a sense of being "gathered" into one mind, becoming of one accord (Phil. 3:15). Thomas Kelly writes: "A quickening Presence pervades us, breaking down some part of the special privacy and isolation of our individual lives and blending our spirits within a superindividual Life and Power. An objective, dynamic Presence enfolds us all, nourishes our souls, speaks glad, unutterable comfort with us, and quickens us in depths that had before been slumbering."[6] When we are truly gathered into worship, things occur that could never occur alone. There is the psychology of the group to be sure, and yet it is so much more; it is divine interpenetration. There is what the biblical writers called *koinonia*, deep inward fellowship in the power of the Spirit.

This experience far transcends *esprit de corps*. It is not in the least dependent upon homogeneous units or even knowing information about one another's lives. There comes a divine melting of our separateness. In the power of the one Spirit we become "wrapped in a sense of unity and of Presence such as quiets all words and enfolds [us] within an unspeakable calm and interknittedness within a vaster life."[7] Such fellowship-in-worship makes vicarious worship via the media tasteless and flat.

The Leader of Worship

Genuine worship has only one Leader, Jesus Christ. When I speak of Jesus as the Leader of worship, I mean, first of all, that he is alive and present among his people. His voice can be heard in their hearts and his presence known. We not only read about him in Scripture, we can know him by revelation. He wants to teach us, guide us, rebuke us, comfort us.

Christ is also alive and present in all his offices. In worship we are prone to view Christ only in his priestly office as Savior and Redeemer. But he is also among us as our Prophet and King. That is, he will teach us about righteousness and give us the power to do what is right. George Fox says, "Meet together in the Name of Jesus . . . he is your Prophet, your Shepherd, your Bishop, your Priest, in the midst of you, to open to you, and to sanctify you, and to feed you with Life, and to quicken you with Life."[8]

Further, Christ is alive and present in all his power. He saves us not only from the consequences of sin but from the domination of sin. Whatever he teaches us, he will give us the power to obey. If Jesus is our Leader, miracles should be expected to occur in worship. Healings, both inward and outward, will be the rule, not the exception. The book of Acts will not just be something we read about, but something we are experiencing.

Finally, Christ is the Leader of worship in the sense that he alone decides what human means will be used, if any. Individuals preach or prophesy or sing or pray as they are called forth by their Leader. In this way there is no room for the elevation of private reputations. Jesus alone is honored. As our living Head calls them forth, any or all of the gifts of the Spirit can be freely exercised and gladly received. Perhaps a word of knowledge is given in which the intent of the heart is revealed and we know that King Jesus is in charge. Perhaps there is a prophecy or an exhortation that puts us on the edge of our seats because we sense that the *Kol Yahweh* has been spoken. Preaching or teaching that comes forth because the living Head has called it forth breathes life into worship. Preaching that is without divine unction falls like a frost on worship. Heart preaching enflames the spirit of worship; head preaching smothers the glowing embers. There is nothing more quickening than Spirit-inspired preaching, nothing more deadening than human-inspired preaching.

With all this lofty talk about Christ as the Leader of worship you might conclude that human leadership is unimportant. Nothing could be further from the truth. If God does not raise up inspired leaders who can guide people into worship with authority and compassion, then the experience of worship will be nearly impossible. This is the reason for the leadership gifts of the Spirit (Eph. 4:11). Worship leaders who are called out by God must not be shy about their leadership. People need to be led *into* worship: from the Outer Court to the Inner Court and finally into the Holy of Holies. God anoints leaders to bring people through this progression into worship.

Avenues into Worship

One reason worship should be considered a Spiritual Discipline is because it is an ordered way of acting and living that sets us before God so he can transform us. Although we are only responding to the liberating touch of the Holy Spirit, there are divinely appointed avenues into this realm.

The first avenue into worship is to still all humanly initiated activity. The stilling of "creaturely activity," as the patriarchs of the inner life called it, is not something to be confined to formal worship services, but is a life-style. It is to permeate the daily fabric of our lives. We are to live in a perpetual, inward, listening silence so that God is the source of our words and actions. If we are accustomed to carrying out the business of our lives in human strength and wisdom, we will do the same in gathered worship. If, however, we have cultivated the habit of allowing every conversation, every business transaction to be divinely prompted, that same sensitivity will flow into public worship. François Fénelon writes, "Happy the soul which by a sincere self-renunciation, holds itself ceaselessly in the hands of its Creator, ready to do everything which he wishes; which never stops saying to itself a hundred times a day, 'Lord, what wouldst thou that I should do?' "⁹

Does that sound impossible? The only reason we believe it to be far beyond us is that we do not understand Jesus as our present Teacher. When we have been under his tutelage for a time, we see how it is possible for every motion of our lives to have its root in God. We wake up in the morning and lie in bed quietly praising and worshiping the Lord. We tell him that we desire to live under his leadership and rule. Driving to work, we ask our Teacher, "How are we doing?" Immediately our Mentor flashes before our mind that caustic remark we made to our spouse at breakfast, that shrug of disinterest we gave our children on the way out the door. We realize we have been living in the flesh. There is confession, restoration, and a new humility.

We stop at the gas station and sense a divine urging to get acquainted with the attendant, to see her as a person rather than an automaton. We drive on, rejoicing in our new insight into Spirit-initiated activity. And so it goes throughout our day: a prompting here or a drawing there, sometimes a bolting ahead or a lagging behind our Guide. Like a child taking first steps we are learning through success and failure, confident that we have a present Teacher who, through the Holy Spirit, will guide us into all truth. In this way we come to understand what Paul means when he instructs us to "walk not according to the flesh but according to the Spirit" (Rom. 8:4).

To still the activity of the flesh so that the activity of the Holy Spirit dominates the way we live will affect and inform public worship. Sometimes it will take the form of absolute silence. Certainly it is more fitting to come in reverential silence and awe before the Holy One of eternity than to rush into his Presence with hearts and minds askew and tongues full of words. The scriptural admonition is, "The LORD is in his holy temple;

let all the earth keep silence before him" (Hab. 2:20). The desert Father Ammonas writes: "Behold, my beloved. I have shown you the power of silence, how thoroughly it heals and how fully pleasing it is to God. . . . It is by silence that the saints grew . . . it was because of silence that the power of God dwelt in them, because of silence that the mysteries of God were known to them."[10]

Praise is another avenue into worship. The Psalms are the literature of worship and their most prominent feature is praise. "Praise the Lord!" is the shout that reverberates from one end of the Psalter to the other. Singing, shouting, dancing, rejoicing, adoring—all are the language of praise.

Scripture urges us to "offer the sacrifice of praise to God continually, that is, the fruit of our lips, giving thanks to his name" (Heb. 13:15, KJV). The Old Covenant required the sacrifice of bulls and goats. The New Covenant requires the sacrifice of praise. Peter tells us that as Christ's new royal priesthood we are to offer "spiritual sacrifices" which means to "declare the wonderful deeds of him who called you out of darkness into his marvelous light" (1 Pet. 2:5, 9). Peter and John left the Sanhedrin with bleeding backs and praising lips (Acts 5:41). Paul and Silas filled the Philippian jail with their songs of praise (Acts 16:25). In each case they were offering the sacrifice of praise.

The mightiest stirring of praise in the twentieth century has been the charismatic movement. Through it God has breathed new life and vitality into millions. In our day the Church of Jesus Christ is coming into a greater awareness of how central praise is in bringing us into worship.

In praise we see how totally the emotions need to be brought into the act of worship. Worship that is solely cerebral is an aberration. Feelings are a legitimate part of the human personality and should be employed in worship. To make such a statement doesn't mean that our worship should do violence to our rational faculties, but it does mean that our rational faculties alone are inadequate. As Paul counsels, we are to pray with the spirit and pray with the mind, sing with the spirit and sing with the mind (1 Cor. 14:15). That is one reason for the spiritual gift of tongues. It helps us to move beyond mere rational worship into a more inward communion with the Father. Our outward mind may not know what is being said, but our inward spirit understands. Spirit touches spirit.

Singing is meant to move us into praise. It provides a medium for the expression of emotion. Through music we express our joy, our thanksgiving. No less than forty-one psalms command us to "sing unto the Lord." If singing can occur in a concentrated manner it serves to focus us. We become centered. Our fragmented minds and spirits flow into a unified whole. We become poised toward God.

God calls for worship that involves our whole being. The body, mind, spirit, and emotions should all be laid on the altar of worship. Often we forget that worship should include the body as well as the mind and the spirit.

The Bible describes worship in physical terms. The root meaning for the Hebrew word we translate *worship* is "to prostrate." The word *bless* literally means "to kneel." *Thanksgiving* refers to "an extension of the hand." Throughout Scripture we find a variety of physical postures in connection with worship: lying prostrate, standing, kneeling, lifting the hands, clapping the hands, lifting the head, bowing the head, dancing, and wearing sackcloth and ashes. The point is that we are to offer God our bodies as well as all the rest of our being. Worship is appropriately physical.

We are to present our bodies to God in a posture consistent with the inner spirit in worship. Standing, clapping, dancing, lifting the hands, lifting the head are postures consistent with the spirit of praise. To sit still looking dour is simply not appropriate for praise. Kneeling, bowing the head, lying prostrate are postures consistent with the spirit of adoration and humility.

We are quick to object to this line of teaching. "People have different temperaments," we argue. "That may appeal to emotional types, but I'm naturally quiet and reserved. It isn't the kind of worship that will meet my need." What we must see is that the real question in worship is not, "What will meet my need?" The real question is, "What kind of worship does God call for?" It is clear that God calls for wholehearted worship. And it is as reasonable to expect wholehearted worship to be physical as to expect it to be cerebral.

Often our "reserved temperament" is little more than fear of what others will think of us, or perhaps unwillingness to humble ourselves before God and others. Of course people have different temperaments, but that must never keep us from worshiping with our whole being.

Having said this, I must hasten to add that the physical response to worship is never to be manipulated in any way. We are to give each other freedom to respond to the moving of God upon the heart. In many worship experiences I have seen, at any given moment, people sitting, standing, kneeling, and lying prostrate, and the Spirit of God resting upon them all. Some evidence deep emotion, others show no outward manifestations whatever, but all are under the brooding Spirit of God. "For freedom Christ has set us free; stand fast therefore, and do not submit again to a yoke of slavery" (Gal. 5:1).

We may, of course, do all the things I have described and never enter into worship, but they can provide avenues through which we place ourselves before God so that our inner spirit can be touched and freed.

Steps into Worship

Worship is something we do. Studying the theology of worship and debating the forms of worship are all good, but by themselves they are inadequate. In the final analysis we learn to worship by worshiping. Let me give a few simple steps that I hope will help in the experience of worship.

First, learn to practice the presence of God daily. Really try to follow Paul's words, "Pray without ceasing" (1 Thess. 5:17,

KJV). Punctuate every moment with inward whisperings of adoration, praise, and thanksgiving. Have personal times of inner worship and confession and Bible study and attentiveness to Christ, your present Teacher. All this will heighten your expectancy in public worship because the gathered experience of worship just becomes a continuation and an intensification of what you have been trying to do all week long.

Second, have many different experiences of worship. Worship God when you are alone. Have home groups not just for Bible study, but for the very experience of worship itself. Gather little groups of two and three and learn to offer up a sacrifice of praise. Many things can happen in smaller gatherings that, just by sheer size, cannot happen in the larger experience. All of these little experiences of worship will empower and impact the larger Sunday gatherings.

Third, find ways to really prepare for the gathered experience of worship. Prepare on Saturday night by going to bed early, by having an inward experience of examination and confession, by going over the hymns and Scripture passages that will be used on Sunday, by gathering early before the actual worship service and filling the room with the presence of God, by letting go of inner distractions so that you can really participate.

Fourth, have a willingness to be gathered in the power of the Lord. That is, as an individual I must learn to let go of my agenda, of my concern, of my being blessed, of my hearing the word of God. The language of the gathered fellowship is not "I," but "we." There is a submission to the ways of God. There is a submission to one another in the Christian fellowship. There is a desire for God's life to rise up in the group, not just within the individual. If you are praying for a manifestation of the spiritual gifts, it does not have to come upon you but can come upon anybody and upon the group as a whole if that pleases God. Become of one mind, of one accord.

Fifth, cultivate holy dependency. Holy dependency means that you are utterly and completely dependent upon God for anything significant to happen. There is inward travail that the evil will weaken and that the good will rise up. You look forward to God acting and moving and teaching and wooing and winning. The work is God's and not yours.

Sixth, absorb distractions with gratitude. If there is noise or distraction, rather than fussing and fuming about it, learn to take it in and conquer it. If little children are running about, bless them. Thank God that they are alive and that they have energy. Become willing to relax with distractions—they may be a message from the Lord. When I am preaching, I love to have babies and little children in the congregation because sometimes they are the only ones that I can be sure are alive! Learn simply to receive whatever happens in a gathered worship experience, rather than feeling that distractions somehow deter you from worshiping God.

Seventh, learn to offer a sacrifice of worship. Many times you will not "feel" like worship. Perhaps you have had so many disappointing experiences in the past that you think it is hardly worth it. There is such a low sense of the power of God. Few people are adequately prepared. But you need to go anyway. You need to offer a sacrifice of worship. You need to be with the people of God and say, "These are my people. As stiff-necked and hard-hearted and sinful as we may be, together we come to God." Many times I do not feel like worshiping and I have to kneel down and say, "Lord, I don't feel like worshiping, but I desire to give you this time. It belongs to you. I will waste this time for you."

Isaac Pennington says that when people are gathered for genuine worship, "They are like a heap of fresh and burning coals warming one another as a great strength and freshness and vigor of life flows into all."[11] One log by itself cannot burn for very long, but when many logs are put together, even if they are poor logs, they can make quite a fire. Remember the counsel of Proverbs 27:17 that "Iron sharpens iron," and even rather dull lives can help each other if they are willing to try.

So go, even if you don't feel like it. Go, even if worship has been discouraging and dry before. Go, praying. Go, expecting. Go, looking for God to do a new and living work among you.

The Fruits of Worship

Just as worship begins in holy expectancy, it ends in holy obedience. If worship does not propel us into greater obedience, it has not been worship. To stand before the Holy One of eternity is to change. Resentments cannot be held with the same tenacity when we enter his gracious light. As Jesus says, we need to leave our gift at the altar and go set the matter straight (Matt. 5:23, 24). In worship an increased power steals its way into the heart sanctuary, an increased compassion grows in the soul. To worship is to change.

Holy obedience saves worship from becoming an opiate, an escape from the pressing needs of modern life. Worship enables us to hear the call to service clearly so that we respond, "Here am I! Send me" (Isa. 6:8). Authentic worship will impel us to join in the Lamb's war against demonic powers everywhere—on the personal level, on the social level, on the institutional level. Jesus, the Lamb of God, is our Commander-in-Chief. We receive his orders for service and go ". . . conquering and to conquer . . . with the word of truth . . . returning love for hatred, wrestling with God against the enmity, with prayers and tears night and day, with fasting, mourning and lamentation, in patience, in faithfulness, in truth, in love unfeigned, in long suffering, and in all the fruits of the spirit, that if by any means [we] may overcome evil with good. . . ."[12] In all things and in all ways we do exactly what Christ says because we have a holy obedience that has been cultivated over years of experience.

Willard Sperry declares, "Worship is a deliberate and disciplined adventure in reality."[13] It is not for the timid or comfortable. It involves an opening of ourselves to the adventurous life of the Spirit. It makes all the religious paraphernalia of temples and priests and rites and ceremonies irrelevant. It involves a willingness to "Let the word of Christ dwell in you richly, as you teach and admonish one another in all wisdom, and as you sing psalms and hymns and spiritual songs with thankfulness in your hearts to God" (Col. 3:16).

12. The Discipline of Guidance

Dwell in the life and love and power and wisdom of God, in unity one with another and with God; and the peace and wisdom of God fill your hearts, that nothing may rule in you but the life, which stands in the Lord God.

—GEORGE FOX

In our day heaven and earth are on tiptoe waiting for the emergence of a Spirit-led, Spirit-intoxicated, Spirit-empowered people. All of creation watches expectantly for the springing up of a disciplined, freely gathered, martyr people who know in this life the life and power of the kingdom of God. It has happened before. It can happen again.

Indeed, in movements all over the world we are now beginning to see the breaking forth of the apostolic church of the Spirit. Many are having a deep and profound experience of an Emmanuel of the Spirit—God with us; a knowledge that in the power of the Spirit Jesus has come to guide his people himself; an experience of his leading that is as definite and as immediate as the cloud by day and the pillar of fire by night.

But the knowledge of the direct, active, immediate leading of the Spirit is not sufficient. Individual guidance must yield to corporate guidance. There must also come a knowledge of the direct, active, immediate leading of the Spirit *together*. I do not mean "corporate guidance" in an organizational sense, but in an organic and functional sense. Church councils and denominational decrees are simply not of this reality.

Much of the teaching on divine guidance in our century has been noticeably deficient on the corporate aspect. We have received excellent instruction on how God leads us through Scripture and through reason and through circumstances and through the promptings of the Spirit upon the individual heart. There has also been teaching—good teaching—on the exceptional means of guidance: angels, visions, dreams, signs, and more. But we have heard little about how God leads through his people, the body of Christ. On that subject there is profound silence.

For this reason I have chosen to list guidance among the Corporate Disciplines and to stress its communal side. God does guide the individual richly and profoundly, but he also guides groups of people and can instruct the individual through the group experience.*

Perhaps the preoccupation with private guidance in Western cultures is the product of their emphasis upon individualism. The people of God have not always been so.

God led the children of Israel out of bondage *as a people*. Everyone saw the cloud and fiery pillar. They were not a gathering of individuals who happened to be going in the same direction; they were a people under the theocratic rule of God. His brooding presence covered them with an amazing immediacy. The people, however, soon found God's unmediated presence too awful, too glorious and begged, "Let not God speak to us, lest we die" (Exod. 20:19). So Moses became their mediator. Thus began the great ministry of the prophets whose function was to hear God's word and bring it to the people. Although it was a step away from the corporate leading of the Holy Spirit, there remained a sense of being a people together under the rule of God. But a day came when Israel rejected even the prophet in favor of a king. From that point on the prophet was the outsider. He was a lonely voice crying in the wilderness; sometimes obeyed, sometimes killed, but almost always on the outside.

Patiently God prepared a people and in the fullness of time

---

*One of the very finest books on the personal side of guidance is *In Search of Guidance* by Dallas Willard (Ventura, CA: Regal Books, 1984).

Jesus came. And with him dawned a new day. Once again a people were gathered who lived under the immediate, theocratic rule of the Spirit. With quiet persistence Jesus showed them what it meant to live in response to the voice of the Father. He taught them that they, too, could hear the heaven-sent voice and most clearly when together. "If two of you agree on earth about anything they ask, it will be done for them by my Father in heaven. For where two or three are gathered in my name, there am I in the midst of them" (Matt. 18:19, 20).

In those words Jesus gave his disciples both assurance and authority. There was the assurance that when a people genuinely gathered in his name his will could be discerned. The superintending Spirit would utilize the checks and balances of the different believers to ensure that when their hearts were in unity they were in rhythm with the heartbeat of the Father. Assured that they had heard the voice of the true Shepherd, they were able to pray and act with authority. His will plus their unity equaled authority.

Although Jesus was an outsider to his own people, being crucified beyond the city gates, some people embraced his rulership. And they became a gathered people. "Now the company of those who believed were of one heart and soul, and no one said that any of the things which he possessed was his own, but they had everything in common. And with great power the apostles gave their testimony to the resurrection" (Acts 4:32, 33). They became a fiery band of witnesses, declaring everywhere that Christ's voice could be heard and his will obeyed.

Perhaps the most astonishing feature of that incendiary fellowship was their sense of corporate guidance. It was beautifully illustrated in the calling forth of Paul and Barnabas to tramp the length and breadth of the Roman empire with the good news of the kingdom of God (Acts 13:1–3). Their call came when a number of people had been together over an extended period of time. It included the use of the Disciplines of prayer, fasting, and worship. Having become a prepared people, the call of God arose out of their corporate worship: "Set apart for me Barnabas and Saul for the work to which I have called them" (Acts 13:2).

With all our modern methods of missionary recruitment we could profit by giving serious attention to this example of corporate guidance. We would be well advised to encourage groups of people to fast, pray, and worship together until they have discerned the mind of the Lord.

Under corporate guidance the early Church faced and resolved its most explosive issue (Acts 15). Some free-lance Christians had gone up to Antioch and had begun preaching the necessity of circumcision for all Christians. The issue was far from trivial. Paul saw at once that it was tantamount to the Jewish cultural captivity of the Church.

Appointed elders and apostles gathered in the power of the Lord not to jockey for position or to play one side against another, but to hear the mind of the Spirit. It was no small task. There was intense debate. Then in a beautiful example of how individual guidance impinges upon corporate guidance, Peter told about his experience with the Italian centurion Cornelius. As he spoke, the ever-brooding Spirit of God did a wonderful work. When Peter finished, the entire assembly fell into silence (Acts 15:12). Finally, the gathered group came into what must be called a glorious, heaven-sent, unified commitment to reject cultural religion and to hold to the everlasting gospel of Jesus Christ. They concluded, "It has seemed good to the Holy Spirit and to us . . ." (Acts 15:28). They had faced the toughest issue of their day and had discerned the voice from on high. This is the high watermark in the book of Acts.

It was more than a victory regarding an issue; it was a victory of the method used in resolving all issues. As a people they had decided to live under the direct rulership of the Spirit. They had rejected both human totalitarianism and anarchy. They had even rejected democracy, that is, majority rule. They had dared to live on the basis of Spirit-rule; no fifty-one percent vote, no compromises, but Spirit-directed unity. And it worked.

No doubt those experiences in discerning the will of God in community contributed greatly to Paul's understanding of the Church as the body of Christ. He saw that the gifts of the Spirit were given by the Spirit to the body in such a way that interdependence was ensured. No one person possessed everything. Even the most mature needed the help of others. The most insignificant had something to contribute. No one could hear the whole counsel of God in isolation.

Sadly, we must note that by the time John received his great apocalyptic vision the believing community was beginning to cool. By the time of Constantine the church was ready to accept another human king. The vision, however, did not die, and there have been groups throughout the centuries gathered together under the rulership of the Holy Spirit. And today we are beginning to see just such a gathering, and for this we can thank God.

Some Models

The apostolic band did not leap from ground zero to the dizzy heights of Spirit-rulership in a single bound. Neither will we. For the most part they moved into that realm one step at a time, sometimes moving forward a bit, sometimes withdrawing. But by the time Pentecost had come, they were a prepared people.

Having once understood the radical implications of being a people under the direct administration of the Holy Spirit, one of the most destructive things we can do is to say, "Sounds wonderful. Beginning tomorrow I'll live that way!" Such zealotry only succeeds in making life miserable for ourselves and everyone around us. So, rather than sally off to conquer the world of the Spirit, most of us need to begin with more modest steps. One of the best ways we learn is from models of people who have struggled corporately to hear the voice from on high.

One of the most delightful examples comes from "the poor little monk of Assisi," St. Francis. Francis, it seems, was in "great agony of doubt" about whether he should devote himself only to prayer and meditation, which was a common practice in those days, or whether he should also engage in preaching missions. Wisely, Francis sought out counsel. "As the holy humility that was in him did not allow him to trust in himself or in his own prayers, he humbly turned to others in order to know God's will in this matter."

He sent messages to two of his most trusted friends, Sister Clare and Brother Silvester, asking them to meet with one of their "purer and more spiritual companions" and seek the will of God in the matter. Immediately, they gathered to pray and both Sister Clare and Brother Silvester returned with the same answer.

When the messenger returned, St. Francis first washed his feet and prepared him a meal. Then, kneeling down before the messenger, St. Francis asked him, "What does my Lord Jesus Christ order me to do?" The messenger replied that Christ had revealed that "He wants you to go about the world preaching, because God did not call you for yourself alone but also for the salvation of others." Receiving the message as the undisputed word of Christ, St. Francis jumped up saying, "So let's go—in the name of the Lord," whereupon he immediately embarked on a preaching mission. That direction gave the early Franciscan movement an unusual combination of mystical contemplation and evangelistic fervor.[1]

In this experience Francis was doing more than seeking out the advice of wise counselors. He was seeking a way to open the windows of heaven to reveal the mind of Christ, and he took it as such—to the great good of all to whom he ministered.

Another model for corporate guidance can be found in what some call "meetings for clearness." Such meetings are called specifically to seek the mind of the Spirit for some individual's question. Once a gifted young man asked my counsel about his future. He had graduated from college and was wrestling with whether or not to go into the pastoral ministry. He had availed himself of all the vocational tests and guidance courses offered and still was undecided. I honestly did not know what was best for him and suggested that he call a meeting for clearness. So he gathered a group of people who knew him well, had spiritual maturity, and were unafraid to be honest and candid with him. There were no earth-shattering visions given to my friend that night, but as this group worshiped and shared they became a supporting community. Over a period of time the gifts and calling of that young man were confirmed, and today he is in the pastoral ministry.

A concept closely akin to this has been pioneered by the Church of the Saviour in Washington, D.C. When any member feels that God has led him or her to establish a particular mission group or to venture into a special area of service, they "sound the call." This is done at the conclusion of a worship service when the member shares the vision that he or she senses. Afterward, all who want to are welcome to meet with the person to "test the call." Together they probe the issue, praying, questioning, searching. Sometimes there is a sense that the idea was the product of false enthusiasm, and it is abandoned. At other times it is confirmed by the prayers and interaction of the group. Perhaps others in the room are drawn into the call and make it their own. Thus a "company of the committed" is formed.

Matters of the highest personal importance can be brought to the believing community for discernment. For example, on one occasion two people came before our community stating that they felt the leading of the Lord to be married and desired the confirmation of a Spirit-directed body. Several people who knew the couple well were asked to meet with them. This is their report:

"The special committee appointed to communicate with Mark

and Becky regarding their plans to marry is happy to return a most positive report.

We met with Mark and Becky and had a most enjoyable evening of fellowship and prayer. We shared our concern for the sanctity of the family which is the heart of God's plan for human relationships. We were impressed with Mark and Becky's dependence upon the Lord's leading, their anticipation of potential problems, and their mature realization that successful marriage depends upon continuing commitment to each other and to the Lord.

We are happy to commend Mark and Becky's plans to the [church]. We feel their home will reflect the prayerful and loving influence of their childhood homes and the church community as they unite their love in that relationship ordained by God.

The committee feels a beneficial, special warmth for Mark and Becky which we anticipate will continue in a shepherding relationship. We recommend this precedent to other couples considering marriage."*

It is possible for business decisions to be made under a sense of the corporate leading of the Holy Spirit. Quakers have done so for years and have demonstrated the feasibility of such an approach. Business meetings should be viewed as worship services. Available facts can be presented and discussed, all with a view to listening to the voice of Christ. Facts are only one aspect of the decision-making process and in themselves are not conclusive. The Spirit can lead contrary to or in accord with the available facts. God will implant a spirit of unity when the right path has been chosen and trouble us with restlessness when we have not heard correctly. Unity rather than majority rule is the principle of corporate guidance. Spirit-given unity goes beyond mere agreement. It is the perception that we have heard the *Kol Yahweh*, the voice of God.

---

*Mark and Becky have given me permission to tell their story.

A classic and dramatic illustration occurred in 1758. John Woolman and others had pricked the conscience of the Society of Friends over their involvement in the demonic institution of slavery. As Philadelphia Yearly Meeting gathered for its business meetings that year, the slavery issue was a major agenda item. A great deal was at stake and the issue was hotly debated. John Woolman, with head bowed and tears in his eyes, sat through the various sessions in complete silence. Finally, after hours of agonizing prayer he rose and spoke. "My mind is led to consider the purity of the Divine Being and the justice of His judgment, and herein my soul is covered with awfulness. . . . Many slaves on this continent are oppressed and their cries have entered into the ears of the Most High. . . . It is not a time for delay." Firmly and tenderly Woolman dealt with the problems of the "private interests of some persons" and the "friendships which do not stand upon an immutable foundation." With prophetic boldness he warned the Yearly Meeting that if it failed to do its "duty in firmness and constancy" then "God may by terrible things in righteousness answer us in this matter."[2]

The entire Yearly Meeting melted into a spirit of unity as a result of this compassionate witness. They responded as one voice to remove slavery from their midst. John Greenleaf Whittier states that those sessions "must ever be regarded as one of the most important religious convocations in the history of the Christian Church."[3]

That united decision is particularly impressive when we realize that the Society of Friends was the only body that asked slaveholding members to reimburse their slaves for their time in bondage.* It is also striking to realize that under the prompting of the Spirit, Quakers had voluntarily done something that not one of the antislavery revolutionary leaders—George

*There are no accurate figures on the amount that was paid though it was common to pay the yearly wage at that time. In an appeal to the House of Commons to abolish slavery, one Mr. F. Buston said that it had cost North Carolina Friends fifty thousand pounds to release their slaves.

Washington, Thomas Jefferson, Patrick Henry—was willing to do. So influential was the united decision of 1758 that by the time of the signing of the Declaration of Independence Quakers had completely freed themselves from the institution of slavery.

Many of the Christian communities springing up around the world have discovered the reality and practicality of business decisions through Spirit rule. Such diverse groups as Reba Place Fellowship in Illinois, Society of Brothers in New York, and the Mary Sisterhood in Darmstadt, Germany, all operate on the basis of Spirit-directed unity. Issues are approached with an assurance that the mind of the Spirit can be known. They gather in Christ's name, believing that his will will be fleshed out in their midst. They do not seek compromise, but God-given consensus.

I once attended a business session of some two hundred people in which an issue had been earnestly debated. Though there was a sharp difference of opinion, each of the members sincerely desired to hear and obey the will of God. After a considerable period of time, a united sense of direction began to emerge among all except a few people. Finally, one person stood and said, "I do not feel right about this course of action, but I hope that the rest of you will love me enough to labor with me until I have the same sense of God's leading as the rest of you or until God opens another way to us."

As an outside observer, I was touched by how tenderly the group responded to that appeal. All over the auditorium little groups began gathering to share, to listen, to pray. By the time they had broken through to a united decision, I had received a far greater appreciation for the way in which Christians are to "maintain the unity of the Spirit in the bond of peace" (Eph. 4:3). Such expressions of the central function of corporate guidance are among the most healthy signs of spiritual vitality today.

The Spiritual Director

In the Middle Ages not even the greatest saints attempted the depths of the inward journey without the help of a spiritual director. Today the concept is hardly understood, let alone practiced, except in the Roman Catholic monastic system. That is a tragedy, for the idea of the spiritual director is highly applicable to the contemporary scene. It is a beautiful expression of divine guidance through the help of our brothers and sisters.

Spiritual directorship has an exemplary history. Many of the first spiritual directors were the desert Fathers and were held in high regard for their ability to "discern spirits." People would often travel for miles in the wilderness just to hear a brief word of advice, a "word of salvation," which summed up the will and judgment of God for them in their actual concrete situation. The *Apophthegmata* or "Sayings of the Fathers" is an eloquent testimony to the simplicity and depth of this spiritual guidance. Also, many of the Cistercian laybrothers in twelfth-century England were distinguished for their ability to read and guide souls.

What is the purpose of a spiritual director? The seventeenth-century Benedictine mystic, Dom Augustine Baker, writes, "In a word, he is only God's usher, and must lead souls in God's way, and not his own."[4] His direction is simply and clearly to lead us to our real Director. He is the means of God to open the path to the inward teaching of the Holy Spirit.

His function is purely and simply charismatic. He leads only by the force of his own personal holiness. He is not a superior or some ecclesiastically appointed authority. The relationship is of an adviser to a friend. Though the director has obviously advanced further into the inner depths, the two are both learning and growing in the realm of the Spirit.

All this talk of "soul" and "spirit" might lead us to think that spiritual direction deals only with a small corner or compartment of our lives. That is, we would go to a spiritual director to care for our spirit the way we might go to an ophthalmologist to care for our eyes. Such an approach is false. Spiritual direction is concerned with the whole person and the interrelationship of all of life. Thomas Merton tells of a Russian spiritual director who was criticized for spending so much time earnestly advising an old peasant woman about the care of her turkeys. "Not at all," he replied, "her *whole life* is in those turkeys."[5] Spiritual direction takes up the concrete daily experiences of our lives and gives them sacramental significance. We learn "the sacrament of the present moment" as Jean-Pierre de Caussade put it.[6] "So, whether you eat or drink, or whatever you do, do all to the glory of God" (1 Cor. 10:31).

Spiritual direction is first born out of natural, spontaneous human relationships. A hierarchical, or even organizational system, is not essential to its function and is often destructive to it. The ordinary kinds of caring and sharing that belong to the Christian community are the starting point for spiritual direction. Out of them will flow "kingdom authority" through mutual subordination and servanthood.

A spiritual director must be a person who has developed a comfortable acceptance of himself or herself. That is, a genuine maturity must pervade all of that person's life. Such persons are unmoved by the fluctuations of the times. They can absorb the selfishness and mediocrity and apathy around them and transform it. They are unjudging and unshakable. They must have compassion and commitment. Like Paul who thought of Timothy as his "beloved child," they must be prepared to take on certain parental responsibilities. Theirs must be a tough love that refuses to give approval to every whim. They should also know enough of the human psyche that they will not reinforce unconscious and infantile needs for authoritarianism.

Spiritual directors must be on the inward journey themselves and be willing to share their own struggles and doubts. There needs to be a realization that together they are learning from Jesus, their ever-present Teacher.

How does such a relationship come about? As with all other things in the kingdom of God, it is arranged by prayer. Bringing and resting our case with God, we wait patiently for his way to be manifest. If he should invite us to speak to someone or make certain arrangements, we gladly obey. Such relationships can be formal as in some of the monastic orders, but they do not need to be. If we have the humility to believe that we can learn from our brothers and sisters and the understanding that some have gone further into the divine Center than others, then we can see the necessity of spiritual direction. As Virgil Vogt of Reba Place Fellowship says, "If you cannot listen to your brother, you cannot listen to the Holy Spirit."[7]

Also, it is helpful to realize that there are many forms of spiritual direction. Preaching is a form of spiritual direction as is the ministry of many small groups. John Wesley established the "class meetings" and the "bands" as forms of spiritual direction. The Bible itself functions as spiritual direction, for as we read it prayerfully we are being formed more and more into the image of Christ.

In reflecting on the value of this ministry for centuries of Christians, Thomas Merton says that the spiritual director was something of "a spiritual father who 'begot' the perfect life in the soul of his disciple by his instructions first of all, but also by his prayer, his sanctity and his example. He was . . . a kind of 'sacrament' of the Lord's presence in the ecclesiastical community."[8]

The Limits of Corporate Guidance

As we all know, dangers exist in corporate guidance as well as in individual guidance. Perhaps the most menacing danger is manipulation and control by leaders. If corporate guidance is not handled within the larger context of an all-pervasive grace, it degenerates into an effective way to straighten out deviant behavior. It becomes a kind of quasi-magic formula through which leaders can impose their will upon individuals, an authorized system through which all differing opinions can be brought into line.

Such manipulative perversion results in the stifling of fresh spiritual vitality. The prophet Isaiah tells us that the coming Messiah "will not break a bruised reed, or quench a smoldering wick" (Isa. 42:3; Matt. 12:20). It is not the way of Jesus to crush the weakest person or to snuff out the smallest hope. Tenderness toward each individual situation must inform all our deliberations. On one occasion George Fox was debating, and roundly defeating, one Nathaniel Stephens. Overwhelmed, Stephens declared that "George Fox is come into the light of the sun, and now he thinks to put out my starlight." Fox writes: "But I said, 'Nathaniel, give me thy hand'; then I told him I would not quench the least measure of God in any, much less put out his starlight."[9]

There is also danger in the opposite direction. It is possible for a hard-hearted and stiff-necked people to hinder Spirit-inspired leaders. While leaders need the counsel and discernment of the believing community, they also need the freedom to lead. If God has called them to lead, they should not have to bring every detail of life to the community. We must never be seduced by Western democratic ideals into believing that every person must have an equal say about every triviality in the community's life. God appoints authoritative leadership in his Church so that his work may be done upon the earth.

Another danger is that corporate guidance will become divorced from biblical norms. Scripture must pervade and penetrate all our thinking and acting. The one Spirit will never lead in opposition to the written Word that he inspired. There must always be the outward authority of Scripture as well as the inward authority of the Holy Spirit. In fact, Scripture itself is a form of corporate guidance. It is a way God speaks through the experience of the people of God. It is one aspect of "the communion of the saints."

Finally, we must recognize that corporate guidance is limited by our finitude. We are fallible human beings and there are times when, despite our best efforts, our own prejudices and fears keep us from a Spirit-led unity. Sometimes we simply see things differently. Paul and Barnabas, for example, could not agree on whether to take John Mark with them on their second missionary journey. Luke says "a sharp contention" developed between them (Acts 15:39). We should not be surprised if we have the same experience in our ministry efforts.

If this happens, my counsel is that we be kind to each other. Ministry teams at times do part ways, and churches at times do split. Let us do all we can to make any such separation as gracious as possible. Let us pray for each other and ask God's blessing upon one another. Let us have the confidence of the apostle Paul that "in every way, whether in pretense or in truth, Christ is proclaimed; and in that I rejoice" (Phil. 1:18).

Dallas Willard states, "The aim of God in history is the creation of an all-inclusive community of loving persons, with Himself included in that community as its prime sustainer and most glorious inhabitant."[10] Such a community lives under the immediate and total rulership of the Holy Spirit. They are a people blinded to all other loyalties by the splendor of God, a compassionate community embodying the law of love as seen in Jesus Christ. They are an obedient army of the Lamb of God living under the Spiritual Disciplines, a community in the process of total transformation from the inside out, a people determined to live out the demands of the gospel in a secular world. They are tenderly aggressive, meekly powerful, suffering, and overcoming. Such a community, cast in a rare and apostolic mold, constitutes a new gathering of the people of God. May almighty God continue to gather such people in our day.

13. The Discipline of Celebration

> The Christian should be an alleluia from head to foot!
> —AUGUSTINE OF HIPPO

Celebration is at the heart of the way of Christ. He entered the world on a high note of jubilation: "I bring you good news of a great joy," cried the angel, "which shall come to all the people" (Luke 2:10). He left the world bequeathing his joy to the disciples: "These things I have spoken to you that my joy may be in you, and that your joy may be full" (John 15:11).

André Trocmé in *Jésus-Christ et la révolution non-violente* and later John Howard Yoder in *The Politics of Jesus* go to some length to demonstrate that Jesus began his public ministry by proclaiming the year of Jubilee (Luke 4:18, 19). The social implications of such a concept are profound.* Equally penetrating is the realization that, as a result, we are called into a perpetual Jubilee of the Spirit. Such a radical, divinely enabled freedom from possessions and a restructuring of social arrangements cannot help but bring celebration. When the poor receive the good news, when the captives are released, when the blind receive their sight, when the oppressed are liberated, who can withhold the shout of jubilee?

In the Old Testament all the social stipulations of the year of Jubilee—canceling all debts, releasing slaves, planting no crops, returning property to the original owner—were a celebration of the gracious provision of God. God could be trusted to provide what was needed. He had declared, "I will com-

---

*Johannes Hoekendijk writes, "Jubilee is exodus spelled out in terms of social salvation. . . ." ("Mission—A Celebration of Freedom," *Union Seminary Quarterly Review*, January 1966, p. 141).

mand my blessing upon you" (Lev. 25:21). Freedom from anxiety and care forms the basis for celebration. Because we know he cares for us, we can cast all our care upon him. God has turned our mourning into dancing.

The carefree spirit of joyous festivity is absent in contemporary society. Apathy, even melancholy, dominates the times. Harvey Cox says that modern man has been pressed "so hard toward useful work and rational calculation he has all but forgotten the joy of ecstatic celebration. . . ."[1]

Celebration Gives Strength to Life

Celebration brings joy into life, and joy makes us strong. Scripture tells us that the joy of the Lord is our strength (Neh. 8:10). We cannot continue long in anything without it. Women endure childbirth because the joy of motherhood lies on the other side. Young married couples struggle through the first difficult years of adjustment because they value the insurance of a long life together. Parents hold steady through the teen years, knowing that their children will emerge at the other end human once again.

We may be able to begin tennis instruction or piano lessons by dint of will, but we will not keep at them for long without joy. In fact, the only reason we can begin is because we know that joy is the end result. That is what sustains all novices; they know there is a sense of pleasure, enjoyment, joy in mastery.

Celebration is central to all the Spiritual Disciplines. Without a joyful spirit of festivity the Disciplines become dull, death-breathing tools in the hands of modern Pharisees. Every Discipline should be characterized by carefree gaiety and a sense of thanksgiving.

Joy is part of the fruit of the Spirit (Gal. 5:22). Often I am inclined to think that joy is the motor, the thing that keeps everything else going. Without joyous celebration to infuse the other Disciplines, we will sooner or later abandon them. Joy produces energy. Joy makes us strong.

Ancient Israel was commanded to gather together three times a year to celebrate the goodness of God. Those were festival holidays in the highest sense. They were the experiences that gave strength and cohesion to the people of Israel.

The Path to Joy

In the spiritual life only one thing will produce genuine joy, and that is obedience. The old hymn tells us that there is no other way to be happy in Jesus but to "trust and obey." The hymn writer received his inspiration from the Master himself, for Jesus tells us that there is no blessedness equal to the blessedness of obedience. On one occasion a woman in the crowd shouted out to Jesus, "Blessed is the womb that bore you, and the breasts that you sucked!" Jesus responded, "Blessed rather are those who hear the word of God and keep it!" (Luke 11:27, 28). It is a more blessed thing to live in obedience than to have been the mother of the Messiah!

In 1870 Hannah Whitall Smith wrote what has become a classic on joyous Christianity, *The Christian's Secret of a Happy Life*. The title barely hints at the depths of that perceptive book. It is no shallow "four easy steps to successful living." Studiously, the writer defines the shape of a full and abundant life hid in God. Then she carefully reveals the difficulties to this way and finally charts the results of a life abandoned to God. What is the Christian's secret to a happy life? It is best summed up by her chapter entitled "The Joy of Obedience." Joy comes through obedience to Christ, and joy results from obedience to Christ. Without obedience joy is hollow and artificial.

To elicit genuine celebration, obedience must work itself into the ordinary fabric of our daily lives. Without that our celebrating carries a hollow sound. For example, some people live in such a way that it is impossible to have any kind of happiness in their home, but then they go to church and sing songs and pray "in the Spirit," hoping that God will somehow give them an infusion of joy to make it through the day. They are looking for some kind of heavenly transfusion that will bypass the misery of their daily lives and give them joy. But God's desire is to transform the misery, not bypass it.

We need to understand that God does at times give us an infusion of joy even in our bitterness and hard-heartedness. But that is the abnormal situation. God's normal means of bringing his joy is by redeeming and sanctifying the ordinary junctures of human life. When the members of a family are filled with love and compassion and a spirit of service to one another, that family has reason to celebrate.

There is something sad in people running from church to church trying to get an injection of "the joy of the Lord." Joy is not found in singing a particular kind of music or in getting with the right kind of group or even in exercising the charismatic gifts of the Spirit, good as all these may be. Joy is found in obedience. When the power that is in Jesus reaches into our work and play and redeems them, there will be joy where once there was mourning. To overlook this is to miss the meaning of the Incarnation.

That is why I have placed celebration at the end of this study. Joy is the end result of the Spiritual Disciplines' functioning in our lives. God brings about the transformation of our lives through the Disciplines, and we will not know genuine joy until there is a transforming work within us. Many people try to come into joy far too soon. Often we try to pump up people with joy when in reality nothing has happened in their lives. God has not broken into the routine experiences of their daily existence. Celebration comes when the common ventures of life are redeemed.

It is important to avoid the kind of celebrations that really celebrate nothing. Worse yet is to pretend to celebrate when the spirit of celebration is not in us. Our children watch us bless the food and promptly proceed to gripe about it—blessings that are not blessings. One of the things that nearly destroys children is being forced to be grateful when they are not grateful. If we pretend an air of celebration, our inner spirit is put in contradiction.

A popular teaching today instructs us to praise God for the various difficulties that come into our lives, asserting that there is great transforming power in thus praising God. In its best form such teaching is a way of encouraging us to look up the road a bit through the eye of faith and see what will be. It affirms in our hearts the joyful assurance that God takes all things and works them for the good of those who love him. In its worst form this teaching denies the vileness of evil and baptizes the most horrible tragedies as the will of God. Scripture commands us to live in a spirit of thanksgiving in the midst of all situations; it does not command us to celebrate the presence of evil.

The Spirit of Carefree Celebration

The apostle Paul calls us to "Rejoice in the Lord alway: and again I say, Rejoice" (Phil. 4:4, KJV). But how are we to do that? Paul continues, "Have no anxiety about anything," or as the King James Version puts it, "Be careful for nothing." That is the negative side of rejoicing. The positive side is "in everything by prayer and supplication with thanksgiving let your requests be made known to God." And the result? "The peace of God, which passes all understanding, will keep your hearts and minds in Christ Jesus" (Phil. 4:6, 7).

Paul instructs us on how we can always rejoice, and his first word of counsel is to be "full of care" for nothing. Jesus, of course, gives the same advice when he says, "Do not be anxious about your life, what you shall eat or what you shall drink, nor about your body, what you shall put on" (Matt. 6:25). In both instances the same word is used, which we translate "anxious" or "careful." Christians are called to be free of care, but we find such a way foreign to us. We have been trained since we were two years old to be full of care. We shout to our children as they run to the school bus, "Be careful," that is, be full of care.

The spirit of celebration will not be in us until we have learned to be "careful for nothing." And we will never have a carefree indifference to things until we trust God. This is why the Jubilee was such a crucial celebration in the Old Testament. No one would dare celebrate the Jubilee unless they had a deep trust in God's ability to provide for their needs.

When we trust God we are free to rely entirely upon him to provide what we need: "By prayer and supplication with thanksgiving let your requests be made known to God." Prayer is the means by which we move the arm of God; hence we can live in a spirit of carefree celebration.

Paul, however, does not end the matter there. Prayer and trust by themselves are not adequate to bring us joy. Paul proceeds to tell us to set our minds on all the things in life that are true, honorable, just, pure, lovely, and gracious (Phil. 4:8). God has established a created order full of excellent and good things, and it follows naturally that as we give our attention to those things we will be happy. That is God's appointed way to joy. If we think we will have joy only by praying and singing psalms, we will be disillusioned. But if we fill our lives with simple good things and constantly thank God for them, we will be joyful, that is, full of joy. And what about our problems? When we determine to dwell on the good and excellent things in life, we will be so full of those things that they will tend to swallow our problems.

The decision to set the mind on the higher things of life is an act of the will. That is why celebration is a Discipline. It is not something that falls on our heads. It is the result of a consciously chosen way of thinking and living. When we choose this way, the healing and redemption in Christ will break into the inner recesses of our lives and relationships, and the inevitable result will be joy.

The Benefits of Celebration

Far and away the most important benefit of celebration is that it saves us from taking ourselves too seriously. This is a desperately needed grace for all those who are earnest about the Spiritual Disciplines. It is an occupational hazard of devout folk to become stuffy bores. This should not be. Of all people, we should be the most free, alive, interesting. Celebration adds a note of gaiety, festivity, hilarity to our lives. After all, Jesus rejoiced so fully in life that he was accused of being a wine-bibber and a glutton. Many of us lead such sour lives that we cannot possibly be accused of such things.

Now I am not recommending a periodic romp in sin, but I am suggesting that we do need deeper, more earthy experiences of exhilaration. It is healing and refreshing to cultivate a wide appreciation for life. Our spirit can become weary with straining after God just as our body can become weary with overwork. Celebration helps us relax and enjoy the good things of the earth.

Celebration also can be an effective antidote for the periodic sense of sadness that can constrict and oppress the heart. Depression is an epidemic today and celebration can help stem the tide. In his chapter titled "Helps in Sadness," François Fénelon counsels those who are bowed low with the burdens of life to encourage themselves "with good conversation, even by making merry."[2]

Another benefit of celebration is its ability to give us perspective. We can laugh at ourselves. We come to see that the causes we champion are not nearly so monumental as we would like to believe. In celebration the high and the mighty regain their balance and the weak and lowly receive new stature. Who can be high or low at the festival of God? Together the rich and the poor, the powerful and the powerless all celebrate the glory and wonder of God. There is no leveler of caste systems like festivity.

Thus freed of an inflated view of our own importance, we

are also freed of a judgmental spirit. Others do not look so awful, so unspiritual. Common joys can be shared without sanctimonious value judgments.

Finally, an interesting characteristic of celebration is that it tends toward more celebration. Joy begets joy. Laughter begets laughter. It is one of those few things in life that we multiply by giving. Kierkegaard says that "humor is always a concealed pair."[3]

The Practice of Celebration

If celebration is primarily a corporate Discipline, and if it brings such benefit to the people of God, how is it practiced? The question is a good one, for modern men and women have become so mechanized that we have snuffed out nearly all experiences of spontaneous joy. Most of our experiences of celebration are artificial, plastic.

One way to practice celebration is through singing, dancing, shouting. Because of the goodness of God, the heart breaks forth into psalms and hymns and spiritual songs. Worship, praise, adoration flow from the inner chambers. In Psalm 150 we see the celebration of the people of God with trumpet and lute and harp, with timbrel and dance, with strings and pipe and loud clashing cymbals.

What do little children do when they celebrate? They make noise, lots of noise. There is not a thing wrong with noise at the appropriate time, just as there is nothing wrong with silence when it is appropriate. Children dance when they celebrate. When the children of Israel had been snatched from the clutches of Pharaoh by the mighty power of God, Miriam the prophetess led the people in a great celebration dance (Exod. 15:20). David went leaping and dancing before the Lord with all his might (2 Sam. 6:14, 16). The folk dance has always been a carrier of cultural values and has been used repeatedly in genuine celebration. Of course, dancing can have wrong and evil manifestations, but that is another matter entirely.

Singing, dancing, and noise-making are not required forms of celebration. They are examples only, to impress upon us that the earth indeed is the Lord's and the fullness thereof. Like Peter, we need to learn that nothing that comes from the gracious hand of God is inherently unclean (Acts 10). We are free to celebrate the goodness of God with all our viscera!

Laughing is another way we practice celebration. The old adage that laughter is the best medicine has a lot going for it. Indeed, Norman Cousins in his book, *Anatomy of an Illness*, discusses how he used the therapy of laughter to help him overcome a crippling disease. In his hospital bed Cousins watched old Marx Brothers films and "Candid Camera" shows, and the genuine belly laughter he experienced seemed to have an anesthetic effect and gave him pain-free sleep. Doctors even confirmed the salutary effect of laughter on his body chemistry.

Why not! Jesus had a sense of humor—some of his parables are positively comical. There is even such a thing as "holy laughter," a frequent phenomenon in various revival movements. Although I have not experienced holy laughter myself, I have observed it in others and its effects appear altogether beneficial. But whether God gives us this special grace or not, we can all experience times of wholesome laughter.

So poke fun at yourself. Enjoy wholesome jokes and clever puns. Relish good comedy. Learn to laugh; it is a discipline to be mastered. Let go of the everlasting burden of always needing to sound profound.

A third way to encourage celebration is to accent the creative gifts of fantasy and imagination. Harvey Cox observes that "man's celebrative and imaginative faculties have atrophied."[4] In another place he writes, "There was a time when visionaries were canonized, and mystics were admired. Now they are studied, smiled at, perhaps even committed. All in all, fantasy is viewed with distrust in our time."[5]

We who follow Christ can risk going against the cultural tide. Let's with abandon relish the fantasy games of children. Let's see visions and dream dreams. Let's play, sing, laugh. The imagination can release a flood of creative ideas, and it can be lots of fun. Only those who are insecure about their own maturity will fear such a delightful form of celebration.

Let us also relish the creativity of others. Those who create sculptures and paintings and plays and music are a great gift to us. We can organize art shows to display their work. We can sing their music in intimate gatherings and formal concerts. We can arrange for dramatic productions of our friend's works. We can have a family art show and feature the kid's paintings from school. Why not! It is great fun and builds community.

Another thing we can do is to make family events into times of celebration and thanksgiving. This is particularly true of the various rites of passage in our culture like birthdays, graduations, marriages, anniversaries. One couple I know plants a tree for every wedding anniversary. On their farm they now have a little forest of some forty trees that bear silent witness to their love and fidelity.

We can also celebrate lesser, but equally important events like finishing a major project, securing a job, receiving a raise. In addition, why not form regular rituals of celebration that are not connected with special events. Spend more time around the piano as a family and sing out! Learn the folk dances of various cultures and enjoy them together. Set up regular times to play games or watch movies or read books together. Turn visits to relatives into celebrations of your relationship. I am sure you can come up with many other ideas that belong to your family alone.

A fifth thing we can do is to take advantage of the festivals of our culture and really celebrate. What a great celebration we can make of Christmas. It does not have to have all the crass commercialism connected to it if we decide that we do not want it that way. Of course the giving of gifts is a great thing, but we can give many kinds of presents. Several years ago our young son Nathan, who was learning to play the piano at that time, gave every member of the family a special gift—playing a song he had learned. He had great fun gift wrapping huge boxes and trying to get everyone to guess what their gift was. And then when they opened it, a note said that he was going to play some little piece for them on the piano. How delightful, how fun!

And what about Easter? Forget the spring style show and celebrate the power of the resurrection. Make family Easter plays. Revive the May Day celebrations. Go pick flowers and deliver them to your neighbors and friends. Rejoice in the beauty of color and variety. Why allow Halloween to be a pagan holiday in commemoration of the powers of darkness? Fill the house or church with light; sing and celebrate the victory of Christ over darkness. Let the children (and adults) dress up as biblical characters or as some of the saints through the centuries.

In the Middle Ages there was a holiday known as the Feast of Fools.[6] It was a time when all "sacred cows" of the day could be safely laughed at and mocked. Minor clerics mimicked and ridiculed their superiors. Political leaders were lampooned. We can do without the excessive debauchery that often accompanied those festivities, but we do need occasions when we laugh at ourselves. Instead of chafing under the social customs of our day, we might do well to find ways to laugh at them.

We are not limited to established festivals; we can develop our own. One fellowship held a celebration night in appreciation of their pastors. Each family designed a homemade card. Various groups prepared skits, plays, readings, jokes. As one of those pastors, I can say that it was a hilarious night. Why do we wait until our pastors are ready to leave before we throw a party for them? If we will show our appreciation more often, they just might be encouraged to stay longer.

I know of one church that has a "festival of lights" for Christmas. They have music, they have drama, and most of all they involve lots of people. I know of another group that meets quarterly to celebrate the foods of other countries. On one occasion they will have a Swedish meal, at another Irish, and at another Japanese.

Where I teach we have an annual event called "Symphony of Spring," and the good it does for the human spirit is impossible to calculate. It is the most anticipated event of the year. Music, costumes, color—it is a mini-extravaganza with all the expertise of a professional production without the plastic superficiality. This event is not cheap. There is a considerable expense in time, energy, and money. But we all need such festivals of joy as together we seek the kingdom of God.

Celebration gives us the strength to live in all the other Disciplines. When faithfully pursued, the other Disciplines bring us deliverance from those things that have made our lives miserable for years which, in turn, evokes increased celebration. Thus, an unbroken circle of life and power is formed.

Finis

We have come to the end of this study, but only to the beginning of our journey. We have seen how *meditation* heightens our spiritual sensitivity which, in turn, leads us into *prayer*. Very soon we discover that prayer involves *fasting* as an accompanying means. Informed by these three Disciplines, we can effectively move into *study* which gives us discernment about ourselves and the world in which we live.

Through *simplicity* we live with others in integrity. *Solitude* allows us to be genuinely present to people when we are with them. Through *submission* we live with others without manipulation, and through *service* we are a blessing to them.

Confession frees us from ourselves and releases us to *worship*. Worship opens the door to *guidance*. All the Disciplines freely exercised bring forth the doxology of *celebration*.

The classical Disciplines of the spiritual life beckon us to the Himalayas of the Spirit. Now we stand at timber line awed by the snowy peaks before us. We step out in confidence with our Guide who has blazed the trail and conquered the highest summit.

In Celebration of
Celebration of Discipline

To honor the tenth anniversary of the publication of *Celebration of Discipline*, a number of church leaders and teachers were asked to reflect on the meaning of the book in their lives and their ministries and on its effect on the teaching and practice of spirituality in the Church as a whole.

Their comments, which invite deeper appreciation of this book and of the centrality of the Spiritual Disciplines to the Christian's life, follow.

"I first heard of *Celebration of Discipline* from a Catholic priest in the Republic of Panama who was recommending the book to his parish. I purchased a copy and immediately made it mandatory reading for all the leadership in our church. . . . Since then, I have been walking out the disciplines as a way of life. . . . I am deeply indebted to Richard Foster for clearly defining on paper those things about which the Spirit has been tugging at my heart."

Jamie Buckingham, editor, *Buckingham Report*

"Richard Foster has impacted my life. As an activist, I have a tendency to get so involved in my own 'good works' that I often neglect the spiritual disciplines that keep me in touch with the sources of my strength and vision. I have so far to go, but *Celebration of Discipline* is a major help for moving me in the direction I ought to go."

Tony Campolo, author of *Who Switched the Price Tags* and *Seven Deadly Sins*

"Richard Foster is a rare and powerful author whose writings are insightful, concisely written, penetrating, thought-provoking, intellectually stimulating, intensely practical, and free of the verbal fluff that seems to characterize so many modern books. *Celebration of Discipline* has been an influential, challenging, and helpful guide in my own spiritual walk. The book is like a much appreciated old friend. I am grateful to God for Richard Foster's deep and powerful contribution to Christian spirituality, and I am encouraged to know that this contemporary Christian classic continues to help generations of readers in their walks with Christ."

Gary R. Collins, professor of psychology, Trinity Evangelical Divinity School

"The past decade has seen a very deep and renewed interest in spirituality in many areas of the church. Those of us who are evangelical Protestants have needed a corrective to our activism and a return to our roots of an authentic walk with God. *Celebration of Discipline* certainly has been one of the key books in this renewal. I personally was greatly helped when I first read it and have recommended it widely. Richard Foster's lucid writing plus his emphasis on disciplined grace have made this one of the notable books of our time. I often refer to it. Those of us who are concerned for world evangelization as we face the end of this century need to recognize that this vast task can never be accomplished apart from an even deeper rootage in Christ, instructed by the Word of God and nurtured by His Spirit. I welcome the new edition of *Celebration of Discipline*."

Leighton Ford, Leighton Ford Ministries

"Richard Foster's *Celebration of Discipline* is one of few books in our generation to earn the title 'classic.' When speaking of Christian 'classics,' we rarely think of any contemporary works.

The assumption is that to be a classic, the work must be very old. In reality, age has little to do with it. A book becomes classic when its primary message has been tested by a sufficient number of people and found to be authentic, wise, and useful.

"*Celebration of Discipline* is a popular book in the best sense of that word—it is for the people. Too often the spiritual disciplines are thought to be reserved either for the spiritual giants, or for those privileged souls who do not have to cope with the 'distractions' of a family or a full-time job. Richard Foster rescues the disciplines from the specialists and the ascetics and returns them to the ordinary disciples for whom they are intended. His vision of a 'disciple in training' embraces both the assembly-line worker and the academic, the harried mother of small children, the office worker, and the cleric."

William C. Frey, bishop, Episcopal Diocese of Colorado

" 'Follow me!' was Christ's call to James and John along the Galilean seashore as he began his earthly ministry. 'Follow me,' continues to be Christ's call to believers today. But heeding this call in the midst of a culture that ignores Christ and embraces materialism is difficult and can easily produce frustration and defeat. *Celebration of Discipline* by Richard Foster carefully explores the biblical means for knowing and following the Savior in contemporary society and offers practical suggestions to believers for everyday living."

Mark O. Hatfield, senator from Oregon

"*Celebration of Discipline* has helped the church today come to a refreshing, in-depth understanding of classical spiritual disciplines. An excitement has swept the country as many Christians have put into practice the life-changing truths found in this book."

Carolyn Koons, author of *Tony: Our Journey Together* and *Beyond Betrayal*

"Upon reading *Celebration of Discipline* nearly ten years ago, I no longer felt so frighteningly alone on the spiritual journey.

Over the years, I have grown to value this book immensely in my work as a writer and teacher. Much like an old and very dear friend, *Celebration of Discipline* gently challenges me to walk steadfastly along the path toward wholeness and God. The force and clarity of Richard Foster's thought and expression lights the way even during the darkest of moments while his lucid prose and keen observations help make the difficult personal and corporate practice of the spiritual disciplines a remarkably joyous experience."

Judith C. Lechman, author of *Yielding To Courage* and *The Spirituality of Gentleness*

"*Celebration of Discipline* won me when it was first published, a fresh voice of reality . . . and there is even more need for Richard Foster's wisdom today. Indeed his offerings to us of the joy of discipline will help us to seek the kingdom of God in a more joyous and less moralistic way than late twentieth century Christendom has tended to urge on us. He sings along the fine line between crippling permissiveness and self indulgence, and equally destructive legalism and fear. Whether he is writing of meditation and contemplation, or of studying, or of fasting, Richard Foster gives us a spiritually healthy and happily robust view of discipline. If everybody in this country could read— and heed—this book, what a difference it would make to the planet—nay, to the cosmos."

Madeleine L'Engle, author of *A Wrinkle in Time* and *The Crosswicks Journals*

"We are an indulgent people in a selfish age. Even as Christians we do not celebrate discipline, whether physical, intellectual, social, or spiritual. But that is the spirit-guided genius of Richard Foster's *Celebration of Discipline.* Out of his own faith and practice he shows what we are missing—the joy of exercising spiritual discipline and finding the fullness of life promised by Christ. Ten years after its publication I still quote from the book, recommend its reading, practice its principles, and cel-

ebrate its timely contribution to lasting Christian literature."
David L. McKenna, president, Asbury Theological
Seminary

"I used to say that the anthem of evangelicalism was 'Amazing
Grace,' lamenting that we evangelicals had never written a
hymn called 'Amazing Discipline.' I no longer say that. Richard
Foster has taught me a more thorough inwardness than I once
knew. *Celebration of Discipline* is a contagion of joy that led me
past cheap grace to a contemplative lifestyle that not only
changed my life, but gave my renovated ministry to a congregation grateful for the changes."
Calvin Miller, author of *The Singer* trilogy and *The
Legend of the Brotherstone*

"Like a child exploring the attic of an old house on a rainy day,
discovering a trunk full of treasure and then calling all his
brothers and sisters to share the find, Richard Foster has
'found' the spiritual disciplines that the modern world stored
away and forgot, and has excitedly called us to celebrate them.
For they are, as he shows us, the instruments of joy, the way
into mature Christian spirituality and abundant life."
Eugene H. Peterson, author of *Reversed Thunder* and *A
Long Obedience in the Same Direction*

"The great lack in the Church today is self-discipline. There is
too little sound instruction as to what Christians must do *after*
being born anew. The great work of sanctification only begins
at conversion. The book, *Celebration of Discipline*, by Richard J.
Foster, has been and continues to be a most valuable celebration of that kind of discipline every Christian must undertake
if he or she would mature in Christ. We highly recommend
Celebration of Discipline to all readers."
John and Paula Sandford, authors of *Transformation of the
Inner Man*

"Where cheap and tawdry values shape our society, Richard
Foster holds up for us a model that is both solid and costly.

The disciplines about which he writes so boldly and clearly are the convincing disciplines practiced by Christ himself. . . .

"One of Foster's most helpful conclusions to me, personally, is that the disciplines in themselves are valueless—they are simply means to a greater end—freedom. . . . [J]ust as the laws (or disciplines) of physics free a sailboat to turn a keen head-wind into forward movement against that wind, so the spiritual and physical disciplines allow us to turn our limitations and liabilities into redemptive freedoms and benefits for ourselves, our churches, society, and God.

"And I've always liked Foster's practicality. There is mystery here, but it is not inaccessible, because we are shown *how* to practice the disciplines in a detailed and concrete way. The spiritual is fused with the physical; the word is again made flesh; heaven and earth seem joined in this writing."

Luci Shaw, author of *Listen to the Green*

"Richard Foster's *Celebration of Discipline* is the best modern book on Christian spirituality. I have read it about a half a dozen times in the last decade and have used it as a text in classes and small groups. . . . No other book apart from the Bible has been so helpful to me in the nurturing of my inward journey of prayer and spiritual growth."

Ronald J. Sider, executive director, Evangelicals for Social Action

"To celebrate the anniversary of Richard Foster's superb *Celebration of Discipline* with a new edition gives us all an occasion of thanking God for this gift, a book that has brought precious new meaning to the living of a Christian life in our sated world."

Lewis B. Smedes, author of *Caring & Commitment* and *Forgive & Forget*

"*Celebration of Discipline* has helped me grow in both understanding and practicing the Christian life. I especially appreciate Foster's sensitivity to community—his focus on the shared disciplines as well as the private ones. *Celebration of Discipline* helps us experience the true reality of the church."

Howard A. Snyder, associate professor of church
renewal, United Theological Seminary

"*Celebration of Discipline* should be in the library of every Christian and should be read and studied on a regular basis. The entire field of spiritual growth is given redemptive interpretation throughout the pages of this book. Richard Foster weds traditional classical and scriptural material with contemporary insight and truly updates the meaning and necessity of a *Celebration of Discipline*. Each reading of this book brings a renewed desire to have one's life conformed to the person of Jesus Christ."

Tommy Tyson, evangelist

"Most books recognized as classic were good books written at the right time. Richard Foster wrote *Celebration of Discipline* at the right time, and many have indeed been calling it a classic. The time was the late 1970s when God was just beginning to move the church in America and in other parts of the world into a new era of heightened spirituality. . . . Richard Foster was one of the first to hear what the Spirit was saying to the churches and to let the rest of the world know what he was hearing through *Celebration of Discipline*. The book was the central hinge on the door to God's new era. Its message has gone far and wide and helped Christians of all walks of life to establish deeper intimacy with their heavenly Father."

C. Peter Wagner, professor of church growth, Fuller
Theological Seminary School of World Mission

"Over the past two decades my own personal spiritual pilgrimage has taken me away from the propositional and rationalistic mind-set that proclaims an intellectualized proof-oriented faith toward a Christianity of practice and experience.

"Richard Foster's *Celebration of Discipline* calls us all to that kind of faith. It says it isn't enough to just believe. What God wants is practice, the practice of worship, the practice of discipline, the practice of an experienced faith. I firmly believe this is a book for our time! It is an oasis in a dry land that can lead us moderns to a fresh spiritual drink from the waters of a spirituality rooted deep in the Christian tradition."

Robert Webber, professor of theology, Wheaton College

"In *Celebration of Discipline* Richard Foster has given us a rare gift. This book has helped me connect with truths I already know but keep forgetting. It has drawn me once again to a treasure that my monastic life has always encouraged me to explore, *my inner life*. Richard Foster beckons me to the deeps with the promise that going to the depths does not require the drudgery of a morbid, gloomy asceticism that breaks my spirit but rather a joyful discipline that opens a door to freedom and becomes a celebration.

"I have long suspected that the best way to authentic joy is through obedience. Obedience, however, is a word that turns stale in our mouths today. How delightful, then, to discover a book that brings a fresh image to obedience. Indeed, the strength of this book is that obedience to the traditional Christian disciplines of prayer, fasting, meditation, simplicity, spiritual guidance, et cetera is presented as a celebration rather than a law. . . .

"Richard Foster has offered us some ways to do the daily things deeply. The celebration of each discipline in this book hands us a tool that can be useful in helping us to integrate our inner and outer lives."

Macrina Wiederkehr, O.S.B., author of *A Tree Full of Angels*

"*Celebration of Discipline* has quietly asserted itself in the lives of multitudes around the globe, and has taken its place as a guide to the uplands of the spiritual life for the late twentieth century. Everywhere I go I meet those whose lives have been changed by encountering it. It places us on the path of life with those who have succeeded in walking with Jesus in every circumstance and shows us accessible patterns of action through which interaction with his Kingdom is assured to us. This is the secret of its power. If you wish to know in your self the reality of the gracious life of God seen in the Bible, you may find no better counselor than Richard Foster."

Dallas Willard, author of *The Spirit of the Disciplines*

"In 1978 Richard Foster's first book, *Celebration of Discipline*, was published with little fanfare. Its initial sales were sluggish at best. Few marketing experts thought that a book calling for discipline and piety would sell to a self-indulgent, self-absorbed, post-sixties generation. After all, this was the advent of yuppies who drove BMWs while sipping Perrier, not cloistered monks in caves on two-week fasts.

"Well, the experts were wrong. Those first few readers of *Celebration of Discipline* began spreading the word; the true door to liberation in Christ is the spiritual disciplines. Foster, reflecting his Quaker heritage, writes about an inner life of piety and self-restraint that is both obtainable and desirable. It can even be fulfilling!

"Since 1978 hundreds of thousands of people around the world have read and re-read *Celebration of Discipline*. I am numbered among them, and my prayer life has been greatly aided because of it. As the book enters its second decade, [the] hope is that a new generation will discover *Celebration of Discipline*'s central message: that cultivating a personal relationship with Jesus Christ is truly the path to spiritual growth."

John Wimber, pastor and founder, Vineyard Christian Fellowship

Notes

Chapter 1

1. John Woolman, *The Journal of John Woolman* (Secaucus, NJ: Citadel Press, 1972), p. 118.
2. Thomas Merton, *Contemplative Prayer* (Garden City, NY: Doubleday, 1969), p. 37.
3. Heini Arnold, *Freedom from Sinful Thoughts: Christ Alone Breaks the Curse* (Rifton, NY: Plough Publishing House, 1973), p. 94.
4. Ibid., p. 64.
5. Ibid., p. 82.
6. Frank S. Mead, ed., *Encyclopedia of Religious Quotations* (London: Peter Davis, 1965), p. 400.

Chapter 2

1. Morton T. Kelsey, *The Other Side of Silence: A Guide to Christian Meditation* (New York: Paulist Press, 1976), p. 83.
2. Madame Guyon, *Experiencing the Depths of Jesus Christ* (Goleta, CA: Christian Books, 1975), p. 3.
3. Timothy Ware, ed., *The Art of Prayer: An Orthodox Anthology* (London: Faber & Faber, 1966), p. 110.
4. Jeremy Taylor, *The House of Understanding: Selections from the Writings of Jeremy Taylor,* ed. Margaret Gest (Philadelphia: Univ. of Pennsylvania Press, 1954), p. 106.
5. Dietrich Bonhoeffer, *The Way to Freedom* (New York: Harper & Row, 1966), p. 57.
6. Guyon, p. 32.
7. Thomas à Kempis, *The Imitation of Christ* (Garden City, NY: Image Books, 1955), p. 85.
8. Thomas Merton, *Contemplative Prayer* (Garden City, NY: Doubleday, 1969), p. 59.
9. Morton Kelsey in *The Other Side of Silence* makes an excellent analysis of Eastern and Christian meditation. See especially pp. 1, 57, 98, and 121.
10. Thomas Merton, *Spiritual Direction and Meditation* (Collegeville, MN: Liturgical Press, 1960), p. 68.
11. Merton, *Contemplative Prayer,* p. 39.
12. William Penn, *No Cross, No Crown,* ed. Ronald Selleck (Richmond, IN: Friends United Press, 1981), p. xii.
13. Merton, *Contemplative Prayer,* p. 29.

14. A. W. Tozer, *The Knowledge of the Holy* (New York: Harper & Brothers, 1961), p. 20.
15. Elizabeth O'Connor, *Search for Silence* (Waco, TX: Word Books, 1971), p. 95.
16. Merton, *Spiritual Direction and Meditation*, p. 98.
17. Ibid., p. 47.
18. Alexander Whyte, *Lord, Teach Us to Pray* (New York: Harper & Brothers, n.d.), p. 249.
19. As quoted in Lynn J. Radcliffe, *Making Prayer Real* (New York: Abington-Cokesbury Press, 1952), p. 214.
20. St. Francis de Sales, *Introduction to the Devout Life*, trans. John K. Ryan (New York: Doubleday, 1955), p. 84.
21. Merton, *Contemplative Prayer*, p. 59.
22. Merton, *Spiritual Direction and Meditation*, p. 75.
23. Bonhoeffer, p. 59.
24. Whyte, pp. 249–50.
25. Ibid., p. 251.
26. Evelyn Underhill, *Practical Mysticism* (New York: Dutton, 1943), p. 90.
27. Merton, *Spiritual Direction and Meditation*, pp. 88–89.

Chapter 3

1. E. M. Bounds, *Power Through Prayer* (Chicago: Moody Press, n.d.), p. 23.
2. Ibid., p. 38.
3. Ibid., pp. 38, 77.
4. Ibid., pp. 41, 54.
5. Ibid., p. 13.
6. Thomas Merton, *Contemplative Prayer* (Garden City, NY: Doubleday, 1969), p. 11.
7. Søren Kierkegaard, *Christian Discourses*, trans. Walter Lowie (Oxford: Oxford University Press, 1940), p. 324.
8. Meister Eckhart, *Meister Eckhart*, trans. C. de B. Evans, Vol. 1 (London: John M. Watkins, 1956), p. 59.
9. As quoted in Lynn J. Radcliffe, *Making Prayer Real* (New York: Abington-Cokesbury Press, 1952), p. 214.
10. Frank C. Laubach, *Prayer the Mightiest Force in the World* (New York: Fleming H. Revell, 1946), p. 31.
11. Frank C. Laubach, *Learning the Vocabulary of God* (Nashville: Upper Room, 1956), p. 33.
12. Bounds, p. 83.
13. Thomas R. Kelly, *A Testament of Devotion* (New York: Harper & Brothers, 1941), p. 124.
14. Ibid., p. 35.
15. Bounds, p. 35.

Chapter 4

1. John Wesley, *The Journal of the Reverend John Wesley* (London: Epworth Press, 1938), p. 147.
2. David R. Smith, *Fasting: A Neglected Discipline* (Fort Washington, PA: Christian Literature Crusade, 1969), p. 6.

3. Arthur Wallis, *God's Chosen Fast* (Fort Washington, PA: Christian Literature Crusade, 1971), p. 25.
4. Dietrich Bonhoeffer, *The Cost of Discipleship* (New York: Macmillan, 1959), p. 47.
5. E. M. Bounds, *Power Through Prayer* (Chicago: Moody Press, n.d.), p. 25.
6. John Wesley, *Sermons on Several Occasions* (London: Epworth Press, 1971), p. 301.
7. Smith, p. 39.
8. Thomas R. Kelly, *A Testament of Devotion* (New York: Harper & Brothers, 1941), p. 35.
9. Wallis, p. 66.
10. Elizabeth O'Connor, *Search for Silence* (Waco, TX: Word Books, 1971), pp. 103, 104.
11. Wesley, *Sermons on Several Occasions*, p. 297.

Chapter 5

1. Martin Buber, *Tales of the Hasidim: Early Masters* (New York: Schocken Books, 1948), p. 111.
2. André Gide, *If It Dies*, trans. Dorothy Bussey (New York: Random House, 1935), p. 83.
3. Evelyn Underhill, *Practical Mysticism* (New York: World, Meridian Books, 1955), pp. 93–94.
4. Fyodor Dostoevski, *The Brothers Karamazov* (Chicago: Encyclopaedia Britannica, Great Books, 1952), p. 167.
5. Charles Noel Douglas, ed., *Forty Thousand Quotations* (Garden City, NY: Halcyon House, 1940), p. 1680.

Chapter 6

1. Richard E. Byrd, *Alone* (New York: Putnam, 1938), p. 19.
2. Arthur G. Gish, *Beyond the Rat Race* (New Canaan, CT: Keats, 1973), p. 21.
3. Ibid., p. 20.
4. Søren Kierkegaard, *Christian Discourses*, trans. Walter Lowie (Oxford: Oxford University Press, 1940), p. 322.
5. Ibid., p. 27.
6. John Wesley, *The Journal of the Reverend John Wesley* (London: Epworth Press, 1938), Nov. 1767.
7. Ronald J. Sider, *Rich Christians in an Age of Hunger* (Downers Grove, IL: InterVarsity Press, 1977), p. 18.
8. Kierkegaard, p. 344.
9. John Woolman, *The Journal of John Woolman* (Secaucus, NJ: Citadel Press, 1972), pp. 144–145.
10. Ibid., p. 168.
11. George Fox, *Works*, Vol. 8 (Philadelphia, 1831), p. 126, Epistle 131.

Chapter 7

1. Elizabeth O'Connor, *Search for Silence* (Waco, TX: Word Books, 1971), p. 132.

2. Dietrich Bonhoeffer, *Life Together* (New York: Harper & Row, 1952), pp. 77, 78.
3. Catherine de Haeck Doherty, *Poustinia: Christian Spirituality of the East for Western Man* (Notre Dame, IN: Ave Maria Press, 1974), p. 23.
4. Thomas à Kempis, *The Imitation of Christ* (New York: Pyramid, 1967), p. 18.
5. John Woolman, *The Journal of John Woolman* (Secaucus, NJ: Citadel Press, 1972), p. 11.
6. Bonhoeffer, *Life Together*, p. 79.
7. Doherty, p. 212.
8. St. John of the Cross, *The Collected Works of St. John of the Cross*, trans. Kieran Kavanaugh and Otilio Rodriguez (Garden City, NY: Doubleday, 1964), p. 296.
9. Ibid., p. 363.
10. Ibid., p. 295.
11. Ibid., p. 364.
12. Ibid., p. 365.
13. Bonhoeffer, *Life Together*, p. 80.
14. Thomas Merton, *The Sign of Jonas* (New York: Harcourt, Brace, 1953), p. 261.
15. Doherty, p. 216.

Chapter 8

1. Thomas à Kempis, *The Imitation of Christ*, in an anthology entitled *The Consolation of Philosophy* (New York: Random House, 1943), p. 139.
2. *Hymns for Worship* (Nappanee, IN: Evangel Press, 1963), p. 248.
3. John Howard Yoder, *The Politics of Jesus* (Grand Rapids, MI: Eerdmans, 1972), pp. 181–82. (I am indebted to Yoder for several of the ideas that follow.)
4. Ibid., p. 181.
5. Ibid., p. 186.
6. Kempis, p. 172.

Chapter 9

1. Thomas R. Kelly, *A Testament of Devotion* (New York: Harper & Brothers, 1941), p. 124.
2. St. Francis of Assisi, *Selections from the Writings of St. Francis of Assisi* (Nashville: Upper Room Press, 1952), p. 25.
3. John Milton, *The Complete Works of John Milton* (New York: Crown, 1936), p. 614.
4. C. H. Dodd, quoted in William Barclay, *The Letters of John and Jude* (Philadelphia: Westminster Press, 1960), pp. 68, 69.
5. William Law, *A Serious Call to a Devout and Holy Life* (Nashville: Upper Room Press, 1952), p. 26.
6. Thomas à Kempis, *The Imitation of Christ*, in an anthology entitled *The Consolation of Philosophy* (New York: Random House, 1943), p. 211.
7. Brother Ugolino di Monte Santa Maria, *The Little Flowers of St. Francis* (Garden City, NY: Doubleday, 1958), pp. 58–60.

8. Dietrich Bonhoeffer, *The Cost of Discipleship* (New York: Macmillan, 1963), p. 188.
9. Jeremy Taylor, *The Rule and Exercises of Holy Living* in *Fellowship of the Saints: An Anthology of Christian Devotional Literature* (New York: Abingdon-Cokesbury Press, 1957), p. 353.
10. Dietrich Bonhoeffer, *Life Together* (New York: Harper & Row, 1952), p. 99.
11. François Fénelon, *Christian Perfection* (Minneapolis: Bethany Fellowship, 1975), p. 34.
12. Ibid., p. 36.
13. Bernard of Clairvaux, *St. Bernard on the Song of Songs* (London: Mowbray, 1952), p. 70.
14. Bonhoeffer, *Life Together*, p. 97.
15. Ibid., p. 98.

Chapter 10

1. Dietrich Bonhoeffer, *Life Together* (New York: Harper & Row, 1952), p. 112.
2. Ibid., p. 118.
3. Agnes Sanford, *The Healing Gifts of the Spirit* (New York: Holman, 1966), p. 110.
4. Bonhoeffer, *Life Together*, p. 116.
5. St. Alphonsus Liguori, "A Good Confession," in an anthology entitled *To Any Christian* (London: Burns & Oates, 1964), p. 192.
6. Douglas Steere, *On Beginning from Within* (New York: Harper & Brothers, 1943), p. 80.
7. Liguori, p. 193.
8. Geoffrey Chaucer, *The Canterbury Tales* (Baltimore: Penguin Books, 1959), p. 23.
9. E. M. Bounds, *Power Through Prayer* (Chicago: Moody Press, n.d.), p. 77.
10. Liguori, p. 195.
11. Bonhoeffer, *Life Together*, p. 118. (The phrase "living under the cross" is Bonhoeffer's.)
12. Sanford, p. 117.

Chapter 11

1. A. W. Tozer, *The Knowledge of the Holy* (New York: Harper & Brothers, 1961), p. 11.
2. Ibid., p. 21.
3. Frank C. Laubach, *Learning the Vocabulary of God* (Nashville: Upper Room, 1956), pp. 22–23.
4. Brother Lawrence, *The Practice of the Presence of God* (Nashville: Upper Room, 1950), p. 32.
5. Douglas Steere, *Prayer and Worship* (New York: Edward W. Hazen Foundation, 1942), p. 36.
6. Thomas R. Kelly, *The Eternal Promise* (New York: Harper & Row, 1966), p. 72.
7. Ibid., p. 74.
8. George Fox, Epistle 288 (1672), quoted in *Quaker Religious Thought* 15 (Winter 1973–74): 23.

216 / NOTES

9. François Fénelon, *Christian Perfection* (Minneapolis: Bethany Fellowship, 1975), p. 4.
10. Thomas Merton, *Contemplative Prayer* (Garden City, NY: Doubleday, 1969), p. 42.
11. As quoted in D. Elton Trueblood, *The People Called Quakers* (New York: Harper & Row, 1966), p. 91.
12. James Nayler, *A Collection of Syndry Books, Epistles, and Papers, Written by James Nayler*, etc. (London, 1716), p. 378.
13. Willard Sperry, "Reality in Worship," in *The Fellowship of Saints: An Anthology of Christian Devotional Literature*, ed. Thomas S. Kepler (New York: Abingdon-Cokesbury Press, 1963), p. 685.

Chapter 12

1. Brother Ugolino di Monte Santa Maria, *The Little Flowers of St. Francis* (Garden City, NY: Doubleday, 1958), pp. 74–78.
2. Rufus M. Jones, *The Quakers in the American Colonies* (New York: Norton, 1921), p. 517.
3. John G. Whittier, ed., *The Journal of John Woolman* (London: Headley Brothers, 1900), p. 13.
4. Thomas Merton, *Spiritual Direction and Meditation* (Collegeville, MN: Liturgical Press, 1960), p. 12.
5. Ibid., p. 8.
6. Jean-Pierre de Caussade, *The Sacrament of the Present Moment*, trans. Kitty Muggeridge (San Francisco: Harper & Row, 1982).
7. Dave and Neta Jackson, *Living Together in a World Falling Apart* (Carol Stream, IL: Creation House, 1974), p. 101.
8. Merton, *Spiritual Direction and Meditation*, p. 9.
9. George Fox, *The Journal of George Fox* (London: Headley Brothers, 1975), p. 184.
10. Dallas Willard, "Studies in the Book of Apostolic Acts: Journey into the Spiritual Unknown" (unpublished study guide available only from the author).

Chapter 13

1. Harvey Cox, *The Feast of Fools* (Cambridge: Harvard University Press, 1969), p. 12.
2. François Fénelon, *Christian Perfection* (Minneapolis: Bethany Fellowship, 1975), p. 102.
3. D. Elton Trueblood, *The Humor of Christ* (New York: Harper & Row, 1964), p. 33.
4. Cox, p. 11.
5. Ibid., p. 10.
6. Ibid., p. 3.

A Brief Bibliography of Recent Works

The notes in the back of this book and the rather extensive annotated bibliography in *Richard J. Foster's Study Guide for Celebration of Discipline* are meant to provide you with resources for further exploration. In addition to those sources, I thought it would be helpful to give an update on books that have been published in more recent years. When I wrote *Celebration*, the contemporary works in Spirituality were slim pickings indeed, especially among Protestants. But in the past ten years a whole spate of new books have been written, some of them quite good, which is a cause for rejoicing. Below is a sample listing of these books that I hope can provide markings for your journey.

Reference Works on Spirituality

Many people have almost no sense of the history of Spirituality, or of the development of spiritual theology, or even of the major figures in the field. The volumes below will help to fill in any gaps you may feel in this regard.

Jones, Cheslyn, Geoffrey Wainwright, and Edward Yarnold, eds. *The Study of Spirituality*. New York: Oxford University Press, 1986. This volume provides an excellent sampling of writers from all of the major traditions in Spirituality. I am especially glad that an entire section is devoted to "Pastoral Spirituality" since this emphasis has been sorely neglected in traditional programs in Pastoral Theology.

Lane, George A. *Christian Spirituality: An Historical Sketch*. Chicago: Loyola University Press, 1984. This book will give you a thumbnail sketch of the historical flow of Christian Spirituality. It provides a nice schematic chronology of the major personalities in the back of the book. (You may also want to be aware of *A History of Spirituality* by Urban Holmes.)

Leech, Kenneth. *Experiencing God: Theology as Spirituality.* San Francisco: Harper & Row, 1985. You may be acquainted with Kenneth Leech through his other books, *Soul Friend* and *True Prayer. Experiencing God* seeks to ground theology in its central role, which is the search for a transforming knowledge of God. The old writers used to speak of "theology habitus", that is, a theology that transforms us at the most basic level of our habits. This is a substantial book that brings theology back into that tradition.

Pennington, M. Basil, Alan Jones, and Mark Booth, eds. *The Living Testament: The Essential Writings of Christianity Since the Bible.* San Francisco: Harper & Row, 1985. A lively selection of writings from The Apostles Creed to Billy Graham.

Ramsey, Boniface. *Beginning to Read the Fathers.* New York: Paulist Press, 1985. All those who have wanted to read the early church Fathers (including the Desert Fathers) but have felt intimidated by the cultural and linguistic gap will be encouraged by this book. It helps to clarify their varied positions on many themes from the "human condition" to "death and resurrection." Fortunately, it has abundant quotations from the actual writings of the Fathers.

Spirituality and Prayer

Since prayer is at the heart of the spiritual life, it makes sense to give particular attention to this topic.

Bloesch, Donald G. *The Struggle of Prayer.* San Francisco: Harper & Row, 1980. In this book an important evangelical theologian wrestles with significant biblical and theological issues related to prayer. While focusing on tough questions, Bloesch also displays a warm-hearted piety.

Griffin, Emilie. *Clinging: The Experience of Prayer.* San Francisco: Harper & Row, 1984. Emilie Griffin knows God and so her warmly-felt invitation to the life of prayer can be taken seriously. This is a slender volume that is worth its weight in gold.

Guyon, Jeanne. *Experiencing the Depths of Jesus Christ.* Goleta, CA: Christian Books, 1975. This is a new edition of an old book (seventeenth century) and we can be glad that the simple—

profoundly simple—teaching on prayer of Madame Guyon is accessible to modern readers.

Hassle, David J. *Radical Prayer: Creating a Welcome for God, Ourselves, Other People and the World*. New York: Paulist Press, 1983. Arising out of insights gained from *The Spiritual Exercises of St. Ignatius*, this book leads us to discover what prayer is before it becomes a technique. Roman Catholic in its orientation, it nevertheless has insights for those from all traditions.

Hinson, E. Glenn. *The Reaffirmation of Prayer*. Nashville, TN: Broadman, 1979. This book takes the traditional forms of prayer—adoration, thanksgiving, confession, intercession, petition, and dedication—and seeks to give them modern adaptation. Those who know Glenn Hinson are struck by his massive intellect and deep piety—twin virtues that are seldom found in the same person.

Peterson, Eugene H. *Earth & Altar: The Community of Prayer in a Self-Bound Society*. Downers Grove, IL: InterVarsity, 1985. No doubt you are familiar with Eugene Peterson for his books *A Long Obedience in the Same Direction* and *Traveling Light*. In *Earth and Altar* he works on the corporate side of prayer and especially focuses on how prayer works to free us from self-centeredness. He utilizes eleven psalms that shaped the politics of Israel as a platform from which he shows us how prayer is to shape the politics of America.

Toon, Peter. *From Mind to Heart: Christian Meditation Today*. Grand Rapids, MI: Baker Book House, 1988. This book introduces us to the Christian discipline of meditation. The author shows how meditation "is related to, but not identical with, either intellectual study or prayer."

General Works on Spirituality

Some excellent books on Spirituality have come out in recent years. Below is a sample listing.

Boyer, Ernest, Jr. *A Way in the World: Family Life as Spiritual Discipline*. San Francisco: Harper & Row, 1984. This book takes the family seriously, not as a hindrance to the spiritual life, but as a God-given way to nurture the spiritual life. "The Sacrament of the Care of Others" and "The Sacrament of the Routine" are two chapters that represent this concern well.

Colliander, Tito. *Way of the Ascetics: The Ancient Tradition of Discipline and Inner Growth*. Trans. by Katherine Ferré. San Francisco: Harper & Row, 1960. If you have ever wanted to learn from the devotional masters of the Eastern Orthodox Church, this little book would be a good place to begin. It contains mainly succinct extracts from the writings of the Orthodox Church fathers with brief commentary and practical applications for daily devotion.

Edwards, Tilden H. *Spiritual Friend: Reclaiming the Gift of Spiritual Direction*. New York: Paulist Press, 1980. For many the concept of Spiritual Direction is vague, foreboding, and shrouded in mystery. *Spiritual Friend* helps clear away the confusion and invites us to see that we do not have to live the spiritual life in isolation. Also, you will want to be acquainted with Edwards' earlier book, *Living Simply Through the Day*.

Foster, Richard J. *The Challenge of the Disciplined Life: Christian Reflections on Money, Sex & Power*. San Francisco: Harper & Row, 1985. While *Celebration* is an attempt to describe how we live devotionally, this book is an attempt to describe how we live ethically—love of God, love of neighbor. In doing so, I key off the monastic vows of poverty, chastity, and obedience as a response to the issues of money, sex, and power and seek to articulate contemporary vows of simplicity, fidelity, and service. You should also be aware of an earlier book, *Freedom of Simplicity*.

Granberg-Michaelson, Wesley. *A Worldly Spirituality: The Call to Redeem Life on Earth*. San Francisco: Harper & Row, 1984. This book calls for a new theological perspective that supports a caring, nurturing fellowship with the whole of God's creation. It seeks to apply the themes of Spirituality to the complex ecological problems we face today.

Holmes, Urban T. *Spirituality for Ministry*. San Francisco: Harper & Row, 1982. Many busy pastors and priests find that the spiritual life is almost the last thing their people encourage them to nurture. Here is a book that seeks to correct this imbalance.

Klug, Ronald. *How to Keep a Spiritual Journal*. Nashville, TN: Thomas Nelson, 1982. A straightforward book about the value and the mechanics of maintaining a spiritual journal.

Leckey, Dolores R. *The Ordinary Way: A Family Spirituality*. New York: Crossroad, 1982. This book attempts to apply the insights gained from the *Rule* of St. Benedict to family life. It covers such issues as intimacy, equality, prayer, play, study, stability, and hospitality.

McNeill, Donald P., Douglas A. Morrison, and Henri J. M. Nouwen. *Compassion: A Reflection on the Christian Life*. Garden City, NY: Image Books, 1983. Here is a book that seeks to apply the Christian virtue of compassion to the pressing social injustices of our day. The authors show how compassion is nurtured in a rightly ordered spiritual life and how it can move us into action on behalf of the bruised and broken.

Macy, Howard R. *Rhythms of the Inner Life: Yearning for Closeness with God*. Old Tappan, NJ: Fleming H. Revell, 1988. Using the Psalms as a basis, the author identifies seven movements of the heart that help to nurture the spiritual life: longing, waiting, trembling, despairing, resting, conversing, and celebrating.

Nouwen, Henri J. M. *The Way of the Heart: Desert Spirituality and Contemporary Ministry*. New York: Seabury, 1981. Nouwen has nurtured many of us in the spiritual life through such books as *The Wounded Healer, The Genesee Diary*, and *Making All Things New*. In *The Way of the Heart* he applies the insights of desert spirituality to the contemporary scene. He focuses particularly upon the Spiritual Disciplines of solitude, silence, and prayer.

Stringfellow, William. *The Politics of Spirituality: Spirituality & the Christian Life*. Richard H. Bell, ed. Philadelphia: Westminster, 1984. To have met William Stringfellow is to be delivered from the temptation to divorce the spiritual life from the pressing social issues of the day. This book treats Spirituality as an elementary political reality in the sense that it is intended to affect the whole person—body, mind, soul, place, relationships, institutional structures, and more. Throughout his active life Stringfellow wrote fourteen books, among them *Conscience and Obedience* and *An Ethic for Christians and Other Aliens in a Strange Land*.

Willard, Dallas. *The Spirit of the Disciplines: Understanding How God Changes Lives*. San Francisco: Harper & Row, 1988. If I were to list the single most important book of this decade in Spirituality, this would be the book. It sets forth a clear theology for the Spiritual Disciplines as the means by which we are transformed into the likeness of Christ.

Woodbridge, Barry A. *A Guidebook for Spiritual Friends*. Nashville, TN: Upper Room, 1985. This is a simple but helpful book on how to go about the business of Spiritual Direction.

Scripture Index

Subject Index

THE CHALLENGE OF THE DISCIPLINED LIFE

Christian Reflections on Money, Sex & Power

Richard J. Foster

PREVIOUSLY PUBLISHED UNDER THE TITLE
Money, Sex & Power

Unless otherwise indicated, all scriptural quotations are from the
Revised Standard Version of the Bible.

In memory of David M. Leach

faithful minister of Christ and
dear friend to our family

CONTENTS

ACKNOWLEDGMENTS

The sacrifice my family has endured to see this book to completion is considerable. My heartfelt thanks to Carolynn, my wife, who bore the burden with me and gave me many insightful suggestions that have made the book far better than it would have been otherwise. Joel and Nathan, our children, were exceedingly understanding through the obsessive months of writing. Nathan, especially, sacrificed our reading time together at night—happily, I can now return to this as well as many other family joys.

Lynda Graybeal, my associate, has done far more than enter, print out, and proofread the manuscript. She has been an invaluable source of wisdom. Many of her comments opened up whole new creative directions for the book.

Some years back I spoke at a retreat outside of Washington, D.C., sponsored by The Ministry of Money, and it was there that I met the director, Don McClanan. It was through Don that I first saw the connection between the money-sex-power issue and the monastic vows; I am indebted to him.

Kathy Gaynor, reference librarian at Friends University, was especially helpful in my research. She found "unfindable" books with amazing speed, at times scouring the countryside for an obscure reference. My thanks to her.

Over the months, I read the entire manuscript to a literary group here at Friends University of which I am a member. They made many useful suggestions. Several others read all or part of the manuscript, and their comments helped me a great deal. They include Vivian Felix, George Fooshee, David Holley, and Richard Sosnowski. Roy M. Carlisle, my editor at Harper & Row, San Francisco, has been deeply involved in the development of this book from the first day I mentioned it to him as an embryonic idea several years ago. I have appreciated his patience and encouragement.

This is my known list of indebtedness. There are many others who have helped me write this book who will forever remain unknown. A phrase here or an experience there has sharpened my thinking and created a new idea. I could never trace these ideas to their sources, for they have merged with the flow of ideas from a thousand others. But even if I cannot thank everyone individually, I can express indebtedness—and I do.

PREFACE

A special concern has surrounded the writing of this book. To the popular mind, topics like prayer and worship carry an aura of spirituality, whereas the themes of money, sex, and power sound terribly "secular" at best. My longing throughout the writing has been to help people sense that as we come to these "secular" issues we are treading on holy ground. To live rightly with reference to money and sex and power is to live sacramentally. To misuse and abuse these is to desecrate the holy things of God.

I have sought to write in a spirit of reverence and worship, knowing that I was handling sacred themes. Each day of the writing I began with a time of meditation upon one of the psalms, and in this way I read through the entire psalter. My desire was to be baptized into the hopes and aspirations of the psalm writers, for the psalter is the prayer book of the Church. With the cadence of joy and beauty, worship and adoration that comes from the psalms I was able to look with new eyes at the issues of money, sex, and power. Then, and only then, was I prepared to write on these themes that are so close to the heart of God. My hope and prayer is that reading these words will help you as the writing of them has helped me.

I should, at the outset, note the special problem of the personal pronoun when referring to God. I think it is obvious to all that God is not a male deity as opposed to a female deity. God is beyond and includes our distinctions of sexuality. As long ago as the fourteenth-century,

Juliana of Norwich declared, "As truly as God is our Father, so truly is God our Mother." The Bible is full of both feminine and masculine imagery for God. However, when we come to the personal pronoun for God, it is difficult to express God's greatness in this regard. The problem is not with God, but with us. Our language is simply too limited. The attempt to solve this problem with dashes and slashes is semantically awkward and aesthetically abhorrent. I have, therefore, chosen to follow the standard usage of the masculine pronoun "he" and "him," although I am keenly aware of the inadequacies of this approach.

Richard J. Foster
February 1985
Friends University

1. Money, Sex and Power in Christian Perspective

> It is vanity to seek riches that shall perish and to put one's hope in them. It is vanity also to aspire to honours and to climb to high degree. It is vanity to follow the lust of the flesh.
> —THOMAS à KEMPIS

The crying need today is for people of faith to live faithfully. This is true in all spheres of human existence, but is particularly true with reference to money, sex, and power. No issues touch us more profoundly or more universally. No themes are more inseparably intertwined. No topics cause more controversy. No human realities have greater power to bless or to curse. No three things have been more sought after or are more in need of a Christian response.

The issues of money, sex, and power catapult us into the arena of moral choice. In this book I am seeking to describe how we are to live ethically, but I am not attempting to cover the waterfront of ethical inquiry, as one might do in a textbook on ethics. Instead, by dealing with three issues of such importance in modern society I hope to give clues for how we, as followers of Christ, are to handle the many ethical choices we must face daily.

In doing this I believe I am following the pattern of Christ himself. Jesus did not give detailed instruction on how we are to live in every corner of life. Instead he took the crucial issues of his day and showed how the gospel message bears upon them. And in this way he gave us paradigms for conjugating the many other verbs of ethical choice.

Jesus gave considerable attention to the themes of money, sex, and power. Of the three, he spoke more about money and power than he did about sex, for the simple reason that sex was not the burning issue then that it has become in our day. Today, however, we must deal vigorously with the sex issue for there is obvious misery in modern society from a lack of subordination of eros to agape.

WHY MONEY, SEX AND POWER?

You may well wonder why I would choose to write a book on the specific topics of money, sex, and power. The answer is simple. Throughout history, and in our own experience, these issues seem inseparably intertwined. Money manifests itself as power. Sex is used to acquire both money and power. And power is often called "the best aphrodisiac." We could discuss at length the interlacing connections. There is, for example, an important relationship between sex and poverty: sex is the poor man's holiday and the poor woman's disaster. Note also the connection between power and wealth: power is frequently used to manipulate wealth, and wealth is used just as frequently to buy power. And on it goes. The truth is that it is not really possible (or even desirable) to unravel all the intricate ways money, sex, and power intertwine.

Another reason for writing on these themes is that the need is great today. We have gone through upheavals in our culture with regard to each of these issues. The time is right for an attempt to respond to the money—sex—power question. Christians need a fresh articulation of what it means to live faithfully in these areas, and those who are considering the Christian faith deserve some indication of what they might expect if they become followers of Christ.

I have a third reason for writing about these themes. Historically it seems spiritual revivals have been accompanied by a clear, bold response to the issues of money, sex, and power. This is true whether we think of the Benedictine movement, the Franciscan movement, the Cistercian movement, the Reformation movement, the Methodist movement, the modern missionary movement, or any number of other groups. When these revivals occur in a culture, there is a renewal of both devotional experience and ethical life. We need a modern-day renewal of spiritual experience that is ethically potent.

SOCIAL IMPLICATIONS

It is important right at the outset that we see the far-reaching social implications of the issues with which we are dealing. These are matters that profoundly affect corporate and institutional, as well as private, life. The social dimension to money is "business"; for sex it is "marriage"; for power it is "government."[1]*

I am using the terms *business, marriage,* and *government* in their broadest sense. Business refers to the task of bringing forth the goods and services of the earth either to bless or oppress humankind. Marriage refers to the human relationship par excellence that creates the context for either the deepest possible intimacy or the greatest possible alienation. Government refers to the enterprise of human organization that can lead toward either liberty or tyranny. Instantly you can sense that money, sex, and power are vital issues, not only to each of us as individuals, but to all human society.

Business, marriage, and government can be either a supreme benefit or a plague of monstrous proportions.

---

* All strictly bibliographical information is placed in the Notes at the back of the book. Other commentary notes are placed at the bottom of the individual pages.

And the variables that tip the scale one way or the other are more numerous and more complex than merely the character of the individuals involved. Our problems will not be solved simply by getting the "right" kind of people in business or government. That is certainly a good thing, but it does not guarantee that these institutions will serve humankind. Inherent within the institutional structures themselves are destructive forces that need to be transformed by the power of God if they are to benefit human society.

THEMES OF THE CENTURIES

Money, sex, and power are three of the great ethical themes that have concerned human beings throughout the centuries. It was these three things that Dostoevsky dealt with so sensitively in his masterpiece *The Idiot*.[2] In this novel the Christ-figure, Prince Myshkin, is thrust into a culture obsessed with wealth, power, and sexual conquest. But the prince himself has no pride, no greed, no malice, no envy, no vanity, and no fear. His behavior is so abnormal that people do not know what to think of him. They trust him because of his innocence and simplicity, yet his lack of ulterior motives causes them to conclude that he is an idiot.

Skillfully Dostoevsky weaves the themes of money, sex, and power through the story, contrasting the spirit of the prince with all those around him. Of him, the narrator notes, "He did not care for pomp or wealth, nor even for public esteem, but cared only for the truth!"[3] In a letter, Dostoevsky himself said of the prince, "My intention is to portray a truly beautiful soul."[4]

The aristocratic society of Dostoevsky's time could not comprehend an individual like Prince Myshkin, but then neither can modern society. Imagine Myshkin making a guest appearance in a television soap opera. The script writers simply would not know what to do with a person who had no desire for possessions, no craving for sexual conquest, no need for domination.

Of course, the real question throughout the novel is, Who really is the idiot? Perhaps the true fool is the person whose life is dominated by greed and power and sexual conquest.

Of course, Dostoevsky is only representative of a long line of individuals and groups who have given serious and sustained attention to the themes of money, sex, and power. Virtually every major thinker and every great movement have wrestled with these issues. The ancient monastic vows of poverty, chastity, and obedience were a direct response to the issues of money, sex, and power. Or think of the Puritans, who answered the question with their emphasis upon industry, faithfulness, and order. We can learn much by giving attention to their efforts.

THE HISTORIC VOWS: MONEY

Compulsive extravagance is a modern mania. The contemporary lust for "more, more, more" is clearly psychotic; it has completely lost touch with reality. The chasm between Third World poverty and First World affluence is accelerating at an alarming rate. And many earnest believers are at a loss to know what to do in the midst of these perplexing realities.

The monastic response to money is seen in the ancient vow of *poverty*. Intense renunciation was their way of shouting no to the prevailing values of their society. They were, however, giving far more than a negative word. They were saying no in order to say yes. They renounced possessions in order to learn detachment.

The lovable (and sometimes frustrating) Franciscan Brother Juniper had so learned the meaning of detachment that many thought he was a fool. On one occasion he came across an elaborate altar that had silver ringlets hanging from the frontal. He took one look at them and announced, "These ringlets are superfluous," and proceeded to cut them off and give them to the poor. The village priest, of course, was outraged. Poor Juniper simply could not understand the priest's anger, for he assumed he had done him a great service by freeing him from this "display of worldly vanity."[5] Saint Francis was so moved by the spirit of detachment he saw in Brother Juniper that on one occasion he cried out, "My brothers, if only I had a great forest of such junipers!"[6]

We need to hear their word today: we who love greed more than we love the gospel, we who live in fear, and not in trust. We need to hear their word today: we who define people in terms of their net worth, we who push and shove to gain an ever larger piece of the consumer pie.

The Puritan response to the issue of money is seen in their stress upon *industry*. The Puritans emphasized industry because they believed intensely in the sanctity of all honorable work. They completely rejected the ancient division between things sacred and things secular. For them, vocation was an expression of one's spiritual life. In *The Tradesman's Calling*, Richard Steele declared that it is in the shop "where you may most confidently expect the presence and blessing of God."[7]

Their vocation was a calling of God. Cotton Mather declared, "Oh, let every Christian walk with God, when he works at his calling, act in his occupation with an eye to God, act as under the eye of God."[8] Work was an opportunity to glorify God and to serve one's neighbor.

They also stressed moderation in work. They scorned the mentality of the workaholic as much as they did sloth. Since work was to honor God rather than to make money, too much work could be as evil as too little work. Richard Steele notes that a person should not "accumulate two or three callings merely to increase his riches."⁹

We need to hear their word today: we who find work meaningless and dull, we who are tempted by sloth and laziness. We need to hear their word today: we who are workaholics, we who take multiple jobs in order to move up the economic ladder.

We can be glad for the monastic vow of poverty and the Puritan "vow" of industry, but we today need a new "vow" that responds creatively and boldly to the money issue. It must be a vow that will reject the modern mania for wealth without a morbid asceticism. It must be a vow that calls us to use money without serving money. It must be a vow that brings money into obedience to the will and ways of God.

THE HISTORIC VOWS: SEX

People today are hopelessly confused about their sexuality. For vast numbers the word *love* means nothing more than a tumble in some bed. Many look upon an affair as a badge of honor. All the old foundations for permanence and fidelity seem to have eroded away. Bewildered by the modern confusion, many sincere people today struggle to define their own sexuality.

The vow of *chastity* was the monastic response to the issue of sex. They were saying far more than a negative word. They renounced marriage in order to learn vacancy. Chastity arose as a witness for a holy empty space in a world overcrowded with interpersonal relationships. Thomas Aquinas called celibacy a *vacare Deo*, "a vacancy for God." "To be a celibate," notes Henri Nouwen, "means to be empty for God, to be free and open for his presence, to be available for his service."¹⁰

The vow of chastity also witnesses against unrestrained self-indulgence. It reminds us that discipline and denial are gospel imperatives. You see, our sexual intoxication is only representative of an all-pervasive mood of intemperance that dominates the world in which we live today. The Franciscan Brother Giles once said, "By chastity I mean to keep guard over all the senses with the grace of God."[11] If we need anything today, it is to learn how "to keep guard over all the senses by the grace of God," and if the vow of chastity can remind us of this need, it has done us an immense service.

We need to hear their word today: we who are desperately afraid to be alone, we who try to replace God with interpersonal relationships. We need to hear their word today: we who are caught up in the modern mania of narcissism, we who avoid discipline as if it were a plague.

Faithfulness was the Puritan response to the issue of sex. Unfortunately the wholesomeness of their approach has been obscured for us by complete distortions of their thought. In fact, the misapprehension has gone so far that the word *Puritan* can function today as a noun defining someone plagued with sexual taboos and unhealthy inhibitions. Actually, that definition fits better the more squeamish nineteenth-century Victorians than the seventeenth- and eighteenth-century Puritans. No rigid ascetics, these were people who knew how to laugh and how to love. In 1660 Fritz-John Winthrop commissioned John Haynes to buy a pair of garters for Winthrop to present to his fiancée. In a letter enclosed with the garters Haynes teased Winthrop that "you would be glad to have a Lady leggs and all."[12] In a wedding sermon in 1694 John Cotton told the story of a couple who determined to live a contemplative life without sexual relations, and he assessed their decision as "blind zeal," noting that it was "not of that Holy Spirit which saith *It is not good that man should be alone.*"[13]

They sought to think through to a serious Christian basis for marriage and family life. Perhaps their most radical departure from the Catholic-Anglican view was

their conviction that companionship was the primary purpose of marriage and healthy sexuality within marriage
was a vital part of this companionship. Francis Bremer
has observed, "The stereotype of the Puritan as having
been prudish and condemnatory about sex has no basis in
fact. . . . As their diaries, letters, and other writings make
evident, the Puritans were a good deal more comfortable
discussing sexual matters than many of their descen-
dants."[14]

They also labored to construct a Christian basis for divorce and remarriage. On this issue the Puritans were
actually the liberals of their day. They rejected the medieval church's ban on divorce on both biblical and practical
grounds. William Perkins advocated divorce for infidelity,
desertion, disease, and insanity, with equal rights for
men and women.* John Milton argued for incompatibility
as valid grounds for divorce, since Puritan theology
placed companionship as the primary purpose of marriage.[15]

We need to hear their word today: we who flit from
marriage to marriage with the greatest of ease. We need
to hear their word today: we who lay impossible burdens
upon people in our frantic zeal to stem the tide of
divorce.

We can appreciate the monastic vow of chastity and
the Puritan "vow" of faithfulness, but we today urgently
need a contemporary "vow" that responds forthrightly
and compassionately to the sex issue. It must be a vow

---

* M. M. Knappen, *Tudor Puritanism: A Chapter in the History of Idealism*
(Chicago: The University of Chicago Press, 1939), pp. 459–61. This
chapter in Puritan history is really quite interesting and not without
its controversies. An interesting sample of the debates that raged
over this issue can be seen by reading John Rainolds, *A Defence of the
Judgment of the Reformed Churches: That a Man May Lawfullie Not Only
Put Awaie His Wife for Her Adulterie But Also Marrie Another* (1609) and
the response of Edmund Bunry, *Of Divorce for Adulterie and Marring
Again* (1610).

that will affirm our God-given sexuality without encouraging promiscuity. It must be a vow that gives wholeness to the marriage experience without depreciating the single life. It must be a vow that defines the moral parameters of our sexuality and also calls us to joyful expression within those parameters.

THE HISTORIC VOWS: POWER

The idolatry of today is the idolatry of power. Books by the score appeal to our Machiavellian passions. Today, by and large, political leaders give more energy to jockeying for position than to serving the public good; business executives care more for keeping on top of the heap than for producing a useful product; university professors seek sophistication more than truth; and religious leaders care more for their image than for the gospel. And in the midst of this power-crazed society many Christians wonder how to live with integrity.

The vow of *obedience* was the monastic response to the issue of power. They renounced power in order to learn service. Now, if the vows of poverty and chastity are incomprehensible to modern men and women, the vow of obedience is utterly reprehensible. The very idea of somebody—anybody—having any kind of say in our lives runs so counter to everything in our society that anger and even hostility is our almost automatic response.

The monastics, however, were trying to learn service through the vow of obedience. Obedience was an intense way of confessing their corporate life. They were accountable to each other and responsible for each other. Through obedience they sought to be receptive to the rightful rule of God through others. On one occasion Saint Francis asked Sister Clare and Brother Masseo to seek the mind of the Lord regarding his ministry. When they returned, Saint Francis knelt and said, "What does my Lord Jesus Christ order me to do?"[16] You see, he did not ask for their opinion or their counsel but for his marching orders. Under "holy obedience" he let go of his way in order to hear Christ's way, and on this occasion at least he learned to hear it through others.

Leonardo Boff put it well when he said, "Obedience is the greatest free decision one makes for God."[17] Perhaps the vow of obedience can help us see more fully that to lose ourselves is the only way to truly find ourselves.

We need to hear their word today: we who want to be accountable to no one, we who want to be responsible for no one. We need to hear their word today: we who lust for power and status, we who find serving others demeaning.

Order was the Puritan response to the issue of power. In the church order was built around their concept of "the Visible Covenant," which was a mutual commitment of support and accountability. The purpose of this mutual responsibility and care was to give "Church-power over one another mutually."[18] And when the purpose of this "Church-power" was to stir one another to love and good works, it helped immensely.

In government order was built around the idea of "the Holy Commonwealth." The vision was certainly ambitious: a government based upon the Bible with magistrates to execute the will of God. To their credit, the Puritans sought to use the power of the state to bring moral fiber to public as well as private life.*

We need to hear their word today: we who reject all

---

* The Puritan vision of order also had very negative consequences. When this "Church-power" was turned toward routing out heretics, as in the Salem witch trials, we see a Church-power gone sour. We can, of course, discover many of the same shortcomings in the monastic vows. Money, sex, and power are very seductive things, and even in religious garb, the temptations to manipulate and control, to suppress and oppress are very great.

order and all authority. We need to hear their word today: we who love our own way more than we love the divine fellowship.

Clearly the monastic vow of obedience and the Puritan "vow" of order can teach us many things, but the crying need today is for a new "vow" that responds creatively and positively to the issue of power. It must be a vow that is able to harness the good side of power without being obsessed by its shadow side. It must be a vow that will bring authority and submission into proper balance. It must be a vow that models leadership within the context of servanthood.

WHEN GOOD THINGS GO BAD

There is, of course, a proper place in Christian life and experience for money, sex, and power. When properly placed and effectively functioning, they have the ability as nothing else does to enhance and bless life. Money, for example, can enrich human life in wonderful ways. Food, shelter, education—these are things that money can help us acquire. More than once I have watched students literally jump for joy when a way has been found to finance their education. Or in the area of sex, I have counseled and prayed with young couples who have been wonderfully transformed by the inner healing of an old sexual hurt or by a new insight into their sexuality. Power can be used by individuals of genuine spiritual authority to bless and liberate virtually everyone around them. I have witnessed people whose very presence was enriching.

Again, when properly placed and effectively functioning, money, sex, and power have enormous ability to bring goodness into human life. Exactly what that place is and how they function there will be the enduring task of this book.

Having said this, however, we must also underscore

to ourselves again and again that we are dealing with explosive themes that easily turn into "demons" that make of our lives one great sorrow.

The demon in money is greed. Nothing can destroy human beings like the passion to possess. In *The Idiot*, Dostoevsky has one of his characters observe, "Every one is possessed with such a greed nowadays, they are all so overwhelmed by the idea of money that they seem to have gone mad."[19]

The demon in sex is lust. True sexuality leads to humanness, but lust leads to depersonalization. Lust captivates rather than emancipates, devours rather than nourishes.

The demon in power is pride. True power has as its aim to set people free, whereas pride is determined to dominate. True power enhances relationships; pride destroys them.

The demons of greed, lust, and pride can be exorcised, but let me warn you that the exorcisms will not come easily or quickly.* Hasty exorcisms almost always drive out angels as well as demons. And once the demons are gone, we had better be clear about what is to fill the vacancy, for empty spaces never remain empty for long (Matt. 12:43-45).

We must understand that these are not matters we can be neutral about and hope they will go away. If we fail to exorcise the demons of greed, lust, and pride, we are doomed to eventually be dominated by them. They may take on the appearance of angels, but they will be demonic powers nonetheless.

We may take money and use it to help people, but if it has within it the demon seed of greed, we will put people into our debt in ruinous ways. And when greed is tied to

---

* My reference here to "demons" and exorcism is purely metaphorical. I am *not* suggesting that anyone who evidences characteristics of greed or lust or pride is "possessed" and needs exorcism.

giving, it is particularly destructive because it appears so good, so much like an angel of light. When we give out of a spirit of greed, an all-pervasive attitude of paternalism poisons the entire enterprise. When greed motivates our giving, we are still trying to profit from the transaction. That is why the apostle Paul says that we can give away everything but if we lack love we "gain nothing" (1 Cor. 13:3).

When we turn to the sexual experience, we discover that lust, too, can appear as an angel of light. Lust imprisons the other person, and yet the incarceration can look good from many angles. It promises security and safety from a hostile world. In fact, many people will enter a marriage relationship based upon lust rather than love simply because the two often look so much alike. But the end result of lust is dehumanization, in which the important thing is not the person but the possession of that person. People become things to acquire, prizes to win, objects to control. "My wife" or "my husband" becomes "my toy."

Or we may take power and use it in such good ways, but if the demonic force of pride still resides, the end result will be manipulation, domination, and tyranny. The Jonestown tragedy is a blatant example. Here was an enterprise that began as a noble ministry but ended in destruction. Power infested with pride will surely give rise to egomania.

A NEW CALL TO OBEDIENCE

How do we live faithfully today with regard to the issues of money, sex, and power? This is *the* question that demands an answer today. The answer will not come quickly or easily; it will require our best thinking and our greatest devotion.

The monastic movement, with its vows of poverty,

chastity, and obedience, was an attempt to answer this question within the context of one culture. The Puritan efforts to bring monastic conviction into common life through their concerns for industry, faithfulness, and order was an attempt to answer this question within the context of a quite different culture. The issue that we must now face is how to answer this question within the context of our own culture.

We can learn much from the many groups in the past who have sought to live obediently, but we cannot deal with the issues of money, sex, and power in precisely the same way they did. We live in another era. We face many problems that did not even exist for them. New situations demand new responses. And so we are faced with the necessity for framing a contemporary response to the issues of money, sex, and power.

Today we need a new articulation of Christian "vows." Such vows will constitute a new call to obedience to Christ in the midst of contemporary society. The need is great. The task is urgent. Our century longs for a new demonstration of joyful, confident, obedient living. May we be just such a demonstration.

PART I
Money

2. The Dark Side of Money

Money has demonically usurped the role in modern society which the Holy Spirit is to have in the Church.

—THOMAS MERTON

Martin Luther astutely observed, "There are three conversions necessary: the conversion of the heart, mind, and the purse."[1] Of these three, it may well be that we moderns find the conversion of the purse the most difficult. It is hard for us even to talk about money. In fact, I recently heard of a couple, both psychologists, who would speak openly and frankly in front of their children about sex, death, and all manner of difficult subjects, but would go into the bedroom and close the door when they wanted to talk about money. In a survey of psychotherapists in which they listed things they should not do with their patients, it was found that lending a client money was a greater taboo than touching, kissing, or even sexual intercourse. For us, money is indeed a forbidden subject.

And yet Jesus spoke about money more frequently than any other subject except the kingdom of God. He gave an unusual amount of time and energy to the money question. In the moving story about the "widow's mite," we are told that Jesus intentionally sat in front of the treasury and watched people putting in their offerings (Mark 12:41). By design, he saw what they gave and discerned the spirit in which they gave. For Jesus, giving was not a private matter. He did not—as we so often do today—glance away embarrassed at prying into someone's personal business. No, Jesus considered it public business and used the occasion to teach about sacrificial giving.

Jesus' careful attention to the money question is one of the truly amazing things about the Gospel narratives. The range of his concern is startling: from the parable of the sower to the parable of the rich farmer, from the encounter with the rich young ruler to the encounter with Zacchaeus, from teachings on trust in Matthew 6 to teachings on the dangers of wealth in Luke 6.

TWO STREAMS

In my book *Freedom of Simplicity* I went into detail about the biblical perspective on money in both Old and New Testaments; I will not retrace my steps here.* We do, however, need to be aware of the two major streams of teaching regarding money that we find in the New Testament and, indeed, throughout the Bible.

These two divergent streams of teaching are certainly paradoxical, and sometimes they seem downright contradictory. This should not surprise us. God so superintended the writing of the Scriptures that they accurately reflect the real world in which we live, and most of us are so well acquainted with paradox and perplexity in our own experience that we understand. Only the arrogant and the dogmatic find paradox hard to accept.

THE DARK SIDE

The first stream of teaching we find is what I have chosen to call the dark side of money. I am referring both to the way in which money can be a threat to our relation-

---

* See *Freedom of Simplicity* (San Francisco: Harper & Row, 1981). Note especially chapters 2 and 3. In that book I was dealing with the issue of Christian simplicity, which is a larger question than money, but you will find most of Jesus' teaching regarding money there. Also, I devote chapter 6 of *Celebration of Discipline* (San Francisco: Harper & Row, 1978) to that question.

ship with God and to the radical criticism of wealth that we find so much of in Jesus' words. The warnings and exhortations are repetitious, almost monotonous. "Woe to you that are rich" (Luke 6:24). "You cannot serve God and mammon" (Luke 16:13). "Do not lay up for yourselves treasures on earth" (Matt. 6:19). "It is easier for a camel to go through the eye of a needle than for a rich man to enter the kingdom of God" (Matt. 19:24). "Take heed, and beware of all covetousness" (Luke 12:15). "Sell your possessions, and give alms" (Luke 12:33). "Give to every one who begs from you; and of him who takes away your goods do not ask them again" (Luke 6:30). And, of course, many more statements could be added to this sample listing.

The point is that the teaching is very clear and very severe. Right at this juncture we face a real temptation to tone down the criticism immediately, or at least to try to balance it with more positive biblical statements. But this is the very thing we must not do, at least not yet. First we are obliged to allow Scripture to speak to us on this issue. We must not take the sting out of the teaching too quickly. Before we try to explain why it cannot apply to our day, before we insert a dozen qualifications, before we try to interpret or explain or resolve the problem in any way, we simply need to *hear* the word of Scripture.

The truth is that it is not really difficult to discover what the Bible teaches about money.* If we will simply read it through with honest hearts, we can come to a rather clear sense of the direction of Scripture on this subject. The Bible is much more clear and straightforward about money than it is about many other issues. Our difficulty is not in understanding the teaching; our

---

* I am well aware of the difficulties posed, for example, by the differing emphasis of Old and New Testament regarding money but those problems should not keep us from acknowledging the overall clarity of the biblical witness.

problem lies in another direction. The most difficult thing we have to deal with when we begin to look at the dark side of money is fear. If we have any sense at all, these words of Jesus really do frighten us. They frighten me. And we will not be able to hear the Scripture on this issue until we come to terms with our fear.

There is good reason for fear. These statements of Jesus fly in the face of virtually everything we have been taught about what constitutes an abundant life. Their implications are staggering for us, for the Church, and for the wider world of economics and politics. They challenge our privileged status in the world and call us to vigorous sacrificial action. There is indeed good reason for fear.

But the reason for fear is yet more complicated. We may fear being without money because our parents were without money. We may fear failure. We may fear success. Our parents may have had anxieties about money that we have made our own. We may have fears that stem from watching the absurdities to which some people have taken the teachings of Jesus.

I do not want to make light of these fears of ours in any way. Many of them are completely justified, and all of them need to be dealt with. In due time I will be discussing how we can come to terms with our fears. For now, it is enough to know that as the spirit of fear is replaced with the spirit of trust we will become more and more able to hear Jesus' radical criticism of wealth.

THE LIGHT SIDE

If we focused our attention exclusively on the warnings, we would have a distorted picture of the New Testament teaching. There is another stream of teaching that stresses what I have chosen to call the light side of money. I am referring to the way in which money can be used to enhance our relationship with God and bless humankind. A giving spirit can enhance the life of prayer and devotion. When Zacchaeus was freed to begin transferring his treasure from earth to heaven, Jesus joyfully announced, "Today salvation has come to this house" (Luke 19:9). The anointings of Jesus were each extravagant and each praised (Matt. 26:6–12; Luke 7:36–50; John 12:1–8). The good Samaritan used money generously and drew close to the kingdom of God.

The teaching on the light side goes further still. At times there seems to be a carefree, almost nonchalant attitude toward wealth. Jesus allowed well-to-do women to support his ministry (Luke 8:1–3). He ate with the rich and privileged (Luke 11:37; 14:1). He joined in the lavish wedding feast of Cana (John 2:1). The apostle Paul was as content with abounding as he was with being abased, as content with plenty as he was with hunger (Phil.4:12). And this, of course, is only a sample of the teaching.

How do we resolve the apparent conflict between the dark side and the light side? My attempt to do so will come later, in chapter 4. Besides, an instant resolution is probably not desirable, for it would keep us from hearing Jesus' teaching about the dark side of money.

PREVAILING DISTORTIONS

Our desire to resolve the problem quickly—and our consequent failure to hear the dark side—has brought about two prevailing distortions. The first is that money is a sign of God's blessing, and hence poverty is a sign of God's displeasure. This has been turned into a religion of personal peace and prosperity: crudely stated, "Love Jesus and get rich." Many churches are saturated with readily available gimmicks for blessedness, all the way from exact mathematical formulas (God will bless you sevenfold) to much more subtle but equally destructive forms. The distortion, of course, rests upon a piece of important biblical teaching, namely, the great generosity of God. But it is a distortion because it turns one aspect of the Bible's teaching on money into the whole message. This distortion fails to hear money's dark side.

Even the disciples struggled with this distortion. Remember how astonished they were when Jesus declared that a camel could slip through the eye of a needle more easily than the wealthy could enter the kingdom of God. Their amazement was primarily due to their belief that the wealth of the rich young ruler was a sign of God's special favor upon him. No wonder they exclaimed, "Who then can be saved?" (Matt. 19:25). Or think of Job's comforters—their firm conviction that he must have sinned stemmed from the obvious fact of his economic misfortune. Repeatedly Jesus opposed this false and destructive doctrine, showing instead that in the economy of God the poor, the bruised, the broken were special objects of his blessing and concern (Matt. 5:1–12). He made it quite clear that wealth itself was no assurance of God's blessing (Luke 6:24).*

A second distortion about money is found in the prevailing view of stewardship today. Discussions of stewardship, almost without exception, view money as completely neutral and depersonalized. It is merely "a medium of exchange," as we say. God has given us money to use, to administer, to put into service, goes the teaching. And so the emphasis is always placed upon the best use, the proper stewardship, of the resources God has entrusted to us.

What all this talk about stewardship fails to see is that money is not just a neutral medium of exchange but a

---

* Donald Kraybill, in chapter seven of his book *The Upside Down Kingdom* (Scottdale, Penn.: Herald Press, 1978), discusses ten different attempts to evade Jesus' hard teachings on money. Nearly all ten stem from this fatal distortion of the biblical witness.

"power" with a life of its own. And very often it is a "power" that is demonic in character. As long as we think of money in impersonal terms alone, no moral problems exist aside from the proper use of it. But when we begin to take seriously the biblical perspective that money is animated and energized by "powers," then our relationship to money is filled with moral consequence.

MONEY AS A POWER

The New Testament teaching on money makes sense only when we see it in the context of the "principalities and powers." The good creation of God has both "visible" and "invisible" realities (Col. 1:16). To describe certain aspects of the invisible realities the apostle Paul uses such terms as "principalities," "powers," "thrones," "dominions," and "authorities."* Originally part of God's good creation, these powers have, because of sin, lost their proper relationship to God. They have fallen and are in revolt against their creator. This is why the powers bring with them such mixed results—good and evil, blessing and cursing. This is why Paul can speak of the powers (*exousia*) as both the stabilizing forces in the Roman government (Rom. 13:1) and the demonic forces we are to wage war against (Eph. 6:12). The conviction was that in back of earthly rulers, social institutions, and many other things were invisible spiritual authorities and powers that were of an angelic or demonic nature.

Money is one of these powers. When Jesus uses the Aramaic term *mammon* to refer to wealth, he is giving it a personal and spiritual character. When he declares, "You cannot serve God and mammon" (Matt. 6:24), he is personifying mammon as a rival god. In saying this, Jesus is

---

* See, e.g., Col. 1:16; 2:15; Rom. 8:38; 1 Cor. 15:24–26; Eph. 1:21; 2:2; 3:10; 6:12; etc.

making it unmistakably clear that money is not some impersonal medium of exchange. Money is not something that is morally neutral, a resource to be used in good or bad ways depending solely upon our attitude toward it. Mammon is a power that seeks to dominate us.

When the Bible refers to money as a power, it does not mean something vague or impersonal. Nor does it mean power in the sense we mean when we speak, for example, of "purchasing power." No, according to Jesus and all the writers of the New Testament, behind money are very real spiritual forces that energize it and give it a life of its own. Hence, money is an active agent; it is a law unto itself; and it is capable of inspiring devotion.

It is the ability of money to inspire devotion that brings its dark side to the forefront. Dietrich Bonhoeffer has rightly said, "Our hearts have room only for one all-embracing devotion, and we can only cleave to one Lord."[2] What we must recognize is the seductive power of mammon. Money has power, spiritual power, to win our hearts. Behind our coins and dollar bills or whatever material form we choose to give to our money are spiritual forces.

It is the spiritual reality behind money that we want so badly to deny. For years I felt that Jesus was exaggerating by fixing such a huge gulf between mammon and God. Couldn't we show how advanced we are in the Christian life by giving each his due, God and mammon? Why not be joyful children of the world just as we are joyful children of God? Aren't the goods of the earth meant for our happiness? But the thing I failed to see, and the thing that Jesus saw so clearly, is the way in which mammon makes a bid for our hearts. Mammon asks for our allegiance in a way that sucks the milk of human kindness out of our very being.

That is why so much of Jesus' teaching regarding wealth is evangelistic in character. He calls people to turn away from the mammon god in order to worship the one true God. When a would-be disciple told Jesus of his determination to follow him anywhere he went, Jesus responded, "Foxes have holes, and birds of the air have nests; but the Son of man has nowhere to lay his head" (Matt. 8:20).

The rich young ruler asked Jesus how he could have eternal life and received the startling reply, "Go, sell what you possess and give to the poor, and you will have treasure in heaven; and come, follow me" (Matt. 19:21). The instruction makes sense only when we see that the rich young ruler's wealth was a rival god seeking his complete devotion. And note that when this young man went away sorrowful Jesus did not run after him and suggest that he only meant it metaphorically, that all that was really required was a tithe. No, money had become an all-consuming idol, and it had to be rejected totally.

Jesus' lunch with Zacchaeus had a remarkable outcome. This chief tax collector, for whom money was everything, was so freed by the life and presence of Christ that he declared, "Half of my goods I give to the poor; and if I have defrauded any one of anything, I restore it fourfold" (Luke 19:8). But even more striking is Jesus' response, "Today salvation has come to this house" (Luke 19:9).

Do you see what an utter contrast this is to the normal means of evangelism today? Our method is to get them "saved," and then later on instruct them in "Christian stewardship." For us, salvation usually consists in assenting to three or four statements and saying the prescribed prayer. But Jesus warns people to count the cost of discipleship before they ever enter into it. Not to do so would be as foolish as a construction company starting a skyscraper without calculating the expense, or a military dictator beginning a war without assessing his chances of winning (Luke 14:25–32). Jesus concludes this sobering teaching with such disturbing words that we find it hard to believe he could possibly mean what he says: "So therefore, whoever of you does not renounce all that he has cannot be my disciple" (Luke 14:33). I have yet to go to an evangelistic meeting and hear that kind of statement made before the invitation is given. But that is exactly what Jesus did, not just once but repeatedly.

For Christ money is an idolatry we must be converted *from* in order to be converted *to* him. The rejection of the god mammon is a necessary precondition to becoming a disciple of Jesus. And in point of fact, money has many of the characteristics of deity. It gives us security, can induce guilt, gives us freedom, gives us power and seems to be omnipresent. Most sinister of all, however, is its bid for omnipotence.

It is money's desire for omnipotence, for all power, that seems so strange, so out of place. It seems that money is not willing to rest contented in its proper place alongside other things we value. No, it must have supremacy. It must crowd out all else. This is, I say, the strange thing about money. We attach importance to it far beyond its worth. In fact, we attach ultimate importance to it. It is tremendously instructive to stand back and observe the frantic scramble of people for money. And this does not occur just among the poor and starving. Quite to the contrary—the super-wealthy, who have really nothing to gain by more money, still seek it furiously. The middle class, who are really quite adequately cared for (and who are from a global perspective the wealthy), continue to buy more houses than they need, to acquire more cars than they need, to have more clothes than they need. Many of us could live on half what we now receive without much serious sacrifice, yet we feel we are just barely making ends meet—and we feel this way whether we are earning $15,000 or $50,000 or $150,000.

Think of the symbols we attach to money—symbols

that are unrelated to its true value. If money were only a medium of exchange, it would make no sense at all to attach prestige to it, for example. And yet we do. We value people in relation to their income; we give people status and honor in relation to how much money they have. We dare to ask that question of questions that always reveals far more about ourselves than about the other person, "How much is he (or she) worth?" Dr. Lee Salk, a professor of psychology at the New York Hospital Cornell Medical Center, declared, "People jockey to find out what other people earn because, in our society, money is a symbol of strength, influence and power."[3]

In this century we have witnessed some of the most massive efforts in history to break the power of money through political means, but they have all failed. Both China and Cuba, for example, got rid of money as a means of exchange and then made it impossible to save money, to build up capital. But in time these imperatives had to be abandoned, and first money as a means of exchange, then money as a means of savings, reappeared. Finally, cash production bonuses were reinstated. Now, I give this example, not as a criticism of communist regimes, but as an example of what Jacques Ellul calls "the incredible power of money, which survives every trial, every upset, as if a merchant mentality has so permeated the world's consciousness that there is no longer any possibility of going against it."[4]

These strange facts make sense only as we come to understand the spiritual reality of money. Behind money are invisible spiritual powers, powers that are seductive and deceptive, powers that demand an all-embracing devotion. It is this fact that the apostle Paul saw when he observed that "the love of money is the root of all evils" (1 Tim. 6:10). Many have rightly observed that Paul did not say "money" but "the love of money." Given the almost universal love of money, however, they are often the same in practice.

Paul saw the same thing Jesus was dealing with in his many statements about money, namely, that it is a god that is out to gain our allegiance. By saying that the love of money is the root of all evils he does not mean in a literal sense that money produces all evils. He means that there is no kind of evil the person who loves money will not do to get it and hold onto it. All restraint is removed; the lover of money will do anything for it. And that is precisely its seductive character; for the person who loves money, no half measures will do. The person is hooked. Money becomes a consuming, life-dominating problem. It is a god demanding an all-inclusive allegiance.

This is why Jesus' cleansing of the temple was so pivotal. It was a deliberate act to symbolize that in the coming of the Messiah the religion of Israel was to be purged of its mammon worship. We must remember that the temple trade was good business in many ways. A valuable service was being provided, and although the prices were inflated, it was no more than what the market would bear. But Jesus saw through all that to the idolatry, the threat to the worship of the one true God.

As we come to understand better the dark side of money—its demonic tendency—we have a greater appreciation of Jesus' radical criticism of wealth. Without this insight it would be very easy for us to make Jesus' critical statements regarding money apply only to the dishonest rich. Certainly those who have obtained their money honestly and use it wisely are not included in his criticism—are they? But much of Jesus' teaching cannot be confined to the dishonest wealthy, for it speaks with equal severity to those who have acquired their wealth justly. There is every indication that the rich young ruler had gained his wealth honestly (Luke 18:18–30). In the story of the rich man and Lazarus there is no hint of dishonesty related to the condemnation of the rich man (Luke 16:19–31). In the parable of the rich farmer who tore down his barns to make way for expansion, we have every indication of honesty and industry (Luke 12:16–21). We would call him prudent—Jesus called him a fool.

This radical criticism of wealth makes no sense to us at all unless we see it in the context of its spiritual reality. It is one of the principalities and powers that must be conquered and redeemed through the blood of Jesus Christ before it can be usable for the greater good of the kingdom of God.

CONQUERING THE DARK SIDE

How is the god mammon conquered? Do we embrace it and try to use it for good purposes? Do we flee from it in total renunciation and divestiture?

Part of the reason these are difficult questions to answer is that the Bible does not offer us a Christian doctrine of money. It is a misuse and abuse of the Bible to make it yield some economic theory or give us ten rules for financial rectitude. But what it does offer us is even better: a perspective from which to view all life's economic decisions and a promise of dialogue, personal counseling in all life's financial decisions. The Holy Spirit is with us; Jesus is our present Teacher, and he will guide us through the money maze in all its personal and social complexity.

With that understanding, I would like to share several practical suggestions, knowing that they must be sifted through the filter of your own unique personality and circumstances. Perhaps they can serve in some way as signposts to encourage you in your journey.

First, let us get in touch with our *feelings* about money. For most of us the biggest obstacle to overcome is not that of understanding what the Bible teaches about money but that of coming to terms with our fear, insecurity, and guilt about money. We really are threatened by the subject of money. We are afraid that we have too little, and we are afraid that we have too much. And our fears are often irrational. For example, people who earn twenty times the average income of a citizen of Kenya are afraid of being on the brink of starvation. Or some of us are terrified of the possibility that others might overestimate our wealth and conclude that we are greedy.

These feelings are real and need to be taken seriously. Often they stem from childhood memories. I remember as a child having one ability that gave me unusual "wealth"; I could play marbles better than any other kid in the school. Since we always played for "keeps," I could often wipe out another boy's fortune before the noon recess was over. On one occasion I remember taking a huge sack of marbles, throwing them one by one into a muddy drainage ditch, and watching with delight as the other boys scrambled to find them. Through that single experience I began to sense something of the power wealth can give and the manipulative ends to which it can be put.

Some of us grew up during the depression years and know firsthand the pervasive anxiety of scarcity. Because of that experience, a holding, hoarding spirit is almost instinctive in us, and the very idea of letting go of a possession is frightening. Others of us grew up in an era of affluence and are keenly aware of the spiritual dangers of too much; the notions of conserving and being frugal feel like vices rather than virtues. It is only as we come to terms with these and the many other feelings that have shaped our understanding of money that we can act upon the biblical call to faithfulness.

Second, by a conscious act of the will, let us stop denying our wealth. Let us look at the large picture. Rather than comparing ourselves to others like ourselves, so that we can always claim comparative poverty, let us become world citizens, looking at ourselves in relation to all humanity.

Those who own a car are among the world's upper class. Those who own a home are more wealthy than 95 percent of all the people on this planet. The very fact that you were able to purchase this book probably puts you among the world's wealthy. The very fact that I had the time to write this book puts me in the same category. Let us get away from our pervasive dishonesty and frankly admit our wealth. Although most of us have a difficult time balancing our budgets, we must recognize that as world citizens we are among the very wealthy.

But please note that this is not intended to make us feel guilty; it is intended to help us capture an accurate picture of the real situation in the world. We are wealthy. The very fact that we have the leisure time to read a book or watch television means that we are wealthy. We do not need to be ashamed of our wealth or try to hide it from ourselves and others. It is only as we admit our wealth and quit trying to run from it that we are in a position to conquer it and use it for God's good purposes.

Third, let us create an atmosphere in which confession is possible. Much of our preaching on money has been either to condemn it or praise it but not to help each other relate to it. Many of us feel isolated and alone, as if we were the only ones who count our gold in the night. How much better it would be to create a climate of acceptance in which we can talk about our mutual problems and frustrations, confess our fears and temptations. We can listen with empathy to the confession of someone who has been seduced by sex; let us just as freely hear the confession of someone who has been seduced by money. Let us learn to receive from each other the heart cry, "Forgive me, for I have sinned; money has captured my heart!"

We need others who will hear our fear and hurt, accepting it and lifting it on our behalf into the arms of God. For the Church to function as the Church, it needs to create an environment in which our failures over money can come to the surface and we can be healed.

Fourth, let us discover one other person who will struggle with us through the money maze. If it could be our husband or wife, that, I think, would be ideal. Together we covenant to help each other detect when the seductive power of money is beginning to win. This needs to be done in a spirit of love and graciousness, but it does need to be done. Anything that is made totally private and is never open to public correction will be distorted. All of us need as much help as possible to unearth our blind spots. Perhaps we want more things than are good for us—we need someone to help us face that fact. Perhaps we need to venture forth courageously into the business world for Christ and his kingdom—we need those who will encourage us in this ministry. Perhaps a spirit of greed has crept into our business dealings—we need people who will help us see it. Perhaps our fears keep us from the joyful life of trust—we need those who will prod us into faith.

Fifth, let us discover ways to get in touch with the poor. One of the most damaging things affluence does is allow us to distance ourselves from the poor so we no longer see their pain. We then can create an illusionary world that prevents us from evaluating life in the light of "love of neighbor."

What can we do? We can make a conscious choice to be among the poor, not to preach to them but to learn from them. We can read books, like *The Grapes of Wrath* and *Songs from the Slums*, that capture the smell and texture of life on the other side. We can stop watching the television programs that concentrate exclusively on the plastic world of the affluent. (If we do watch them, we can do so with discernment, knowing that it is a dream world that can easily insulate us from the pain and suffering and agony of the vast majority of humanity.)

Sixth, let us experience the meaning of inner renunciation. Abraham was asked to sacrifice his son, Isaac. And I can well imagine that by the time he came down from the mountain, the words *my* and *mine* had forever changed their meaning for him. The apostle Paul speaks of "having nothing, and yet possessing everything" (2 Cor. 6:10). As we enter the school of inner renunciation we come into that state in which nothing belongs to us and yet everything is available to us.

We badly need a conversion in our understanding of ownership. Perhaps we need to stamp everything in our possession with the reminder "Given by God, owned by God, and to be used for the purposes of God." We need to find ways to remind ourselves over and over again that the earth is the Lord's, not ours.

Seventh, let us give with glad and generous hearts. Giving has a way of routing out the tough old miser within us. Even the poor need to know that they can give. Just the very act of letting go of money, or some other treasure, does something within us. It destroys the demon greed.

Some will be led, like Saint Francis of Assisi, to give away everything and embrace "Lady Poverty." That is not a command for all, but it is the word of the Lord for some, as Jesus' encounter with the rich young ruler testifies. We must not despise people called to this form of giving but rejoice with them in their growing freedom from the god mammon.

The rest of us can find other ways to give. We can find needy people who have no way to repay us and give to them. We can give to the Church. We can give to educational institutions. We can give to missions. We can take the money we want to give and throw a high holy party for those who need to celebrate: the idea has good biblical precedent (Deut. 14:22–27). But whatever we do, let us give, give, give. Gordon Cosby has noted that "to give away money is to win a victory over the dark powers that oppress us."[5]

Perhaps you have found this a difficult chapter to read; I found it a difficult one to write. I so much wanted to get on to the good, the positive, the light side of money! We all like the affirmative viewpoint, so it is natural to downplay the negative, critical aspects. And yet, we really need to come to terms with the indisputable fact that, by far, most of Jesus' statements regarding money are about the dark side. And now we understand why this is so: only until we have faced and conquered the hellish character of money are we candidates for receiving and using its beneficial side. We now turn our attention to the light side of money.

3.   The Light Side of Money

The only right stewardship is that which is tested by the rule of love.

—JOHN CALVIN

The issue of money would be much easier to deal with if it were all bad. Our task then would be to denounce it and withdraw from it. That, however, is the one thing we cannot do if we want to be faithful to the biblical witness. Though the Bible gives repeated warnings about the dark side of money, it also contains a stream of teaching on the light side of money. In this tradition, money is seen as a blessing from God and, even more startling, as a means of enhancing our relationship with God.

THE OLD TESTAMENT WITNESS

The Old Testament bears repeated witness to this reality. In the creation story we are struck by the refrain that this world that God created is good. The garden of Eden was a lavish provision for the original pair.

God's great generosity can be seen in his care for Abraham. God said that he would make Abraham's name great and prosper him. And he kept his word, for we read that "Abram was very rich in cattle, in silver, and in gold" (Gen. 13:2). Isaac was blessed in a similar fashion, so much so that we are told that because of his great wealth "the Philistines envied him" (Gen. 26:14).

We are told that Job was a man of great wealth and that he was "blameless and upright, one who feared God, and turned away from evil" (Job 1:1). After his trial by fire, God restored Job's fortunes twofold (Job 42:10).

Solomon's great wealth was not viewed as something to be embarrassed about; rather, it was considered as evidence of God's favor (1 Kings 3:13). The Bible gives considerable space to cataloging Solomon's riches and then concludes, "Thus King Solomon excelled all the kings of the earth in riches and in wisdom" (1 Kings 10:23). The famous pilgrimage of the queen of Sheba to the court of Solomon underscores his prosperity. The queen exclaims, "I did not believe the reports until I came and my own eyes had seen it; and, behold, the half was not told me; your wisdom and prosperity surpass the report which I heard" (1 Kings 10:7).

The list could go on for some time, from the promise of a land flowing with milk and honey to the promise of the windows of heaven opening to pour out a material blessing beyond what we could contain (Mal. 3:10). Material things are neither antithetical nor inconsequential to the spiritual life but intimately and positively related to it.

THE NEW TESTAMENT WITNESS

Nor is the New Testament devoid of this emphasis. Money is often seen as a way of enhancing our relationship with God and expressing our love for our neighbor. The wise men brought their wealth to the Christ child as a means of worship. Zacchaeus gave generously, and the poor widow gave sacrificially. Wealthy women helped support the band of disciples (Luke 8:2-3). Both Joseph of Arimathea and Nicodemus used their wealth in the service of Christ (Matt. 27:57-61; John 19:38-42).

By teaching us to pray for daily bread, Jesus brought the concern for material provision into intimate relationship with the spiritual life. Material things are not to be despised or thought of as something outside the parameters of true spirituality. Indeed, material provisions are the lavish gifts of a bountiful God.

In Acts we are told of Barnabas, who was a true son of encouragement when he used his land investments to aid the early church (Acts 4:36-37). We are given the wonderful story of Cornelius, who "gave alms liberally to the people, and prayed constantly to God" (Acts 10:2). We are reminded of Lydia, the seller of purple, who used her status and resources to benefit the early church (Acts 16: 14).

The apostle Paul uses the collection for the saints in Jerusalem as an opportunity to teach the spiritual benefits of cheerful giving (2 Cor. 8 and 9). He even lists giving as one of the spiritual gifts (Rom. 12:8).

From this brief overview it is clear that the New Testament contains a stream of teaching that views money in a positive way. Let us now focus our attention on how money can enhance our relationship with God.

THE GOOD EARTH

Throughout Scripture the provision of those things necessary to carry on human life adequately is seen as the gracious gift of a loving God. Everything that God created is good, very good. It is meant to bless and enhance human life. How thankful we can be for these bountiful signs of God's goodness! As I write these words, the birds outside are singing, perhaps in thanksgiving for the bounty and beauty of sky and sea and land. We can join with them in cheerful song, for God has indeed given us a good world to enjoy. The very bounty of the earth can draw us closer to God in thanksgiving and praise.

Most wonderful of all is how so much of what comes is not the result of our doing but a gift, unearned and unearnable. God told the children of Israel that he was going to give them "great and goodly cities, which you did not build, and houses full of all good things, which you did not fill, and cisterns hewn out, which you did not hew, and vineyards and olive trees, which you did not plant" (Deut. 6:10b-11). Cities they did not build, wells they did not dig, orchards they did not plant—this is God's way with his people.

We do not need to look very deeply into our own experience to know that this is so. Many times all our hard work and clever scheming yield little or nothing, and then all of a sudden we are flooded with good things from completely unexpected sources. Many factors in our business and economic lives are completely beyond our control.

The farmers of ancient Israel had a keen sense of this reality. They worked, to be sure, but they also knew that they were helpless to grow grain. Drought, fire, pestilence, and a hundred other things could wipe them out in an instant. They knew and understood on a very deep level that a good harvest was the gracious provision of a loving God.

This is, of course, nothing more than the confession that we live by grace. Though it is a wonderful truth to know that we are saved by grace, it is equally wonderful to know that we live by it as well. Though we labor, just as the birds of the air labor, we do not need to grasp and grab frantically, because we have One who cares for us just as he cares for the birds of the air.

And so, as we learn to receive money and the things it buys as gracious gifts from a loving God, we discover how they enrich our relationship with God. Our experience resonates with the words of Deuteronomy, "God will bless you in all your produce and in all the work of your hands, so that you will be altogether joyful" (Deut. 16:15). Doxology becomes the posture of our experience. Joy, thanksgiving, celebration—these mark our lives. One reason so many of the ancient Jewish worship festivals revolved around thanksgiving was because of their experience of the gracious provision of God.

GOD'S OWNERSHIP

Closely tied to God's provision is God's ownership. There is hardly anything more clear in the Bible than God's absolute right to property. To Job, God declares, "Whatever is under the whole heaven is mine" (Job 41: 11). To Moses, he says, "All the earth is mine" (Exod. 19:5-6). And the psalmist confesses, "The earth is the LORD's and the fulness thereof" (Ps. 24:1).

We moderns find it difficult to identify with this teaching. Much of our training draws from the Roman view that ownership is a "natural right." Hence the very idea that anything or anyone can infringe upon our "property rights" feels alien to our world view. This, coupled with our seemingly innate self-centeredness, means that, for us, "property rights" tend to take precedence over "human rights."

In the Bible, however, God's absolute rights as owner and our relative rights as stewards are unmistakably clear. As absolute owner, God put limits on the individual's ability to accumulate land or wealth. For example, a percentage of the produce of the land was to be given to the poor (Deut. 14:28-29). Every seventh year the land was to lie fallow, and whatever volunteer grain came up was for the needy, so that "the poor of your people may eat" (Exod. 23:11). Every fiftieth year was to be a Jubilee year, in which all slaves were to be set free, all debts were to be canceled, and all land was to return to its original owner. God's rationale for so violently upsetting everyone's economic applecarts was—very simply—that "the land is mine" (Lev. 25:23).

God's ownership of all things actually enhances our relationship with him. When we know—truly know—

that the earth is the Lord's, then property itself makes us more aware of God. For example, if we were staying in and caring for the vacation home of a famous actress, we would be reminded of her daily by the very fact of living in her home. A thousand things would bring her presence to mind. So it is in our relationship with God. The house we live in is his house, the car we drive is his car, the garden we plant is his garden. We are only temporary stewards of things that belong to Another.

Being aware of God's ownership can free us from a possessive and anxious spirit. After we have done what we can to care for those things that have been entrusted to us, we know that they are in bigger hands than ours. When John Wesley heard that his home had been destroyed by fire, he exclaimed, "The Lord's house burned. One less responsibility for me!"[1]

God's ownership of everything also changes the kind of question we ask in giving. Rather than, "How much of my money should I give to God?" we learn to ask, "How much of God's money should I keep for myself?" The difference between these two questions is of monumental proportions.

THE GRACE OF GIVING

The grace of giving is often a tremendous stimulant to the life of faith. This is why the offering is correctly placed as part of the worship experience.

In Isaiah 58 we read of a very religious people whose pious devotion counted for nothing because it was not matched with active caring for the poor and the oppressed. "Is not this the fast that I choose," proclaims God, "to loose the bonds of wickedness, to undo the thongs of the yoke, to let the oppressed go free, and to break every yoke?" (Isa. 58:6). Religious piety is bankrupt without justice. If you want your fasting to have true spiritual content, then you are to "share your bread with the hungry, and bring the homeless poor into your house" (Isa. 58:7).

If our spiritual vitality seems low, if Bible study produces only dusty words, if prayer seems hollow and empty, then perhaps a prescription of lavish and joyful giving is just what we need. Giving brings authenticity and vitality to our devotional experience.

Money is an effective way of showing our love to God because it is so much a part of us. One economist put it this way: "Money as a form of power is so intimately related to the possessor that one cannot consistently give money without giving self."[2] In a sense, money is coined personality, so tied to who we are that when we give it we are giving ourselves. We sing, "Take my life and let it be, consecrated, Lord, to Thee." But we must flesh out that consecration in specific ways, which is why the next line of the hymn says, "Take my silver and my gold, not a mite would I withhold." We consecrate ourselves by consecrating our money.

Dr. Karl Menninger once asked one wealthy patient, "What on earth are you going to do with all that money?" The patient replied, "Just worry about it, I suppose!" Dr. Menninger went on, "Well, do you get that much pleasure out of worrying about it?" "No," responded the patient, "but I get such terror when I think of giving some of it to somebody."[3]

Now, this "terror" is real. When we let go of money we are letting go of part of ourselves and part of our security. But this is precisely why it is important to do it. It is one way to obey Jesus' command to deny ourselves. "If any man would come after me, let him deny himself and take up his cross daily and follow me" (Luke 9:23).

When we give money we are releasing a little more of our egocentric selves and a little more of our false security. John Wesley declared that "if you have any desire to escape the damnation of hell, give all you can; otherwise I can have no more hope of your salvation than that of Judas Iscariot."[4]

Giving frees us from the tyranny of money. But we do not just give money; we give the things money has purchased. In Acts the early Christian community gave houses and land to provide funds for those in need (Acts 4:32-37). Have you ever considered selling a car or a stamp collection to help finance someone's education? Money has also given us the time and leisure to acquire skills. What about giving those skills away? Doctors, dentists, lawyers, computer experts, and many others can give their skills for the good of the community.

Giving frees us to care. It produces an air of expectancy as we anticipate what God will lead us to give. It makes life with God an adventure of discovery. We are being used to help make a difference in the world, and that is worth living for and giving for.[5]

CONTROLLING AND USING

Although giving must have a large place in Christian experience, the control and use of money must have an even larger place.[6] Believers who are rightly taught and disciplined are enabled to hold possessions without corruption and use them for the greater purposes of the kingdom of God.

The truth is that total divestiture is usually a very poor way to help the poor. Certainly it is vastly inferior to the proper management and use of resources. How much better to have wealth and resources in the hands of those who are properly disciplined and informed by a Christian world view than to abandon these things to the servants of mammon!

Abraham managed large holdings for the glory of God and the greater public good. So did Job and David and

Solomon. In the New Testament Nicodemus used both his wealth and his high position for the good of the Christian fellowship (John 7:50; 19:39). Because Barnabas had done well in managing his property holdings, he was able to help the early church when the need was acute (Acts 4:36–37).

Jesus gave us the parable of the talents (Matt. 25:14-30). Think of it: Jesus, who had spoken so severely of the danger of riches, now compares the kingdom of God to a man who entrusts his wealth to servants, fully expecting them to use it to make a profit. A talent was worth about a thousand dollars, and the man who had been given five thousand doubled his investment, as did the man with two thousand. But the poor fellow who had been given only one thousand was so afraid of losing it in the rough and tumble of the marketplace that he did nothing, and gained nothing. Jesus' words to this over-conservative servant are harsh indeed, "You wicked and slothful servant! You knew that I reap where I have not sowed, and gather where I have not winnowed? Then you ought to have invested my money with the bankers, and at my coming I should have received what was my own with interest. So take the talent from him, and give it to him who has the ten talents" (Matt. 25:26-28).

Now, it is not wrong to make spiritual applications of this parable, but it is wrong to completely divorce it from its economic context. Christians are to immerse themselves in the world of capital and business. That is a high and holy calling. It is a good thing for those under the rule of God to make money. We should not hide from these opportunities to labor for the sake of the kingdom of God.

Believers can and should be called into positions of power, wealth, and influence. It is a spiritual calling to take leadership roles in government, education, and business. Some are called to make money—lots of money

—for the glory of God and the larger public good. Others are called into positions of immense power and responsibility for the same purpose. Banks, department stores, factories, schools, and a thousand other institutions need the influence of Christian compassion and perspective.

But as I noted earlier, all this must be done in the context of a people who are "rightly taught and disciplined." You see, we need instruction on how to possess money without *being* possessed *by* money. We need help to learn how to own things without treasuring them. We need the disciplines that will allow us to live simply while managing great wealth and power.

The apostle Paul said that he had learned to be abased and that he had learned to abound; he could live in abundance, or in want, because "I can do all things through Christ who strengthens me" (Phil. 4:13, NKJV). It takes as much grace to abound as it does to be abased. If God chooses to bring us into great wealth or power, we are to humbly confess, "I can do all things through Christ who strengthens me," just as we do if severity and deprivation come.

The call of God is upon us to use money within the confines of a properly disciplined spiritual life and to manage money for the good of all humanity and for the glory of God. And when this is done we are drawn deeper into the divine Center. We stand amazed that God would use our meager efforts to do his work upon the earth. Resources are channeled into life-giving ministry. The helpless are helped. Projects that advance Christ's kingdom are financed. Great good is accomplished. Money is a blessing when it is used within the context of the life and power of God.

We can control and use money while we are alive: we can also control and use money at our death. A compassionate will is a good thing; it gives joy to know that our wealth will bless many after our death.

THE LESSONS OF TRUST

Another example of the light side of money is the way it can be used by God to build trust. When Jesus teaches us to pray for daily bread he is teaching us to live in trust. Huge stockpiles and elaborate backup systems are not necessary, because we have a heavenly Father who cares for us. When the children of Israel gathered manna in the wilderness they were allowed only a daily supply. Any more than the daily allotment would spoil. They were learning to live in trust, daily trust, upon Yahweh.

In giving these examples I am not speaking against retirement plans or savings accounts. What I am stressing is the way in which money can be used by God to build a spirit of trust within us.

During my senior year in high school I was invited to go on a summer mission venture among the Eskimo people of northern Alaska. Over the months I grew in my conviction that this was God's will for my life, yet I had no funds to make it a reality. Both my parents were seriously and chronically ill, and all the family's money had gone to pay medical bills.

In April I went on a weekend retreat with the other team members to make further plans for the trip. Over the weekend my conviction that I should go grew even stronger—but how? On my return home I discovered a letter in the mail with a thirty-dollar check. The letter was from someone who knew nothing of my summer hopes, but the note read simply, "For your expenses this summer." I took this check as God's gracious confirmation that I should go. I followed George Mueller's principle of telling no one my need except God, and it was a beautiful experience to watch over the ensuing months God's provision for every need for the trip. That was very faith-building for me as a young teenager.

But the story does not end there. When I returned

home my hopes for college were dim. All the money I had painstakingly saved through high school had gone for hospital care for my parents. Now the summer had been used, not to earn money, but to minister among the Eskimo people. A bit sad but still confident I had made the right decision, I applied for and was offered a job working for an insurance company. But before I could begin work, a series of events occurred that I could never have anticipated and for which I never had asked.

On Sunday, one week before fall college classes were to begin, I spoke in my home church on the experiences of the summer. After the service a couple in the congregation took me to their home for lunch and during the course of the afternoon inquired into my college plans. Within a few days this couple had formed a support group that helped me financially through four years of college and three years of graduate school. God had taken people and their sanctified use of money to teach me trust. And as is characteristic of the ways of God, it was above all I could ask or think.

That was my first experience in learning to trust God with money matters. Since that time, he has graciously used money to teach me more about trust and faith. You, I am sure, could relate similar experiences. Think of it, God takes so ordinary a thing as money, the very thing that so often rears its ugly head as a rival deity, and uses it to lead us forward in the kingdom of Christ.

PRACTICING THE LIGHT SIDE

We celebrate the light side of money by learning to cultivate a spirit of thanksgiving. I say "learn to cultivate" because it seems that thanksgiving does not come naturally to human beings. (Anyone who has children needs no further elaboration on that point.) However, we do need ways to help each other grow in gratitude. Often we miss the lavish provision of God—the air, the sunshine, the rain, the magnificent colors that delight our eyes, the many friendships that enrich our lives. The very rhythms of the earth are gracious gifts from the hand of the Creator.

Can we learn to wake up in the morning rejoicing in the miracle of sleep? Anyone who suffers from insomnia knows what a great gift sleep is. Perhaps at night we could go to the rooms of our sleeping children and sit down and watch them, all the time giving thanks. We can also look at our possessions and, without treasuring them, give thanks for them.

When we have a spirit of thanksgiving we can hold all things lightly. We receive; we do not grab. And when it is time to let go, we do so freely. We are not owners, only stewards. Our lives do not consist of the things that we have, for we live and move and breathe in God, not things. And may I add that this includes those intangible "things" that are often our greatest treasures—status, reputation, position. These are things that come and go in life, and we can learn to be thankful when they come and thankful when they go.

Perhaps we could discover new wineskins that would incarnate the Old Testament notion of the thank offering. Few of us are farmers, so fall harvest festivals are not as meaningful for us as they were for ancient Israel. But perhaps we can discover corresponding events that mark our economic lives. Maybe some payday we should convert our entire paycheck into dollar bills and then spread the money out on the living room floor just to help us visualize all that God has given us. We could then take what we plan to give away and actually give it in dollar bills, making the act visual to us in the way that grain was visual to the ancient Israelite making a thank offering.

Perhaps we could establish a Christian thanksgiving celebration for the signing of significant contracts. Maybe we could establish a consecration service for those called into the world of business. Whatever the ideas, the key is to continually discover a deeper, richer life of thanksgiving.

So far, we have sought to understand the two major streams of teaching in the Bible regarding money: the dark side and the light side. What we have not done yet is to merge the two streams together and show how they function in a working harmony in contemporary life. It is now time to attempt such a merger.

4. Kingdom Use of Unrighteous Mammon

Gain all you can, save all you can, give all you can.
—JOHN WESLEY

To my knowledge no one has attempted to reconcile Jesus' statement that we cannot serve God and mammon (Matt. 6:24) with his concern that we are to make friends by means of "unrighteous mammon" (Luke 16:9). This reconciliation, however, is precisely what is necessary if we are to rightly understand the Bible's witness to both the dark and the light side of money.

LUKE 16

In the opening verses of chapter 16 of Luke, Jesus tells a parable that has tied commentators into knots and puzzled ordinary Christians for centuries (Luke 16:1-13). And well it should, for the story is indeed an unusual one. However, it contains tremendous significance for our present study and holds the key to unlocking our understanding of both sides of money.

The parable itself is simple enough. A wealthy man discovers that his steward or business manager has been mishandling his funds and promptly fires him. But before his termination becomes final, the steward devises an ingenious plan to ensure his future. He calls in his employer's debtors, and one by one he writes off 20 to 50 percent of their debts. These people will thus be so indebted to him that when he is out of a job they will feel obliged to help him out.

The plan is obviously clever and just as obviously dishonest. When the master finds out what his steward has done, rather than throw him into prison as we might expect, he is so impressed by the man's ingenuity that he commends him on his prudence.

One reason we find this passage difficult is that Jesus uses what is so clearly a dishonest act to teach an important spiritual truth. However, Christ never commends the steward's dishonesty. Rather, he highlights his shrewdness in using economic resources for noneconomic goals —that is, using money to make friends so that when he needed it he would have a place to go.

Our biggest difficulty is with Jesus' own comments following the parable. He first notes that "the sons of this world are wiser in their own generation than the sons of light" (Luke 16:8). Next, he makes a most startling statement: "And I tell you, make friends for yourselves by means of unrighteous mammon, so that when it fails they may receive you into the eternal habitations" (Luke 16:9). In short, Jesus is telling us to use money in such a way that when it fails—and it will fail—we are still cared for.

Two things shock us in these words of Jesus: first, that mammon is unrighteous, and second, that we are to use it to make friends. The two ideas seem so opposed to each other that we find it hard to believe that Jesus could have meant them both.* The language, however, is clear enough—he did indeed mean to say that mammon is unrighteous *and* that we are to make friends with it.

---

* I am well aware of the various attempts to explain away the idea that mammon is unrighteous. The most argued position recently is that Jesus was using the term *unrighteous mammon* to refer to the practice of charging interest, which was prohibited to Jews and hence "unrighteous." Those who take this position include Dan Otto Via, Jr., in *The Parables: Their Literary and Existential Dimension* (Philadelphia:

When Christ spoke of "unrighteous mammon" he was underscoring the inherent fallenness of money. Unrighteousness is a necessary attribute of mammon. The word Jesus uses here (*adikos*) is very strong. Some translations render it "the mammon of iniquity," which perhaps best captures the odious character of the word. Commenting on this passage, Jacques Ellul has written, "This means both that Mammon generates and provokes iniquity and that Mammon, symbol of unrighteousness, emanates from iniquity. In any case, unrighteousness, the antithesis of God's word, is Mammon's trademark."[1]

The inherent unrighteousness of mammon is a hard pill for us to swallow. We so badly want to believe that mammon has no power over us, no authority of its own. But by giving the descriptive adjective *unrighteous* to mammon, Jesus forbids us from ever taking so naive a view of wealth. We must be more tough-minded, more realistic.

And in fact, those who work with money all the time know better than to think of it in neutral terms. As Jesus told us, in such matters the children of this world are wiser than the children of light (Luke 16:8). They know that money is far from harmless: money is poison, and if it is used in the wrong way, it can destroy as few things can. But they also know that once you conquer money

---

Fortress, 1967), and Donald Kraybill, in *The Upside Down Kingdom* (Scottdale, Penn.: Herald Press, 1978). To do this, however, not only takes the sting out of the parable, it makes it meaningless. The whole point of the teaching is that we are to take what is essentially "of this world" and use it in the service of God. This interpretation of "unrighteous mammon" is in complete accord with Jesus' other numerous negative statements regarding mammon.

Perhaps it should also be noted that some have sought to divorce the comments of Luke 16:8b–13 from the parable itself, viewing them as random pericopes that were gathered together and placed here. The statements, however, make sense *only* in relation to the parable as Jesus' commentary upon it.

and learn how to use it, its power is virtually unlimited. Money has power out of all proportion to its purchasing power. Because the children of this world understand this, they can use money for noneconomic purposes. And use it they do! Money is used as a weapon to bully people and to keep them in line. Money is used to "buy" prestige and honor. Money is used to enlist the allegiance of others. Money is used to corrupt people. Money is used for many things; it is one of the greatest powers in human society.

And this is precisely why Jesus tells us to "make friends" by means of this "unrighteous mammon." Rather than run from money, we are to take it—evil bent and all—and use it for kingdom purposes. We are to be absolutely clear about the venomous nature of money. But rather than reject it we are to conquer it and use it for noneconomic purposes. Money is to be captured, subdued, and used for greater goals. We are called to use money to advance the kingdom of God. What a tragedy it is if all we do is use money in the ordinary ways and not make any greater use of it.

MATTHEW 6

It is exactly this "greater use" that Jesus gives attention to in the sixth chapter of Matthew. He begins by warning us against "laying up treasures on earth"— mainly because it is such an insecure investment, for moth and rust will consume it, or thieves will steal it (Matt. 6:19). Rather, we are to lay up for ourselves "treasures in heaven," and we are to do so for two reasons. First, it is an investment that guarantees far greater security—neither moth, rust, thieves, nor any other thing can get to it. Second, it draws our affections—indeed our whole being—into the kingdom of God: "Where your treasure is, there will your heart be also" (Matt. 6:20-21).

Treasure in the bank of heaven is an investment with a high return.

It is often said of money that "you can't take it with you!" Jesus, however, is saying that if we know what we are doing we can take it with us after all. But how do we deposit treasure in heaven? We cannot deposit a check there.

One question to ask is, What will be in heaven? Obviously, there will be people in heaven; thus one way we lay up treasure in heaven is to invest in the lives of people. That kind of investment we will indeed take with us. Money invested in people is the best possible investment.

Suppose that the United States decided to change over its entire currency to British pounds, that the moment it did all American currency would be worthless, but that we were not told when the monetary conversion would take place. In that situation, the wise course would be to turn our money into British pounds, keeping only enough American currency to live day to day.

Now this gives us something of the picture Jesus means to convey when he tells us to lay up treasure in heaven and to make friends with unrighteous mammon. The proper use of money is not for living high down here; that would be a very poor investment indeed. No, the proper use of money is for investing as much of it as possible in the lives of people, so that we will have treasure in heaven. Of course, we need to keep a certain amount of money in order to carry on the day-to-day business of life, but we want to free up as much as we possibly can in order to place it where the return is eternal.

The children of light are faced with the great challenge of finding ways to convert "filthy lucre" into kingdom enterprises. Money, evil tendency and all, is to be mastered and turned into kingdom opportunities. Perhaps there is a needy neighbor next door, or a famine in the Sudan, or an opportunity to spread the gospel to a hitherto unreached group of people, or a chance to invest in the future of a bright young student. These are all wonderful investment opportunities.

USING, NOT SERVING

We can now bring into harmony the commandment of Matthew 6 that we are not to serve mammon and the counsel of Luke 16 that we are to make friends by means of unrighteous mammon. The Christian is given the high calling of *using* mammon without *serving* mammon. We are using mammon when we allow God to determine our economic decisions. We are serving mammon when we allow mammon to determine our economic decisions. We simply must decide who is going to make our decisions— God or mammon.

Do we buy a particular home on the basis of the call of God, or because of the availability of money? Do we buy a new car because we can afford it, or because God instructed us to buy a new car? If money determines what we do or do not do, then money is our boss. If God determines what we do or do not do, then God is our boss. My money might say to me, "You have enough to buy that," but my God might say to me, "I don't want you to have it." Now, who am I to obey?

Most of us allow money to dictate our decisions: what kind of house we live in, what vacation we will take, what job we will hold. Money decides.

Suppose Carolynn says to me, "Let's do this or that," and I complain, "But we don't have enough money!" What has happened? Money decided. You see, I did not say, "Well, honey, let's pray together and see if God wants us to do it." No, money made the decision. Money is my master. I am serving money.

J. Hudson Taylor would never have launched the great chapter in mission history called the China Inland Mission if he had let money decide. He was an ordinary person with few resources, yet once he had determined that God wanted him to go, he went. God had made the decision, not money. His master was God, and it was this master that he served.

Over the course of his effective ministry, God channeled very large sums of money through Hudson Taylor, enough to care for the needs of well over a thousand missionaries. But from his earliest days in the slums of London, Taylor had learned to understand money in the light of the cross. He had learned to use money without serving it.

And so the conflict we feel between Luke 16:9 and Matthew 6:24 is answered by learning to use money without serving money. But we must not be fooled: in the rough and tumble of life we find that the conflict is not resolved quickly or easily. Very often those who try to make friends by using mammon are soon serving mammon. We cannot safely use mammon until we are absolutely clear that we are dealing, not just with mammon, but with *unrighteous* mammon. The spiritual powers that stand in back of money and through which money lives and moves and has its being need to be conquered and subdued and made subservient to Jesus Christ. The conquest must go forth on all fronts at once, both inwardly and outwardly. We are seeking the overthrow of not only the spiritual power of mammon but the mammon spirit within us as well. The more we conquer money's evil side, the more money is used rather than served—and the more it is a blessing, not a curse.

MASTERING MAMMON

Just to say that we must master mammon does not make it happen. There are definite things we must do if we expect to defeat the tough old miser within and the spiritual powers without. The following steps in mastering mammon are given in the hope of starting you on your way.

The first step is to listen to the biblical witness about money. Begin with the Gospels. You may want to use a marking pen to highlight any reference to money and possessions. The purpose is to bathe in the biblical truth of Jesus' second most recurring theme. Next, turn to the Epistles with the same goal in mind. Then go back through all you have read and type up separately every reference to the dark side of money and every reference to the light side of money. Now that you can read the New Testament witness in one sitting, see what conclusions you can come to about money and write them down. Add any Old Testament passages about money that can give you added insight.

The second step is to consider money from a psychological and sociological perspective. We seek to understand ourselves better. Do we fear money? Do we hate money? Do we love money? Does money produce pride or shame in us?

We seek to understand our world better. What are the causes of Third World poverty and First World affluence? What responsibility do we bear for hurting, bleeding humanity? What resources are available to us?

As we grow in our understanding of the biblical, psychological, and sociological perspectives, we are able to turn to the third action step, which is the technical side, money management. Courageously we can take up such important items as family budgeting, estate planning, investments, deferred giving, and more. Now we can plan our budgets responsive to God's concern for the poor. Now we can evaluate our expenditures sensitive to a just sharing of the world's resources. Now we can write our wills unafraid of our own frailty. Now we can look at our giving in light of Christ's great missionary mandate. Now we can control and manage money to the glory of God and the good of others.

A fourth action step is to gather a community of support that will stand with us in our struggle and affirm us in life-style changes. Those who are rich and powerful need understanding and compassion as much as those who are poor and hungry.

A loving community of support can be found in many ways, and it does not always need to be formal or to take immense amounts of time. One January day I was having a brown-bag lunch with a judge and a businessman in our city, when the businessman pulled out a sheet of paper and began sharing with the two of us his giving goals for the next ten years. What fun to listen to his plans and sense his excitement in making his money count for the kingdom of God!

Husbands and wives can help each other. Home study groups can support one another. It is important, however, that such groups be quick to listen and slow to advise. Often an understanding heart is the greatest help we can give.

Such a community of creative, challenging, and affirming love may be slow in developing. Our wealth makes us lonely and isolated. What is needed is patience with each other and patience with ourselves. Our desire is to experience together the grace of a growing discipleship.

A fifth action step is to bring the ministry of prayer to bear directly upon money matters. Money *is* a spiritual issue, and prayer is our chief weapon in the life of the spirit. Let us learn to pray for each other for the binding of greed and covetousness and the releasing of liberality and generosity. In prayer, through the imagination, let us see the power of money broken. Let us picture the spiritual powers behind money brought under the lordship of Christ. Let us visualize money being channeled into

needy lives, providing necessary food and medical supplies. Let us imagine Christians in business controlling,
investing, and channeling money in new, creative, life-
enhancing ways. Let us see the governments of the world
diverting their vast resources away from bombs and into
bread.

Let us pray for each other. We need wisdom to be
faithful with our resources. It is a great service to lay
hands on one another and pray for an increase of the gifts
of wisdom and giving. Pray over how to budget money.
Pray for freedom from money's power. Pray for money to
be provided to those who need it. Before giving money
away pray over it, asking God to use it for his good purposes: do the same for money that is invested in some
enterprise.

Learn to pray preventive prayers. Rather than waiting
until there is a financial problem, pray for protection of
those who are doing well. If they have no money problems, pray that they will continue to know freedom. If
they show the grace of giving, pray that the grace will
increase. If they are called to manage and use money,
surround them with the strong light of Christ so that they
will be free from greed and avarice.

A sixth action step is to dethrone money.* By inner
attitude and outward action, we must defile money's
sacred character. Money is too high on our list of values.
As Thomas Merton observed, "The true 'law' of our day
is the law of wealth and material power."[2] For Christians,
this giving of high priority to money is not just
unfortunate, it is idolatry. For the sake of faithfulness to
Christ, we need to find ways to shout no to the god money.
We must dethrone it. One of the best ways is by showing

---

* See Jacques Ellul, *Money & Power* (Downers Grove, Ill.: Inter-Varsity
Press, 1984), pp. 109–16, for more on this subject.

our disrespect for it. When we trample it under our feet we remove its power.

When Paul ministered the word of God in Ephesus, many people who had practiced "magic arts" brought their books and other objects and made a huge bonfire. Luke calculated that the estimated value of that act came to "fifty thousand pieces of silver" (Acts 19:18–20).

What they had done was profane something that in their world had become sacred. Without question, money has taken on a sacred character in our world, and it would do us good to find ways to defame it, defile it, and trample it under our feet.

So step on it. Yell at it. Laugh at it. List it way down on the scale of values—certainly far below friendship and cheerful surroundings. And engage in the most profane act of all—give it away. The powers that energize money cannot abide that most unnatural of acts, giving. Money is made for taking, for bargaining, for manipulating, but not for giving. This is exactly why giving has such ability to defeat the powers of money.

Not long ago we had a swing set, not one of those store-bought aluminum things but a real custom-made job—huge steel pipes and all. But our children would soon be beyond swing sets, so we decided that it would be good to sell it at a garage sale. My next decision was what price to put on it. I went out in the backyard and looked it over. "It should bring a good price," I thought to myself. "In fact, if I touched up the paint just a bit I could up the ante some, and if I fixed the seat on the glider I could charge even more . . ."

All of a sudden I began to monitor a spirit of covetousness within me, and I became aware of how really dangerous it was spiritually. Well, I went into the house and rather tentatively asked my wife, Carolynn, if she would mind if we gave the swing set away rather than selling it.

"No, not at all!" she responded quickly. I thought to myself, "Rats!" But before the day was out we had found a
couple with young children who could make good use of
it, and we gave it to them—and I didn't even have to
paint it! The simple act of giving crucified the greed that
had gripped my heart, and the power of money was broken—for the time being.

A seventh action step is to side with people against
money and things. The biblical witness to this perspective
is impressive. The Bible forbade charging interest on
loans, because it was viewed as an exploitation of another's misfortune (e.g., Exod. 22:25). Wages were to be
paid daily, because many people lived hand-to-mouth
and needed the money (Deut. 24:14-15). When a coat was
given as a pledge for borrowed tools, it was to be returned at night even if the tools had not been given back,
because the nights were cold and the coat was needed
(Deut. 24:6-13).

There are many things we can do to declare that we
value people above things. We can be willing to lose
money rather than a friendship. We can side with the
"use" of church facilities over the "preservation" of facilities. We can provide wages that respond to human need
as well as human productivity. We can always remember
that the child who breaks the toy is more important than
the toy. We can give up a major purchase to feed hungry
people. The possibilities are endless.

One final action step: root out all favored treatment of
people based upon money. James counsels us to "show
no partiality" (James 2:1). He adds, "If a man with gold
rings and in fine clothing comes into your assembly, and
a poor man in shabby clothing also comes in, and you
pay attention to the one who wears the fine clothing . . .
have you not made distinctions among yourselves, and
become judges with evil thoughts?" (James 2:2-4). Perhaps it is acceptable for political parties to give special

privileges to generous benefactors, but such a practice can never be allowed in the community of faith. For believers, money can never be a bargaining tool or a way to gain status.

In the world money means access to the corridors of power; in the Church money should mean nothing. Money should not make people think better of us, for we are part of the fellowship of sinners. Money should not win us leadership roles, for those are determined by spiritual giftedness alone. Money should not make us more necessary to the fellowship, for our dependency is upon God, not money. In the fellowship of the Church money should mean nothing.

MONEY AND BUSINESS

In the first chapter I noted that business is the social side of money. In light of our analysis of money, what conclusions can we draw with regard to business?

As believers we affirm the goodness and necessity of work. Before the fall, Adam and Eve had generous work to do in the care of the garden. The curse that came from the fall was not work but work that was by the "sweat of your brow" (Gen. 3:19, KJV). That is, before the fall the fruits were commensurate to the effort, whereas after the fall the effort far exceeded the fruit gained.

When the apostle Paul said, "If any one will not work, let him not eat." (2 Thess. 3:10), he was not so much speaking against some welfare system as he was speaking for the goodness of work. We need to work. Work is creative, life-giving.

When Saint Benedict coined the phrase *Ora et labora,* Pray and work, he was calling attention to the intimate connection between the life of devotion and the life of labor. Work is essential to a spiritual life, and a spiritual life gives meaning to work.

As believers we affirm work that enhances human life and shun work that destroys human life. This brings us face-to-face with issues of immense importance and controversy. Is our ever increasing technology life-enhancing or dehumanizing? Can a Christian have any part in a military-industrial complex that produces weapons with obvious first-strike capability? Should we engage in occupations whose very nature involves compromises of many kinds? Is it ethical to work for companies that directly or indirectly destroy the ecological balance on the earth?

You can see that the vocational question is much broader than whether or not a Christian should be a bartender. In the first church I pastored, a faithful member—a brilliant Ph.D. in physics—came to me deeply disturbed because he had just learned that 80 percent of the research at the think tank where he worked ended up being used for military purposes. The job was death-giving! Yet it was the very work for which he had given half his life to become qualified to perform. Difficult decisions indeed!

Many jobs are clearly more life-enhancing than others. Teaching, counseling, pastoring—these obviously place us smack in the middle of human need and afford precious opportunities to bring a redemptive touch. But there are many more possibilities. All the people-related tasks—from child care worker to medical doctor—provide excellent opportunities to enhance human life. Often these helping professions pay less, have less prestige, and are more demanding, but they should be highly valued in the Christian fellowship because of their life-changing potential. A preschool teacher is doing much more than making a living; he or she is molding lives. Purpose and meaning in one's work can be fringe benefits of the highest order.

All the occupations that provide needed services and manufacture needed goods are life-enhancing. Farmers, carpenters, electricians, grocery store clerks, and many others enrich us in innumerable ways. We need them all.

The arts is another life-enhancing field. Music and drama, film and sculpture, literature and art enrich the human experience and need to be captured for the cause of Christ. The day is long overdue for the Christian fellowship to once again gain an exalted view of the arts.

We could profit from a fresh look at the Puritan emphasis upon "calling" in our vocation. Prayer groups and "clearness meetings" could be gathered to help *all* the members of the fellowship—not just potential pastors—find their vocational place.

There are many other jobs I could have mentioned and many questions related to the jobs I did mention. Computer technology, law, science, and many other fields need to be studied in the light of this affirmation.

As believers we affirm human value above economic value. For the Christian, the bottom line can never be the bottom line. An employee is more than just the cost of production. There are human needs that take precedence over monetary needs.

Business people face many tough questions. Return on investment must be given careful attention, for no business can survive long if it sees only red on the ledger sheet. To go bankrupt helps no one. But profits must be brought into perspective alongside many other equally important values.

The principle of human value above economic value will have a lot to say about how we organize a business. For example, some businesses organize in such a way that periodic layoffs are virtually guaranteed. Recognizing this as a human problem, we might place a higher priority on trying to balance contracts so as to achieve greater stability.

Many American corporations are set up on the assumption of high employee turnover. Some companies even build-in a high turnover rate on purpose so that wages can be kept lower. Japanese corporations, on the other hand, tend to organize for low employee turnover. It is not easy to deal with the problem of mobility in a culture, but if we begin with a different set of assumptions, we might well make a big difference.

If we assume longer employee tenure, that will affect how we handle wages, employee benefits, and retirement programs. Even more, it will mean that we will place a high priority on people developing friendships and establishing networks of support.

The Japanese model has shown us that long-term stability does not need to conflict with profits; in fact, in many ways it seems to enhance them. But even if that were not the case, Christians have an obligation to place concern for human beings into their ledger calculations.

As believers we affirm the need to enter into each other's space in the employer–employee relationship. Let us not fool ourselves: employers and employees are involved in a power relationship. Employers have the power to fire and hire, to raise or lower wages, to control benefits and working conditions. The employee has the power to frustrate or enhance the working relationship and, in some cases, to undermine the effective functioning of the company.

Employers need to *feel* the insecurity of employees. Very often employees feel dehumanized and used, and very often they are. Mechanization that is done to ensure efficiency can depersonalize the entire enterprise.

In an act of Christian identification, employers can stand in the place of their employees. They can try to feel what it is like to have someone else controlling their future. Do you buy the new refrigerator if a layoff is impending? Do you add on the extra bedroom if there is the possibility of a transfer? Asking themselves questions like these can help employers feel what it is like to be an employee.

This does not mean that painful decisions cannot be

made. Employers must still look at income and expenses and overall production. Decisions may look terribly cold at the time, yet if they are made in the context of an ongoing identification with the employee's vulnerability, a measure of grace can permeate the situation, and wrong and harmful decisions often can be avoided.

Employees, in turn, need to *feel* the isolation of employers. Leadership and responsibility set a person apart in many ways. Everyone knows that criticism is the price of leadership, but that does not make it hurt less. The old adage that sticks and stones may break our bones but names will never hurt us is simply not true.

As employees seek to stand in the shoes of employers, questions begin to surface. If I had to be concerned for the good of the entire enterprise, would my evaluation of what needs to be done change? How would it feel to live with a business around the clock rather than merely eight to five? In what ways do status and wealth decrease life's pleasures?

Trying to understand the dilemmas of employers does not mean that criticism should be avoided. For the good of employers, criticism is necessary. A perceptive challenge to a long-standing practice can lead to creative new ideas. But once we have entered into the lonely space of our superiors, our criticism will be tempered with understanding.

As believers we refuse to buy or sell things frivolous. Fads will come and go; there is no need for the follower of Christ to participate.

John Woolman, who owned and operated a retail goods store, wrote of his own struggles with this. In 1756 he noted in his Journal, "It had been my general practice to buy and sell things really useful. Things that served chiefly to please the vain mind in people, I was not easy to trade in; seldom did it; and whenever I did I found it weakened me as a Christian."[3]

Our refusal to merchandise in the frivolous is directly connected to the high value we place upon human life. It is a wrong use of the world's resources to fritter them away on trivialities when human beings need to be fed, clothed, and educated. We value people more than ostentatious clothes and gaudy homes. So long as the gospel needs to be preached, so long as children need to be fed, Christians cannot afford to have any part with the "Vanity Fairs" of this world.

However, no clear lines can be drawn between things frivolous and things essential. What is an unnecessary luxury to one person is a necessity to another. What is superfluous at one time becomes indispensable in another context.

Though the difficulties are genuine, they should not obscure the fact that many issues are really quite clear. In many cases we need, not more insight, but strength to obey what we already know is right. We can quickly turn away from many things as evidences of the old life. In the few cases in which we have honest questions, we may ask guidance of the Lord, who gives his wisdom liberally, and we may also ask discerning members of the Christian fellowship, who can often bring us the word of the Lord. Of course, we will have to struggle with many money matters, holding in creative tension the many needs, opportunities, and responsibilities that make up our world. Only fools imagine that it could or should be otherwise.

As believers we refuse to take advantage of our neighbor. How to hammer this out on the hard anvil of the business world is no small task, but hammer it out we must. Yet many of the situations we face are completely unambiguous. Recently my wife and I sold a car that had chronic carburetor problems. Both of us were clear that whoever looked at it had to be told of the problem and encouraged to have a mechanic give an evaluation. We probably sold it for considerably less than perhaps we could have, but integrity and friendship are worth a great deal. The point is to stick to plain statements without attempts to embellish or obscure the truth.

In many business situations contracts are good and help us to keep from taking advantage of our neighbor. A contract accomplishes several things. It puts the agreement into writing, so that miscommunication is minimized. The lawyers who help draft the contract often can see potential problems that we who are not schooled in "legalese" have missed. Also, a contract forces us to clarify in our own minds what we are doing.

Contracts, therefore, are good, but trust is better. Contracts are a witness to the fall and the natural tendency to sin. Trust is a witness to grace and the supernatural tendency toward righteousness. One of the greatest evils of a contract is its tendency to breed distrust and suspicion that often ends up in lawsuits. Paul counseled against going to court to settle disputes and we would be wise to avoid it whenever possible (1 Cor. 6:1-11).

Trust, by contrast, builds community. To be sure, when we trust, we run the risk of having others take advantage of us. However, note that I did not state the principle to our defense but to the defense of others. We refuse never to take advantage of our neighbor; that is no guarantee that our neighbors will not take advantage of us. In fact, they *will* take advantage of us. But trust is worth the risk because of its power to build community. Besides, as Paul put it, "Why not . . . suffer wrong? Why not . . . be defrauded?" (1 Cor. 6:7). And why not? After all, it is only money, and there are many things of far greater value than money.

As Christians our word is as good as our bond. Others may well take advantage of us, but perhaps, just perhaps, our willingness to be defrauded rather than to break the bonds of community can witness to a better way.

These six principles, then, can frame the beginning of

a growing understanding of the role of the Christian in business:

—As believers we affirm the goodness and the necessity of work.

—As believers we affirm work that enhances human life and shun work that destroys human life.

—As believers we affirm human value above economic value.

—As believers we affirm the need to enter into each other's space in the employer-employee relationship.

—As believers we refuse to buy or sell things frivolous.

—As believers we refuse to take advantage of our neighbor.

UNITY AT THE MANGER

We have seen that the Bible emphasizes both a dark and a light side with regard to money. The gulf between the two can seem very large indeed, but we have worked to bridge the gap.

Now come with me to the manger in Bethlehem. Notice the worshipers—humble shepherds and regal magi. Here we see poverty and wealth both brought to the manger. The kingly gifts of gold, frankincense, and myrrh are given freely in the service of the messianic King. Shepherds who have been closed out of life's money channels give their presence and their worship. Both are called, the poorest of the poor and the richest of the rich. Both come, both kneel, both give Christmas worship.

5. The Vow of Simplicity

Simplicity is an uprightness of soul.
—FRANÇOIS FÉNELON

In the past three chapters we have been dealing with the difficult—our wealth. We have been learning to overcome our resistance, to claim our richness, and to share it with new freedom and joy.

Our study of money leads us to one inescapable conclusion: we who follow Jesus Christ are called to a vow of simplicity. This vow is not for the dedicated few but for all. It is not an option to take or leave depending on our personal preference. All who name Christ as Lord and Savior are obliged to follow what he says, and Jesus' call to discipleship in money can be best summed up in the single word *simplicity*. Simplicity seeks to do justice to our Lord's many-faceted teachings about money—light and dark, giving and receiving, trust, contentment, faith.

Simplicity means unity of heart and singleness of purpose. We have only one desire: to obey Christ in all things. We have only one purpose: to glorify Christ in all things. We have only one use for money: to advance his kingdom upon the earth. Jesus declares, "If thine eye be single thy whole body shall be full of light" (Matt. 6:22, KJV).

Simplicity means joy in God's good creation. Oscar Wilde once said that people do not value sunsets because they cannot pay for them. Not so for us! We cherish all the free gifts of the good earth: sunset and sunrise, land and sea, colors and beauty everywhere.

Simplicity means contentment and trust. "Have no anxiety about anything" counsels Paul (Phil. 4:6). "Having nothing, and yet possessing everything" (2 Cor. 6:10). "I have learned, in whatever state I am, to be content" (Phil. 4: 11). This is the way Paul lived, and so do we.

Simplicity means freedom from covetousness. Paul's confession is ours, "I coveted no one's silver or gold" (Acts 20: 33). We no longer "pant after the possessions of others," as John Calvin put it![1]

Simplicity means modesty and temperance in all things. Paul calls us to be "sober, just, holy, temperate" (Titus 1:8, KJV). And so we are. Our lives are marked by voluntary abstinence in the midst of extravagant luxury. We refuse to indulge in elegance and display in clothing or manner of life. Our use of resources is always tempered by human need.

Simplicity means to receive material provision gratefully. Through Isaiah, God promises, "If you are willing and obedient, you shall eat the good of the land" (Isa. 1:19). We are not rigid ascetics who cannot abide a land flowing with milk and honey. Rather, we rejoice in these gracious provisions from the heart of God. Complete personal deprivation is not a good thing, and we reject it as a sign of duplicity, not simplicity.

Simplicity means using money without abusing money. In the power of the Holy Spirit we conquer and capture money and put it into service for Christ and his kingdom. We know that well-being is not defined by wealth, and so we can hold all things lightly—owning without treasuring, possessing without being possessed. We use money within the confines of a properly disciplined spiritual life, and we manage money for the glory of God and the good of all people.

Simplicity means availability. Freed from the compulsions of ever bigger and ever better, we have the time and energy to respond to human need. Some, like pastors and others, are freed full-time so they can minister the word of life. Others will release blocks of time to further advance the kingdom.

· *Simplicity means giving joyfully and generously*. We give ourselves, and we give the product of our life's work. "First they gave themselves," said Paul of the churches of Macedonia (2 Cor. 8:5). The matter of giving is so central to our entire relationship toward money that I would like us to turn our attention to a more detailed discussion of this aspect of simplicity.

GUIDELINES FOR GIVING

When we read the teaching of the Bible concerning money we see very quickly that giving figures very prominently. We would be hard pressed to find a teaching on money that does not somehow mention giving. Whether we think of the tithe, the law of gleaning, the Jubilee principle, the story of Zacchaeus, the story of the rich young ruler, the parable of the good Samaritan, the parable of the rich fool, or any number of other passages, we find a strong emphasis upon giving.

If we take the biblical witness seriously, it seems that one of the best things we can do with money is to give it away. The reason is obvious: giving is one of our chief weapons in conquering the god mammon. Giving scandalizes the world of commerce and competition. It wins money for the cause of Christ. Jacques Ellul has noted, "We have very clear indications that money, in the Christian life, is made *in order* to be given away."[2] Hence the guidelines that follow are an attempt to help us in our giving.

First, with glad and generous hearts let us give proportionately, beginning with a tithe of our incomes. Neither Jesus nor any of the apostles confined giving to the tithe—they went beyond it. In all their teachings, generosity and sacrifice loom large. This is true whether we are looking at the poor widow giving her mite or Barnabas giving a parcel of land to the early church (Mark 12:41-44; Acts 4:36-37).

The tithe, therefore, is an Old Testament principle that should be a standard we will not go below except in the rarest of circumstances. This is not a rigid law, but a starting point for organizing our economic lives.

Now it takes no financial wizard to determine 10 percent of our gross income, but it demands a deep sensitivity to the Spirit of God to know what proportionate giving means. In wrestling with this matter, Elizabeth O'Connor has written: "Proportionate to what? Proportionate to the accumulated wealth of one's family? Proportionate to one's income and the demands upon it, which vary from family to family? Proportionate to one's sense of security and the degree of anxiety with which one lives? Proportionate to the keenness of our awareness of those who suffer? Proportionate to our sense of justice and of God's ownership of all wealth? Proportionate to our sense of stewardship for those who follow after us? And so on, and so forth. The answer, of course, is in proportion to all of these things."[3]

To help us think through what proportionate giving might mean, Ron Sider has suggested the concept of the graduated tithe.[4] Very simply, one decides on a standard of living and tithes 10 percent on that amount. Then, out of every thousand dollars of additional income, one gives 5 percent more. With this arrangement, once we have reached eighteen thousand dollars of income above our standard, we give away 100 percent of all additional income.

One man I know has another approach. He owns a business and has put himself on a salary that he has determined as his standard of living. Of this salary he tithes 15 percent. He then gives away 25 percent of the profits that the company generates above his salary. He also has income from book and film royalties and speaking honorariums; he gives away a hundred percent of this money.

Perhaps some of us with ample resources should try living on 10 percent of our income and giving away 90 percent. R. G. LeTourneau, owner of a large earth-moving business, did this very thing.

But please, do not be intimidated by these examples. They are only illustrations of ways we can come to terms with proportionate giving in an affluent culture. Many of us need to take smaller, more humble steps. Some have disciplined themselves to match dollar for dollar what they spend on lawn fertilizer with fertilizer for Third World food production. Others might want to match money spent on eating out with giving to famine-relief projects or match money spent on clothes with giving to a relief agency. The idea is simply to inform our spending with a sensitivity to the needs of others.

Perhaps none of these ideas are right for you. Many people feel so strapped financially that the idea of giving "above and beyond" seems ludicrous. And yet many of us can do much more if we begin to think in creative new ways.

One word of caution: some people need to give *less* than they do now if they are to be faithful to God. You may need to care for your children or your parents or your spouse—or even yourself—more adequately. Do not excuse your responsibility on religious pretenses. Jesus, you remember, had very strong words for such a practice (Mark 7:9-13).

Second, with glad and generous hearts, let us keep in creative tension "reasoned" giving and "risk" giving. There is one kind of giving that carefully evaluates the track record of organizations and individuals, and another that gives without calculation. Both kinds of giving are essential.

A good percentage of our giving should be reasoned and responsible. If we are giving to organizations, many questions need to be asked. Does the organization to which I am giving have a good record of responsible use of money? How much goes to overhead, and how much gets to the project to which I am giving? Does the organization have a responsible board that monitors the use of money? Is there an annual audit? Is the organization a member of the Evangelical Council for Financial Accountability?

If our giving is to individuals, another set of questions needs to be considered. Will my giving be helpful, or harmful? What is the right amount for that person to receive? Does he or she have an overall budget? Is this to be a one-time gift, or a regular monthly gift? What other sources of income does this person have or should have? Can I give to someone without controlling that person?

However, there is a danger in too much calculation in our giving. That danger is the subtle tendency to call the shots. The warm openness that once characterized our giving can gradually turn into tightfistedness. A miserly spirit becomes justified in the name of prudent and responsible giving.

To overcome this soul-destroying bid for power we need to give with lavish abandon, like the woman with the alabaster jar (Matt. 26:6-13). In an act of uncalculated generosity she broke it and poured its treasure on Christ's head. The disciples saw it as an act of waste; Jesus saw it as an act of beauty.

For the sake of our own souls there are times when we need to throw caution to the winds and give, just give. We need to risk giving to individuals, not because they have proven that they can handle money well, but because they need it. In so doing, we give love and trust as well. And we free ourselves from that clutching, holding spirit that spells spiritual ruin.

Third, with glad and generous hearts let us seek out and give to individuals and organizations that lack celebrity status. We are so often prone to champion causes that already have thousands of champions. But among the disciples of Christ this is not to be. We are to seek out and generously support the disenfranchised and the disinherited.

Let us discover the politically uninteresting, the "newsworthyless," and lend our hand of support. These are not found on television or in newspapers or in magazines. These are found by prayerfully walking into the press of humanity. Ask God to give you eyes to see and ears to hear the little ones of the kingdom—the ones others normally pass by without a second thought.

We need a divine sense of foresight rather than hindsight when it comes to supporting God's servants. George Mueller began giving to support J. Hudson Taylor long before Taylor won fame as a pioneer missionary. There were no enthusiastic cover stories in the Christian magazines about Taylor's outlandish proposal to go into the interior of China with an army of missionaries. But Mueller found in this young man a soul hard after God. We now look back at Hudson Taylor as inaugurating the second great wave in the modern missionary movement.

To have the foresight that Mueller had demands a spiritual perception born out of intimate communion with the Heavenly Monitor and the courage to go into the highways and byways of life to discover the work of God.

How do we get beyond the media propaganda machine into places of kingdom need and action? Begin by inviting every missionary you can into your home to share their insights and broaden your cross-cultural vision. These faithful workers are a tremendous resource of wisdom and experience, but often they are neglected because we confine them to the one forum they are least prepared for—public speaking. But bring them into your home and ask them where God's work is going forward, and these quiet, mild-mannered folk turn instantly into fiery orators.

As you go about your daily routine, listen prayerfully to people—ideas and needs crop up in the strangest places. Gather in small study groups and ask, What is God doing in our world? As you gather with others for worship, invite those with prophetic insight to help you see the direction you are headed, show you where that leads, and give you a value judgment upon it. Take your summer vacation among the huddled masses of Haiti instead of on a cruise to Puerto Vallarta. In these and many other ways, we can try to find the unsung heroes and the unrecorded places where the battle is hottest.

Fourth, with glad and generous hearts, let us give without seeking power. We do not need to control, to manage, or to influence. Freely we have received, freely we give.

In Acts we see the generous giving of the early church that broke the cycle of tyranny by which benefactors dictated terms to the poor and powerless. Money was used by the early church, not as an instrument of control, but as an instrument of love. All the subtle tricks were gone. And when someone did attempt a financial power play, it was quickly revealed for the sin it was and speedily dealt with (Acts 5:1-11). It should be so among us.

As disciples we reject money's manipulative capacity. We refuse to use money to jockey for position or to maneuver ourselves into favor. We will not pull strings or put anyone into our debt with money. We reject money's power for evil; we affirm money's power for good.

Our pastors and others need to know of our faithful support, even if they do and say things we do not like. They can thus be encouraged to fulfill their prophetic ministry. Otherwise, they will hesitate to speak unpopular words and to espouse unwelcome programs for fear of crippling the work economically. They need to know that our giving is not determined by the latest public opinion poll. We will not hold the Church ransom because we disagree with this or that decision.

There may, of course, come a time when it is appropriate to withhold our giving out of concern for the direction of our local congregation, but that comes a long way down the road. The normal pattern is to give freely without any need to direct how the Church is using the money. I can well imagine that the poor widow could have thought of plenty of reasons to withhold her "mite" from the temple treasury. Yet she gave, and Jesus honored the act (Mark 12:41-44).

Fifth, with glad and generous hearts, let us give ourselves as well as our money. "First they gave themselves," declared Paul (2 Cor. 8:5). And so must we.

Someone I know who always has given of his resources generously is attempting now to give more of himself. He decided that he needed a closer personal tie to the poor, so instead of just writing checks to organizations that work among the poor, he decided to make a commitment to one family. This family has known little stability over the years, because of drugs and related problems. But with this man's help, the husband has secured a job and the family has learned to live by a monthly budget and a weekly food menu. My friend meets with the family every week to review their budget with them and evaluate their goals. He also has had to invest some of his own resources in the family (none of it is tax deductible). This kind of giving is much more costly than writing a check, yet giving oneself along with money can produce dramatic results.

Someone else I know has used his resources to establish a Christian film company, a publishing house, and a seminary. These projects take up a tremendous amount of his time and energy, but he does it because he wants to give himself as well as his money.

These two examples may seem more than most of us can do. But there are many simple and humble ways to give ourselves. In Acts we read of Tabitha, who made "coats and garments" for the widows of her village. Luke describes her as "full of good works and acts of charity" (Acts 9:36-43). Perhaps we also can discover ways to give ourselves by meeting the needs of those around us, so that we too will be full of good works and acts of charity.

Sixth, with glad and generous hearts, let us seek out advisers who can help us in our giving.[5] It is responsible stewardship to seek out the finest expertise available to guide us with regard to outright cash gifts, deferred giving, wills, planned giving, and more so that our total estate is seen in perspective. This can be done informally through Sunday school classes and casual visits or formally through hired financial planners.

One warning is in order. Most financial advisers are by temperament and spirit conservative and technical in orientation. Their technical knowledge of the money world is vitally important, but, for the believer, facts and figures can never speak the last word. A free and liberated spirit is essential throughout the process. Very few lawyers and trust officers—even those with a Christian orientation—understand the spiritual nature of money or the spirit of carefree unconcern that is to characterize our lives. And so, though we can be grateful for their counsel and advice, we cannot be bound by it.

Remember that laying up treasure in heaven is a major business investment. As in any serious venture, we want to do the very best we can. Most of us will have hundreds of thousands of dollars flowing through our hands in the course of our employable years. As stewards we have a responsibility to use this bounty in ways that will reap the greatest benefit for Christ and his kingdom. Each of us will have to work through our own priorities for kingdom investments, and advisers can help us find our way.

By these comments I do not in the least mean to depreciate the use of money in the service of one's family. Quite to the contrary, I think one of the finest investments I can make for advancing the kingdom of God upon the earth is that of investing in my own children. Enriching experiences that broaden their perspective and sensitize their spirit are well worth the investment.

Seventh, with glad and generous hearts, let us make out caring wills that express our concern for the kingdom of God. It is understandable that people hesitate to make out a will. It shouts out to us about our finitude and makes specific our resources—realities most of us would like to avoid. But the failure to draw up a will is the worst possible stewardship. Our denial of our wealth has been so constant and so total that most of us would be astonished at the resources we could potentially make available to the world upon our graduation into heaven. I say "potentially" because without a will those resources will be lost to the work of God.

So if you have no will, make an appointment to draw one up before you finish this chapter. Do not excuse yourself on the grounds that you are too young to die or do not have enough money to make any difference. Both statements are false, so draw up a will right away.

The Church could do an immense service by offering instruction sessions in how to handle this matter. It is the best possible context in which to face up to both our wealth and our impending death. Besides, many questions could be meaningfully addressed in a Christian context. Do I leave all my resources to my children, or only a percentage? What organizations could I include in my will that would best advance the cause of Christ? Are there ways I could give to the poor in death that I cannot do in life?

In our will, Carolynn and I have included our children, to be sure. But we have also included educational institutions, mission organizations, relief organizations, and churches. Many others have done much more. Some have even left an intangible witness. Patrick Henry wrote into his will that if he had left nothing in terms of worldly riches but had given his heirs a faith in Jesus Christ, then they were of all people most wealthy. Conversely, he added that if he had left them all the wealth in the world but had not left them a faith in Jesus Christ, they would be of all people most destitute.

Please believe me, wills are nothing to fear. You can help so many with so little effort that I cannot conceive of a valid reason to postpone writing one.

Giving is a glad and generous ministry to which we are all called. In times of persecution Christians give their lives; in times of prosperity Christians give the fruit of their life's work. William Law said of the early Christian fellowship that they "were glad to turn their whole estates into a constant course of charity."[6] How wonderful if that could be a description of us as well!

As we learn and grow in the ministry of giving, I do want to raise a word of warning. Money, like crabgrass, has a way of rerooting itself in our hearts. We think we have dethroned it and made it an obedient servant, and then all of a sudden it subversively attempts a coup. At its core money seems to have a rebellious nature.

Over the years my friend Don has had an effective ministry with money—earning and giving.* A few years ago he decided to make his giving a capital enterprise. He would buy a piece of property for, say, five thousand dollars and later resell it for perhaps ten thousand and thus be able to give twice as much as he would have otherwise. He was managing money for the greater gain of Christ and his kingdom.

In time, however, Don noticed that he was beginning

---

* The name has been changed to maintain confidentiality.

to be captivated by an investment mentality—a kind of greed for the kingdom. The sense of warmhearted giving began to dry up and become utilitarian giving. Beyond this, giving of long-term capital gains meant that he had to hold onto the property for at least one year, and as he told me, "In that year of waiting you begin to be attached to the money." Don is still working through the spiritual barrenness that has resulted from this process.

Don began this ministry with the most honorable of intentions. And fortunately, he has a sensitive enough spirit to know when the power of money is reasserting itself. We all need to be forewarned and equipped as we enter this dangerous ministry. Money—unrighteous mammon—is poison, and like poison, it is a blessing only when it is used properly and with great care.*

CHILDREN AND MONEY

As disciples of Christ, we cannot avoid the task of teaching our children and the children in our fellowship about money. We cannot hide them from money, for it permeates the very atmosphere of the world in which they live. Some parents may find it embarrassing to talk to their children about sex, but that is nothing compared to our reluctance to openly confront the issue of money.

The truth is, of course, that we *will* teach our children about money. Our very reluctance teaches. Who we are and the daily transactions of ordinary life form the content of our teaching. Our children will pick up from us an all-pervasive attitude toward money.

> Should I fear money?
> Should I love money?
> Should I respect money?

---

* Those who invest money will find a helpful guide to justice in investments in the July 1984 issue of *The Other Side* magazine.

Should I hate money?
Should I use money?
Should I borrow money?
Should I budget money?
Should I sacrifice everything for money?

All these questions and more are answered for children as they watch us. Albert Schweitzer once observed, "There are only three ways to teach a child: the first is by example, the second is by example, the third is by example."[7]

If we are free from the love of money, our children will know it. If apprehension is our automatic response to money, we will teach them worry and fear.

Children need instruction in both the dark and the light side of money. Without this, teaching them how to make a budget and write checks is of little value.

It is not difficult to instruct children about the light side of money. They quickly learn of its ability to bring them many good things. We help them see how money can also be a blessing to others. We give them jobs to do, provide an allowance, teach them to tithe and to save, show them how to use money wisely. Slowly we give them increased control and liberty as they learn how to deal responsibly with money. This—and much more— forms the curriculum for our instruction on the light side of money.

Instruction on the dark side of money is more difficult. For children, the power to buy is heady stuff. Children from poor backgrounds know the evil of too little and cannot imagine too much having an evil side. Children from affluent backgrounds find tremendous power in humiliating their less fortunate friends, never imagining they themselves are also just as unfortunate. The very idea that money is a spiritual power seeking to enslave seems ludicrous to them.

But we must teach them. And more than teach, we

must pray for their deliverance from money's domination. This is no light matter. Money is not just a thing—it is a power. The moment we expose our children to money—and expose them we must—we should pray for their protection.

We also teach. When children fight over money, we can use the opportunity to help them see money's power. We can show them real poverty and help them consider the causes of inequity in the world.

We teach them by word and deed that money is neither respectable nor contemptible. We owe money no honor, but neither do we despise it. Money is useful, even necessary, but it is not to be esteemed or admired. In short, we try to show children how to use money without serving money (e.g., Luke 16:9 and Matt. 6:24).

This distinction is difficult to teach children mainly because so few adults know the difference. We live in an age in which right discipline and control over one's life are so little understood that obsession and abstinence are the only categories that make sense for the modern mind. Either we reject a thing out of hand or we accept it without reservation. This is why dogmatism is so popular today—whether in religion, politics, or economics.

It is precisely this that makes it so incumbent upon us to teach children *use without abuse* in all of life. We show them by example that it is quite possible to watch a single television program and then turn the set off, to eat what is required for good health and then stop, to enjoy good music and then experience silence.

Once children see from us that it is possible to exercise restraint over human passions, then it will be possible to convey the notion of money as servant rather than master. That is the first step, but only the first. Much more must be taught.

For example, children need to know how to exercise authority over the spiritual power of money. We need to help them flesh out answers to many questions. What actions defeat selfishness? How do you effectively pray against greed? How do you release the spirit of generosity and compassion?

Most of all, we are to teach children how to profane money without rejecting it. Let us learn to laugh at its pious religiosity. Let us desecrate its sacred shrines. How? One way is to despise and utterly reject the propaganda that "more is better." Here is where, as parents, we must really fight the battle. A child tends to feel that, if one toy is satisfying, two or three or four will be more satisfying. But we know that this is not necessarily the case. And in this regard we must learn to be as tough as nails, knowing that no is a good answer. Enough is enough, and we should say so to ourselves and to our children. We buy something because we need it, not because we want it, and our children need to learn the difference.

Money does not deserve our respect. It deserves to be conquered in the power of the Spirit. Once defeated and converted to the way of Christ, it can then be used without being served.

GENEROSITY, MAGNANIMITY, AND SHALOM

The dark side of money inevitably leads to greed, which leads to vengeance, which leads to violence. The light side of money inevitably leads to generosity, which leads to magnanimity, which leads to shalom.[8]

The great moral question of our time is how to move from greed to generosity, and from vengeance to magnanimity, and from violence to shalom. The vow of simplicity points the way. Simplicity gives us the perspective and the courage to stand against greed, vengeance, and violence. Simplicity gives us the framework to experience generosity, magnanimity, and shalom. Saint Francis de Sales said, "I recommend to you holy simplicity. . . . In everything, love simplicity."[9]

PART II
Sex

6. Sexuality and Spirituality

Sexuality and spirituality are not enemies but friends.
—DONALD GOERGEN

One of the real tragedies in Christian history has been the divorce of sexuality from spirituality. This fact is all the more lamentable since the Bible holds such a high celebrative view of human sexuality. Let us look at some of the biblical windows onto human sexuality.

MALE AND FEMALE

In the first chapter of Genesis we have a brief, yet magnificent, comment on the meaning of human sexuality. The narrative opens in majesty as God brings the universe into existence by speaking the creative word. And this universe that he created is good, very good. (Please, let us get it straight once and for all: the material world is good and not to be despised. We urgently need to recover a doctrine of God as Creator and of a creation that is good, very good.)

Human beings are the apex of God's creation. In simple, yet noble, language we are told that the human creation is set apart from all others, for it is in the *imago Dei*, the image of God. Notice how closely related our human sexuality is to the *imago Dei*: "So God created man in his own image, in the image of God he created him; *male and female he created them*" (Gen. 1:27, emphasis mine). Strange as it may seem, our sexuality, our maleness and femaleness, is somehow related to our creation in the image of God.

Karl Barth was the first major theologian to help us see

the implications of this tremendous confession of Scripture that human sexuality is grounded in the *imago Dei*. What he has helped us understand is that relationship is at the heart of what it means to be "in the image of God" and that the relationship between male and female is the human expression of our relationship with God.

Our human sexuality, our maleness and femaleness, is not just an accidental arrangement of the human species, not just a convenient way to keep the human race going. No, it is at the center of our true humanity. We exist as male and female in relationship. Our sexualness, our capacity to love and be loved, is intimately related to our creation in the image of God. What a high view of human sexuality!

Notice too that the biblical stress upon relationship helps to enlarge our understanding of human sexuality. The problem with the topless bars and the pornographic literature of our day is not that they emphasize sexuality too much but that they do not emphasize it enough. They totally eliminate relationship and restrain sexuality to the narrow confines of the genital. They have made sex trivial.

How much richer and fuller is the biblical perspective! To chat over coffee, to discuss a great book, to view a sunset together—this is sexuality at its best, for male and female are in intimate relationship. To be sure, genital sex is a part of the total picture, but human sexuality is a far larger reality than merely coitus.

NAKED AND NOT ASHAMED

God spoke all of the creation into existence except for human beings.* To create Adam he took the dust of the

---

* Barth feels that the second creation narrative (Gen. 2:18-25) has as its basic purpose to fill out the theme of our creation as male and female, so that in a sense it is a commentary upon Gen. 1:27.

earth and breathed life into it (Gen. 2:7). And that union of earthy dust and divine breath gives us one of the finest descriptions of human nature. God did not speak Eve into existence as though she were a part of nonhuman reality, nor did he breathe into dust as though she were a creation unrelated to man. God used the rib of Adam to underscore their interdependence—"bone of my bones and flesh of my flesh," as Adam expressed it. The two of them interwoven, interdependent, interlaced: no fierce rivalry, no hierarchical one-upmanship, no independent autonomy. What a beautiful picture.

Next we are given the confession of covenant fidelity that sets the pattern for mature marriage: "Therefore a man leaves his father and his mother and cleaves to his wife, and they become one flesh" (Gen. 2:24). This is really an extraordinary statement. Given the intensely patriarchal culture, it is genuinely phenomenal for a biblical author to speak of the man "leaving" and "cleaving." Then the Bible describes their joining as a "one flesh" reality, a phrase to which Jesus gives depth and richness in his teaching.

Finally, the scene closes with the most refreshing comment of all: "And the man and his wife were both naked, and were not ashamed" (Gen. 2:25). Here we have an idyllic picture of two whose sexuality was integrated into their entire lives. There was no shame because there was wholeness. There was an organic unity within themselves and with the rest of creation. Lewis Smedes has written, "There are two situations in which people feel no shame. The first is in a state of wholeness. The other is in a state of illusion."[1] Naked and not ashamed—a magnificent scene.

Did you notice that unashamed eroticism existed before the fall? The fall did not create eros; it only perverted it. In the creation story we find the man and the woman drawn to each other, naked and not ashamed. They know their masculinity and femininity are the handiwork of God, as is their passionate affection. Their differences also unite them; they are male and female but also one flesh. The two of them in relationship, in love—why should there be shame? Their sexuality is the creation of God.

We all know the tragic conclusion to the story, how the man and the woman rejected God's way. And the venom of that fall poisoned everything. It ruptured the relationship between God and Adam and Eve. It even soured the marriage relationship. In the language of the curse, the man "shall rule over you" (Gen. 3:16). We must never forget that the domination of women by men that fills our history books and our current events is not a part of God's good creation but a result of the fall; hence the tension, the conflict, the hierarchy. As David Hubbard has noted, since the fall "human life has vacillated between the grasping femininity which competes with man and man's blind dominion over woman which degrades personality and destroys partnership."[2]

The result for human sexuality has been, as Karl Barth put it, a vacillation between evil eroticism, on the one hand, and an evil absence of eroticism, on the other. How tragic! However, the Christian witness is that with the present coming of the kingdom of God we are (in some measure) enabled to pass through the flaming sword into the paradise of God and live in righted erotic relations.*

---

* The qualifier "in some measure" is a recognition of the complexity and tragedy of the human situation. Though the kingdom of God is "already here," it is also "not yet." Though in many areas of life we have experienced the redemptive touch of God, other areas remain untouched, and we must live in anticipation of the continuing "salvation of the Lord." This is as true in our sexuality as it is in every other area of life.

In Christ we affirm our full sexuality and, through the power of the gospel, turn away from its perversion.

LOVE CELEBRATED

If Genesis affirms our sexuality, the Song of Solomon celebrates it. Karl Barth has called the Song of Solomon an expanded commentary upon Genesis 2:25—"And the man and his wife were both naked, and were not ashamed." And indeed it is! There is nothing else in our Bible that quite compares with its lavish celebration of human sexuality. That it is in Scripture at all is an elegant testimony to the Hebrew refusal to chop life into things sacred and things secular.

What a beautiful window the Song of Solomon is into eros as it should be! There is sensuality without licentiousness, passion without promiscuity, love without lust. Let me lift up four great themes in this book.

The first is love's intensity. The singer goes to great lengths, piling superlative upon superlative, to show the extravagance of their love. "Sustain me with raisins, refresh me with apples; for I am sick with love," cries the woman (Song of Sol. 2:5).

At another point the singer describes the woman in bed longing for her lover. She gets up in the middle of the night and roams the deserted streets looking for "him whom my soul loves" (3:2). She even accosts the watchmen, pleading for knowledge of her lover's whereabouts. Finally, "I found him whom my soul loves. I held him, and would not let him go" (3:4), a beautiful opening onto love's intensity. It is, indeed, eros without shame.

Alongside love's intensity we need to see love's restraint. There is no crude orgy here, no pawing and pounding. Love is too high, sex is too deep, for such leering and lusting.

In chapter 8 the woman remembers what her brothers said of her when she was a child. "We have a little sister, and she has no breasts." (That is, she has not yet matured.) "What shall we do for our sister, on the day when she is spoken for? If she is a wall, we will build upon her a battlement of silver; but if she is a door, we will enclose her with boards of cedar" (8:8-9). In essence, the brothers protectively ask, "Was our sister a wall? Did she keep herself pure? Did she keep her erotic passions in control, reserving herself for her loyal, permanent lover? Or was she a door? Was she violated by temporary lovers?"

Fully matured, the woman gladly announces to her lover, "I was a wall, and my breasts were like towers" (8:10). She had not given in to unrestrained passion.

The man, too, knew the lessons of restraint. In chapter 6 he recalls the numerous opportunities he could have had to show his sexual prowess. In what is perhaps a bit of Hebrew hyperbole he mentions sixty queens, eighty concubines, and "maidens without number" that could have been his, yet he said no to them all, for "I am my beloved's and my beloved is mine" (6:3, 8).

Love in the Song of Solomon is restrained also in that it refuses to be rushed. This is captured well by the chorus that threads its way through the book: "I adjure you, O daughter of Jerusalem . . . that you stir not up nor awaken love until it please" (3:5; 5:8; 8:4). And if it was important for ancient Israel to hear that counsel of patience and restraint, how much more important for our society, which takes even children and makes them sex symbols.

Such a beautiful combination—this intensity and restraint. Erotic passion is celebrated, but it also has an exclusive character. No passage illustrates this better than the wedding scene. The man describes his bride-to-be as "a garden locked, a fountain sealed" (4:12). She has said no to capricious sex; she has kept her garden locked. But then we come to the wedding night, when the woman calls out: "Awake, O north wind, and come, O south wind! Blow upon my garden, let its fragrance be wafted abroad. Let my beloved come to his garden, and eat its choicest fruits" (4:16). Love's intensity. Love's restraint.

A third theme that weaves its way through the Song of Solomon is love's mutuality. Nowhere in this book do you find the dull story of the man acting and the woman being acted upon—quite the contrary! Both are intensely involved; both initiate; both receive. It is as if the curse of man's domination that resulted from the fall has been surmounted by the grace of God.

Even the literary structure of the book emphasizes that love is reciprocal. The man speaks; the woman speaks; the chorus sings the refrain. There is open-hearted dialogue. The woman is open and unashamed in her expressions of love and passion: "My beloved is a sachet of myrrh lying between my breasts," "My beloved is like a gazelle, like a young stag" (1:13; 2:9, Jerusalem Bible).

In Genesis we are told only of Adam's attraction to Eve, but here the accent is upon the lovers' mutual attraction. Both are constantly giving and receiving in the act of love, love's mutuality.

The final theme we should see is love's permanence—no promiscuity here, no running away when bills and boredom set in. Toward the end of the Song the woman cries out:

> Set me as a seal upon your heart,
>   as a seal upon your arm;
> for love is strong as death,
>   jealousy is cruel as the grave.

> Its flashes are flashes of fire,
> a most vehement flame.
> Many waters cannot quench love,
> neither can floods drown it.
> If a man offered for love
> all the wealth of his house,
> it would be utterly scorned. (8:6-7)

Their love is ongoing and strong. It transcends the hot-cold fluctuations of erotic passion. It is as strong as death; it cannot be bought at any price. Indeed, these words of fidelity and permanence remind us of the love-hymn of the apostle Paul in 1 Corinthians 13—"Love never ends."

How telling is this word of love's permanence! David Hubbard comments, "The loyalty pictured in the Song should remind [us] that there's no way out of this. There's no rip cord that can be pulled, no ejection seat that can be triggered. They are in it together, bound to each other forever with covenantal loyalty."[3]

Love's intensity, love's restraint, love's mutuality, love's permanence—all marvelous windows onto human sexuality.

JESUS AND SEXUALITY

We now turn our attention to Jesus' own affirmative attitude toward sexuality. Actually, we have very little direct teaching from Jesus on sexuality, no doubt primarily because his teachings were in organic unity with the Old Testament's insights and he felt no need to elaborate further upon them. However, what we do have underscores Jesus' high view of sex and of marriage.

Jesus had a high view of sex. The Scribes and Pharisees taught that as long as you stayed away from adultery you were okay. But Jesus saw beyond the externalities of law to the internal spirit in which people live. "I say to you that every one who looks at a woman lustfully has already committed adultery with her in his heart" (Matt. 5:28).

Lust produces bad sex, because it denies relationship. Lust turns the other person into an object, a thing, a nonperson. Jesus condemned lust because it cheapened sex, it made sex less than it was created to be. For Jesus, sex was too good, too high, too holy, to be thrown away by cheap thoughts.

Jesus also evidenced a high view of marriage.* In Matthew 19 we see the Pharisees attempting to trap him by embroiling him in the raging debate of the day about the grounds for divorce. Jesus responded by appealing to the "one flesh" teaching of the creation narrative, adding, "So they are no longer two but one. What therefore God has joined together, let no man put asunder" (Matt. 19:6). In these words of Jesus we are confronted with the great mystery of the life-uniting reality of "one flesh." There is a merger of two that, without destroying individuality, produces unity. The two become one flesh! What a wonder! What a mystery! It is a spiritual reality that we will want to look at again and again.

PAUL AND SEXUALITY

The apostle Paul likewise honored marriage, by comparing it to the covenant relationship between Christ and his Church. After quoting the Genesis passage about the husband leaving father and mother and cleaving to his wife so that the two become one flesh, Paul adds, "This is

---

* Jesus gave a valid place for the single life, too. We will look at this aspect of his teaching in Chapter 7.

a great mystery, and I take it to mean Christ and the church" (Eph. 5:32).

To be sure, Paul spoke with favor and zeal about the value of the single life (1 Cor. 7). But even there, he affirmed marriage and counseled mutual sexual fulfillment, "The husband should give to his wife her conjugal rights, and likewise the wife to her husband" (1 Cor. 7:3).

What have we seen in this brief biblical overview? From the Old Testament to the New Testament, from the Gospels to the Epistles, we have heard the call to celebrate our sexuality. Our sexuality is intimately tied to who we are as spiritual persons. The spiritual life enhances our sexuality and gives it direction. Our sexuality gives an earthy wholeness to our spirituality. Our spirituality and our sexuality come into a working harmony in the life of the kingdom of God. So runs the witness of the Bible.

THE JUDGMENT OF HISTORY

I wish I could speak as warmly about the witness of the Church through the centuries. Two major departures from the biblical perspective began to develop soon after the apostolic age. The first is the view that physical pleasure is bad, and the second is that sexual intercourse should be reserved for procreation. Sexual pleasure began to be looked upon as the enemy of the spiritual life.

Perhaps no one did more to bring these teachings into the heart of the Church than Saint Augustine. No doubt his own sexual escapades as a youth help to account for his negative attitude toward sexuality after his conversion. In *The City of God,* he refers to "the shame which attends all sexual intercourse."[4]

Even within marriage he saw sexual intercourse, except for the sake of begetting children, to be venial sin. Of his influence in these matters, Derrick Bailey has noted,

"Augustine must bear no small measure of responsibility for the insinuation into our culture of the idea, still widely current, that Christianity regards sexuality as something peculiarly tainted with evil."[5]

Many theologians, however, went even further than Augustine. Some warned couples that the Holy Spirit left the bedroom whenever they engaged in sexual intercourse. One Yves of Chartres counseled the devout to abstain from sexual intercourse on Thursdays in remembrance of Christ's rapture, on Fridays in remembrance of Christ's crucifixion, on Saturdays in honor of the Virgin Mary, on Sundays in commemoration of Christ's resurrection, and on Mondays out of respect for departed souls.[6]

The Protestant Reformers were more accepting of human sexuality but were worried about lust in a fallen world and so urged sexual restraint both in and out of marriage. Some, however, had a more positive approach. Jeremy Taylor, in *The Rule and Exercise of Holy Living and Dying*, encouraged sexual intercourse "to lighten and ease the cares and sadnesses of household affairs, or to endear each other."[7] Contrary to popular belief, the Puritans had quite a positive and healthy perspective on sexuality. They saw sexual intercourse as essential to marriage, and it was encouraged as a gift of God. Edward Morgan, in "The Puritans and Sex," noted that "the Puritans showed none of the blind zeal or narrow-minded bigotry which is too often supposed to have been characteristic of them."[8]

Overall, however, we have to recognize that the Church has not maintained the high celebrative view of sexuality that is characteristic of the Bible. How tragic it is that the Church has often ignored the unashamed eroticism of the creation story and the sensual joy of the Song of Solomon. How sad it is that the New Testament's affirmation of sex and marriage has often been twisted into a denial of our sexuality. We must turn again to a more biblical, more Christian posture.

DISTORTED SEXUALITY

Though the Bible celebrates our sexuality, it also provides warnings.* This side of the fall, we often understand our sexuality through a glass darkly. Our task as Christians is to pick our way through sexuality's distortions and into sexuality's wholeness. Sin has distorted sexuality in many ways.

Pornography is a distortion of sexuality. That pornography cannot be defined in absolute terms should not obscure its existence. There is a world of difference between the nude figures in the Sistine Chapel and those in a "skin" magazine, and any reasonable person knows the difference. "Pornography is harmful," says Lewis Smedes, "because it makes sex trivial, uninteresting, and dull."[9] Art or literature moves closer to pornography the more it cuts off our sexuality from the full range of human activity and feeling. In pornography we see a truncated sexuality concerned only with the physical as an activity of lust and a dehumanizing exercise of power over others. Pornographic art cheapens and dehumanizes; true art lifts and ennobles.

One feature of the pornographic business is the fantasy world it creates. Staged photo sessions and the miracle of dye-transfer printing can cover a multitude of flaws. The slick film, with its carefully packaged titillations, can make an otherwise wholesome marriage relationship seem tedious and drab by comparison. What woman can

---

* The views of sexuality we have just seen in the history of the Church stem, in part at least, from a concern for taking the warnings of Scripture seriously. The problem is that their exclusive attention to the warnings produced an inability to appreciate the positive, celebrative side of sexuality.

compare favorably day in and day out with the voluptuous breasts, sparkling smile, and sensuous legs seen on
the screen today? What man can match the bulging biceps
and suntanned body portrayed in the modern media?

The answer is that no one can, not even the people
who stage the phony show. It is a dream world—a deceptive, beguiling, artificial dream world. The sex of the pornographic trade is too slick, too wonderful, too ecstatic.
Sex in the real world is a mixture of tenderness and
halitosis, love and fatigue, ecstasy and disappointment.
When people believe the dream world, they begin to cast
a disparaging eye at the flaws of the real world; indeed,
they begin to seek a flawless fantasy world. Such make-
believe is genuinely destructive to both true sexuality and
true spirituality.

All this is destructive enough, but perhaps the most
destructive aspect of pornography is the twisted forms of
power it portrays. Hard-core pornography is far more
than titillation; it is violent and sick. It appeals to raw
power, sadistic and destructive.

Lust is also a distortion of sexuality. When I speak of
lust, I am not referring to the casual glance or the fleeting
thought but to a condition in which a person lives in a
perpetual sexual stew. Lust is runaway, uncontrolled sexual passion.

Because of sin, our sexual appetites have been distorted. In some cases, they have become obsessive and all-
consuming. C. S. Lewis graphically illustrates the twist-
edness of our sexual instinct: "Or take it another way.
You can get a large audience together for a strip-tease
act—that is, to watch a girl undress on the stage. Now
suppose you came to a country where you could fill a
theatre by simply bringing a covered plate on to the stage
and then slowly lifting the cover so as to let every one
see, just before the lights went out, that it contained a
mutton chop or a bit of bacon, should you not think that

in that country something had gone wrong with the appetite for food?"[10]

Lewis is right; something has gone wrong with the sexual appetite, and it is a tremendous burden for some. There is the feeling of being trapped, plagued and guilt-ridden. The pious platitudes of religion do not chase away these morbidly inflamed instincts. Frederick Buechner, an acclaimed author and Presbyterian minister, has written, "Lust is the ape that gibbers in our loins. Tame him as we will by day, he rages all the wilder in our dreams by night. Just when we think we're safe from him, he raises up his ugly head and smirks, and there's no river in the world flows cold and strong enough to strike him down. Almighty God, why dost thou deck men out with such a loathsome toy?"[11]

All of us can identify with Buechner's plaintive query. But some identify more deeply, more desperately, than others. They cry out for deliverance, but heaven seems to turn a deaf ear. They feel plagued by sexual temptation all the day and all the night. They reject adultery out of Christian conviction but feel driven to pale voyeurism to satisfy the inner craving. But rather than satisfy, it only serves to inflame the desires all the more, a little like leading a starving person past a bakery. Indulgence is followed by guilt and remorse, which is followed by more indulgence and more guilt and more remorse.

We must be slow to condemn and quick to listen to all who are plagued by lust. The temptations are great in our sex-soaked culture. The distortion of our sexuality into lust can take a very tangled, twisted route. Only by the grace of God and the loving support of the Christian fellowship can our lust-inflamed sexuality be straightened upright again.

The strange twists and quirks of sexuality sometimes wind down the paths of *sadism* and *masochism*. The sadist enjoys giving pain, and the masochist enjoys receiving it.

Both are far from the warm, mutual sexuality of the Song of Solomon. Now, I am not talking about the sexual arousal that couples experience with a hard kiss or scratch. The eccentricities of a spouse can be borne within the context of responsible loving and caring.

In sadism and masochism the movement is not toward, but away from, responsible loving and caring. The focus is upon the pain rather than the building of a relationship. Lewis Smedes has noted, "Here a person is not feeling pain *within* a sexual relationship but is experiencing pain as a *substitute* for a sexual relationship."[12]

What is it that leads human beings to enjoy giving and receiving abuse, humiliation and pain? At its extreme sadism takes the form of rape or even murder. The very thing that was created to give joy and life has been twisted and used to bring misery and death. Why? What heinous quirks of sexuality would drive a person to want to dominate and humiliate and even destroy another? No one can adequately answer such questions. We can only say that sexuality's distortions can become demonic indeed. Sin is real; evil is real; the powers and principalities are real and can lead us to the very brink of hell itself.

But we must not be quick to cast stones. Within all of us lurks the potential to dehumanize and destroy. If our temptations do not come in the form of sadism or masochism, they still come and they can still destroy. These realities should humble us beneath the cross and cause us to pray for one another that health and wholeness may abound.

Sexism is yet another distortion of our sexuality. In reality, sexism is merely another side of sadism. It is the drive to dominate, to control, to hold under one's thumb. History bears the sad record of this cruel domination, primarily by men over women. Even in the Old Testament community, women were often treated as property to be protected and disposed of at male discretion.

The notion of female inferiority is a false and soul-destroying doctrine. And if we reject the inherent inferiority of the woman, we must also reject the inherent subordination of the woman. The argument that, although the woman is not inferior to the man she is different from him and therefore necessarily subordinate to him, is not compelling. Differences are obvious, but they do not necessarily entail hierarchical arrangements.

We need to be reminded that the rule of the male *over* the female is not a description of pristine sexuality before the fall but of the curse of the fall; "Yet your desire shall be for your husband, and he shall rule over you" (Gen. 3:16). Sexism is sexuality's distortion, not its wholeness. In the power of Christ's death and resurrection, we have overcome the curse of the fall, we are overcoming the curse of the fall, and we will overcome the curse of the fall.

HOMOSEXUALITY AND THE CHRISTIAN

For many reasons, I genuinely wish I could avoid the subject of homosexuality. For one thing, anything I can say in a few short pages will be wholly inadequate. Also, heterosexuals are, by the very nature of things, terribly ignorant of the homosexual experience. This is true no matter how hard we may try to understand the homosexual milieu and no matter how much we may read in order to inform ourselves about the issues involved. And then, of course, homosexuality is so volatile a matter right now in the Christian community that whatever is said will be severely criticized—and probably for good reason. However, none of this is sufficient cause for me to remain silent, and besides, the matter of homosexuality has caused so much suffering and hurt today that if anything can be said that would be helpful—perhaps even healing —it would be well worth any risk involved.

Because this issue has wounded so many people so deeply, the first word that needs to be spoken is one of compassion and healing. Those who are clearly homosexual in their orientation often feel misunderstood, stereotyped, abused, and rejected. Those who believe that homosexuality is a clear affront to biblical norms feel betrayed by denominations that want to legislate homosexuality into church life.

There is a third group that has been hurt by the contemporary battle over homosexuality: I refer to those who agonize over their own sexual identity, those who feel torn by conflicting sexual urges and wonder if perhaps they are latent homosexuals. Perhaps this group suffers the most. They are cast into a sea of ambiguity because the Church has given an uncertain sound. On their right, they hear shrill denunciations of homosexuality, and, though they appreciate the concern for biblical fidelity, they have been offended by the brash, uninformed, pharisaical tone of the pronouncements. From their left, they hear enthusiastic acceptance of homosexuality and, though they appreciate the compassionate concern for the oppressed, they are astonished at the way the Bible is maneuvered to fit a more accommodating posture.

All who are caught in the cultural and ecclesiastical chaos over homosexuality need our compassion and understanding. We need to ask forgiveness of all homosexual persons who have been discriminated against and persecuted. We need to listen with empathy to all who feel the Church is losing its moral fiber. All who are struggling with their own sexual identity need our understanding, counsel, and sober moral judgment.

Does the Bible give us any guidance on the question of homosexuality? Yes, the Bible is quite clear and straightforward. From beginning to end it views the heterosexual union as God's intention for sexuality and sees homosexuality as a distortion of this God-given pattern. Now, this conclusion is not built simply on the specific references to homosexuality in the Bible, though these passages are, I think, clear enough in their disavowal of homosexual practice.* But it is the larger biblical context that is most persuasive. That context makes it quite clear that heterosexual union is the norm. God created them "male and female" with the intent that they should become "one flesh." That conviction undergirds all the biblical teaching about human sexuality.

Now, it is quite possible to argue that the biblical authors did not understand the distinctions between homosexual lust and homosexual love or between confirmed constitutional homosexuals and those with only inclinations toward homosexuality. But it is not really possible to say that the Bible is ambiguous about this matter. Homosexuality is rejected as "unnatural" and a departure from God's intention. The notion that homosexuality is merely a special form of normal sexuality is unthinkable from a biblical perspective.

To be clear about the Bible's assessment of homosexuality does not mean that we jump to the conclusion that it is simply self-chosen. The idea that all homosexuals freely choose the form their sexuality takes and freely choose homosexual activity is neither good science nor good theology. It is not even good sense. Homosexuality comes in many degrees and has various causes, many of them beyond the individual's control. A person with a 20 or 30 percent inclination toward homosexuality finds it much easier to be "converted" to a full heterosexual orientation than a person with an 80 or 90 percent homosexual inclination. The factors that contribute to a person's sexual orientation are often deep-seated and complex. Hence,

---

* See for example, Lev. 18:22; 20:13; Rom. 1:21–27; 1 Cor. 6:9; and 1 Tim. 1:10. I am well acquainted with the various attempts to reinterpret these passages in a new light, and some of these efforts are quite sophisticated. I do not, however, find them compelling.

though we want to confess heterosexuality as the Christian norm, we also want to empathize and stand with those who find such an orientation foreign and difficult.

Simple sexual attraction to a person of the same sex is a very different thing from homosexuality. Such attraction can be triggered by various things, acceptance, affection, and caring, for example. This is quite different from true homosexuality.

You see, a woman is not a lesbian just because she feels sexually attracted to another woman. A man is not a homosexual just because he is aroused by other men. Sexual arousal is not uncommon in a context of intimacy and affection. It is not abnormal or unusual. And in our day, when so much emphasis is placed upon sex, it is quite possible for heterosexual persons to become so obsessed with sex in general that they seek to express it in both heterosexual and homosexual ways. Such drives do, however, need positive control and redirection.

A person who has experienced same-sex arousal need not be frightened that he or she is destined for a life of homosexuality. The experience is quite common but needs to be responded to firmly and appropriately. A theological, sociological, and psychological framework is needed to help channel sexuality. That framework can be used to say a firm no to homosexual activity in much the same way that a married person uses a Christian framework to say a firm no to extramarital sexual activity.

Sex is like a great river that is rich and deep and good as long as it stays within its proper channel. The moment a river overflows its banks, it becomes destructive, and the moment sex overflows its God-given banks, it too becomes destructive. Our task is to define as clearly as possible the boundaries placed upon our sexuality and to do all within our power to direct our sexual responses into that deep, rich current.

Up to this point I have dealt with those who have

same-sex *responsiveness* but not those who have firmly established patterns of same-sex *preference*. These latter individuals we call constitutional homosexuals. Try as they might, they are simply not aroused by the opposite sex; and try as they might, they seemingly cannot avoid being aroused by the same sex. Social scientists tell us that about 5 percent of all males and about half that percentage of all females have a confirmed sexual drive toward persons of their own sex. What is to be said for those who, as best we can determine, are confirmed constitutional homosexuals?

The first thing that needs to be said is that they did not choose their homosexuality any more than a clubfooted child chose clubfootedness. Both are distortions of God's intention, but neither are blameworthy. We live in a fallen world, and many are trapped by the condition of sin that plagues the human race. Such persons deserve our understanding and empathy, not our condemnation.

But although homosexuals are not responsible for their homosexuality, they are responsible for what they do. Choices must be made, and for Christians who find themselves with a homosexual orientation, those choices must be made in the light of God's truth and God's grace.

In general there are three basic options for homosexuals: to change their homosexual orientation, to control their homosexual orientation, or to practice their homosexual orientation.

Can a constitutional homosexual develop a heterosexual orientation? This question is hotly debated. Verifiable evidence is extremely hard to find. Many of the so-called conversions to heterosexuality are probably of people with leanings toward homosexuality rather than true constitutional homosexuals. Some studies do, however, give hope. Pattison and Pattison, writing in the *American Journal of Psychiatry*, conclude, "The data provide a substantial body of evidence for the plausibility of change from exclusive homosexuality to exclusive heterosexuality, which is in accordance with the Kinsey statistical probabilities for such change, the Masters and Johnson data, and the clincial or observational anecdotes of such change."[13]

Certainly we want to avoid a naive optimism, but we should always hold high the hope of genuine permanent change. Those who work for a change in their sexual orientation need the prayerful support and love of the Christian fellowship. Their way is not easy, and we in the Christian community need to stand with them through times of frustration, discouragement, and failure. Our concern, our prayer, our hope is to bring the life-changing power of God into their situation. And every single time this occurs, we can rejoice with those who rejoice. But we must also be prepared to weep with those who weep.

There are those who have cried out to God and done everything they know to do and yet have experienced no change in their sexual orientation. We who work with them have also done everything we know to do but to all appearances have failed. What happens then? A second option is to control homosexual behavior. Faced with their homosexuality, some have chosen celibacy as the route of moral integrity. These individuals need our warmest support and encouragement. Behavior modification, personal discipline, and wise judgment will be needed. The church community should surround such persons with earnest prayer that they can be faithful to their calling of celibacy.*

The third option homosexuals have is to practice their homosexuality. At this point, it would be very easy to close the discussion by declaring that the practice of

---

* Celibacy is a valid calling for homosexuals, but I am not suggesting that all celibate people are homosexuals.

homosexuality is sin and therefore not an option for Christians. The practice of homosexuality is sin, to be sure, but that does not mean we can therefore wash our hands of the matter. We live in a catastrophically fallen world, and sin's distortions can at times entangle us in tragic ways. Human strength may not always permit the ideal. We are finite; there are limits to our knowledge and power. Of course, we hope for God's power to come; we pray for God's power to come; we expect God's power to come. When it does, it is a wonderful occasion for doxology. But there are other times, times of frustration and discouragement and failure, and when those times come, we must manage as best we can.

The Christian fellowship cannot give permission to practice homosexuality to those who feel unable to change their orientation or to embrace celibacy. But if such a tragic moral choice is made, the most moral context possible should be maintained.

An analogy may be helpful. If a war is entered into when it should have been avoided, there are still moral constraints upon the combatants. Just because the ideal has been violated does not mean that anything goes. A person continues to have moral responsibilities even when driven to engage in an activity that is less than the best. If we cannot condone the choice of homosexual practice, neither can we cut off the person who has made the choice. No, we stand with the person always ready to help, always ready to pick up the pieces if things fall apart, always ready to bring God's acceptance and forgiveness.

We have had two objectives in this chapter. The first was to understand the biblical vision of human sexuality. The second was to see some of the distortions of this vision so that we can know better how to bring our lives into conformity with the ways of God. We now want to turn our attention to how this vision of wholeness in sexuality works its way out in the single life.

7. Sexuality and Singleness

Hell is the only place outside heaven where we can be safe from the dangers of love.

—C. S. LEWIS

One of the great challenges for the Christian faith today is to integrate sexuality and spirituality within the context of the single life. We are fast approaching the day when single people will be in the majority. There are, of course, the young who are still anticipating marriage. Also, there are many who are unwillingly hurled into single life by the tragic death of a spouse. The even greater tragedy of divorce casts untold millions more into the world of the single.

The Church can make an enormous contribution by helping singles grapple with their sexuality with honesty and integrity. But in order to do this we must stop thinking of single persons as somehow devoid of sexual needs. Singles—especially those with a serious Christian commitment—really struggle with their sexuality. They face many troubling questions. Is masturbation a legitimate expression of sexuality for a Christian? How do I deal with the feelings of lust that often seem to dominate my thinking? What is lust, anyway, and how is it different from appropriate sexual desire? What about physical affection? Is it an appropriate means of building a healthy relationship, or is it only a one-way street to sexual intercourse? And speaking of intercourse, why is so much significance given to the insertion of the penis into the vagina? Are there really valid biblical reasons for the ban on intercourse outside of marriage, or are these just social customs? These and many similar questions are faced by all singles who are seeking to integrate their Christianity and their sexuality.

SEXUALITY AND SEXUAL INTERCOURSE

Perhaps it is best to begin by seeking to grasp a Christian perspective on sexuality and sexual intercourse. Sometimes a person will ask, "Do you believe in premarital sex?" The answer to that question is, "yes and no." Christianity says a clear yes to that question insofar as it refers to the affirming of our sexuality as human beings. Christianity says a clear no to that question insofar as it refers to genital sex. Let us try to understand the reasoning behind both the yes and the no.

We are sexual persons. We must never try to deny or reject that in any way. We are created in the image of God, male and female. In an important sense all that we are and all that we do has sexual implications. I am trying here to overcome the really silly notion that single persons are somehow asexual.

The single person's sexuality is expressed in his or her capacity to love and to be loved. Not all experiences of intimacy should eventuate in marriage or in genital sex. Loving does not need to be genital to be intimate, and the capacity to love is vital to our sexuality. And so the single person should develop many relationships that are wholesome and caring. Deeply affectionate but nongenital relationships are completely possible and should be encouraged.

The single person's sexuality is expressed in the need to experience emotional fulfillment. The decision to reserve genital sex for marriage is not a decision to remain emotionally unfulfilled. Warm, satisfying friendships are legitimate ways single people can express their sexuality. Emotional fulfillment is completely possible for the single person, and the Church can help here by providing a context for happy and satisfying friendships to develop.

The single person's sexuality is expressed in learning to accept and control his or her sexual feelings. Individuals outside the covenant of marriage should not deny or repress their sexual feelings. Donald Goergen has noted that "feelings are meant to be felt, and sexual feelings are no exception."[1] When we try to deny these feelings we cut ourselves off from our humanity.

I hear a lot more talk about platonic love than I see in experience. Most intimate heterosexual friendships have erotic dimensions to them. And it does us no good to deny that fact of life. Rather we should accept these feelings. But to accept them does not mean to act upon them. Sexual feelings are not to control us; we are to control them. It is an illusion to think that sexual desires are uncontrollable. Just because we may feel angry enough to want to murder someone does not mean that we will do so. We control our feelings of anger so that we do not kill, and in the same way we bring our sexual feelings under our authority.

So far we have tried to show ways by which singles should say yes to their sexuality. What about the no side of the answer to the question of sex outside of marriage?

There is no getting around it: biblical teaching places a clear veto on sexual intercourse for single people. The question is, Why? The biblical writers were not in the least prudish about sex. God's very creation of human beings as male and female suggests a wholehearted approval of exciting sexual experience. The Song of Solomon celebrates sex as a voluptuous adventure. Paul warns spouses against withholding "conjugal rights." Why, then, would sexual intercourse be reserved for the covenant of marriage?

The Bible's ban on sexual intercourse for the unmarried is based upon a profound positive insight. According to the biblical authors, sexual intercourse creates a mysterious, unique "one flesh" bond. In the creation narrative we are told in simple, yet profound, words, "Therefore a man leaves his father and his mother and cleaves to his wife, and they become one flesh" (Gen. 2:24). When the Pharisees sought to embroil Jesus in the contemporary controversy over the grounds for divorce, he appealed to the "one flesh" concept of Genesis and added, "So they are no longer two but one flesh. What therefore God has joined together, let no man put asunder" (Matt. 19:6). In Ephesians, Paul quotes the "one flesh" account to urge husbands to love their wives, because "he who loves his wife loves himself" (Eph. 5:28). His point is a simple one: marriage creates such a bonded union that to do violence to one's spouse is to do violence to oneself.

For our purposes, however, the most graphic passage of all is found in Paul's teaching in 1 Corinthians 6. Paul is dealing with the case of a man in the Christian fellowship who had been involved with a prostitute. He writes: "Do you not know that he who joins himself to a prostitute becomes one body with her? For, as it is written, 'The two shall become one flesh' " (1 Cor. 6:16). This passage makes it unmistakably clear that Paul sees sexual intercourse as the act par excellence that produces a "one flesh" bond.

We are now in a position to see why biblical morality reserves sex for the covenant of marriage. Sexual intercourse involves something far more than just the physical, more than even the emotions and psyche. It touches deep into the spirit of each person and produces a profound union that the biblical writers call "one flesh." Remember, we do not *have* a body, we *are* a body; we do not *have* a spirit, we *are* a spirit. What touches the body deeply touches the spirit as well.

Sexual intercourse is a "life-uniting act," as Lewis Smedes calls it.[2] And Derrick Baily has added, "Sexual intercourse is an act of the whole self which affects the whole self; it is a personal encounter between man and woman in which each does something to the other, for good or for ill, which can never be obliterated. This remains true even when they are ignorant of the radical character of their act."[3]

Thus the reasoning behind the biblical prohibition of sexual intercourse for the unmarried goes beyond the common practical concerns of pregnancy or veneral disease or whatever. Genital sex outside of marriage is wrong "because it violates the inner reality of the act; it is wrong because unmarried people thereby engage in a life-uniting act without a life-uniting intent. . . . Intercourse signs and seals—and maybe even delivers—a life-union; and life-union means marriage."[4]

Therefore, Paul is saying no to sexual intercourse outside of marriage because it does violence to the very nature of the act itself. The act draws us into the profound mystery of a "one flesh" reality. It unites and bonds in a deep and wonderful way, wonderful, that is, when it is linked to a covenant of permanence and fidelity. When it is not, it becomes "a hollow, ephemeral, diabolical parody of marriage which works disintegration in the personality and leaves behind a deeply-seated sense of frustration and dissatisfaction—though this may never be brought to the surface of consciousness and realized."[5]

The Hebrew word for intercourse means "to know." The biblical writers understood that in sexual intercourse a special kind of knowledge was conveyed, a special kind of intimacy came into being. This reality they called "one flesh." This then is why the Bible reserves sexual intercourse for the covenant of marriage.

Where does this leave those who have engaged in intercourse outside of marriage but who now recognize that what they have done is really and truly wrong? Is the bonded reality of intercourse utterly irreversible? No, it is not irreversible, but it does demand the healing touch of God. To engage in a life-uniting act without a life-uniting intent wounds the inner spirit. Such wounds often fester and become infected so that they poison the entire spiritual life. At best, they leave ugly scar tissue.

But the wonderful news is that healing is possible. The grace of God can flow into the wounded spirit, healing and restoring. Sometimes, however, individuals are not able to do this by themselves. In such cases it is best for them to seek out a wise and compassionate physician of the soul—someone who is experienced in spiritual direction and healing prayer—who can pray for them and set them free.

In whatever way it is done, healing prayer does need to be given. We cannot just pretend that the affair never happened, no matter how casual it was. If it is not dealt with and healed, it will surface sooner or later. A friend of mine once counseled a 78-year-old woman. She had been a missionary for fifty years, but now her life, it seemed, was in shambles. She had fears day and night. She was afraid of crowds; she was afraid of stairs; she was afraid of everything. And she was depressed; a deep sadness hung over her entire life. So total was her misery that she was preparing to have shock treatments.

My friend, who is very wise in the care of souls, asked if she had been happy as a child. "Oh, yes!," she responded. The next question was a simple one, "When did you begin to feel this sadness and depression?" The reply was quick, "When I was sixteen." And so my friend asked, "Why? What happened when you were sixteen that caused the sadness?" For the first time in her life, this woman admitted that at sixteen she had had an affair with a young man. Fortunately she did not become pregnant, and the young man soon went away, but she had carried this deep wound in her spirit for over sixty years.

My friend prayed for the inner healing of this dear

woman, and, wonderfully, within a matter of weeks, the fears and depression began to disappear, so that, as she put it, "I am able to remember that I used to be afraid and depressed, but I can no longer remember what it felt like!"

This ministry of forgiving and healing through the power of Christ is the common property of the people of God. We can bring so much help, so much healing, if we are willing. It is a gracious ministry that needs to abound in the fellowship of the faithful.

SEXUAL FANTASY

Jesus, of course, made it abundantly clear that sexual righteousness was a far deeper issue than merely avoiding sex outside of marriage. He went right to the heart of the matter by speaking of the adultery of the heart, "Every one who looks at a woman lustfully has already committed adultery with her in his heart" (Matt. 5:28). This statement was a profound advance over the external righteousness of the scribes and Pharisees. It has also caused a great deal of concern and confusion about sexual fantasies.

The single person who genuinely wants to be a disciple of Christ and who therefore reserves sexual intercourse for the covenant of marriage is often confused about how to deal with sexual fantasies. Sexual fantasies delight—they also trouble and disturb. And the confusion they cause is only heightened by the ambivalence of the Christian community. When singles turn to the Church for direction, they are usually met with either stony silence or the counsels of repression. Now, silence is no counsel, and repression is bad counsel. Desperate, however, they try to repress their sexual feelings, but their efforts always end in disappointment. The result is guilt, followed by bitterness and disillusionment. The need is great for solid practical guidance on how to deal with sexual fantasies.

At the outset we must make as clear a distinction as possible between lust and sexual fantasy. I say "as clear a distinction as possible" because we simply must admit that the lines that divide the two are sometimes shrouded in ethical mists and fogs. Although all lust involves sexual fantasy, not all sexual fantasies lead to lust. How do we know the difference?

In chapter 6 I defined lust as "runaway, uncontrolled sexual passion." Lewis Smedes has articulated the difference between the two quite well: "When the sense of excitement conceives a plan to use a person, when attraction turns into scheme, we have crossed beyond erotic excitement into spiritual adultery."[6] Lust is an untamed, inordinate sexual passion to possess, and this is a very different thing from the usual erotic awareness experienced in sexual fantasy.

Hence, the first thing that believers should do is to refuse to bear the heavy burden of self-condemnation for every erotic image that floats through their minds. Sometimes sexual fantasies signify a longing for intimacy; at other times, they express attraction toward a beautiful and winsome person. Sexual fantasies can mean many things, and we must not automatically identify them with lust.

It is also helpful to recognize the positive function of fantasy. Through fantasy we are able to hold reality at bay while we allow the imagination to roam freely. Mature people are able to utilize the imagination without ever losing touch with the real world. Some of the world's finest music and greatest inventions have come in this way.

Certainly one of the distinguishing characteristics of our human sexuality, as opposed to the rest of the creation, is our ability to reflect upon our sexuality. We can write love letters, remember the warm kiss many times over, and anticipate love's tender moments yet to come. These are sexual events, erotic experiences, and they should not be classified as lust. In fact, in marriage sexual fantasy is vitally important in awakening sexual expression. Perhaps one reason many couples are bored with sex is atrophy of their imagination.

But if sexual fantasy has its positive side, it also has its destructive side. It can be a substitute for warm friendships, which carry with them the demands and disappointments of real life. It can lead to obsession with the sexual. It can easily become a truncated preoccupation with the physical. It can be a prelude to illicit behavior.

The problem of sexual fantasies is genuinely intensified in our day because of the modern media blitz. It is virtually impossible to get away from the media's constant appeal to our sexual fantasies. Advertisers know well the power of sexual fantasy and constantly exploit that power.

However, we need to realize the authority we can have over our sexual fantasies. The imagination can be disciplined. In our better moments we can choose to place our minds on true and honorable and just and pure and lovely and gracious things. And even in our bad moments we can confess with Paul, "It is no longer I that do it, but sin which dwells within me," and know that a deeper experience of obedience is coming (Rom. 7:17).

You see, when bad people do evil they do exactly what they want to do. But when people who are seeking to follow Jesus Christ do evil they are doing precisely what they do not want to do. As Paul put it, "I do not do what I want, but I do the very thing I hate" (Rom. 7:15). When we are faced with such a condition, we say by faith, "That is not me doing it; it is sin in me, and by the grace of God and in the timing of God I shall be rid of it."

One of the most healing ministries we can render to

each other is to learn to pray for one another about our sexual fantasies. In this realm I have a friend who prays for me and I for him. The sharing is confidential, of course. The praying is spiced with laughter and joy, for it is a happy ministry to which we are called. We pray that we will be protected from sexual influences that will be destructive and harmful. We pray that Christ will enter our sexual fantasies and fill them with his light. We pray that our sexuality will be whole and full and pure. It is a gracious, wholesome, happy ministry, and I would commend it to you.

MASTURBATION

Masturbation is so closely related to the issue of sexual fantasy that it deserves attention at this juncture. Ethical judgments about masturbation run all the way from viewing it as a sin more serious than fornication, adultery, or rape to placing it in the same category as head scratching.*

One thing that is certainly uncontested is the almost universal experience of masturbation. James McCary, author of *Human Sexuality*, has found that about 95 percent

---

* In the Middle Ages the Roman Catholic church stressed the evils of masturbation because of its distance from procreation, which was thought to be the only function of sex, and even the most recent Vatican statement on the subject declares that "masturbation is an intrinsically and seriously disordered act." And in the Evangelical Protestant wing of the Church, Erwin Lutzer, in *Living with Your Passions*, comes very close to a direct identification of masturbation with sin. By contrast, most in the medical profession today regard it as normal and not harmful. James Dobson, in his popular "Focus on the Family" film series, accepts it as a normal part of growing up unless it becomes excessive. Charlie Shedd, in *The Stork Is Dead*, speaks of it as "a gift from God," since it can help to avoid promiscuous sex. The comparison of masturbation with head scratching comes from James McCary, in *Human Sexuality*, 3d ed. (New York: D. Van Nostrand, 1978), pp. 293-94.

of men and between 50 and 90 percent of women masturbate.[7] It has been said that "no other form of sexual activity
has been more frequently discussed, more roundly condemned, and more universally practiced, than masturbation."[8] Nearly all adolescents masturbate and many adults
masturbate from time to time throughout their lives.

The issue of masturbation is particularly acute for single people who, out of Christian conviction, have said no
to sexual intercourse outside of marriage. Many important questions surface: Is masturbation a morally acceptable activity for a disciple of Christ? Even more, could it
be a "gift from God," as some have suggested, to help us
avoid promiscuous sex? What about the sexual fantasies
that invariably crowd into the landscape of masturbation?

These questions—and many more—are of concern to
all believers, but they are especially urgent to singles.
Deeply concerned to do what is right, many singles find
their experiences of masturbation plagued by guilt, defeat, and self-hatred. They determine never to do it again.
But they do. And the pit of self-condemnation deepens.

Let us begin with a couple of indisputable facts. First,
masturbation is not physically harmful in any way. On
this, all medical experts agree. The old myths that masturbation will cause everything from pimples to insanity
are just that—myths.

Second, the Bible nowhere deals directly with masturbation. There are no injunctions against it, as there are
against homosexuality, for example. The Bible's silence
on masturbation is not because it was unknown, since
there are references to it in the Egyptian literature of the
period. It certainly is not because the Bible is squeamish
about sexually explicit topics. Now, the Bible's silence
does not mean that masturbation is not a moral issue, but
it does mean that any biblical help we receive will be in-
direct rather than direct.

Three concerns heighten the moral question of masturbation. The first is its connection with sexual fantasies. Masturbation simply does not occur in an imageless void. And many are deeply distressed by the images that do come, feeling that they qualify as the lust of the heart that Jesus spoke against (Matt. 5:28).

The second concern relates to masturbation's tendency to become obsessive. People who masturbate can become compulsive in it. They feel trapped; the practice becomes an uncontrollable habit that dominates everything. Perhaps the most distressing aspect of this obsessive process is the sense of being undisciplined and out of control.

The third concern has to do with masturbation's depersonalization. Masturbation is sexual solitaire. True sexuality leads us to a deep personal relationship with another, but masturbation is "sex on a desert island," to use the phrase of John White.

On the positive end of the spectrum, masturbation does help compensate for the uneven development that many adolescents experience in their physical, emotional, and social maturation. Many teenagers are physically ready for sex far sooner than they are for social intimacy and the responsibilities of marriage. Masturbation provides a natural "safety valve" while nature is synchronizing growth in the various aspects of life.

For married couples, masturbation can often be a mutually enriching experience when done together. Within the context of married lovemaking, it has been called "an exciting excursion into shared pleasure."[9] In fact, some couples find mutual masturbation a crucial element in the development of their full sexual potential.

What should we say to all this? Well, the first thing we should say is that masturbation is not inherently wrong or sinful. In the main, it is a common experience for most people and should be accepted as a normal part of life.

The second thing we can emphasize is its value in providing a potentially healthy genital outlet when sexual intercourse is not possible. We simply must not lay impossible moral burdens upon people, especially when we have no specific biblical teaching against masturbation. Many honest folk, told of the evils of masturbation, have prayed desperately to be set free, and in reality have been expecting God to take away their sexual desires. These expectations are completely unrealistic, and, in fact, if God were to oblige, he would be doing violence to his own creation. Sexual desire is good and needs to be affirmed, not denied.

But sexual desire also needs to be controlled, which leads us to a third affirmation: the more masturbation tends toward obsession, the more it tends toward idolatry. God is our only legitimate obsession. The body needs to be under our discipline; this is true whether we are talking about sloth, gluttony, or masturbation. The uncontrolled practice of masturbation undermines our confidence and self-esteem. Obsessive masturbation is spiritually dangerous. But we must also be aware of the opposite obsession—the obsession to quit. This obsession is especially painful because one failure can cast a person into despair. It becomes a desperate, all-or-nothing situation. And this is sad, because it is really unnecessary. We do not need to put people into impossible either/or binds. What we are after is control, balance, perspective.

Closely tied to this is a fourth affirmation: masturbation's sexual fantasies are a very real part of human life that needs to be disciplined, not eliminated. Erotic imaginings will come; the real ethical question is how to deal with them. Will they dominate every waking moment, or can they be brought into proper perspective within the far greater matters of love and human relationship? We like fantasies because they idealize life. In our fantasies we are the paradigm of sexual prowess, our partner is desirable beyond compare, and, best of all, he or she says what we want, does what we want, and never makes demands on our time and energy. This is precisely why fantasies need discipline: they can divorce us from the real world of human imperfection. And Jesus' word about adultery of the heart must never be taken lightly.

The final thing we should say about masturbation is that, although it may electrify, it can never fully satisfy. Orgasm is only a small part of a much larger whole. And that larger whole encompasses the entire range of personal human relationship. A cup of coffee together in the morning, a quiet talk in the evening, a touch, a kiss—this is the stuff of our sexuality. Masturbation will always fall short, because it seeks to perpetuate the myth of the self-contained lover.

PASSION UNDER CONTROL

Most cultures in the history of the world have not known the many expressions of courting that are so familiar to us. Marriages were arranged. Abraham sent his servant to find a bride for Isaac, and the choice was made before Isaac and Rebekah ever set eyes on each other (Gen. 24). And so it has been in many cultures. Love and intimacy came after marriage rather than before it. But this is not how it for us, not in our culture. For us, there are elaborate rituals of acquaintanceship and courtship. Many of these rituals seem innocent enough—talking together, holding hands, kissing. Others seem dangerously erotic—necking, caressing, petting.

These rituals hold no moral dilemma for those who allow sexual intercourse to run free. For them, these things can be a prelude to intercourse if the conditions are right and all things work out well. But for those who reserve genital sex exclusively for the covenant of marriage, these matters are filled with moral consequence. It is to these people that the counsel that follows is addressed.

The first question that must be answered is whether or

not there is any place at all within the context of Christian sexual behavior for the many expressions of love and affection. I am going to answer yes to that question, but first let us see why many people, to one degree or another, have tended to answer no. The main reason for a no answer is that the kissing and hugging are considered the first steps toward sexual intercourse, a process that, once begun, cannot be stopped. Now, if that is the sole purpose of these rituals of acquaintanceship and courtship, then it makes all the sense in the world to put up plenty of stop signs and barriers.

However, it is possible for the many acts of affection that accompany courtship to have an altogether different agenda. They can also serve the purpose of tender caring and sharing, of mutual endearment and intimacy. They can be enjoyed for their own sake without necessarily leading to sexual intercourse.

The purpose of the many acts of mutual affection should be to convey closeness without sexual intercourse as the goal. Singles need to understand this purpose with absolute clarity, because the pressure of society and the pressure of friends and the pressure of body chemistry will all push toward intercourse.

I am suggesting that, instead of denying our passions, we need to control our passions. Obviously, there are very real risks. Sexual passion is very powerful, and it can easily carry people beyond the point of no return before they know it. This gives rise to a second major question, If we accept the acts of mutual affection within the context of Christian ethics, are there any guidelines for their practice? These acts can range from simple hugging and kissing all the way to direct stimulation of the breasts and the genitals. What counsel can be given that might help singles find their way along this continuum?

Responsible passion should be guided by one basic principle: *increased physical intimacy in a relationship should always be matched by increased commitment to that relationship.* A diagram[10] might help illustrate this principle:

We build a solid foundation for love by moving toward commitment at the same rate we move toward physical intimacy. As intimacy grows, so does our commitment to each other. As our commitment grows, so does our intimacy. If our mutual commitment is shaky, we had better ease up on the intimacy. The early stages of commitment include such things as exclusively dating one person. Deeper levels of commitment involve such things as engagement. All along the way the privileges of growing intimacy carry with them the responsibilities of growing commitment, so that the ultimate intimacy in sexual intercourse coincides with the ultimate commitment in the covenant of marriage.

The diagram on the following page illustrates what happens when intimacy runs ahead of commitment.

When people move one inch toward commitment and a mile toward intimacy, everything is thrown off balance. There is no solid foundation for love, and the result is frustration and chaos.

I have sought to present a general principle for responsible passion that I hope will provide guidance without legalism. I would like to add to this two opinions of my own: if these are helpful, good; if not, forget them, for they are certainly not essential to the general principle.

My first suggestion is this: since our purpose is to convey personal closeness and sharing without sexual intercourse, I think it would be wise to make the genitals and the woman's breasts off limits until marriage. These areas are just too explosive to be part of a mutual expression of affection and caring short of intercourse.

My second suggestion is that the engagement period not be too long—certainly not more than six months. By the time a couple reaches the point of engagement, they are entering levels of intimacy that should not be sustained for long without expression in sexual intercourse. For Carolynn and me the engagement period, while in many ways very wonderful, was in other ways the most difficult. Our love for each other, our caring, our sharing, was at an apex. We have always been glad that we waited until marriage for sexual intercourse, but we were also glad that the final waiting period was not unduly long.

THE SINGLE LIFE

Some have a special call of God to a single life, as both Jesus and Paul taught. This was a genuine contribution, since before this time there was no theology of sexuality that really allowed for the single life.*

Jesus declared that there were those who were single "for the sake of the kingdom of heaven" (Matt. 19:12).† And Paul builds on this foundation by suggesting that the unmarried can focus their energies toward the work of God in a way that the married simply cannot (1 Cor. 7:32-35).

Some have railed at Paul for urging people to seriously consider the single life, but the truth is that his words are filled with practical wisdom. He was not against marriage —in fact his great contribution to Christian sexual theology is the way he compares the sexual union in marriage to the union of Christ and his Church. But Paul did insist that we count the cost. You see, no one should enter the covenant of marriage without realizing the immense time and energy required to make that relationship work.

---

* In the main, Judaism looked upon celibacy as an abnormal state. Eunuchs, for example, were forbidden to act as priests (Lev. 21:20). The only exception I am aware of to this general rule was the Essene community of Qumran. There celibacy did exist, and Jesus was likely aware of this group since his cousin, John the Baptist, was probably involved with the Essenes.

† The biblical term is *eunuchs*, and there is considerable debate over whether this refers to a person who has never married or to a married person whose partner has left for a pagan life who does not remarry and hence is a "eunuch for the sake of the kingdom." Whichever interpretation is correct, the practical outcome is the same—the person lives a single life for the sake of the kingdom of heaven.

"The unmarried man is anxious about the affairs of the Lord, how to please the Lord; but the married man is anxious about worldly affairs, how to please his wife, and his interests are divided" (1 Cor. 7:32-34).

Therefore, in the Christian fellowship we need to make room for the "vocational celibate"—the person who has chosen a single life in order to focus his or her energies more narrowly on the service of the kingdom of God. Jesus himself is an example of this, as is Paul. Vocational celibacy is not an inferior or a superior way of life—it is simply a different calling.

In *Freedom of Simplicity* I have written, "We do people a disservice when we fail to proclaim the single life as a Christian option. Marriage is not for everyone, and we should say so."[11] Those who are called to the single life should be welcomed into the life and ministry of the church. They are not half-people or folk who somehow cannot snag a mate. They have made a positive choice of the single life for the sake of Christ and in response to the call of God. And as Heini Arnold has noted, "It is possible for everyone to find the deepest unity of heart and soul without marriage."[12]

Before concluding this section I want to speak a special word about those who are single but feel no special calling to be single. Perhaps they are widowed or divorced or have not had a chance to marry but wish they were married. The Christian community needs to have a special tenderness for these who feel shoved aside and left behind in our couple-oriented world.

In many cases their situation has arisen from circumstances completely beyond their control. For example, we tell people to marry "only in the Lord," but because of our mechanisms of evangelism and Christian nurture, we have more women than men in the Church. What are the women to do?

Or consider the plight of the divorcées in our

churches. In many cases we are not sure whether to welcome them or to ostracize them. They sense our ambivalence, and in some ways it is worse than outright rejection.

To the unwilling single I would like to speak the words of trust and hope. Do not harden your heart. God is still sovereign no matter what the frustrations of your life may indicate. He can bring about that "wonder of wonders and miracle of miracles" that Motel Kamzoil sang about in *Fiddler on the Roof*. Trust in him, do all you can yourself, and live in hope. And even if marriage does not come, you can know that his grace is sufficient even for that.

In writing this chapter I have been keenly aware that it is quite easy for me to pontificate on the conditions for sexual purity for singles from the warm confines of a satisfying marriage. To put it bluntly, I do not have to face an empty bed at night or mounting sexual frustrations during the day. But whatever our station in life, we can trust the goodness of God and learn to live in his power.

8. Sexuality and Marriage

Christianity does not depreciate marriage, it sanctifies it.
—DIETRICH BONHOEFFER

Marriage is a great gift of God. It ushers us into the strange and awesome mystery of "one flesh" in all its fullness. It is a gift to be received reverently and to be nurtured tenderly. To be sure, we must not elevate the gift of marriage above the gift of the single life, but neither should we underestimate its importance. Martin Luther declared, "Ah, dear Lord, marriage is . . . a gift of God. It is the sweetest and dearest, yes, purest life."[1]

In the Genesis account we are told that the bond of marriage is greater even than the bond of child to parent. "Therefore a man leaves his father and his mother and cleaves to his wife, and they become one flesh" (Gen. 2:24). Jesus refers to this Genesis passage and then adds, "So they are no longer two but one. What therefore God has joined together, let no man put asunder" (Matt. 19:6). And the apostle Paul elevates marriage to a place of high spirituality by declaring it to be a reflection of Christ and his Church (Eph. 5:21–32). The Bible, therefore, sees marriage as a great calling indeed. So much so, in fact, that Helmut Thielicke can speak of marriage as pre-eminently "the covenant of agape."[2]

CHRIST AND MARRIAGE

What constitutes an adequate basis for Christian marriage?[3] Couples of all ages struggle with this question. Are romantic feelings and the sense of mutual attraction enough? Certainly they are important, but they are not enough. It may surprise you to realize that the New Testament regards romantic love as such a minor factor in marriage that it does not even mention it. That does not mean that romantic love is without significance, but its significance must be brought into perspective with the larger considerations for marriage. One of the great tragedies of our day is the way people drop in and out of marriage solely on the basis of romantic love and sexual attraction. Eros is running amuck today because it is not subordinated to agape.* Sexual attraction and romantic love are good things to have in a marriage, but we cannot build a marriage upon them alone.

If not romantic love, then what does constitute a Christian basis for marriage? *The basis for getting married that conforms to the way of Christ is a regard for the well-being of ourselves and others and a regard for the advancement of the kingdom of God upon the earth.* Without question, this takes into account romantic love and sexual gratification (1 Cor. 7), both of which are God's creation and both of which are limited—limited in the sense that we cannot make a life out of them. Both sex and romance are elements to consider and may even be the deciding consideration in whether or not to marry a particular person, but they can never serve as *the* basis for marriage among those who follow Christ.

The point is that Christian marriage is far more than a private undertaking or a way to personal fulfillment. Christians contemplating marriage must consider the larger questions of vocation and calling, the good of others, and the well-being of the community of faith, and, most of all, how their marriage would advance or hinder the work of the kingdom of God.

---

* In simple terms, eros refers to romantic love and agape refers to divine love or charity.

I can well imagine that all this may sound terribly devoid of moonlight and rhapsody to you. And in one sense it is, because the Bible rejects the romantic-novel paradigm for conjugating the verbs of marriage. Eros simply must stand under the discipline of agape if we expect to give strength and permanence to marriage.

On the other hand, there is plenty of room for romance and rhapsody within the Christian basis for marriage. In fact, the goodness that is in romance and sex is available to us only within homes and communities ruled by agape.

Marriage, you see, must be understood within the larger context of the law of love (agape). Love, from a biblical perspective, is a well-reasoned concern for the well-being of all. A vital consideration in the decision to marry is whether our well-being, the well-being of our partner, and the well-being of others would be enhanced by it.

Marriage must also be understood within the larger context of discipleship. Christian marriage does not stand outside our obedience to Christ; indeed, it is to be an evidence of it. A vital consideration in the decision to marry is whether a greater discipleship to Christ and a further advancement of his kingdom will result from it.

Now, although this general principle can be helpful, it can also cause problems. Life seldom comes so neatly packaged. A potential marriage could enhance the well-being of the couple and could at the same time be destructive for relatives. Who can accurately determine the effect a marriage will have upon Christian discipleship? And after all, aren't romantic feelings and sexual desires at such a fever pitch for couples contemplating marriage that all other considerations seem ludicrous?

Here is where we need the help of the Christian fellowship. We are not left to flounder on our own in these matters. There are others who can lovingly and compassionately help to bring us perspective and discernment. Besides, I have found that even the simple recognition of a larger, more Christian basis for marriage has a way of bringing romantic feelings and sexual desires into better perspective.

Please do not think I am opposed to romantic love. It is of vital importance in enhancing a marriage relationship. It may even be the deciding factor in who specifically to marry. But it is only one factor in deciding whether or not to marry, and not the most important factor at that. My plea is for a greater balance today.

MARRIAGE'S COVENANTAL CHARACTER

When we confess that Christian marriage initiates us into a "one flesh" reality, we are not being merely sentimental. The two become one functional reality a little like the way a computer disk drive and its disk form one functioning unit or the way a bow and arrow are essential to each other.

The result of this reality is the Christian confession that marriage is meant to be for life. It is to be a permanent covenant "for richer for poorer, in sickness and in health till death do us part." We will look at the matter of divorce in a moment, but for now, notice the advantage the permanence of marriage gives us.

Because of the covenant we have made, because of the "one flesh" reality we have experienced, we are able to transcend those times when romantic love cools. Romantic love will cool, you know. No one can maintain the intensity of eros forever; it is in the nature of eros to wax and wane. But as C. S. Lewis has noted, "Ceasing to be 'in love' need not mean ceasing to love."[4] When such times come (and they will come), agape disciplines and nurtures eros. Agape has the staying power that can fan the embers of eros into flame once again.

The moment we call for permanency in the covenant of marriage, we are calling for many other things to happen in concert with it. For example, we are calling for a commitment to make the marriage covenant work. Serious efforts to improve a marriage are tasks as sacred as Bible study or prayer. Indeed, to neglect a marriage relationship in favor of Bible study or prayer is sin, because it violates the covenant we have made in our marriage vows. Attention to our marriage is an act of obedience to God. It is one concrete way we can put the kingdom of God first in our lives. We are serving Christ when we are investing time and energy in the marriage relationship.

When we join in the covenant of marriage we join a lifelong communion with another person. And that communion, in all of its intimacy and mystery, will demand our most skillful efforts. We are committing ourselves to gladly give our best hours and our peak energy to this most taxing and rewarding effort.

CELEBRATION IN THE BEDROOM

Frankly, sex in marriage should be a voluptuous experience. It is a gift to celebrate, excellent in every way. We join in the celebration of the Song of Solomon:

> I come to the garden, my sister, my bride,
> I gather my myrrh with my spice,
> I eat my honeycomb with my honey,
> I drink my wine with my milk.
>
> Eat, O friends, and drink:
> drink deeply, O lovers! (Song of Sol. 5:1)

Gladly we respond to the counsel of Proverbs: "May her breasts satisfy you always" (Prov. 5:19, NIV).

Those who try to limit sex to procreation are simply ignoring the Bible. Scripture enthusiastically affirms sex

within the bonds of marriage. Frequency of sex and variations of sexual technique simply are not moral issues, except in the sense of consideration for one another. In
other words, married couples are free in the Lord to do
whatever is mutually satisfying and contributes to the relationship. There is nothing inherently wrong with oral
sex or mutual masturbation or many other ways to give
pleasure to each other if they are mutually agreed upon.

There is an abundance of literature on sexual technique, so I will refrain from dealing with it in this book. It
is enough to say that believers are free within marriage to
explore the sexual realms of tenderness and delight that
can lead them into deeper experiences of love.

I would, however, like to comment on the mutual
rhythms of our sexuality. Sexual intercourse is not a giv-
en, something that somehow miraculously takes care of
itself once we enter marriage. It needs nurture, tenderness, training, education and much more. When two persons enter into sexual intimacy, there must be a lot of
emotional, spiritual, and physical give-and-take.

Men and women respond differently in the sexual
experience, and we had better learn the differences. You
can find them cataloged in any number of books. But
what you cannot find is the unique differences that exist
between you and your spouse. The books can only provide hints to point you in the right general direction. It is
up to you to explore the unique and mysterious ways of
your partner.

Women, the experts tell us, respond to sex more in
terms of relationship, of caring, of sharing, than do men.
But it is my God-given responsibility to learn the specific
rhythms of my wife. How often, how intense, how slow,
how fast, what gives pleasure, what offends—these and a
thousand other things form the vocabulary of love. I must
learn to read the language of her heart and soul, and she
must learn to read mine.

This is the agony and the ecstasy of sexual intimacy. But we cannot avoid it even if we want to. Besides, it is the very thing that provides such infinite variety and life-long pleasure in our sexual experience. No wonder the Creator made marriage permanent—after a lifetime we have only just begun to understand the marvelous inner clockwork of each other.

The reason many people become bored with sex is that they sever it from the mysterious, wondrous challenge of human personality uniting in one flesh. After all, if the only thing we see in sex is the insertion of a penis into a vagina, then it soon becomes wearisome indeed. But if the Christian witness to a "one flesh" reality is true, then nothing could be more wonderfully challenging.

So it is a spiritual undertaking to learn the ebb and flow of one another's sexuality. Our spiritual growth helps to enhance our sexual intimacy. Christian meditation often helps to sensitize us to the inner rhythm of each other. God, it seems, is keenly interested in helping us experience the full reality of "one flesh." In meditative prayer we are sometimes given a new insight into how to strengthen our sexual intimacy. Why not! God cares about such matters. We will become better, more sensitive lovers if we will give more attention to his guidance through listening prayer.

It was Dr. Norman Lobenz who said, "There is no better safeguard against infidelity than a vital, interesting marriage."[5] And certainly one place in marriage where we want to keep the mystery, the excitement, the fascination—the zip, zam, and zowie—is in sexual intimacy.

CHRIST AND DIVORCE

It is a thrilling thing to soar among the high and lofty peaks of marital success; it is quite another thing to descend into the valley of marital defeat. It is a little like the valley of the shadow of death. All marriages face times of sorrow and pain, but sometimes the sorrow seems too heavy and the pain too great. What should believers do when they are faced with the valley of the shadow in marriage?

The answer to this question is hotly debated today. Interestingly enough, it was hotly debated in Jesus' day. In the Hebraic society of the Old Testament divorce was a common practice, and so Moses set forth legislative guidelines in an attempt to humanize it (Deut. 24:1-4). But even these guidelines were fiercely debated. In Jesus' day there was one school of rabbis, led by Rabbi Hillel, who held that a man could divorce his wife for *any* reason. For example, if she burned the toast that morning, or if he saw another woman that pleased him more—these were sufficient grounds for divorce for the school of Hillel. Another group, led by Rabbi Shammai, felt that marital unfaithfulness was the only allowable grounds for a man to divorce his wife. (You notice that divorce was a male prerogative only—women had no say in the matter.)

The Pharisees sought to bring Jesus into this debate, and so they asked him, "Is it lawful to divorce one's wife for any cause?" (Matt. 19:3). The school of Hillel said yes; the school of Shammai said no. Who would Jesus side with? But rather than side with one group or the other, Jesus brought them back to God's intention from the beginning, "Have you not read that he who made them from the beginning made them male and female, and said, 'For this reason a man shall leave his father and mother and be joined to his wife, and the two shall become one'? So they are no longer two but one. What therefore God has joined together, let no man put asunder" (Matt. 19:4-6).

God's intent is for marriage to be a permanent "one flesh" reality. But this, of course, raised the issue of the Mosaic legislation, and so the Pharisees asked, "Why then did Moses command one to give a certificate of divorce, and to put her away?" (Matt. 19:7). Now, please notice Jesus' answer to that question, "For your hardness of heart Moses allowed you to divorce your wives, but from the beginning it was not so" (Matt. 19:8).

Do you see what Jesus is saying? He is talking to men, and he says that Moses allowed divorce in order to protect women from hard-hearted men! It was better for the man to divorce his wife than to bash her head against a wall. But as Jesus said, divorce was not God's intent from the beginning.

Jesus opposed the divorce practices of his day for exactly the same reason that Moses first instituted a bill of divorcement—to protect the woman, who was utterly defenseless and trapped by a destructive and evil practice. There was great harm done to women in Jesus' day by divorce. The very word for divorce means literally "to throw away," and women could be thrown away by a very simple procedure that did not involve a court of law or even a religious organization. Only witnesses were involved, and they could be the husband's witnesses. No legal charges needed to be brought; it was simply a matter of handing the woman a bill of divorcement that said she was divorced for certain reasons, and those could be almost anything, from speaking out of turn to kicking the dog.

The woman was trapped in the patriarchial world of the first century. And Jesus was opposing this evil practice of throwing women away. He even said that any man who divorces his wife "makes her an adulteress" (Matt. 5:32). What he was getting at was that a woman who was thrown out into the street had only one way to make a living. She could not go out and get a job somewhere. She had only one thing to sell, and that is why prostitution was tolerated in first-century culture.

The one thing we need to see from all this is that Jesus

was not trying to set down a legalistic set of rules to determine when a divorce was allowable. The fact that in Matthew 5:32 Jesus seems to lend support to the school of Shammai about adultery as grounds for divorce does not mean that this is to be the one and only allowable basis for divorce, or even that adultery should mean divorce in every case.* He was not establishing rules at all: he was striking at the spirit in which people live with each other. And so when we study Jesus' teaching on divorce we must not look for the one or two or three things that make divorce allowable. No, we are to see to the heart of Jesus' teaching on human relationships within the context of first-century Palestine and seek to interpret those insights in the context of our world.

That is precisely what the apostle Paul did with regard to Corinthian society. The problem there was that many individuals had come into faith in Christ but had marriage partners who remained pagans. What was the status of that marriage relationship? And what should a believer do if the unbelieving spouse wanted to dissolve the marriage? If Paul had viewed Jesus' teaching legalistically, he would have had to tell Christians that they were bound to the marriage relationship unless there was adultery, since that is the one ground Jesus mentions for divorce (Matt. 5:32). But Paul did not do that. Instead, he instructed believers to stay in the marriage wherever possible. "But if the unbelieving partner desires to separate, let it be so; in such a case the brother or sister is not bound. For God has called us to peace" (1 Cor. 7:15).

What had Paul done? Had he ignored Jesus' teaching about divorce? No, not at all! He saw that the law of love

---

* See Matt. 5:32 and 19:9. But compare this with Mark 10:11 and Luke 16:18, where the same saying is given but without the exception clause about adultery. There is considerable debate over whether the exception clause in Matthew was a later addition to the text, since it seems to blunt the point of the teaching.

stood at the heart of Jesus' instruction on marriage and divorce, and he brought that central truth to bear on the Corinthian situation.

We must not turn Paul's counsel to the believers at Corinth into a new legalism, either. For example, some will teach that there are two and only two allowable grounds for divorce: adultery, because of Jesus' statement in Matthew 5:32, and desertion, because of Paul's statement in 1 Corinthians 7:15. Then if a woman comes in telling of marital rape and every other conceivable inhumanity, she is simply and grandly told that unless there is adultery or desertion she has no "biblical" basis for divorce. Such is the mentality (and the fatal weakness) of all attempts to turn the words of Jesus and Paul into a new legalism.

But if we are not given a set of rules, what guidance are we given on the question of divorce today? The first thing we can say is that God's intention from the beginning is for marriage to be a permanent "one flesh" reality. God created us male and female, and we are made to go together. We are complementaries—lifelong, permanent complementaries—and anything short of that violates God's intent.

So, although Christians may disagree on the allowable grounds for divorce, we can all agree that divorce is akin to cutting into a living organism.⁶ We are not talking about dissolving a convenient partnership that has gone sour; it is more like amputating an arm or losing a lung. Divorce cuts into the heart and soul of a "one flesh" unity. It is possible to survive the operation, but let us be unmistakably clear that we are talking about radical surgery, not just minor outpatient care.

This being the case, believers need to see divorce as an absolutely last-ditch solution after every possible means of grace has been exhausted. Divorce is not something we turn to just because we are having trouble in our marriage or because we have "fallen in love" with someone else. No, Christian marriage is a "one flesh" union, a single organism, and we split it asunder only when no other option is open to us. Chuck Swindoll wisely notes, "Two processes ought never be entered into prematurely: embalming and divorce."[7]

We must not give up too soon. The Bible literally bristles with the hope of forgiven and redeemed relationships. God is vitally interested in the success of our marriages. The resources of a caring Christian community are available to us. The love and care of friends and neighbors are at our disposal. The wise counsel of professionals and the healing prayer of those skilled in spiritual direction can be ours.

But we live in a fallen world, and there are times when, despite all our efforts, the marriage enters the valley of the shadow of death. Every resource has been used. Every possible way to bring healing and wholeness has been tried. Still the marriage is immersed in destruction and bitterness. When such is the case, the law of love (agape) dictates that there should be a divorce. If, indeed, divorce is understood as a consequence of the law of love, the evil that is present in most divorces will be absent, and, indeed, few divorces will occur. But believers will make sure of their obedience to the law of love in any divorce by making God their lawyer and judge through prayer.

The basis for divorce that conforms to the way of Christ is, therefore, precisely the same as the basis for marriage. When it is clear that the continuation of the marriage is substantially more destructive than a divorce, then the marriage should end.

If, as the final, radical solution to an unbearable situation, divorce *is* chosen, it must not be the cruel "throwing away" that Jesus condemned. Provision must be made for the equitable division of property and other resources so that neither partner is left destitute. Further, we must not "throw away" one another emotionally but seek to diminish bitterness and enhance cordiality in every way possible.

Now, there are those who in faithfulness to God choose to stay in a bad marriage. Their decision is not wrong, but it is extremely difficult. They need the prayer and support of the Christian community. We are to suffer with them, to bear them up, and to pray for the inbreaking of God's life and light. Should they later choose divorce, they have not failed or done wrong, and they need our generous love and acceptance.

I want now to speak a word to those of you who are divorced and who fear that you did not work hard enough to save your marriage. When I spoke earlier of divorce as the "absolutely last-ditch solution after every possible means of grace has been exhausted," your heart probably sank. Deep down you wonder whether you turned to divorce too quickly. "Perhaps," you think, "perhaps, if I had stayed with it a little longer, if I had tried one more time, things would have turned out differently." If that describes your quandary, I want to ease your mind *and* your heart. Perhaps you *have* failed—we all fail—but God is greater than our failure. His mercy and forgiveness and acceptance cover it all. You cannot reclaim the past, but you can be set free from its dominion. Stay where you are. Bathe in his love and care. Accept his offer of forgiveness and his invitation to a hopeful tomorrow.

CHRIST AND REMARRIAGE

What "hopeful tomorrow" is there for those who are divorced? Can they or should they look forward to the possibility of remarriage? These are perplexing questions for those who sincerely want to do what is right.

For example, many are genuinely troubled by Jesus' statement in the Sermon on the Mount that "whoever marries a divorced woman commits adultery" (Matt. 5:32; see also Mark 10:11-12; Luke 16:18; and Matt. 19:9). Does this mean that remarriage is never allowed for believers? The language seems straightforward enough, yet why would Jesus make such a stringent prohibition? What was he striking at by forbidding remarriage?

Jesus was dealing with the aggressiveness of the male in the context of first-century culture. In that day a man could drop a woman or take up a woman at a whim, and Jesus was striking at this destructive attitude of male domination. That is why we need to look very carefully, for example, at Jesus' visit with the woman at the well (John 4). He notes that she had had five husbands and that the man presently living with her was not her husband. Jesus, you see, was making a statement of fact—there was no note of condemnation in his words, for the woman had had no say in those divorces. She had been "thrown away" five times, and she had become such "used property" that a man no longer needed to marry her to have her. And Jesus was condemning the callousness by which a man would marry and divorce and remarry with the same ease as he might buy and sell cattle. (In fact, in Jesus' day a good cow would bring a higher price than a woman on the open market!)

In his teaching on remarriage Jesus was calling attention to the degraded relationship that existed between a man and a woman when the woman had been previously married. And in his day it was indeed a degraded and degrading relationship. It was something that kept the woman in perpetual fear, constantly in a corner. The man had her under his power, which made it easy for him to abuse her. In first-century culture the divorced woman was viewed as a "secondhand woman," and Jesus was saying that when a man thinks of a woman as a cheap commodity he has her in a vicious relationship. And that still persists today, doesn't it? Many women live through hell in our day simply because their husbands treat them as "used women."

Jesus therefore spoke of remarriage as adultery, not because there was anything inherently wrong with it, but because of the attitude of contempt with which the man lived with the woman. He used the word "adultery" to refer to the kind of sexual relationship that is wrong and damaging. He did the same thing when he described the lust of the heart as "adultery" (Matt. 5:28). In both instances Jesus was pointing to the destruction done to the relationship and was condemning it.

What we must *not* do is to turn these perceptive words of Jesus about remarriage into another set of soul-killing laws. We would not even consider doing that with Jesus' other sayings. If we took as law his words about eyes and hands that offend us, we would all have truncated bodies (Matt. 5:29–30). None of us would even think of turning into a new legalism Jesus' instruction not to invite friends or relatives or neighbors when we give a banquet (Luke 14:12). And we should not do that with his teaching on remarriage, either. It is true that in the absolute will of God his creative intent is for marriage to be a permanent "one flesh" reality that should never be severed. But in the absolute love of God, his redemptive intent covers the brokenness of our lives and sets us free.

Therefore, the basis for remarriage that conforms to the way of Christ is precisely the same as the basis for marriage and divorce. When the persons involved would be substantially better off and the kingdom of God more effectively advanced by remarriage, then the law of love indicates that remarriage can and even should occur.

In the context of remarriage the practical problems of how to deal with sexual hurts and emotional wounds must be considered. Often these are not things that an individual can handle alone. There are reasons why marriages fail, and seldom is the failure exclusively one-sided. And even if it were one-sided, there would still be wounds that need healing. A remarriage is unwise without substantial movement toward such wholeness.

The Christian fellowship can often help. Compassionate listening and healing prayer can do much. Resources such as counseling and good books to read can also help. Most of all, we can provide a context for intimacy—a womb of compassion in which it becomes safe to feel and to care and to risk loving once again.

Where have we come? We have sought to understand our sexuality within the light of the biblical vision of wholeness. We have endeavored to see what this vision might look like for the single person. We have tried to understand the context in which marriage, divorce, and remarriage conform to the way of Christ. We are now prepared to focus all that we have learned on the vow of fidelity.

9. The Vow of Fidelity

Fidelity is the ethical element which enhances natural love.
—EMIL BRUNNER

The sex issue demands a new and vigorous response. It cannot be a negative or reactionary response; rather, it must be active, creative, positive. We need a response that bears witness to the rich, positive attitude of Scripture toward human sexuality. We need a response that is for all Christians and can be experienced in ordinary life. And we need a response that deals compassionately and forthrightly with our distortions of sexuality's God-given functions. That response is best crystallized in the vow of fidelity. All believers—whether male or female, whether single, married, divorced, widowed or remarried—are called to fidelity in their sexual relationships.

Fidelity means to affirm our sexuality in all its manifold complexity. We celebrate the fact that we are sexual beings with needs for tenderness and compassion, love and friendship. We stoutly refuse to think of ourselves in nonsexual terms. We know that to make a person sexless is to dehumanize that person, and we will not do that to ourselves or anyone else. We will be faithful to our God-created nature as sexual beings.

Fidelity means loyalty to our calling. Some are called to the single life. When that call is given by God and is confirmed in the community of faith, then the disciple of Christ can rest contented in this provision of God's grace. There is no need to fret and stew or cast about for other options. The believing community welcomes this calling and gift without casting disparaging innuendos about the failure to find a mate.

Others are called to marriage. They welcome their calling and do not begrudge the time and energy needed to fulfill it. The Church understands and seeks to enhance their efforts to cultivate a strong marriage and family. The Church refuses to frustrate these goals by proliferating meetings and commitments that separate the family unit.

Fidelity means directing genital sex into its God-given channel in the covenant of marriage. We say no to promiscuity before marriage and adultery after marriage. We scorn the modern myth that sexual prowess is validated by sexual conquest. We confess the wholeness, the fullness, of sexual expression found in a permanent "one flesh" relationship in marriage.

Fidelity means an enduring commitment to the well-being and growth of each other. We commit ourselves to our partner's wholeness and happiness. We desire that every gift, every talent, every ability be given every opportunity to blossom and flower. Husband and wife are each called to sacrifice for the advancement of the other.

Fidelity means mutuality. Our faithfulness means a refusal to lord it over one another. No power plays, no phony superiority, no artificial hierarchy.

Fidelity means honesty and transparency with each other. Our commitment is to take off our masks, to come out from behind our facades. Our sharing is no "trivial pursuit," but a willingness to speak the deep inner language of the heart.

Fidelity means to explore the interior world of the spiritual life together. We pledge ourselves to pray together, to worship together, to celebrate together. We invite our mates into the inner sanctuary of our own soul. We invite them to be witnesses to our struggles, our doubts, our breakthroughs, our growth.

THE MEANING OF FIDELITY FOR SINGLES

Human sexuality has many aspects, only one of which is genital intercourse. If single persons will nurture and cultivate the many other aspects of their sexuality, the genital needs will come into perspective.

In fact, what we call sexual needs are not really needs at all but wants. The body needs food, air, and water—without these human life cannot long survive. But no one has yet died from a lack of sexual intercourse. Many have lived quite full and satisfying lives without genital sex—including Jesus!

So sexual intercourse is a human want, not a human need, and the difference is significant. To understand this difference can be tremendously liberating for singles. They are not half people, unfulfilled and incomplete. They do not need sexual intercourse to experience wholeness in their sexuality.

The apostle Paul dealt specifically with this matter of "sexual needs" in his Epistle to the Christians at Corinth. They lived in a sexually charged environment, and some, sensing the liberty that is in the gospel, assumed that this meant total sexual freedom, including sexual relations with prostitutes. Evidently their slogan was "All things are lawful in Christ." Paul responded, " 'All things are lawful for me,' but not all things are helpful. 'All things are lawful for me,' but I will not be enslaved by anything" (1 Cor. 6:12).

The Corinthians then raised the issue of sex as a normal physical need, just like food. In other words, if sex is a natural physical appetite like the appetite for food, what is wrong with satisfying our sexual need whenever the urge arises? Paul's answer was that "food is meant for the stomach," but "the body is meant for the Lord" (1 Cor. 6:13). He went on to argue that the digestive system is temporal and biological and has meaning only in earthly existence. But the body is the temple of the Holy Spirit and is destined for resurrection and filled with eternal significance. Therefore, we should "shun immorality." Promiscuous sex is such a travesty of the "one flesh" principle that it violates the spiritual aspect of our bodies. "Do you not know that he who joins himself to a prostitute becomes one body with her? For as it is written, 'The two shall become one.' But he who is united to the Lord becomes one spirit with him" (1 Cor. 6:16–17). Paul's word to us, then, is that sexual intercourse is so filled with eternal significance that it should always be reserved for the permanency of marriage. Therefore, believers who are single will want to abstain from genital sex; at the same time, they will want to develop fully the many other aspects of their sexuality.

Intimacy is one facet of our human sexuality that singles should nurture. The giving and receiving of love is essential; in fact, people have literally died from its absence. We need to find friendships that are caring and life-giving. Loneliness is epidemic today, and many singles suffer from it because they have tended to equate intimacy with coitus. But the truth is that many intimate and affectionate relationships can be cultivated without sexual intercourse.

Singles can find intimacy with people by entering into their lives on many different levels. Sharing books, ideas, goals, conversation, and much more helps us to become intimate with one another. Friendships can be with both men and women, both single and married. People are rich tapestries, and learning the varied and intricate weave of each life can be great fun.

Closely associated with intimacy is that aspect of our sexuality that is revealed by touch. Touching, holding, stroking—these are valid aspects of our sexuality that should not necessarily be tied to genital sex. In fact, Ashley Montagu, in his book *Touching*, has noted that, "In the Western world it is highly probable that sexual activity, indeed the frenetic preoccupation with sex that characterizes Western culture, is in many cases not the expression of a sexual interest at all, but rather a search for the satisfaction of the need for contact."[1]

Singles should welcome the touch, the hug, the warm embrace. These are essential ingredients in our human sexuality, and it is not wise to cut ourselves off from them. Nonerotic touching is of growing interest to those in the healing professions. Nurses are learning how to stroke and cuddle babies; psychiatric workers are learning the power of simply holding a hand; and people like Mother Teresa of Calcutta have helped us all discover the healing power of the compassionate touch.

Older singles especially need the life-giving experience of touch. Many go for months without ever being touched by another human being. If people in the churches, for example, were to go to the older members of the fellowship and simply give them a friendly hug or a backrub, they would be astonished at the emotional boost they would be providing.

Another aspect of our sexuality is the appreciation of beauty and physical attractiveness. Many single people draw back from the natural appreciation we have for a handsome man or a beautiful woman for fear that it will lead to the lust of the heart that Jesus condemned. But that is not necessary. It is quite possible to admire beauty of face and figure without lust. We can learn to enjoy the eyes, the hair, the smile, the strength of shoulders and arms, the curve of hips and legs, without leering and lusting. They are lovely gifts from the Creator's hand. How dare we despise them!

The enjoyment of beauty does not need to be wicked; it simply needs to be controlled. And it can be. We can appreciate the lovely curve of bicep or breast without falling headlong into uncontrolled passion. Just because the media tries to tie every attractive figure and every sensuous move to erotic sexuality does not mean that we have to buy into such a fantasy world. As children of the light, let us have beauty without lust and sensuousness without sensuality.

Still another aspect of our sexuality is the experience of communication. Initially this takes the form of simply talking about big and little things. Often it includes laughing. There are times too when it goes beyond human speech, so that quietly sitting together becomes a profound experience of communication.

In my first pastorate there was one individual whose home I would frequent just for conversation. We would often sit in his study and talk over great ideas and dream about what could be. Sometimes we would pause and pray together; often we would laugh together. But what I remember most are the times we would simply stop talking and sit together in profound silence. Enduring bonds are built through such experiences of communication, and they broaden and enhance our ability to be intimate.

Very often we in the Church place single people in a real bind regarding their sexuality. We hang them on the horns of a genuine dilemma: either marry, or bury your sexuality. But that dilemma is false, and they do not need to break it by opting for genital sex outside of marriage. There is another option. It is possible to affirm and celebrate one's sexuality and still reserve genital sex for the covenant of marriage.

Singles have the freedom in Christ to bring to the fore and develop to the full sexuality's many other aspects of intimacy and fellowship. This is the meaning of the vow of fidelity for single people.

THE MEANING OF FIDELITY FOR THE MARRIED

Marriage that is Christian is covenantal.[2] A covenant is a promise—a pledge of love, loyalty, and faithfulness. A covenant involves continuity—the sense of a common future to look forward to and a history to look back on together. A covenant means belonging—a commitment to a rich and growing relationship of love and care. Let us seek, then, to flesh out the meaning of fidelity within the covenant of marriage.

First, fidelity in marriage means monogamy. We argue for monogamy and against polygamy, but not on the basis of biblical laws on the subject. In fact, some people would be surprised to realize that for every verse of Scripture we could marshal in the defense of monogamy we could find two for polygamy. No, the Christian witness to monogamy is based upon the revelation of agape that we have in Jesus Christ. The love that Christ bequeathed to us is an "existence-for-the-other-person" reality.[3] To be blunt, polygamy dehumanizes the woman.* The woman is made to be part of the herd for the pleasure of the man. Polygamy is an affront to the law of love. Even in the Old Testament, we can see some of the harmful results of such an arrangement.

This does not mean that we insist that people in polygamous situations immediately change to monogamy upon conversion. I know a bright student from Nigeria who has a wife and four lovely children. His father, however, had seven wives. Recently his father died, and by custom the seven wives reverted to the son. Now, for my friend to throw these women out would be terribly destructive, and so he has decided to keep all of them as his wives. He will be a husband to them in the sense of providing for their physical needs; however, he has told all seven that he will not be a husband to them sexually and

---

* I am aware that technically *polygamy* refers to multiple mates of either sex. (*Polyandry* means many husbands and *polygyny* means many wives.) Most people, however, think of polygamy in terms of multiple wives, and the practice of polygamy in most cultures has been in that direction.

therefore has given them freedom for sexual expression outside of marriage. If later they have a chance to marry someone else, he will give them a divorce—an "honorable discharge," if you will. These are certainly difficult decisions for a Christian caught in a polygamous culture, but I, for one, applaud his efforts.

Second, fidelity in marriage means a lifelong pledge to love and loyalty. Disciples must refuse to look for a way out of the covenant just because difficulties arise or romantic love cools. Difficulties are not a sign of a bad marriage; indeed, they often indicate health in the marriage. People who care for each other will have arguments and disagreements because they prize the relationship. If there never are any, it may be an indication that they just do not care anymore.

The disagreements and the arguments are not the problem but how we handle them. In *Letters to Karen*, Charlie Shedd has given his "Seven Official Rules for a Good Clean Fight" that have guided him and Martha throughout their marital disagreements, and I recommend them to you.[4] To this wise counsel I would add only one comment: never, but never, allow the conflict to become physically violent. Physical abuse damages the relationship far more deeply than we know. (And if one is looking for biblical grounds for divorce, certainly physical abuse should rank at the top.)

There are times when the conflict that a couple experiences seems unbearable. "Why try any longer?" they ask. We keep trying longer because the stakes are so high, the reward of success is so great! And if we value a long life together, we will believe that our marriage is worth a great deal of effort and struggle. Our love is too good a thing to lose.

Having said this, I also know that in certain situations there may come a time when the conflict not only seems unbearable, it is unbearable. In such circumstances, fidelity suggests that wherever it is feasible the question of divorce be brought before the Christian fellowship for loving counsel and discernment. The Church is supposed to be in the business of healing ruptured marriages, or failing that, of healing the wounds of divorce.

No one is more keenly aware than I that many churches simply could not handle such a delicate and awesome responsibility. Often elders or other officially designated leaders are so divided on the issues of divorce and remarriage that they cannot help at all. Prejudice often reigns and blots out spiritual insight. Many leaders honestly feel that the business of the Church is to monitor budgets and maintain buildings, not to be amateur marriage counselors.

Yet amazing healing can come from a loving fellowship that is allowed to put its arms around a broken and bleeding marriage. It must be done with tenderness and humility. There can be no arrogance, no gossip, and no moralistic advice. The couple must feel assured that the fellowship accepts them and stands with them in their pain whatever the outcome. The main means of support are sympathetic listening and empathetic prayer. Sometimes what emerges from such experiences seems almost as real a resurrection as when Lazarus walked out of the tomb. Not always, but sometimes!

Third, fidelity in marriage means mutual subordination out of reverence for Christ. The apostle Paul places the principle of mutual subordination over all family relationships: "Be subject to one another out of reverence for Christ" (Eph. 5:21). He then proceeds to explain the details of how mutual subordination is to operate within the Christian household. It is truly amazing the responsibility for submission that Paul places upon the male, who, after all, stood at the top of the Hebrew patriarchial society. Paul calls for Christly submission through sacrificial love. First-century marriage customs did not view a woman as a full person, much less as someone to whom sacrifical love was due.

To be sure, Paul places a special responsibility for submission upon the wife: "Wives, be subject to your husbands, as to the Lord" (Eph. 5:22). He also places a special function upon the man: "The husband is the head of the wife as Christ is the head of the church" (Eph. 5:23).* There are those who wish Paul had not put it quite that way, since so often this teaching has been twisted into a way of keeping women under the male thumb. However, we must remember that here Paul is using the teaching approach of connection that is so common in Scripture. He is connecting with where people are and moving them to where he would like them to be.†

What Paul is doing in this passage is really quite astonishing. Informed by the gospel liberty that came from the example of Christ, he makes a radical break with the authoritarian, hierarchical system of the past—"be subject to one another out of reverence for Christ." But in the next breath he connects with the tradition of the past—"wives be subject . . . for the husband is the head." Regarding

---

* There have been more recent attempts to translate *kephale* not as "head" but as "source" and therefore distance the passage from a hierarchial model for the husband-wife relationship. Also, the verb "to submit" does not appear in verse 22; it says simply "wives to your husband." Obviously the verb must be supplied from verse 21 and therefore is precisely the same kind of submission that is required of all believers. For a thoughtful study of this issue, see Berkeley and Alvera Mickelsen, "The 'Head' of the Epistles," *Christianity Today,* 20 Feb. 1981, pp. 20-23.

† Jesus, for example, used this principle of connection when he said, "Think not that I have come to abolish the law and the prophets" (Matt. 5:17). But given what he had just been teaching them they could not think anything other than that he had come to abolish the law and the prophets! So without backing down on his radical disjuncture with the past, Jesus proceeds to show how his teaching connects with the past and fulfills it. Paul is doing the same thing in the Ephesians passage.

this passage, Elizabeth Achtemeier has noted: "The passage is ingenious. It has preserved the traditional view of the male as the head of the family, but that headship is a function only, not a matter of status or superiority. The understanding of the headship and of the wife's relation to it has been radically transformed. There is no lording it over the other here, no exercise of sinful power, no room for unconcern or hostility toward the other. Instead there is only the full devotion of love, poured out for the other, in imitation of Christ's faithfulness and yearning and sacrifice for his church, and of the church's like response to him."[5]

In all honesty, I think it must be said that the apostle Paul does not rush into the arms of egalitarian marriage. But neither does he fit in the embrace of authoritarian, hierarchical marriage. Certainly his strong words of mutual subordination and mutual marital responsibility are moving his readers, and us, along a continuum from a patriarchal or authoritarian approach toward a partnership or companionship approach. And all of us must find our marriage place somewhere along this continuum.

The direction Paul is heading in all of this is most clearly seen in his famous statement of Galatians 3:28, "There is neither Jew nor Greek, there is neither slave nor free, there is neither male nor female; for you are all one in Christ Jesus." In the Jerusalem Council of Acts 15, the Church dealt with the issue of cultural religion —"neither Jew nor Greek." Over many painful centuries the Church finally dealt with the issue of chattel slavery—"neither slave nor free." We can hope and pray that in the providence of God the Church will soon be able to deal successfully with the issue of sexism—"neither male nor female."

What does all this mean to you and me in a practical sense? Well, to borrow from Paul's language, each of us must work out our own marriage style in fear and trembling (see Phil. 2:12). Disciples of Christ are free and equal in the gospel to work through the meaning of mutuality and submission. But there must be no lording it over one another and no headstrong rebellion. Tenderness, love, and mutual respect must govern all decisions. Always remember that the "one flesh" experience of "bone of my bones and flesh of my flesh" gives us a predisposition to walk through life's decisions in concert. Mutuality is one of fidelity's many facets.

Fourth, fidelity in marriage means sexual restraint outside of the marital covenant. When I speak of sexual restraint I mean two things: one, no extramarital genital sex and, two, expression of nongenital sexuality that is controlled by the good of the marriage and the well-being of the spouse.

The first statement needs little clarification. Adultery is not acceptable in any form for those who are followers of Jesus Christ. It does violence to the "one flesh" reality of the marriage covenant and damages the marriage relationship.

The second statement may need to be explained a bit more. Although "all things are lawful . . . not all things are helpful," as Paul put it (1 Cor. 6:12). In one sense, after marriage we are no longer our own, no longer free to choose and act as we please. Every choice, every act, affects our spouse and our marriage. Now, we may not like that, but it is a fact of life and we might just as well make peace with it. Our spouse and marriage are more profoundly affected for good or for ill by the way we express our sexuality than by nearly anything else in our lives.

This does *not* mean that we repress our sexuality outside marriage. Oh, no, hardly anything will damage the marriage more. We must be human; we need intimacy, touch, meaningful conversation, and much more outside the marriage bonds. Otherwise we will be asking the marriage to carry more than is reasonable for even the healthiest relationship.

But we really must be sensitive to how our actions and even our thoughts affect our marriage. For example, if I give all my emotional energy and attention to counseling and other relationships so that I come home with no emotional reserves for my wife and children, I am committing "emotional adultery." Both Carolynn and the boys need and deserve my emotional energy. If I am not giving Carolynn what she needs from me emotionally, I must make whatever changes are necessary to better fulfill the vow of fidelity.

Now Carolynn is involved in some things in which I have no interest. I discuss with friends some issues that she finds boring. That's fine. We want to give each other plenty of freedom and flexibility. But we also want to be sensitive to how our actions and activities affect each other. We need to maintain open and free communication —listening, not just to each other's words, but to feeling tones, body language, the language of the heart and of the spirit. As we listen, we are predisposed to restrain anything that would detract from the marriage. As Francis Moloney has noted, "The external restraint which love practises is often a mark of its freedom from internal limit."[6]

All of which leads to the fifth mark. Fidelity in marriage means sexual liberty within the marital covenant. Here we must truly let the liberty bells ring! When sex is in its own free, full channel of marriage, it is a rich and fulfilling adventure. At times the channel is fast and exciting, like the Colorado River. At other times it is quiet and placid, like the Mississippi. Often it is deep and strong, like the Columbia.

Paul sounded the high note of sexual liberty within marriage when he declared, "The husband should give to his wife her conjugal rights, and likewise the wife to her husband" (1 Cor. 7:3). Now, you might be thinking that that sounds a lot more like obligation than liberty, but I can tell you the women in Paul's day saw liberty in every word of that command, and so did the men, I'm sure, once they understood all that it meant. The call is to give ourselves sexually to each other freely and without reserve. Note the equality of rights. It is not the husband's rights and the wife's duties. There is mutual giving and receiving. Men, your wife deserves to be satisfied sexually. You are free within the covenant of marriage to do whatever would delight, whatever would please, whatever would satisfy. And women have the same liberty.

Coitus has larger purposes than procreation. Children are great, to be sure, but we must never confine sex to "baby making." Intimacy, self-disclosure, vulnerability, recreation—these and more all inform the sexual experience.

One of the great things about sex is the warmth, the love, the indefinable sense of knowing someone in the most intimate way possible. It is no accident that the Hebrew term for coitus is *yada'*, "to know." The sexual experience somehow ushers us into the subterranean chambers of each other's being.

No doubt the experience of self-disclosure and vulnerability that goes hand in hand with sexual intercourse contributes to this mysterious sense of knowing. There is something to the unashamed nakedness, the total giving of oneself that allows a couple to crash through the sound barrier of external niceties and into the inner circle of nearness. There is a sense in which the physical coupling is indicative of a deeper coupling—a uniting of heart, mind, soul, and spirit. It's wonderful, it's good, and even more, it's fun.

It is this aspect of fun, of recreation, that is, in many ways, the richest experience of all. Sex at its best, at its highest, at its holiest, is play. It is festivity; it is delight.

As C. S. Lewis said, "Banish play and laughter from the bed of love and you may let in a false goddess."[7]

We get to know each other in recreation in a way that is not possible when we are serious. Sex is an adventure; it is also a game. We delight in each other's bodies in a light, airy, happy way. We play together; we romp and frolic together. This is an essential element in our celebration of sex.

THE MEANING OF FIDELITY FOR THE CHURCH

We have tried to consider what the vow of fidelity might mean to single people and to married couples, but what about the corporate fellowship of believers? What does fidelity mean to the Church?

The first thing that we need to say to that question is that our understanding of what fidelity means must be drawn from the model we are given in God's covenant relationship with his people, and specifically Christ's fidelity to the Church. God's dogged faithfulness to his children in the Old Testament and Christ's tenacious love of his Church in the New Testament give us the content for the vow of fidelity. Our understanding of marriage must always be brought back to and judged by this paradigm. Paul puts it most graphically when he is dealing with the marriage union, "This is a great mystery, and I take it to mean Christ and the church." (Eph. 5:32).

When we understand marriage in light of God's covenant love for us, we are catapulted onto a new, positive level. Lewis Smedes writes, "The Christian concept of fidelity is based on the model offered to us by the marriage between God and his people. . . . If we use this model, we will avoid the sterile, passive caricature of fidelity that is mere absence of adultery. We will have a picture of someone who makes a solemn vow to enduring partnership and whose fidelity is measured in terms of creative love for his partner."[8] This model, however, can never remain theoretical. It must work its way into our practice. Let us turn, then, to the practical implications in the life of the Church.

The Church is first called to a ministry of prayer and spiritual direction. This is the business of the Church. Would to God that the Christian fellowship could provide an environment in which, for example, young couples could bring their questions about marriage and their leanings toward marriage to the fellowship for discernment, counsel, and blessing.

Not long ago I was part of a "meeting for clearness" for a young couple.* They were in love and everyone had encouraged them to get married, and yet they were not sure. They sought guidance from a group of spiritually discerning persons, and so we met together in our home for an afternoon. It was a precious time of laughing and praying and sharing with each other. During the course of the afternoon, the young woman, who was a "preacher's kid," shared that everything she had done all her life was, at least in part, because others wanted her to do it. She was always doing things to please her parents or to please the congregation, and she was afraid that she was entering into this marriage only because everyone else thought they were the "ideal couple." This, of course, was the key to the problem, and once it surfaced we were all able to look at it and deal with it. The final prayer of blessing that a woman minister in our group gave to the couple was deeply moving. She went over to them, laid her hands upon them, and prayed in such

---

* In simple terms a "meeting for clearness" is a gathering of spiritually discerning people to help an individual or couple discern the mind of God about a matter of concern to them. Corporately we are seeking "clearness" from the Lord. The most common matters that are brought to clearness meetings are marital decisions and vocational choices.

tender and edifying words that I thought surely we were in heaven . . . and perhaps in a way we were. The two are now married and are vital members of our church fellowship. This was only one small event for a single couple, but this experience needs to be multiplied tens of thousands of times in churches everywhere.

There is so much more that we can do. We can all be glad for the good that has come from the Marriage Encounter movement that exists in many denominations, and we can only hope that it will increase. Here at the university, we have a program for engaged couples adapted from Marriage Encounter called Fit to Be Tied. As I write today, over fifteen couples are participating in this weekend experience and have just walked by my window on their way to the dining commons. Inwardly I pray for these marriages-to-be. What a wonderful ministry this program is! In this city we also have a program for people whose marriages are near shipwreck. We call it Recovery of Hope. It has been so well received that plans are now being made to establish it nationally. But these programs are only a drop in the bucket. The work is great and the laborers are few.

Church, do you get the idea? Stop wasting precious time and energy on committee meetings that discuss nothing. Stop carrying on business meetings that deal with everything except the business of the Church. Those marriages, those precious lives are the business agenda for the Church! Let us get on with it!

And then there are weddings. Even in our day of secularization, the Church still plays a prominent role in many weddings. Let us do something really significant with the opportunity. Let us have weddings that are genuine invitations to fidelity, to a lifetime call to marriage. Then the gathered fellowship can truly be "witnesses" to the rightness of marriages.

A few years back, I was at the wedding of a lovely

couple who had gone through a clearness meeting and who had asked the church to approve their intention for marriage which was done in a regularly called business session. Then at the wedding, rather than having the customary guest book, the couple had a large document that they asked all three hundred guests to sign as legal witnesses at the appropriate time in the ceremony. It was touching to walk to the front of the church and declare my conviction, both verbally and in writing, that I believed this marriage to be "in the Lord."

For the Church to "witness" and "bless" a marriage involves ongoing accountability for its success. We have dozens of useless committees; how about a useful one charged with encouraging the healthy growth and maturing of young marriages? Visiting homes, suggesting reading material, friendship counseling, and much more could make up the committee's agenda. And why not have another committee concerned with the health of established marriages?

We have a special service to begin marriages, why not a special service for the healing and blessing of existing marriages? Couples could come to the altar together; ministers could lay hands on them and offer prayers for the marriage to go from strength to strength.

C. S. Lewis has suggested that we need two kinds of marriages: one civil that is governed by the state and one Christian that is governed by the Church.[9] I agree. In this way the Church would be responsible for overseeing the health and success of Christian marriages. Marital problems, divorce, remarriage, and more would be issues for the community of faith to lovingly deal with. The believing fellowship would need to oversee the care of widows, widowers, divorcées, and the victims of desertion. In short, the care of Christian marriages would be the business of the Church.

THE SEXUALLY DISENFRANCHISED

We have been looking at what it means to be faithful before God with regard to our sexuality. In every case, we have taken for granted the fact that we are sexual beings. At no point did we need to convince ourselves of this fact. There are people, however, that have been shoved outside the world of sexualness. They have been thought of, by and large, as nonsexual beings. The vow of fidelity means a new awareness of and responsibility to the sexually disenfranchised.[10]

The physically disabled are considered nonsexual persons by many. The myth that the physically disabled are totally incapable of any sexual expression and therefore uninterested in sex only serves to isolate them all the more. However, studies have shown that even people with spinal cord injuries are often capable of *"achieving orgasm in spite of complete denervation of all pelvic structures."*[11]

How can we respond to the needs of the physically disabled? We can refuse to ignore their sexuality. We can recognize the wholesome value of fantasizing that can be so important to the sexual expression of the disabled. We can encourage couples to use a wide range of pleasuring techniques, all the way from stroking the face to oral-genital sex. One of the most valuable capabilities of the disabled is the ability to provide sexual pleasure to a spouse. Even if the individual is unable to experience orgasm, it is tremendously rewarding and stimulating to be able to give an orgasm to one's spouse.

Nor should we regard the seriously ill as nonsexual beings. The fact that death may be drawing near does not mean that all sexual interest and activity should or will disappear. "Indeed, the patient may often feel the desire for increased sexual activity with the spouse, as a way of clinging to life's vitalities and as a way of coping with death's anxieties."[12]

In spite of all the difficulties that the terminally ill face in carrying on a sexual life, it is often immensely rewarding. "Patients and their spouses report the deepening of their bonds and the clarifying of their real values. They report a more intense orientation to the possibilities of the present moment with each other, and the graceful appreciation of just being, not always doing."[13]

What can the Church do? Much. Let us train our pastors and chaplains to deal frankly and compassionately with this aspect of life rather than avoiding it. Let us encourage hospitals and other facilities to set aside rooms for conjugal visits. Maybe the Church could even volunteer to furnish rooms with large beds, soft lights, and comfortable furniture. Let us train ordinary folk in the pew in the healing art of touch—rubbing the back, combing the hair, holding the hand—intimate experiences all.

James Nelson tells the story of a colleague in the clergy that is a helpful illustration of the concern we should have for the need for intimacy of the seriously ill. " 'His mother was dying of cancer. Her body was clearly showing the ravages of the disease, and she was distressed by her altered appearance. On the one hand, she was resistant to the visits of those close to her because of her disfigurement. Yet, at the same time, her need for physical closeness and personal intimacy was great. Her son came to the hospital to visit, and as they talked, he rubbed her back to relieve some of the pain. After a time, sensing her need for even greater closeness, he lay down on the hospital bed beside her and held her closely in his arms. They talked for a long time that afternoon, sharing thoughts and feelings more deeply than ever before. Later that night she died.' It was, said my friend, clearly . . . an experience of physical closeness which deepened love's bonds and eased the pain of impending death."[14]

The aging is another group that we see as nonsexual. Our contemporary mania for identifying sex with youth and physical attractiveness only accentuates the problem. Yet the older members of our community continue to have sexual desires. The notion that the sex drive plummets rapidly to zero sometime after the age of sixty-five is simply false. Studies show that many people remain sexually active into their eighties and beyond.[15]

How can the Church respond? We can insist that nursing homes and retirement centers have facilities with beds large enough to allow married couples to sleep together. We can encourage widowed persons to remarry if they wish to rather than stay "faithful" to the dead spouse. We can work to change the Social Security laws so that remarriage for the elderly will not be an economic liability. We can give social permission for masturbation and allow for the needed privacy. We can encourage touching, holding, hugging.

Lastly, there is the mentally retarded. Often we think of these good people as nonsexual beings, but research indicates just the opposite. The overwhelming majority are keenly aware of their own sexuality, and most are very aware of their own genital needs and desires. Unfortunately, the institutional environment is usually not conducive to wholesome sexual development. Men and women are frequently segregated; there is seldom any privacy.

What can we do? We can insist that the mentally retarded receive as much sex education as is feasible. Studies show keen interest by the mentally retarded in learning about their sexuality. They are left out of so much of life; it is wrong to withhold sex education if we can possibly do otherwise.

The question of sterilization of the mentally retarded must be handled with great sensitivity. On the one hand, individual rights must be protected and, on the other hand, genetic mental retardation needs to be curbed. If the matter of unwanted pregnancy can be resolved, we can encourage the possibility of marriage. The mentally retarded have as great a capacity for love and relationship as you or I, perhaps greater. We should not deny them this opportunity. When marriage is undertaken, then allowance should be made for the couple to live together, even if it is within the institution.

FIDELITY IN PERSPECTIVE

We have sought to travel a long way. We have looked at the vow of fidelity for the single, for the married, and for the Church. We have considered a few ways we can respond to the sexually disenfranchised. Always remember, fidelity is not a static set of regulations; it is a vibrant, living adventure. It is not so much a way to suppress lust as a way to orient our lives toward a unifying goal. Fidelity is the sine qua non of unity and focus.

PART III
Power

10. Destructive Power

We live in a world possessed. And we know it.
—JOHAN HUIZINGA

If money hits us in the pocketbook, and sex hits us in the bedroom, power hits us in our relationships. Power profoundly impacts our interpersonal relationships, our social relationships, and our relationship with God. Nothing touches us more profoundly for good or for ill than power.

Power can destroy or create. The power that destroys demands ascendency; it demands total control. It destroys relationship; it destroys trust; it destroys dialogue; it destroys integrity. And this is true whether we look through the macrocosm of human history or the microcosm of our own personal histories.

What does the power that destroys look like? Think of Adam and Eve in the garden—given every pleasure, every delight, everything necessary for a good life. Yet they wanted more; they grasped and grabbed in a headlong rush to be like God, to know good and evil. *The sin of the garden was the sin of power.* They wanted to be more, to have more, to know more than is right. Not content to be creatures, they wanted to be gods.

That spirit festers within us, doesn't it? For us, it is never enough to enjoy good work. No, we must obtain supremacy; we must possess; we must hoard; we must conquer. The sin of power is the yearning to be more than we are created to be. We want to be gods.

Philosophy professor Arthur Roberts speaks of the little tin idols we make of ourselves in type and the colored mirror, television.[1] We chase our reflected image down broad highways and fling our metal birds at the planets. "Hallelujah to us!" we shout. But the sounds hurt our ears, and the sights burn our eyes, and the ashes fill our mouths, and the whole thing stinks to high heaven. And God, watching, weeps.

For Adam and Eve, the will to power meant a rupture in their relationship with God. The experience of communion and dialogue with God was broken. They hid from him. We, too, hide from God. The will to power ruptures our relationship with him. Our headstrong determination to do it our way makes God's voice distant and his word hard to hear.

What does the power that destroys look like? Think of King Saul and his insane envy of David. Saul was the king; he was supposed to wield the power. But power cannot command affection, and the people loved David. Saul was powerless to control the hearts of people, so he turned in rage against David. He would rather have murdered than allow power to slip through his fingers. How tragic to see the relationship between Saul and David destroyed because of Saul's lust for power. It even destroyed Saul's relationship with his own son Jonathan.

Power destroys relationships. Lifelong friends can turn into mortal enemies the moment the vice-presidency of the company is at stake. Climb, push, shove is the language of power. Nothing cuts us off from each other like power. Even ordinary human conversation is destroyed by it. Paul Tournier writes, "Power is the greatest obstacle in the way of dialogue. . . . We pay dearly for our power; we live the drama of the lost dialogue."[2] And we see this tragic drama everywhere: between husband and wife, between parent and child, between employer and employee. Power's ability to destroy human relationships is written across the face of humanity.

What does the power that destroys look like? Think of

the disciples arguing bitterly over who would be the greatest in the kingdom of God. These arguments must have been intense, because they are mentioned in all four Gospels. The end result of this constant bickering and jockeying for position was the undermining of harmony among the apostolic band. From that point on, they would have been suspicious of each other's motives.

Amazing isn't it, grown-up people deeply exercised over who is at the top of the heap! Of course, whenever we are deciding who is the greatest, we are also deciding who is the least. This is the problem for us, isn't it? To be the least means to be helpless. If we are at the "bottom rung" of a company, we are completely without authority, completely without power.

Whenever this argument came up among the disciples, Jesus would sit a child in the middle of the group and teach them about greatness. What was he doing? He was pointing to the ability of children to work and play without the need for supremacy. Have you ever watched little children in the backyard making mud pies? You see, they are simply content to make mud pies while the rest of the world goes on in its mad rush for "greatness." It reminds me of Tolkien's description of Aüle, one of the original eight guardians and governors of Middle Earth, "But the delight and pride of Aüle is in the deed of making, and in the thing made, and neither in possession nor in his own mastery; wherefore he gives and hoards not and is free from care, passing ever on to some new work."[3] You see, in the kingdom of God the issue of greatness is an issue that is beside the point. Others may fight and struggle over the question of who is the greatest, but for the disciple of Christ it is a virtue to ignore the question. Paul says, "There is great gain in godliness with contentment" (1 Tim. 6:6).

What does the power that destroys look like? Think of Simon Magus and his desire to merchandise the Holy

Spirit (Acts 8:9-25). Simon was a magician in Samaria who evidently had considerable power, because the people said of him, "This man is that power of God which is called Great" (Acts 8:10). Simon, however, came under the influence of Philip's preaching and was converted to faith in Jesus Christ. Later Peter and John came to Samaria and laid hands on the people, and they received the Holy Spirit. When Simon saw the power that came through the laying on of hands, he "offered them money, saying, 'Give me also this power, that any one on whom I lay my hands may receive the Holy Spirit'" (Acts 8:18-19). Peter, of course, rebuked him for thinking he could merchandise the power of God, and we are given indication that Simon repented of his evil intent.

The sin of Simon Magnus was to try to use the power of God for his own ends. This is the sign of all false religion, but it is exactly this mentality that has come over so much of Christianity in our day. Cheryl Forbes writes, "The cassock of righteousness becomes the vestment of power."[4]

Power can be an extremely destructive thing in any context, but in the service of religion it is downright diabolical. Religious power can destroy in a way that no other power can. Power corrupts, and absolute power corrupts absolutely; and this is especially true in religion. Those who are a law unto themselves and at the same time take on a mantle of piety are particularly corruptible. When we are convinced that what we are doing is identical with the kingdom of God, anyone who opposes us *must* be wrong. When we are convinced that we always use our power to good ends, we believe we can never do wrong. But when this mentality possesses us, we are taking the power of God and using it to our own ends.

Those who are accountable to no one are especially susceptible to the corrupting influence of power. It was precisely this problem that caused Saint Benedict to establish the rule of stability. In the sixth century there were many wandering prophets and monks with no one to hold them accountable for what they said or did. But with the rule of stability they were drawn into communities in which mutual encouragement and discipline were possible. Today, most media preachers and itinerant evangelists suffer from exactly the same lack of accountability that the wandering prophets of the sixth century did. What is needed today is a modern Benedictine rule that would draw these powerful leaders into a disciplined and accountable fellowship.

What we must see is the wrongness of those who think they are always right. Jesus Christ alone is always right. The rest of us must recognize our own foibles and frailties and seek to learn from the correction of others. If we do not, power can take us down the path of the demonic.

PRIDE AND POWER

There is an intimate connection between pride and the destructive character of power. Samson was a man of immense power, power that was given by God. But pride filled his heart, and not only pride but arrogance as well. Before his enemies Samson boasts, "With the jawbone of an ass have I slain a thousand men" (Judg. 15:16). This unholy trinity of pride, arrogance, and power contributed to Samson's downfall.

Power is insidious when it is coupled with pride. Among the most dangerous people in our media-soaked culture are leaders who believe their own press releases. I remember once being honored at a large conference. I could only stay for twenty-four hours because of family commitments. The time was full of special luncheons and autograph parties and media interviews. By the end of the twenty-four hours, I told Carolynn, "We have to get out of here; I'm beginning to believe all these things people are saying about me." One can quickly lose all perspective. That is why those in positions of leadership must root themselves deeply in the experiences of ordinary life.

Of course, all of us suffer from vanity's lures, not just leaders. But leaders are especially susceptible today because of our infatuation with the media. Isn't it strange, for example, that we unquestionably assume that being on television is some kind of honor? Somehow we feel that television defines who the important people are. The idea is really silly, of course, but we hold to it nonetheless. In *Christ and the Media*, Malcolm Muggeridge suggests that if Jesus were going through the wilderness temptation today Satan would add a fourth temptation, namely, to appear on national television.

All of this makes pride one of the monumental problems of our day. Isn't it instructive that in a day when so many people struggle desperately for self-esteem we also have an abundance of people with over-inflated egos? When pride is mixed with power the result is genuinely volatile. Pride makes us think we are right, and power gives us the ability to cram our vision of rightness down everyone else's throat. The marriage between pride and power carries us to the brink of the demonic.

THE PRINCIPALITIES AND THE POWERS

The demonic is precisely where destructive power reaches its apex. The Bible speaks of very real cosmic spiritual powers that manifest themselves in the very real structures of our very real world. The apostle Paul's favorite term to describe this spiritual reality is "the principalities and powers," though he uses other terms as well—"authorities," "dominions," "thrones," "rulers," "the elemental spirits of the universe," "princes of this world," and still others. These "powers" account for the destructive bent of power that we see all around us. Indeed, it is only as we begin to understand what the Bible calls "the principalities and powers" that we can truly confront the power issue in our own lives.

We must not dismiss this teaching as the relic of a prescientific era. The Bible is dealing with a far more profound reality than forked-tailed demons in red pajamas or benign ghosts. The powers are not spooks floating around in the air preying on unwary individuals but spiritual realities that play a definite role in the affairs of human beings.

The powers are created realities. Paul tells us that in Christ "all things were created, in heaven and on earth, visible and invisible, whether thrones or dominions or principalities or authorities—all things were created through him and for him" (Col. 1:16). The powers were once related to the creative will of God; however, we no longer see them in this role. They are in revolt and rebellion against God their Creator. Our warfare, says Paul, is "against the principalities, against the powers, against the world rulers of this present darkness, against the spiritual hosts of wickedness in the heavenly places" (Eph. 6:12). Indeed, the Bible speaks of the powers as gods that seek to enslave and destroy (Gal. 4:8-10).

The powers are incarnational. They are the energizing forces behind human beings and social structures. When Paul tells us that the powers "crucified the Lord of glory," he is emphasizing that the crucifixion of Christ was far more than the work just of human personalities (1 Cor. 2:8). *

---

* First Corinthians 2:8 reads, "None of the rulers of this age understand this; for if they had, they would not have crucified the Lord of glory." "The rulers of this age" is a phrase that Paul uses to describe the powers. Almost all commentators agree that Paul here is not speaking of human beings but of superearthly realities. See Chapter 2 of *Christ and the Powers* by Hendrik Berkhof for more information (trans. John H. Yoder [Scottdale, Penn.: Herald Press, 1962]).

The powers, however, do not "possess" just individuals but organizations and whole structures of society. Institutions can and do often become nothing more than organized sin. There are fundamental spiritual realities that underlie all political, social, and economic systems. In back of brutal dictators and unjust policies and corrupt institutions are spiritual principalities and powers. Walter Wink writes, "the 'principalities and powers' are the inner and outer aspects of any given manifestation of power. As the inner aspect they are the spirituality of institutions, the 'within' of corporate structures and systems, the inner essence of outer organizations of power. As the outer aspect they are political systems, appointed officials, the 'chair' of an organization, laws—in short, all the tangible manifestations which power takes. Every Power tends to have a visible pole, an outer form—be it a church, a nation, or an economy—and an invisible pole, an inner spirit or driving force that animates, legitimates, and regulates its physical manifestation in the world."[5]

When the apostle Paul says that our warfare is not against flesh and blood but against the principalities and powers, he does not mean that flesh and blood are unimportant. Not at all! He means that the real focus of our battle should be the powers that stand in back of the person or institution.

Organizations and whole nations are often defined and controlled by particular concepts and ideologies. There is a prevailing mood or spirit that gives unity and direction to whole groups of people. These moods are not created in a vacuum, but are closely tied to very genuine spiritual realities. Hence, when we speak of "the spirit of a group" we are perhaps saying more than we know.

For example, when Ku Klux Klan members gather together, the collective hatred is something that is greater than the sum of its parts. When a certain critical flashpoint of prejudice and ruthlessness is reached, a "mob spirit" erupts that no single individual is able to control. Spiritual powers are involved in the creation of such realities.

This is a terribly difficult concept for us to comprehend in our modern society. We are accustomed to viewing institutions as sterile, neutral structures that have nothing to do with the spiritual life. There has been, however, one outstanding historical event that can help us develop a new appreciation for the biblical emphasis upon the powers. When Adolf Hitler took over Germany, the powers of state and race took on hideous new dimensions. In the Third Reich the very idea of *volk*—race—became captive to the egomania of Aryan supremacy. Those who have seen the crematories of Dachau and Auschwitz do not find it hard to believe in the demonic powers.

What does this mean to us on a practical level? Well, when we look at our own insane drive to make it to the top, we must confront the powers of pride and prestige that grip our hearts. When there is a school board decision that does a disservice to children, we must confront the powers of vested interest and self-seeking that stand behind that decision. We must seek out the "spirit" that energizes the unjust law or the unjust corporate structure and seek to defeat *it* in the power of Christ.

DISCERNING THE POWERS

Amazing as it may seem, it is the Church's awesome responsibility to discern these spiritual powers. Among the gifts that the Holy Spirit gives to the people of God is the discernment of spirits (1 Cor. 12:8-10). We are given the ability to recognize the powers for what they are and to understand their hostility to the way of Christ.

Discerning the powers is not as easy as we may think at first. For example, when Hitler began his rise to power in Germany, he campaigned on a 25-point platform that included a vigorous German nationalism, a pledge to improve educational opportunities, a concern for "raising the standard of health in the nation," and a belief in "positive Christianity."[6] Now, you and I can look back on the Third Reich and easily see its demonic perversion, but in the midst of that wrenching experience virtually the only Christians who had eyes to see the hellish powers behind the Third Reich were the Confessing Church.* Pastor Martin Niemöller saw; Reich Bishop Müller did not.

This ministry of discerning the powers, fraught as it is with frustrations and pitfalls, is given to you and to me. We are to discern what is truly happening today, understand where it could lead us, and give a value judgment upon it.

Saint Francis of Assisi saw the people of his day in the grip of the power of mammon, and he joyfully called them to a new way. Once a man named Silvester saw Francis and Bernard distributing money to the poor; he was "seized with greed" and said to Francis, "You did not pay me all you owe me for those stones you bought from me to repair the churches." Saint Francis just stood there "marveling at his greed" and finally reached both hands into the money bag and gave to Silvester all the money his hands could hold. He then said, "If you ask for more, I will give you still more." Silvester went home with the money, but he soon "reproached himself for his greed." For three nights straight he had a

---

* The "Confessing Church" (Bekennende Kirche) was composed of Christians in Germany who opposed the takeover of the Church by Hitler's ecclesiastical puppet, Reich Bishop Müller. They drafted the famous Barman Confession of May 1934 which categorically rejected the supremacy of the state over the Church and confessed the Lordship of Jesus Christ. Among their leaders were Karl Barth, Martin Niemöller, and Dietrich Bonhoeffer.

vision from God telling him that Saint Francis was the one who had the true wealth. In the end, Silvester was freed from the spirit of greed and was enabled to give generously to the poor; in time he became "so holy and filled with grace that he spoke with God as one friend to another."[7]

What happened? Saint Francis had discerned the spiritual power of greed that possessed Silvester, and he was able, in the power of God, to free him from it.

How desperately we need to be freed from greed today! It is a spiritual power that grips us. The whole ethos of our nation is possessed by it. It exists at every level of society. If Christians would take the initiative in bringing about a national exorcism of greed, we might be able to open our hearts and hands to a hungry world once again.

Nearly a hundred and fifty years before the Civil War, John Woolman saw dire consequences for our bondage to the powers of racism and oppression. "I saw a dark gloominess hanging over the Land," he wrote. If people were not willing to "break the yoke of oppression," he saw that "the Consequence will be grievous to posterity."[8] It is a genuine tragedy that we as a nation were unwilling to heed his prophetic discernment. As G. M. Trevelyan has said, "Close your ears to John Woolman one century, and you will get John Brown the next, with Grant to follow."[9]

How desperately we need to be free of the spiritual powers of racism and oppression! These demons of the spirit are on the rise today. We can all be glad for the advances made during the civil rights movement, but we are now seeing alarming reversals. Would to God that Christians could lead the way to a new day of justice and brotherhood. It will happen if we can discern the powers and seek their defeat in the strength of the Lamb.

NAMING THE POWERS

"Test the spirits," says John (1 John 4:1). This is a task fraught with pitfalls, but one we cannot avoid. How do the powers manifest themselves today?

Mammon is one of the powers. Paul Tournier notes that, "the GNP is the modern Golden Calf."[10] Our wealth is not neutral. It is not sterile or inanimate. It is alive with spiritual power; it seeks to possess us. In Part I we took a long look at how we can conquer mammon in the power of the Lamb and bring it back to its divine intent.

Sex is one of the powers. Sex in our day is not just a need, like cheerful surroundings or friendly conversation. It is a power energized by lust, sensuality, and uncontrolled carnality. For untold millions it is an all-consuming passion. We cannot hear the old cliché, "Keep her barefoot in the winter and pregnant in the summer," without recognizing the language of power. We cannot look at the crimes of incest and rape without realizing that these are crimes of power. Sex is power, real power. There is nothing neutral or passive about it. It is alive with spiritual energy seeking to make a bid for supremacy over the hearts of men and women. In Part II we dealt with ways we can defeat the carnality of sexuality and bring it back to its God-given function of enriching human relationships.

Religious legalism is one of the powers. Paul declares, "If with Christ you died to the elemental spirits of the universe, why do you live as if you still belonged to the world? Why do you submit to regulations, 'Do not handle, Do not taste, Do not touch' . . . according to human precepts and doctrines?" (Col. 2:20-22). These "elemental spirits" are religious and ethical rules. Paul's point is that behind the religious traditions and regulations are spiritual powers, powers that have claimed autonomy and have made obedience to them the highest good.

The tragedy here is that the very thing that is designed

to lead us to God does exactly the opposite. The divine function of moral law is to bring us into obedience, but when it becomes an end in itself the demonic perversion called legalism rears its ugly head. These rules and regulations become rival gods holding us captive and demanding our total allegiance.

Religious legalism is one of the heaviest burdens human beings ever have to bear. Jesus warns us of those who will "bind heavy burdens, hard to bear, and lay them on men's shoulders; but they themselves will not move them with their finger" (Matt. 23:4).

Technology is one of the powers. In the broad sense, technology standardizes procedures and behavior in order to produce efficiency. In fact, efficiency is the sacred law of technology. Of course, there is nothing wrong with efficiency and productivity—not until it becomes an ultimate value. "Technology tends more and more to become a new god," notes John Wilkinson.[11]

When efficiency becomes a new god, we have the supremacy of standardization over spontaneity. We all feel this, don't we? When we receive a telephone call from a computer we know that efficiency has won over spontaneity. When we fill out punch cards that ask for numbers rather than names, we know that standardization has won over individuality. We have become things and we sense deep inside that our personhood has been violated.

When we say, "If it is efficient it *must* be good," we have given ultimate significance to technology. For the Christian, other questions must counterbalance the question of efficiency: Will human beings be crushed in the process? Will it damage individual self-esteem? These and many other questions need to be considered as we seek to discern the spirituality of technology and to respond to it appropriately.

Narcissism is one of the powers. Narcissism is excessive self-love, and it is the dominant mood of our age. Pleasure seeking and self-satisfaction are at the top of the priority list. Advertisers scream, "Grab all the gusto you can get," and we sing, "I did it my way." The very idea of sacrifice for the good of others seems ludicrous.

We must reject the narcissism of our age. We as believers know that the good life is not found in selfishness but in self*less*ness. We who follow the crucified Christ know that to lose ourselves is to find ourselves (Luke 9: 24–25).

Militarism is one of the powers. The divine purpose of military power is to restrain chaos, but in our day militarism is doing precisely the opposite. Today the purpose is not to prevent chaos but to promote it. Military strategists plot, not how to make the world more stable, but how to make it less stable. Terrorism and spy networks are the order of the day.

In saying this, I am not criticizing any particular nation or institution or group. In our day the creation of chaos has become an all-pervasive mood of militarism. The final end of this demonic perversion is the ultimate exercise of power in destroying the world. Christians must call militarism away from its evil bent.

Absolute skepticism is one of the powers. Absolute skepticism is so pervasive a belief in university life today that it must be considered a spiritual power hostile to an honest search for truth. The task of the university is to pursue truth—all truth—and yet in many cases precisely the reverse is happening today. What was once a humble position of genuine agnosticism has been turned into the arrogance of absolute skepticism. Not knowing, not being sure, becomes the final dogma that must never be violated.

C. S. Lewis, in his novel *That Hideous Strength*, depicts the ultimate destructiveness of the university when it is given over to deception and a desire to obscure the truth.

We must call the university back to its humble mission of truth seeking. The university should be the place par excellence where the big questions of purpose, meaning, and values are relentlessly pursued, and when answers are found they should be embraced and not denied.

Demonic spiritual powers have a pronounced impact upon the world in which we live. They stand behind, influence, and energize evil individuals and institutions. They manifest themselves in such things as mammon, sex, religious legalism, technology, narcissism, militarism, and absolute skepticism.

DEFEATING THE POWERS

We must never fool ourselves. The powers against which we wage the Lamb's war are very strong. Satan prowls about like a "roaring lion" seeking those whom he may devour (1 Pet. 5:8). This is no minor league game we are playing; we are in the major leagues, and the stakes are high. The principalities and powers do not just have power—they *are* power. They exist as power; power is how they manifest themselves. To dominate, to control, to devour, to imprison, is their very essence. How then do we defeat the demons without and the monsters within?

First, we must recognize that Christ has already defeated the powers. In his death and resurrection, Christ "disarmed the principalities and powers and made a public example of them, triumphing over them in him" (Col. 2:15). On the cross Christ could have summoned ten thousand angels to his aid, but instead he renounced the mechanisms of power in order to defeat the powers of the abyss. In the death and resurrection of Jesus Christ, the powers were defeated here in our time-space-energy-mass world.

Second, we defeat the powers by cultivating the gift of

discernment. Any serious engagement with the powers necessitates the "discerning of spirits" (1 Cor. 12:10, KJV). Until we have eyes to see the spiritual powers that energize a family, a corporate structure, or a government agency we do not fully understand it.

You may wonder how such a discerning spirit is obtained. It comes first by asking for it. "You do not have, because you do not ask," said James (James 4:2). We ask. We also listen: listen to God, listen to those around us, listen to what is occurring in our world. And we invite God to teach us what it all means. We also gather in groups of faithful believers to share insights and to listen together, for no single individual can know all of God's will. We do all this with a good deal of humor and humility: humor, because we must never take ourselves too seriously; humility, because we must take God's word through others with utmost seriousness.

Third, we defeat the powers by forthrightly facing the "demons" within. Right at the outset, we all need to see and to address the powers that nip at our own heels. Otherwise we will utilize the tactics of the very powers we oppose and, in the end, become as evil as they. We must look squarely into the face of our own greed and lust for power and see them for what they are. We must look at ourselves spiritually and discern ourselves spiritually.

The glory is that we do not do this alone. The blessed Holy Spirit comes alongside of us and comforts and encourages as he convicts and reproves. He leads us into the inner solitude of the heart where he can speak to us and teach us. Sometimes this will take the form of private retreat for prayer and reflection. More often it will be an inner retreat of the heart in the midst of life's many activities and demands. In this interior silence we hear the *Kol Yahweh*, the voice of the Lord. Hearing, we turn from our violence, our greed, our fear, our hate. Hearing, we turn to Christ's love and compassion and peace. We rejoice over every conquest of the Lamb, and as the Lamb conquers and wins our hearts, every victory feast has a place setting for our enemies.

Fourth, we defeat the powers by an inner renunciation of all things. In a posture of total renunciation, we have nothing to lose; the powers have no control over us. Suppose the powers take our goods and possessions—no matter, our possessions are only on loan from God; protecting them is more his business than it is ours. Suppose the powers seek to destroy our influence by defaming our reputation—no matter, our reputation is not ours to protect, and we could not do it even if we wanted to. Suppose the powers throw at us the fear of death itself—no matter, we belong to One who can lead us through death's dark pathway into greater life. So, you see, we simply have nothing to lose. We are positionless and possessionless, and this complete and total vulnerability is our greatest strength. You cannot take something from someone who has nothing.

Fifth, we defeat the powers by rejecting the weapons of power of this world. We stop trying to manage and control others. We refuse to dominate or intimidate. As Walter Wink has written, "The direct use of power against a Power will inevitably be to the advantage of The Powers That Be."[12]

The only way we can battle the principalities and powers is in the life and power of the Holy Spirit. Now, in saying this I am not trying to catapult this entire issue into the realm of the pietistic or the theoretical. Quite the contrary. The Holy Spirit wants to be an active agent in our lives in the most practical and socially concrete way.

If we attack the form of power alone without defeating the angel or spirit that energizes that form, we have accomplished nothing. For example, most revolutions in the world have struggled to throw out one corrupt and self-serving government only to have another corrupt and self-serving government take its place. The failure is to understand that the real battle has more to do with the powers of greed, vested interest, and egomania than with actual persons and structures of government. We must focus our attention on both the institution *and* the spirituality of the institution.

Sixth, we defeat the powers by using the weapons of Ephesians 6. To reject the weapons of this world does not leave us defenseless. Far from it! Who needs guns and tanks and MX missiles when we are given the far greater weapons of truth, righteousness, peace, faith, salvation, the word of God, and prayer (Eph. 6:10-18)! These weapons are more powerful than we can possibly imagine. Paul insists that "the weapons of our warfare are not worldly but have divine power to destroy strongholds" (2 Cor. 10:4).

Often we have rendered these spiritual weapons harmless by ignoring the social context of the Ephesians passage. We have turned them into pietistic weapons that have nothing to do with the world of mammon or militarism. We talk glibly of Roman shields and helmets and never once guess that we are called to arm ourselves for a real battle against the spirituality of institutions and cultures and all forms of demonic incarnation.

Another way we have sought to sterilize these weapons is by teaching that they are all "defensive." This is simply not the case. The Roman military was the most powerful and ruthless killing machine of that day. The equipment Paul describes was not solely for standing one's ground, but for advancing against the enemy. No doubt Paul had in mind the "Roman wedge," which was an effective V-shaped formation that made full use of a specially designed, elongated shield with which a soldier covered two-thirds of his own body and one-third of his comrade to the left. This ingenious arrangement forced soldiers to work together for mutual protection and attack. It was "the most efficient and terrifying military formation known up to that time and for some thousand years after."[13]

Paul's military metaphor is a wonderful picture of the company of the committed working in concert, advancing against the powers, conquering in Christ's name. The gates of hell cannot stand against such a unified and determined offensive. James Nayler writes, "He [Christ] puts spiritual weapons into their hearts and hands. . . . to make war with his enemies, conquering and to conquer, not as the prince of this world . . . with whips and prison, tortures and torments on the bodies of creatures, to kill and destroy men's lives . . . but with the word of truth . . . returning love for hatred, wrestling with God against the enmity, with prayers and tears night and day, with fasting, mourning and lamentation, in patience, in faithfulness, in truth, in love unfeigned, in long suffering, and in all the fruits of the spirit, that if by any means he may overcome evil with good."[14]

A PERSONAL REFLECTION

C. S. Lewis notes that "there are two equal and opposite errors into which our race can fall about the devils. One is to disbelieve in their existence. The other is to believe and to feel an excessive and unhealthy interest in them. They themselves are equally pleased by both errors and hail a materialist or a magician with the same delight."[15] If we err today it is usually in the direction of the materialist, for that is the dominant mood of our age. Normally I am hesitant to interject personal experiences but in this case I think it might be helpful.

Although I had finished writing this book, I did not feel satisfied with these last chapters on power. So I sent the first nine chapters to my editor, explaining that I had decided to rewrite the final four. By Wednesday of the first week of rewriting I began to sense a heaviness and darkness come over me. I am sure it was partly due to emotional and physical weariness with the task, for I had been writing for nine months with hardly a break and had done considerable research before that. (I had, however, been very careful to discipline myself to obtain adequate sleep and exercise.)

By Friday the darkness was nearly overwhelming. I felt as though I never wanted to write again, speak again or teach again. I would look over a chapter and want to throw it away. I tried to think of some way to cancel the entire project. Even now, I cannot fully explain what I was feeling. To use the words of George Fox, I was nearly overcome by an "ocean of darkness."[16]

Anyone who has studied psychology will know that what I am describing shows telltale signs of the beginning stages of exhaustion. That was certainly a factor in my experience, but it did not seem to account for everything I felt. There seemed to be more to it, some deeper greater foreboding.

On Saturday I went to my office to write, but with no hope of producing anything worth reading. During a period of meditation and prayer, I thought of the time Martin Luther threw his ink bottle at the devil. Instinctively I grabbed my pen and threw it against the wall, breaking it. I said to myself, "Well, if the devil is here I probably missed him!" I tried to arm myself with the weapons of Ephesians 6, but it seemed to do little good.

In the late morning a group of five friends came to pray for me. We talked only briefly, and then they prayed quietly. Though I cooperated with their efforts, I had absolutely no expectation that it would do any good. I felt nothing at all.

After they left, however, the heaviness began to lift just a bit. As the day went on, things got brighter and brighter, until by evening the darkness was completely gone. I was able then to finish my task without further oppression.

A few days later one member of the group that had come Saturday morning told me that during the prayer she had seen the entire room being filled with the light of Christ and the evil powers being thrust outside. I did not see anything, but I do not doubt her word, for she is a spiritually alert person and not in the least given to mystic fantasy. I believe her also because the ocean of darkness was indeed overcome by the ocean of light and life.

All of this may sound strange to you, but it did happen, and perhaps it can stand as a witness that the principalities and powers are real and do indeed wage war against us. It can also witness to the importance of having others who can help us as we do battle against the powers in this dark, evil age.

The powers are strong, but Christ is stronger still. The defeat of the powers is sure. We live in that life that overcomes the world, and we should expect to see the overthrow of the kingdom of darkness and the inauguration of the Lamb's rule of righteousness wherever we go.

11. Creative Power

The only cure for the love of power is the power of love.
—SHERRI MCADAM

There is a power that destroys. There is also a power that creates. The power that creates gives life and joy and peace. It is freedom and not bondage, life and not death, transformation and not coercion. The power that creates restores relationship and gives the gift of wholeness to all. The power that creates is spiritual power, the power that proceeds from God.

What does the power that creates look like? Think of Joseph sold into slavery, thrown into prison without hope but later rising to a position of great power and influence in the mightiest nation of the time. What a pilgrimage! In this position Joseph was able to combine spiritual discernment with political clout to avert a disastrous famine. Then the fateful day arrived when his brothers— the very ones who had sold him into slavery—came seeking famine relief. Joseph was faced with the great test of power. It would have been a perfect opportunity for revenge, but instead he chose to use his power for reconciliation. Scripture tells us that Joseph was overcome with emotion and compassion for his brothers. Joseph "could not control himself" and "wept aloud," and finally "he fell upon his brother Benjamin's neck and wept; and Benjamin wept upon his neck. And he kissed all his brothers and wept upon them" (Gen. 45:1-15). This is a beautiful story of relationships restored by the exercise of creative power.

The power that creates is the power that restores relationships. William Wilburforce was a Christian politician who used the power of his position to help abolish the slave trade in the British Empire. The good of his prolonged efforts is beyond calculation. Families throughout Africa remained together because the gruesome British slave trade had been stopped. Talk about preserving relationships! And this is a story that could be repeated many times over as faithful believers have sought to apply God-given power creatively in the arena of politics and business.

The use of power to restore relationships is also a part of our personal, everyday world. The mother who rights a wrong between children is using her authority to restore broken relationships. The school principal who changes soul-destroying rules in the school system is breathing life into the hearts of students. The pastor who helps feuding committee members settle their differences is using power for healing in the community of faith. The company president who corrects the cost overruns of the project manager is using power to restore integrity and wholeness to the world of business. All of us in daily life encounter thousands of opportunities to enlist power in the service of reconciliation.

What does the power that creates look like? Think of Moses, who understood as few did the might and power of Egypt and who was forced to flee that power. In the desert he came to experience a new kind of power, the power of Yahweh. By the time Moses returned to face down the power of Egypt, he was a different person. Gone was the old arrogance; in its place was a new combination of meekness and confidence. The strong imperative "Let my people go" was backed up by the mighty acts of God, which brought even mighty Pharaoh to his knees. The result was the most dramatic release of captives ever known in human history.

Creative power sets people free. When Martin Luther

King, Jr., stood firm against America's racism, millions were set free. When teachers unlock the joy of discovery in the minds of students, they are using the power of their position to liberate. When an older brother uses his superior status to build the self-esteem of younger siblings, he is using power to set them free. When the old destructive habit patterns of depression or fear are transformed by the power of God, the result is liberation.

What does the power that creates look like? Think of Jeremiah, who remained true to the word of God in the most discouraging of circumstances. We call him the weeping prophet and for good reason. In a day when the religious leaders were catering their message to fit the prevailing political winds, Jeremiah spoke the *Dabar Yahweh*, the word of the Lord. That word was a discouraging one at best, a word of defeat and not of victory. And the people rejected Jeremiah's word of warning and even persecuted him. At one point he was thrown down a cistern and left to die. We are told that "Jeremiah sank in the mire" (Jer. 38:6). In many ways this simple statement is a good description of Jeremiah's entire ministry. He had to watch his beloved country overthrown and ravaged and his own people deported as spoils of war.

But it was the teaching of Jeremiah—the very teaching that the people had rejected—that enabled Judah to hold onto faith in Yahweh throughout the long years of exile. You see, the people had elevated their belief in the invincibility of Zion into a cardinal doctrine of their faith. And when Zion was destroyed, their whole belief system came crashing down. Hadn't God promised them Jerusalem would not fall? Where was God when the Babylonian hoards ravaged their land?

But Jeremiah had insisted over and over that Zion's invincibility was predicated upon obedience to the Mosaic Covenant, and because they had disobeyed the covenant, Zion would fall. God had not failed them by allowing

Jerusalem to fall; they had failed God by disobeying his covenant. Finally, Jeremiah spoke the words of hope and restoration and pointed to a new covenant, a covenant written not on tablets of stone but on the fleshy tablets of their hearts. "But this is the covenant which I will make with the house of Israel after those days, says the Lord: I will put my law within them, and I will write it upon their hearts, and I will be their God, and they shall be my people" (Jer. 31:33). It was Jeremiah's tenacity to the truth of Yahweh that enabled the people of Judah to keep faith in God when all the confident words of the false prophets were revealed as spurious.

Jeremiah reminds us that spiritual power sometimes looks like weakness. Faithfulness is more important than success, and the power to remain faithful is a great treasure indeed. Perhaps Jeremiah's word to his servant Baruch is good counsel for us today, "And do you seek great things for yourself? Seek them not" (Jer. 45:5).

Dietrich Bonhoeffer knew the power of God that looks like weakness to the world. "When Christ calls a man," he said, "he bids him come and die."[1] Bonhoeffer knew what it meant to die; he died to self, he died to all his hopes and dreams, and he died at the hands of Hilter's SS Black Guards. But as the Scripture reminds us, a grain of wheat that falls to the ground and dies bears much fruit (John 12:24). The fruit of Bonhoeffer's life and death is beyond calculation. We are all in his debt. As G. Leibholz has said, "Bonhoeffer's life and death has given us great hope for the future. . . . The victory which he has won was a victory for us all, a conquest never to be undone, of love, light and liberty."[2]

What does the power that creates look like? Think of the early church gathered at the Jerusalem Council (Acts 15). They had gathered to answer a momentous question: Can Gentiles have genuine faith in Christ without conformity to Jewish religious culture? It was an issue that could have easily split the Christian fellowship right down the middle. Yet as they gathered, as they talked, as they listened, the power of God broke through in a Spirit-led unity of heart and mind. Miraculously they saw that Gentiles could live faithfully before God within the context of their own culture and that Jews could do likewise. So the cultural captivity of the Church was broken, and believers everywhere could receive one another without needing to proselytize for their own culture. They experienced the power of unity in the Holy Spirit.

The power that creates produces unity. When John Woolman stood before the annual conference of the Quakers in 1758 and delivered his moving plea against slavery, the entire body, without spoken dissent, agreed to remove slavery from its midst. This unity of heart and mind is not easy to come by, but it is worth the effort. If we would learn to listen to the Lord together in our homes, in our churches, and in our businesses, we would see more of this unity of the Spirit. The family is the best place to begin. Father and mother can do much by leading the way in these matters.

What does the power that creates look like? Think of Jesus and his ministry of teaching and healing. Here we find the perfect display of perfect power. Everywhere he went, the powers of darkness were defeated, people were healed, relationships were restored. People came alive to God and alive to each other through the life-giving ministry of Jesus.

In the crucifixion the power that creates reached its apex. At the cross Satan sought to use all the power at his disposal to destroy Christ, but God turned it into the ultimate act of creative power. The penalty for sin was paid; the justice of God was satisfied. Through the cross of Christ, you and I can receive forgiveness and know the restoring of our relationship to God. Christ died for our sins, and in that death we see the power that creates.

Our response to this supreme act of power is gratitude. It is "love divine, all loves excelling." We can never hope or want to duplicate this act of power. We simply thank God for what he has done. Real forgiveness brings doxology. To know that God truly forgives all our sins and welcomes us into his presence is "joy unspeakable and full of glory." Doxology itself is power. As we live thankfully for God's great gift, others are drawn to know this joy of the Lord that overcomes all things.

THE MARKS OF SPIRITUAL POWER

The power that creates is spiritual power, and it is in stark contrast to human power. The apostle Paul spoke of the "flesh," and by it he meant human-initiated activity without the aid of divine grace. People can do many things in the power of the flesh, but they cannot do the work of the Spirit of God. The power of the flesh relies upon such things as proper pedigree, positions of status, and connections among those in the power structure. But Paul, you see, had given up on the flesh. He said that he counted those things as "dung," for his sights were set on a greater power, "that I may know him and the power of his resurrection, and may share his sufferings, becoming like him in his death, that if possible I may attain the resurrection from the dead" (Phil. 3:10–11).

Now, when we see people desperately scrambling for the "dung"— human power—we can be sure that they know precious little of the "power of his resurrection." What, then, are the marks of this power that proceeds from God?

Love is the first mark of spiritual power. Love demands that power be used for the good of others. Notice Jesus' use of power —the healing of the blind, the sick, the maimed, the dumb, the leper, and many others. Luke, the physician, observes that "all the crowd sought to touch him, for power came forth from him and healed them all" (Luke 6:19). Notice in each case the concern for the good of others, the motivation of love. In Christ, power is used to destroy the evil so that love can redeem the good.

Power for the purpose of advancing reputations or inflating egos is not power motivated by love. When God used Paul and Barnabas to heal a cripple at Lystra, the astonished people tried to turn them into Greek gods, but they tore their clothes and shouted out, "We also are men, of like nature with you" (Acts 14:15). Many of us might not find the idea of deity status so reprehensible. Think of the power over people we would have, and, after all, we would use the power to such good ends! But power that is used to advance reputations destroys the user, because with it we aspire to be gods.

This leads us to the second mark of spiritual power, humility. Humility is power under control. Nothing is more dangerous than power in the service of arrogance. Power under the discipline of humility is teachable. Apollos was a powerful preacher, but he was also willing to learn from others (Acts 18:24-26). In the course of his powerful ministry, Peter made some serious mistakes, but when confronted with his errors he had the humility to change (e.g., Acts 10:1-35; Gal. 2:11-21).

Believe me, this is no small matter. Many have been destroyed in their walk with God simply because their exercise of power was not controlled by humility. Power without humility is anything but a blessing.

James Nayler was one of the greatest of the early Quaker preachers. But he got carried away by his exercise of power, and in 1656 some of his wilder followers persuaded him to re-enact at Bristol Jesus' Palm Sunday ride into Jerusalem. This act proved to be his undoing. He was tried and convicted of blasphemy. The story does have a happy ending, for in time Nayler repented of his presumption, but he had lost his effectiveness in the service of Christ. Power destroys when it is not coupled with the spirit of humility.

To really know the power of God is to be keenly aware that we have done nothing more than to receive a gift. Gratitude, not pride, is our only appropriate response. The power is not ours, though we are given the freedom to use it. But when we truly walk with God, our only desire is to use power in the service of Christ and his kingdom.

This leads into the third mark of spiritual power, which is self-limitation. The power that creates refrains from doing some things—even good things—out of respect for the individual. Have you ever noticed the number of times Jesus refused to use power? He refused to dazzle people by jumping off the pinnacle of the temple (Matt. 4:5). He rejected the temptation to make more "wonder bread" to validate his ministry (John 6:26). He refused to do many wonderful works in his own hometown because of the unbelief of the people (Luke 4:16-27). He said no to the Pharisees' demand that he give a sign to prove he was the Messiah (Matt. 12:38). At his arrest, Jesus reminded Peter that he could have summoned a whole army of angels to his rescue, but he did not (Matt. 26:53).

The power that comes from the Holy Spirit is not to be used lightly. Paul said, "Lay hands suddenly on no man" (1 Tim. 5:22, KJV). We do people a disservice if we bring them into the power of God before they are ready. Those who live and move in God know that there is a time to withhold the hand of power just as there is a time to use it.

Joy is the fourth mark of spiritual power. This is no grim-faced, dour effort! Far from it! To see the kingdom of Christ break into the midst of darkness and depression is a wonderful thing. M. Scott Peck writes, "The experience of spiritual power is basically a joyful one."[3]

When the lame man was healed, he went "walking

and leaping and praising God" (Acts 3:8). That is a good description of our spontaneous reaction to the work of God. I once prayed with a veteran missionary over some deep inner hurts that stemmed from the tragic death of her son. As we prayed there was a very special sense of God's presence and then the clear release of the powers of fear and guilt. The Presence was so real, the release so definite, that we were both filled with a sense of wonder and awe. The time that has passed since those first prayer sessions has only validated what we experienced then. Months later, she wrote, "I have such peace. Rich, beautiful, holy joy lives inside me and just bubbles out. Finally, I know what Jesus meant when he said there would be rivers of living water flowing in us and through us. This is something I have looked for all my life."

I hope you understand that I am referring to something more profound than the bubbly "joy" of the superficial. The rich inner joy of spiritual power knows sorrow and is acquainted with grief. Joy and anguish often have a symbiotic relationship.

Vulnerability is the fifth mark of spiritual power. The power that comes from above is not filled with bravado and bombast. It lacks the symbols of human authority; indeed, its symbols are a manger and a cross. It is power that is not recognized as power. It is a self-chosen position of meekness that to human eyes looks powerless. It is the power of the "wounded healer," to use the phrase of Henri Nouwen.

The power from above leads from weakness. It is in contradiction to the society of the strong and the capable. Once when the apostle Paul was struggling with his own vulnerability the word of God came to him, saying, "My power is made perfect in weakness," and so he saw that "when I am weak, then I am strong" (2 Cor. 12:9-10).

What we often call the parable of the prodigal son might be more aptly called "the parable of the powerless almighty father."⁴ In the father we see the power that does not dominate, the power that patiently waits. The parable is about God, of course: it is also a parable that was lived out in the life of Jesus. Look at him working patiently with stubborn, rebellious disciples. Look at him at his trial, speaking not a word. Look at him hanging on a wooden throne in total helplessness. These, I submit to you, are acts of spiritual power of the highest order.

In prison, Alexander Solzhenitsyn discovered that, whenever he tried to maintain a measure of power over his own life by acquiring food or clothing, he was at the mercy of his captors. But when he accepted and even embraced his own vulnerability, his jailers had no power over him. In a sense, he had become the powerful, they the powerless.⁵

We who understand the power of defenselessness may well have a genuine advantage. As our world becomes more complicated, the feeling of being powerless has become the order of the day. People we do not even know make decisions that affect us profoundly; we are not in control, and we know it. But the normal reactions of anger and resignation do not need to be ours, because we know what Jürgen Moltmann calls "the power of the powerless."⁶

The sixth mark of spiritual power is submission. Jesus knew what it meant to submit to the ways of God: "The Son can do nothing of his own accord, but only what he sees the Father doing; for whatever he does, that the Son does likewise" (John 5:19). As we learn to experience on a personal level this same kind of intimate cooperation with the Father, we will enter more deeply into the meaning of true power.

There is a power that comes through spiritual gifts, and there is a power that comes through spiritual positioning. The two work in unison. Submission gives us spiritual positioning. We are positioned under the leadership of Christ and under the authority of others. We find others in the Christian fellowship who can further us in the things of God. We submit to Scripture to learn more perfectly the ways of God with human beings. We submit to the Holy Spirit to learn the meaning of obedience. We submit to the life of faith in order to understand the difference between human power and divine power.

"Be subject to one another out of reverence for Christ," said Paul (Eph. 5:21). Paul himself was in submission to the church council at Jerusalem (Acts 15). Peter and Barnabas came under submission to Paul's correction when they failed to extend the right hand of fellowship to the Gentiles (Gal. 2:11-21). Apollos submitted to Aquila and Priscilla when it was clear that they knew more than he in the things of Christ (Acts 18:24-26).

Submission is power because it places us in a position in which we can receive from others. We are impoverished people indeed if our world is narrowed down to ourselves. But when, with humility of heart, we submit to others, vast new resources are opened to us. When we submit to others, we have access to their wisdom, their counsel, their rebuke, their encouragement.

Freedom is the final mark of spiritual power. People were set free when Jesus and the apostles exercised power. The lame could walk; the blind could see; the guilty knew forgiveness; and most wonderful of all, the demon-possessed were released. The powers of this dark evil age were defeated, and the captives were set free.

There is more, however, to this matter of freedom. Notice how Jesus worked with people. "He will not break a bruised reed or quench a smoldering wick," prophesied Isaiah (Matt. 12:20). And it was true. Jesus never ran roughshod over the weak. He never snuffed out even the smallest flicker of hope. He never used his power to exploit or to control others. It would have been easy for him to do otherwise. The poor who heard him so gladly would have done anything for him because they were so grateful just to have someone pay attention to them. But Jesus refused to exploit the power he had over them. No, he freed them to be themselves, fully and uniquely.

I once experienced this power that frees in an especially vivid way. I had just returned from a conference where I had made some rather significant decisions, and I was telling a friend who was a spiritual mentor about the experience. At one point I exclaimed, "Oh, by the way, I made one decision that I know you have been wanting me to make for a long time . . ." My friend interrupted, "Wait just a minute! Let's be clear about one thing. My business, my only business, is to bring the truth of God as I see it, and then to simply love you regardless of what you do or don't do. It is not my business to straighten you out or to get you to do the right thing." After our visit I thought about the significance of this simple statement. His care and compassion had always been evident, but in those words I discovered a new dimension of freedom—a freedom that allowed intimate friendship without a slavish need to please on either side. His power in my life is real, but it is a power that frees, not binds. Human power is power *over* someone, divine power has no such need to control — "*sine vi humana sed verbo*, 'without human power, simply by the word.' "[7]

POWER IN THE MARKETPLACE

This life-giving spiritual power is of value to us only as it is fleshed out in ordinary life. It will never do to speak piously of love, joy, and humility without rooting those realities in home, office, and school. What does spiritual power look like in the marketplace of life?

In the individual, power is to be used to promote self-control, not self-indulgence. Self-control is at home with both self-esteem and self-denial. Robert Schuller calls self-esteem *"the human hunger for the divine dignity that God intended to be our emotional birthright as children created in His image."*[8] Self-denial is the way this human hunger for self-esteem is satisfied, and self-control embraces them both.

Discipline is the language of self-control. The disciplined person is the person who can do what needs to be done when it needs to be done. The disciplined person is the person who can live appropriately in life. Such a person can laugh when laughter is appropriate, weep when weeping is appropriate, work when working is appropriate, play when playing is appropriate, pray when praying is appropriate, speak when speaking is appropriate, and be silent when silence is appropriate. Jean-Pierre de Caussade beautifully describes the life of self-control, "The soul, light as a feather, fluid as water, innocent as a child, responds to every movement of grace like a floating balloon."[9]

We experience control over self-indulgence by the power of God. Saint Francis called the human body "Brother Ass," because we are supposed to ride the ass rather than the ass riding us. It is self-control that gives us authority over "Brother Ass." From self-control comes freedom, for we are becoming what we were created to be.

In the home, power is to be used to nurture confidence, not subservience. How crucial it is for parents to use the authority they have over their children to build them up rather than tear them down, to encourage them rather than discourage them. A very wise parent once said to me, "Every 'No, no' must be matched by ten 'Atta boys.'" Criticism and correction is certainly necessary, but it must never be allowed to become destructive. As James Dobson says, we are "to shape the will of the child . . . *but to do so without breaking his spirit."*[10] The use of power in the home can be a blessing if it is surrounded by a spirit of caring.

In the marriage, power is to be used to enhance communication, not isolation. Husbands and wives have power over each other, and they know it. All of us have certain things within us that will trigger utterly irrational reactions. When our spouse even comes near one of these issues, it is as though he or she has tripped a high-voltage lever. Knowledge is power, and in the intimacy of marriage we learn in explicit detail the nature of each other's "high-voltage levers." A particular topic or phrase, a certain way of acting, a particular tone of voice, even something as simple as the lift of an eyebrow or the shrug of a shoulder, can trigger these levers and start World War III.

These levers are real dynamite. Many times they have to do with old hurts and wounds in the marriage, and they have the power to block all genuine love and communication. But in the power of God we learn to lovingly avoid things that can be destructive to each other. We can also ask God to rewire our internal circuitry in such a way that these old hurts, these old wounds, are desensitized and no longer control us.

Our intimate knowledge of each other also means that we know what will enhance the relationship and encourage communication. We make use of this knowledge to open wide the channels of love and compassion.

In the Church, power is to be used to inspire faith, not conformity. Bishops, pastors, elders, deacons, and others have real power over people and should use it for life, not death. In matters that are essential to our spiritual growth, we want to do all we can to rouse people to action. But we must frankly admit that many things in our church life have little to do with righteousness, peace, and joy in the Holy Spirit. We do not need to proselytize people for our culture where it is not *necessary* as an expression of love of God and neighbor. In such matters we give people freedom in the gospel to be themselves without cultural conformity.

I remember so well "my pastor." I was young in both years and faith. I was also shy, and to compensate I would often show off and act boisterous. My pastor, however, bore patiently with me through those years of growing. He never tried to make me conform to the religious culture in the trivial matters of dress or speech. He gave me plenty of opportunity to struggle with theological issues, while at the same time setting forth clearly the fundamental tenets of the faith. I was inspired toward faith without conformity, a legacy for which I will always be grateful.

In the school, power is to be used to cultivate growth, not inferiority. Let us not kid ourselves; teachers and students are in a power relationship, but it can be a power to lift, not to destroy, if they understand their purpose. When teachers use their authority to stimulate children to learn, to think, to go on an adventure of discovery, they are engaging in a life-giving ministry. But it is very easy for a teacher to push too hard and to criticize too severely; when this happens, the child feels worthless. Teachers need to prod without demeaning, encourage excellence without depreciating those who fall short.

I vividly remember a teacher who prodded me to excellence without demeaning my shortcomings. He was a philosophy professor, and although I cannot remember all he taught me about Plato and Kierkegaard, I will never forget his love of words. He handled words in a way that was new for me: as a treasure to be cherished rather than propaganda to be maneuvered. He had a special regard for the mystery and power of words. In fact, words seemed to usher him into another world, a world in which I was a foreigner. I was very clumsy with words, so his skill with language frightened me as much as it intrigued me. He never depreciated me for my clumsiness but always urged me to try again. And I did try again, until I became at home in this world of words—a world in which zeal and insight meet in friendship, a world in which truth and beauty kiss each other. He was a teacher who saw past my feelings of inferiority and encouraged me to grow.

On the job, power is to be used to facilitate competence, not promote feelings of inadequacy. The business world is one place in which a Christian witness to creative power is desperately needed. Subordinates often feel helpless and manipulated, but it does not need to be this way. One thing all of us want to do is a good job. We want to know that we have made a genuine contribution, and we want to be competent in our area of service. Employers have the power to help realize this deep desire by providing opportunities for advanced training, by carefully delegating increased responsibility, and by helping employees realize their full potential. In fact, one definition of management is *"meeting the needs of people as they work at accomplishing their jobs."*[11]

The employee also has power, the power of encouragement. It may be hard for us to believe, but it is lonely at the top. Executives find that genuine friendships are hard to come by, because people fear their power. And those who do not fear it often are hoping to use it.

Employees who follow the way of Christ will reach out to their employers. They discern the hurt and loneliness of those who are over them. They give their friendship with no strings attached. They pray for their superiors and encourage them in every way possible. This, too, is a ministry of power.

THE POWER TO LIBERATE

We all exercise power over others. We are all affected by the power others exercise over us. We can choose the destructive power that is used to dominate and manipulate, or we can choose the creative power that is used to lead and liberate. It is only through the grace of God that we are able to take something as dangerous as power and make it creative and life-giving.

12. The Ministry of Power

In the mighty power of God go on!
—GEORGE FOX

Power touches us all. We cannot get away from it even if we wanted to. All human relationships involve the use of power. Therefore, rather than seek to run from it or to deny that we use it, we would do well to discover the Christian meaning of power and learn how to use it for the good of others. All who follow Christ are called to the "ministry of power."

POWER IN THE MINISTRY OF JESUS

Nothing is more clear than Jesus' consistent use of power to overthrow the kingdom of darkness and confirm his message that the kingdom of God has arrived. The Gospels are redundant with Jesus' ministry of casting out demons, healing the sick, and taking control over nature. Such demonstrations of kingdom power were not lost on the crowds: "When the multitudes saw it, they marvelled, and glorified God, which had given such power unto men" (Matt. 9:8, KJV).

Jesus' ministry was marked with authority. Spiritual power and spiritual authority are inseparable. In his Gospel, Mark tells of Jesus' healing of a demon-possessed person, adding that the people "were all amazed, so that they questioned among themselves, saying, 'What is this? A new teaching! With authority he commands even the unclean spirits, and they obey him'" (Mark 1:27). Jesus was not giving a new teaching; he was demonstrating a new power. He not only proclaimed the presence of the kingdom of God, he demonstrated its presence with power.

Now if Jesus had been the only one who exercised the ministry of power, we might be able to dismiss it as the privileged domain of the Messiah, but he delegated this same ministry to others. "And he called the twelve together and gave them power and authority over all demons and to cure diseases, and he sent them out to preach the kingdom of God and to heal" (Luke 9:1-2). That is precisely what they did, "And they departed and went through the villages, preaching the gospel and healing everywhere" (Luke 9:6).

"But," we may think to ourselves, "after all, they were the Twelve; perhaps this ministry of power is part of the apostolic call—certainly it is not for us." Jesus, however, delegated this same ministry to the Seventy, saying to them, "Heal the sick . . . and say to them, 'The kingdom of God has come near to you' " (Luke 10:9). And the Seventy did exactly as they were told, and they return thrilled, saying "Lord, even the demons are subject to us in your name!" (Luke 10:17). These were ordinary people, yet they were entrusted with extraordinary power.

Finally, we are given those startling words of Jesus in the Upper Room; "Truly, truly, I say to you, he who believes in me will also do the works that I do; and greater works than these will he do, because I go to the Father" (John 14:12). There is no way to get around it: the ministry of power is the common property of the people of God.

"OFFICIAL-LESS" POWER

This is nowhere more evident than in the book of Acts. How little the disciples really understood the matter of power, even after the resurrection, is seen in their initial question to Jesus, "Lord, will you at this time restore the kingdom to Israel?" (Acts 1:6). They wanted a kingdom so they could exercise a little power. "Is this the time when we can have the kingdom, the authority, the position, so we can really show those Romans what power looks like?" But Jesus made it quite clear to them that the matter of the kingdom was none of their business; he would give them power, spiritual power: "But you shall receive power when the Holy Spirit has come upon you; and you shall be my witnesses in Jerusalem and in all Judea and Samaria and to the end of the earth" (Acts 1:8). He gave them power without a kingdom, power without a position.

We are so often just like the disciples. We think the position guarantees the power. Give someone a Ph.D., a professorship, and then he or she will be able to teach! But we all know people with Ph.D.'s and professorships who cannot teach worth a lick. The position does not guarantee that the power is there. The world is full of people who will do anything to get the position so they can have power over others. That is the kind of power that belongs to this world system. It is dependent upon human authorization, and its power is the power to dominate others.

But to the eye of faith positions in the human order themselves are really powerless, ignorant of the way of God and the life of spiritual power. Throughout the book of Acts, we see repeatedly the clash between powerless officials and official-less power.

The authority of Peter, John, and the others was shocking to everyone because they had no human credentials of authority. They had no degrees, no titles of distinction, no human authorization. Since their ability (power) came from God, human authorization was irrelevant. Hence their authority flew in the face of the vested interests of those in power. Since the disciples had no need to be authorized, they could not be controlled.

Here we see uneducated common people standing before the "powerful" declaring, "Whether it is right in the sight of God to listen to you rather than to God, you must judge; for we cannot but speak of what we have seen and heard" (Acts 4:19–20). Here we see "officialdom" powerless to stop the healing of the sick and the preaching of the good news. Repeatedly, the official-less power of the disciples confronted the powerless officials of the religious and civil establishment, and repeatedly they won. They won because they operated out of a power that came from above.

One of the most humorous contrasts between human systems of power and spiritual power occurred in the ministry of Paul. He had been casting out many demons and in general exercising a ministry of power. Some professional Jewish exorcists saw Paul's work and decided to use his "technique," so at the next opportunity they tried to exorcise a demon, saying, "I adjure you by the Jesus whom Paul preaches" (Acts 19:13). But instead of obeying, the evil spirit answered, "Jesus I know, and Paul I know; but who are you?" And according to the Scripture, the man with the evil spirit "leaped on them, mastered all of them, and overpowered them, so that they fled out of that house naked and wounded" (Acts 19:15-16). What a contrast between official-less power and powerless officials!

HIDDEN PREPARATION

If we expect to engage in the ministry of power, we must understand the hidden preparation through which God puts his ministers. Moses thought he would set the world's wrongs right by the use of human power when he killed an Egyptian. What he thought would be creative power was in the end destructive power. There was a hidden preparation that was essential before Moses was ready for the ministry of power. He had to go into the desert for forty years to learn the difference between human manipulation and divine power. By the time Moses stood before God at the burning bush, he was a different man. Gone was the self-assured arrogance of one who could wield power with the wave of his hand. Now we find the meekest of human beings, who learned confidence by trusting in the power of God alone.

The apostle Paul also experienced a hidden preparation for his ministry. He was converted in dramatic fashion on the road to Damascus and later escaped his would-be assassins via a bucket dropped over the wall. He disappeared into the deserts of Arabia for three years, and after a brief visit to Jerusalem, fled to his old hometown of Tarsus for a number of years (Gal. 1:15-18; Acts 9:30; 11:25-26). It was nearly thirteen years from the time of Paul's conversion until he came to Antioch, where he began his missionary career. When we see in the book of Acts the great work of Paul, we must remember the hidden preparation that preceded it.

Today we have forgotten the importance of this hidden work of God. As a result, we immediately thrust people into notoriety, bestowing on them unbelievable power, and then we wonder why they are corrupted. Unless we are ready for it, power will destroy us. This is no small matter in the Church today. Because of our wholesale ignorance of the importance of hidden preparation, we have thrust untold numbers of workers into the limelight before they were ready.

All of us must experience this hidden preparation. Time spent being instructed by God is well spent and never wasted. In hiddenness we learn to see life spiritually—to see what is important and what is of little consequence. Often God completely reverses our priorities.

What we once saw as great and wonderful shrinks down to trivial and insignificant. Gaining recognition, success, wealth, and autonomy no longer attracts us. We learn to let go of all humanly initiated bids for power. Things we once considered unimportant and beneath us become matters of genuine consequence. We begin to value simple acts of kindness and neighborliness. Small ordinary tasks become genuinely significant to us.

THE MINISTRY OF SMALL THINGS

In experiences of hiddenness we learn that the ministry of small things is a necessary prerequisite to the ministry of power. Tabitha was a woman "full of good works and acts of charity" who gave her life to making "coats and garments" for the widows (Acts 9:36-42). She was exercising the ministry of small things. Barnabas shared his wealth with the struggling community, befriended Paul when others had given him the cold shoulder, and patiently nurtured John Mark when even Paul had decided he was unreliable (Acts 4:36–37; 9:27; 15:36–41). Barnabas too was exercising the ministry of small things.

When the people asked John the Baptist what they should do to exhibit true repentance, he counseled, "He who has two coats, let him share with him who has none; and he who has food, let him do likewise." To tax collectors he said, "Collect no more than is appointed you." To soldiers he counseled, "Rob no one by violence or by false accusation, and be content with your wages" (Luke 3:10-14). The point of his teaching is its triviality—small, simple ordinary things. John was calling people to the ministry of small things.

The ministry of small things is among the most important ministries we are given. In some ways it is more important than the ministry of power. The work of power occurs now and again, but the work of small things occurs repeatedly throughout the course of our days. Because our daily tasks afford us constant opportunity to engage in the ministry of small things, it is through this work that we become most intimately acquainted with God. No doubt this is one reason the prophet Zechariah counsels us not to despise the day of small things (Zech. 4:10).

Small things are the genuinely big things in the kingdom of God. It is here we truly face the issues of obedience and discipleship. It is not hard to be a model disciple amid camera lights and press releases. But in the small corners of life, in those areas of service that will never be newsworthy or gain us any recognition, we must hammer out the meaning of obedience. Amid the obscurity of family and friends, neighbors and work associates, we find God.

And it is this finding of God, this intimacy with God, that is essential to the exercise of power. The ministry of small things must be prior to and more valued than the ministry of power. Without this perspective we will view power as a "big deal." Make no mistake, the religion of the "big deal" stands in opposition to the way of Christ. It is this spirit that leads to the cruelest excesses. It is one of the greatest hindrances today to a free exercise of the ministry of power.

When power is seen as a "big deal," we want to draw attention to what we have done. We put up our signs and carry on our advertising campaigns in a frantic attempt to show that we are important. The one thing we cannot abide is for this great work of God (and ourselves) to go unnoticed.

The Bible tells us that after God used Peter to raise Tabitha from the dead Peter "stayed in Joppa for many days with one Simon, a tanner" (Acts 9:43). Now, what would we do if God had just used us to raise someone from the dead? I know what most of us would do: first we would go on a speaking tour, and then we would write a book about it! But Peter was content to do nothing, because he had no need to impress anyone. Power was no "big deal."

The ministry of small things can save us from the distortions of the "big deal." Under its authority power assumes its proper place as simply another normal aspect of the work we are given to perform. Power takes on a certain naturalness—the thing one would expect to see among the people of God—and it is experienced and reported in modesty and with humility. If small things become a glad and frequent ministry, we will discover that God is near us, and then the exercise of power will be a blessing and not a curse. Jean-Pierre de Caussade writes, "To discover God in the smallest and most ordinary things, as well as in the greatest, is to possess a rare and sublime faith."[1]

THE ALONENESS OF SPIRITUAL POWER

Those who exercise spiritual power must be prepared for aloneness. Please note that I did not say loneliness, for such persons will have many clamoring for their attention. Aloneness means having to decide and act alone, for no others can share the burden or even understand the issues involved. Wise counselors, friends, the community of faith—all are helpful, but only to a certain point. Most people have good intentions, but they simply do not understand spiritual power, and it is neither kind nor wise to ask them to help with decisions they can neither understand nor appreciate. We walk alone—well, not quite alone, for we have One who walks with us, but alone as far as human wisdom is concerned.

One of the most touching themes in the Gospels is Jesus' aloneness. The multitudes could not understand; even the disciples were thick of head and heart. Jesus tried to bring the Three—Peter, James, and John—along with him into the inner sanctuary of power, but they seldom could follow. They missed the whole point of the experience on the Mount of Transfiguration and could only think of how to set up an appropriate memorial. Most poignant of all is the scene in the garden of Gethsemane where Jesus singled out the Three to watch and pray with him. On that holy night they abandoned their Master for sleep, and Jesus was forced to wrestle with the powers alone.

We too must wrestle alone. We cannot even depend upon our husband or wife to understand what is occurring in the inner sanctuary of our soul. More than three hundred years ago James Nayler wrote of the aloneness of divine intimacy and power, "I found it alone, being forsaken. I have fellowship therein with them who live in dens and desolate places in the earth, who through death obtained this resurrection and eternal holy life."[2] Aloneness is the price of spiritual power.

THE PRACTICE OF POWER

It is one thing to applaud a true life-giving ministry of power and to see biblical models of power that take our breath away; it is quite another to experience spiritual power in our lives. The issue of real importance is how to bring the lofty talk into daily walk. What are some of the arenas in which the ministry of power needs to be exercised?

I want to be very straightforward with you in describing the first arena. We are to do battle with the Devil, Beelzebul, Apollyon, the Prince of the power of the air. Like Jesus, we go into the desert to meet the demons of the spirit, and if we do not go into a physical desert we do journey into the desert of the heart. We must not assume that we have fought this battle just because we have come into a living experience of faith in Jesus Christ, or just because we have been Christians for many years, or just because we have been active church leaders.

We need divine protection before daring to enter this dark night of faith. We ask for the strong light of Christ to surround us, the blood of Christ to cover us, and the cross of Christ to seal us. As we go into the desert of the heart, we enter with confidence, knowing that God is with us and will protect us.

But we go to the desert to meet, not God, but the Devil. In the desert we are stripped of all our support systems and distractions so that, naked and vulnerable, we face the demons without and within. There in the desert, alone, we look squarely into the face of the seductive powers of greed and prestige. Satan tempts us with wild fantasies of status and influence. We feel the inner pull of these fantasies because deep down we really do want to be the most important, the most respected, the most honored. We fancy ourselves before the cameras, in the judge's seat, at the top of the heap. "After all," we muse, "aren't these things nothing more than the desire for excellence?"

But in time we see through the deception. With a power given from above we shout, "No!" to him who promises the whole world if we will only worship him. We crucify the old mechanisms of power—push, drive, climb, grasp, trample. We turn instead to the new life of power—love, joy, peace, patience, and all the fruit of the Spirit.

Another arena in which the ministry of power needs to be exercised is the physical body. Many of us have so etherealized our spirituality that it is a genuine surprise to us to discover that the body plays an integral part in the life of faith. With the word of power we take authority over our bodies. We discipline the body so that it enters into a working harmony with the spirit. We bring the body into the God-given rhythms of life—eating, sleeping, working, playing.

Inordinate passions are like spoiled children and need to be disciplined, and not indulged. Sexual yearnings that transgress God's revealed will are controlled by the power of the Spirit. Slothful tendencies are restrained, tenderly but firmly. The same is true for a superheated zeal for work. Through prayer and faith we make food our servant and not our master. In the power of God we stoutly refuse to delay sleep at night in the pretense that our bodies are invincible. We exercise for health and spiritual alertness.

The healing ministry is part of the authority we are to exercise over our bodies. Jesus healed, and he commissioned us to heal (Mark 16:15-18).* Healing is listed among the spiritual gifts, and there is every indication that it is a valid ministry for today (1 Cor. 12:28). In our day, however, this good ministry has been abused terribly.

Some, for example, posit an absolute dichotomy between healing through medicine and healing through prayer. This is unfortunate and unnecessary! God uses his friends the doctors, who utilize their God-given knowledge and talents to bring health and wholeness. God also uses his friends who know how to pray to bring his life-giving power into hurting humanity. When doctors and nurses and other healing professionals learn to combine prayer with their medical skills, great good can be accomplished.

Another tragic abuse in the healing ministry is the tendency to assign blame if healing does not occur. We blame God, we blame ourselves, we blame the person who is sick. Often, for example, people will tell the per-

---

* I am aware that the authenticity of this passage is disputed, but it is quite consistent with Jesus' other statements and the experience of the church as recorded in Acts.

son who is ill that healing has not occurred because there is sin in his or her life. This is the worst possible counsel and is deeply destructive to the sick person, who wants nothing more than to get well. When the disciples tried to play this guilt game on the man blind from birth, Jesus quickly put a stop to it (John 9:1-3). For the most part, the issue of who sinned is simply beside the point; loving concern for the person is the point. May God raise up many who will bring to the healing ministry a compassionate heart and a good dose of common sense!

At this juncture I want to speak directly to those who have bodies that are frail or in other ways incapacitated. Be tender with yourself—slow to condemn, quick to encourage. Remember that spiritual power is as often gentle as it is dramatic. Give thanks for whatever physical abilities your body may have and concentrate on strengthening those rather than deploring your body's disabilities.

Pray for wholeness and well-being, and rejoice in whatever good comes from that process. If you have asked for healing and it has not come, do not fall into self-pity or self-condemnation. Keep praying, if you can, and remember that healing comes in many ways. Do your best to treat your body as a friend, not an enemy, and certainly in the resurrection, if not before, you finally will have a body that truly is a friend.

A third arena in which we need the exercise of spiritual power is the Church. In recent decades true power has been stifled by entrenched bureaucracies and a system of pastoral training that produces scribes rather than prophets. In order to have more freedom, many parachurch organizations have sprung up, but these seldom have any mechanisms for accountability and usually end up being dominated by a single individual. As a result, we have, in the main, timidity in the churches and egotism in the para-church movements.

What is needed is a new renaissance of leadership

within the Church. We need churches who will call out their most capable men and women for ministry. We need seminaries who will train pastors to walk with God. We need pastors who will hunger for God and who will seek the power of God more than they seek position.

We desperately need pastoral leaders who know God. Their leadership should be both compassionate and strong. They must lead us through a strong pulpit ministry; they also must lead us through compassionate spiritual direction. When their leadership is infused with the joyful power of the Holy Spirit, it is a blessing indeed.

There are many other arenas in which the ministry of power is urgently needed, but I shall confine my discussion to only one more. The state, the arena of politics, needs the life-giving ministry of spiritual power. All believers, but particularly those in democracies, are to call the state to its God-given function of justice for all people alike. We are to commend the state whenever it fulfills its calling and confront it when it fails.

When I speak of the state I am not just referring to national governments, though I certainly mean to include them. By the state I mean all those systems of human organization whereby we empower people to represent and serve the whole. School boards, regulatory agencies, state legislatures, public health organizations, city councils, courts, and many others are all part of the state.

We discern the "angel" of the state through meditative prayer. Contemplation and interior prayer are closely linked with any genuine awakening of a social conscience. Upon receiving insight we "speak truth to power," as the old Quakers used to say.

Where the state genuinely and indiscriminately provides justice for all, we gladly commend it and give it our support. But if the state fails in this, we are to confront it vigorously with every means consistent with the weapons of Ephesians 6. Prayer and fasting, mourning and lamentation are weapons in our struggle for truth, the truth of justice. Vigorous protest, nonviolent confrontation, and civil disobedience are also weapons at our disposal. We serve the state when we refuse to give in to its demonic perversions. The underground railroad was civil disobedience in the nineteenth century; the sanctuary movement is civil disobedience in the twentieth century. In both cases believers declare with Peter and John, "We must obey God rather than men" (Acts 5:29).

Civil disobedience must, however, be done within the confines of spiritual power. There can be no coercion and no retaliation, because it grows out of love, not hate. It eschews the human weapons of violence but instead resorts to the "violence of love"—a firm intransigence to oppression and injustice.[3] The object is to make the evil visible and to prick the social conscience of people.

I have not forgotten that one means of waging the fight of faith is by being a public servant for the state and exerting a Christian influence from within. It is an honorable path, and many have chosen it. May their number increase.

The path of the public servant, however, is fraught with dangers, and not just the ordinary dangers of moral compromise via financial or sexual temptation. The state by definition has been invested with coercive power (that is, it can *demand* obedience), and coercive power is fundamentally at cross purposes with spiritual power. This does not mean that a believer cannot serve in the state; but it does mean that there are likely to be times when the state will make demands of its public servants that violate the Christian witness to love, and at that point the believer will have to decide whether allegiance belongs to Caesar or to God.

BE VALIANT FOR THE TRUTH

Of all people, spiritual people know the dangers of power. The temptations to abuse are everywhere. Yet we must not back away. Christ calls us to the ministry of power. He will give us the compassion and humility to fulfill our ministry. George Fox wrote, "Let all nations hear the word by sound or writing. Spare no place, spare not tongue nor pen; but be obedient to the Lord God and go through the work and be valiant for the Truth upon earth."[4] It is Christ who calls us; he will also empower us.

13. The Vow of Service

A Christian is a perfectly free lord of all, subject to none. A Christian is a perfectly dutiful servant of all, subject to all.
—MARTIN LUTHER

Power is a genuine paradox to believers. We love it and we hate it. We despise its evil and appreciate its good. We would like to do without it, but we know it is part and parcel of human life.

Our ambivalence about power is resolved in the vow of service. Jesus picked up a basin and a towel and, in doing so, redefined the meaning and function of power. "If I then, your Lord and Teacher, have washed your feet, you also ought to wash one another's feet. For I have given you an example, that you also should do as I have done to you" (John 13:14–15). In the everlasting kingdom of Christ, low is high, down is up, weak is strong, service is power. Do you sincerely want to engage in the ministry of power? Do you want to be a leader who is a blessing to people? Do you honestly want to be used of God to heal human hurts? Then learn to become a servant to all. "If any one would be first, he must be last of all and servant of all" (Mark 9:35). The ministry of power functions through the ministry of the towel.

Service means saying no to the power games of modern society. We refute the voices that say, "It's O.K. to be greedy. . . . It's O.K. to look out for Number One. . . . It's O.K. to be Machiavellian. . . . And it's *always* O.K. to be rich."[1] We reject the use of power to dominate and manipulate. We discard the symbols of power and prestige that are used to intimidate others.

Service means saying yes to true power harnessed for the good of all. We affirm power that frees and liberates. We rejoice when power is used in the service of truth. Power made obedient to the purposes and ways of Christ is our delight.

Service means discerning the powers, engaging the powers, and defeating the powers. We serve people when we disarm evil and set the captives free. Through prayers and tears, fasting and lamentation, we wage the peaceable war of the Lamb of God against all that is contrary to God and his way.

Service means obedience. By obedience to the ways of God we come to know the heart of God. By entering the heart of God we are enabled to be of help to people. Wholeness reigns in us, which means effective service for others.

Service means compassion. Compassion puts us in touch with all people. "Compassion requires us to be weak with the weak, vulnerable with the vulnerable, and powerless with the powerless."[2] Compassion gives us the heart to serve others.

Service means "servant leadership."[3] Our management style focuses as much on meeting the needs of people as it does on getting the job done. We are able to bring out the best in others because we value them as individuals. Our leadership flows out of servanthood; our first and primary drive is to serve, and our desire to serve motivates us to lead.

THE VOW OF SERVICE WITHIN THE INDIVIDUAL

The vow of service within the individual begins and ends with obedience to the ways of God. Until the matter of our obedience is settled, we cannot be useful to others, for we will constantly be bringing to that relationship our own agenda, our own opinion, our own human, manipulative ways. A life of obedience ensures that service flows out of divine promptings rather than human ingenuity. "Obedience gives servanthood its deepest dimension."[4]

The words of Samuel to Saul speak to us with prophetic force, "Behold, to obey is better than sacrifice" (1 Sam. 15:22). The greatest of God's demands is not for us to do heroic deeds or to make great sacrifices, but to obey.

Gethsemane gives us the most intimate and anguished model of obedience that we have in the entire Bible. Great drops of sweat like blood fell from Jesus' brow as he uttered the deepest prayer of obedience known to human beings, "Father if thou art willing, remove this cup from me; nevertheless not my will, but thine, be done" (Luke 22:42). Jesus was not trying to get out of drinking the cup—his crucifixion—he was trying to be certain that the cup was God's will. The will of God, not the cup, was the absolute thing. If the cup had not been in the plan of God, to drink it would have been disobedience. This is why when Jesus was finally clear that the cup was the path of obedience he said, "Rise, let us be going" (Matt. 26:46). At every point and in every way, Jesus was the obedient servant who did absolutely nothing except in response to the divine prompting.

I hope you understand that Jesus' obedience flowed out of his intimacy with the Father. Often the idea of obedience conjures up in our minds a hierarchical world of impersonal superiors issuing inane orders that we must obey even if we find no rhyme or reason for them. But Jesus' obedience, and consequently ours, is of a different quality altogether. It is an obedience that flows out of the intimacy that cries, "*Abba*! Father!" There is an inner knowing that God's ways are not only right but good. Knowing by experience the goodness of rightness, we concur with the will of God. It is no order to obey but a divine yes to follow.

The word *obedience* comes from a Latin root that means

"to listen." The good news is that we can live in such intimacy with the infinite Creator of the universe that we can hear his voice and obey his word. And it is our intimacy with the true Shepherd that makes our hearing and obeying possible.

What does this have to do with the vow of service? Service severed from obedience degenerates into spiritual stardom. Service devoid of obedience says, "Look at how wonderful I am, doing all these kind and self-sacrificing things! Look at how much good I am accomplishing." Indeed, the spirit of martyrdom that pervades service that is not in obedience to God often becomes a subtle tool of manipulation. We begin to control others through our service. When this happens, service is transformed into a demonic power and is, in fact, an act of disobedience.

But service that flows out of obedience is of a different quality altogether. When "we discover that our obedient listening leads us to our suffering neighbors, we can go to them in the joyful knowledge that love brings us there."[5] Vainglory, manipulation, coercion are all gone. We can disregard our obsession about the results of our service, since the divine nod of approval is completely sufficient. We can be fully present to people because we know we are living in obedience.

THE VOW OF SERVICE IN THE FAMILY

If the vow of service is to function anywhere, it must function in the family. Within the family unit, the ministry of the towel must be mutual and reciprocal. Respect and compassion should permeate all acts of authority and submission in the Christian home.

How do we as parents serve our children? We serve them by providing purposeful leadership. Children need wise counsel and concrete guidelines. They need loving correction. To lead is to serve.

How do we as parents serve our children? We serve them through compassionate discipline. Children are rendered a serious disservice when we fail to establish reasonable but clear boundaries for acceptable behavior. An early bedtime is important because sleep is important. Good nutrition is important because our bodies are important. Household duties are important because self-worth and a sense of contributing to the welfare of the family are important. Discipline is no small task, but it is one way we serve our children.

How do we as parents serve our children? We serve them by giving them a growing self-government.[6] We need to train our children for increased independence. We do not serve them by placing them under rigid rules until they reach the age of eighteen and then shoving them out the door. Early on, we teach children how to disciminate good from bad. We walk with them through life's decisions, gradually giving them opportunities to learn from their own mistakes. At some point in their growing self-government—certainly by age twenty-one—we relinquish all parental authority. We are available for advice and counsel, but only if they ask for it. Providing the atmosphere for a growing independence is serving children.

How do we as parents serve our children? We serve them by being available and vulnerable. The cliché that it is not the quantity of time but the quality that counts is simply false. Quality in large measure depends upon quantity. We need to give time to our children, and when we are with them we need to be transparent. To go to a child and say, "I was wrong, I'm sorry," is not a sign of weakness but of strength.

How do we as parents serve our children? We serve them by respecting them. Observe any large gathering of people, and see how children are systematically ignored. Their opinion is neither sought nor appreciated. Indeed, afterward, most adults would not be able to name any of the children in the room. We, however, make a point of getting to know children. We listen to what they say and value their contribution. We do not make light of their concerns. The loss of a puppy for a child, or the breakup of a romance for a teenager, is a matter of genuine consequence and should be treated as such.

How do we as parents serve our children? We serve them by introducing them to the spiritual life. If we can be vulnerable enough to share our own pilgrimage of faith, it will go a long way toward making the spiritual life real to our children. And it is our job to instruct them in biblical faith; it is a vital service we owe our children. We must not depend upon the church to do the job of teaching for us.

The obligations of service are reciprocal. How do our children serve us? They serve us by being obedient. They obey not just because the Bible says to obey but because it is good to do so. Children cannot always understand the reasons for what we ask of them, but they can always be assured that their best interest stands behind all we ask. They obey even when it hurts to obey, though, as we shall see presently, obedience cannot be given when it is clearly destructive to do so.

How do our children serve us? They serve us through respect. Respect is due the office of parent even though sometimes the person fulfilling that role is a great disappointment. Parents whose lives show that they are not deserving of respect place a terrible burden upon children, and it is often a cause for their stumbling (Matt. 18:6).

How do our children serve us? They serve us by meekly refusing to do what is clearly destructive. We parents need all the help we can get, and we can learn from our own children, if we are teachable. Children run a terrible risk when they engage in this ministry of service. They risk our anger, and, more importantly, they risk losing our love and support. We must always assure them by word and deed that our love for them is stronger and deeper than any temporary disagreement. It is an unconditional love that is not dependent upon what they do or do not do. The one thing that is more important than their obedience to us is their obedience to the Voice from above.

How do our children serve us? They serve us by caring for our needs when the dependency roles are reversed. For everyone, the time comes when Mom and Dad need help. Aging parents may need their children's financial help, and they need their emotional help. It is not wrong for children to place parents in a nursing home, but their responsibilites do not end there. They also need to give their time, their presence, their attention, and, most of all, their love. Children have an obligation to serve parents in this way. In Jesus' day people tried to get out of this service to parents with religious excuses (Mark 7:9-13). It did not work then, and it does not work now.

All that I have said about the vow of service between parent and child also applies to the relationship of spouse to spouse and child to child. We serve each other in the Christian family because we follow Him who took on the form of a servant (Phil. 2:7). In modern society, one place where a Christian witness to the grace of God is desperately needed is in the home. The vow of service can help realize this witness.

THE VOW OF SERVICE IN THE CHURCH

In the Christian fellowship some serve by leading, others serve by following, and all serve by compassionate caring. Authoritative leadership is essential in the community of faith. It is easy to forget this when we see leadership abused. When we witness people jockeying for position and clamoring for status and using their power to put others into bondage, we are tempted to throw up our hands and try to do away with leadership altogether. But an infantile anarchy in church life is no better than an oppressive dictatorship.

Jesus recognized the need for leadership, but he also gave it an unusual twist. "Jesus called them to him and said, 'You know that the rulers of the Gentiles lord it over them, and their great men exercise authority over them. It shall not be so among you; but whoever would be great among you must be your servant, and whoever would be first among you must be your slave; even as the Son of man came not to be served but to serve, and to give his life as a ransom for many' " (Matt. 20:25-28).

Leadership therefore is an office of servanthood. Those who take up the mantle of leadership do so for the sake of others, not for their own sake. Their concern is to meet the needs of people, not to advance their own reputations. Bernard of Clairvaux wrote, "Learn the lesson that, if you are to do the work of a prophet, what you need is not a scepter but a hoe."[7]

We need leaders with servant hearts. We earnestly petition the Bestower of spiritual gifts to raise up humble men and women to be apostles, prophets, evangelists, pastors, and teachers (Eph. 4:11). We need them, each one. Their authority comes from God, and it is recognized and affirmed by the community of faith. They are our spiritual directors, and we honor them as servants of Christ.

How do spiritual leaders serve their people? They serve them by learning the ways of prayer. People desperately need the ministry of prayer. Marriages are being shattered. Children are being destroyed. People are living in dark depression and misery. And we can make a difference if we will learn to pray. If we genuinely love people, we will desire for them far more than it is within our power to give them, and that will lead us to prayer.

Let me briefly speak directly to pastors and others in positions of spiritual leadership. Your people expect you to bring the ministry of healing prayer. When you go into a home and see people bowed low with the sorrows of life, it is the most natural thing in the world to lay your hands upon them in the sacramental way and pray for their wholeness. Do it with all the confidence and humility, with all the tenderness and boldness, at your disposal. If you will do this day in and day out with a deep dependence upon the Holy Spirit, you will be amazed at the results. Many times there will be substantial improvement, and sometimes the impact will be so dramatic that it feels like a resurrection—and in a way it is. We do not need to be frightened of the few times when no improvement is noticeable, for there are many other times when much good has been done.*

One caution: we must pray for people in the utmost simplicity and joy. We do not try to psychoanalyze them or to figure everything out. We do not even try to correct their theology. We simply invite the Lord to enter the mind and the heart and to heal them both and to restore the God-intended personality.

There have been many who have prayed for me over the years. I remember one individual especially. As a result of three days of fasting and prayer, I felt led to ask this man to come and pray for me. He came, but instead of praying he began sharing his own shortcomings and confessing his sins. I thought to myself, "What is he doing? I am the one in need; he is the spiritual giant," but I said nothing. When he had finished, he looked up at me

---

* As a rough estimate, I find that about 20 percent of those I pray with seem to experience no improvement in their emotional or physical health; another 20 percent experience a little improvement; about 50 percent experience significant improvement; and about 10 percent experience dramatic improvement or total healing.

and asked, "Now, do you still want me to pray for you?" He had seen into my heart. He knew that I had turned him into a spiritual guru. When he finally placed his hands on my head and prayed for me, it was one of the most profound experiences of my life! There was a deep settledness and centeredness, a firmness of life orientation, that entered me at that time, and it has never left. I remember that, without knowing anything of my secret hopes and dreams, he had prayed for "the hands of a writer." Spiritual leaders serve people when they pray for them.

How do spiritual leaders serve their people? They serve them by blazing the trail of inwardness.[8] People today are profoundly interested in the inward nature of the spiritual life. They are also hopelessly confused about what it all means and how it relates to biblical faith. Henri Nouwen says that today's spiritual leader needs to be "the articulator of inner events."[9]

Spiritual leaders must discern the spirits for people. "Test the spirits to see whether they are of God," counsels John (1 John 4:1). Not every supernatural experience is an encounter with the God of Abraham, Isaac, and Jacob, and we had better learn the difference. There is so much foolishness today, so much holy baloney. Spiritual leaders need to help their people distinguish the voice of the true Shepherd from the voice of the evil one.

But even more, leaders serve by plunging into the spiritual depths ahead of their people and interpreting those experiences to them. If by their vulnerability they help us understand some of the dangers and rewards in this interior life hid with God in Christ, then we who are more timid will be able to step out with confidence.

One older woman did this for me. She was the head of the nursery of a large hospital and also the chairperson of the elders in the little church where I pastored. She worked the night shift and would often stop by the church in the morning after work. She read voluminously and would pepper me with questions about the spiritual life, many of which I could not answer. Oh, I could give a textbook answer, but I had no answer from life. More importantly, she would try many adventures in prayer at the hospital and in the congregation, and we would discuss at length what it all meant. What does it really mean to be "in Christ"? How does prayer work? What is the prayer of quiet? The prayer of faith? The prayer of command? How does prayer change others? How does prayer change us? These and many other questions challenged our faith.

She would pray for the babies in the hospital that were in critical condition. She put her hands in the gloves in the incubator and would hold a child, praying, sometimes for an hour or more, and almost always the baby would live.

What was she doing? She was blazing the trail ahead of me and encouraging me to step out into the spiritual life. And so I did. I made many mistakes. Sometimes I would be too bold and run ahead of my leading. More often, I would be too timid and need to be encouraged to step out. At every point, mutual clarification of what was happening enabled us to distinguish between creative and destructive power. She had served me by blazing the trail of inwardness.

How do spiritual leaders serve their people? They serve them by compassionate leadership. People do not need someone who will stand over them and pontificate in authoritative tones about the meaning of life. They need someone who will stand with them and share their excitement, their confusion, their hurt. People need leaders who love them.

I once worked for a psychologist who embodied the meaning of compassionate leadership for me. He was a leader, no doubt about that. He could be very forceful when the occasion demanded it. But his leading drew its strength from his compassion. All of us on the counseling team sensed his love. His clients also felt his kindness and caring. No distant pity for him, no narrow sympathy, but an all-inclusive compassion. In staff meetings he would sometimes read the love hymn of 1 Corinthians 13 and then stop and shake his head as if overwhelmed by the words. He loved to speak to us about love and "the psychic power of change through love," as he put it. All of us on the staff saw the power of that love. Following his leadership was not a burden, but a delight because we knew he loved us.

How do spiritual leaders serve their people? They serve them by being what Henri Nouwen calls "contemplative critics."[10] We live in a disruptive, disoriented time. From the bosom of the Church must emerge perceptive prophets who can help us understand the world. (And I do not mean those narrow-visioned "prophets" who wag their tongues at every news event, certain that it heralds the dawning of doom and the coming of Antichrist.)

Nouwen writes, "The contemplative critic takes away the illusory mask of the manipulative world and has the courage to show what the true situation is."[11] Such leaders are "contemplatives" because the inner silences are necessary to have perspective on this present evil age. Such leaders are "critics" because evil must be named and clearly distinguished from the good.

One contemplative critic I know is a very busy, very good teacher. It is not just the knowledge he displays, which is considerable; it is not even the wisdom and insight that permeate his teaching, though this is immensely helpful. It is the bringing together of all these things with compassion and humility. We would often sit in his study, with its book-lined walls and the grand piano off to one side and talk about the events in the world—not just the big events but also simple, everyday things.

Once, for example, I recall him asking me, "Have you ever noticed how we heat our homes?" He proceeded without expecting me to respond, "There used to be a day when we really did have central heat—the fireplace. Now people can be in the same house all evening and never see each other. Do you realize how much the way we heat our homes affects our family life!" Casual comments like these would often release a flood of ideas in my mind that could take years to process. Repeatedly he helped me see the world with new eyes—he was, and is, a contemplative critic.

How do spiritual leaders serve their people? They serve them by living under authority themselves. Nothing is more dangerous than leaders accountable to no one. We all need others who can laugh at our pomposity and prod us into new forms of obedience. Power is just too dangerous a thing for any of us to face alone. If we will look at the abuses of power in the Church today, very often we will see that behind them is someone who has decided that he or she has a direct pipeline to God and therefore does not need the counsel and correction of the community.

It was no accident that the monastic response to the issue of power was the vow of obedience. (There is even evidence that this was the first of the monastic vows.) Now, we may not feel comfortable with the monastic vow of obedience, but we do need to find ways to live under authority. Living under authority does not necessitate a superior-inferior relationship. Very often it can take the form of mutual accountability. Pastors can gather a small cadre of trusted peers who can share the spiritual journey with one another. The old Methodist class meeting was a way of providing mutual support and accountability, and it could be a helpful model for us today.

I have a pastor friend who helped me in more ways than I can tell. We began meeting when I asked him to teach me to pray. We had wonderful times together— talking, laughing, praying. It was a loving environment in which we could follow the counsel of James to "confess your sins to one another, and pray for one another, that you may be healed" (James 5:16). In a way, we were spiritual directors for each other, though in those days I had never heard of the term. We were living under authority.

In the church, as in the family, the obligations of service run both ways. How do we serve our spiritual leaders? We serve them through glad obedience. Pastors and other leaders are shepherds of the flock; it is their responsibility to help us find the path of faithful living. Their word of counsel or correction or guidance needs to be taken with utmost seriousness. They can be wrong, for they are fallible human beings just like us, but wise leaders are quick to listen and slow to speak, so when they do speak we need to listen. We need to be under their authority.

How do we serve our spiritual leaders? We serve them through constructive criticism. Glad obedience is not blind obedience. There are times when spiritual leaders need our thoughtful and loving correction. This is a service too.

In the past when I traveled and spoke I sometimes took a friend with me to keep me honest. He knew me well, and if my stories were becoming exaggerated, it was his business to correct me. Jesus said that a prophet is without honor in his own country, but sometimes when we are in a far country we have too much honor. My companion helped me keep my perspective under the overzealous praise of well-meaning people.

Ordinary common sense should guide the service of constructive criticism. It should be done in privacy and with tact. It should be accompanied with loving support. It should always aim to build up, and not to tear down.

How do we serve our spiritual leaders? We serve them

through the ministry of prayer. Loving, joyful prayer in behalf of our leaders can do much. When I was a pastor I would ask people to come by any time and give me a "booster shot" of prayer. Now that I teach at a university I encourage students in the same ministry. I don't want people to come to my office only when they are angry or burdened with some great need. I want them to come also when they are doing quite well and would like to minister life to me. It is a wonderful ministry that they perform. People just cannot feel isolated and alone when they are surrounded with that kind of loving support. These are only a few examples of the many ways there are to serve leaders through the ministry of prayer.

THE VOW OF SERVICE IN THE WORLD

It is all well and good to speak of service within the warm confines of the home or the believing fellowship, but what about the rough and tumble of the world of business and politics? To be a servant in a culture predicated upon competition may not be easy, but Jesus never suggested that discipleship would be effortless.

How do we serve others in the world? We serve them by valuing their opinion. We serve them by acts of common courtesy. We serve them by guarding their reputation. We serve them by simple acts of kindness. We serve them by integrity of life. We serve them by honesty, truthfulness, and dependability.

These sound so simple that we are tempted to think of them as unimportant. Simple they are, unimportant they are not. If we will just reflect on those few people who have had significant impact on our lives, we will often discover individuals who have performed simple acts of goodness in our behalf. The friend who takes the time to listen to us, the teacher who encourages us, the boss who recognizes our potential, the spouse who loves us, warts and all—these are those who serve.

How do we serve others in the world? We serve them by preparing ourselves to lead and by accepting the opportunity to lead when it is offered. Our world is hungry for compassionate, servant leaders. Talk about a mission field! Changes in the world will be initiated by those who are on the inside of the great institutions and who seek to lead them into better performance for the public good. For example, I may make some small contribution to the quality of life in this city by standing on the outside of the institutional structures and critiquing them and bringing pressure to bear where I can, but it is the mayor who is really going to have an impact on this city. Corporations, universities, and government posts desperately need skilled leaders who can give them the stamp of their personal values. Sears, Roebuck, the largest merchandising company in America, was significantly influenced by the leadership of Julius Rosenwald, who brought "unusual humanness and trust" to that great institution.[12] Thousands of other institutions need that same kind of leadership.

But the leadership must be *servant* leadership. Servant leaders are people who are servants before they are leaders and will be servants when the tenure of leadership is concluded. In *Celebration of Discipline* I discussed the character of that servanthood. Here I want to stress that this servanthood is the core of who we are as persons. The vow of service has become so much a part of our very nature that the easy thing is to serve, the hard thing would be to keep from serving. Every action arises out of that foundation, including the desire to lead itself.

How do we serve others in the world? We serve them by providing "meaningful work" for employees and performing "honest labor" for employers. Robert Greenleaf, author of *Servant Leadership*, who devoted all of his working years to management positions in AT&T, suggests that the time is right for the emergence of a new business ethic. He writes, "The new ethic, simply but quite completely stated, will be: *the work exists for the person as much as the person exists for the work.* Put another way, the business exists as much to provide meaningful work to the person as it exists to provide a product or service to the customer."[13] Meaningful work is work in which people feel a sense of accomplishment. It is also work in which people feel that they are making a genuine contribution to the good of society. Business managers and institutional trustees serve by helping facilitate this sense of meaningful work. Employees reciprocate by contributing honest work, work that is as good as possible, work that is as productive as possible.

How do we serve others in the world? We serve them by a firm refusal to allow them to misuse and abuse us. To allow people to walk over us as one would a doormat is not service, but subservience. It is not healthy for us or for others. Service must not be identified with a false modesty or a Caspar Milquetoast personality. On the contrary, service resonates well with forthrightness and courageous action.

Therefore, if others try to walk over us and take advantage of our serving spirit, we stand up to the abuse. Our concern is not to defend "our rights," for we have already given those to God. Firmly, we press others to respect all people—including us—as fully human. The issues can be many and varied—low salary, heavy workload, lack of advancement—the resolve is always the same: never to be "thingafied."

THAT SOLITARY INDIVIDUAL

We have come a long way on our journey into the nature of legitimate power and greatness. At times we have wondered if power is too great a danger, too fraught with corruption, to ever be brought into the service of

Christ. But in the end we have discovered that power harnessed to service can be an immeasurable good in human society.

And so we take the risk. We lead, we parent, we serve —always remembering that we do not serve some nameless, faceless humanity, but "that solitary individual."*

There is an old story† of a young fugitive who was taken in by the people of a small village and given a place to stay. Eventually, however, enemy soldiers came and demanded to be told where the young man was hiding. When the people hesitated to tell, the soldiers threatened to destroy the village and kill every man, woman, and child by dawn if the man they sought was not turned over to them. Frightened, the people turned to their beloved pastor for guidance.

Torn between deserting his people and betraying the young man, the pastor went to his room and began reading his Bible in hope of finding an answer before dawn. He read all night, and finally, just before sunrise, he came to the words, "It is better for one man to die for the people, than for the whole nation to be destroyed" (John 11:50, Jerusalem Bible).

Trembling, the pastor walked outside and told the soldiers where to find the youth. As they took the fugitive away to be executed, the people in the village began celebrating and feasting because their lives had been spared. The pastor, however, did not celebrate with them. Instead he went to his room smitten with a deep heaviness. In the evening an angel appeared to him and asked, "What have you done?" The pastor replied slowly, "I be-

---

* The phrase is Søren Kierkegaard's. It was to "that Solitary Individual" that Kierkegaard dedicated his book *Purity of Heart Is to Will One Thing*.

† There are numerous versions of the story, but this particular one is drawn from Henri Nouwen's *The Wounded Healer* (Garden City, NY: Image Books, 1979), p. 25.

trayed the fugitive." "But didn't you know," said the angel, "that the fugitive you betrayed is the Messiah?" "No! No! No!" groaned the pastor, "I didn't know, how could I have known?" The angel spoke: "If you had set down your Bible and gone to the fugitive and looked into his eyes you would have known!"

The vow of service is first and foremost a vow to look into the eyes of that solitary individual. And perhaps, just perhaps, that look will keep us from betraying the Lord of glory. You see, service is not really charts and programs and elaborate strategies to serve humanity. No, it is looking into the fugitive's eyes.

It is easy for us to see enemy soldiers all about us, and their power looks so overwhelming that it threatens everything we hold dear. We become so preoccupied with the enemy that we never see the frightened look in the eyes of this little child or the far-off look in the eyes of that old man. In fact, we do not see them at all—all we can see is the threat to our own security. What we miss is the gaze of Christ.

The vow of service means to see that solitary individual. This is the way of Christ. This is the path of obedience. And I have discovered that regardless of where this path leads us or whatever difficult decisions it thrusts upon us, it is the path of life.

Epilogue: Living The Vows

> You are a Christian only so long as you constantly pose criti-
> cal questions to the society you live in . . . so long as you stay
> unsatisfied with the status quo and keep saying that a new
> world is yet to come.
>
> —HENRI NOUWEN

The vows of simplicity, fidelity, and service are for all Christians at all times. They are categorical imperatives for obedient followers of the obedient Christ. They are the beginning point from which we explore the depths of the spiritual life and discover our mission in the world.

The vows prod us into seeking a deeper spiritual life. We turn our backs on the superficiality of modern culture and plunge into the depths by making use of the classical disciplines of meditation, prayer, fasting, study, simplicity, solitude, submission, service, confession, worship, guidance, and celebration.[1] We help each other move forward in the spiritual life by encouraging those who advance and by comforting those who stumble.

The vows call us to a vigorous social witness. We stand in contradiction to the dominant culture, which has given its soul to the vows of greed, permissiveness, and selfishness. We critique the empty values of contemporary society, and call it to joyful discipleship to Christ.

The vows call us to evangelism and mission-mindedness. They are not ideals that we keep to ourselves and retreat into our cloistered homes to enjoy; they are to be freely shared with all who confess Christ as Lord and King. We have an obligation to win the nations and all peoples of the earth in anticipation of that day when "every knee should bow . . . and every tongue confess

that Jesus Christ is Lord, to the glory of God the Father"
(Phil. 2:10-11).

The time is now for a great new movement of the
Spirit of God. Such movements have emerged in the past.
Think of Abba Anthony and the desert fathers, Bernard
of Clairvaux and the Cistercians, Francis of Assisi and the
Friars Minor, Martin Luther and the Reformers, George
Fox and the early Quaker evangelists, and John Wesley
and the Methodist circuit riders.

It has happened before: it *can* happen again. Such a
movement must be disciplined, evangelistic, socially relevant, and unapologetically Christian. It must take with
utter seriousness the need for spiritual power to sustain
the life of faith and overcome evil with good. It must
combine courageous action with suffering love.

Perhaps the vows of simplicity, fidelity, and service
could form the common commitment of such a movement. The Church could spearhead such an effort by including the vows as the minimum basis for membership.
And the churches, if they are willing, could provide a
context for the living out of the vows.

May a new wave of earnest prayer sweep the community of faith to petition God for the emergence of such a
movement of the Spirit. May powerful servant leaders of
the apostolic mold rise up to lead us into new avenues of
faithfulness. May we be willing to be in the vanguard of
such a new movement toward Christ in our day.

Notes

Chapter 1. Money, Sex and Power in Christian Perspective

1. James O'Reilly, *Lay and Religious States of Life: Their Distinction and Complementarity* (Chicago: Franciscan Herald Press, 1976), p. 22.
2. I want to express my debt to Jim Smith for encouraging me to look at *The Idiot* in light of my work on money, sex, and power.
3. Fyodor Dostoevsky, *The Idiot*, trans. Constance Garnett (New York: Bantam Books, 1981), p. 569.
4. Letter to Apollon Maikov, January 12, 1868, quoted in Konstantin Mochulsky, *Dostoevsky: His Life and Work*, trans. Michael A. Minihan (Princeton, N.J.: Princeton University Press, 1967), p. 344.
5. Brother Ugolino di Monte Santa Maria, *The Little Flowers of Saint Francis*, trans. Raphael Brown (Garden City, N.Y.: Image Books, 1958), p. 227.
6. Ibid., p. 222.
7. Leland Ryken, "Puritan Work Ethic: The Dignity of Life's Labors," *Christianity Today*, 19 Oct. 1979, p. 15.
8. Ibid., p. 16.
9. Ibid., p. 18.
10. Henri J. M. Nouwen, *Clowning in Rome: Reflections on Solitude, Celibacy, Prayer, and Contemplation* (Garden City, N.Y.: Image Books, 1979), p. 45.
11. Brother Ugolino, *Little Flowers*, p. 274.
12. *Massachusetts Historical Society Proceedings*, vol. 21, p. 123, as quoted in Edmund S. Morgan, *The Puritan Family: Religion & Domestic Relations in Seventeenth-Century New England*, rev. ed. (New York: Harper & Row, 1966), p. 64.
13. Ibid., pp. 62-63.
14. Francis J. Bremer, *The Puritan Experiment* (New York: St. Martin's Press, 1976), pp. 177-78.
15. Ibid., p. 177.
16. Brother Ugolino, *Little Flowers*, p. 75.
17. Leonardo Boff, *God's Witnesses in the Heart of the World* (Chicago, Los Angeles, Manila: Claret Center for Researches in Spirituality, 1981) p. 149, as quoted in Francis J. Moloney, *A Life of Promise: Poverty, Chastity, Obedience* (Wilmington, Del.: Michael Glazier, Inc., 1984), p. 152.

18. Thomas Hooker, *The Cambridge Platform*, chap. 4, par. 3, as quoted in Herbert Wallace Schneider, *The Puritan Mind* (New York: Henry Holt, 1930), p. 19.
19. Dostoevsky, *The Idiot*, p. 156.

Chapter 2.   The Dark Side of Money

1. Quoted in Edward W. Bauman, *Where Your Treasure Is* (Arlington, Va.: Bauman Bible Telecasts, 1980), p. 74.
2. Quoted in ibid., p. 84.
3. Quoted in Bernard Gavzer, "What People Earn," *Parade Magazine*, 10 June 1984, p. 4.
4. Jacques Ellul, *Money & Power* (Downers Grove, Ill.: Inter-Varsity Press, 1984), pp. 166-68.
5. Quoted in Elizabeth O'Connor, *Letters to Scattered Pilgrims* (San Francisco: Harper & Row, 1979), p. 8.

Chapter 3.   The Light Side of Money

1. Quoted in Bauman, *Where Your Treasure Is*, p. 73.
2. Ibid., p. 113.
3. Ibid., pp. 89-90.
4. Quoted in Dallas Willard, "The Disciple's Solidarity with the Poor," 1984 (unpublished paper), p. 15.
5. I am indebted to Lynda Graybeal for this insight into the grace of giving.
6. I am indebted to Dallas Willard for insights into the control and use of money.

Chapter 4.   Kingdom Use of Unrighteous Mammon

1. Ellul, *Money & Power*, p. 94.
2. Quoted in Don McClanen, *Ministry of Money Newsletter* (Germantown, Md.: Nov. 1983), p. 4.
3. John Woolman, *The Journal of John Woolman and a Plea for the Poor* (Secaucus, N.J.: The Citadel Press, 1972), p. 41.

Chapter 5.   The Vow of Simplicity

1. John Calvin, *The Institutes of the Christian Religion, Book II*, trans. John Allen (Philadelphia: Presbyterian Board of Publication, 1813), chap. 8, sec. 45.

2. Ellul, *Money & Power*, pp. 110-11.
3. O'Connor, *Letters to Scattered Pilgrims*, p. 7.
4. Ron Sider, *Rich Christians in an Age of Hunger: A Biblical Study* (Downers Grove, Ill.: Inter-Varsity Press, 1977) pp. 175-78.
5. My thanks to Don McClanen for insight on this giving principle.
6. William Law, *A Serious Call to a Devout and Holy Life* (New York: Paulist Press, 1978), p. 60.
7. Quoted in Malcolm MacGregor, *Training Your Children to Handle Money* (Minneapolis: Bethany Fellowship, 1980), p. 111.
8. These ideas grew out of a visit I had with Don McClanen, Director of Ministry of Money.
9. Quoted in Goldian VandenBroeck, ed., *Less Is More: The Art of Voluntary Poverty* (New York: Harper & Row, 1978), pp. 172 & 223.

Chapter 6. Sexuality and Spirituality

1. Lewis B. Smedes, *Sex For Christians* (Grand Rapids, Mich.: Eerdmans, 1976), p. 47.
2. David Allan Hubbard, "Love and Marriage," *The Covenant Companion*, 1 Jan. 1969, p. 2. I am indebted to Dr. Hubbard for his insights both here and later in my discussion of the Song of Solomon.
3. David Allan Hubbard, "Love and Marriage," *The Covenant Companion*, 15 Jan. 1969, p. 4.
4. Saint Augustine, *The City of God*, vol. II of *The Nicene and Post-Nicene Fathers*, 1st series (Buffalo: The Christian Literature, 1887), bk. 14, chap. 18.
5. Derrick Bailey, *Sexual Relations in Christian Thought* (New York: Harper & Brothers, 1959), p. 59.
6. Quoted in Letha Dawson Scanzoni, *Sexuality* (Philadelphia: Westminster Press, 1984), p. 46.
7. Jeremy Taylor, *The Rule and Exercise of Holy Living and Dying*, rev. ed., vol. III of *The Whole Works of the Right Rev. Jeremy Taylor*, ed. Charles Page Eden (London: Longman, Green, Longman & Roberts, 1862), p. 63.
8. Edward S. Morgan, "The Puritans and Sex," *The New England Quarterly*, Dec. 1942, p. 607.
9. Smedes, *Sex for Christians*, p. 49.
10. C. S. Lewis, *Mere Christianity* (New York: Macmillan, 1943), p. 89.
11. Frederick Buechner, *Godric* (New York: Harper & Row, 1980), p. 153.
12. Smedes, *Sex for Christians*, p. 56.

13. E. Mansell Pattison and Myrna Loy Pattison, " 'Ex-Gays': Religiously Mediated Change in Homosexuals," *American Journal of Psychiatry*, vol. 167, no. 12 (Dec. 1980), p. 1553.

Chapter 7. Sexuality and Singleness

1. Donald Goergen, *The Sexual Celibate* (New York: Seabury Press, 1974), p. 181.
2. Smedes, *Sex for Christians*, p. 128.
3. Derrick Sherwin Bailey, *The Mystery of Love & Marriage* (New York: Harper, 1952), p. 53.
4. Smedes, *Sex for Christians*, p. 130.
5. Bailey, *Mystery of Love & Marriage*, pp. 53-54.
6. Smedes, *Sex for Christians*, p. 210.
7. McCary, James, *Human Sexuality*, 3d ed. (New York: D. Van Nostrand, 1978), p. 150.
8. "Autoeroticism," in *The Encyclopedia of Sexual Behavior*, ed. A. Ellis and Aborbanel, vol. I (New York: Hawthorne Books, 1961), p. 204.
9. Smedes, *Sex for Christians*, p. 246.
10. This diagram was first suggested to me by Walter Trobisch, though I have modified it somewhat. His discussion is found in *I Married You* (New York: Harper & Row, 1971), pp. 77-83.
11. Richard J. Foster, *Freedom of Simplicity* (San Francisco: Harper & Row, 1981), p. 137.
12. Heini Arnold, *In the Image of God: Marriage & Celibacy in Christian Life* (Rifton, N.Y.: Plough Publishing House, 1976), p. 161.

Chapter 8. Sexuality and Marriage

1. Arthur Cushman McGiffert, *Martin Luther: The Man and His Work* (New York: Century, 1910), p. 287.
2. See Helmut Thielicke, *The Ethics of Sex*, trans. John V. Doberstein (New York: Harper & Row, 1964), pp. 79-144.
3. I am indebted to Dallas Willard for the insights he has given me into the Christian basis for marriage, divorce, and remarriage.
4. Lewis, *Mere Christianity*, p. 99.
5. Quoted in J. Allan Peterson, *The Myth of the Greener Grass* (Wheaton, Ill.: Tyndale House, 1983), p. 175.
6. I am indebted to C. S. Lewis for this analogy. See *Mere Christianity*, p. 96.
7. Charles R. Swindoll, *Strike the Original Match: Rekindling & Preserving Your Marriage Fire* (Portland, Ore.: Multnomah Press, 1980), p. 136.

Chapter 9. The Vow of Fidelity

1. Ashley Montagu, *Touching: The Human Significance of the Skin*, 2d ed. (New York: Harper & Row, 1978), p. 166.
2. Scanzoni, *Sexuality*, pp. 60-62.
3. Thielicke, *The Ethics of Sex*, p. 90.
4. Charlie Shedd, *Letters to Karen* (New York: Avon Books, 1978), pp. 61-69.
5. Elizabeth Achtemeier, *The Committed Marriage* (Philadelphia: Westminster Press, 1976), p. 86.
6. Moloney, *A Life of Promise: Poverty, Chastity, Obedience*, p. 118.
7. C. S. Lewis, *The Four Loves* (New York: Harcourt Brace Jovanovich, 1960), p. 140.
8. Smedes, *Sex for Christians*, p. 169.
9. Lewis, *Mere Christianity*, p. 102.
10. James B. Nelson, *Embodiment: An Approach to Sexuality and Christian Theology* (Minneapolis: Augsburg, 1978), pp. 211-35. I am indebted to Dr. Nelson for the insights that follow.
11. Ibid., p. 213.
12. Ibid., p. 217.
13. Ibid., p. 219.
14. Ibid., pp. 220-21.
15. Ibid., p. 222.

Chapter 10. Destructive Power

1. The imagery that follows is adapted from a poem by Arthur Roberts entitled "The Age of Metal," in *Listen to the Lord* (Newberg, Ore.: Barclay Press, 1974), pp. 61-63.
2. Paul Tournier, *The Violence Within*, trans. Edwin Hudson (San Francisco: Harper & Row, 1978), p. 128.
3. J. R. R. Tolkien, *The Silmarillion* (New York: George Allen & Unwin, 1977), p. 8.
4. Cheryl Forbes, *The Religion of Power* (Grand Rapids, Mich.: Zondervan, 1983), p. 85.
5. Walter Wink, *Naming the Powers: The Language of Power in the New Testament*, vol. 1 (Philadelphia: Fortress Press, 1984), p. 5.
6. Roselle Chartock and Jack Spencer, eds., *The Holocaust Years: Society on Trial* (New York: Bantam Books, 1978), pp. 132-36.
7. Brother Ugolino, *The Little Flowers*, pp. 44-45.
8. John Woolman, *The Journal and Essays of John Woolman* (New York: Macmillan, 1922), p. 167.

9. Quoted in Thomas E. Drake, "Cadwalader Morgan—Antislavery Quaker of the Welsh Tract," *Friends Intelligencer,* vol. 98, no. 36 (1941), p. 200.
10. Tournier, *Violence Within,* p. 119.
11. Quoted in Jacques Ellul, *The Technological Society* (New York: Alfred A. Knopf, 1970), p. xi.
12. Wink, *Naming the Powers,* p. 130.
13. Ibid., p. 86.
14. James Nayler, *The Lamb's War* (1658), in Hugh Barbour and Arthur Roberts, *Early Quaker Writings* (Grand Rapids, Mich.: Eerdmans, 1973), pp. 106-7.
15. C. S. Lewis, *The Screwtape Letters* (West Chicago: Lord & King, 1976), p. 17.
16. George Fox, *The Journal of George Fox,* rev. John L. Nickalls (Cambridge: Cambridge University Press, 1952), p. 19.

Chapter 11.   Creative Power

Sherri McAdam, a former student of mine, wrote the sentence used as the epigraph on Chapter 11 on a final exam for the course "Pioneers in the Spiritual Life."

1. Dietrich Bonhoeffer, *The Cost of Discipleship,* trans. R. H. Fuller (New York: Macmillan, 1963), p. 7.
2. Quoted in ibid., p. 35.
3. M. Scott Peck, *The Road Less Traveled* (New York: Simon & Schuster, 1978), p. 286.
4. Moloney, *A Life of Promise: Poverty, Chastity, Obedience,* p. 128.
5. See Aleksander I. Solzhenitsyn, *The Gulag Archipelago,* trans. Thomas P. Whitney (New York: Harper & Row, 1973). See also Cheryl Forbes, *The Religion of Power,* p. 35.
6. See *The Power of the Powerless* by Jürgen Moltmann, trans. Margaret Kohl (San Francisco: Harper & Row, 1983).
7. Martin Hengel, *Christ and Power,* trans. Everett R. Kalin (Philadelphia: Fortress Press, 1977), p. 81.
8. Robert H. Schuller, *Self Esteem: The New Reformation* (Waco, Tex.: Word Books, 1982), p. 15.
9. Jean-Pierre de Caussade, *The Sacrament of the Present Moment,* trans. Kitty Muggeridge (San Francisco: Harper & Row, 1982), p. 22.
10. James Dobson, *The Strong Willed Child* (Wheaton, Ill.: Tyndale House, 1978), p. 76.
11. Myron Rush, *Management: A Biblical Approach* (Wheaton, Ill.: Victor Books, 1983), p. 13.

Chapter 12. The Ministry of Power

1. Caussade, *Sacrament of the Present Moment*, p. 64.
2. *Christian Faith and Practice in the Experience of the Society of Friends*, London Yearly Meeting of the Religious Society of Friends, ed. (Richmond, Ind.: Friends United Press, 1973), No. 25.
3. Jacques Ellul, *Violence: Reflections from a Christian Perspective* (New York: Seabury Press, 1969), p. 166.
4. Fox, *The Journal of George Fox*, p. 263.

Chapter 13. The Vow of Service

1. Michael Korda, *Success!* (New York: Random House, 1977), p. 4.
2. Donald P. McNeill, Douglas A. Morrison, and Henri J. M. Nouwen, *Compassion: A Reflection on the Christian Life* (Garden City, N.Y.: Image Books, 1982), p. 4.
3. See *Servant Leadership: A Journey into the Nature of Legitimate Power and Greatness* by Robert K. Greenleaf (New York: Paulist Press, 1977).
4. McNeill, Morrison, and Nouwen, *Compassion*, p. 35.
5. Ibid., p. 40.
6. Charlie Shedd, *Promises to Peter* (Waco, Tex.: Word Books, 1970), pp. 17-59.
7. Quoted in Richard J. Foster, *Celebration of Discipline* (San Francisco: Harper & Row, 1978), p. 110.
8. I am indebted to Henri Nouwen for the analysis that follows. See *The Wounded Healer* (Garden City, N.Y.: Image Books, 1979), pp. 25-47.
9. Ibid., p. 36.
10. Ibid., pp. 43-46.
11. Ibid., p. 45
12. Greenleaf, *Servant Leadership*, p. 139.
13. Ibid., p. 142.

Epilogue

1. See Foster, *Celebration of Discipline*.

Scripture Index

Subject Index

Freedom of
SIMPLICITY

Richard J. Foster

To
Dallas Willard

whose life reflects
the grace of simplicity
in all its manifold complexity

Designed by Donna Davis

CONTENTS

PREFACE

This is not a book that I was automatically drawn to write. I was, in fact, brought all but kicking and screaming to this task. I did in the end write it, but it is perhaps not irrelevant to note the reasons for my hesitancy.

First, there was the matter of my own experience in simplicity, or lack thereof. Did I know enough of the inner reality of simplicity to write with any degree of integrity? How deeply rooted was I in this life of unhurried peace and power? And then there was the matter of lifestyle. My family and I still struggle with decisions about money and possessions. By no stretch of the imagination do we have the final answer on what to buy or what to do without. And what about the corporate nature of simplicity? How could I, with any measure of competence, address the tangled issues of economics and world hunger and international trade? I felt, and do feel, like a beginner in all the varied aspects of simplicity.

Second, I hesitated because I know that Christian simplicity is a terribly complex matter. That is understandable, if paradoxical. Seldom in life is there any issue of significance that will yield to easy answers. Not only must we understand the biblical witness to simplicity and the rich tradition of the devotional masters, but we must interact with the contemporary issues. Further, it is necessary to boil all these matters down into the practical world in which we live—a world of schedules and demands, a world of bills and budgets. And this is no simple task.

Third, I was concerned about the danger of legalism. Simplicity is the most outward of all the Disciplines, and hence the most susceptible to corruption. How could I be specific without being rigid? How could I call people from greed without introducing a new pharisaism?

I had a fourth reason that made me cautious about writing a book on simplicity. Of the four, this one was my greatest concern, and the one to which I give attention in Chapter 1.

ACKNOWLEDGMENTS

Anyone who writes knows that an author's family always bears the greatest burden of sacrifice in the publication of a book. My wife, Carolynn, bore patiently my year-long obsession with the topic of simplicity. During the final months of writing, she took over all of my responsibilities at home and literally was mother and father to our boys. I thank her. Joel and Nathan were keenly interested in the progress of the book, and somehow always seemed to understand when the soccer game with Dad had to be cut short. I now look forward to many exciting and lengthy soccer games, even if I continue to lose every one of them.

The relationship between an author and an editor is unique. Roy M. Carlisle, my editor at Harper & Row, has an unusual ability to guide without dominating, to encourage without flattering, and to correct without discouraging. On several occasions his perceptive comments have opened up an entirely new creative direction for the book, for which I am grateful.

I was privileged to attend the International Consultation on Simple Lifestyle held at Hoddesdon, England, in March of 1980. The many Christian friends from around the world whom I met at that gathering helped me to see the infinite variety of faithful witnesses to the life of simplicity.

My deep appreciation goes to Dorothy Craven, Professor of English, Emeritus, at Friends University, who read the entire manuscript and made many helpful suggestions. My thanks also to a small literary group at Friends University who listened as I read much of the text of this book and encouraged me in its writing.

Numerous people read all or part of the manuscript and gave valuable suggestions. They include Kenneth Boulding, Harold Friesen, Verlin Hinshaw, Howard Macy, Raymond Nelson, and Tom Rozof. My thanks to Leroy Brightup and Harold Cope, who encouraged me throughout this project; and to Marilyn Pitts and Wanda Payne, who did the typing.

These and the many others who have surrounded my life have helped give shape to this book. I owe them an immense debt. They are the living voice of the Church—*vita vox ecclesiae*.

PART I

The Foundation

1. THE COMPLEXITY
OF SIMPLICITY

Seek simplicity—and distrust it.
—Alfred North Whitehead

Contemporary culture is plagued by the passion to possess. The unreasoned boast abounds that the good life is found in accumulation, that "more is better." Indeed, we often accept this notion without question, with the result that the lust for affluence in contemporary society has become psychotic: it has completely lost touch with reality. Furthermore, the pace of the modern world accentuates our sense of being fractured and fragmented. We feel strained, hurried, breathless. The complexity of rushing to achieve and accumulate more and more frequently threatens to overwhelm us; it seems there is no escape from the rat race.

Christian simplicity frees us from this modern mania. It brings sanity to our compulsive extravagance, and peace to our frantic spirit. It liberates us from what William Penn called "cumber." It allows us to see material things for what they are—goods to enhance life, not to oppress life. People once again become more important than possessions. Simplicity enables us to live lives of integrity in the face of the terrible realities of our global village.

Christian simplicity is not just a faddish attempt to respond to the ecological holocaust that threatens to engulf us, nor is it born out of a frustration with technocratic obesity. It is a call given to every Christian. The witness to simplicity is profoundly rooted in the biblical tradition, and most perfectly exemplified in the life of Jesus Christ. In one form or another, all the devotional masters have stressed its essential nature. It is a natural and necessary outflow of the Good News of the Gospel having taken root in our lives.

While it is important to stress that Christian simplicity is more than a mere reaction to the modern crisis, it should also be underscored that simplicity is keenly relevant to the massive problems of our world. We are witnessing poverty and starvation on a scale unprecedented in human history. By the time we fall asleep tonight another ten thousand individuals will have died of starvation—over four hundred per hour. Many more millions live on the brink of extinction—malnourished, aimless, desperate. It is difficult to relate to statistics, even when we know they represent precious ones for whom Christ died. But it is not hard to relate to the story of a man such as Kallello Nugusu, who had to sell his two oxen in order to buy food to keep his wife and six children alive when the famine struck Ethiopia. He then had no way to plow his fields and plant his crops, and the food was gone. When asked what he would do, he responded that he didn't know. Then, dropping his head into his hands, he said, "When my children cry because they are hungry, then it is very hard to be a father."[1]

Though such accounts touch us deeply, we often feel helpless to do anything. How can we respond with any degree of integrity and effectiveness? It is the Discipline of simplicity that gives us the basis for developing a strategy of action that can address this and many other social inequities. Individual, ecclesiastical, and corporate action can spring from the fertile soil of simplicity.

We also struggle with the problem of competing responsibilities that all demand our attention. Like Jack's beanstalk, our obligations seem to grow overnight. We are trapped in a rat race, not just of acquiring money, but also of meeting family and business obligations. We pant through an endless series of appointments and duties. This problem is especially acute for those who sincerely want to do what is right. With frantic fidelity we respond to *all* calls to service, distressingly unable to distinguish the voice of Christ from that of human manipulators. We feel bowed low with the burden of integrity.

But we do not need to be left frustrated and exhausted from the demands of life. The Christian grace of simplicity can usher us into the Center of unhurried peace and power. Like Thomas Kelly, we can come to know by experience that God "never guides us into an intolerable scramble of panting feverishness."[2] In simplicity, we enter the deep silences of the heart for which we were created. Pope John XXIII declared, "The older I grow the more clearly I perceive the dignity and winning beauty of simplicity in thought, conduct, and speech: a desire to simplify all that is complicated and to treat everything with the greatest naturalness and clarity."[3]

Complex Simplicity

While simplicity provides an answer to the modern dilemma, it does not provide an *easy* answer. We must never confuse simplicity with simplism. If you came to this book in the hope of finding four easy steps to total simplicity, you will be sadly disappointed. Simplistic answers, by their very nature, fail to perceive the rich, ordered complexity of life.

Whether we peer into the universe of the telescope or the universe of the microscope, we cannot help being amazed at the varied complexity of the created order. From galaxy to ant to atom we are awed by the intricate mosaic. The apparatus inside our head is literally inconceivable in its complexity, containing perhaps a hundred billion neurons. And beyond that is the mystery of human consciousness, which baffles the imagination. As the Psalmist declared, we are indeed "fearfully and wonderfully made."

Christian simplicity lives in harmony with the ordered complexity of life. It repudiates easy, dogmatic answers to tough, intricate problems. In fact, it is this grace that frees us sufficiently to appreciate and respond to the complex issues of contemporary society. The duplicitous mind, on the other hand, tends to confuse and obscure. While the dogmatic person cannot understand the diversity in simplicity, the double-minded person cannot perceive the unity in complexity.

This brings us to the central paradox of our study: the complexity of simplicity. The fact that a paradox lies at the heart of the Christian teaching on simplicity should not surpise us. The life and teachings of Christ were often couched in paradox: the way to find our life is to lose it (Matt. 10:39); in giving we receive (Luke 6:38); he who is the Prince of Peace brings the sword of division (Matt. 10:34). Those with simplicity of heart understand the Lord, because much of their experience resonates with paradox. It is the arrogant and the obscurant who stumble over such realities.

Paradoxes, of course, are only apparent contradictions, not real ones. Their truth is often discovered by maintaining a tension between two opposite lines of teaching. Although both teachings may contain elements of truth, the instant we emphasize one to the exclusion of the other the truth becomes distorted and disfigured. We can see this easily enough when we insist—rightly I think—that God is both imminent and transcendent, both in the created order and beyond the created order. If we stress imminence to the exclusion of transcendence, we end up with some form of pantheism. Conversely, if we stress transcendence to the exclusion of imminence, we will end up with a detached, disinterested, wind-the-clock-up kind of God. If we embrace either end of the teaching exclusively, we get a distortion; if we hold both in tension, we find the God of Abraham, Isaac, and Jacob. We could just as easily take concepts such as the love and justice of God, the deity and humanity of Christ, or any one of the number of examples that abound in the Scripture.* Let us consider some of the complex aspects of simplicity that we must keep in proper tension if we are to enter into this important Christian virtue.

A pivotal paradox for us to understand is that simplicity is both a grace and a discipline. An old Shaker hymn articulates this double reality with amazing clarity. Joyfully, there is the affirmation,

> 'Tis a gift to be simple,
> 'Tis a gift to be free.

---

* Though not central to the present discussion, it should nevertheless be noted that some paradoxes involve keeping more than two lines of teaching in tension. The doctrine of the Trinity, for example, involves three separate teachings which must be kept in undivided tension if we are to do justice to the biblical record. Incidentally, it is only in this perfect tension that we see the profound unity in the Godhead. It is the example *par excellence* of complex simplicity.

as well as the assertion that we must,

> Turn and turn,
> Till we turn 'round right.

Simplicity is a grace because it is given to us by God. There is no way that we can build up our willpower, put ourselves into this contortion or that, and attain it. It is a gift to be graciously received. By way of illustration, the story is sometimes told of Hans the tailor. He had quite a good reputation, and so when an influential entrepreneur in the city needed a new suit he went to Hans requesting one be tailor-made. But the next week when he came to pick it up, the customer found that one sleeve twisted this way and the other that way, one shoulder bulged out and the other caved in. He pulled and struggled until finally, wrenched and contorted, he managed to make his body fit the strange configuration of the suit. Not wanting to cause a scene he thanked the tailor, paid his money, and caught the bus for home. A passenger on the bus, after surveying the businessman's odd appearance for some time, finally asked if Hans the tailor had made the suit. Receiving an affirmative reply, he remarked, "Amazing! I knew that Hans was a good tailor but I had no idea he could make a suit to fit perfectly someone as deformed as you." Just like the entrepreneur, we often get an idea of what simplicity should look like and then we proceed to push and shove until, bruised and battered, we "fit." But that is not the way simplicity comes. It slips in unawares. A new sense of wonder, concentration, even profundity steals into our personality. We change our lifestyle, even taking up the ministry of poverty when it is clearly right and good, out of inner promptings, knowing that when the call is made the power is given. The tailor-made fit is perfect. Simplicity is a grace.

Of course, we must not forget the other pole of our tension, for simplicity is also a discipline. It is a discipline because we are called to do something. Simplicity involves a consciously chosen course of action involving both group and individual life. What we *do* does not give us simplicity, but it does put us in the place where we can receive it. It sets our lives before God in such a way that he can work into us the grace of simplicity.

It is a vital preparation, a cultivating of the soil, a "sowing to the Spirit," as Paul put it.

Perhaps we need to learn to speak of "disciplined grace." Isn't that the profound reality which underlies the symbiotic alliance between faith and works? Our salvation is *sola fide,* by faith alone, but without works faith is dead. The Gospel reality comes to us by pure grace, but it bears the mark of spiritual discipline.

A second, closely aligned paradox regarding Christian simplicity is that it is both easy and difficult. It is easy in the same way in which all Christian graces, having once worked their way into the ingrained habit structure of our lives, are easy. It is easy in the way that breathing is easy. "Virtue is easy," say the moral philosophers, and so it is once it is embedded in the personality. The playing of Tchaikovsky's *Pathétique* is easy to the accomplished musician who has labored until it flows out in his very body language; but until then it is difficult, painfully difficult. And in simplicity there are times of struggle and effort, times when we despair of ever having our lifestyles where we feel they should be, times when we wonder if our lives will ever be of one piece. But occasionally, in the middle of the struggle, we have a sense of entering in, and spontaneously we glorify our Father in heaven because we know that we have done no more than to receive a gift.

A third tension we must work to keep in balance is between the inner and outer dimensions of simplicity. Simplicity is an inward reality that can be seen in an outward lifestyle. We must have both; to neglect either end of this tension is disastrous.

If simplicity were merely a matter of externals, things would be quite easy. We would then need only to formulate the system (no small trick to be sure) that defines the boundaries— Christian faithfulness would allow us to live in this income bracket but not that one, to purchase this house but not that one. We would have a clearly definable arrangement, even if it would need periodic adjustment to keep abreast of inflation. It would be clear who is in and who is out, who is faithful and who is not. Presto, a new pharisaism. Very fine, thank you.

Sometimes I genuinely wish it were that way. And I have no

desire to speak disparagingly of the many groups who have developed such systems. In fact, I envy them at times, because the clarity of that approach has immense power to motivate and change behavior. But as we all know, its end result is bondage and death. The letter always kills; the Spirit alone gives life. Gospel simplicity gives freedom and liberation.

The outer expression of simplicity must flow from the inner resources. It is learning to walk in the Spirit that builds the life of purity, unity, and grace. There is an inwardness that is central to our task; without it all is lost. We delude ourselves, however, if we think we can possess the inner reality of simplicity without its having a profound effect upon the way we live; the tension must be maintained.

Perhaps you have noted that I have been dealing with the age-old continuum of legalism to license. We reject legalism because it leads to spiritual suicide, and we reject license for the same reason. There is another way—the life of the Spirit. The Apostle Paul gives the classic formulation of this reality in his Epistle to the Galatians. There he came down about as hard as he possibly could against casuistic legalism and for the glorious freedom that we know in Christ, perceptively adding that we must not allow our freedom to be an opportunity of the flesh. He concludes, "If we live by the Spirit, let us also walk by the Spirit" (Gal. 5:25). If we possess the inward reality, it must manifest itself in an outward lifestyle.

A fourth paradox in simplicity is seen in the affirmation of both the goodness and the limitation of material things. The material world is good, but it is a limited good—limited in the sense that we cannot make a life out of it. To deny the goodness of the created order is to be an ascetic. To deny the limitation of the created order is to be a materialist.

The Christian faith views material things as created goods God has given us to enjoy. It does not dismiss material things as inconsequential, or worse yet, as evil. The material world is good and meant to make life happy. In fact, adequate provision is an essential ingredient in the good life. In human society today, misery often arises from a simple lack of provision.

Misery also arises when people try to make a life out of provision. While it is an essential ingredient in the good life, it is by no means the only ingredient, nor is it even the most important one. So often the biblical teaching on provision has been taken and twisted into a doctrine of gluttonous prosperity. All the subtle, and sometimes not so subtle, coaxing to "love Jesus and get rich" reflects our failure to see the biblical limitation upon things. Incarnated into our theology are covetous goals under the guise of the promises of God. And the interesting thing about all these little gimmicks to blessedness is that they work, they really do work. That is, they work if what we want is a little money; but if we desire the abundance which God gives, they fail.

Again, we see that Christian simplicity does not yield to simplistic answers. The tension must be maintained: things are good, but that good is limited.

Perhaps one more example of paradoxical tension will be sufficient to emphasize the fact that our journey into simplicity will be as intricate, varied, and rich as human personality itself. I refer to the attractive ability to be single-hearted and at the same time sensitive to the tough, complex issues of life. It is a strange combination and quite difficult to explain, though quite easy to recognize. There is focus without dogmatism, obedience without over-simplification, profundity without self-consciousness. It means being cognizant of many issues while having only one issue at the center—holy obedience.

Jesus spoke to the heart of the matter when he taught us that if the eye were single, the whole body would be full of light (Matt. 6:22). Dietrich Bonhoeffer, before he died at the hands of the Nazis, said, "To be simple is to fix one's eye solely on the simple truth of God at a time when all concepts are being confused, distorted, and turned upside down."[4] Such focus makes one decisive and able to cut through the Gordian knots of life.

But we must never confuse the clear decisiveness of the single-hearted with the simplistic decisiveness of the propagandist. While propagandists have a singleness of purpose that is often quite amazing (and baffling), they do not enter it by the same path as the single-hearted. In joyful abandon they pontificate on politics, religion, and philosophy, without the slightest awareness or concern for the intricacies involved. At times they may come to exactly the same conclusion as the single-hearted, and may even express it in the same words and with the same conviction. But they came to the conclusion too quickly, too easily. It is hollow because it lacks the integrity of painful struggle.

Have you ever experienced this situation? One person speaks, and even though what he or she is saying may well be true you draw back, sensing the lack of authenticity. Then someone else shares, perhaps even the same truth in the same words, but now you sense an inward resonance, the presence of integrity. What is the difference? One is providing simplistic answers, the other is living in simplicity.

The Part and the Whole

Oversimplification is a danger in any field of study. But the danger is especially insidious in the study of Christian simplicity, because it can so easily be viewed as a virtue. We have touched on a few pitfalls; however, we have not yet mentioned the area of greatest peril: the danger of assuming that simplicity can function independently of the rest of Christian devotion. Simplicity is the most outward of all the Spiritual Disciplines and therefore the most susceptible to corruption, and the greatest corruption is to isolate it. It was this danger that prevented me for many months from consenting to write a full-length book on the subject. I had written about simplicity before, but always in the context of the Classical Disciplines of the Spiritual Life.[5] There it was integrated into the whole of Christian devotion; it was only a part, howbeit a vital part, of something much larger, more comprehensive.

Simplicity needs to be seen in the light of the whole. For example, there is an intrinsic relationship between simplicity and prayer, especially that central aspect of prayer which is trust. My children love pancakes, so once in a while I get up early to fix them a batch. It is interesting to watch those boys. They wolf down pancakes as if there were an endless supply. They are not worried one whit about the price of eggs or my ability to provide them with pancakes. Not once have I seen them slipping some into their pocket thinking, "I don't know about Dad; I had better put away a little stash so that I can be sure of pancakes tomorrow." As far as they are concerned, the reservoir of pancakes is infinite. All they need to do is ask and, if it is in their best interest, they know they will receive. They live in trust. And without this spirit of trust we will find it exceedingly difficult (should I say impossible?) to live on the basis of prayer for daily bread. No, we will need an adequate stash somewhere, just in case—and be assured that what we now have is *never* adequate.

Paul counseled Christians to live free from anxiety. That, of course, is more easily said than done. Everything in our training and in our culture combats a carefree spirit of unconcern. How can we be free from anxiety? What resource is available to us? Paul perceived the resource to be prayer: "Have no anxiety about anything, but in everything by prayer and supplication with thanksgiving let your requests be made known to God" (Phil. 4:6). Prayer frees us from anxiety because it teaches us trust. And the result is peace: "And the peace of God, which passes all understanding will keep your hearts and minds in Christ Jesus" (Phil. 4:7). Prayer and simplicity are intertwined.

Again, simplicity and solitude walk hand in hand. Solitude refers principally to the inward unity that frees us from the panicked need for acclaim and approval. Through it we are enabled to be genuinely alone, for the fear of obscurity is gone; and we are enabled to be genuinely with others, for they no longer control us.

It is not difficult to see how dependent simplicity is upon solitude. Enslavement to the opinions of others is the source of a great deal of duplicity in modern society. How often we discover our action to be prompted, not by the divine Center, but by what others may say or think. Sadly, we must confess that our experience is all too frequently characterized by endless attempts to justify what we do or fail to do. And how violently this problem rears its ugly head the moment we seek a simpler lifestyle. Whereas before we were tyrannized by the desire to look affluent, now we are tyrannized by the desire to look scant. If what we own can look slightly austere and unvarnished, then perhaps others will think we live in simplicity. Painfully, we know we are too dependent upon the approval of others. We sincerely want to do what is right, but our own self-consciousness betrays our lack of true simplicity. Our struggle affirms the observation of François Fénelon, "These people are sincere, but they are not simple."[6] The grace of solitude must be rooted deep within if we are to know simplicity of heart.

And so it is with all the Christian Disciplines. If we detach simplicity from them, we will turn it into something other than what it is. But when we view it within the landscape of the whole of Christian spirituality, we gain balance and perspective.

It is not wrong for us to isolate some aspect of the spiritual walk for the sake of study, as long as we understand the artificiality of the isolation. And we must always come back to the whole. Perhaps the technical sciences can ignore the whole for the part,* but in the spiritual walk it is ruinous. The life with God, hid in Christ, is a unity, a seamless robe. That, of course, is the essence of its simplicity and the cause of its complexity.

We might be tempted to discouragement by the apparent intricacies of a subject we thought would be straightforward and easy to grasp. At times simplicity seems as elusive as humility; the moment we think we have it we have lost it. It seems fraught with hidden crevices and box canyons. How can we ever expect to pick our way through these perplexing catacombs?

If, in a small way, this describes your feelings and fears and even frustrations, I would like to bring you a word of encouragement. The very sense of awe you feel at the immensity of the task is the first requirement for entering the grace of simplicity. Those who come bolting in discover not simplicity, but arrogance.

Beyond that, you will be encouraged to discover that simplicity is much more tangled in analysis than it is in practice. If you desire Christ and his way with sincerity of heart, he will faithfully teach you. He will not let you stray far. Lovingly, tenderly, he will always bring you back to the straight gate and the narrow way. You need not worry if you find it difficult to ex-

---

* This is called specializing, and I have my reservations about it even in the technical sciences.

plain exactly what this virtue is. We could well say of simplicity what Thomas à Kempis said of compunction of heart, "It is better to practice it than to know how to define it."[7]

Models of simplicity are desperately needed today. Our task is urgent and relevant. Our century thirsts for the authenticity of simplicity, the spirit of prayer, and the life of obedience. May we be the embodiment of that kind of authentic living.

2. THE BIBLICAL ROOTS: THE OLD COVENANT

All plenty which is not my God is poverty to me.
—*St. Augustine*

Simplicity is deeply rooted in the Old Testament revelation. In it, God revealed both what he is like and how people are to live. The two ideas are inseparable. The more clearly we understand the nature of God, the more clearly we understand how we are to live.

The pressing question today is not, "Is there a God?" but, "What kind of God is there?" Few seriously champion atheism because of its obvious intellectual vulnerability, but many have searching questions about what God is like. Is God cruel or is he good? In short, can God be trusted? Simplicity of heart can flourish only in the fertile soil of trust, and it is the Old Testament's revelation of the faithfulness and goodness of God that opens the door to that trust.

We also struggle to understand how we are to live. Few of us would buy into the naive notion that the accumulation of bigger and better things will give us joy or purpose. Yet neither are we comfortable with the rigid ascetic who thunders down denunciations on the evil of possessions. We don't want to be materialists, ever acquiring and ever hoarding. And yet, John the Baptist with his skins and wild honey doesn't quite seem the model either. How can we put material things in a proper perspective in a world of dental bills and piano lessons? How do we decide for or against a new microwave oven or a dishwasher? This ancient record of God's revelation to his people, Israel, provides us with important hints for answering such questions.

It is, of course, a long journey from Kadesh-barnea to London or Chicago in both space and time. The cultural distance might tempt us to wonder if instruction about lifestyle—even divine instruction—given to shepherds and farmers would have any relevance to modern urbanites. What does the law of gleaning have to do with the consumer price index? How can the year of Jubilee possibly relate to the international trade deficit?

The problem is a real one, but thoughtful people realize that though specific legislation often has only parochial application, the principles inherent in that legislation are timeless. In fact, the Old Testament revelation provides us with some of the most profound perceptions into life to be found anywhere. That, of course, does not solve the hermeneutical question of how to understand the perceptions, or the practical question of how to apply the perceptions, but it does save us from temporal snobbishness.

Radical Dependence

The creation story is the starting point for our understanding of simplicity. At center stage is God, who speaks, and at his word the entire universe comes crashing into being. The high point of his creative effort is humanity, whom he made male and female.

The radical dependence of the entire creation upon God is a central teaching of this breathtaking narrative, and certainly the pivotal notion for our understanding of simplicity. We have no independent existence, no self-sustaining ability. All we are and all we possess is derived.

We need to lift high the biblical doctrine of creation today, particularly our own creatureliness. We are not the captains of our souls nor the masters of our fates. We are part of the created order and hence totally dependent. Our posture is not one of arrogant acquisition, but of simple trust. What we have or ever will have comes from his gracious hand.

We are dependent upon God for even our sense of worth as individuals. Our uniqueness and dignity is rooted in our creation in the image of God. Our value is not tied to wealth, status, accomplishments, or position. It is a gift. Obviously, this wonderful truth flies in the face of the modern tendency to define people by what they produce or what they have.

The terrible reality of the fall was nothing more than a repudiation of our dependence upon God. Adam and Even took to themselves what God had forbidden. They said, in effect, "We will provide for ourselves." They mistrusted the goodness of God by believing the serpent's lie that God was holding back from them something good. And when they did, they realized that they were naked. The nakedness in question was not so much a lack of clothes as it was the awful vulnerability which they assumed in repudiating their dependence. Independence always comes at a high price, and especially so when it involves a rejection of the gracious provision of God.

Simplicity means a return to the posture of dependence. Like children we live in a spirit of trust. What we have we receive as a gift.

Radical Obedience

If the first insight into simplicity that we receive from the Old Testament is radical dependence, the second is radical obedience. Perhaps nowhere is this more graphically seen than when Abraham was called upon to surrender his most priceless treasure—his son Isaac. God spoke, Abraham obeyed. No contingency plans, no skirting around the issue, no ifs ands or buts. Through a long painful process Abraham's life had been honed down to one truth—obedience to the voice of Yahweh. This "holy obedience" forms the grid through which the life of simplicity flows.

Radical obedience is possible only when God has our supreme allegiance. The Ten Commandments begin with three staccato warnings against idolatry. Idolatry is, of course, the attempt to erect an allegiance higher than God. "No," shouts the Decalogue; the one true God must be the heart of our devotion.

Today we need to hear again that God alone is worthy of our worship and obedience. The idolatry of affluence is rampant. Our greed for more dictates so many of our decisions. Notice how the fourth commandment of the Sabbath rest strikes at the heart of this everlasting itch to get ahead. We find it so very hard to rest when, by working, we can get the jump on everyone else. There is no greater need today than the freedom to lay down the heavy burden of getting ahead.

The prohibition against covetousness is the tenth commandment. At the heart of the sin of covetousness is the inner lust to have. Obviously, there is nothing wrong with having things; it is the inordinate desire, the inner compulsion, the undisciplined craving that is condemned. Covetousness is the idolatrous worship of things. But, and here comes the rub, all of us feel that we are in complete control of our desire for things. We would never admit to an ungovernable spirit of covetousness. The problem is that we, like the alcoholic, are unable to recognize the disease once we have been engulfed by it. Only by the help of others are we able to detect the inner spirit that places wealth above God. And we must come to fear the idolatrous state of covetousness because the moment things have priority, radical obedience becomes impossible.

The Generosity of God

A dominant note in the Old Testament witness is the generosity of God, who freely gives to his children. Repeatedly in the creation story we have the confession that the earth is good. God lavished abundant provision upon the original pair.

God called Abram from Ur of the Chaldeans to be the father of a new nation. With that call was the promise to make Abram's name great and to prosper him in material ways (Gen. 12:1–7). This pledge was certainly fulfilled, for we are informed that "Abram was very rich in cattle, in silver, and in gold" (Gen. 13:2).

Abraham's son of promise, Isaac, was likewise showered with material provision: "The Lord blessed him [Isaac], and the man became rich, and gained more and more until he became very wealthy. He had possessions of flocks and herds, and a great household, so that the Philistines envied him" (Gen. 26:12–14). Even Jacob, who received the parental blessing through deceit, was indeed blessed. When he sought to return to his homeland he offered to Esau, his brother, a tribute that only the genuinely wealthy could afford—490 costly animals, including thirty camels with their young (Gen. 32:13–21). Joseph and Job both went through the crucible of obedience and both were rewarded handsomely in the end. Solomon chose wisdom above wealth, but received both in abundance.

The book of Deuteronomy is peppered throughout with promised blessing, and we do the text a grave injustice if we seek to spiritualize the blessing. It was literal land and flocks with which God said he would bless the people: "He will love you, bless you, and multiply you; he will also bless the fruit of your body and the fruit of your ground, your grain and your wine and your oil, the increase of your cattle and the young of your flock" (Deut. 7:13). Deuteronomy 16:15 is typical of so much in this echoed law code: "God will bless you in all your produce and in all the work of your hands, so that you will be altogether joyful." Note that the rejoicing is *because* of the abundant provision from the hand of God.

Even the Book of Amos, which lashed out so viciously at the uncompassionate accumulation of wealth, saw a day:

> When the plowman shall overtake the reaper
>   and the treader of grapes him who sows the seed;
> the mountains shall drip sweet wine,
>   and all the hills shall flow with it.
> I will restore the fortunes of my people Israel . . .
>   says the Lord your God. (Amos 9:13–15)

And Malachi flatly declared that, if only the people would open their hearts in obedient giving, God would open the windows of heaven and pour out upon them material blessing beyond what they could possibly contain (Mal. 3:10).

We do need to stress that the promise of material blessing was a conditioned promise. It was no blank check. There was the stipulation, "If you are willing and obedient you shall eat the good of the land" (Isa. 1:19). That is to say, there was the strong emphasis upon the inward nature of simplicity—holy obedience—that conditioned all the promised provision. And a vital aspect of that obedience was compassionate provision for the poor and needy.

And why shouldn't the high note of obedience have among its secondary notes the promise of blessing? After all, it would be a strange kind of God who would always repay obedience by withholding the good of the earth. Such did sometimes happen, as the Psalmist testified, but even so he was puzzled by the prosperity the wicked enjoyed while he suffered (Ps. 73). God at times does withhold material blessing for our greater good, but that is the exception to the rule of gracious provision, which is also for our good. It is like God to want to give us good things.

The connection between obedience and blessing is genuinely significant, and the significance is not primarily in the notion of being rewarded for doing what is right. That has its place, but it is a minor place, almost a childish place. *The deeper reality in obedience is the kind of spirit it works into us.* It is a spirit that crucifies greed and covetousness. It is a spirit of compassion and outreach. It is a spirit of sensitivity and trust. Once this inner disposition has taken over our personality, material blessings cannot hurt us, for they *will* be used for right purposes. We will recognize material goods to be not for us alone, but for the good of all.

This leads to another important factor in understanding the Old Testament emphasis upon material blessings. Almost without exception the promised provision was for the community rather than the individual. The stress was upon the good of the nation, the tribe, the clan. The idea that one could cut off a piece of the consumer pie and go off and enjoy it in isolation was unthinkable.

Generosity Begets Generosity

God's great generosity to us sets us free to model that generosity toward others. Because he gave, we are enabled to give.

This celebration of the generosity of God and freedom to give in return is clearly seen in the year of Jubilee (Lev. 25). The Jubilee was a call to a divinely enabled freedom from possessions and an equitable restructuring of social arrangements.

Once every fifty years, on the Day of Atonement, the loud trumpet was to sound proclaiming "liberty throughout the land to all its inhabitants" (Lev. 25:10). All slaves were to be set free. All debts were to be canceled. All land was to be returned to the original owner.

Inherent in the concept of the Jubilee was a carefree spirit of joyous trust. God could be relied upon to provide what was needed. He had promised, "I will command my blessing upon you" (Lev. 25:21). It was this inner spirit of trust that gave the ability to meet the stipulations of the Jubilee.

There was an important social principle in the Jubilee. If faithfully executed (which it was not), it would have utterly eliminated the age-old problem of the rich becoming richer and the poor becoming poorer. It was, in effect, legislative justice on behalf of the poor; an institutionalized legal mechanism for solving a social and spiritual problem. The vicious cycle of poverty could be broken. Parents who had lost everything and were forced to sell themselves into slavery to survive knew that their children need not be crushed with their economic legacy. They could have a fresh start. Conversely, the wealthy could not forever lord it over those less fortunate. Their advantaged position was not perpetual.

We would do well today to take a thoughtful look at this unique approach for curbing social injustice. We live in a world in which the gulf that separates the haves and the have-nots is widening at a phenomenal rate. It is, of course, the height of simplistic thinking to assume that you can take an ancient and local law and attempt to universalize it and apply it to the complex international scene. But neither is the Jubilee principle totally irrelevant to our day. In fact, it just might give us some important clues into ways we could have a saner, more just world.

Another interesting thing about the Jubilee was the perspective it gave on the land, a perspective that was characteristic of Old Testament thought. The land did not have value in and of itself, but only in terms of the number of crops it would produce until the Jubilee (Lev. 26:16). Land was not used as an investment as is common today. The point was that the children of Israel did not own the land; they were merely given the use of it. God was the sovereign of the land: "The land shall not be sold in perpetuity, for the land is mine" (Lev. 25:23). Like the treasurer of a company or the housekeeper of a mansion, human authority over the land was one of supervision. God had so parceled out the land that all the people could benefit from its produce.

This principle of equitable distribution rather than hoarding, and managership rather than ownership, was as revolutionary then as it is now. What would happen if this idea—that the purpose of the land is to serve the needs of humanity rather than provide the means of self-aggrandizement—were to be accepted today? What would that say to our real estate investments? Perhaps such an approach would not meet with general approval, but what if Christians were to believe that the land was for the good of all people alike? Is it possible that this group alone could unleash resources that would amputate starvation from the face of the earth?

We have no historical evidence that the children of the covenant ever implemented the Jubilee. However, that tells us only that they were often a stiff-necked and disobedient people; it provides no light on the rightness or workability or even desirability of such an arrangement. What the Jubilee principle does show us is God's deep abiding concern for justice and equity.

The law of the first fruits also illustrates how our generosity flows out of God's generosity. This law stipulated that the first of the crop to ripen was to be given to God. It was, in effect, an act of trust in the generosity of God. They gave in confidence that they would be able to bring in the rest of the harvest. It was an acted-out confession of God as the gracious Giver of all good things.

Similar to the law of first fruits, the tithe was a concept of joyful celebration. By Jesus' day this delightful rule had become as twisted and abused as it has in our own day. It is sad to think that tithing, which was intended to express liberation and freedom, has been so often turned into another way to put people into bondage.

The custom of tithing is first mentioned in the Bible in connection with Abraham. Upon his return from a retaliation raid, Abraham joyfully gave Melchizedek a tenth of the spoils and gave 100 percent of the remainder to the King of Sodom. Although the King objected, Abraham insisted, "Lest you should say, 'I have made Abram rich'" (Gen. 14:17–24). Abraham gave lavishly in celebration of God's power over his enemies. He was not counting each shekel to ensure his fair share—he wanted to get rid of it all. There was a spirit of joy and freedom connected with the giving.

The Mosaic law maintains this sense of joyful festivity. A full tenth of the Israelite's income, beyond the first fruits, was to be given away in celebration of the gracious provision of God. The money was used to care for the Levites, the sojourner, and the poor and needy. It was also used to underwrite the expenses of the festivities involved in celebrating God's generosity:

> You shall tithe all the yield of your seed . . . and before the Lord your God . . . you shall eat the tithe of your grain, of your wine, and of your oil, and the firstlings of your herd and flock; that you may learn to fear the Lord your God always . . . and spend the money for whatever you desire, oxen, or sheep, or wine, or strong drink, whatever your appetite craves; and you shall eat there before the Lord your God and rejoice, you and your household. And you shall not forsake the Levite who is within your towns, for he has no portion or inheritance with you. (Deut. 14:22–27)

In effect, this amounted to an all-expense-paid religious holiday. Tithe money used for a glorious holy party! At the heart of the tithe was a joyous spirit of generosity, worship, celebration.

Nor is that all. In the regulations regarding the tithe we can see God's special concern for the helpless and the needy, which is always an important ingredient in simplicity. Every third year the tithe money was to be gathered together and used specifically for those who were unable to care for themselves. "At the end of every three years you shall bring forth all the tithe . . . and the Levite . . . the sojourner, the fatherless, and the widow . . . shall come and eat and be filled" (Deut. 14:28–29). In an agrarian society, land was the principal means of support, and so the Levite and the sojourner stood outside the normal means of earning a living. In a patriarchal culture the fatherless and the widows also stood outside the ordinary means of support. Given the make up of Jewish culture in that period, these four groups of people were the least able to care for themselves. And because of God's compassionate concern for them, this provision was written into the tithe.

We would do well to consider, given the shape of modern society, whether there are people today that parallel the Levites, the sojourners, the fatherless, and the widows. By the very nature of our culture, are there groups that are left outside the normal means of self-supporting income? If so, do not the rest of us have an obligation to respond to their need?

It should be noted that the New Testament does not make use of either the tithe or the first fruits. Jesus had a great many things to say about our attitude toward possessions but he mentions the tithe only twice, in both cases negatively (Luke 18:21, Matt. 23:22). The Apostle Paul had a good deal to say about giving, but any reference to the law of the tithe is conspicuously absent. Neither Jesus nor Paul ever made the tithe the basis for Christian stewardship. The reason for this will be discovered in Chapter 3.

Perhaps the patriarch Abraham should be the paradigm for our understanding of the principle of generosity. Here was a man who was given great wealth. However, it was never a wealth to be hoarded; rather, it was freely shared with the clan. Indeed, Abraham exhibited an unusual posture of relaxed nonchalance toward possessions. When the covetous spirit of Lot brought them into conflict, Abraham literally gave him the pick of the land (Gen. 13:5–12). Freely he received, freely he gave.

The Call for Justice

The call for justice is one of the great themes that echoes throughout the Old Covenant. We gain insight into this cry for justice through the Hebrew word *mishpat* (מִשְׁפָּט). This was a frequently used word, rich in meaning; a legal term that also carried ethical and religious connotations. *Mishpat* involved a morality over and above strict legal justice; it included observance of good custom or established practice, especially the practice of an equitable distribution of the land. It was used so

constantly in conjunction with the Hebrew word for righteousness that the biblical scholar Volkmar Herntrich believes the
two concepts should be viewed as virtually synonymous.[1] This
is vividly seen in the impassioned plea of Amos, "Let justice
roll down like waters, and righteousness like an everflowing
stream" (Amos 5:24).

In Deuteronomy we are told that Yahweh "executes justice
for the fatherless and the widow, and loves the sojourner, giving
him food and clothing" (Deut. 10:18). And again the Psalmist
declares, "The Lord works vindication and justice for all who
are oppressed" (Ps. 103:6).

This justice involved the wisdom to bring equitable, harmonious relationships between people. Solomon prayed to receive
wisdom to govern the people and God responded, "You have
asked for yourself understanding to discern what is right [mish-
pat]" (I Kings 3: 11).

Political leaders were to exercise this quality of ethical compassion on behalf of all people. Micah accuses the rulers of Israel of economic cannibalism for their brutal injustice. They "eat
the flesh of my people" and "chop them up like meat in a kettle," laments Micah (Micah 3:1–3). Jeremiah was brokenheart-
ed that justice could not be found anywhere in Jerusalem,
though a person would search every street (Jer. 1:5).

There were repeated warnings against the failure to provide
justice: "Cursed be he who perverts the justice due to the sojourner, the fatherless, and the widow" (Deut. 27:19).* Great
was the blessing promised to those who did exercise justice:
"Happy is he . . . who executes justice for the oppressed; who
gives food to the hungry" (Ps. 146:7).

The prophets spared no quarter in denouncing the blatant
failure of the people to do justice. The scathing denunciations
of Amos are legion. Echoing throughout the book is the charge
that "They sell the righteous for silver, and the needy for a pair
of shoes" (Amos 2:6). He charges that the women "oppress the
poor" and "crush the needy" in their lust for an ever higher
standard of living (Amos 4:1). The people were so filled with

---

* Also note Exodus 23:6; Deuteronomy 24:17; Job 36:6; Isaiah 10:2; Jeremiah
5:28.

greed that they could hardly wait for the end of the Sabbath so that they could "make the ephah small and shekel great, and deal deceitfully with false balances (Amos 8:4–6). Bribery was the order of the day, and just judges who spoke the truth were despised (Amos 5:10, 12). Is it any wonder that Amos cried out, "Let justice roll down like waters, and righteousness like an everflowing stream" (Amos 5:24)?

While Amos was lashing out against Israel in the north, Isaiah, in the southern kingdom, lamented, "Everyone loves a bribe and runs after gifts" (Isa. 1:23). Isaiah depicts a courtroom scene in which God is the prosecuting attorney who exposes the unjust practices of the rulers: "What do you mean by crushing my people, by grinding the face of the poor?" (Isa. 3:13–15).

Judah's oppression had extended all the way to official decrees and law books. Just as God had institutionalized a system of compassionate justice, the rulers had institutionalized a system of hardened injustice: "Woe to those who decree iniquitous decrees, and the writers who keep writing oppression" (Isa. 10:1–2). We are told that God abhorred all of Judah's pious rituals because they lacked social relevance. The life pleasing to God is not found in a series of religious duties but in obedience. The fast that God desired was for the people to "loose the bonds of wickedness" and to "let the oppressed go free." God's words to them were these: "Share your bread with the hungry" and bring the "homeless poor into your house" (Isa. 58:5–7).

Among the prophets there was no more plaintive or heartfelt cry than the voice of Jeremiah. He was called the weeping prophet, and with good reason. How he loved the great city of Jerusalem. He agonized over the sin of her people, he pled with them to repent. How broken-hearted he was when his own prophecies of destruction were fulfilled. He is a sad, yet faithful figure in desperate times.

Like the others before him, Jeremiah called the people back to the ancient covenant with its stipulation to "do justice and righteousness, and deliver from the hand of the oppressor him who has been robbed" (Jer. 22:3). Repeatedly he called them to plead the "cause of the fatherless," and to "defend the rights of the needy" (Jer. 5:28, 22:15). But sadly he had to admit, "You have eyes and heart only for your dishonest gain, for shedding innocent blood, and for practicing oppression and violence" (Jer. 22:17).

The tragedy was that the Exile could have been avoided if the people had turned in repentance to God: "If you truly execute justice one with another . . . then I will let you dwell in this place, in the land that I gave of old to your fathers forever" (Jer. 7:5–7). But the Exile did occur and the tragedy of it echoes through the centuries. Injustice, intertwined with idolatry, forced God to send Israel into captivity.

The Call for Compassion

The theme of compassion weaves its way throughout the Old Testament and can be vividly seen in the theologically rich word *hesed* (חֶסֶד). *Hesed* is so laden with meaning that the translators struggle to find an English equivalent, often rendering it "loving kindness" or "mercy." But *hesed* also carries with it the idea of endurance or faithfulness. It is most frequently used in reference to God's unwavering compassion for his people. His wonderful *hesed* is from everlasting to everlasting (Ps. 103:17). It endures forever (Ps. 106:1). It was this quality of limitless mercy which God revealed to Moses when he had asked to see God's glory: "The Lord passed before him, and proclaimed, 'The Lord, the Lord, a God merciful and gracious, slow to anger, and abounding in steadfast love [*hesed*] and faithfulness, keeping steadfast love [*hesed*] for thousands, forgiving iniquity and transgression and sin' " (Exod. 34:6–7).

However (and here is the great challenge), this covenant love, this durable mercy, which is so central to the character of God, is to be reflected in our lives as well. God declares through Hosea the prophet, "I desire steadfast love [*hesed*] and not sacrifice, the knowledge of God, rather than burnt offerings" (Hos. 6:6). And the wisdom of Proverbs counsels, "He who pursues righteousness and kindness [*hesed*] will find life and honor" (Prov. 21:21).

But most amazing of all is the way in which the biblical writers bring together the justice of *mishpat* and the compassion of *hesed*. To give people what is due them is one thing; the quality of spirit through which we relate to them is quite another. Zechariah received this mighty word of the Lord, "Thus says the Lord of hosts, Render true judgments [*mishpat*], show kindness and mercy [*hesed*] each to his brother, do not oppress the widow, the fatherless, the sojourner, or the poor; and let none of you devise evil against his brother in your heart" (Zech. 7:9–10). In his call to repentance, Hosea tenderly pled with the people, "So you, by the help of God, return, hold fast to love [*hesed*] and justice [*mishpat*], and wait continually for your God" (Hos. 12:6). And in what must be considered one of the most insightful summations of our task in all the Old Testament, we have again the outward demand of justice combined with the inward spirit of compassion:

> He has showed you, O man, what is good:
>   and what does the Lord require of you
> but to do justice [*mishpat*], and to love kindness [*hesed*],
>   and to walk humbly with your God? (Mic. 6:8)

Compassion and justice blended call us to simplicity of life.

Sprinkled throughout the Old Covenant is what I call its laws of compassion and concern. Perhaps the one most quickly recognized is the law of gleaning (Lev. 19:9–20; 23:22, Deut. 24:19–20). In harvesting, the farmer was to leave some of the crop along the borders and the grain which fell as he worked, so that the poor could gather it. "And when you reap the harvest of your land, you shall not reap your field to its very border, nor shall you gather the gleanings after your harvest; you shall leave them for the poor and for the stranger: I am the Lord your God" (Lev. 23:22). Likewise, the vineyards and the olive groves were not to be stripped bare so that there could be provision for the needy. The book of Ruth gives a vivid portrayal of the tenderness in this law. Naomi and her daughter-in-law, Ruth, had returned to Israel husbandless and landless and hence helpless, but they were able to gather the gleanings from the field of Boaz (Ruth 2:1 ff.).

At the heart of God is compassionate concern for the broken and desperate. By means of the law of gleaning, he placed into the economy of Israel provision for those who, for whatever reason, had become disadvantaged. There seemed to be an almost holy indifference about whether or not the person deserved to be poor; the simple fact that the person was without was sufficient reason to provide for his or her need.

Consider the tenderness in the old laws of giving and taking a pledge. If a neighbor borrowed your oxcart and left his coat in pledge, you had to be sure to give the coat back before sunset, even if he hadn't finished with the oxcart. Why? Because the night air was cold and he needed the coat for warmth. If you refused and your neighbor cried out to God in the chilly night, God warned, "I will hear, for I am compassionate" (Exod. 22:26–27). Deuteronomy made this rule especially binding if the pledge had been given by a poor person, since in all likelihood he had no other coat with which to keep warm (Deut. 24:12). A widow's coat could not be taken as a pledge—she was helpless enough as it was (Deut. 24–17). A millstone could not be taken as a pledge—it was a man's livelihood (Deut. 24:6). It was forbidden to barge into a neighbor's house to get a pledge; you were to wait at the front door until he brought it out (Deut. 24:10–11). Graciousness and common courtesy were to penetrate all human relationships, even business dealings.

Note the approach to the giving of loans. Since it was assumed that debtors would be among the poor and vulnerable, the charging of interest on loans was forbidden. It was viewed as an unbrotherly exploitation of another's misfortune and only served to deepen his dependency (Deut. 23:19).

Wages were to be paid to the poor on the day the work was done, undoubtedly because the money would be needed for supper (Deut. 24:14–15). If you were hungry you could eat from your neighbor's vineyard or grainfield, but you were not allowed to put any in a bucket (Deut. 23:24). And on it goes. Tender commands. Wise empathetic instruction on interpersonal relationships.

This quality of compassion and concern extended even to the animals and the land. We often forget that the Sabbath rest principle included the needs of the livestock: "Six days you shall do your work, but on the seventh day you shall rest; that your ox and your ass may have rest" (Exod. 23:12). The land itself needed "a year of solemn rest" (Lev. 25:5). Every seventh year there was to be no planting and no harvesting, for "the land shall keep a sabbath to the Lord" (Lev. 25:2). Even the soil of the vineyards was not to be overtaxed by planting other crops between the rows (Deut. 22:9). The oxen that trod out the grain should not be muzzled in order to allow them to eat while they worked (Deut. 25:4). Baby birds might be taken, but the mother bird must be left to care for remaining eggs and to produce future young (Deut. 22:6–7).

The whole point of this instruction is that our dominion over the earth and the little creatures that creep upon it is to be a compassionate dominion. We are not to rape the earth but to care for it—kindly, lovingly, tenderly.

These old laws, regulations, and moral judgments temper and tender our aggressiveness. Like the mysterious manna from heaven, there is always enough to care for one's needs, but never any for hoarding. There is a limit to a good thing, and whenever that limit is transgressed a good thing turns into a bad thing. Our task is to bring things into their God-ordained perspective, and these Old Testament laws give us intriguing hints at what that perspective should be.

The Call for Wholeness

The vision for wholeness and peace, which shines like a beacon of light through the Old Covenant, gives us important insights into Christian simplicity. This theme is wonderfully gathered up in the Hebrew word shalom, שָׁלוֹם,[2] a full-bodied concept that resonates with wholeness, unity, balance. Gathering in (but much broader than) peace, it means a harmonious, caring community with God at its center as the prime sustainer and most glorious inhabitant. This great vision of shalom begins and ends our Bible. In the creation narrative, God brought order and harmony out of chaos; in the Apocalypse of John, we have the glorious wholeness of a new heaven and a new earth. The messianic child to be born is to be the Prince of Peace (Isa. 9:6). Justice and righteousness and peace are to characterize his unending kingdom (Isa. 9:7). Central to the dream of shalom is the wonderful vision of all nations streaming to the mountain of the temple of God to be taught his ways and to walk in his paths; to beat their swords into plowshares and their spears into pruning hooks (Isa. 2:2–5; Mic. 4:1–4). *Shalom* even carries the idea of a harmonious unity in the natural order: the cow and the bear become friends, the lion and the lamb lie down together, and a little child leads them (Isa. 11:1–9). We are in harmony with God—faithfulness and loyalty prevail. We are in harmony with our neighbor—justice and mercy abound. We are in harmony with nature—peace and unity reign.

Economically and socially, the vision of *shalom* is captured in what Bishop John Taylor calls "The Theology of Enough." The greed of the rich is tempered by the need of the poor. Justice, harmony, equilibrium prevail. "It meant a dancing kind of inter-relationship, seeking something more free than equality, more generous than equity, the ever-shifting equipoise of a life-system."[3] Excessive extravagance, vaunting ambition, ravaging greed—all are foreign to the complete contented brotherhood of *shalom*. Under the reign of God's *shalom* the poor are no longer oppressed, because covetousness no longer rules.

In a particularly tender scene, Jeremiah lamented the fraud and greed of prophet and priest, saying, "They have healed the wound of my people lightly, saying, 'Peace, peace,' when there is no peace" (Jer. 6:14). In essence, Jeremiah had filed a malpractice suit against the self-styled religious quacks. They had put a Band-Aid over a gaping social wound and said, "*Shalom, shalom*—all will be well." But Jeremiah thundered, in effect, "*En shalom*—all is not well. Justice is spurned, the poor oppressed, the orphan ignored. There is no wholeness or healing here!"

But the healing peace of God will not be spurned forever. Isaiah saw a day when the reconcilation between people will be a reality, a day when justice and righteousness will reign, a time when the wholeness of God's peace will rule and people will "walk in the light of the Lord" (Isa. 2:4–5).

In an especially poignant passage, Scripture brings together the three Hebrew concepts we have studied: justice, compassion, and peace. The Psalmist points to the day when "Steadfast love and faithfulness will meet; righteousness and peace will kiss each other" (Ps. 85:10).

What is God's word for the world in which we live? Does he

see justice and righteousness increasing among us? Is he saddened by our lack of compassion? Are there any who embrace his peace as a way of life?

I am not posing these questions only to the world at large. I query us who own Christ as our life. Can God be pleased by the vast and increasing inequities among us? Is he not grieved by our arrogant accumulation, while Christian brothers and sisters elsewhere languish and die? Is it not obligatory upon us to see beyond the nose of our own national interest, so that justice may roll down like waters and righteousness like an everflowing stream? Is there not an obligation upon us to do justice, and to love mercy, and to walk humbly with God if we want to live in his wonderful peace?

These are tough questions, I know. But they are questions we must ask if we are to take seriously God's word to us through the Old Covenant.

3. THE BIBLICAL ROOTS: THE NEW COVENANT

I place no value on anything I possess, except in relation to the Kingdom of God.

—David Livingstone

In his manifesto on the poor, Jesus declares his intention to "set at liberty those who are oppressed" (Luke 4:18). And as he went among people teaching and healing, he observed the many oppressions that bore down upon them. He sought to lift their burdens, and as he did he spoke repeatedly and vigorously of one of the greatest burdens they bore—the burden of providing for themselves against tomorrow.

He saw how people were broken by the effort to attain riches. He perceived their awful vulnerability in believing that it was their responsibility to provide for themselves, to watch out for number one. The Apostle Paul said that those who desire wealth have "pierced their hearts with many pangs" (I Tim. 6:9–10). And Jesus observed the pangs that had pierced the hearts of so many, the pangs of striving for riches.

Jesus also saw how people were crushed by the failure to obtain riches. In his day it was considered a mark of God's displeasure to be poor. And those who had failed to receive the goods of this world could not help feeling that somehow God was against them. Remember how baffled the disciples were when Jesus told them that a camel could slip through the eye of a needle more easily than the wealthy could enter the Kingdom of God (Matt. 19:24)? This astonishment was due primarily to their belief that the wealth of the rich young ruler was a sign of God's special favor upon him. No wonder they exclaimed, "Who then can be saved?" (Matt. 19:25). And Jesus perceived how bruised and trampled in spirit people were because they were poor and felt God was displeased with them. Repeatedly he opposed this false and destructive doctrine, showing instead that in the economy of God, the poor, the broken, the halt were special objects of his blessing and concern (Matt. 5:1–12). By word and deed he sought to lift the burden of the discouraged and disheartened.

Jesus further saw the wearisome burden upon those who had gotten riches and were trying to hold onto them. He knew the cancerous nature of wealth and often warned of its dangers. He spoke of the "deceitfulness of riches" (Matt. 13:22, KJV). Riches are deceitful precisely because they lead us to trust in them, and Jesus saw that trap and the spiritual destructiveness which attends it. This was the burden that bore down upon the rich young ruler. Not only did he have great possessions, but more significantly, the great possessions had him. Of all oppressions his was the most spiritually debilitating.

To all those weighted down by the burden of tomorrow, or any other burden, Jesus extends a gracious invitation, "Come to me, all who labor and are heavy laden, and I will give you rest. Take my yoke upon you, and learn from me; for I am gentle and lowly in heart, and you will find rest for your souls. For my yoke is easy, and my burden is light" (Matt. 11:28–30). Our task in the pages that follow is to seek an understanding of the teaching which undergirds this call to liberation, this summons to simplicity of life.

Christ the Center

The most radiant passage on Christian simplicity in all the Bible must be Matthew 6.[1] It simply sparkles with joy and trust. Earlier, Jesus announced that the Kingdom of God has burst upon the human scene. Hence we can live in a new glorious inner liberty in alms giving, praying, and fasting without any need for human approval. We can obey the trenchant command, "Do not lay up for yourselves treasures on earth" (Matt. 6:19). We can live lives focused upon stockpiling "treasures in heaven" (Matt. 6:20). We can be scandalously free from anxiety, because we are under the watchful eye of him who richly cares for the birds of the air and the lilies of the field. No longer do we need to bear on our backs the soul-crushing gentile burden of the world of tomorrow. With focused eye and centered heart we can freely "seek first his Kingdom and his righteousness," knowing that all things needful will be provided (Matt. 6:33).

Jesus teaches us with a negative and a positive command: "Do not lay up for yourselves treasures on earth," but "do lay up for yourselves treasures in heaven" (Matt. 6:19). The "treasures" in view here are not just great riches, but all those things that we trust in and cling to. My boys, for example, have some very special treasures. When I begin to look into what they are, I am frequently amazed, for they may be only some shiny stones, or an odd looking stick, or a pile of rubber bands. But for my children these are coveted treasures. Jesus is warning us that, no matter what our earthly treasures may be, we have to be very careful about holding too tightly to them because they are bound to disappoint us and to keep us from living in the Kingdom of God in the freedom and power we desire. He knows that we have an almost compulsive need to secure ourselves by means of earthly things, but tells us not to do that, and proceeds to give three reasons why we should not amass earthly treasure but should store up heavenly treasure.

The first reason is that this world is a very uncertain place (Matt. 6:19–20). There simply is "no hidin' place down here." Now, today we may not have a problem with moths and rust corrupting our treasure, but it is certainly difficult to find a situation where inflation does not "break in and steal" it. Jesus is forcing us to see that, regardless of how secure our treasure may be, it will ultimately fail us.

The second reason Jesus points to is the fact that whatever we fix as our treasure will obsess our whole life: "For where your treasure is there will your heart be also" (Matt. 6:21). He was not saying that the heart should or should not be where the treasure is, but that it *will* be.

There is no option in this matter: our whole mind will be fixed around our treasure. When Jesus said that "no one can serve two masters," he did not mean that it was unwise to serve two masters, but that it was impossible. If our treasure is in our bank account, or an educational diploma, or any other earthly thing, our mind will not be on God.

Jesus illustrates this fact in the most profound way: "The light of the body is the eye: if therefore thine eye be single, thy whole body shall be full of light" (Matt. 6:22, KJV). If all within us is honed down to the single treasure of Christ and his Kingdom, then we are living in the light of simplicity. The ancient term "single eye" (ὁ ὀφθαλμός ἁπλοῦς) has a rich connotation, which our English has difficulty capturing. It refers both to a single aim in life and to a generous unselfish spirit. The two ideas have such a close connection in the Hebrew mind that they can be expressed in a single phrase. Singleness of purpose toward God and generosity of spirit are twins. The single eye is contrasted with the "evil eye," which is a Semitic expression for a covetous nature.[2]

Jesus lived in this singleness of purpose with God so perfectly that he could say without embellishment that he did nothing of his own accord (John 5:19). His words were the words of the Father, his deeds the deeds of the Father. And, astonishingly, he calls us in our small way to enter this unity of purpose. He invites us to the life of the "single eye" through which the entire personality is bathed in light and unity. With our eye focused on Christ the Center, we are to live with glad and generous hearts. This is simplicity.

The third reason Jesus gives for not laying up treasure on earth is that provision has already been made. The birds of the air and the lilies of the field all witness to an order in the Kingdom of God, in which adequate provision is made for everyone and everything. God provides for us according to our needs, just as he does for the plant and the animal life.

Jesus is not telling us to refrain from making provision. We miss the point of the teaching if, when the family gathers for supper, we announce, "Now, the Bible says to take no thought for supper and so we haven't." No, we work, but we work in faith, not in the anxious concern of distrust. On a practical level it is at this point that the nagging problem of "faith versus works" is resolved. We live centered in trust and faith and all our action and work arises out of that center. It is not fear and anxiety over tomorrow that prompt us to work, but obedience to the divine command. We make provision as it seems right and good (just as the birds do), but what comes to us is not so much the result of our labor as it is the gracious gift of God. We live the carefree life of unconcern for possessions in the midst of our work.

When this spirit of trust pervades all of our efforts, we understand the unwisdom of borrowing evil from tomorrow. No longer distracted by concerns for tomorrow, we seek first Christ's Kingdom and his righteousness. The focus of our thought, speech, and action is Christ the Center.

Identification with the Poor

The life of Christian simplicity is necessarily tied to a concern for the poor and defenseless. We cannot live at the divine Center for long without being compelled to care for our neighbor. For Christ, love of God and love of neighbor were two sides to the same door—we must do both to get through the door. And like the Samaritan, we soon discover that our path often leads to the bleeding and broken of humanity.

Perhaps no book in the New Testament gives a more sustained and passionate plea for the disadvantaged and dispossessed than the Gospel of Luke. Luke is the Gospel of the poor, the voice of the voiceless. Any statistical accounting would demonstrate that Luke gives the most attention to the poor and needy. But beyond sheer scoreboard count, it seems that Luke has a special sensitivity to the hurting and the helpless. This Gospel, then, provides us with a valuable departure point in understanding the New Testament summons to simplicity.

Luke alone records Mary's *Magnificat* with its lovely magnification of the Lord. Its very beauty may cause us to miss its strong advocacy of the lowly and needy:

He has shown strength with his arm,
he has scattered the proud in the imagination of their hearts,
he has put down the mighty from their thrones,
    and exalted those of low degree;
he has filled the hungry with good things,
    and the rich he has sent empty away. (Luke 1:52–53)

The birth story itself is told with stark simplicity: the obedience of Mary, the humility of a manger, the faithfulness of Simeon and Anna. How often we have marveled at God's choosing unpretentious Bethlehem and simple shepherds as the court scene for the regal birth. Perhaps God is teaching us something central about the nature of the Gospel life in the way his only begotten son was born.

Consider the simple counsel John the Baptist gave the common folk: "He who has two coats, let him share with him who has none; and he who has food, let him do likewise." To the tax collectors he urged honesty: "Collect no more than is appointed you." To soldiers he counseled contentment: "Rob no one by violence or by false accusation, and be content with your wages" (Luke 3:11-14). The point of the instruction is its elementary nature—small, simple items that accent the welfare of others.

Again, Luke alone records Jesus' proclamation at Nazareth with its tender advocacy of the poor and oppressed.

The Spirit of the Lord is upon me,
because he has anointed me to preach good news to the poor.
He has sent me to proclaim release to the captives
 and recovering of sight to the blind,
to set at liberty those who are oppressed,
 to proclaim the acceptable year of the Lord. (Luke 4:18-19)

Note the helpless nature of each group—the poor, the captive, the blind, the oppressed. Certainly this shouts to us something of the burden of Jesus Christ. Certainly it must also be the burden of all who follow him.

The beatitudes of Luke are distinguished by their pointed economic perspective: "Blessed are you poor.... Blessed are you that hunger.... Blessed are you that weep.... Woe to you that are rich.... Woe to you that are full.... Woe to you that laugh" (Luke 6:20-21, 24-25). The poor, the hungry, the sad are contrasted with the rich, the full, the happy. It is as if all those classes of people we feel are unblessed and unblessable are showered with special honor. And if that is not enough, those people we would consider to be well off have woes pronounced upon them. Blessings upon the poor, woes upon the rich.

Do these beatitudes mean that God has no concern for the wealthy and self-sufficient? Is God opposed to people of means? The moment we pose the question we sense its absurdity. Deep down we know that God's love is indiscriminate. But how are we to understand these beatitudes? Clearly Jesus was making use of the common Jewish teaching technique of hyperbole to accent God's identification with the weak and the destitute. There is a special divine caring for those who cannot care for themselves. In these beatitudes, Jesus is expressing his burden for the bruised and broken and he invites us to share that burden.

This tenderhearted compassion for the defenseless is again seen in Christ's instructions to his dinner host to invite the poor, the maimed, the lame, and the blind when he gives a banquet (Luke 14:12–14). The purpose of inviting such folk, of course, is not to get one's name in the social register, but because they need help.

Luke's account of the rich man and poor Lazarus underscores the same perspective (Luke 16:19–31). The rich man was not an evil person as we normally think of evil. He had not caused Lazarus' poverty, at least not directly. He did not even chase Lazarus away from his gate as many of us might be tempted to do. He merely ignored him. But that was the great offense! According to Christ, torment in Hades is a just recompense for the failure to respond to the plight of poor Lazarus.

Following a luncheon with Jesus, Zacchaeus exclaimed, "Half of my goods I give to the poor; and if I have defrauded anyone of anything, I restore it fourfold" (Luke 19:8). Honesty, generosity, and concern for the poor belong together. It was this act alone that caused Christ to remark, "Today salvation has come to this house" (Luke 19:9).

The Epistles expressed the same concern. According to the Apostle Paul, the Jerusalem council urged those ministering among the Gentiles to "remember the poor" (Gal. 2:10, but see also Acts 15:35). Former thieves are to learn to labor with their hands in order to "be able to give to those in need" (Eph. 4:28). Even widows are to be characterized by generosity to the afflicted (I Tim. 5:9).

According to the Apostle James, the definition of pure and undefiled religion is "to visit orphans and widows in their affliction, and to keep oneself unstained from the world" (James 1:27). The wealthy are not to receive preferred treatment in the Christian fellowship (James 2:2–9). If a brother or sister is in need, we are to meet that need rather than piously say "Be warmed and filled" (James 2:15). And John, the Apostle of love, reminds us that if we close our hearts to the obvious need of another when we have the ability to help, we do not possess the love of God (I John 3:17).

The Dangers of Wealth

The New Testament consistently and vigorously warns of the dangers of wealth. Many of Jesus' statements on riches and caring for the needy come to us in staccato commands that frighten us. With seemingly reckless abandon, we are advised to "Give to everyone who begs from you; and of him who takes away your goods do not ask them again" (Luke 6:30). And again we are to "Lend, expecting nothing in return" (Luke 6:35). If someone takes our outer cloak we are to surrender our coat as well (Luke 6:29). In terse, pointed language Jesus commands, "Sell your possessions, and give alms" (Luke 12:33). It was not sufficient for the rich young ruler to have an inner spirit of detachment from his possessions; he was commanded literally to sell everything if he wanted the Kingdom of God (Luke 18:22). And with broad strokes the Lord declares, "Whoever of you does not renounce all that he has cannot be my disciple" (Luke 14:33).

If we are shocked by these strong words of Christ and try to retreat from his direct commands to his more general instruction, we find little comfort. To would-be disciples he warned, "Foxes have holes and the birds of the air have nests; but the Son of man has nowhere to lay his head" (Luke 9:58). He told the parable of the rich farmer whose life centered in hoarding, and called him a fool (Luke 12:16–21). He counseled the disciples to travel light: "Take nothing for your journey, no staff, nor bag, nor bread, nor money; and do not have two tunics" (Luke 9:3, but also see Luke 22:36). Jesus said, "Take heed, and beware of all covetousness; for a man's life does not consist in the abundance of his possessions" (Luke 12:15). He declared war on the materialism of his day. The Aramaic term for wealth was "mammon," and Jesus condemned it as a rival god: "You cannot serve God and mammon" (Luke 16:13). Graphically, he depicted the difficulty of the wealthy entering the Kingdom of God to be like a camel attempting to get through the eye of a needle. With God, of course, all things are possible, but Jesus clearly understood the difficulty because he saw the grip that wealth can have on a person.

The Epistles are characterized by the same uncompromising language. Paul declared that "Those who desire to be rich fall into temptation, into a snare, into many senseless and hurtful desires that plunge men into ruin and destruction" (I Tim. 6:9). With embarrassing vigor James denounced the wealthy: "Come now, you rich, weep and howl for the miseries that are coming upon you. Your riches have rotted and your garments are moth-eaten. Your gold and silver have rusted, and their rust will be evidence against you and will eat your flesh like fire" (James 5:1–3). Earlier he had blamed killings and wars on the lust for possessions: "You desire and do not have; so you kill. And you covet and cannot obtain; so you fight and wage war" (James 4:1–2).

Paul said a bishop should not be a "lover of money" (I Tim. 3:8). A deacon should not be "greedy for gain" (I Tim. 3:8). The writer to the Hebrews counseled, "Keep your life free from love of money, and be content with what you have; for he has said, 'I will never fail you nor forsake you'" (Heb. 13:5). Paul called covetousness idolatry and commanded the Corinthian church to exercise stern discipline against anyone guilty of greed (Eph. 5:5, I Cor. 5:11). He listed greed alongside adultery and thievery and declared that those who live in such things would not inherit the Kingdom of God. Paul counseled the wealthy not to trust in their wealth but in God, and to share generously with others (I Tim. 6:17–19). The Spirit had stern words for the lukewarm church in Laodicea which rested in self-sufficient ease: "For you say, I am rich, I have prospered, and I need nothing; not knowing that you are wretched, pitiable, poor, blind, and naked" (Rev. 3:17). Strong, powerful, stringent words indeed!

We sense in these statements an uncompromising and frightening call to discipleship. They are words that do not admit to "easy Christianity" or "cheap grace," as Bonhoeffer put it. But this is not the only reason they frighten us (and may I add, just so that you understand, I too am frightened by this fierce language). These words terrorize us because we read them as laws that are to be adhered to in every circumstance. Hence we see no way to limit them. But we simply must understand that the writers of the New Testament did not intend to give us a new set of laws. The limit inherent in all these teachings is built into the simple principle of love of God and neighbor. Dr. Dallas Willard has said, "Love is a well-reasoned concern for the good of all."[3] Love does not have tunnel vision. If I bring the needy into my home and destroy my own family in the process, I am driven by something other than love. These commands of Jesus must be understood within the broader context of the law of love. This biblical instruction is not meant to destroy us, but to set us free. It is the glad trumpet call of liberation to all who are oppressed by reputation, wealth, and power.

We must not overstate the New Testament criticism of wealth. Though far from rich, Jesus himself did not come from the poor masses of Israel. New Testament scholar Martin Hengel surmises that, as a carpenter, Jesus came from "the middle class of Galilee, the skilled workers."[4] The twelve came from basically the same background. Zebedee, the father of James and John, evidently owned the family fishing business, which employed other laborers beside his sons (Mark 1:20). Matthew apparently held a rather prestigious position in the tax collecting business before his call by Christ (Mark 2:14). Although they had left their regular occupations to follow Jesus, the disciples received support from well-to-do women, "who provided for them out of their means" (Luke 8:3).

Jesus was often among the poor, but he was also frequently in contact with the rich and privileged. More than once he was found dining at the banquet table of wealthy Pharisees (Luke 7:36, 11:37, 14:1). Joseph of Arimathea was both a wealthy man and a disciple of Jesus (Matt. 27:57). Also Nicodemus, who had come to Jesus at night and later had become a disciple, evidently had considerable means (John 19:39).

Jesus was so far from being a rigid ascetic that he was accused of being a glutton and a drunkard (Luke 7:34). The accusation was obviously a malicious smear, but it pointed to the fact that joyous celebration was an important element in his life. He could rejoice with a young couple in a week-long wedding festival and even provide extra drinks for everyone (John 2:1–11). The Lord could allow the lavish expenditure of perhaps a year's wages to be poured over his head and feet while the disciples grumbled about the needs of the poor (Matt. 26:6–12). The Apostle Paul could rest contented with much as well as little.

What we discover from the New Testament witness is the combination of a penetrating criticism of wealth with a carefree, almost light-hearted attitude toward possessions. It is a combination seldom found today.

The Incendiary Fellowship

When the life and power of the Kingdom of God burst upon the human scene at Pentecost, it was the catalyst for a powerful expression of Christian simplicity. The infant Jerusalem Church is eloquent testimony to that reality. Until then the disciples were a motley crew—bickering, backbiting, jockeying for position, always squabbling over who was to receive top billing. Unfocused, they did not know simplicity of life. But in the course of time Jesus had formed a community of people who would live in holy obedience (always the most distinguishing characteristic of simplicity). Finally a people had been gathered who, when God said, "Wait," would wait, when God said, "Go," would go, when God said, "Give," would give. Rugged men and women who had been seasoned by many failures and some successes, imperfect and ignorant of many things, they were nevertheless a prepared people. And God said, "Wait." Disciplined, obedient, simple, they waited. And the fire fell!

The report of the economic repercussions of that incendiary life burning throughout the fellowship still throbs with joy and freedom: "And all who believed were together and had all things in common; and they sold their possessions and goods and distributed them to all, as any had need" (Acts 2:44–45). The principle was that "as any had need" the others would share of their resources until the need was met.

There was a beautiful, almost unconscious integration of economic sharing with other spiritual disciplines, such as teaching and prayer: "And they devoted themselves to the Apostles' teaching and fellowship, to the breaking of bread and the prayers" (Acts 2:42). Barnabas became something of a paradigm of spontaneous generosity by selling a field to provide for the needs of the fellowship (Acts 4:36–37).

Please remember, we have no indication that what occurred in the early days of the Church was commanded or that it was even the right thing to do. This is not some pattern to be slavishly imitated. What we do see is an incredible freedom to experiment with practical ways to flesh out the meaning of love for God and neighbor. Under the authority of Christ they were freed to try new ways to love one another.

Isn't this the model for us? Not a legal system, but a fresh freedom to discover what it means to live as Christ's disciples together. And the caring we see in Acts gives us significant clues as to which direction the winds of the Spirit desire to blow in our day.

It is important for us to understand the interwoven connection between the fellowship's economic liberality and divine power. In one breath we hear of "wonders and signs" being done by the Apostles, and in the next breath we discover that "All who believed were together and had all things in common" (Acts 2:43–44). We read of the marvelous prayer meeting where the building shook and the people "were all filled with the Holy Spirit and spoke the word of God with boldness" and in the very next verse we discover that "the company of those who believed were of one heart and soul, and no one said that any of the things which he possessed was his own, but they had everything in common" (Acts 4:31–32). As if that were not enough, the very next sentence once again takes up the theme of power: "And with great power the Apostles gave their testimony to the resurrection of the Lord Jesus, and great grace was upon them all" (Acts 4:33). And the next verse echoes their generous sharing. And on it goes, back and forth, interwoven like a tapestry, braided together like a rope.

These passages are not meant to be a systematic theology, and I have no desire to squeeze some kind of normative teaching from them that is universally binding upon the Church. What I am trying to express is that these people were being taken over by the life of the Spirit, which transformed them at every point. They were living on a new level of experience. Signs and wonders and miracles of all kinds abounded. The power of the Holy Spirit was felt and seen. And in the context of that wonderful outpouring of God's life, the sharing of resources was free and generous. And why not? People were being healed, relationships righted, servant leadership exhibited. To be quite honest about it, sharing is not difficult when the power of God is manifest in the midst of his people. His mighty hand and outstretched arm are there to sustain them. Who is there to fear? What better economic security could they have? And if there is ever any instance of deception, as was the case with Ananias and Sapphira, it is cared for quickly through spiritual discernment and the power of God (Acts 5:1–11).

Sometimes people find the joyous sharing of the Jerusalem Church hard to believe. The reason is understandable: they have never seen anything like it in their own experience. But in my small way, and through my limited experience, I want to testify to this reality. When the dynamic presence of God breaks in upon a *sufficiently prepared people,* there is an unguarded sharing that is thrilling, almost frightening. I stress the need for sufficient preparation because, like the early experiences of the disciples, it is possible to know mighty experiences of God's power without it having a lasting impact on the self-centered nature (compare, for example, Luke 9:1 with 9:54). But when a people are gathered who live under the cross and in holy obedience, then the incendiary power of the Holy Spirit can ignite everything, including all economic relationships.

By now you may be wondering, "Why all this talk about miracles, divine power, and spiritual preparation? Can't we just get on with the business of simplifying our lifestyles without all the God talk?" I answer that you are welcome to try, and God help you—because you will sorely need it. Although I deeply empathize with this "holy impatience" to get on with the task, the clear witness of Scripture is that something beyond good intentions and will-power is needed to transform our egocentric, greed-captivated personalities into an all-inclusive community of loving, sharing persons.

There once was a time when I urged simplicity of life upon people indiscriminately. I would cajole, shove, push, and often they would indeed change their lifestyle, but I found that it was all quite destructive. I discovered that simplicity is just another anxiety-laden burden until people have experienced God's gracious power to provide them with daily bread. Only as Kingdom power breaks in are we free to live in trust.

Have you not found it so? Perhaps out of concern for the terrible iniquities in the world, you have sought to open your heart and your pocketbook to needy brothers and sisters. Perhaps you have led the fight for certain causes of compassion in your church and community. You may even have attempted a common purse or some other form of economic sharing. But somehow, deep down inside, it all seems so dry and artificial. There is no oil of the Spirit to heal wounded relationships. Giving is done, but it lacks warmth and vibrancy. Like Moses of old you see the oppression of the people, but also like Moses you have tried the arm of flesh and find it failing you as it did him. For all the good that has been done, you have the uneasy sense that something central is lacking. Could it be that we need to follow the lead of the disciples, who through bitter experience were taught that their first priority was to seek hard after the Kingdom of God, and once baptized into its life and power that they were liberated to care for one another in unprecedented ways?

Freedom to Surrender Our Rights

The attractive ability to surrender our rights for the good of others is central to everything about simplicity. This reality burst forth repeatedly in the experience of the early Christian community. It was based firmly upon the example of Christ who, though rich, for our sakes became poor, and was "obedient to death, even death on a cross" (II Cor. 8:9, Phil. 2.8).

Consider the compassionate manner in which the problem of the neglected Hellenistic widows was resolved (Acts 6:1–7). The Hellenists were Greek-speaking Jews who were quite different culturally from their Hebrew counterparts. Evidently, in the rush of activities, the Greek-speaking widows were overlooked in the daily distribution of food and other goods. No doubt the oversight was completely unintentional, but it produced the potential for a serious split in the infant Church. But under the mighty power of the Spirit it was resolved in the most tender fashion. Wisely, the Apostles refrained from arbitrating the matter and asked that seven be chosen who were filled with the Holy Spirit and wisdom. So tender, so gracious was the spirit of this group that all seven who were chosen were from the aggrieved party—every single one of them had Greek names! The Hebrew believers had given up their own rights. They did not have to have things their own way. They were released from greedy self-serving one-upmanship. And because this freedom from self-interest abounded among them, the widows were cared for, justice prevailed, severed relationships were healed.

How heartening and how instructive! It is an example of simplicity of heart at its best. Perhaps, like me, you have often longed for an increase of this ability to lay down the terrible burden of always needing to get your own way. Often you have prayed for its enlargement among the Christian fellowship. Doesn't our own failure make the Spirit-led experience of that pristine community all the more impressive? And the result is so uplifting: "And the word of God increased; and the number of the disciples multiplied greatly" (Acts 6:7).

This principle of giving way for the good of others is at the heart of Paul's ethical teaching. He counseled the believers at Corinth that, whenever there was a grievance among them, they should give in to each other rather than disgrace the name of Christ by taking the matter to a court of law. He queried, "Why not rather suffer wrong? Why not rather be defrauded?" (I Cor. 6:7). And why not? Christ suffered wrong for us and we are called to "follow in his steps. . . . When he was reviled, he did not revile in return; when he suffered, he did not threaten; but he trusted to him who judges justly" (I Pet. 2:21, 23).

Paul had earned the credentials to urge the Corinthians to surrender their own rights for the good of Christ and his Kingdom. He had done exactly the same among them. He had every right to receive financial support during the one and one-half years that he ministered among them. Pointedly he asked them, "Do we not have the right to our food and drink? ... If we have sown spiritual good among you, is it too much if we reap your material benefits? If others share this rightful claim upon you, do not we still more?" Of course he did, and he knew it and they knew it. But he added, "Nevertheless, we have not made use of this right, but we endure anything rather than put an obstacle in the way of the Gospel of Christ" (I Cor. 9:4, 11–12). Rather than take advantage of his legitimate claim upon them, he provided for his needs through tent-making so that the word of Christ might abound in that city.

Having given these two examples, I hasten to warn that they can be easily twisted and turned into a new law that binds rather than liberates. I hope we will resist the temptation. There may well be times when going to court is the right and good thing to do, and often support for Gospel ministry should be freely given and graciously received. Paul was not giving a law but setting forth a perception into exactly how we can prefer one another in love (Rom. 12:10).

For Paul, the reason for acquiring money was not to build a nest egg but so he could share with others in need (Eph. 4:28). He urged the Corinthian believers to excel in giving to the Macedonian relief fund for the Christians at Jerusalem (II Cor. 8). James urged merchants to subordinate their buying and selling to the greater purposes of God. He wanted them to see that life was larger than business deals and accumulated wealth. He counseled perspective: "What is your life? For you are a mist that appears for a little time and then vanishes" (James 4:14).

Both Peter and Paul encouraged the practice of hospitality, which as any homemaker knows often involves considerable inconvenience for the sake of others (I Pet. 4:9, Rom. 12:13, I Tim. 3:2, I Tim. 1:8). James made it quite clear that if we discover brothers or sisters who are ill clad and lack daily food, we must give them what they need (James 2:14–17).

We are told in John's first Epistle that Christ laid down his life for us and that we ought to lay down our lives for the brethren. He then proceeded to describe in a concrete way how they were to lay down their lives for each other: "If anyone has the world's goods and sees his brother in need, yet closes his heart against him, how does God's love abide in him?" (I John 3:17). The question is obviously a rhetorical one. God's love is made flesh through these simple practical deeds in which we "by love serve one another" (Gal. 5:13, KJV).

Note how over and over the interest of others is the controlling principle. Banished is the obsession to demand one's own rights. Uppermost is the good of the fellowship and the advancement of Christ's Kingdom.

The Scandalous Invitation

Jesus Christ and all the writers of the New Testament call us to break free of mammon lust and live in joyous trust. Their radical criticism of wealth is combined with a spirit of unconditional generosity. They point to us a way of living in which everything we have we receive as a gift, and everything we have is cared for by God, and everything we have is available to others when it is right and good. This reality frames the heart of Christian simplicity. It is the means of liberation and power to do what is right and to overcome the forces of fear and avarice.

In our consideration of the Old Testament law of tithing, I promised to deal with the reason why none of the New Testament writers ever made the tithe the basis for Christian giving. That fact is quite conspicuous and quite startling, especially in the case of Paul. The relief fund for Jerusalem would have given him ample opportunity and reason to insist upon the tithe if he had wanted to make it normative for the Church. Why did Jesus, Paul, and all the Apostles refrain from making use of that well-established biblical tradition?

After having read through the New Testament witness to simplicity, and specifically its statements on wealth, the answer to that question is probably obvious to you. The tithe simply is not a sufficiently radical concept to embody the carefree unconcern for possessions that marks life in the Kingdom of God. Jesus Christ is the Lord of all our goods, not just ten percent. It is quite possible to obey the law of the tithe without ever dealing with our mammon lust. We can feel that our monthly check to the Church meets the new law of Jesus, and never once root out reigning covetousness and greed. It is quite possible to tithe and at the same time oppress the poor and needy. Jesus thundered against the Pharisees, "Woe to you, scribes and Pharisees, hypocrites! for you tithe mint and dill and cummin, and have neglected the weightier matters of the law, justice and mercy and faith; these you ought to have done, without neglecting the others" (Matt. 23:23). Mint, dill, and cummin were herbs of the kitchen garden, and hence any tithe on them would be infinitesimally small. How tragic to be meticulously trivial in the tithe and blind to justice and mercy and faith.

No doubt you noted that Jesus did not condemn the tithe as such: "These you ought to have done, without neglecting the others."* The tithe is not necessarily evil; it simply cannot provide a sufficient base for Jesus' call to carefree unconcern over provision. It fails to dethrone the rival god of materialism. It can never bring the freedom and liberality which is to characterize economic fellowship among the children of the Kingdom. Perhaps the tithe can be a beginning way to acknowledge God as the owner of all things, but it is only a beginning and not an ending.

When Jesus watched the voluntary offerings made in the temple treasury, he was moved by the sacrificial gift of the poor widow. What was it about her giving that touched him so? Jesus' comment on that simple act was, "For they all contributed out of their abundance; but she out of her poverty has put in everything she had, her whole living" (Mark 12:44).

Her giving had a certain reckless abandon to it. She evidenced an undivided devotion that fulfilled the command to

---

* Some scholars have felt that this phrase was a gloss, since it seems to spoil the point of the saying. There is, however, no manuscript evidence for this contention.

love God with all the heart, soul, mind, and strength. In fact, in Mark's Gospel this story follows closely on the heels of the two great commandments, as if to be a commentary upon them. A simple act, but one that crystallized the Christian witness. Here was a woman free from idolatry to mammon, devoid of greed and avarice. Here was a person in whom extravagant giving exceeded prudent thrift. Here was a widow, helpless and defenseless, who had learned to trust the Father in heaven for her needs day by day, one who sought first the Kingdom of God and his righteousness. Dare we follow her lead?

4. SIMPLICITY AMONG
THE SAINTS

I recommend to you holy simplicity.
—*Francis de Sales*

History has a wonderful way of freeing us from the cult of the contemporary. It opens to us rich new vistas of "the communion of saints." We realize more pointedly than ever before that God has spoken in the past, and that we are not the only ones who have sought to live in faithful conformity to his word. It is humbling to be writing on Christian simplicity and to discover a fifteenth-century tome by Girolamo Savonarola entitled, *The Simplicity of the Christian Life.* Such experiences have a way of destroying all contemporary arrogance.

One remarkable feature of the devotional masters is the incredible sense of uniform witness in the midst of such diverse personalities. In the words of William James, "There is a certain composite photograph of saintliness."[1] People from different cultures and centuries exhibit a mutual verification that is well nigh amazing. And the necessity of Christian simplicity is one of their most consistent themes. People as divergent as Augustine of Hippo and Francis of Assisi, Blaise Pascal and Robert Barclay, Richard Baxter and John Wesley all called for simplicity of life.

We need to give attention to these voices rising out of the past, hear their witness, and follow their lead. We will investigate six different "models" of Christian simplicity. Obviously, they are only representative of the rich witness of Christians throughout the centuries.

There is no perfect model of anything. As long as we are

finite human beings we are bound to make mistakes and distort the truth. Movements throughout the history of the Church are no exception. Each group we will investigate evidenced deficiencies in one form or another. But this fact of human existence should in no way hinder our appreciation for their bright witness to a way of walking with God that is "free from outward cumbers."[2] In each case, particular attention will be given to the most prominent contribution to simplicity found in each movement. Finally, all of the concerns will be brought together by looking at three classical pieces of literature in the field of Christian simplicity.

Exuberant Caring and Sharing

In the period directly following the Apostolic Age there was an exuberant caring and sharing on the part of Christians that was unique in antiquity. Julian the apostate, an enemy of Christianity, admitted that "the godless Galileans fed not only their [poor] but ours also."[3] Tertullian wrote that the Christians' deeds of love were so noble that the pagan world confessed in astonishment, "See how they love one another."[4] Exactly what is it that these Christians did which elicited such a response from their enemies?

There was, first of all, an exceptional freedom to care for the needs of one another in the believing community. The *Didache* admonished Christians: "Thou shalt not turn away from him that is in want, but thou shalt share all things with thy brother, and shalt not say that they are thine own."[5] By A.D. 250 Christians in Rome were caring for some fifteen hundred needy people. In fact, their generosity was so profuse that Ignatius could say that they were "leading in love," and Bishop Dionysius of Corinth could note that they were sending "supplies to many churches in every city."[6] When Marcion, a well-to-do ship-owner from Asia Minor, joined with the Christians at Rome, he gave them the substantial sum of 200,000 sesterces.

We gain a helpful glimpse into the caring Christian community from I Clement, "Let everyone be subject to his neighbor. ... Let the rich man provide for the wants of the poor; and let the poor man bless God, because He hath given him one by whom his needs may be supplied."[7] Tertullian catalogued a long list of groups that were cared for by the Christian believers. They supported and buried the poor, supplied the needs of the boys and girls destitute of means, cared for the elderly that were confined to the house, provided for those who had suffered shipwreck, and gave to those who had been banished to islands or mines for their fidelity to Christ's cause.

Those who could work were encouraged to do so, in order that they might help those in need. The Pseudo-Clementine literature said that those who could work should do so, those who were unskilled should be helped to learn a skill, and those who could not work should be cared for by the fellowship.[8]

Christians also provided for those who lost their jobs because of their faith in Christ. It was assumed, for example, that an actor who became a Christian, and had to give up his profession because of its involvement in pagan mythology, would be cared for by the Church.

Christians were eager to help in other emergencies as well. When the Christians of Numidia were left homeless in A.D. 253 by invading nomads, Cyprian collected a spontaneous contribution for them of 100,000 sesterces from a small group in Carthage.

But their joyful sharing was not confined to Christians. These believers lived in such trustful simplicity toward God that they were liberated to share with any and all in need. Bishop John Chrysostom witnessed, "Every day the Church here feeds 3,000 people. Besides this, the church daily helps provide food and clothes for prisoners, the hospitalized, pilgrims, cripples, churchmen, and others."[9] When epidemics broke out in Carthage and Alexandria, Christians rushed to aid all in need. Justin Martyr said that the believing community gathered money in order to care for orphans, widows, the sick, those in prison, strangers, and "in a word takes care of all who are in need."[10]

These repeated and sustained sacrificial acts of charity cannot be explained in terms of ecclesiastical or secular politics. They grew out of a deep commitment to Christ and his call to care for the needy. These Christians genuinely believed that

God was the owner and giver of all good gifts. Their generosity was an imitation of God's generosity. They were free from anxiety because they knew that tomorrow was in God's hands. They lived in simplicity.

Perhaps no one has captured the exuberant spirit of simple caring and sharing better than the Christian philosopher Aristides, whose words (written in A.D. 125) are so moving that they are best quoted in full:

> They walk in all humility and kindness, and falsehood is not found among them, and they love one another. They despise not the widow, and grieve not the orphan. He that hath distributeth liberally to him that hath not. If they see a stranger, they bring him under their roof, and rejoice over him as if he were their own brother: for they call themselves brethren, not after the flesh, but after the Spirit of God; but when one of their poor passes away from the world, and any of them see him, then he provides for his burial according to his ability; and if they hear that any of their number is imprisoned or oppressed for the name of their Messiah, all of them provide for his needs, and if it is possible that he may be delivered, they deliver him. And if there is among them a man that is poor and needy, and they have not an abundance of necessaries, they fast two or three days that they may supply the needy with their necessary food.[11]

This model of simplicity speaks to our condition. How desperately we need today to discover new creative ways of caring and sharing with any in need.

The Power of Renunciation

The power of renunciation as seen in the Desert Fathers is a second model of Christian simplicity.

As the persecution of the early Christians began to die out, it was no longer possible to witness for Christ by martyrdom. But the world had not changed its antipathy to the Gospel message, only its tactics. Persecution was replaced by assimilation.

For the Desert Fathers, the flight to the desert was a way of escaping conformity to the world. The world, including the Church, had become so dominated by secular materialism that, for them, the only way to witness against it was to withdraw from it. Thomas Merton writes in the introduction to his *Wisdom of the Desert*, "Society ... was regarded by the Desert Fathers as a shipwreck from which each single individual man had to swim for his life."[12]

They were seeking to revive true Christian devotion and simplicity of life by intense renunciation. Their experience has particular relevance, because modern society is uncomfortably like the world that they attacked so vigorously. Their world asked, "How can I get more?" The Desert Fathers asked, "What can I do without?" Their world asked, "How can I find myself?" The Desert Fathers asked, "How can I lose myself?" Their world asked, "How can I win friends and influence people?" The Desert Fathers asked, "How can I love God?"

Anthony, the "father of monks" (A.D. 251–356), was about eighteen years old when he heard the Gospel words, "Go, sell what you possess and give to the poor ... and come, follow me" (Matt. 19:21). Going out from the church, he immediately gave away his inherited land, sold all of his possessions, and distributed the proceeds among the poor, saving only enough to care for his sister. After living at the edge of his village for a time, he retreated into the desert, where for twenty years he lived in complete solitude. In the solitude he was forced to face his false, empty self. He learned to die to the opinions of others. He came out of a bondage to human beings. Violent and many were the temptations he faced.

When he emerged from the solitude of the desert, he was marked with graciousness, love, kindness, endurance, meekness, freedom from anger, and the practice of prayer. People recognized in him a unique compassion and power. Many sought him out for spiritual counsel and healing prayer. Even the Emperor Constantine sought his advice. For many years he had an effective and varied ministry. In the final years of his life he retreated again to the solitude of the desert, where he died in his 105th year.

The Desert Fathers renounced things in order to know what it meant to have the single eye of simplicity toward God. They were the *Athletae Dei*, the athletes of God, who sought to strip away all hindrances. There is no question that there were excesses in the monasticism of the Desert Fathers, but no more so than the excesses evidenced in the Church of today in the opposite direction.

The renunciation of the Desert Fathers had great transforming power. They renounced possessions in order to learn detachment. These men and women of the desert gained a great freedom when they surrendered the need to possess. Among the sayings of the Fathers is the story of an important dignitary who gave a basket of gold pieces to a priest in the desert, asking him to disperse it among the brethren. "They have no need of it," replied the priest. The wealthy benefactor insisted and set the basket of coins at the doorway of the Church, asking the priest to tell the brethren, "Whoso hath need, let him take it." No one touched it, or even cared enough to look at it. Edified, and no doubt astonished, the man left with his basket of gold.[13]

Detachment frees us from the control of others. No longer can we be manipulated by people who hold our livelihoods in their hands. Things do not entice our imaginations, people do not dominate our destinies.

The Desert Fathers renounced speech in order to learn compassion. A charming story is told of Abbot Macarius, who said to the brethren in the Church in Scete, "Brethren, flee." Perplexed, one of the brothers asked, "How can we fly further than this, seeing we are here in the desert?" Macarius placed his finger to his mouth and said, "Flee from this." When Arsenius, the Roman educator who gave up his status and wealth for the solitude of the desert, prayed, "Lord, lead me into the way of salvation," he heard a voice saying, "Be silent."[14]

Silence frees us from the need to control others. One reason we can hardly bear to remain silent is that it makes us feel so helpless. We are accustomed to relying upon words to manage and control others. A frantic stream of words flows from us in an attempt to straighten others out. We want so desperately for them to agree with us, to see things our way. We evaluate people, judge people, condemn people. We devour people with our words. Silence is one of the deepest Disciplines of the Spirit simply because it puts the stopper on that.

When we become quiet enough to let go of people, we learn compassion for them. We can be with people in their hurt and need. We can speak a word out of our inner silence that will set them free. Anthony knew that the true test of spirituality was in the freedom to live among people compassionately: "With our neighbor there is life and death: for if we do good to our brother, we shall do good to God: but if we scandalize our brother, we sin against Christ."[15]

The Desert Fathers renounced activity in order to learn prayer. Prayer was at the heart of the desert experience. These athletes of God sought to strip away all superfluous things, so they could concentrate on the one thing most needful. Prayer was the great work of their lives. Abbot Agatho declared, "There is no labor so great as praying to God. . . . With any other labor that a man undertakes in the life of religion, however instant and close he keeps to it, he hath some rest: but prayer hath the travail of a mighty conflict to one's last breath."[16]

Prayer frees us to be controlled by God. To pray is to change. There is no greater liberating force in the Christian life than prayer. To enter the gaze of the Holy is never to be the same. To bathe in the Light in quiet wonder and glad surrender is to be slowly, permanently transformed. There is a richer inward orientation, a deeper hunger for communion. We feel as if we are being taken over by a new control Center, and so we are.

Few if any of us will be led to the forms of renunciation that characterize the Desert Fathers. But all of us need to seek God for "wineskins" that will build into our lives the simplicity of detachment, compassion, and prayer.

The Joy of Simplicity

The poor little monk of Assisi, St. Francis, and his jubilant band comprise yet another model of Christian simplicity. They tramped the earth inebriated with the love of God, and filled with ecstasy. Buoyant joy was the hallmark of their simplicity.

Francis (A.D. 1182–1226) is one of the most winsome figures

in the history of the Christian faith. Born in the ancient Italian town of Assisi of wealthy parents, his adolescent years were spent as a charming and carefree playboy. A leader among the local young aristocracy, he often initiated their fun-loving revelries.

Illness and a military disappointment were among the influences that began to lead the sensitive Francis through a lengthy series of intense struggles of the spirit. The climax came in 1206 when his enraged father brought him before the bishop, to disinherit him. Francis stripped himself naked and walked away determined to follow the Lord's bidding into apostolic poverty.

Moved by his joyousness under oppression and his espousal of Lady Poverty, many flocked to the young Francis. Three years after the decisive call had come to Francis, a young girl of sixteen, Clara, sought to join the movement. Thus a woman's branch of the Franciscans, the Poor Ladies or Poor Clares, came into being. In time, this jubilant group of men and women became one of the largest and most influential orders in the Catholic faith.

The early Franciscan movement had an unusual combination of mystical contemplation and evangelistic fervor. Paul Sabatier, perhaps the most authoritative biographer of St. Francis, wrote of Francis' missionary zeal, "Perfectly happy, he felt himself more and more impelled to bring others to share his happiness and to proclaim in the four corners of the world how he had attained it." [17] Enthusiastically, he traversed much of Italy, preached to the Sultan in Egypt, and sought to engage in ministry among the Moslems in Spain. He was a captivating speaker, and his deep conviction and radiant love aroused an almost delirious enthusiasm on the part of the people. [18]

He sent out his Brothers Minor—Little Brothers—all over Europe and to Morocco. He referred to his humble band as "God's jugglers," whose task was to "revive the hearts of men and lead them into spiritual joy." [19]

The Friars Minor not only preached, but also sang. Exuberant and joyful, they were often caught up in ecstasy as they worshiped. With the soul of a poet, Francis would improvise their hymns. Best known is his *Canticle of the Sun,* with its celebration of Brother Sun and Sister Moon, Brother Wind and Sister Water. It is a joyous adoration of God as the Creator of all good things.

A love for the creation certainly marked these simple Friars. They lived close to the earth and took special joy in it. On one occasion Francis and Brother Masseo went begging bread in a small village. Returning with a few dried crusts, they searched until they found a spring for drinking and a flat rock for a table. As they ate their meager lunch Francis exclaimed several times, "Oh Brother Masseo, we do not deserve such a great treasure as this!" Finally, Brother Masseo protested that such poverty could hardly be called a treasure. They had no cloth, no knife, no dish, no bowl, no house, no table. Elated, Francis replied, "That is what I consider a great treasure—where nothing has been prepared by human labor. But everything here has been supplied by Divine Providence, as is evidenced in the baked bread, fine stone table, and the clear spring." Joyfully they finished their meal and then journeyed on toward France "rejoicing and praising the Lord in song."[20]

A joyous trust characterized their simplicity. At one time Francis gathered some five thousand Friars in an open plain for something akin to a camp meeting among the Brothers. Saint Dominic and several other prominent people had come to watch the event. At one point Francis rose and delivered a moving sermon concluding with the command that the Friars not have "any care or anxiety concerning anything to eat or drink or the other things necessary for the body, but to concentrate only on praying and praising God. And leave all your worries about your body to Christ, because He takes special care of you."

Hearing this, Dominic was distressed at the seemingly imprudent order. However, within a short period of time people from all the surrounding towns began arriving, bringing with them generous supplies of food. A great celebrative feast followed as the monks rejoiced in this provision of God. Dominic was so moved by the scene that he meekly knelt before Francis and said, "God is truly taking care of these holy little poor men, and I did not realize it. Therefore I promise henceforth to observe the holy poverty of the Gospel."[21]

Francis knew joy, but it was the joy rooted in the Cross, not in escape from it. The delightful story is told about how Francis taught Brother Leo the meaning of perfect joy. As the two walked together in the rain and bitter cold, Francis reminded Leo of all the things that people believed would bring joy, adding each time, "Perfect joy is not in that." Finally, in exasperation Brother Leo asked, "I beg you in God's name to tell me where perfect joy is." Whereupon, Francis began enumerating the most humiliating, self-abasing things he could imagine, adding each time, "Oh, Brother Leo, write that perfect joy is there." To explain and conclude the matter he told him, "Above all the graces and gifts of the Holy Spirit which Christ gives to His friends is that of conquering oneself and willingly enduring sufferings, insults, humiliations, and hardships for the love of Christ."[22]

The life of St. Francis gives us a healthy model of celibacy. (Examples of unhealthy celibacy abound in the history of the Church.) This matter of the single life should not be taken lightly. To be quite blunt about it, celibacy is necessary for some forms of simplicity. Francis could not have done what he did if he had not been single. Nor could Jesus.

Celibacy is not essential to simplicity, but it is essential to some expressions of simplicity. If we want to live like Francis, we had better not be married. If we want to be married, we had better not try to live like Francis. The failure to understand this simple fact has caused a great deal of misery in human society.

Francis and his Friars Minor knew the joy of the Lord. They were stamped by simple love and joyous trust. They led a cheerful, happy revolt against the spirit of materialism and double-mindedness. Nothing is more needed today than a simplicity distinguished by triumphant joy.

Theology in the Cause of Simplicity

The Protestant Reformation provides a crucial insight into the theological foundation for simplicity. Luther saw that the encrusted traditions of the Middle Ages undermined the authority of Scripture, and so lifted high the principle of *sola scriptura,* Scripture alone. He sought to cut down the complex system of merit that had arisen in the Roman Catholic Church with the Scriptural principle of *sola gratia,* grace alone. He endeavored to provide a basis for faithful living that stood over against the works righteousness of his day, by insisting on the biblical principle of *sola fide,* faith alone. The result was a simplification in both doctrine and life.

Martin Luther dealt with the matter of simplicity in the most profoundly practical way in his book *The Freedom of a Christian.* What he saw in such sharp focus was that the liberty of the Gospel sets us free to serve our neighbor with singleness of purpose. If our salvation is by grace alone we no longer need to keep juggling a myriad of religious duties to get right with God. We are free from constantly taking our own spiritual temperature.

Our freedom from sin allows us to serve others. Before, all our serving was for our benefit, a means to somehow get right with God. Only because the grace of God has been showered upon us are we enabled to give that same grace to others. Luther expresses this thesis in his famous paradox: "A Christian is a perfectly free lord of all, subject to none. A Christian is a perfectly dutiful servant of all, subject to all."[23] Through the grace of God alone, and not by any work of righteousness on our part, we come into the glorious liberty of the Gospel. We are all lords and kings and priests, as Luther put it. We are set free from the law of sin and death.

But this freedom is not for our sake alone—it is also a freedom to serve others. Until we are righteous we cannot really do righteous deeds no matter how hard we try. Luther said, "Good works do not make a good man, but a good man does good works; evil works do not make a wicked man, but a wicked man does evil works."[24]

Let's illustrate this matter in a simple way. A poor artist may paint many pictures, but he will not paint any good pictures. An inferior contractor may build many homes, but he will not construct any good homes. The person who is still bound to sin and enslaved to others is not free to truly love his neighbor.

A moment's reflection on our part confirms the truth of Luther's insight. If we are still in bondage to sin, our serving will flow out of that center. We will not have the single eye that gives light to all we do. Pride and fear and manipulation will control our actions. We will not be free to serve our neighbor in simplicity. If we are still in bondage to others, our serving will flow out of that center. We will be controlled by a desire to impress them, or receive their help. Without Gospel liberty, we will forever measure who we are by the yardstick of others. We will not be free to serve our neighbor in simplicity.

But once the grace of God has broken into our lives, we are free. When we are free from the control of our neighbor, we are able to obey God. And as we obey God with a single heart, we are given a new power and desire to serve our neighbor, from whom we are now free. We have become "servants of our neighbors, and yet lords of all."[25] We know simplicity of life. Luther concludes, "A Christian lives not in himself, but in Christ and his neighbor. Otherwise he is not a Christian."[26]

John Calvin developed a theology of the state that was the source of tremendous social power. While Luther tended to separate the Church from the state, Calvin tried to integrate them, and to produce a just social order by giving the controlling power to the righteous. He viewed Christians as the instruments of God in the transformation of the entire society.

This approach took seriously the role of Christian political activism. Christians must concern themselves with matters of justice and service. A social order that caters to the privileged elite, while masses of its people are deprived of necessities, cannot be tolerated. Christians have a responsibility to bring social justice into realization. These are concerns close to the heart of Christian simplicity. Concerning government authorities, Calvin could say, "They are not to rule for their own interest, but for the public good; nor are they endued with unbridled power, but what is restricted to the wellbeing of their subjects."[27] In other words, the state has a God-given task to provide justice for all people alike, and Christians have a responsibility to see that it fulfills this function.

Christians are to commend the state when it does justice, and condemn it when it fails to bring justice. More than that, Christians are to actively involve themselves in the state to work for the cause of justice. However much we may debate the specific means Calvin himself used to realize this conviction, we must join him in the conviction.

Luther and Calvin help us to understand the importance of

both liberty and justice in our search for Christian simplicity. We need to join with Luther in seeking the freedom of the Gospel which allows us to serve our neighbor in love. We need to join with Calvin in seeking social justice in all of society, which allows human beings to live in peace.

Hearing and Obeying

Holy obedience to the living voice of Christ brought birth to a vigorous form of simplicity among seventeenth-century Quakers. Offense at the gluttonous excess of his day led young George Fox (A.D. 1624–1691) to seek after God, a seeking that reached an important turning point when he heard a voice which said, "There is one, even Christ Jesus, that can speak to thy condition."[28] And so from the very outset Quakerism centered in the conviction that the voice of Christ could be heard and his will obeyed. This listening to Jesus Christ is what led the early Quakers to a radical simplicity testimony.

If the early Quaker preaching were to be brought into one sentence, it would be, "Christ has come to teach his people himself." These people were convinced that Christ was the fulfillment of the "prophet like unto Moses" who had been prophesied (Deut. 18:15–18, KJV). As prophet, Christ is able to teach us the righteousness of God. We can hear his voice if we will listen. His teaching will always be consistent with the Scriptures, since the Scriptures give us a faithful record of Christ's teaching to the Apostles and Prophets.

Not only does Christ our Prophet teach us, but he gives us the power to obey. George Fox declares that "God doth draw people from their unrighteousness and unholiness to Christ the righteous and holy one, the great prophet whom Moses said God would raise up whom people should hear in all things," and he urges all Christians to consider "whether you do believe that God raised up this prophet Christ Jesus? And if so, whether you do hear him?"[29]

A simplicity that took exception to many of the customs of the day resulted from this hearing and obeying the word of Christ. The early Quakers witnessed to simplicity in their attire: they rejected the gaudy superficial fashions that abounded in that day, and instead adopted the plain clothing of the working class. They refused to remove their hats in deference to the nobility, because they were convinced that all people deserved equal honor.

They witnessed to simplicity in their speech, in which honesty and integrity were the distinguishing characteristics. It was said that a Quaker's word was as good as his bond. "Thee" and "thou," which at the time were used for everyone but the elite, they used when speaking to peasant and king alike. They refused to take oaths because it implied a double standard of truth. They needed no oath to guarantee that they spoke the truth—their Yes was Yes, and their No was No.

They witnessed to simplicity by vigorously opposing injustice and oppression. They condemned the "price fixing" of the day, which discriminated against the poor and needy, and insisted instead on a one-price system for all. Their writings were shot through with outraged cries against the conspicuous consumption of the wealthy because of its connection with the poverty that was rampant in the land. In *No Cross, No Crown*, William Penn scathingly denounced the practice of 95 percent of agriculture going to feed "the inordinate lusts and delicious appetites" of 5 percent of the population.[30] When the wealthy rationalized their extravagance under the excuse that it provided employment for the poor, George Fox rebutted, "If you say how shall the poor live if you do not wear that; give them all that money which you bestow upon all that gorgeous attire, and needless things, to nourish them, that they may live without making vanities."[31]

These early "Publishers of Truth," as they called themselves, took with utter seriousness the task of hearing the voice of Christ and obeying his word. They would ask, "What does it mean to live faithful lives in our day?" and they fully expected to receive an answer. Christ spoke to them through the Scripture, he also moved directly upon the heart of the attentive listener, and he spoke most powerfully when they were gathered together in worship. The corporate commitment to listen to Christ produced corporate convictions, for their Teacher promised to create unity among them (Matt. 18:18–20).

But to hear Christ's word was not enough. They also waited

to receive the power to obey that word. And it was the conviction that they would actually receive the power to obey the instruction given them which gave early Friends such vitality. They walked cheerfully upon the earth in the power of the Lord. They called their struggle "the Lamb's War," and fully believed the Lamb of God would give them victory over all "vanity, customs, and fashions of this generation." [32] In every detail they sought to live in holy obedience.

We who live in a world of half-truths and rationalizations and intellectual gymnastics that keep us from hearing and obeying the word of Christ need to hear their witness. Because we live in a different culture, we must once again ask what it means to live faithful lives in our day. But we must ask fully expecting to receive an answer and fully expecting to be given the power to obey the call.

Simplicity in Action

Examples abound of Christian simplicity in the task of evangelism, in the service of the poor, and in the cause of social justice. The vigorous evangelistic efforts of John Wesley and the early Methodists are well known. The simplicity of their lifestyle gave integrity to the Gospel they preached. Wesley is reported to have told his sister, "Money never stays with me. It would burn me if it did. I throw it out of my hands as soon as possible, lest it should find its way within my heart." He told everyone that, if at his death he had more than ten pounds (about $23) in his possession, people had the privilege of calling him a robber. [33] Near the end of his life he wrote in his journal very simply, "I left no money to anyone in my will, because I had none." [34]

Francis Asbury, the "Apostle of American Methodism," remained single all of his life and lived on a very meager income in order to devote all his energies to the advancement of Christ's cause in America. His single-hearted devotion is evidenced from a notation in his journal as he sailed to the Colonies, "Whither am I going? To the new world. What to do? To gain honor? No, if I know my own heart. To get money? No. I am going to live to God and to bring others so to do." [35] Such simplicity of life in the task of evangelism could be multiplied a thousand fold among the faithful army of itinerant Methodist preachers.

No one can read the Journal of David Brainerd without being struck by the utter simplicity of his life, and his single-minded devotion to bring Christ to the American Indian. Obsessive status seeking and compulsive extravagance were antithetical to his life and message.

From its inception, the modern missionary movement was rooted in sacrifice and simplicity. From William Cary to Adoniram Judson, from J. Hudson Taylor to C. T. Studd, they leave us a legacy of commitment to simplicity. As Hudson Taylor prepared to bring the Gospel to the great throngs of inland China, he taught himself to endure hardness and to economize in order to help people in need. He said, "I soon found that I could live upon very much less than I had previously thought possible. Butter, milk and other luxuries I ceased to use, and found that by living mainly on oatmeal and rice, with occasional variations, a very small sum was sufficient for my needs." In this way he was able to use two-thirds of his income for other purposes. He wrote, "My experience was that the less I spent on myself and the more I gave to others, the fuller of happiness and blessing did my soul become."[36]

In our own century, consider the example of Sadhu Sundar Singh, the man who has done more than any other to incarnate the Christian faith into the life and culture of India. Adopting the saffron robe of the Indian Sadhus, or holy men, Sundar Singh lived a life of extreme simplicity as he tramped the length and breadth of India. His bearded figure, radiant smile, and compelling preaching became widely known in many countries. He disappeared in 1929 while on an evangelistic mission into Tibet, presumably martyred for his faith in Christ.

Christians have also raised the standard of simplicity in the service of the poor. At the early age of twenty, Antoine Frédéric Ozanam persuaded some of his fellow students to help him in serving the destitute and underprivileged of France. It was the beginning of the St. Vincent de Paul Society. Begun in 1833, it quickly spread to many countries.

William Booth established the Salvation Army out of a

burning desire to help the dregs of the industrial urban civilization. Ministering among the worst slums of London, Booth first sought to bring these broken and dispossessed people into the churches. Unwilling to receive them, the churches rejected Booth and his followers. Booth turned to unconventional open-air meetings on the streets, complete with drums, tambourines, and trumpets. His book, *In Darkest England and the Way Out,* is a scathing exposé of the economic, social, and moral conditions in the slums, and in it Booth made daring proposals to overcome these conditions. Along with other things he called for a poor man's bank, rescue homes for prostitutes, and model suburban villages.[37]

Robert Raikes established the Sunday School movement in an attempt to provide educational opportunities for the extremely poor on the only day they did not have to work—Sunday. George Müller has inspired many to faithful ministry by his homes for the orphans of Bristol, which were begun and maintained entirely through prayer for their material means. George Williams founded the Young Men's Christian Association (YMCA) to provide evangelistic, social, and athletic opportunities for the lower income levels of the white collar class.

In the twentieth century, one thinks immediately of Albert Schweitzer. Extremely versatile, Schweitzer was a New Testament scholar, a distinguished organist and authority on Bach, and an accomplished philosopher and theologian. He chose, however, to give the bulk of his adult career to serving the people of French Equatorial Africa as a medical missionary.

Simplicity also has been a vigorous force in the cause of social justice. David Livingstone is well known for missionary exploits and especially for his determined efforts to abolish what he called "the open sore of the world," the African slave trade. Living in great simplicity, both in inward spirit and in outward lifestyle, he persistently pleaded the cause of the helpless of Africa. The horrors of the slave trade, said Livingstone, were beyond exaggeration. "To overdraw its evils is a simple impossibility."[38] Among the last words which he was to write in his journal were these: "I will forget all my cold, hunger, suffering and trials, if I can be the means of putting a stop to this cursed traffic."[39]

Clarence Jordan has made an important imprint upon twen-
tieth-century America by his courageous life of simplicity in the
cause of social justice. The founder of Koinonia Farm and author of the Cotton Patch version of the New Testament, he has
sometimes been called a theologian in overalls. He withstood
harassment, economic boycott, and gunfire from nightriders in
order to make a bold social witness for peace, community, and
racial equality.

Jordan began his experiment in racial reconciliation in 1942
on a farm near Americus, Georgia, and he remained there until
his death in 1969. In everything he was marked by simplicity of
spirit and life. His call for justice and peace and simplicity in
the context of authentic Christian community is a challenge to
our perennial culture-conforming tendencies.[40]

And today many groups have arisen which have battled for
justice out of Christian conviction. Among some of the better
known of these groups are the Berkeley Christian Coalition in
Berkeley, California, which publishes *Radix;* Voice of Calvary
in Mendenhall, Mississippi, which publishes *The Quiet Revolution;* Jubilee Fellowship in Philadelphia, Pennsylvania, which
publishes *The Other Side;* the Catholic Worker Movement in
many American urban centers, which publishes *The Catholic
Worker;* and The People's Christian Coalition in Washington,
D. C., which publishes *Sojourners.* Whatever may be the shortcomings of these many movements, certainly one of their greatest assets has been their understanding of how intrinsic
Christian simplicity is in the cause of justice.

Words to Live By

No investigation into simplicity in the history of the Church
is complete without at least a brief perusal of its literature. We
possess a rich heritage of writings on this topic from Clement's
The Rich Man's Salvation and Cyprian's *On Good Works and
Alms Giving,* to the *Letters of St. Jerome* and the works of
Eckhard, Tauler, and Suso; from the writings of the Radical
Reformation to the *Epistles of George Fox* and William Penn's
No Cross, No Crown. And, of course, many modern writers
have addressed this subject with new vigor, including Francis

Florand in *Stages of Simplicity*, Arthur Gish in *Beyond the Rat Race*, and Ronald Sider in *Rich Christians in An Age of Hunger*.

I have chosen to look at three representative writings which, taken together, give us a composite picture of the concern for Christian simplicity in the history of the church: *The Simplicity of the Christian Life*, by Girolamo Savonarola; *Purity of Heart Is to Will One Thing*, by Søren Kierkegaard; and *The Journal* and *A Plea for the Poor* by John Woolman.

Girolamo Savonarola's *The Simplicity of the Christian Life* is actually a discussion of the nature of the good life. He is seeking to answer the question, "What makes people happy?" Of all created beings, writes Savonarola, only humans have to struggle to discover their proper role in the whole scheme of things. We are the only ones who seek for meaning, purpose, happiness. The blessed life, says Savonarola, is not found primarily in sensual pursuits nor in intellectual pursuits nor even in spiritual pursuits, as normally understood. No, the happy life is rooted in the grace of God and discovered in imitating the life and teachings of Jesus. The main means through which this simple life of the *Imitatio Christi* occurs are prayer and love.

Having laid the foundation, Savonarola proceeds with two crucial chapters: "Simplicity of the Heart" and "Exterior Simplicity." "Each Christian," declared Savonarola, "ought to try to come to perfect simplicity" of the heart.[41] Even the natural order witnesses to the fact that the more inwardly simple or unified something is the more perfect it is. In the spiritual realm, this inner heart simplicity is discovered in having the crucified Christ as the unifying force of all our affections and aspirations.

Exterior simplicity flows from this true interior simplicity. We can see this in the creation, says Savonarola. A tree or flower is pleasing to the eye because it reflects an inner harmony and unity. The same is true of our lives. If we enter into the simplicity of God we will have an exterior quality of life marked by unity and peace. "The true Christian greatly loves and adores exterior simplicity," comments Savonarola. In even stronger language, he goes on to add, "He who does not love exterior simplicity is not able to live the Christian life."[42]

But we must remember, counseled Savonarola, that simplicity in exterior things does not come to all equally. Some occupations demand a greater use of material goods. Also, there needs to be a certain ordinary common sense (he uses the word "prudence") employed in deciding what we should do without. In fact, Savonarola adds, it is not wrong to seek those things necessary for a "decent state," and if we have simplicity of heart we can distinguish between those things that are necessary for a decent state and those things that are superfluous. The best guides in these decisions, says Savonarola, are the Sacred Scriptures and spiritual discernment. He then concludes with a chapter on the danger of wealth, and a chapter on the happiness of the Christian life.

Kierkegaard's *Purity of Heart Is to Will One Thing* stands as a vigorous statement of inward simplicity. While Descartes said, "I think, therefore I am," Kierkegaard said in effect, "I am, therefore I must decide." Slowly, carefully he strips away all of our rationalizations and barriers to willing one thing until we stand as a single individual at the crossroads. Significantly, the book itself is dedicated to "that solitary individual," and relentlessly it forces us to come, naked and alone, before God, where we must decide how to live. In reality, the book is an extended commentary on words of the Apostle James, "Draw near to God and he will draw near to you. Cleanse your hands, you sinners, and purify your hearts, you men of double mind" (James 4:8).

Some have misunderstood the message of *Purity of Heart* by assuming that it is possible to will one thing, and that unspeakably evil, as in Adolf Hitler. On the contrary, says Kierkegaard, "the person who wills one thing that is not the Good . . . does not truly will one thing. It is a delusion, an illusion, a deception, a self-deception that he wills only one thing. For in his innermost being he is, he is bound to be, double-minded."[43] His point is a simple one. God is the only whole, satisfying, unifying reality in the universe. Only God is one, and he alone encompasses the good. To desire anything outside of God is not to will *one* thing but "a multiple of things, a dispersion, the toy of changeableness, and the prey of corruption!" No desire can be fully satisfied when it is outside of God, and the individual becomes "not merely double-minded but thousand-minded, and at variance with himself."[44]

Purity of heart, then, is found in willing only the good, which is God. To do so unifies and simplifies everything. But Kierkegaard warns that to desire the good for the sake of the reward is not to will one thing, to desire the good out of fear of punishment is not to will one thing, to desire the good out of self-centered willfulness is not to will one thing, to desire the good with a half-hearted commitment is not to will one thing. Utter abandonment, absolute commitment to the good, to God, is the requirement for willing one thing, for purity of heart.

Kierkegaard has pressed home for us how essential inner simplicity is to our task. Even when we are seeking God, but doing so out of a duplicitous motivation, though our words and deeds may seem virtuous we will be double-minded at best. No, Kierkegaard makes it clear; our inward disposition must be centered, focused, synoptic if we want to know that purity of heart that is Christian simplicity.

The Journal of John Woolman has stood the test of time and is now universally recognized as one of our great devotional classics. Often published with *The Journal* is *A Plea for the Poor*. Together they stand as a witness to the necessity of both inward and outward simplicity, the one flowing from the other. It would be hard to imagine a more eloquent testimony to the grace of Christian simplicity.

Woolman first dealt with the issue of simplicity on a personal level. A businessman in retail goods, a tailor, and a nurseryman, he soon found that his trade "increased every year, and the way to large business appeared open, but I felt a stop in my mind." The hesitancy he felt was not due to a fear of entering into too affluent a lifestyle. That matter had been settled long ago as he witnessed, "I had, in a good degree, learned to be content with a plain way of living."

The real problem was two-fold. First, there was the issue of compromise found in marketing items that catered to people's vanity more than they served real needs. He writes, "Things that served chiefly to please the vain mind in people, I was not easy to trade in; seldom did it; and whenever I did I found it weakened me as a Christian."[45] The second and deciding issue was the need to be free from "cumbers" in order to give uninhibited attention to the Lord's call upon him. Finally, he felt he must cut back his business. This set him free to engage in a remarkable traveling ministry that was to be a major force in causing Quakers to rid themselves of slavery before America had gained independence from the British Empire.

Passage after passage is filled with tender references to the plight of slaves and slave-owners alike. He saw with unusual clarity the connection between covetousness and slavery.

> The Lord . . . is graciously moving in the hearts of people to draw them off from the desire of wealth and to bring them into such a humble, lowly way of living that they may see their way clearly to repair to the standard of true righteousness, and may not only break the yoke of oppression, but may know him to be their strength and support in times of outward affliction.[46]

His *Plea for the Poor* is a tract for our times. In it, Woolman addresses affluent America and asks us to tender our hearts to the needs of the poor. It is filled with practical suggestions on how we can identify with the poor and needy of the earth, especially those who "labor for us out of our sight."[47] He even recommends that we take up the work of the poor for a time in order to *feel* their burdens.

In a small way, we have entered the "communion of saints" in this chapter. We have heard the witness of men and women throughout the centuries who have sought to walk with God faithfully and simply. Their message is clear, and is perhaps best summed up in the words of Francis de Sales, "In everything, love simplicity."[48]

PART II

The Practice

5. INWARD SIMPLICITY:
THE DIVINE CENTER

Oh, blessed simplicity, that seizes swiftly what cleverness, tired out in the service of vanity, may grasp but slowly.
—Søren Kierkegaard

In his lofty mythology, *The Silmarillion*, J. R. R. Tolkien gives a penetrating picture into the effects of inward simplicity, "But the delight and pride of Aüle is in the deed of making, and in the thing made, and neither in possession nor in his own mastery; wherefore he gives and hoards not, and is free from care, passing ever on to some new work."[1] What an inviting picture of movement and work in harmony with the divine Center of the universe. And what a contrast to the frantic and often frustrated rush of our daily lives.

We dash here and there desperately trying to fulfill the many obligations that press in upon us. We jerk back and forth between business commitments and family responsibilities. While we are busy responding to the needs of child or spouse, we feel guilty about neglecting the demands of work. When we respond to the pressures of work, we fear we are failing our family. In those rare times when we are able to juggle the two successfully, the wider issues of nation and world whisper pestering calls to service. If anyone needs a simplification of life, we do.

What will set us free from this bondage to the ever spiraling demands that are placed upon us? The answer is found in the grace of Christian simplicity. This virtue, once worked into our lives, will unify the demands of our life. It will prune and trim gently and in the right places. It brings a liberty of soul that eliminates constant reversions to ourselves.

Life at the Center

I still remember the rainy February morning inside a Washington, D.C., airport many years ago. Exhausted, I slumped into a chair to wait for my flight. As always, I had brought reading material in order to make good use of free moments. For the first time in my life I opened Thomas Kelly's *Testament of Devotion*.

Immediately, he caught my attention by describing perfectly my condition and the condition of so many I knew: "We feel honestly the pull of many obligations and try to fulfill them all. And we are unhappy, uneasy, strained, oppressed, and fearful we shall be shallow."[2] Yes, I had to confess I was in those words. To all who saw me I was confident and in command, but inwardly I was tired and scattered. Then my eyes came upon words of hope and promise, "We have hints that there is a way of life vastly richer and deeper than all this hurried existence, a life of unhurried serenity and peace and power. If only we could slip over into that Center!"[3] Instinctively, I knew that he was speaking of a reality beyond what I had known. Please understand me, I was not ungodly and irreverent, just the opposite. My problem was that I was so serious, so concerned to do what was right, that I felt compelled to respond to every call to service. And, after all, they were wonderful opportunities to minister in Christ's name.

Then came the sentence that was to prompt an inner revolution: "We have seen and known some people who seem to have found this deep Center of living, where the fretful calls of life are integrated, where No as well as Yes can be said with confidence."[4] This ability to say Yes and No out of the divine Center was foreign to me. I had always prayed over decisions, and yet I too often responded on the basis of whether or not the action would put me in a favorable light. To say Yes to pleas for help or opportunities to serve usually carried an aura of spirituality and sacrifice. I could say Yes easily, but I did not have the ability to say No. What would people think of me if I refused?

Alone, I sat in the airport watching the rain splatter against the window. Tears fell on my coat. It was a holy place, an altar, the chair where I sat. I was never to be the same. Quietly, I asked God to give me the ability to say No when it was right and good.

Back home, I was once again caught up into a flurry of activity. But I had made one decision—Friday nights were to be reserved for the family. It was a small decision at the time; nobody but I really knew about it. I had told the family in a casual, off-hand fashion; they did not know it was a covenant commitment, a crossroads decision. Nor did I, really. It just seemed the right thing to do, hardly what one would call a God-given directive.

But then the phone call came. It was a denominational executive. Would I be willing to speak to this group on Friday night? There it was, another wonderful opportunity. My response was casual, almost unconscious, "Oh, no, I can't." The reply was also casual, "Oh, do you have another commitment?" I felt trapped. (In those days I did not know that I could quite legitimately say that I did indeed have a very important commitment.) Cautiously but purposefully, I answered simply, "No," with no attempt to justify or explain my decision. There followed a long period of silence which seemed to last an eternity. I could amost feel the words, "Where is your dedication?" traveling through the telephone wires. I knew I had made a decision that made me seem less spiritual to one for whom I genuinely cared. After a moment we shared a few pleasantries and then hung up; but as the phone hit the receiver, inwardly I shouted, "Hallelujah." I had yielded to the Center. I had touched the margin of simplicity, and the effect was electrifying.

The incident was so small and insignificant that it is almost embarrassing to relate it to you. I'm sure my denominational friend does not even recall the phone conversation. And yet somehow I had turned a corner. Even now I sometimes wish I could say that something terribly important precipitated the change. But there it was, a trivial event, yet it had changed everything. Perhaps it has been that way for you also. At least I know that often the genuinely important issues are decided in the small corners of life.

I mention these little incidents of the airport and the phone conversation only because they were the first opening to me of what it meant to respond to the demands of life from the divine Center. But it is this reality that lies at the heart of all Christian simplicity. As we yield to the Center everything about us becomes focused, synoptic. This yielding is nothing more than the experience of the great commandment to love God with all our being. A French Christian, Marie of the Incarnation, wrote in 1628, "My spirit was more and more being simplified. . . . In the depths of my soul . . . these words were continual; 'Ah! My Love, my Well-Beloved! Be blessed, O my God!' . . . And since that time my soul has *remained in its center* which is God."[5]

I hope you understand what I mean when I speak of living out of the Center. I am of course referring to God, but I do not mean God in an abstract theoretical sense, nor even God in the sense of One to be feared and revered. Nor do I mean God only in the sense of One to be loved and obeyed. For years I loved him and sought to obey him, but he remained on the periphery of my life. God and Christ were extremely important to me but certainly not the Center. After all, I had many tasks and aspirations that did not relate to God in the least. What, for heaven's sake, did swimming and gardening have to do with God? I was deeply committed, but I was not integrated or unified. I thought that serving God was another duty to be added onto an already busy schedule.

But slowly I came to see that God desired to be not on the outskirts, but at the heart of my experience. Gardening was no longer an experience outside of my relationship with God—I discovered God in the gardening. Swimming was no longer just good exercise—it became an opportunity for communion with God. God in Christ had become the Center.

Our Many Selves[6]

You may be wondering what all this has to do with simplicity. Perhaps I could explain it this way. Within all of us is a whole conglomerate of selves. There is the timid self, the courageous self, the business self, the parental self, the religious self, the literary self, the energetic self. And all of these selves are rugged individualists. No bargaining or compromise for them. Each one screams to protect his or her vested interests. If a decision is made to spend a relaxed evening listening to Chopin, the business self and the civic self rise up in protest at the loss of precious time. The energetic self paces back and forth impatient and frustrated, and the religious self reminds us of the lost opportunities for study or evangelistic contact. If the decision is to accept an appointment on the human services board, the civic self smiles with satisfaction, but all the excluded selves filibuster. No wonder we feel distracted and torn. No wonder we overcommit our schedules and live lives of frantic faithfulness. But when we experience life at the Center, all is changed. Our many selves come under the unifying control of the divine Arbitrator. No longer are we forced to live by an inner majority rule which always leaves a disgruntled minority. The divine Yes or No settles all minority reports. Everything becomes oriented to this new Center of reference. The quiet evening can be enjoyed to the fullest because our many selves have been stilled by the Holy Within. The business self, the religious self, the energetic self, all are at peace because they know we are living in obedience. There is no need to wave the flag of self interest, since all things good and needful will be given their proper attention at the appropriate time. We enter a refreshing balance and equilibrium in life.

Until we begin to move into this way of living we cannot possibly make sense out of Jesus' startling statement, "Let what you say be simply 'Yes' or 'No'; anything more than this comes from evil" (Matt. 5:37). When all of life's motions are governed by the heavenly Monitor, then we speak and make decisions in simplicity. Before, when asked to lead a campaign for minority rights (or teach a Sunday School class or whatever), our competing selves engaged in vigorous debate. "It's the right thing to do!" "But really now I am just too busy." "The need is so great, and besides think of all those who will approve of the action . . . but then what of those who will disapprove." "And what if I become entangled with the authorities, perhaps thrown into prison." And on it went. We jerked back and forth between Yes and No, indecisive, confused. From earliest days we had been taught that God is not the author of confusion, but there we sat in inward disarray.

But when we live out of the divine Center, thoughts and decisions flow from the Fountainhead. All relevant data are considered, to be sure, but decisions stem from a source deeper than facts and figures. Once we have understood the mind of the Father, we can speak our Yes or No with confidence. We will have no need to reverse our decision if the winds of opinion change, for we have spoken out of a deeper Reality than the latest Gallup poll.

Earlier I spoke of God on the periphery of my life. Actually, it would be more accurate to say that I was on the periphery of his Life. It was I who needed to come into the Center, the Core. It is one thing for God to come into us (and a very necessary thing), but it is quite another for us to come into God. In the first instance we are still the center of attention; in the second God is the focal point. When God comes into us we still have a certain autonomy; when we come into God we have come IN. He is in all and through all and above all. This is no infantile pantheism, as if God could be captured in his creation; it is a marvelous majestic monotheism—one God from whom all life is sustained. It is life out of the divine Center.

The focus of Christian simplicity becomes more clear when we change the image flow from God coming into us to our coming into God. "Christ in you" was certainly an important theme in Paul's teaching, but his favorite and most frequent image was of us "in Christ." In the latter case, Christ has become the reference point and we are making the movement into him. When we are in Christ, truly in Christ, our deeds and words are of one piece, because they both flow from a single Spring.

A Perpetual Communion

You may well ask if such a life is possible. Can we really hear God in such a way that each decision can be ordered and governed by him? Can we live in virtually constant communion with the divine Center of the universe? Can Christ truly be present among his people so that he can be heard? Oh, yes! His voice is not hard to hear. His vocabulary is not hard to understand.

Through his illustrious missionary and literary career, Frank Laubach bore repeated witness to this reality. His diaries and books on prayer are peppered with his many experiments to remain in constant communion with God. On the first day of 1937 he wrote in his diary, "God, I want to give you every minute of this year. I shall try to keep You in mind every moment of my waking hours. . . . I shall try to let You be the speaker and direct every word. I shall try to let You direct my acts. I shall try to learn Your language."[7] What a marvelous resolve for the new year! Three months later, he noted his progress in learning to practice God's presence: "Thank Thee . . . that the habit of constant conversation grows easier each day. I really do believe *all* thought can be conversations with Thee."[8]

Think of the number of people who have been encouraged in this way by the simple writings and profound life of Brother Lawrence. How vastly enriched we are that he was finally persuaded, almost against his will, to write down how he had learned *The Practice of the Presence of God*. His famous words still throb with life and joy, "The time of business does not with me differ from the time of prayer; and in the noise and clatter of my kitchen, while several persons are at the same time calling for different things, I possess God in as great tranquillity as if I were upon my knees at the blessed sacrament."[9] Every thought, every decision, every action stemmed from the divine Root. A simple kitchen monk, who meekly referred to himself as the "lord of all pots and pans," found it to be possible. We can too!

But we fool ourselves if we think that such a sacramental way of living is automatic. This kind of living communion does not just fall on our heads. We must desire it and seek it out. Like the deer that pants for the flowing stream, so we thirst for the living Spring. We must order our lives in particular ways. We must take up a consciously chosen course of action that will draw us more deeply into perpetual communion with the Father.

I have discovered one delightful means to this end to be prayer experiments that open us to God's presence every waking moment. The idea is extraordinarily simple. Seek to discover as many ways as possible to keep God constantly in mind. "There is nothing new in that," you may say. "That practice is very ancient and very orthodox." Exactly! This desire to practice the presence of God is the secret of all the saints. "Pray constantly," urged Paul (I Thess. 5:17). "In everything by prayer and supplication with thanksgiving let your requests be made known to God" (Phil. 4:6). "For all who are led by the Spirit of God are sons of God" (Rom. 8:14). Of course it is not new. Countless millions have shown it to be a practical living reality.

Have you ever tried to live out your day so that you fill each moment with the thought of God? I do not mean that you are to cease normal activity. Oh no! Just the opposite. Bring God into each activity, infusing it with the divine Light.

One night I made a high resolve: every person whom I saw the next day I would consciously try to lift into the light of Christ. In the morning I jumped up, had breakfast, and was on my way to work before I realized I had not prayed at all for the family. One by one I sought to immerse them in the Light. Once at the office I rushed in, gave the day's work to my secretary, and was walking out the door before I realized my omission once again. I prayed for the joy of the Lord to enter her day. By now I was beginning to realize how far my life was from constant communion. I became more collected within. Then as I went through the routine of my day I sought to beam prayers at each one I met. I asked for discernment to perceive what was in people, inviting Christ to comfort those who seemed hurt, encourage those who seemed weary, challenge those who seemed indifferent. It was a wonderfully happy day. Sometimes people I would pass on the street would turn, smile, and wish me a good day.

We can help people immensely in this secret ministry. Once, in an ordinary committee meeting, I felt moved to pray for one member who seemed weighted with sorrow, even bitterness. I, of course, participated in the discussion, but all the time inwardly I sought to bathe this person in the light of Christ. The meeting was somewhat difficult due to her rather caustic remarks, especially toward two others in the group. But as we prepared to dismiss, this person suddenly began to weep and finally said to the group, "I wish you would pray for me." After she had shared the source of her hurt and anger, the two who had been verbally attacked gathered around her and prayed the most tender prayer of healing and release. The room seemed full of power and joy.

Frank Laubach spoke of his "Game with Minutes." The idea is to take a given hour each day and see how many minutes during that hour you can be conscious of God's presence. At first you will find the practice difficult and your "score" will be low. That is all right; you are developing new spiritual muscles. With practice, the habit will become more and more ingrained. Make your first experiment in a worship service and hopefully that will be an aid to your concentration. In time extend the experiment to the whole of your day.

When I first began reading Laubach's journals, I was puzzled by the notations at the top of each day: "Conscious 50% ... Conscious 25% ... Conscious 80%." No explanation whatever was given and I would wonder, "Conscious of what?" Finally I realized that he was playing his little game with minutes and recording the percentage of each day that he felt he was living conscious of God's presence.

I'm glad he called it a game, because it is a delightful spiritual exercise. Besides, there needs to be a certain joyful light-heartedness about our task. Otherwise we will become overly serious and dreadfully boring. Meister Eckhart remarked, "The soul will bring forth person if God laughs into her and she laughs back into Him."[10] Our work is no grim duty. It is a delightful privilege. We are engaged in a joyous adventure, not a sourfaced penance. God is no killer of happiness. In this little exercise we are coming alive to God. Every person, every tree, every flower, every color is alive with God for those who know his language. Kagawa said that every scientific book was a letter from God telling us how he runs his universe.

And the glory of this experiment is that it works best when we concentrate not upon ourselves but upon others. We miss the point if we are taking our spiritual temperature every few moments to see if we are concentrating upon God enough. How much better if we try every moment to give God to someone else. It is wonderful to walk onto a grade school playground and inwardly lift every child into the arms of Christ. Or to ride in the back of a bus and invite Christ to visit with each person that boards. Carpenters and plumbers and electricians can fill the homes in which they work with the light of Christ, praying for each member of the family, or if it is a new home for the family which will live there. Grocery store clerks and retail checkers can pray for each person who passes through the line, imagining him or her drawing closer to God. In my work I write many letters, and so each time I sign my name I try to pray for the person to whom the letter is addressed. It is great fun to imagine the recipient opening the letter and being strengthened with a fresh sense of God's presence. There are thousands of these little experiments you can try, and very often you will be startled by the results.

And most wonderful of all is what happens inside us. More and more we develop what Thomas á Kempis called a "familiar friendship with Jesus."[11] No longer is "Jesus, Lover of My Soul" a quaint song—it is an amazing experience. To our astonishment we find that we are walking with God. His thoughts are becoming our thoughts, his desires our desires. Increasingly, old ugly thoughts melt away and our minds become pure as a mountain stream. Proof upon proof begins to pile up that God is at work in our daily lives, until we become certain of God, not from books or preachers, but from experience. The old strain and indecision are replaced by a greater ease and confidence.

Of all the inward changes we experience, the most awesome is that we begin to know his Voice. We become inwardly acquainted with the language of the true Shepherd. Humbled under the cross, we are able increasingly to discern the true Spirit from the clatter and clamor of human voices, and even the hollow voice of the enemy who comes under the guise of an angel of light. We begin to live in guidance. Inward promptings give unity to our decisions. All the demands for service are somehow filtered through the Light. Our lives are being simplified because we are giving attention to only one Voice, and our Yes and No arise from that Center. We no longer rush puffing and panting through our jam-packed day, yet somehow we accomplish more. Thomas Kelly witnessed, "Life from the Center is a life of unhurried peace and power. It is simple. It is serene. It is amazing. It is triumphant. It is radiant. It takes no time, but it occupies all our time. And it makes our life programs new and overcoming."[12]

The Principle of Contentment

One of the most profound effects of inward simplicity is the rise of an amazing spirit of contentment. Gone is the need to strain and pull to get ahead. In rushes a glorious indifference to position, status, or possession. Living out of this wonderful Center causes all other concerns to fade into insignificance. So utterly immersed was St. Paul in this reality that from a Roman prison he could write, "I have learned, in whatever state I am, to be content" (Phil. 4:11). To be abased or to abound was a matter of indifference to him. Plenty and hunger, abundance and want were immaterial to this little Jew with the Titan soul. "I can do all things through Christ who strengthens me," he said, and so he lived (Phil. 4:13, NEW KJV).

How cleverly Paul turned the tables on all those who taught that "godliness is a means of gain" by replying that "there is great gain in godliness with contentment" (I Tim. 6:5, 6). He saw that the problem with material gain is its inability to bring contentment. John D. Rockefeller was once asked how much money it would take to be really satisfied. He answered, "Just a little bit more!" And that is precisely our problem—it always takes a little more; contentment always remains elusive.

But the wonderful thing about simplicity is its ability to give us contentment. Do you understand what a freedom this is? To live in contentment means we can opt out of the status race and the maddening pace that is its necessary partner. We can shout "No!" to the insanity which chants, "More, more, more!" We can rest contented in the gracious provision of God.

I still remember the day this reality struck me with unusual force. I was passing by some very expensive homes, and began pondering our perennial tendency to want something bigger, better, and more plush. At the same time, I was monitoring the rise of covetousness in my spirit as I admired those homes. I carried on a little inward dialogue. Was it possible, I wondered, to come to the place where you do not desire more house even if you can afford it? Couldn't you decide on a particular economic livability level and rest contented with that, even if your income exceeded it considerably? The response was swift: "Oh yes! It is not necessary to always crave more. You *can* live contented with what you have, with no further desire to accumulate more." I'm quite sure I have not attained this holy contentment, but from time to time I have known a measure of its liberating graces and have found it a wonderful resting place.

Think of the misery that comes into our lives by our restless gnawing greed. We plunge ourselves into enormous debt and then take two and three jobs to stay afloat. We uproot our families with unnecessary moves just so we can have a more prestigious house. We grasp and grab and never have enough. And most destructive of all, our flashy cars and sports spectaculars and backyard pools have a way of crowding out much interest in civil rights or inner city poverty or the starved masses of India. Greed has a way of severing the cords of compassion. How clearly the Apostle Paul saw this when he warned that our lust for wealth causes us to fall into "many senseless and hurtful desires that plunge men into ruin and destruction" (I Tim. 6:9).

But we do not need to be imprisoned to avarice. We can be ushered into a life of peace and serenity. With Paul we can say, "If we have food and clothing, with these we shall be content" (I Tim. 6:8).

I wish I could end our discussion of contentment on this high note. But as you have probably already realized, contentment has certain difficulties. The great problem with a principle of contentment is its tendency to baptize the status quo, to give religious sanction to present conditions. It is the kind of counsel that the powerful enjoy giving to the poor and defenseless. Often it is the very spirit of *discontent* that has prompted wonderful changes for good. There is a kind of holy restlessness that inspires important social advances. And so we are faced with the practical issue of knowing when our disquiet stems from a God-given concern to improve conditions, and when it is the result of self-serving greed. There are, of course, no foolproof answers, but I share the following guidelines in the hope that they may at least turn us in the right direction.

First, we can share the concern with other brothers and sisters whose discernment we respect. Second, if our restlessness has its root in anguish over the plight of those whose condition is clearly desperate, most likely it is of the Lord. Third, if the concern involves the well-being of our children, it is often right. Fourth, if we are wanting to improve our own state, we should not automatically assume that it is wrong. Fifth, let us consider if our discontent has its source in a lack of inward peace with Christ. Sixth, we need to learn to distinguish a genuine psychological need, such as cheerful surroundings, from an obsession. Seventh, we must grow in our discernment between desires that spring from Heavenly Love and those arising from the love of money. Eighth, by an act of the will we must still every motion that is centered in greed.

Moving Up and In

The inner integration I have described is the longing of many. We weary of competing commitments and exhausting schedules. We desire to be obedient to God in all things, and have a growing knowledge that this frantic scramble is not his will. We yearn to enter the deep silences that give unity and force to our service.

Desire, however, is not enough. If we expect to enter the inward simplicity for which we were created, we will need to order our lives in specific ways. The things we do will not give us simplicity of heart, but they will put us in the place where we can receive it.

One way to nurture simplicity is through the discipline of silence. Society is dominated by the inane notion that action is the only reality. Please, for God's sake and your own, don't just do something, stand there! Come in and enjoy his presence. Sink down into the light of Christ and become comfortable in that posture. Open the subterranean sanctuary of your soul and listen for the *Kol Yahweh*, the voice of the Lord. To do so gives us focus, unity, purpose. We discover serenity, unshakableness, firmness of life orientation.

At first we will hesitate to do this. It is strange territory and, as Blaise Pascal said, "The eternal silence of the infinite spaces terrifies me."[13] But if we will once overcome our fear and quiet ourselves we will discover that Christ is our Friend who desires our company. Our fear comes from our unfamiliarity with centering down our lives. In his book *Nurturing Silence in a Noisy Heart,* Wayne Oates says, "Silence is not native to my world. Silence, more than likely, is a stranger to your world, too. If you and I ever have silence in our noisy hearts, we are going to have to grow it. . . . You *can* nurture silence in your noisy heart if you value it, cherish it, and are eager to nourish it."[14]

Yes, we can have a holy silence within, but we need to nurture it. And when we do, miracles occur. If we are assailed by temptation, all we need to do is quiet ourselves into the power of God and watch the good rise up and the evil dissipate. It is wonderful—this resting in God, this stilling of frantic activity, this seeking first his Kingdom.

At all times, but especially in the beginning, we need to find a specific time and place to nurture silence. As a teenager I used to go out behind the garage and sit on a wall with my feet on the trash cans. It was a quiet sanctuary there, and I learned to commune with the Father. One May day Frank Laubach wrote, "The day had been rich but strenuous, so I climbed Signal Hill back of my house talking and listening to God all the way up, all the way back, all the lovely half hour on the top."[15] Some draw near in the recreating silences of the early morning, others quiet themselves best in the deep quiet of the night, still others retreat from the blast of the day for a time of attentive, listening silence. We must have a time to still the churning, to quiet the restlessness, to meditate on the almighty God who dwells in our hearts.

Another important ingredient in opening the way for interior simplicity is to get in tune with the God-given cycles of life. There are cycles of eating, cycles of sleeping, cycles of work, cycles of play. And when these God-appointed cycles are broken, misery is the result. My students often suffer from a simple denial of the normal cycle of sleep. Large numbers of Americans endure immense heartache (and heartburn) from the failure to respond correctly to the cycle of eating. Finitude is a cycle, the cycle of growing old. And what a terrible burden we place upon ourselves and others in our desperate attempt to stay young. On the other end, of course, children struggle to be twenty-one and hence independent. People are in misery because they are not yet twenty-one, and people are in misery because they are past twenty-one, and that leaves most of us in misery most of the time.

Many of us would find great relief in discovering our own cycles of activity and quiet. For example, I function best when I alternate between periods of intense activity and of comparative solitude. When I understand this about myself I can order my life accordingly. After a certain amount of immersion in public life, I begin to burn out. And I have noticed that I burn out inwardly long before I do outwardly. Hence, I must be careful not to become a frantic bundle of hollow energy, busy among people but devoid of life. I must learn when to retreat, like Jesus, and experience the recreating power of God. We are told that Peter tarried in Joppa for many days with one Simon, a tanner (Acts 9:43). And along our journey we need to discover numerous "tarrying places" where we can receive heavenly manna.

This knowledge is a wonderful freedom. No longer do I rebuke myself that I am not giving enough attention to study and meditation in the days of intense activity among people. Nor do I any longer malign periods of quiet reflection or vacation as unproductive sloth. I can understand and value the hidden preparation through which God puts his ministers. I am free from desiring public gaze when I need hiddenness.

Still another step toward simplicity is to refuse to live beyond our means emotionally. In a culture where whirl is king, we must understand our emotional limits. Ulcers, migraines, nervous tension, and a dozen other symptoms mark our psychic overload. We are concerned not to live beyond our means financially; why do it emotionally? Let us repudiate the modern success image of the person "on the go," whose workload is double what any single person can possibly accomplish. Let us reject the delusions of grandeur that say we are the only ones who can save the world. We must learn our emotional limits and respect them. Our children and spouses will love us for it.

Is there anything more we can do? Yes, much! We can keep a record of all our activities for one month. Then we should rank them in the following way: absolutely essential—number 1, important but not essential—number 2, helpful but not necessary—number 3, trivial—number 4. Next, we must ruthlessly eliminate all of the last two categories and 20 percent of the first two. We are too busy only because we want to be too busy. We could cut out a great deal of our activity and not seriously affect our productivity.

Purposefully, we can cultivate the life of reflection. We need not merely listen to the news or read the paper, we can ponder its significance. Let's get the broad picture on the events of our time and evaluate them. The real prophets of our day are those who can perceive what is happening in modern society, see where it will lead us, and give a value judgment upon it. Let's wrestle with "existence clarification"—who we are and what our purpose for being is. We can take a one-day retreat just to reflect on our direction in life. We should not just absorb facts, but think about their significance. When a brilliant philosopher friend of mine went on a one-year sabbatical, I asked him what he would do. "For the first three months I plan to do nothing but think," was his reply. Most of us cannot be unencumbered for three months, but we can think. Thinking is the hardest work we can do, and among the most important.

Another step that opens us to heart simplicity is the commitment to a previously agreed rule. The covenant of marriage is perhaps the clearest example of this. Think of the host of costly and painful decisions that are avoided by this commitment. No flirting with divorce, no casting about for better options—marriage becomes a *decision* to love and cherish each other until death. In our family we have decided how much per month we will spend on entertainment. That simple commitment greatly reduces the strain and stress of decision-making. I have set a limit on the number of speaking engagements I can accept that will allow me to maintain my other obligations with integrity. When that limit has been reached, I can decline even "wonderful opportunities" with amazing speed, because I feel God has called me to that limit. I have been saved enormous frustration and over-commitment by the simple rule of *never* accepting a speaking engagement over the telephone. By the time a letter has arrived, my enthusiasm has been tempered by realism. A mother or father who has decided to stay at home until the children are school age eliminates many wonderings and vacillations about this or that job. Patterns are, of course, not always perfect, and they sometimes need to be broken, but for the most part they economize greatly the frustration of numerous decisions.

Of all the virtues, simplicity is the most inviting because it brings such inward unity. François Fénelon put it most emphatically: "O, how amiable this simplicity is! Who will give it to me? I leave all for this. It is the pearl of the Gospel."[16]

6. INWARD SIMPLICITY:
HOLY OBEDIENCE

The fruit of holy obedience is the simplicity of the children of God.   *—Thomas Kelly*

T. S. Eliot speaks of Christianity as "A condition of complete simplicity / (Costing not less than everything)."[1] Holy obedience is stamped with that enormous price tag. Holy obedience is the insatiable God-hunger that will make a person dissatisfied with anything less than the pearl of great price. Holy obedience is the joyful abandon of the person who will sell absolutely everything to buy the field. It is the obedience of an Abraham willing to plunge the knife into his own dear son at the *Kol Yahweh,* the voice of the Lord. It is three Hebrew children who refused to bow the knee to the golden image. It is a Daniel who would die before he would stop praying to the one true God.

Holy obedience is the single eye that bathes the entire personality in light. It is the purity of heart that can desire only one thing—the good. It is a God-intoxicated life that can embrace wealth or poverty, hunger or plenty, crucifixion or acclaim with equal ease at the word of Christ.

Dr. Graham Scroggie, a gifted preacher of another generation, preached on the Lordship of Christ at a huge Keswick Convention in England. A great orator, he spoke powerfully. After the crowd had left, he saw a young college student seated alone. He went to her, asking if he could help. "Oh, Dr. Scroggie," she blurted out, "your message was so compelling, but I am afraid to truly make Christ Lord, afraid of what he will ask of me!" Wisely, Graham Scroggie turned his worn Bible to the story of Peter at Joppa, where God had taught him about his racial and cultural discrimination. Three times God brought down a sheet laden with animals unclean to orthodox Judaism and said, "Rise, Peter; kill and eat." Three times Peter responded, "No, Lord." Tenderly, Dr. Scroggie said, "You know it is possible to say 'No,' and it is possible to say 'Lord,' but it is not really possible to say, 'No, Lord.' I'm going to leave my Bible with you and this pen and go into another room and pray for you, and I want you to cross out either the word 'No' or the word 'Lord.'" He did so, and when in prayer he felt that the matter had been settled he slipped back into the auditorium. The young woman was weeping quietly, and peering over her shoulder he saw the word 'No' crossed out. Softly she was saying, "He's Lord, He's Lord, He's Lord." Such is the stuff of holy obedience.

Going Deeper

We must be more precise, more concrete about this matter of holy obedience. Otherwise it will remain forever a pious-sounding theoretical ideal that does not much affect the way we live. Meister Eckhart wrote, "There are plenty to follow our Lord half-way, but not the other half. They will give up possessions, friends, and honors, but it touches them too closely to disown themselves."[2] As we cross over the line and venture into this second half, we find ourselves in the land of holy obedience. To gladly disown ourselves, to live in joyful self-renunciation, is the other half from which we so often draw back. Jesus declared, "If any man would come after me, let him deny himself and take up his cross and follow me" (Mark 8:34). Harsh demand, this self-denial. We would much prefer more comforting words like "self-fulfillment" and "self-actualization." Self-denial conjures up in our minds all sorts of images of groveling and self-hatred. We imagine that it most certainly means self-contempt and will probably lead to various forms of self-mortification.

What we have failed to see is this amazing paradox: true self-fulfillment comes only through self-denial. There is no other way. The most certain way to miss self-fulfillment is to pursue it. "He who finds his life will lose it, and he who loses his life for my sake will find it" (Matt. 10:39).

It is wonderful, this losing of one's self through a perpetual vision of the Holy. We are catapulted into something infinitely larger and more real than our petty existence. A blazing God-consciousness frees us from self-consciousness. It is freedom. It is joy. It is life.

I cannot stress enough how essential this quality is to true simplicity of life. It is the only thing that will allow us to hold the interest of others above self-interest. It saves us from self-pity. It lifts the burden of concern over having a proper image. It frees us from bondage to the opinions of others.

No one has written with greater vigor or more perception on the connection between selflessness and simplicity than the seventeenth-century Archbishop of Cambrai, François Fénelon. In his sensitive little book *Christian Perfection,* Fénelon identifies three stages through which we travel on our way into the simplicity of self-blindedness. The first stage involves freeing ourselves from an "intoxication" to material or outward things and becoming sensitive to the things of the spirit, especially our own inward condition. We are no longer dazzled by the outward, the superficial. Impressive buildings, bulging budgets, flashy programs simply fail to move us. We give up on all the outward human systems to accomplish the work of God. Our attention is drawn to the more internal work of the Spirit. We become absorbed with the work of God upon the soul. It is a good and healthy step, but deeply self-centered and far from genuine simplicity. "It is a wise self-love, which wants to get out of the intoxication of outside things."[3]

In the second stage we move away from total absorption in ourselves and our eternal destiny to being centered in the fear of God. It is a step forward but it is, as Fénelon said, "a weak commencement of true wisdom," since we are "still wrapped up in self."[4] In this stage it is not enough for us to fear God, we must be *sure* that we fear him. We fear not-fearing. We have a kind of spiritual rigor that is determined to obey God. We are constantly returning to our own behavior to see if we can find any dregs of pride or avarice. There is a great longing for humility, and we work with all our might to attain it. There is a keen sensibility of sin within. A strong identity is felt with St. Paul who, regardless of what others had done, could feel in the depths of his being that he was the "chief of sinners" (I Tim. 1:15).

This stage is one of great honesty and sincerity, but it is not yet true simplicity. "Sincerity is a virtue below simplicity,"[5] said Fénelon. The reason is easy to see. The sincere have a deep concern for honesty and truth. Rectitude, fidelity, conscientiousness, impeccability—these all mark the sincere. And although all of these are great virtues, they have a certain self-consciousness about them: a concern to do right, to be right, to look right. Of the sincere, Fénelon says, "They are always studying themselves, going over all their words and all their thoughts, and going back over all that they have done, afraid of having said or done too much."[6]

The sincere are not yet simple. They have a kind of artificial rigor that makes us feel uncomfortable, though we cannot fault the virtue. They put us on edge and make us feel ill at ease. This often concerns us because they seem so spiritual, so determined to know God. We wonder if our discomfort stems from a resistance to God and his way. In reality, however, it is due to the fact that these deeply committed folk are trying too hard. They lack the ease, freedom, and naturalness that mark true interior simplicity. We would prefer less perfect people who are more at ease with themselves.

This stage in the spiritual walk must never be despised. It is, in a certain sense, necessary as we are coming into God. In the Christian fellowship there needs to be a sufficient measure of grace and latitude to allow our brothers and sisters and ourselves to travel through these experiences. Nor must we hurry people through this stage too quickly. People who see the peace and liberty that comes from simple love often try to push themselves (and everyone else) into it before they are ready. This is a grave mistake. As the wise preacher of Ecclesiastes said, there is a time and a season for everything under heaven, and there must be times of inward struggle and penitence. When the time is right, the spirit is nourished by the bread of careful introspection. There is a proper place for inner disturbance and rigorous examination. Brother Lawrence witnessed to ten years of this inner turbulence.[7]

Having cautioned you about too brief a sojourn in this stage, I must hasten to add that neither must we become too attached to this period, for we are only pilgrims through the land. We were never meant to set up permanent residence there. An inward resting in the midst of strife is the rightful inheritance of the children of the Kingdom (Heb. 4). When God begins to open us to something more pure, we are to follow promptly and never lose time in backward glances.

As we move along, God will lead us into the third stage, in which our attention becomes more and more drawn to the divine Center. "It begins to consider God more often than it considers self, and insensibly it tends to forget self in order to become more concerned with God with a love devoid of self-interest."[8]

Please understand, this is not the destruction of self or the loss of individuality in some sort of "cosmic consciousness." This is the discovery of the self achieved by focusing our attention on the Creator of the self. It is losing the self in order to find it. Only in this way can the true self blossom and flourish.

This third stage is a marvelous virtue, and something sublime. It is the natural charm and unpretentious exuberance of simplicity. We admire people who walk in this way, and enjoy their company. Gone is the forced behavior and sticky righteousness.

Do you know the wonderful new freedom this simplicity brings? No longer is there the stifling preoccupation with ourselves. Now there are new liberating graces to care deeply for the needs of others. And most wonderful of all, we can lay down the crushing burden of the opinions of others. Fénelon witnessed, "With this purity of heart, we are no longer troubled by what others think of us, except that in charity we avoid scandalizing them."[9] We do not *have* to be liked. We do not *have* to succeed. We can enjoy obscurity as easily as fame.

We have also a curious liberty to speak about ourselves, not excessively but naturally. I say "curious" because most people assume that those who are truly unself-conscious would never talk about themselves. That approach belongs to an earlier period in which, out of false modesty, we try to quell any rise of pride. We are afraid that maybe we have said too much. We slip an example or word about ourselves into the conversation and immediately worry that it was inspired by vanity. We determine that we will never speak of ourselves, neither our accomplishments nor our failures, lest in either case *we* become the center of attention. At many points this is indeed good counsel, but it is a strained humility and contrary to simplicity. In time, however, we begin to relax, and are enabled to speak of ourselves with the same candor as we do of others. "Simplicity consists of not having any wrong shame, or false modesty," writes Fénelon.[10]

The Apostle Paul knew this freedom to an amazing degree. He could assert his Roman citizenship and his Hebrew lineage when it was needed. He could boast of his many sufferings for Christ's cause: beatings and stonings, shipwrecks and sleepless nights, hunger and thirst (II Cor. 11:24–29). He received his Apostleship and teaching from Christ alone, and even opposed Peter for his cultural Jewish Christianity (Gal. 1, 2). He was so free and unpretentious that he could boldly urge believers, "Be imitators of me, as I am of Christ" (I Cor. 11:1).

Here is language that most of us would not dare utter. On our lips it would seem like the height of arrogance, and probably that is exactly what it would be. But Paul was beyond such petty self-admiration. He had passed through all that long ago. The hidden preparation through which God had put this man had changed him. We cannot understand the things that Paul said and the life that Paul lived until we see that he had given up on all the little human systems of self-aggrandizement. Without exaggeration he could call it all "dung," because he was living in a greater Power. And when we see ourselves desperately struggling for the "dung," we can be fairly certain that we know little of this "power of his resurrection, and the fellowship of his sufferings, being made conformable unto his death" (Phil. 3:10). Paul knew what it meant to be free from himself. What a desperately needed freedom it is today!

Throughout history there have been various traditions which, in one form or another, have advised verbal debasement of ourselves in order to gain mastery over reigning pride. We can remember this tendency in some of the ascetic practices of the Middle Ages, but it is also in evidence today in what I have sometimes called "worm theology." "Without God I am nothing, I am no good, I am a worm!" Whatever merit such statements have theologically, I honestly doubt that they have much value in increasing selflessness. Fénelon is, I think, far wiser when he says simply, "Self-love prefers injury to oblivion and silence."[11] To be silent is probably the best way to deal with self-love.

In simplicity we are also free to let others speak well of us when it is appropriate. I still remember the day I was with a group of friends and one person paid me a sincere compliment. With self-conscious modesty I blushed, hemmed and hawed, and tried to shrug off the remark. A very perceptive friend in the group looked me straight in the eye and said, "Foster, you don't know how to take a compliment, do you?" That was a turning point for me. I realized that a compliment, if given in honesty and not to impress, should be taken seriously. I had no right to affront people by rejecting their gift of love. Over the years since that incident, God has given me a measure of freedom in that regard, and it is a happy freedom.

In all of this we can sometimes get the mistaken impression of uninterrupted progress forward. Even the use of the term "stages" can unwittingly convey the idea of leaving one level for a higher one never to return again. I have not found it to be so. My experience has been much more fluid and undulating. One day I may be experiencing an intimate attention to Christ's presence that is well nigh amazing, and the next day I am in the "Slough of Despond." I can alternate between being meekly submissive and stubbornly rebellious with surprising speed. And I find many of the devotional masters record similar experiences. The stages are not hard and fast. There is a lot of movement back and forth, up and down.

But it is not a spiritual roller coaster either, because through all the motion there is a sense of progress and growth. The feeling of intermittent communion begins to give way to more sustained fellowship. Whereas before the hard thing was to seek his face, more and more the hard thing is to refrain from seeking him. Slowly and certainly, howbeit with many reversals, knowing God moves from obligation to delight. Although many times we do not pay attention to the holy Whisper, increasingly we do. We are less and less discouraged by our many wanderings in the wilderness because, having tasted the land of promise, we desire it more and more. As much as we may flirt with double-minded living, our real love is singleness of purpose and increasingly it is capturing our heart. We cannot help being drawn toward this way of life when we read the inviting words of our mentor, François Fénelon, "When we are truly in this interior simplicity our whole appearance is franker, more natural. This true simplicity ... makes us conscious of a certain openness, gentleness, innocence, gaiety, and serenity, which is charming when we see it near to and continually, with pure eyes." [12]

Joy the Hallmark

Does all this sound difficult to you? Perhaps you are saying to yourself, "I thought I was doing well to get to stage one, and now I discover that it is the bottom rung! It sounds like too much work for me." Yes, it is work—but then again, it isn't. Once we begin, we discover that Someone is working on our behalf, and carrying the bulk of the load. It is the easy yoke and the light burden of which Jesus spoke. The Hound of Heaven is doggedly after us to do us good.

Actually this reality is not something we can bring about by gritting our teeth and fortifying our will. There are things for us to do, as we shall see, but they are more like getting in step with the Leader than blazing the trail for ourselves. There is a quality of yieldedness, a living in the passive voice. Fénelon observed, "The more docile and yielding a soul is in letting itself be carried away without resistance or delay, the more it advances in simplicity." [13]

I often have students who are keenly conscientious and determined to come into God. Sometimes I need to counsel them to relax and quit trying to be so religious. Recently, I had one such student who was struggling desperately and praying fervently over an internal matter. I shocked him when I said, "Please stop praying. You are working at this too hard; let me do the praying for you." Such a small word, and yet it set him marvelously free.

Joy, not grit, is the hallmark of holy obedience. We need to be lighthearted in what we do to avoid taking ourselves too seriously. It is a cheerful revolt against self and pride. Our work is jubilant, carefree, merry. Utter abandonment to God is done freely and with celebration. And so I urge you to enjoy this ministry of self-surrender. Don't push too hard. Hold this work lightly, joyfully.

The saints throughout the ages have witnessed to this reality. Think of St. Francis, the poor little monk of Assisi, inebriated with the love of God and filled with ecstasy. Those early Franciscans walked in holy obedience with the most incredible exuberance and merry abandon. Jubilant, they lived rapt in God by the overflow of divine grace that descended upon them. Juliana of Norwich in her beautiful *Revelations of Divine Love* said that she was filled with "delight and security so blessedly and so powerfully that there was no fear, no sorrow, no pain, physical or spiritual, that one could suffer which might have disturbed me." [14] Blaise Pascal wrote, "Certitude. Certitude. Feeling. Joy. Peace. . . . Forgetfulness of the world and of everything, except God. . . . Joy, joy, joy, tears of joy." [15] And on and on march the witnesses.

You know, of course, that they are not speaking of a silly, superficial, bubbly kind of joy like that flaunted in modern society. No, this is a deep, resonant joy that has been shaped and tempered by the fires of suffering and sorrow—joy through the cross, joy because of the cross.

The Rise of Humility

Of all the theological virtues, humility is one of the most coveted. No one enjoys people who are consumed with themselves. Smug arrogance is always distasteful. Genuine humility, on the other hand, has a gentleness about it that is delightful. There is an unpretentiousness in true humility that all people appreciate.

But humility is as elusive as it is desirable. We all know that it can never be gained by seeking it. The more we pursue it the more distant it becomes. To think we have it is sure evidence that we don't. But there is a way for humility to come into the habit patterns of our lives. Holy obedience opens the door. It is a central means of God's grace to work humility into us.* It is not hard to see how this can be. When the whole of our vision is filled with the Holy, petty selfishness is squeezed out. Perpetual God-consciousness of necessity eliminates self-consciousness. Thomas Kelly wrote, "Humility rests upon a Holy blindedness, like the blindedness of him who looks steadily into the sun. For wherever he turns his eyes on earth, there he sees only the sun. The God-blinded soul sees naught of self, naught of personal degradation or of personal eminence, but only the Holy Will."[16]

For the Christian, this comes as wonderful news. How many times we have longed to be free of our own self-conceit and domineering pride. What needless anguish we have borne simply because we were not noticed. We puff and strut to get a little attention, and later deplore our vanity. Wistfully we have seen the humility of others and ached to know its ease and freedom. How deeply we have desired to obey the word of Scripture to take on the mind of Christ, who though God the Son did not grasp for equality, but rather "emptied himself, taking the form of a servant. . . . And being found in human form he humbled himself and became obedient unto death, even death on a cross" (Phil. 2:7–8).

How wonderful now to see the connection between humility and obedience. Jesus "humbled himself and became obedient." There is a way into humility, and it is through holy obedience. The God-possessed soul knows only one purpose, one goal, one desire. God is not some figure in our field of vision, sometimes blurred, sometimes focused; he IS our vision. Our eye is single, our whole body is full of light. Selfishness cannot find a toehold.

---

* In *Celebration of Discipline* I mention that the Spiritual Discipline of service is also used by God to bring us humility. Service is, of course, an outflow of holy obedience. This again demonstrates the interdependence of the Disciplines.

First Steps

You may feel that the way of living we have been considering is a quantum leap from your present experience. Not only do you feel that you are in left field; you are in another ballpark, maybe another league. That probably overstates the case, but even if it is an accurate description of your situation you need not be discouraged. You do not have to be advanced in the intricacies of sainthood to begin to move into holy obedience. You do not even need to know all of the problems or pitfalls. You need only one thing: a desire to know God and to walk with him. And even if you do not desire God but wish you did, you may ask him for the desire and he will give it to you. Indeed, I would go so far as to say that the very fact that you are reading this book is desire enough for God to begin bringing the grace of holy obedience into your life.

Holy obedience does not just fall upon our heads. There are things we can do that will draw us into this sacred sanctuary. So I share the following "first steps" but I share them only as suggestions of the direction we need to travel, not as laws to encompass the journey. You can trust God to individualize the teaching: some things he will no doubt urge you to ignore; certainly he will teach you many personalized steps I do not mention. Above all, seek to be attentive to your present Teacher, whether through these words or beyond these words.

The first step I want to give you is not something to do at all. It is something to refrain from doing. Very simply, we should not try to be less egocentric. The attempt would be self-defeating. The more we work at being unconcerned about ourselves, the more conscious of ourselves we become. And so what are we to do? Nothing. Let the matter drop. It is one of those things in life that will never yield to a frontal attack. Concentration upon the problem redoubles its strength. This matter will be cared for in due time, but only if we first forget it and turn our attention to other things.

The second step is rather like the first in that it is less a plan for action and more a call to focus our field of vision. We are to discipline ourselves to "seek *first* the Kingdom of God." This focus must take precedence over absolutely everything. We must never allow anything, whether deed or desire, to have that place of central importance. The redistribution of the world's wealth cannot be central, the concern for ecology cannot be central, the desire to get out of the rat race cannot be central, the desire for simplicity itself cannot be central. The moment any of these becomes the focus of our concern, it has become idolatry. Only one thing is to be central: the Kingdom of God. And, in fact, when the Kingdom of God is genuinely placed first, the equitable distribution of wealth, ecological concerns, the poor, simplicity, and all things necessary will be given their proper attention.

In a particularly penetrating comment on this verse of Scripture, Søren Kierkegaard considered what sort of effort should be done to pursue the Kingdom of God. Should a person get a suitable job in order to exert a virtuous influence? His answer: no, we must *first* seek God's Kingdom. Then should we give away all our money to feed the poor? Again the answer: no, we must *first* seek God's Kingdom. Well, then perhaps we are to go out and preach this truth to the world that people are to seek first God's Kingdom? Once again the answer is a resounding: no, we are *first* to seek the Kingdom of God. Kierkegaard concludes, "Then in a certain sense it is nothing I shall do. Yes, certainly, in a certain sense it is nothing, become nothing before God, learn to keep silent; in this silence is the beginning, which is, *first* to seek God's Kingdom."[17]

And so I urge you to still every motion that is not rooted in the Kingdom. Become quiet, hushed, motionless until you are finally centered. Strip away all excess baggage and nonessential trappings until you have come into the stark reality of the Kingdom of God. Let go of all distractions until you are driven into the Core. Allow God to reshuffle your priorities and eliminate unnecessary froth. Mother Teresa of Calcutta said, "Pray for me that I not loosen my grip on the hands of Jesus even under the guise of ministering to the poor."[18] That is our first task: to grip the hands of Jesus with such tenacity that we are obliged to follow his lead, to seek first his Kingdom.

The third step is so simple I am almost embarrassed to mention it, and yet it is so important that I must. Begin now to obey him in every way you can. Start right where you are, in the midst of all the tasks that press in upon you. Do not wait for some future time when you will have more time or be more perfect in knowledge. The Roman governor Felix wanted to wait for a more "convenient season," but we all know that there is no more convenient season. "Today when you hear his voice, do not harden your hearts," warned the author of Hebrews (Heb. 3:7–8). Right now, as you read these words, ask for an increase of the light of Christ. Ask that the Shekinah, the glorious radiant presence of God, which once filled the mercy-seat, fill your heart. In every task of your day seek to live in utter surrender, listening and obedient.

Allow me to share with you a very small experience, but one that may help you to see what I mean. This occurred at an especially busy time in my year. I was preparing for a weekend trip that involved speaking at three different churches. The financial arrangement was for each church to take up a little offering on my behalf when I had finished speaking. As I was meditating on what God desired of me for that weekend, I had the strong impression that I was not to take any money at all from these churches. For some time I struggled over this directive, for we were counting on the money to meet several obligations. The struggle further revealed an inward greed that I thought had been exorcised long ago. Finally, I felt clear that this was what I had to do if I was to be obedient. I shared this with my wife, for I felt we had to be in unity on the matter. She released the money much more easily than I, noting that perhaps there would be some people in the meetings who needed to know that ministers of Christ were not always after their pocketbooks.

I told the pastors of the first two churches that any offering should be given to the poor or disposed of in whatever way they saw fit. Although surprised at my unorthodox request, they were congenial to the idea. But I arrived at the third church just as the service began, and so had no opportunity to explain my concern. I was relieved, however, when they did not take up an offering for me, and assumed that the matter was settled.

It was late when I finally arrived at the home where I was to stay the night. As I walked in the door my host handed me a check of an amount that was, for me, considerable. It was from the church. I protested, but they mistook my concern for modesty and insisted with such vigor that I let the matter drop.

I wish I could express to you the experience I went through that night. There was the check lying on the nightstand, mine to take. I did not want to cause offense or seem ungrateful; after all, the money had been given for me. Maybe this last church should be considered an experience separate from the others. But what about the earlier directive—it *had* seemed quite clear. Back and forth I went. Finally, I had about decided that I really should take the money rather than cause any trouble, but I determined to review my decision once more in the morning when I was rested. I invited God to teach me while I slept if he desired.

When I opened my eyes the next morning it was unmistakably clear to me that I could not—must not—take the money. A period of meditation only intensified the conviction. With considerable trepidation I explained to my hosts as best I could why I was not able to accept the gracious gift. The moment I finished there rushed into me an unspeakable joy. Though outwardly I tried to remain calm, I was being filled with an overwhelming sense of the glory of God. Once alone in the car I shouted and sang and blessed God. I did not have to be controlled by money! I could live in obedience! It was wonderful, jubilant ecstasy, and although the profuse exuberance lasted for perhaps twenty minutes, the sense of deep warm joy flowed over me all day long. (I was pleased to learn later that the church decided to give the money for refugee work in Cambodia.)

It was such a small matter, and yet obedience was so important, so necessary. And you can obey him right where you are with the light you now have. Begin today, this moment.

A fourth advice in holy obedience is to get up quickly and keep going if you stumble and fall. You will fall, you know. I shared one incident of victory, but I could also tell you of so many times when stubborn self-will would shake its defiant fist at the gentle Voice: times when I simply didn't want to listen so that I would not receive any disturbing instruction; neglect of whispered urgings to visit a neighbor or write a letter.

But when we do fail we do not need to give excessive time

mourning the loss. We need to make confession, get up, and start again immediately. Nor should we linger long at the site of battles won. The issue in holy obedience is not whether we failed or succeeded yesterday or this morning, but whether we are obedient *now*. Does heaven's light blind us to all other affections *now*? Is our eye single, are we living in simplicity *now*?

A fifth counsel in holy obedience is to still all vain talk about ourselves and others. I am not referring to gossip—I'm sure you ended that long ago. I mean the subtle mutual backscratching that is profoundly dishonest, the strokes we give people, not to encourage them but to win them to our side. These over-flattering compliments are seldom thought to be deceitful, but they are. It is not the straightforward speech that Jesus said would characterize the children of the Kingdom (Matt. 5:33–37). And I have discovered that it does not really promote the honest warm relationships we seek. Instead, it places an extra burden upon our brothers and sisters who are truly seeking to know humility of heart and now have to deal with our zealous misrepresentation of them.

In a public meeting I once spoke of a fellow pastor as "the most capable and compassionate pastor I know." Later this good friend confronted me about the statement, saying that he did not feel compassion was yet a distinguishing characteristic of his ministry. He was helping me to see the difference between a true compliment and sheer flattery. A compliment affirms what is already there or coming into being. Flattery degrades us by saying something is that isn't.

We would do well to discipline our words to what is actually the case without embellishment or overstatement. A commending word fitly spoken can be a special benediction, but we need to be careful not to offend propriety.

I shall mention a sixth word of counsel in this walk, which many have found especially helpful. I refer to the practice of keeping a spiritual journal. It is something of a book of remembrances, a personal Ebenezer to say, "Hitherto the Lord has helped us" (I Sam. 7:12).

A journal is immensely encouraging, for we often forget over the years from what petty self-centered depths God has brought us. We tend to be so immersed in the tussle of the moment that we fail to see that the issues over which we now struggle are vastly more significant and substantial. Many matters are settled and behind us.

Beyond this, a journal has the added merit of focusing and concentrating our thinking. Writing out our concerns helps to clarify things and keeps us honest. Self-centered prayers become manifestly self-centered, even to us, when seen on paper. Insights that are hazy figures on our horizon sometimes become crystal clear when committed to a journal. Vacillating indecision can be turned into marching orders.

Many have been helped by sharing their journal notations with each other, thus providing mutual accountability and encouragement. None of us can live in holy obedience on our own. We need the help and encouragement, and even rebuke, of our brothers and sisters.

In our day a great crowd of concerns presses into our little lives, demanding attention. Neighbors are lonely, marriages are floundering, social injustice is prolific, world hunger is escalating. We are pulled, pushed, torn. We need not answer these concerns by rushing out in double-minded obedience. With our eyes blinded to all else by a flaming vision of God, we may respond decisively in holy obedience.

7. OUTWARD SIMPLICITY: BEGINNING STEPS

There are two ways to get enough: one is to continue to accumulate more and more. The other is to desire less.
—G. K. Chesterton

Personal finance is the new forbidden subject of modern society. Once we were afraid to discuss sex in public, but no more. Now we flaunt our newfound freedom like an adolescent first learning to smoke. Then death was the subject no one dared discuss above a whisper. That day is gone too. Seminars on death and dying abound. We can buy tapes, films, and books on how to die gracefully. Gerontology is fast coming into prominence as a major science.

The great taboo today is personal finances. How we spend our money is our business, and nobody is going to tell us what to do with it. Vigorously we resist any public airing of so private a subject. When laws are passed to force public officials to give an open accounting of their stewardship, they still find ways to obscure the truth. Sermons on lifestyle or our obligation to the poor are viewed as a personal affront, a breach of private boundaries. We pull down the shades over our financial affairs; we balance our budgets and shuffle our credit cards behind closed doors.

Today there is a heretical teaching that is an absolute plague in American Christianity. It is the dogmatic and unexamined credo that whatever we gain is ours to do with as we please. If we earn $50,000, how we spend it is our private affair. Perhaps we will concede that it is legitimate for the church to talk about tithing, but the other 90 percent is none of its business.

How utterly self-consumed and provincial! In no way can we

twist the Scripture to justify such a belief. Our lifestyle is *not* our private affair. We dare not allow each person to do what is right in his or her own eyes. The Gospel demands more of us: it is obligatory upon us to help one another hammer out the shape of Christian simplicity in the midst of modern affluence. We need to love each other enough to sense our mutual responsibility and accountability. We are our brother's (and our sister's) keeper.

Precision without Legalism

In attempting to determine what simplicity might look like in the marketplace, we are accepting a massive assignment, one fraught with difficulties. We are now moving out of the realm of interpretation and into the realm of application, and that is always risky business. No longer is our primary question "What does the Bible say?" We must now concentrate on the question, "What does the Bible say to us?" As you know, we have been working on this second question all along, but it now becomes the center of our attention. It is wise to begin such a difficult task by setting forth some foundational building blocks which will undergird our effort.

The first such overarching principle is the necessity of precision without legalism. No one knows more keenly than I the grave danger in giving specific outward application to simplicity. How do you address such a wide variety of people with different needs and vastly different circumstances?

Some have large families, others have small families or no children. Still others are single. Some children have unusual needs that increase significantly the demands of time and money. The needs of teenagers are different from the needs of children.

We come from varying backgrounds. Some grew up during the depression, and felt keenly the evil of too little. Others grew up in post–World War II affluence, and felt keenly the evil of too much. It is not hard to see why the accumulation of possessions would be called prudent by the first group and hoarding by the second.

We are different emotionally. One needs privacy, another

thrives on crowds. One is sensitive to beauty and symmetry, another has no interest in such matters. One person may need a variety of new wallpaper or paint, while another person could not even tell you the color of the living room after five years.

Different jobs make different demands. The president of the university where I teach needs a larger house than I do. He regularly entertains groups of forty to fifty people; I panic if we top six. Some jobs are so publicly oriented that absolute privacy in the home is a psychological necessity.

There is also the problem of personal bias. In issues such as these it is always easy for an author to ride a favorite hobby horse or grind the proverbial axe. At the very least, you can be assured that I am keenly aware of the problem of personal prejudice and desire very much to avoid it.

That is not all. We also have the difficulty of the changing culture and world scene. We cannot—we must not—live in isolation from our world. What was a prophetic expression of simplicity in one generation may become only quaint in the next. Time changes issues and we dare not close our eyes to that fact if we hope to be redemptive.

And most dangerous of all is our tendency to turn any expressions of simplicity into a new legalism. How quickly we calcify what should always remain alive and changing. How soon we seize upon some externalism in order to judge and control others. How much we like these nice easy ways to determine who is in and who isn't, who has it and who doesn't.

Is it any wonder that we struggle and strain in an attempt to express exterior simplicity? Unquestionably, this enterprise is fraught with many pitfalls and dangers.

But we must not shrink back from our task. We must risk the danger of legalism, because to refuse establishes a legalism in defense of the status quo. Until we become specific we have not spoken the word of truth that liberates.

The writers of Scripture repeatedly took the risk of being specific. Over and over they fleshed out the meaning of simplicity with frightening precision. The difficulty with such precision is obvious: the specific application to one culture and time is seldom transferable to another culture and time. Peter forbade braided hair and wearing of robes because in his day those things were signs of ostentatious elitism (I Pet. 3:3). Few today would bat an eyelash at the rather ordinary practice of braiding hair, and no one even wears the lavish Roman robe. We understand that he spoke to the particular issues of his day; our task is to discern what constitutes ostentatious elitism today, and speak to that situation.

The Old Testament forbade the charging of interest on loans because it was viewed as an unbrotherly exploitation of another's misfortune (Deut. 23:19). In a world of soaring inflation, the question of unbrotherly exploitation could just possibly go the opposite direction—the person who gives a loan without interest may be the one being exploited. Be that as it may, the issue we must struggle with is how we can care for one another today without exploitation.

The law of gleaning was a compassionate piece of legislation appropriate for the Palestinian agrarian culture, whose principal source of livelihood was small family-owned farms. A tender, gracious command, but totally irrelevant for today. The poor are concentrated in our cities and could not possibly get to the farms to glean the grain. Who would want to legalistically attempt to enforce this divine command today? No, we understand that it was a specific and appropriate application of the law of love in that society. Our task is to discover specific and appropriate ways to care for the poor and defenseless today.

Therefore, let us dare to be specific and at the same time always remember that the exterior expression we give to simplicity today may not be appropriate tomorrow. Our task is to walk the narrow path of precision without legalism.

Accommodation without Compromise

The second principle that will guide our journey into outward simplicity is practical accommodation without ethical compromise. We are dealing with the ancient tension of being in the world without being of it. And this tension has extremely practical implications.

We *are* in the world. The truth of the matter is that our lifestyle *is* affected by the culture in which we live. We may dislike that, chafe under it, but we cannot get around it. For example, I take the bus to work. To do so costs 50 cents per ride or $1.00 a day. That computes to $5.00 a week or approximately $250.00 per year. Hence, the single decision to ride the bus to work amounts to more than twice the annual income of one-third of the world's people. The point is that, while you may shout at me that the average annual income in India is $200.00 or that 900 million people in the world subsist on less than $75.00 a year, you have not helped me much except to increase my guilt. I simply cannot live on $200.00 a year. The very fact that I live in a particular society necessitates a certain economic accommodation to that society.

Now I know that these words go down very hard with purists. They would argue strenuously that we must never accommodate ourselves under any circumstances. They would respond to my little bus illustration that I should live closer to my work, or ride a bicycle to work, or quit my work. I, of course, need to take these counsels seriously, but seldom do people get around the problem. In fact, I find that even those who take a vow of poverty make rather substantial accommodations to the culture in which they live, and I mean that in no derogatory sense at all. Accommodation is part and parcel of what it means to be *in* the world. And there are many practical, economic ways in which we accommodate ourselves to our society: swimming lessons for the children, some new books for Mom, a power saw for Dad.

But we can come to the place where right and necessary accommodation crosses over into wrong and unnecessary compromise. We are not to be *of* the world. And the main problem in the church today is our failure to see where proper accommodation leaves off and where compromise begins.

To know the distinction is admittedly a difficult task. We are vastly different people, with vastly different circumstances, and vastly different needs. Obviously we will never find a clear line of demarcation, but that must never stop us from attempting to help one another know when we are crossing over the line.

This task is enormously complicated by modern media propaganda. When taken as a whole, the media commercials constitute a world view, a rival religious philosophy about what constitutes blessedness. We are told by television that the most idiotic things will make us insanely happy. They may well make us insane, but it is genuinely doubtful that they will ever make us happy.

The purpose of all this media bombardment is to increase desire. The plan is to change "That's extravagant" into "That would be nice to have," and then into "I really need that," and finally into "I've got to have it!"

We are taken in, duped, brainwashed. But it is done in such subtle ways that we do not realize what has happened. We think we are wise because we can easily see through the childish logic of the commercials. But the ad writer never intended us to believe those silly commercials, only to desire the product they advertise. And sure enough we buy, because the commercials accomplish their goal of inflaming our desire.

And most diabolical and manipulative of all is the way in which the same company will manufacture competing products. They know that consumers feel they have power if there is a choice, and that feeling of power will cause them to buy, buy, buy. We love the power of refusing to buy one detergent with its stupid brightening crystals, and instead choose another. The choice, however, was really no choice at all, since both brands were made by the same corporation and were basically the same anyway. The apparent cutthroat competition is usually nothing but a phony war to make us think we are getting a better buy. The intention of advertising is not to persuade the viewer to buy a particular brand of this or that, but to create a consumer mood. More luxurious gadgets, more comfortable sofas, more prestigious cars, more . . . more . . . more. The goal is to increase desire.

We need to make firm concrete moves if we ever expect to counter this massive assault of materialism. To obey St. Paul's command "Do not be conformed to this world" (Rom. 12:2) takes deliberate and sustained effort.

We understand the need for a certain adaptation or accommodation to be in the society in which we live, but we want to grow in our perception of when that turns into conformity or compromise. We seek to be in the world without being of the world.

Voluntary Poverty

Serious consideration should be given to voluntary poverty as an important beginning step into external simplicity. "Why," you ask, "would you list poverty as a potential first step into simplicity? Certainly it is the last, most radical step one would take, certainly not something for the beginner." Quite to the contrary, voluntary poverty can be the easiest step of all. Drastic measures are often less painful, a little like tearing off the Band-Aid quickly rather than pealing it back slowly, painfully. This drastic step can sometimes lance the ugly infection of covetousness more readily than anything else. Nothing can strike at the heart of the love of money quite like severing a relationship with money.

In many other respects it is less difficult. The break with possessions is clear and clean-cut. Gone is the struggle about this or that—all of it is forbidden. You own nothing. How much easier, how much simpler than our world of endless decisions between acquiring and not acquiring. Think of young Francis of Assisi throwing away everything and walking naked down the road. Joyfully he tramped the earth, trusting in God and begging for his food. He was free from any need to work through the knotty problems of stewardship of goods. He had no bothersome budget, bank account, or income tax report. In many ways, poverty is the easiest step of all.

The call to voluntary poverty is not obligatory upon everyone, but it is God's word to some. It was this call that the rich young ruler rejected. But there are many who have accepted it and made it their own.

Voluntary poverty provides a crucial identification with the poor and needy. Toyohiko Kagawa made a profound impact for Christ upon Japan; indeed, his witness rose to worldwide fame in Protestantism. A prolific writer, this brilliant young man lived in Franciscan-like love and poverty in one of the worst slums in Japan. His *Songs from the Slums* is an eloquent testimony of one who walked among the poor as poor himself. And in our day, the simple witness of Mother Teresa of India has had worldwide impact. Her compassionate identification with the sick, starving masses of Calcutta has touched us all. And who could count the untold thousands of faithful servants of Christ that these two examples represent?

On a practical level, voluntary poverty is most easily accomplished in groups, the Roman Catholic orders being the most prominent example. In that way provision is made for the individual by the community, and the individual is freed to fulfill his or her calling without economic considerations. As you know, there are many variations upon this approach by many different groups.

Voluntary poverty does not need to be a lifetime commitment. I know of one couple in Colorado who felt the call of God to give up all their possessions. In a simple act of holy obedience they sold their house and gave away everything. In the process of time they have felt clear about acquiring various possessions, but you can well imagine that their spirit about those possessions can never be the same. Today they own a large house near a state university and rent out most of the house to university students in order to facilitate a ministry among them. We can never know for certain, but it is entirely possible that Jesus' call to the rich young ruler to sell all that he had was exactly this kind of one-time only command.

Never forget that poverty is not simplicity. Poverty is a word of smaller scope. Poverty is a means of grace; simplicity is the grace itself. People can live out all their lives in poverty and never know the grace of simplicity. It is quite possible to get rid of things and still desire them in your heart. But there is also a poverty that can be used of God to throw open the windows of heaven to the fresh life of simplicity. How can we know the difference? We are to live listening, attentive, and open. If the word of command comes, then joyfully we obey.

I would like to give a word of counsel to those who are not called to voluntary poverty: do not despise the call of those who are. In our rush to be prudent and reasonable we can sometimes hinder the word of God. Let us be slow to condemn, slow even to give advice. First let us listen tenderly, patiently. It was said of Jesus that he would "not break a bruised reed, or quench a smoldering wick" (Matt. 12:20). And like him we must be careful lest we trample upon the tender spirit of those who are just learning to hear God, or snuff out their beginning insights. And so prayerfully we listen to see if they have indeed received a word from God. As we learn to walk with the Lord and know his ways, it is seldom difficult to distinguish youthful idealism from the call of Yahweh. Likewise, those who are called to poverty must not reject those who have not received that call.

Finally, I suggest one tiny experiment in voluntary poverty that many of us could do with genuine profit as God prompts us. We can go through our home, find one possession that we value, and consider, "Am I growing too attached to this object? Is it becoming a treasure to me?" Having examined our hearts before the Lord, let us give it away. We must not rationalize by saying, "But after searching my heart I know that it is clearly not a treasure to me, and so I don't need to give it away." If it is truly not our treasure we will not mind in the least giving it away, and if it has become our treasure we will want to give it away for our soul's sake. Also we will pray for the person who receives our little gift that it will be a blessing, and not a hindrance, to his or her walk with God.

Planned Spending

By now we could well be feeling that all this lofty talk of resistance to the consumer mentality and of voluntary poverty completely misses our situation. To be quite blunt, we are trying to figure out how to pay the monthly bills, not whether we should give everything away. We are deeply moved by the wretched squalor of Brazil's 35 million poor, but feel helpless to respond. It is almost all we can do to make ends meet as it is. It seems like every time we turn around the children have outgrown their shoes. Our teenagers "dollar" us to death—"It's only a dollar." Escalating food prices, gas prices, property taxes; we just can't seem to keep up.

And most frustrating of all, we cannot see for the life of us where it all goes. Always there seems to be more month than money. We wonder how in the world the paycheck can slip through our fingers so quickly. What happens to it all?

And that is exactly where we must begin. We cannot hope to deal seriously with exterior simplicity until we know what happened to it all. I am constantly amazed that people do not know where their money goes. If people ask us exactly how much we spent on entertainment or clothes or gifts, could we tell them, not in some round figure, but exactly? If not, we need to find a way to know where our money goes. Most of us would be absolutely astonished at how much we spend in certain categories if we would keep a careful record for one year.

This is the most crucial accountability point in a budget. We will design budgets galore, but have no way to see if we actually keep within that budget. So the first ingredient in planned spending is to know where our money goes. There is absolutely no way we can control it unless we know where it is spent.

If we feel this is a lot of unnecessary work, since it involves so little money anyway, we are dead wrong. Forty years of gainful employment times an annual income of $15,000 would amount to $600,000 for which we are responsible. And that doesn't include any increase of salary. We are accountable for the stewardship of that money. How dare we even think of handling such a tremendous resource without careful records.

We have a very practical way to accomplish this in our home. In our budget book we have twenty separate expenditure categories.* When any money is spent we record what it was and how much it cost in the appropriate category. Simple. Bothersome? Sometimes, but even this simple recordkeeping can encourage us to make fewer purchases.

The second step in planned spending is the development of a budget. A budget is nothing more than making the decision where our money goes. Without a budget we forfeit the ability to make that decision. A budget merely controls how much goes where. It keeps us honest with ourselves.

Of one thing we can be certain: our wants will always exceed both our needs and our funds. If our own egocentric greed does not ensure that, then advertising will. If we allow our wants to determine our buying patterns, the result will be chaos—and

---

* Giving, shelter (house payments, utilities, household items, misc.), food, transportation, medical needs, health insurance, life insurance, education, clothing, house improvements, business expenses, gifts, entertainment, savings, income tax savings, investments, vacations, allowances, special needs, miscellaneous.

considerable debt. A friend of mine who is the president of a credit agency tells me, out of considerable experience, that seldom does he find a couple in financial trouble who have been operating with a well-designed budget.

This book is not the place to go into the details of forming a budget; there are many good guides on the market.¹ I would, however, like to make several observations about the task of budget making.

First, it is almost universally true that in the initial attempt to put a realistic budget onto paper, expenses will exceed income. No budget will ever work until the flow *in* exceeds or equals the flow *out*. Something has to change. And I would suggest that you first look at ways to cut back expenses rather than ways to increase income. This is a time for a couple to experience tears and prayer and tenderness. It is not easy to say No to hoped for vacations or Yes to a smaller food budget. But whatever you do, balance that budget.

Second, never go into debt for ordinary expenditures. An investment is one thing, that new tea set you just can't do without is quite another. Remember, deficit spending will work no better for you than it does for the federal government. Perhaps it is permissible to take out a loan to secure a house, but I can hardly think of anywhere else it would be justified, including the purchase of a car. If you need a car, put it in your budget and begin building the fund until you can pay for the car in cash.

Third, build accountability into your budget. Our system is simple: in our budget book I treat each of our twenty budget categories as if it were a separate bank account. At the beginning of each month I record the allotted "deposit" and then deduct expenditures as they are made. For example, our monthly family budget for clothing is $50.00. The first of each month I record a $50.00 deposit in that category. Then, when the question arises as to new shoes for the kids or whatever, the answer is easy: if there is a sufficient balance in the clothes budget, go ahead; if not, wait. The same holds true in all other categories as well.

Fourth, if you exceed your budget don't be discouraged. At least you know where your money is going and are beginning to have some control over it. You will get better and more realistic as you go along.

Fifth, put the giving of money to Christ and his Kingdom in a different financial frame of mind from other budget items. What I mean is this: most budget items we hope to hold down, but our desire is to see giving increase as much as possible. I have one friend who has a financial goal to always give away more than he spends on himself. So we are to work to decrease our operating budget and increase our giving budget.

Unplugging from the Consumptive Society

The Madison Avenue hucksters are working day and night to squeeze us into their mold. They have launched a concerted effort to capture our minds, and the minds of our children. Christian simplicity demands that we break free of this "thingification." But how do we do it? Here are some suggestions. They are not meant to be rules, for some will speak to your condition and others will not.

First, join the joyful happy revolt against the modern propaganda machine. We need to greet with sarcastic laughter all those patently phony television commercials. In unison the family should shout, "Who do you think you are kidding!" List obviously dishonest ads and boycott their products. Write the networks and companies and let them know what you think of their ads. Help your children to see the attempts of commercials to identify status and prestige with their product. Pray for your children and for yourselves to be protected from the subtle drive to always acquire more. Resist obsolescence. Trinkets are added to products to make you unhappy with the old model. Who in the world needs a new model automobile every single year? Significant safety and efficiency changes occur much less frequently. Why not make a car that would last for the lifetime of the owner? Let the industry know you don't want the costly new design every single year, and urge them to put their money into more meaningful tasks.

Use postage paid envelopes of direct mail advertisers to object to unscrupulous ads. Reject any junk mail you can. Resist all those contests that promise free vacations and dream homes to the winner. Nothing is free! All the people who are buying that product are paying for that $200,000 home and all-expense paid trip to Tahiti, plus the multimillion dollar costs of the contest. How much better to dispense with the contests and have less expensive products that the poor could afford. If enough of us saw the evil of them, we could put a stop to those contests. The only reason companies have contests is that people respond to them. What would happen if next year they had a fifty percent reduction in response to their silly games? At any rate, Christians should have no part in this greedy madness. In every way we can, we must do all we can to refuse to be propagandized.

Second, I propose an exercise which many have found liberating. When you decide that it is right for you to purchase a particular item, see if God will not bring it to you without your having to buy it. I have a close friend who needed a pair of gloves for work. Rather than rush out to the store to buy them he gave the matter over to God in prayer. Although he had not spoken to anyone about this need, in a couple of days someone gave him a pair of gloves. How absolutely marvelous! The point is not that he was unable to buy the gloves; he could have done that quite easily. But he wanted to learn how to pray in ways that might release money for other purposes.

Literally dozens of experiments can be made in this realm. Even the rich can do it. Once a decision is made to secure a particular item, hold it before God in prayer for perhaps a week. If it comes, bless God; if not, reevaluate your need for it; and if you still feel that you should have it, go ahead and purchase the item.

One clear advantage to this approach is that it effectively ends all impulse buying. It gives time for reflection so that God can teach us if the desire is unnecessary. Another obvious benefit is the way in which it integrates the life of devotion with the life of service. The supply of our material needs becomes an exciting venture of faith. What better way to learn to pray for daily bread! One small counsel: it is probably wise to give the money you would have spent on the object to the poor in order to avoid the slightest thought of this as a means of material gain.

Third, stress the quality of life above the quantity of life. Refuse to be seduced into defining life in terms of *having* rather than *being*. Cultivate solitude and silence. Learn to "listen to God's speech in his wondrous, terrible, gentle, loving, all-embracing silence."[2] Develop close friendships and enjoy long evenings of serious and hilarious conversation. Such times are far more rewarding than all the plastic entertainment that the commercial world tries to foist upon us. Value music, art, books, significant travel. If you are too busy to read, you are too busy. Discover prayer as an evening entertainment.

Learn the wonderful truth that to increase the quality of life means to decrease material desire; not vice versa. Close your ears to the ads that bellow their four letter obscenities, "more, more, more!" Listen instead to the life-giving words of St. John of the Cross, "Let your soul turn always not to desire the more, but the less."[3] Richard E. Byrd recorded in his journal after months alone in the barren Arctic: "I am learning . . . that a man can live profoundly without masses of things."[4]

Turn your back on all high pressure competitive situations that make climbing the ladder the central focus. The fruit of the Spirit is not push, drive, climb, grasp, and trample. Don't let the rat-racing world keep you on its treadmill. There is a legitimate place for blood, sweat, and tears; but it should have its roots in the call of God, not in the desire to get ahead. Life is more than a climb to the top of the heap.

Never put happiness at center stage. It is the by-product of a life of service, never the chief end of life. Happiness is not a right to be grasped, but a serendipity to be enjoyed.

Fourth, make recreation healthy, happy, and gadget-free. You don't need an expensive jogging suit to run around the block. Walking, jogging, and swimming are among the best forms of human exercise and they require a minimum of equipment. Get close to the earth with hiking, camping, and backpacking.

The bicycle is a wonderful form of transportation that uses renewable energy. The faddish and expensive sports models are unnecessary, and often too complicated for us to repair. I finally got wise and quit seeking after the ten-speeds and asked God for a sturdy, work-horse model. Now I am as delighted as a child with a new toy. Ride together as a family in the evenings.

Repudiate "spectatoritus." The modern spectator sports programs are obscene in their waste of human and material resources. Sports conglomerates know they have Americans trapped, and so they boldly extend the season with pre-season games, and bowl games, and super bowl games, and post-bowl games, and all-star games! Enough is enough. Don't get me wrong, it is a joy to watch some games; but abject slavery is another thing altogether. Many couples have constant fights because one spouse prefers Monday night football to live conversation. Can you imagine?

Encourage cooperative games and play. Why must winning *always* be uppermost? It is quite possible to have fun without winners or losers. Western society has been seduced to believe that competition is the only way to play. Competition has its place; but cooperation also has its place. Balance is what we need.

Fifth, learn to eat sensibly and sensitively. Reject products shot full of poisonous chemicals, artificial colors, and other questionable means used to produce engineered food. Eliminate pre-packaged dinners. Become sensitive to the whole bio-food chain and eat foods that do not do violence to that balance, such as fruits and grain. Grain-fed animals are a luxury that the bio-food chain cannot sustain for the masses of humanity.

Get in on the joy of a garden, even if it consists of pots in a window sill. Can, preserve, dry, and freeze your foods. Thanks to the faithful efforts of my wife, our children eat dried fruit all winter in place of candy, and like it just as well. With several dwarf fruit trees in a back yard you can have fruit fit for a king.

As much as possible, buy more locally produced foods to save the energy required for transportation. Explore producer and consumer cooperatives. Compost all the garbage you can. Recycle all the items you can. Grow all the fresh food you can.

Eat out less. When you do, make it a celebration. An apple and milk is faster than the fast-food "restaurants" and much tastier, not to mention more nutritious. Go without food one day a week and give any money saved to the poor. Have joyful potluck meals with friends. Buy less food rather than more diet pills.

Sixth, know the difference between significant travel and self-indulgent travel. To begin with, refuse to be conned into believing that you have missed half your life if you haven't seen all the glamour spots of the world. Many of the wisest and most fulfilled people in the world never traveled anywhere, including Jesus Christ. If you do travel, give it purpose. Go beyond the splashy travel brochures with their sights of tinselled affluence, and get to places of anguish and pain and human need. Stay in places that identify with the common people of a country. When Albert Schweitzer visited America, newspaper reporters asked him why he traveled in the third class section of the train. He answered, "Because there is no fourth class!"

Become as acquainted with people as you do with places. Make a genuine effort to communicate; you will be enriched by the experience. Why must we always view folks from other cultures as oddities to be examined? I once saw a man grab the camera of someone trying to take his picture and angrily smash it on the ground shouting, "I am a man, not a picture!"

Seventh, buy things for their usefulness rather than their status. In building or buying homes, thought should be given to livability rather than to how much it will impress others. Don't have more house than is reasonable. After all, who needs seven rooms for two people? Do you live alone after raising a large family? Rather than leaving your spacious home, filled with its wonderful memories, consider inviting another single person or some college students to join you. It just might once again fill the rooms with laughter and ordinary squabbles, and help to ease the loneliness you feel.

Consider your clothes. Most people have no need for more clothes. They buy more not because they need clothes, but because they want to keep up with the fashions. Hang the fashions. Buy only what you need. Wear your clothes until they are worn out. Stop trying to impress people with your clothes and impress them with your life. If you are able to, learn the joy of making clothes. Have clothes that are practical rather than ornamental. John Wesley declared, "As for apparel, I buy the most lasting and, in general, the plainest I can."[5]

Now I know that this matter of fashion is much more difficult for teenagers than for adults. Most adults have come into a measure of inward security, and are no longer so vulnerable to the opinions of others; hence they are free from the need to impress them unduly. Teenagers (and some teenage adults), however, have not yet developed this inner sense of place, and feel keenly the need for acceptance and love. Correct fashion is, of course, a cultural means of inclusion and exclusion. And while we must always be cognizant of the potential evil in this superficial form of judgment, neither should we force our children into positions that will mean unnecessary ridicule. These are matters which we must work through with one another in tenderness and love, teaching and encouraging each other.

Furniture can have beauty and usability without costing the world. There is not a thing wrong with the styles of "early attic" and "late basement." Be creative. Your furniture should reflect you, not some stuffy showroom. Build furniture or refinish good used pieces.

Learn to find bargains. Shop at garage sales and Salvation Army Stores. One caution: sales can be cancerous and inflame a covetous spirit. To acquire an unneeded item at a ridiculously low price is no bargain. Pray for inner detachment before ever venturing out into this world of auctions and sales.

One final word needs to be said. Simplicity does not necessarily mean cheapness. Simplicity resonates more easily with concerns for durability, usability, and beauty. Though I built the beds for our children, we purchased the mattresses, and we chose ones that would last for as long as the boys would live in our home. (And I can bear witness that they were not cheap!) Many items should be chosen to last our entire lifetime and beyond, and should be chosen with great care.

Our task is not easy. Often we will wonder what to do in a given situation. We will struggle for integrity as we feel pressures from all sides. Most likely the greatest and most constant pressures, however, will be to ever acquire, ever possess. As we labor to know what to do in each situation, we would do well to keep before us the astute observation of Mark Twain, "Civilization is a limitless multiplication of unnecessary necessities."[6]

8. OUTWARD SIMPLICITY: LONGER STRIDES

To have what we want is riches, but to be able to do without is power.
　　　　　　　　　　　　　　　　—George MacDonald

Simplicity is the new necessity of the modern era. Our little planet simply cannot sustain the gluttonous consumption of the wealthy West. Mahatma Gandhi said once that the world has enough for everyone's need but not for everyone's greed. It simply is not a matter of somehow raising the standard of living of the poor of the world to that of the affluent West. America has 6 percent of the world's population and consumes 33 percent of the world's resources. If the rest of the world were to attempt to live on our level of consumption, it is projected that all known world resources of petroleum, tin, zinc, natural gas, lead, copper, tungsten, gold, and mercury would be exhausted in ten years.[1] Even if we made a generous allowance for scientific breakthroughs, we still must confess that our planet simply cannot support the overload were the starving masses raised to our level of consumption. Put simply, the earth cannot afford our lifestyle. No, the answer is clear: we must cut back our standard of living if there is ever to be anything approaching a just distribution of the world's resources.

But that is not all. The imperative of simplicity is further heightened when we couple the call for justice with a compassionate concern for evangelism. Precious lives all over the face of the earth are living without hope. People hungry of heart and weary in spirit are longing for the word of Truth. Two-thirds of the people of this earth have not heard the wonderful news of Christ's liberating Gospel. Are you not moved with the desire to do more than ever before to reach out to help? This is no time for business as usual. Nearly two and one-half billion people stand culturally outside the reach of a Christian witness. These "hidden peoples'" will never be reached through the Church as it now stands. No Christian is within their cultural sphere of influence. We must find new creative ways to reach out to the hidden peoples if we ever hope to fulfill Christ's commission to disciple all nations. Such a task will demand vast outlays of time and resources.

The Covenant that came out of the 1974 International Congress on World Evangelism held in Lausanne, Switzerland, states, "The goal should be, by all available means and at the earliest possible time, that every person will have the opportunity to hear, understand, and receive the good news." Our hearts resonate with this high and holy goal. But it will never be realized without drastic and sacrificial lifestyle changes. The Covenant continues, "We cannot hope to attain this goal without sacrifice. All of us are shocked by the poverty of millions and disturbed by the injustices which cause it. Those of us who live in affluent circumstances accept our duty to develop a simple life-style in order to contribute more generously to both relief and evangelism."[2]

Ecologists and economists shout out to us that simplicity is a new necessity. The great host of hidden peoples shout out to us that simplicity is a new necessity. Will we hear their cry?

The Gift of Giving

Wealth is a dangerous thing. The entire biblical tradition underscores that truth. Therefore, I know that the proposal which I will now make is a risky one, but one which is also deeply rooted in Scripture. There are those who are called to the ministry of money. The gift of giving is a vital and valid spiritual gift, and essential to it is the task of using money for the common good. Jesus told us to make "friends of the mammon of unrighteousness" (Luke 16:9, KJV); that is, make Kingdom use of material goods. It is a much needed ministry among us.

Simplicity always calls us to a simple lifestyle, but it does not always call us to a reduction in income. God calls some to increase their income in order to use it for the good of all.

Again, I emphasize the danger of this ministry. We are deal-ing with dynamite. Wealth is not for spiritual neophytes; they will be destroyed by it. Only the person who has clean hands and a pure heart can ever hope to handle this "filthy lucre" without contamination. Gluttony, pride, greed, covetousness, and avarice can slip in unawares. This path is fraught with great frustrations and temptations, and those who walk it have to face perplexing decisions and tragic moral choices that most people will never have to consider. In many ways our life will be immensely more complex, though it does not need to be com-plicated. We will need the prayer and support of the people of God who must stand by us, counsel us, guide us. We will be living close to hell for the sake of heaven.

The most subtle and dangerous aspect of the ministry of money is the false sense of power it gives. We begin to feel in control. Others begin to seek us out, not because of who we are, but because of what we have. They begin to look to us in spiri-tually destructive ways. In one important sense money *is* pow-er, and we have the power to determine the future of this project or that cause, and they know it. And most destructive of all, we know it. Spiritual pride rears its ugly head as the thought seeps in that we are in charge, we call the shots. The degenerative slide continues until a new pseudo-saviour has been born.

Only veteran soldiers can take up this work successfully. Only those who have been disciplined under the Cross qualify. That is why I waited for this chapter to discuss the ministry of money. This is no beginning step, no easy work. Only one skilled in spiritual warfare should ever attempt it. A person is needed who can receive $50,000 from the hand of God one day, and at the divine prompting give it all away the next. (I did say *all* of it, not just a tithe.)

I would never ask anyone to take up this important and haz-ardous ministry without the aid of spiritual guidance. Clement of Alexandria counseled that the wealthy servant of God should never attempt to work out his salvation alone, but rather should seek advice of a spiritual director. I concur wholeheartedly.

Choose someone or some small group with whom you can share intimately, someone wise in the things of the Spirit—a person who is not impressed by money, and able to speak the word of Truth with tenderness. Seek his or her counsel and advice. Share your spiritual goals, including a detailed accounting of your financial goals. Be open, listening, teachable. If he or she detects in you a spirit of possessiveness and shares that with you, do not become defensive. Listen eagerly to these words of life. You desperately need this help. The work you have undertaken puts you in constant spiritual danger. It is entirely possible to become disqualified from this high holy work.

But it is a wonderful work. Immense good can come of it. I think of innumerable servants of Christ who quietly and unpretentiously have been the channel through which huge sums of money have flowed. Released from any need to hold on to or control it, they have been able to freely receive and freely give.

The historically rich building in which I write this book was constructed in 1886 as Garfield University. Massive stonework and beautiful turrets give it a castle-like appearance that can be seen for miles around. But in 1897 it was empty and deserted. It was then that James Davis read the advertisement offering the defunct campus for sale, and said to his wife, "Anna, I believe this is our chance to give a college to the world."[3] That is exactly what he did. He bought the magnificent building and then gave it to the Quakers for the development of a Christian university. Think of the thousands of lives that have been enriched simply because one man was free to make Kingdom use of material goods! And think of the innumerable places this story can be retold, with a thousand variations, throughout the world, wherever faithful people advance Christ's Kingdom through the ministry of money.

Does it sound to you as if I am speaking only of the wealthy, who out of a vast financial store underwrite great enterprises throughout the world? They have their place, to be sure; but the ministry of money is more often expressed in more simple ways. This work is usually engaged in by ordinary people with limited budgets. The requirement is not great resources, but a humble willingness to be an unhindered channel.

Here is one simple "wineskin" for this ministry. Together the family prayerfully decides on the budget for that year. It is lean, trim, realistic. Provision is made in the budget for retirement and other similar concerns. Included in the budget is a tithe on the budget. Then any money which comes to us in excess of that budgeted figure is given in its entirety to Kingdom purposes. In this way God can trust us to be an unimpeded conduit. We can be the joyful channel for God's resources. The money may come through salary or it may come in completely unexpected ways. We will marvel that God is using us, trusting us.

As a young man, John Wesley calculated that twenty-eight pounds a year (about $65) would care for his own needs. Since prices remained basically the same, he was able to keep at that level of expenditure throughout his lifetime. When Wesley first made that decision, his income was thirty pounds a year. In later years sales from his books would often earn him fourteen hundred pounds a year, but he still lived on twenty-eight pounds and gave the rest away.[4] Wesley, of course, was single much of his life and never had children, so he did not deal with the financial problems engendered by a family; but the idea is a sound one. We can do the same thing. Obviously we have to make adjustments for growing children, savings for college, and inflation, but the principle remains firm.

Here is another wineskin. If both the wife and the husband desire to work, discipline yourselves to live on one salary and give the other away. In this way, one couple could potentially support an entire missionary family. Why not? What better investment opportunity could there be than that? Think what would happen to the worldwide missionary enterprise if each Christian couple would determine to give every second salary to missions.

Try still another model. Take a careful look at your income. Are there ways to so simplify your lifestyle that you can live on half of what you make? If so, rather than quit your job so that your earnings drop to half, plan to give away half of your earnings.

Here is still another approach. Rather than just giving the money away, invest it for the Kingdom of God. It is usually best to set up a separate checking or savings account. Money put into this account is to be used entirely for Kingdom causes.

Then, as you are led, invest the money in ways consistent with
Christian principles. The total earnings are either reinvested or
given away. At all times hold firm to the policy that the money,
including any and all earnings, belongs entirely to God.

Investments consistent with Christian principles can be a
terribly complex matter. I am not just referring to items that
are obviously unchristian. The deeper issues of justice, ecology,
and violence must be considered. What about real estate investments that have little regard for a proper stewardship of
the earth? What about a company's tie to the military industrial complex? What about corporations who have links to repres-
sive and unjust regimes abroad? Some companies oppress the
poor, others pollute the environment, and on it goes. As I noted
earlier, the ministry of money is fraught with complexity.

The ministry of giving is a good context in which to consider
the tithe. While tithing is not a New Testament measure for
giving, it can sometimes be a helpful starting point from which
to begin giving. In the early days, the Church of the Saviour in
Washington, D.C., struggled with the place of the tithe as one
of their corporate disciplines. They sought the counsel of theologian Reinhold Niebuhr, who suggested that they commit
themselves not to tithing but to "proportionate giving, with
tithing as an economic floor beneath which you will not go unless there are some compelling reasons." As a result, the discipline to which they all now agree reads, "We covenant with
Christ and one another to give proportionately beginning with
a tithe of our incomes."[5]

This approach has one wonderful advantage: it has a minimum discipline which is not intended to become the standard.
All members know the starting point, but understand it to be
only the beginning of the journey. Individually and corporately
they must wrestle with what it means to give proportionately.
That is no small issue. Elizabeth O'Connor has stated the difficulty well when she writes:

Proportionate to what? Proportionate to the accumulated
wealth of one's family? Proportionate to one's income and
the demands upon it, which vary from family to family?
Proportionate to one's sense of security and to the degree

of anxiety with which one lives? Proportionate to the keenness of our awareness of those who suffer? Proportionate to our sense of justice and of God's ownership for those who follow after us . . . ? The answer, of course, is in proportion to all of these things.[6]

With all of its difficulties, this grace of giving is a happy ministry. So much good can be done. So many lives can be helped. Stanley Mooneyham tells of his visit to the small village of Singhali, in India, a village suffering from a severe drought that plagued that region. He spoke with one Moslem landowner whose well was nearly dry. Though this man was facing disaster himself, he continued to share his water with Moslem and Christian alike. When Stanley Mooneyham told him that through World Vision's relief funds his well would be deepened, his speech stopped in mid-sentence, and he stood with mouth open. "No words came, but his soul spoke richly through the pools which formed in his eyes. With no attempt to wipe them dry, he just stood there and sobbed. He clutched my hand and would not let go. In his eyes I saw the response to love—and his response was love also."[7]

The Gift of Service

A simple lifestyle can also open to us vast new areas of service. It becomes possible to cut back our needs drastically so that we can devote time to important tasks. John Woolman cut back his business ventures in order to give attention to a traveling ministry. He said, "A way of life free from much entanglement appeared best for me, though the income might be small." Though he had several business offers, he refused them all because of the "outward care and cumber" that would divert his energies. Remember, Woolman was not a professional minister in the sense of being free from the concerns of the marketplace in order to preach. He was a businessman, and that was how he earned his living. He simply determined to "live on a little" in order that "nothing might hinder me from the most steady attention to the voice of the true Shepherd."[8]

Many do the same today. One professional carpenter I know

supports his family by working two days a week. The rest of the week is then devoted to the cause of justice for the poor in the city. A citrus rancher friend of mine sold his ranch at such a profit that he and his wife were able to serve for many years on the mission field without any expense to anyone. (They did this later in their lives, after the children were grown.) Many teachers keep their needs pared down enough so that they do not have to earn money in the summer, and can devote their time to ministry among the poor and needy. Many families engage in extensive weekend ministries at considerable expense to themselves in both time and money. And on it goes.

The possibilities are limitless. Many opportunities open up when we believe they are possible. Some situations do not allow us this flexibility, but many more than we think will. We are close to a family who gave this idea a try. The husband is a construction superintendent, and they have the normal responsibilities that come with four children. Over a period of time they began to sense the call of God to give help to a Christian work in New Guinea. Prayerfully and tactfully, the husband was able to arrange for a two-month leave of absence. To be quite honest, the venture involved a considerable expenditure of their personal money in order for the family to be involved in this two-month ministry. And yet the value for all concerned was enormous, well worth the investment, they told me. They are now listening to God to see if they should involve themselves more extensively in the New Guinea work.

One does not need to go to New Guinea, of course. Free time for service is desperately needed anywhere there are people. Crisis centers, counseling services, hospitals, all need our help. The ordinary ministry of local churches could be greatly enhanced if numerous members were free to invest their lives in the work. In one metropolitan city a small fellowship was able to find homes for some 350 homeless children. But to do such things demands a substantial investment of time, and some of us need to find ways to release ourselves. In our day many need to rearrange their lives in specific ways if they hope to engage in the ministry of service.

However, we must not concentrate exclusively upon the financial aspects of service. It is commendable to pare down our needs in order to release time to serve, but Christian simplicity adds another important ingredient. With self-interest rooted out, we have become free to serve as servants. Self-righteous service is banished. We do not have to lord it over others or make them feel indebted to us. Service can be rendered freely and without manipulation. We can joyfully surrender our own rights for the good of others. This is a great liberty in the work of service. It gives us the ability to prefer one another in love.

I would like to give one specific word of counsel in the context of the ministry of service. I think it is important that we find specific ways to serve our neighbors. We need to experience the ministry of small things for those who live near us.

Why would I mention such an insignificant matter? The answer is that it is far from insignificant. To be content with a life of simple goodness among our neighbors demands a total reorientation of values. It involves a whole restructuring of our perspective about what is important in life. Only the grace of simplicity can inform us with that perspective.

To value our neighbor does not put us in the headlines of any publication. It does not give us any advantaged position at work. It is not even valued in many churches, simply because it takes time away from important ministries there. To rake our neighbor's leaves, to babysit their children, to take the time to visit with them is the stuff of service to our neighbor. And until we learn to live in simplicity we will find it hard to believe it is an important ministry. John Woolman spoke of being "weaned from the desire of outward greatness."[9] Without that weaning process we will not know simplicity, nor will we find much place in our lives for our neighbors.

The Gift of Sacrifice

There is a need today for what I call prophetic simplicity. We need voices of dissent that point to another way, creative models that take exception to the givens of society. Obviously, prophetic simplicity runs the risk of excess; but the danger is no greater than the excess of the status quo.

Often these men and women speak to us in hyperbole and exaggeration. We label them hopelessly utopian and idealistic.

All the same, we need their word to jar us loose. Our consciences need to be pricked by their sharp barbs. We need to understand the relevance of their impossible ideal.

Prophetic simplicity is often expressed in ways that make many of us uncomfortable: models that are certainly not obligatory upon all Christians at all times. And yet they are not in opposition to the way of Christ either. They become open windows and swinging doors onto new options, new possibilities. They are participants in the ministry of sacrifice.

Our temptation to reject prophetic simplicity out of hand must be held in abeyance. After all, John the Baptist *is* in the Bible. And although Jesus did not go in much for animal skins and wild honey, that does not mean we shouldn't. At the word of God Elijah lived by a desert stream for three years, and we may be given a similar call. At the heart of prophetic simplicity is self-renunciation for the cause of Christ.

Some have chosen the single life in order to advance the Kingdom of God. In our day many have faulted the Apostle Paul because he urged the unmarried to consider the single life as a genuine option (I Cor. 7). They miss the profound wisdom in his counsel. Marriage of necessity divides one's loyalties. To be faithful to the marriage covenant, the husband and wife must concern themselves with a whole host of personal and financial matters. The single person can concentrate with abandon on the advancement of the Kingdom of God. Every married person with any kind of sensitivity understands very well that this is the case.

Paul was not against marriage, but he did insist that people should count the cost. No one should enter the covenant of marriage without understanding the immense amount of time and energy involved in making that relationship work. We need to face the fact that we cannot do many of the kinds of things which Paul did and be married.

One of the great tragedies of our day is the number of Christian leaders who have given themselves unselfishly to the cause of Christ, but have destroyed their marriages and their children in the process. And it was all so unnecessary. Many of them simply needed to understand that their sense of call was incompatible with the responsibilities of marriage, and to choose the single life. Paul's caution has the ring of practical wisdom. Jesus Himself said that some have become eunuchs for the sake of the Kingdom of God (Matt. 19:12).

We do people a disservice when we fail to proclaim the single life as a Christian option. Marriage is not for everyone, and we should say so. A single person can venture into forms of simplicity that are closed to the rest of us. By word and deed the Church should encourage these faithful servants of Christ. They should never be looked down upon or viewed as somehow odd. We should do all that we can to be with those who have chosen the single life, because they need our friendship and we need their wisdom.

Others who are married have voluntarily chosen to go without children. To be sure, some have made the decision from purely selfish motives; but others have done so in order to be free to care for the children of the world. I am very close to a couple who have consciously chosen not to have children so that they may have a more effective ministry among teenagers. Their home is open to young and old day and night. Although one night in their home is enough to drive me crazy, I must confess that their ministry is an extraordinarily effective one.

A couple must be in covenant unity with one another in any decision of this nature. This is no place for a husband to try to exercise some kind of "headship" over the wife. Such a decision takes time. The feelings of each spouse must be given full expression. At no time should there be conveyed a sense of spiritual inferiority if children are desired. This is a matter of calling, not spirituality.

Most couples will want and should have children, but again we should know the commitment that entails. We must be prepared to pay the financial and emotional price.

Perhaps some will remonstrate, "I wish that I had counted the cost, but I didn't. I now have a family, but still feel called to a ministry that does not have time for marriage and family obligations." I answer that your calling is now to your family. You are to fulfill the covenant made with your spouse. To jump into some kind of ministry that ultimately would be destructive to your marriage is sin. Be content to invest your life in your spouse and your children. If the ministry is important, God will either raise up others to do it, or in his time will arrange your situation so that this work is compatible with your family responsibilities.

Another aspect of the ministry of sacrifice is in the area of Christian fasting. Many have advocated a weekly fast as a means of releasing funds for the world's hungry. This practice is in every way commendable, but I want here to deal with fasting on a deeper level.

Fasting helps to give us balance. It makes us more keenly sensitive to the whole of life, so that we do not become obsessed with our consumer mentality. It is something of an inner alarm to help us hold our priorities straight, to give us a sense of spiritual sensitivity.

Fasting reveals the things that control us. We cover up what is inside us with food and other good things, but in fasting these things come to the surface. The first truth that was revealed to me in my early experiences in fasting was my lust for good feelings. It is certainly not a bad thing to feel good, but we must be able to bring that feeling to an easy place where it does not control us. So many attitudes strive to control us: anger, pride, fear, hostility, gluttony, avarice. All of these and more will surface as we fast. It is a blessed release to have these things out in the open so that they can be defeated, and we can live with a single eye toward God.

The central idea in fasting is the voluntary denial of an otherwise normal function for the sake of intense spiritual activity. Remember, there is nothing wrong with these normal functions in life—it is simply that there are times when we set them aside in order to concentrate. Viewed from this perspective we can see the reasonableness of fasting, and also its broader dimensions. For example, there is a great need today to learn to fast from people. Most of us have a tendency to devour others, and usually we get severe heartburn from it. I suggest that we experience times of fasting from people not because we are antisocial, but precisely because we love people intently and when we are with them we want to be able to do them good, and not harm. Thomas Merton said, "It is in deep solitude that I find the gentleness with which I can truly love my brothers. . . . Solitude and silence teach me to love my brothers for what they are, not what they say." [10]

We also need to have times when we fast from the media. It is amazing to me that many people are incapable of going through an entire day concentrating on one thing. Their train of thought is constantly broken by this demand or that interruption. The newspaper, the radio, the television, magazines—everything interrupts their concentration. Some people are so enslaved to television that if it were taken away they would go through withdrawal. Obviously, there is a time for the various media, but there is also time to be without them.

We can also learn to fast from the telephone. This instrument is a wonderful invention, but it controls many people. Some people will stop praying in order to answer the telephone. Can you imagine anything more absurd? I want to let you in on a secret: we do not need to answer that gadget every time it rings. We are not its slave, but its master. When people come to visit us, we should not insult them by interrupting our conversation to answer the telephone. In our home, when we are eating or when I am reading stories to the children, we do not answer the phone. I want my children to know that they are more important than any phone call. People will call back if they genuinely need to reach us.

Earlier I dealt with voluntary poverty, but I now would like to take up one further aspect of it, namely communalism. Communalism is nothing more than the renunciation of private ownership for the sake of the wider community.

Throughout history, utopian movements have arisen and disappeared in the same way that many ruthless competitive societies have arisen and disappeared. Permanence is not an important criterion; faithfulness is. Many have attempted communal living and found it terribly complicated; others have found it liberating. As a prophetic model for our day it probably allows for the simplest standard of living. Goods that would normally serve one nuclear family can now accommodate perhaps two dozen people.

Although communal approaches to life have existed for many centuries—the most notable being the Roman Catholic monasteries—there has been a recent surge of interest by Christian groups in this expression of faithfulness. The Word of God community in Ann Arbor, Michigan, Reba Place Fellowship in Chicago, Illinois, and the Church of the Redeemer in

Houston, Texas, are a few of the better known examples. The reasons for this revival of interest are not hard to discover. The feelings of alienation and loneliness, the concern for ecological responsibility, the desire for a just distribution of the world's resources, and the joyful freedom to share resulting from the charismatic renewal are a few of the causes. We should also recognize that the size and shape of the nuclear family makes communal arrangements more feasible and desirable. It was not so many years ago that large extended families were commonplace. When you have parents with half a dozen children combined with grandparents and another extra person or two thrown in, you have a community of considerable size and complexity. Today's family of three or four often gains a great deal from sharing with others.

Communal arrangements have many difficulties: how to provide for privacy, how to handle money matters, how to discipline children, and so on. And although communalism has a great deal of historical precedence, there is not much biblical basis for it. Perhaps the greatest value of the Christian commune is its symbolic importance. Quietly, it questions society's affluence, and points to another way.

Identification with the Poor

Another way in which simplicity takes outward shape is through conscious identification with the poor and forgotten. Jesus Christ did so repeatedly, and so must we. The exact expression of our identification will have infinite variety, but there is no doubt that we ought to engage in this loving work.

Many of us need to champion the cause of the oppressed, witness to their misery, and call for justice. We are to plead their cause before the powerful. The Christian is to be the voice of the voiceless, the face of the faceless, before authorities. Is this not precisely what Moses did before Pharaoh? When we represent the poor before the powerful, we are ambassadors of Christ. Quakers on the American frontier would often attend treaty negotiations between the federal government and the Indian tribes in order to plead for justice. Jacques Ellul says, "I hold that in every situation of injustice and oppression, the

Christian—who cannot deal with it by violence—must make himself completely a part of it as representative of the victims."[11]

But a warning is needed here. The Christian must advocate the cause of those who are truly poor and forgotten. So often it seems as if Christians have a particular knack for joining causes that are nearly over and championing issues that have thousands of champions. We must go beyond newspaper accounts (in fact, newspapers are usually a hindrance in this work) to find the genuinely dispossessed. If we desire to identify with the poor we will be concerned to be informed, really informed. Ellul reminds us that Christians "must be so concerned about human misery that they take pains to discover the really lost before it is too late."[12]

This is a thankless ministry. We are seeking to be led by the Holy Spirit to the truly abandoned and defenseless. We will defend the cause of people who are not politically "interesting." We will be bringing before mayors and city councilmen issues that all others would like to sweep under the rug. We will be making people uncomfortable over matters they deem "trivial." But that is what is asked of us if we are to identify with the genuinely poor and forgotten.

Another way we identify with the poor is to be among them. There are some who are led to take this up as a vocation: living among the poor, suffering with the poor, praying for the poor. Albert Schweitzer lived this vocation in Africa as did Toyohiko Kagawa in Japan.

Many of us, however, will be called to be among the abandoned of the earth in less dramatic ways. We will respond to Divine promptings to visit prisons and hospitals, rest homes and mental institutions. We will tutor little ones deprived of basic skills. We will take time to play with the child down the street that sits on the curb alone.

Our children need to join us in this ministry of identification. We do them no favor by hiding them from suffering and need. If we imprison them in ghettos of affluence, how can they learn compassion for the broken of the world? So, let us walk hand in hand with our children into pockets of misery and suffering.

One specific means of identification with the poor is discovered in our approach to education. Do we see a college education, for example, as a ticket to privilege or as a training for service to the needy? What do we teach our teenagers in this matter? Do we urge them to enter college because it will better equip them to serve? Or do we try to bribe them with promises of future status and salary increases? No wonder they graduate more deeply concerned about their standard of living than about suffering humanity.

As we seek to follow in the steps of Jesus, we will be drawn to identify with the poor. As we do, perhaps a valuable question to keep before us is whether we are as willing to evaluate our living standards by the needs of the poor as we are by the lifestyle of our neighbors.

Reachable Handles

It is entirely possible that you have found this chapter extremely frustrating, maybe even irrelevant. Grand ideas of giving and serving, celibacy and communal living, have left you in the dust. You are not certain that you desire those things, let alone do them. I too have felt, and do feel, the same way.

We must not despair that we are still in the foothills. The heights are seldom scaled in a single bound. And so I close this chapter with some practical handles that are within reach of us all.

First, develop a habit of plain honest speech. Strike "I am starved" from your speaking vocabulary. It is not true and obscures the fact that many indeed are starving. When you are hungry say that you are hungry and reserve the word "starvation" for the real thing. Make honesty and integrity the distinguishing characteristics of your speech. Reject jargon and abstract speculation, the purpose of which is to obscure and impress rather than to illuminate and inform.

We have simplicity of speech when our words come from only one Source. Søren Kierkegaard wrote, "If thou art absolutely obedient to God, then there is not ambiguity in thee and . . . thou art mere simplicity before God. . . . One thing there is which all Satan's cunning and all the snares of temptation cannot take by surprise, and that is simplicity." [13]

Second, write out a money autobiography.* Consider the place of money in your childhood. What view of money did your parents have? Did you feel deprived or privileged? How are those influences affecting you today?

Consider your changing attitudes toward money over the years. What influences have affected the change? Have the changes been good or detrimental?

Consider your own feelings. Are you fearful of the future? Is money a security to you? Do you feel guilty about the money you spend?

Consider your personality. Are you a "nothing ventured nothing gained" person or a "better safe than sorry" person? How does that influence your approach to money?

Third, find new creative ways to get in touch with the earth. Revel in the infinite variety of colors around you. Listen to the birds—they are God's messengers. Walk whenever you can. Enjoy the texture of grass and leaves. Grow flowers or plant trees and discover once again that "the earth is the Lord's and the fullness thereof" (Ps. 24:1).

Fourth, learn to enjoy things without owning them. Possession is an obsession in our culture. If we own it we feel that we can control it; and if we control it, we feel that it will give us more pleasure. The idea is an illusion. Many things in life can be enjoyed without possessing or controlling them. We gain great benefit from "common ownership" of many things: schools, public buildings, parks, rivers, public beaches, roads. Let's learn to enjoy the beauty of the beach without the compulsion to buy a piece of it. Many things can be shared among neighbors or friends. Some cultures even have common ownership of land. Many agricultural kibbutzim of Israel are successful and efficiently run. Give some things away just for the freedom it brings.

Fifth, develop the habit of homemade celebrations. There is an infinite variety of things you can do. It is great fun and draws you closer together. Talk to each other; even little ones can tell the most entertaining stories if we will listen. Read

---

*The concept of a money autobiography is considered in some detail in Elizabeth O'Connor's *Letters to Scattered Pilgrims* (pp. 28–30). I have taken the idea from that source.

books out loud to each other. Such times together make the entertainment extravaganzas of modern society seem cheap and hollow by comparison, and they are.

Invite neighbors and other lonely folk to join you—they won't bite! And please, do not make such a fuss over having guests in that you drop exhausted at the end of the evening and determine never to do that again. How can you enjoy people if you are always trying to impress them? Genuine hospitality is more simple, more relaxed.

Sixth, teach your children by word and deed about the varied aspects of simplicity, including the use of money. In regard to expenditures, draw clear, hard lines beyond which you will not go. Our culture is training them to desire everything in sight when they enter a store. You do them no favor when you give in to their incessant demands. You must protect them, tenderly, firmly. Spoiled children need discipline, not pampering. It is a terrible disservice to fail to set the limits. Get them what they need, not what they want; and in time they will come to want what they need.

Provide your children the experience of a growing self-government. Our children receive an allowance in order to give them the experience of managing money. (We pay twice their age—the six-year-old gets 12 cents per day, the nine-year-old gets 18 cents per day.) But they have to work for that money. They lose 5 cents for every job left undone, though they cannot go below zero. We also decided that it was important for the boys to have jobs they did because they were a part of the family and for which there was no pay. Each child has three banks—one for spending, one for savings, one for giving away. They are required to save 10 percent and give away 10 percent: the rest we decide together how to spend. Presently I pay for their necessities, they pay for their luxuries. In time I will hike up their allowance and go half with them on necessities; eventually they will pay for everything themselves. As we work to give them a growing self-government, our hope and plan is that by the age of sixteen each boy will be managing all his own income and expenses, except for housing and food. By the time they are eighteen, we hope that they will have had enough counsel and experience to make wise and responsible use of their money. (And we hope that we will be wise enough to keep our hands off their decisions, refraining even from giving advice unless it is sought.)

We have no ideal arrangement. Even now we sometimes fight over what is a luxury and what is a necessity. We make many mistakes, but our desire is to help them grow in their understanding of money and its proper use.

Seventh, seek to obey the counsel of John Woolman, "Silence every motion proceeding from the love of money."[14] The love of money is a tricky thing—often those who have it the least love it the most. Watch for that rise within that signals danger. When it comes, be still in the power of God until it is defeated. Do not try to argue down the desire; be silent and quiet. Allow the ocean of love and light to overcome the ocean of greed and fear. If you remain hushed and calm in the grip of Christ, you will discover the good rising and the evil receding.

In attempting to hammer out the outward expression of simplicity, we are undertaking no small task. It will be easy to make mistakes in both restraint and excess. Perhaps the counsel of William Penn will help us to cut back our margin of error: "Frugality is good if Liberality be join'd with it. The first is leaving off superfluous Expenses; the last bestowing them to the Benefit of others that need."[15]

9. CORPORATE SIMPLICITY:
THE CHURCH

*I have felt tender breathings in my soul after God
. . . and strong desires have attended me that his
family, who are acquainted with the moving of the
Holy Spirit, may be so redeemed from the love of
money and from that spirit in which men seek hon-
or one of another, that in all business, by sea or
land, they may constantly keep in view the coming
of His Kingdom on earth as it is in heaven.*
                                        —John Woolman

    While individual effort is good, it is always limited. There
are things that we can do together that we cannot possibly do
alone. God has so arranged human life that we are dependent
upon one another to come into all that he desires of us. We
need each other's help in order to know how to love God. We
need each other's help in order to know how to love our neighbor. Lone Ranger Christianity is a contradiction in terms.
    In the twelfth chapter of Romans, Paul sets forth a lovely
picture of a community of people living in simplicity. Placed in
the context of teaching on the gifts of the Holy Spirit, Paul
provides a profoundly practical understanding of how we are to
live. We are to give freely to the needs of the saints and to
practice ordinary hospitality. We are to enter into the needs of
one another—rejoicing with those who rejoice and weeping with
those who weep. We are to deal with class and status distinction to the extent that we can freely be among the lowly. We
are to surrender the need to have our own way, and instead
concern ourselves with what will build the fellowship. We are to
live in peace and harmony, never avenging ourselves, always
trusting in God. What an inviting paradigm of simplicity by
which to conjugate our lives!

The Teaching Ministry of the Church

One of the most urgent needs in the contemporary struggle for simplicity in the church is the ministry of teaching. There is a dismal ignorance of the simplest truths about both inward and outward simplicity. People need to know the truth if they are to be set free by the truth. Those of us in the congregation can make a valuable contribution in this direction by encouraging our pastors to dare to address such subjects. We can let them know that we are personally struggling with what it means to be a responsible citizen in a hungry world, and would welcome their instruction and insight. By our own honesty and openness we let our pastor know our willingness to have him or her deal with controversial issues. We are willing to be challenged at the point of our own vested interests, because we desire truth more than our vested interests.

This encouragement can be most helpful. Pastors do not enjoy declaring unpopular messages any more than the rest of us. How encouraging to know of even a few who would welcome thoughtful, prayerful truthgiving.

Pastors also need to take courage and share boldly and tenderly. People need the truth. It does them no good to remain ignorant. They need the freedom that comes through the grace of simplicity. And if we are to bring the whole counsel of God, we must give attention to these issues that enslave people so savagely. Martin Luther is reported to have said, "If you preach the Gospel in all aspects with the exception of the issues which deal specifically with your time you are not preaching the Gospel at all."[1] Given the contemporary milieu, several dimensions of simplicity seem to me to need careful attention in the teaching ministry of the Church.

We must boldly teach the essential connection between the inner and outer aspects of simplicity. We can no longer allow people to engage in pious exercises that are divorced from the hard social realities of life. Nor can we tolerate a radical social witness that is devoid of inward spiritual vitality. Our preaching and teaching needs to hold these elements in unity. If our teaching is centered in the biblical text, we will find literally hundreds of examples—from Abraham to St. John, from the wisdom literature to the apocalyptic writings.

By now you may have grown weary of my constant stress upon this matter, but the need for such a holistic message today is as obvious as the lack of it is terrifying. It is by far the most distinguishing feature of the classical literature on this subject, and the most lacking feature in the contemporary literature. Take, for example, Francis de Sales' *Introduction to the Devout Life,* which has instruction on meditation, prayer, humility, and solitude combined with counsel on wealth, poverty, attire, and simplicity of speech. Or consider William Law's *A Serious Call to a Devout and Holy Life,* which has three chapters on economics set in the middle of a discussion on devotional exercises. Or think of Richard Baxter's *A Christian Directory,* which gives practical instruction on prayer and faith, love and submission, as well as condemning the sin of oppression and boldly setting forth a scheme of economic ethics. This superb balance in the ancient writings between the inward and the outward, between devotion and action, is epitomized so well in the words of Bernard of Clairvaux, "Martha and Mary are sisters."[2] In fact, one of the best ways to help us see the fundamental connection between interior and exterior simplicity is to study in our churches some of the classical Christian writings on this theme.

A second theme that needs to be taught in our churches is the biblical and theological foundations for justice. The message of the prophets must be given new attention. Are we willing to have the scathing social critique of Amos applied to our day? Can we listen to Isaiah's impassioned plea on behalf of the poor and defenseless? Will we give attention to Micah's thundering denunciation of injustice and corruption? Are we willing to hear Jonah's call to worldwide citizenship and missionary responsibility? To hear the biblical message on justice, really hear it, will drive us into the contemporary problems of hunger and poverty.

Another issue that needs earnest study and teaching is the missionary obligation of the Church of Jesus Christ. Despite numerous church mission conferences, there remains a tragic lack of knowledge in this field. Missionaries need to quit boring us with technicolor travelogues and plunge us into an understanding of the theology of missions, the sociology of people movements, and the anthropology of cross-cultural evangelism.

Nothing could motivate us to simplify our lifestyles more than a clear understanding of our responsibilities to the many "hidden cultures" of the earth that have no Christian witness.

A fourth issue that demands thoughtful study is the relationship between simplicity and peace, or conversely, between covetousness and war. Does our luxury and wealth accumulation sow the seeds of revolution and desolation? To what extent is military might used to protect the privileged position of the wealthy, and keep the poor out of the profit-making cycle? Is peacemaking the natural outflow of simplicity? These and many similar questions need careful and prayerful thought.

In our ministry of teaching we also need to rethink our doctrine of work. The goal of work is not to gain wealth and possessions, but to serve the common good and bring glory to God. Even the Puritans, who have often been accused of espousing an unhappy work ethic, saw work as an opportunity to enhance the public good rather than gratify selfish ambition. The great Puritan divine Richard Baxter urged the choosing of an employment in which we could be the most serviceable to God. "Choose not," says Baxter, "that in which you may be most rich or honorable in the world; but that in which you may do most good, and best escape sinning."[3]

Simplicity takes vigorous exception to both the slothful and the workaholic. Diligence and faithfulness are to be praised, but slavish addiction is sin. Simplicity calls us off of a lifestyle of go, go, go. And if we are to teach this reality of unhurried peace and power, we had better demonstrate it in the life of the Church. If we believe in family solidarity, we had better find ways to help families to be together in the evenings rather than in twenty-five different committee meetings. Such frantic hyperactivity is sin, and we should be willing to say so. To be spent in the cause of Christ is a very different reality from the frenzied activity of the modern Church.

If we are serious about teaching Christian simplicity, we will have to address the prevalent theology of wealth. This theology takes many forms, but its point is always the same: God will bless us materially beyond our wildest dreams. This teaching does contain an important truth—God does indeed want to bless his children. The real issue, however, is the purpose for which God blesses us. God's blessing is not for personal aggrandizement, but to benefit and bless all the peoples of the earth. To understand the distinction makes all the difference in the world. The theology of wealth says, "I give so that I can get." Christian simplicity says, "I get so that I can give." The difference is profound.

The fatal flaw in all these little schemes, in which we give to Jesus in order to get rich from Jesus, is the same as that in "chain letters"—someone has to pay. In a world of limited resources, our wealth is at the expense of the poor. To put it simply, if we have it, others cannot.

The Sacred Cow

I have often pondered the perennial desire for bigger and better in the church. I do not say that this is bad, but I wonder about it. I listen, as I am sure you do, to the radio and TV evangelists' constant appeals for money. I receive, as I am sure you do, numerous letters describing the wonderful work God is doing through them, and appealing for more money to increase this good work. Always God is leading these groups to ask for more. I want to speak this tenderly because, quite frankly, I am not saddled with the responsibility of raising vast amounts of money, but isn't it possible that sometimes God would lead us to ask for less? Just once I would like to hear a Christian leader say, "Folks, God has been good to us in many ways, and as we were praying over the future, it seemed as if he desired us to tell you to take the money that you would normally give to us this month and give it to the poor." Isn't it possible that God would lead in this way at times? Such an idea sounds naive, I know, and clearly it is not an effective fund-raising technique. But then obedience is a higher priority than any program or budget, and the advancement of Christ's Kingdom is of greater consequence than our little projects.

I must also give a word about our fund-raising techniques. It is one thing to inform people of legitimate needs; it is quite another to purposely calculate emergency appeals so as to gain the largest response. It is one thing to teach about the spiritual necessity of giving; it is quite another to make use of psychological techniques that are proven to increase giving but have no regard whatsoever for the spiritual state of the individual. It is one thing to help people understand their responsibility for justice and evangelism; it is quite another to persuade and cajole and manipulate the emotions.

Christian fund raising has reached the end of its tether after it has adequately informed us of the need. Convincement is the proper terrain of the Holy Spirit, and we dare not abrogate his work. To be quite honest, I will no longer read appeal letters that have the appropriate sentences underlined in red, and promise to give me a special trinket if I give, and enclose a hand-written (though printed) final note of appeal just in case I have decided to say No. It is with sadness that I refuse to read them, because I am certain that they are often for very good causes; but the approach has moved from information to psychological manipulation.

In our concern for simplicity of speech, I would also like to raise the matter of the naming of our church buildings. There is, I think, an inherent honesty in naming our facilities after the town or street where they reside. All our descriptive adjectives such as "Open Bible" or "Full Gospel" imply that everyone else is "closed Bible" or "half Gospel." Besides, a name such as Maple Street Episcopal Church or Salem Baptist Church helps give us an identity and commitment to the area to which we seek to minister.

I would further caution us in the naming of our fellowship groups. A person once asked me what we called a little group to which I belonged that was attempting to experience a deeper sense of community. I answered, "I think we had better have the reality before we try to name it." I soon discovered that this response was particularly appropriate, as this individual belonged to a group called "Unity House," which had known anything but unity.

I know that naming is a way of describing the distinctive emphasis of a group, but I am concerned that we do not claim more than we can possibly deliver. The usual pattern in the Scripture is to give a new name to someone after his or her transformation has occurred.

Simplicity in speech also deals with the issue of titles of distinction. On this matter Jesus was straightforward: "But you are not to be called rabbi, for you have one teacher, and you are all brethren. And call no man your father on earth, for you have one Father, who is in heaven. Neither be called masters, for you have one master, the Christ" (Matt. 23:8–10).

Does this mean that we can never use the term "father" even in reference to the male parent? Of course not! What Jesus was pointing to is the destructive way we use titles to control and manipulate others. If the rabbi (or professor, or doctor) said it, no one can dispute it. The practical wisdom in Jesus' words is so easy to see in academic institutions. When professors are having a particularly difficult time convincing students, subtle appeals to technical knowledge and advanced degrees usually silence all discussion. Such manipulative control is inconsistent with Christian simplicity. Obviously, some people have more authority to speak on some issues than others, but I have found that that authority has precious little to do with titles of distinction.

It is one thing to teach respect for elders and those in authority, it is quite another to manage and maneuver people by our titles of Doctor, Reverend, Professor, Your Honor, and so on. The title "Reverend" is singularly inappropriate. The term means "one who is to be revered," and that is a distinction that belongs to God alone.

Christian simplicity does not demand a slavish use or disuse of titles. What it does demand is a careful examination of the spirit in which we hold one another, and a willingness to be servants in word as well as in deed.

Aesthetics and Utility in Creative Tension

Any attempt to deal with simplicity in the church cannot avoid the issue of buildings and architecture. This is not an issue that yields to an easy answer, but I would propose that we must hold the concerns for aesthetics and utility in creative tension.

I imagine my little principle is not a very helpful guide to a building committee that is trying to hammer out the size and shape (and cost) of a new sanctuary, but I do think that it can provide some guidance. We need to be concerned for both use-fulness and beauty, efficiency and artistry.

In the final analysis, our decisions about architecture and buildings will be determined by our theology of the church, and that is a topic far beyond the scope of this small book. But I present the following suggestions as one attempt to hold aesthetics and utility in creative tension.

One question to answer is the function we want the building to have, since form should always follow function. If worship and adoration is the central concern, then the form articulated in stone or wood or concrete should address that idea. If the primary concern is fellowship, then a different kind of architecture is appropriate. The high arching ceiling is more conducive to adoration, the circle more suggestive of fellowship.

A second suggestion is that we face with brutal honesty the issue of whether our building project is for prestige or the glory of God. I heartily recommend to any group planning to build that they meet together *as a group* for worship and adoration with the single purpose of listening to God about the proposed plan.

I learned the value of this experience in the first building program in which I was involved. It was actually a rather small project—an educational unit that was to double as a day-care center. We had all the right reasons for needing such a facility. We had gone through all the appropriate committees. We had the architect's drawings and had even launched a fund drive. But at that time I was also learning many things about the work of prayer, and finally realized that this was a matter over which we should pray together *as a people*. A meeting for worship was called for that purpose. We met with no pressure to make a decision, for we already had official church approval for the project. We read Scripture, we prayed, we sang, we shared, we listened quietly. It was a wonderful experience. I went into the meeting thinking that probably we should build, and left certain that we should not. The crucial turning point came when I saw the driving force behind my desiring that building to be my unarticulated feeling that a building program was the sign of a successful pastor. Theologically and philosophically, I did not believe that, but as we worshiped the Lord, the true condition of my heart was revealed. Eventually we decided against building, a decision now validated by hindsight.

And so we must find ways to ask if our projects signal money, success, and prestige or service, caring, and the glory of God. "But people won't come unless we dazzle them," you remonstrate. Perhaps, but remember that cuts both ways: many (myself included) will not go to a church that is purposefully trying to dazzle them.

Another suggestion is to call for a revival of the artisan and craftsman. Perhaps someone in the fellowship can carve a beautiful door or altar to the glory of God. Paintings, mosaics, tapestries can be made with care and prayer by fellow worshippers. Sculptures and pottery can be created *soli deo gloria*.

Still a fourth suggestion is to remember that beauty is expressed in many ways other than brick and stone. Flowers and grass and majestic trees can all enhance our sense of color and symmetry. I have often strolled through the Spanish Missions of California and marveled at the lovely quadrangles with their gardens and fountains. If we value fellowship, then we should provide quiet places of beauty and color where friends can sit and visit. Often a tranquil fountain can quiet our inner rush, and drown out street noises as well.

Extravagant, you say. Perhaps, but then maybe it is an extravagance that has a kinship to the spilled spikenard of Mary.

Of course, we need to consider the matter of what will fit the geographic and cultural context of the area. And then there is the important issue of cost efficiency. Further, there should be concern for quality and durability. Also, we will want to ask if our facilities are encouraging a lifestyle consistent with the life and teachings of Jesus. These and many more issues grow out of the creative tension between aesthetics and utility.

The Care of Souls

Probably the most significant lack in modern church life is in the ministry of eldering. When Paul gathered the Ephesian elders at the Aegean port of Miletus, he told them to watch over the flock of God which the Holy Spirit had given to them (Acts 20:17–35). This ministry of watching over one another in love is as important now as it was then. Christian simplicity is advanced through the ministry of eldering.

The first thing that must be done if we are to take this work seriously is to provide settings where it can happen. Caring for one another in most churches is quite impossible, simply because we don't know each other well enough to help. A pastor cannot possibly hope to provide adequate shepherding care to a group of any significant size. The answer is for people with the spiritual gift of eldering (whether officially designated as such or not is of little consequence) to give oversight and counsel to the people of God. But elders must get to know their flock if they hope to provide spiritual direction. The class meetings that John Wesley instituted provided this kind of oversight. Converts were divided into small groups that met weekly for mutual accountability and support. Many churches have formed "care groups" or "mini-churches" with the same concern in mind.

What does all this have to do with simplicity? The answer is easy to see: we cannot enter simplicity of life without the help of one another. We need the benefit of people with insight and discernment. For example, there are some people that really need to take a sabbatical leave from their labors in the church. But they will never do it unless someone tenderly urges them to take this step of simplification. Others need to be encouraged out of their sloth and self-interest.

In the early days of Koinonia Farm, a wealthy woman expressed an interest in joining. Clarence Jordan, the founder and spiritual leader of Koinonia, told her to first dispose of her money. "How?" she asked. Jordan replied, "Give it to the poor, give it to your relatives, throw it over a bridge—but you must enter the fellowship without it." She asked if she could give the money to Koinonia Farm. Perceptively, Jordan saw the danger of that act. He accurately discerned her to be a lonely person, lonely because every friend she had was after her money. "If you put that money here," said Jordan, "you would think we courted you for your money and that we loved you for your money." The wealth would become a further barrier to fellowship, Jordan noted, because she would begin to view herself as the great benefactor of the group and feel that they should forever feel indebted to her. Jordan concluded "For your sake and our sake, you get rid of that money and come walk this way with us."⁴ What a beautiful example in action of a wise and discerning eldership.

Please do not read these words in too structured a way. I am not dealing with a rigid church policy, or giving license for some demigod of an elder to lord it over everyone else. This is something much less formal and authoritarian. I am only suggesting that we should find ways to receive the help and counsel of those who are endowed by God with the spiritual gifts of discernment and wisdom.

One way many of us have found to allow this gracious ministry to occur is through what is sometimes called "meetings for clearness." They are nothing more than bringing together people whom we respect for their spiritual wisdom, and sharing a matter in the desire to gain "clearness." The issue can be anything from employment decisions (my decision to move from the pastorate to college teaching and writing came out of a meeting for clearness), to sharing budgets for mutual evaluation, to a decision about marriage, or any number of other items.

A decision does not need to be made in the meeting; in fact, it is often best to wait a bit to see if any direction sensed in the group experience is confirmed. An individual shares his or her concern, and then together the group seeks to understand the mind of Christ in the matter. There are questions and discussion, but also prayer and worship. Advice should never be given in haste, lest it distract from the truth rather than lead into it. Words should arise out of the power of God in the midst of the group. Every individual must have the inward discipline to never, never, never interject merely personal bias. People who cannot control their tongue do not belong in such a gathering.

What happens? Often—not always, but often—there begins to emerge a clearer, more certain sense of direction. There is, certainly, the normal sense of assurance that comes from mutual evaluation, but something more occurs—something that does not easily yield to sociological cataloging. It is a reality that I have never known in the ordinary experiences of gathering data, evaluating, discussing and voicing opinions. I have no way to validate it conclusively, but I wonder if the difference is not in the fact that when Christians gather with a commitment to hear the voice of Christ, they receive the direction for which they seek.

Such a group experience can help us keep our eye single. Christian brothers and sisters may warn us if we are taking on too many activities, or if we are getting too puffed up, or both, as one friend said to me once, "You need to lay low in the Lord." They may encourage us that we are moving in the right direction. They may stir us up to love and good works.

The group can also be the catalyst for ministry, and provide a basis for emotional and even financial support. When the word of the Lord came to the "meeting for clearness" at Antioch instructing Paul and Barnabas to go to the Gentiles, they did not need to go to twenty churches to drum up support. The fellowship at Antioch was their base of support: spiritually, emotionally, economically (Acts 13:1–3, 14:27–28).

Suppose in your congregation there is a widowed woman with two small children.[5] She works as a lawyer and is actively involved in your church. But a conviction grows within her that she is to use her profession as a ministry among the city's poor. She calls a group together to help her discern the Lord's will in the matter. What will such a decision mean? First, because of the time commitment of this proposed ministry, she would have to resign from the choir and the nominating committee. Second, the loss of salary would mean that she could no longer give to the church budget as generously as before. Third, and perhaps most crucial, she would experience such a drastic cut in pay that financial assistance would be necessary if she were to engage in this ministry. What happens? Any group which confirms her sense of call would also be committed to helping her find the means for it to happen. Sometimes the group can carry the entire support of the work, other times they become the catalyst for involving others. In either case it is astonishing how often impossible dreams become realizable when a group of people, even a very small group, genuinely believe God is directing them.

The care of souls is an ancient and time-honored ministry. May God grant us new "wineskins" for its fulfillment in our day.

Economic Equipoise

The Apostle Paul set before Christians of all generations a challenging economic principle in his efforts to gather an offering for the poor Christians at Jerusalem (Rom. 15:25–27). He saw the situation in Jerusalem as a wonderful opportunity to express Christian brotherhood across cultural and racial lines.

What a rare privilege for Gentiles to show Christian love to their Jewish brothers and sisters who were in need. Paul spent no small effort to bring this mission of mercy to pass, and we catch important glimpses into it in his second letter to the Corinthians.

He first cites the heartwarming response of the Macedonian believers who recently had been through severe financial difficulties themselves, and still had given with great liberty and joy: "For they gave according to their means, as I can testify, and beyond their means, of their own free will, begging us earnestly for the favor of taking part in the relief of the saints" (II Cor. 8:3).

Here was lavish joyful giving. No mechanical tithe, no calculated attempt to give the least possible amount. They were delighted for the opportunity to share. And Paul encouraged the Corinthians to "excel in this gracious work also" (II Cor. 8:7).

Do you sense the spirit of joy and abandon? This was no time to worry about investment plans and financial security. Here was an opportunity to help Christians in need. Here was an opening to follow in the steps of Christ who, "Though he was rich, yet for your sake he became poor, so that by his poverty you might become rich" (II Cor. 8:9). Only a fool would fail to seize so wonderful an opportunity.

But I have yet to mention Paul's most shocking statement: "I do not mean that others should be eased and you burdened, but that *as a matter of equality* your abundance at the present time should supply their want, so that their abundance may supply your want, *that there may be equality*" (II Cor. 8:13–14, emphasis mine). What an astonishing principle for modern ears. In essence, Paul is suggesting a certain economic balance among the Christian community. It is, as he put it, "a matter of equality." Now Paul is not seeking some kind of precise financial leveling. Gospel liberty was too deeply embedded within him for such pharisaical gymnastics. But he is pointing to a generosity of life that cannot rest in abundance while others suffer in need. Extremes of wealth and poverty are a scandal to Christian brotherhood. They must not be allowed.

To buttress this principle, Paul cited the story of the miraculous feeding of the children of Israel with manna: "As it is written, 'He who gathered much had nothing over, and he who gathered little had no lack' " (II Cor. 8:15).

This Old Testament reference is particularly instructive. Each morning, God graciously provided the children of Israel a supply of the mysterious flake-like material called manna (Exod. 16:9–36). To deal with their insatiable greed and to teach them trust, God commanded that only one-day's supply was to be gathered. True to form, however, some gathered more than allowed; but amazingly, when it was measured with the four-pint omer, "He that gathered much had nothing over, and he that gathered little had no lack" (Exod. 16:18). But some never learn, and they decided to ration out the day's supply so that they could build up a little security for tomorrow. After all, God might not provide them with manna tomorrow. Actually, it was quite prudent and frugal of them. But God wanted to teach them about daily bread, so the stored manna "bred worms and became foul" (Exod. 16:20).

The lessons of the manna were clear: trust God implicitly, no hoarding permitted, and—most pointed of all—no greed allowed. *There were to be equal portions for all.* The reason for equal portions is so practical: it eliminates the occasion for covetousness, jealousy and division. And it is this principle of equality that Paul stresses so vigorously.

What should the principle mean for us today? Inequity in the Christian fellowship is so blatant as to need no demonstration. Millions of our Christian brothers and sisters in Asia, Africa, and Latin America barely escape starvation—many do not escape—not to mention their lack of health care and education. Dare we sit back in our comfort and ease, debating the color of our padded pews, while this scandal exists?

No, of course we must do something. But the real difficulty is exactly how to respond to the problem. Is the early Franciscan fidelity to "Lady Poverty" the best approach? Some have said Yes and have called the church to a radical divestiture of holdings. Some churches may be called to such a step, but many will not. For those who do not feel total divestiture is right for them, I offer three suggestions.

First, we could establish as a budget policy a goal of giving as much to others as we spend on ourselves. I know that this has many difficulties. Is the salary for a Minister of Evangelism giving to others? Is a VBS budget that reaches many new children giving to others? What about a building program that may open the way for many new members? As difficult as the idea admittedly is, still it is a policy worth considering. If nothing else, it would continually force us to ask how much we care about the needs of Christians in other places.

Second, we could develop an ongoing relationship with an economically poor church. This might be an inner city church, or one in another country. When I pastored in Southern California, we developed a relationship with a fellowship in the Los Angeles inner city. When we gathered a "collection for the saints in Los Angeles," we actually appointed people who would take it to them in person. This recommendation also has difficulties. It becomes easy to think of ourselves as God's guardian angel for the other congregation, and expect them forever to be grateful to us. But given all of its dangers, it can still provide benefit to all concerned if done with sensitivity.

Third, we could set aside one special year as a Jubilee, in which we try to give all we possibly can to a particular work. Perhaps we might choose the churches of the Sudan Interior Mission, or the Evangelical Church of India, or our denominational mission program. Individuals may adopt families or local churches. For one year we find as many ways as possible to give as much as possible. Some may sell property holdings, others will have garage sales, still others will sell their car. For one year the budget committee will make an unprecedented outward thrust. And this Jubilee will be proclaimed so that our Christian brothers and sisters in other lands who speak other languages may know of our love. As a "matter of equality" our abundance shall supply their want.

Unrealistic? Utopian? I suppose so, but some congregations will dare it—why not yours?

Practical Helps

It is good to seek broad sweeping reform; it is also important to find small ways to stimulate one another to love and good works. I therefore conclude this chapter with some simple counsels for the Christian fellowship.

Let us seek to live in compassion and patience with one another. Grace and latitude should mark our relationships. All too often we can injure each other unduly in our zeal for justice and truth and righteousness. The spirit of condemnation can creep into our relationships so subtly. We can begin to look at each other's possessions with a mental calculator. But there is a more excellent way: we simply need to be with one another, loving, supporting, caring. Of course, we live and speak the truth as it has been given to us, but the business of straightening each other out belongs to God, not us.

Let us seek to do "ecclesiastical mercy-killing" wherever we can. Committees and programs that have outlived their usefulness should be given a proper burial. There is no need to complicate the lives of our people with unproductive meetings. Annual reviews that can cut and streamline the church organization will do much to simplify our lives.

Let us seek simple ways to help one another. Many churches have arrangements where people can bring quite good clothing that the children have outgrown so that it can be passed on to families with younger ones. Some churches have food pantries where canned goods and other staples are available to those in need. At harvest time a table can be set out for people to share their surplus garden produce. Some churches have a weekly or monthly "need sheet" where items to sell, buy, or give away can be listed.

Let us seek ways to resurrect the old practice of community "barn-raising." Roofs can be reshingled together. Skills in plumbing, electricity, and carpentry can be swapped. I have seen entire homes built out of the loving labor of the fellowship.

And with the escalating costs of financing today, this may be the only way the younger couples in our fellowship can own a home.

Let us seek to pay our pastors well. Do we fear that they will be taken over by the spirit of greed? No one who has a weakness toward the love of money should be in a pastoral position in the first place (I Tim. 3:3). Let's be known for our gracious generosity to our pastors. It is one way we show our love. It also provides them with the joy of giving to people and causes which they feel are important.

Let us seek to develop many corporate celebrations and feast days. We are enriched by celebrating the goodness of God and our life together. Many such festivals need not be expensive, but some of them should be. We need times when our frugality gives way to the joyous slaying of the "fatted calf." Where I teach we have an annual event called "Symphony of Spring," and the good it does for the human spirit is impossible to calculate. It is the most anticipated event of the year. Music, costumes, color—it is a mini-extravaganza with all the expertise of a professional production, without the plastic superficiality. This event is not cheap. There is a considerable expense in time, energy, and money. We all need such festivals of joy as together we seek the holy simplicity so inherent to the Kingdom of God.

10. CORPORATE SIMPLICITY: THE WORLD

On our crowded planet there are no longer any internal affairs! —*Alexander Solzhenitsyn*

As we face the close of the twentieth century, we need the courage to see the world as it truly is. Many lack this courage. An educated and prosperous professional woman articulated the feelings of vast numbers, "Global consciousness is what I really hate. . . . It is spoiling my life. I can't stand to have all those pictures of misery, violence and injustice in the world dumped into my living room through the TV."[1] At times we all feel that way. We are overwhelmed by the immensity of the problem and feel helpless to respond.

But we must never succumb to the temptation to self-centered provincialism. We dare not close our eyes to world events by relegating them into neatly packaged eschatological schemes that relieve us of any responsibility. We dare not stop our ears to the sobbing moan of the world's hungry by the insulated assertion that these things must occur before the return of Christ. May God give us eyes to see and ears to hear the world in which we live.

What is our world like? Three billion people have yet to hear the redemption that is in Jesus Christ. Nearly two and one-half billion are culturally outside the present scope of Christian witness. They die without hearing, without knowing. Business as usual will never accomplish the great irrevocable mandate to world evangelization.

What is our world like? We are split between the fat, prosperous affluent and the weak, hungry poor. The gap is widening with alarming speed. Two-thirds of the world, over one hundred nations, suffer chronic food deficiencies while a handful of wealthy nations have attained the highest peaks of material abundance known in the history of humankind.

What is our world like? Nations are irreversibly interdependent. The United States now imports nearly 50 percent of its vital resources, and exports vast amounts of food and technology. Any national decision anywhere sends repercussions throughout the globe. Ready or not, like it or not, we are a married world with no divorce possible.

What is our world like? Our planet is plagued by overpopulation and over-consumption. The net increase in world population now stands at about two hundred thousand a day or seventy-three million per year.[2] No one knows the carrying capacity of our globe but it is likely that we are pushing the limits. Overpopulation is the problem of the third and fourth World; over-consumption is the problem of the West. The average American child this year will consume as much of the world's resources as twenty children born in India.[3] Deliberate and calculated waste is the central aspect of the American economy.[4] We over-eat, over-buy, and over-build, spewing out our toxic wastes upon the earth and into the air.

But this gloomy picture is not the final word. Hope has the final word. We are not locked into a prison of determinism: change is possible. Ruthless inequities can be eradicated. The hungry can be fed. Millions can be reached with the message of life in Christ. He whose power is over all desires to use his people as agents of change. We are to walk cheerfully over the face of the earth, conquering evil with good in the power of the Spirit.

The Principalities and Powers

We who are Christians have a unique contribution to make in solving the vexing global problems, because we have a unique perception of the central issue involved. At the heart of all these complex difficulties is a fundamental spiritual reality. We are not just dealing with facts and figures, people and issues, but with spiritual principalities and powers.

When I speak of these issues as primarily a spiritual reality,

I do *not* mean that all we are to concern ourselves with is saving souls and with personal piety. Far from it! I mean that in back of brutal dictators and unjust policies and corrupt institutions are spiritual principalities and powers. I mean that evil can and does incarnate itself into human structures. I mean that institutions can become nothing more than organized sin.[5]

The reverse is also true. By the power of the Spirit, institutions and structures can be the means of bringing great good and blessing into the lives of human beings. Behind just policies and equitable laws are profound spiritual realities. The spiritual powers or "authorities" (ἐξουσίαις) can be either good as in Romans 12, or evil as in Ephesians 6.

Once we perceive the fundamental spiritual reality which underlies all political, social, and economic issues, we understand why we cannot be indifferent to these matters. We dare not confine our efforts to the private sector of life if we desire to bring the whole Gospel that is in Jesus Christ. Jesus addressed nearly every major social issue of his day in one form or another. If we are to be faithful, we must do the same.

The Apostle Paul calls us to wage the peaceable war of the Lamb against evil principalities and powers. We war against all demonic structures and unjust powers in a manner consistent with the strong weapons of Ephesians 6. We attack sin on every level—personal, social, structural, institutional. Like any war it is waged on all fronts at once. The perimeter of our concern encompasses 360 degrees.

Because we understand that the central issue in all these problems is spiritual and moral, we have a tremendous advantage. We are not distracted by the diversionary skirmishes of the enemy. When we approach an absentee landlord of ghetto apartments, we can speak with authority to the issue of greed, because by the power of Christ we are defeating the demonic powers behind the greed. When we confront political policymakers or corporate executives, we do so with an inward strength born out of prayer and fasting, simplicity and submission.

I do not mean that we are to go around quoting Bible verses at people, or even saying anything religious in the conventional sense. I recall well the meeting five of us had with a senior

White House official over the terribly difficult issues relating to war and peace. We gathered for prayer before the meeting and sought the mind of Christ. In the conference itself no "religious" language was used, but there seemed to be a special sense of the presence of Christ, and truth was spoken, I believe, in the power of God. Did our little meeting change government policy? I do not know, but I do believe that far more was accomplished than if we had come barging in with our own little plans and demands couched in pious platitudes.

To know the underlying spiritual nature of the problem we face gives us hope and courage. From the Gospels to the Epistles to the Apocalypse we are told that Christ has conquered, is conquering, and will continue to conquer all evil powers. Colossians especially lifts high the victory of Christ over all satanic forces: "He disarmed the principalities and powers and made a public example of them, triumphing over them in him" (Col. 2:15).

We are to go in the mighty name of Christ conquering and to conquer, not with the weapons of this evil world—guns and tanks and Trident missile systems—but with the greater weapons of truth and righteousness, peace and faith, prayer and fasting. And we need to understand that these are incredibly strong weapons, "For the weapons of our warfare are not worldly but have divine power to destroy strongholds" (II Cor. 10:4).

Now I have no naive optimism that we are going to solve every problem and eliminate all injustice—that must await the return of Christ. But we have a mandate to invade this present evil age and establish beachheads of light and hope everywhere. And we are promised that the gates of hell will not be able to withstand the onslaughts of the Church.

To know that we are dealing primarily with a spiritual reality also gives us important clues as to our strategy. The work of prayer, for example, should not be shoved off into some pious corner to be used only in connection with devotional concerns. Far from it! When we confront structural evil we do so in a power drawn from divine resources. We go to Congressional hearings on world hunger or town hall hearings on zoning laws praying for the power of the Lord to be over all. When we speak, it is out of the deep reservoir of prayer, which gives both humility and authority to our words.

We now turn our attention to a few of the battle fronts in the Lamb's war that have specific bearing on the Discipline of simplicity: world evangelization, world hunger and overpopulation, over-consumption and pollution, and multinational corporations. We must approach these topics with humility, because they are issues upon which earnest Christians have honest differences. That should not keep us from addressing the issues boldly, but it should keep us from arrogance.

World Evangelization

"Of all the tragic needs of human beings none is greater than their alienation from their Creator and the terrible reality of eternal death for those who refuse to repent and believe." So reads the statement coming out of The Consultation on World Evangelization held in Pattaya, Thailand, in June of 1980. This international gathering of over eight hundred Christian leaders who met as a follow-up to the Lausanne Congress of 1974 continues, "If therefore we do not commit ourselves with urgency to the task of evangelization, we are guilty of an inexcusable lack of human compassion."[6]

They have spoken the truth to us. If we have a Christian world view, we are concerned that people everywhere come to accept Christ as their life. And such phenomenal gains have been made in the past two hundred years that the Church is now firmly established in every continent of the world. But if we are to take seriously the task of world evangelization, we must grapple with a sobering statistic from the U.S. Center on World Mission. They tell us that of the two and one-half billion people yet to be reached, nearly all—five out of six—come from cultural groupings where the church does not have an effective witness. "Culturally distant non-Christians," is the term which they use. They estimate some 16,750 such social groupings. No existing missionary agency or evangelistic work is now reaching these "hidden cultures."

The implication is obvious: we need a great new surge of

cross-cultural evangelism. It happened once in the outbreak of the modern missionary movement with William Carey and others. It happened again at the turn of the twentieth century with the Student Volunteer Movement. It can—it must—happen again.

Today we could be on the brink of a new surge in frontier missions. Inter-Varsity's Mission Convention at Urbana has witnessed a dramatic increase in interest in cross-cultural missions. The number of students who have indicated a willingness to seek God's will concerning their involvement in missions has risen steadily from 1,764 in 1970 to 7,979 in 1979.

The economic resources to match this new wave of missionary interest are available if we will commit ourselves to a simpler lifestyle. Missiologist Ralph Winter tells us that if American Presbyterians would live on the salary of the average Presbyterian minister, two billion dollars would be available, almost three times the present U.S. expenditure for missions.[7] We can do it if we have the will. This is no time for limited vision and pygmy plans. We need resources that will triple our missionary force in order to make a massive assault on this last frontier in Christian missions. Gottfried Osei-Mensah, a leading third world figure in the Lausanne Congress, has called for every one thousand Christians to send one missionary to the unreached peoples. Ralph Winter has proposed that Christians in America voluntarily adopt the same level of support accorded missionaries on furlough and give the extra to frontier missions. He has developed the Order for World Evangelization with exactly that objective in mind. Through this means, a family could actually affiliate themselves with a mission agency and help provide resources to reach the Hidden Peoples of the earth.[8]

As we go, let us clearly understand that global justice places some new requirements upon global evangelism. The Good News must be contextualized into the culture in which it is proclaimed. The Gospel of Jesus Christ has no cultural presuppositions. It welcomes those elements of the culture that are not offensive to the Gospel message and rejects those that are. The enduring task of cross-cultural evangelism is to hammer out the difference.

The Good News must be free of all racism and nationalism. We are global citizens with a global Gospel. Our concern is for the well-being of all peoples of the earth, not the selfish interests of any nation-state.

The Good News must be free of all militarism. It matters little whether the militarism is in defense of the vested interests of the privileged elite or is a modern Zealot movement seeking justice through revolution. We dare not allow the little tin gods of our modern nation-states to draw us into their blasphemous intertribal wars.

The Good News must be given to Christ's favorites, the poor and the helpless. We must go, like the Samaritan, among the bruised and half-dead—to the ghettos of America, to the slums of Brazil, to the refugee camps of Cambodia, to every hovel and hut of the earth.

The Good News must liberate—truly liberate. Those who are in bondage to sin, those who are in bondage to poverty, those who are in bondage to brutal social conditions need to be set free. The liberating Gospel of Christ has not fully come until there is freedom from sin, freedom from economic injustice, freedom from structural evil.

The Good News must come in the power of God. No smooth words, no easy cliches, no enticing gimmicks! All slick image-making advertising campaigns are an offense to the Gospel. Paul said, "The Kingdom of God does not consist in talk but in power" (I Cor. 4:19).

The Good News must be backed by integrity in our lives. We cannot proclaim his love if we close our hearts to the hungry. We cannot proclaim his salvation if we have not been saved from our own greed. Flamboyant, prosperous Christians are an offense to third world peoples by their insensitivity to poverty and human deprivation, whether they come as traveling evangelists or sight-seeing vacationers.

World Hunger

How do you say the word *hunger*? Stop awhile and listen to the inner sob of Carolina Maria de Jesus when her daughter pleaded, "Mama, sell me to Doña Julita, because she has delicious food." Now say the word *hunger*. Step into the hovel of Sebastian and Maria Nascimento and look around. The three-year-old twins lie naked and unmoving on the small cot. They will soon die, the victims of malnutrition. Like me, you want to turn away, but stay and see the quiet little boy. He is a two-year-old whose brain is already vegetating from marasmus, a severe form of malnourishment. Maria tries to speak to you but cannot. The tears of a broken-hearted mother spill down her cheeks.[9] Now say the word *hunger*.

We know little of the world of hunger. We can still choose to escape its sights and sounds. But over half of the world's people are intimately acquainted with its horror—indeed, 460 million people are victims of acute hunger. Ten thousand will die by tomorrow. A million hogs in Indiana have superior housing to a billion humans on this planet. In Calcutta alone 600,000 are perpetually homeless.

The terrible, obscene tragedy in all this is that it is preventable. There is almost unanimous agreement among the experts on world hunger that we can alleviate hunger if we are willing to make the necessary sacrifices. We have the resources. We have the technology. It can be done if we have the will.[10]

However, it cannot be done easily. Major obstacles block the way.

The changes in climate can wreak havoc with whole cultures. The most serious drought in living memory has hit Africa's Sahel. The Sahara Desert has been advancing southward at an estimated four to thirty miles a year. No African country between the tenth and twentieth parallels of latitude has escaped. And Northern Africa is only an extreme example of a pervasive dry-weather pattern that has affected parts of the Middle East, India, South Asia, Northern China, and even Central America.

A gradual cooling trend of the surface temperature of the earth has also been well documented. Since the peak high in 1945, the average surface temperature has fallen about 2.7 degrees Fahrenheit. If the trend continues, scientists are concerned that it could produce agricultural disaster. Scientists are widely divided as to why the change is occurring and whether it is only a temporary cycle or more permanent, but the fact of the change is undisputed.

The capricious decisions of political rulers can mean economic ruin and starvation for millions. Dispossessed men, women, and children flood into refugee camps, the tragic victims of war. Refugees are not new to the human scene, but what is new is the increased numbers. Overconcentrations of population have conspired with the increased savagery of modern warfare upon noncombatants to produce more than fourteen million displaced persons.

Unjust social structures perpetuate a hungry world. In many places the powerful privileged elite manipulate land, money, and political decisions to their advantage. Often foreign aid is given or cut off out of political expediency. International trade and the operations of The International Monetary Fund can contribute to affluence in some countries and poverty in others.

Perhaps one of the most formidable problems in world hunger is overpopulation. If you were born in 1930 and live to the end of this century, the earth's living population will have more than tripled in your lifetime. We grow in numbers the equivalent of the entire U.S. population every three years.

Most of the growth has occurred in the poorer countries. It is estimated that, by the turn of this century, four-fifths of the human race will be living in these countries. This has led the Environmental Fund to propose that food and technical assistance should be suspended from any country that does not control its population growth. The extreme expression of this concern was stated by Johnson Montgomery in the so-called "Lifeboat Theory." In short, this theory maintains that affluent nations, which are obviously in the lifeboat, cannot—indeed, should not—aid population-expanding countries for fear they will overload and sink the boat.

This all sounds quite reasonable until we try to understand the underlying causes of overpopulation. One of the most widely documented concepts in social science is what is called the demographic transition. All of the industrialized countries have experienced this transition, and many of the more advanced third world countries are in the final transition. In brief, it describes the three stages involved in the transition from high birth and death rates to low birth and death rates. The first stage, which is characteristic of all pre-industrial societies, is one of a high birth rate matched by a high death rate. As the society experiences improved health and nutrition it enters the second stage, which maintains a high birth rate but a decreasing death rate resulting in a population explosion. In the third stage, birth rates decrease to match the death rate, resulting in zero population growth. Developing countries are now clearly in the second stage, which is the cause for the population boom.[11]

The reasons for demographic transition are hotly debated among social scientists. But one partial answer is simply that parents depend upon children both to perpetuate the family and to provide for economic and old age security. Once it becomes clear that nine children are not required to ensure that two will live to adulthood, there is a dramatic decrease in the birthrate. But the security to have small families will come only as the benefits of healthy economic growth are spread among the poor. The rise of public education is also cited by many as a crucial factor. The idea that poor countries can attain zero growth by an influx of birth control technology without dealing substantially with the issues of economic and educational well-being is a myth of the privileged elite. Arthur Simon, Executive Director of Bread for the World, says, "Adequate nutrition, health care, literacy, and improved incomes for the poor emerge as the most fundamental remedy to the population problem."[12]

The task is massive, but it is not impossible. Repeatedly, world hunger specialists say that it can be done if we will set ourselves to the task. Wonderful strides have been made by Christian relief organizations such as World Vision, World Concern, Food for the Hungry, and many others. These efforts are good and should receive our generous support. But relief alone will not solve the problem—we need public policies that speak to world hunger.

The 1980 Presidential Commission on World Hunger has urged, as its major recommendation, "that the United States Government make the elimination of hunger *the primary focus of its relationships with the developing countries,* beginning with the decade of the 1980s."[13] Their report has far reaching implications and would mean a major shift in U.S. policy priorities. Among other things, they call for a more liberal trade policy toward developing nations, which would include price stabilizing agreements, a reduction of tariffs, and a Trade Adjustment Act that would make provision for U.S. industries adversely affected. Responding to the commission's concern, Bread For The World has initiated "The Hunger and Global Security Bill," which among other things would provide "U.S. development aid only to countries clearly committed to overcoming hunger and poverty."[14] All these recommendations are sound and the bare minimum we should be doing to solve the hunger problem.

Can more be done? Yes, and it should be. We need to initiate a bold new food policy to answer the cry of world hunger and the need for global security. We need to call upon the United Nations to establish world food banks throughout the earth in which world grain reserves could be gathered and dispersed in emergencies. We need to call upon the United States and other developed nations to make a major shift away from meat and alcohol production and consumption in order to release massive amounts of protein rich grain. We need to call upon the International Fisheries Commissions of the world to search for creative new ways to channel fishing catches into human consumption rather than animal consumption. And we need to call upon the developed nations to share freely and rapidly their intellectual resources, especially in the area of intermediate technology.[15]

In his well-known statement on hunger Jesus said, "I was hungry and you gave me food, I was thirsty and you gave me drink. . . . Truly, I say to you, as you did it to one of the least of these my brethren, you did it to me" (Matt. 25:35, 40). The implication of that passage is devastating: Jesus Christ is starving! Of all people, Christians cannot close their ears to the cry of the hungry, for to feed them is to feed Christ.

Runaway Desire

In *Alice in Wonderland*, there is this significant dialogue between Alice and the Dormouse.

"I wish you wouldn't squeeze so," said the Dormouse, who was sitting next to her. "I can hardly breathe."

"I can't help it," said Alice very meekly: "I'm growing."

"You've no right to grow here," said the Dormouse.

"Don't talk nonsense," said Alice more boldly: "You know you're growing too."

"Yes, but I grow at a reasonable pace," said the Dormouse: "not in that ridiculous fashion."[16]

While the third world must struggle with the problem of unchecked growth, the developed countries must struggle with the problem of unchecked desire.

The idea of unlimited growth and expansion is deeply imbedded in the American psyche. William Ophuls says, "Growth is the secular religion of American society."[17] For us, expansion is always desirable, more is always good, bigger is always better. It pervades all of our thought from our view of the gross national product to the size of our homes.

Economically, the concept of expansion as necessarily desirable has its roots in the philosophic work of Adam Smith and especially his *Wealth of Nations*, published in 1776. For Smith, the purpose of economics was a constantly expanding market, hence anything that would stimulate growth was welcome. In effect, this removed any notion of ethics or morality from economics and replaced it with the concept of an "invisible hand," which would guarantee that the good of the whole was insured if all people would pursue their own self-interest.[18] In Christian theology, of course, the only "invisible hand" is God's, and once we grasp it we discover that it leads away from self-interest to justice and compassion for the poor and oppressed.

The expansionist economy that has grown out of this foundation has four crucial assumptions about the world. First, it is assumed that the pursuit of self-interest will necessarily lead to ultimate social good. Purpose and values should be defined in terms of economic growth. Second, there is hardly any limit to nature's generosity. If the economic balloon is to get bigger and bigger, the good earth must constantly yield the needed amounts of new wealth for expansion to continue. Third, the pursuit of economic self-interest of necessity places a higher priority upon those who are alive than it does on generations yet to be born. Besides, if by its very nature economic expansion is good, then future generations will benefit from our continued growth. Fourth, since constant economic expansion is by definition good, then any negative side effect is a mere externality. Massive industrial pollution is only an unhappy side effect; it does not call into question the economic theory itself.[19]

The effect of all this has been to define success in terms of an ever increasing gross national product and to react negatively to anything that would retard growth. It has also predisposed us to look favorably upon any growth producing incentive. For example, planned obsolescence has become a way of life in American society, because we have found that it produces economic growth. We are a throw-away culture. Industrial designer Brooks Stevens says, "Our whole economy is based on planned obsolescence."[20]

Vance Packard's *The Waste Makers* makes it indisputably clear that deliberate and calculated waste is a central ingredient in our economy. Many products are "death-dated," that is, they are designed to fall apart or become unrepairable at a specific time. In 1960 the average life expectancy of an American car was about ten years, or roughly half the expected life of a Volkswagen.[21] A major steel company has made available a lead-coated steel which, at an increased cost of eight cents per muffler, would give a product which would last the lifetime of the automobile. Instead, auto makers continue to install mufflers that will need to be replaced in two years.[22] At one point a major light bulb producer made a calculated decision to reduce the life span of one of its bulbs from 1000 to 750 hours.[23]

Where planned obsolescence fails, psychological obsolescence takes over. This has been done with unusual success in the clothing and automobile industry, but is also used with many other products. The sole purpose of psychological obsolescence is to make us want to get a product before the old one has ended its usefulness. Back in 1929, General Motors executive Floyd Allen said, "Advertising is in the business of making people helpfully dissatisfied with what they have in favor of something better. The old factors of wear and tear can no longer be depended upon to a create a demand. They are too slow."[24] In the 1920s, Detroit began pioneering in the concept of the annual model change and has not stopped since. Added to this is the endless variety of products that are virtually the same. We can buy 551 brands of coffee, 177 brands of salad dressing, and 249 brands of soap.[25]

The result of this intentional expendability of items to increase economic growth is the most massive solid-waste disposal problem ever known to humankind. Harry Rothman tells us that, "if the American people and their solid wastes were spread evenly over the United States there would be in each square mile of the nation 56 people surrounded by 54 tons of rubbish which would include: 3 junked cars, 25 discarded tires, 8,500 bottles, 17,000 cans, one ton of plastics, and 8½ tons of paper." The American people are now producing a total of 340 million tons of solid wastes per year.[26]

As you know, that is only the tip of the iceberg. In one short generation we have moved from the steel age to the synthetic age. The world of plastics, chemicals, and pesticides is making a profound and irreversible impact upon our ecosystem. According to *Time* magazine there are now 50,000 chemicals on the market, and almost 35,000 of those used in the United States are classified by the federal Environmental Protection Agency (EPA) as being definitely or potentially hazardous to human health.[27] The Surgeon General of the United States recently reported to the Senate that, "The public health risk associated with toxic chemicals is increasing, and will continue to do so," and buttressed his remarks with a Library of Congress study which concluded that toxic chemicals "are so long lasting and pervasive in the environment that virtually the entire population of the nation, and indeed the world, carries some body burden of one or several of them."[28]

Perhaps one of the most dangerous results of all this is the toxic pollutants that we dump into the atmosphere, and which fall back to the earth as "acid rain." Acid rain is destroying forests, crops, even sea life. According to some studies in the United States, acid rain has reduced cotton yields by 33 percent and tomato harvests by 21 percent."[29] Leon S. Dochinger of the United States Department of Agriculture has said that acid rain "is perhaps the most serious environmental dilemma of this century."[30]

Beyond that is the great danger of destroying the earth's

ozone layer. The National Academy of Sciences warns of a future depletion of the ozone layer of up to 16.5 percent as a result of pollutants dumped into the biosphere.[31]

In spite of all the shortcomings of *The Limits of Growth* report of the Club of Rome, they did shout to us one devastatingly undeniable truth: our "growthmania" must stop or it will destroy us.

We simply must understand that the wonderful resources of the earth are limited. We are now entering the age of scarcity. Jeremy Rifkin, in *The Emerging Order*, goes into extensive detail and documentation to demonstrate that our energy resources are severely limited. He explodes the myth that nuclear energy or solar power or some new technological breakthrough will allow our highly prized expansionism to continue unimpeded. We are reaching the limits of our oil, minable coal, and minerals. Many experts now predict that within seventy-five years or less at current consumption rates we will have "exhausted presently known recoverable reserves of perhaps half the world's now useful metals."[32] Rifkin argues persuasively that even our renewable resources—water, forests, fisheries, crop land, and grazing land—are seriously threatened and being depleted.[33]

The message from all quarters is the same: *our undisciplined consumption must end.* If we continue to gobble up our resources without any regard to stewardship and to spew out our deadly wastes over land, sea, and air, we may well be drawing down the final curtain upon ourselves.

I need to add a reason for curbing our gluttonous consumption that Christians should consider very seriously. Overconsumption is a "cancer eating away at our spiritual vitals."[34] It cuts the heart out of our compassion. It distances us from the great masses of broken bleeding humanity. It converts us into materialists. We become less able to ask the moral questions. For example, just because we have the economic muscle to buy up vast amounts of the world's oil, does that give us the right to do so? When the poor farmer of India is unable to buy a gallon of gasoline to run his simple water pump because the world's demand has priced him out of the market, who is to blame? You see, our sensitivities have been dulled by our over-consumption. Our undisciplined squandering is destroying us spiritually. Walter Harrelson, professor of Old Testament at Vanderbilt University, says, "Overeating and overconsumption, gross inequity in the control of wealth, and a desire to maintain one's own style of life irrespective of world famine clearly constitutes sin in the biblical perspective."[35]

What is urgently needed is a bold new move from a consumer economy to a conserver economy in all of the developed countries, and particularly in the United States. It would mean gargantuan policy shifts in industry and government. It would call for a massive reorientation in the mind-set of the American populace. It would demand a conviction that slowing down (and in certain places cutting back) our growth rate would be advantageous. I am not advocating a "zero-growth economy," but I am suggesting that we need a good dose of temperance.

The task will admittedly be formidable. While it is difficult to control a growth economy, the problems are even greater when attempting to control deliberate economic restraint. I am not an economist, and although I have consulted two highly respected economists in the preparation of this chapter,[36] I do not know all of the problems that a conserver economy would engender. Probably no single individual can understand the full dimensions of this problem.

Therefore, I believe it would be wise at this point in our history for the Christian community to convene an International Congress on Economics and Social Justice. The 1974 Lausanne Congress on World Evangelization has had an important and positive impact. We need a similar gathering of Christian leadership to bring our faith to bear on this issue. We need the insight and guidance such an international gathering could provide. Perhaps they could hammer out some ethical guidelines that would inform our policies and practices. Economists from the various Christian colleges and elsewhere could give significant leadership to such an enterprise.

Christians can make, I think, a unique contribution to this issue, because biblically and theologically we have a vital interest in both stewardship of the earth and economic justice for the poor. And because our allegiance to God is higher than to any nation-state, we have a commitment to global citizenship that can help us transcend the provincial claims of national interest.

Multinational Corporations

At this point, any number of issues could be considered with profit. We could look at the proposals for a New International Economic Order that came out of the General Assembly of the United Nations in May of 1974. We could study the question of international trade as it applies to social justice. We could explore the matter of foreign aid and the policies that could be designed to help the bottom 60 percent of the world. All of these matters are worthy of careful study and thought. I have, however, chosen to deal with the issue of multinational corporations, because they pose both the gravest danger to a more just and equitable world, and potentially the most powerful force for realizing a more just and equitable world.

The era of multinational corporations interjects a new reality into human society. We have always had global visionaries, and businessmen have ventured abroad at least since the Phoenicians began selling glass to their Mediterranean neighbors. What makes the global corporations unique is that for the first time in history, organizations have arisen that have both the ideology and the technology to bring about Wendell Willkie's dream of "One World." Richard Barnet and Ronald Müller, in *Global Reach,* their authoritative study of multinationals, state, "The global corporation is the most powerful human organization yet devised for colonizing the future."[37] And Aurelio Peccei, a director of Fiat and organizer of the Club of Rome, says that the multinational corporation "is the most powerful agent for the internationalization of human society."[38]

Arising out of the post–World War II technological explosion, multinational corporations have had a spectacular growth rate. The Club of Rome reports that, "of the 100 wealthiest entities on the international scene, well over half are corporations."[39] The most successful of the multinational organizations have an annual growth rate that is two to three times that of most industrial countries, including the United States. Barnet and Müller have compared the annual sales of multinational corporations with the gross national product of countries for 1973, and discovered that "GM is bigger than Switzerland, Pakistan, and South Africa; that Royal Dutch Shell is bigger than Iran, Venezuela, and Turkey; and that Goodyear Tire is bigger than Saudi Arabia."[40] Seven oil companies, known as the "Seven Sisters," control over two-thirds of the world's oil and natural gas supply. Professor Howard Perlmutter, of the Wharton School, estimates that by 1986, two to three hundred global corporations will control eighty percent of of all productive assets of the non-Communist world.[41]

The global corporations can exert tremendous political and economic clout throughout the world. The economic sanctions, for example, of the countries of the world against the Chilean junta of Augusto Pinochet has had little effect because the multinational banks have loaned the Chilean government some one billion dollars. Hence, the junta has been able to laugh at the international human rights campaign that had been mounted against its brutal violations of civil liberties.[42] Because the multinational corporations often function as monopolies or oligarchies, they can control the supply of resources that is crucial to the survival of nations even as large as the United States.

These corporations are highly mobile, and often build duplicate production facilities in different countries in order to move quickly to avoid stringent antipollution laws, high wage demands, or other economically disadvantageous situations. While such mobility works to the economic benefit of the corporation, it can be devastating to a local economy. In the early 1970s, General Instruments cut its New England labor force by three thousand and increased its force in Taiwan by almost five thousand. Singer Sewing Machine reduced its main American plant in New Jersey from ten thousand employees to two thousand.[43] Their mobility has robbed labor of its traditional bargaining powers, which explains why organized labor has been consistently critical of multinationals.

The most distinctive feature of what Barnet and Müller call "the World Managers" is not their size, but their ability to transcend any given nation-state. The concerns for growth and profits take precedence over the interests of any nation, including the country of their origin. Antitrust regulations and other laws designed to regulate what occurs within a nation prove worthless in controlling the activities of multinationals. Hence, national governments find it increasingly difficult to keep these global corporations from determining what goes on in the world.

Multinationals are not accountable to any nation, nor do they feel a responsibility for the welfare of any nation. They can buy up huge, tillable land masses to grow sugar cane for export without any regard for what that might mean in terms of food production for the people. They can launch large advertising campaigns to convince the poorest of the world that formula milk is to be preferred to breast milk without regard for sanitary conditions among the poor, or for the couple's ability to buy an adequate supply of milk for their child.[44]

The global corporations respond that they are the architects of world peace and prosperity. By interlinking the economies of the earth, they feel they are producing a world that is so interdependent that war is an increasing impossibility. They claim to be producing job markets and increased wealth throughout the world.

Will the era of global corporations institute a new form of imperial domination, or will it usher in a new golden age? No one knows for certain, but two things are clear. First, multinational corporations have the resources and the organization to bring immeasurable benefits to the human family. Second, this will never occur unless some form of strict accountability is placed upon multinationals.

There is need for an international monitoring of the activities of global corporations, perhaps through the United Nations. They must be forced by law to reveal all the relevant facts of their operations which are now concealed. An international Code of Conduct needs to be developed to regulate the operations of multinationals. For example, a policy should be adopted which would insist that there be an economic inflow into a country to match what is extracted from it. Also, the cost of raw materials should have an equitable tie to the purchase price of the finished product.

Strict *international* environmental standards must be set to govern the activities of multinational corporations. Environmental impact studies must be mandatory, with strict and universal antipollution regulations.

These and many more areas of accountability are needed if the global corporations are to benefit society with a generosity equal to their profit margin.[45]

How Can I Help?

It is easy to feel that these issues are far beyond our small abilities, but there is much that we can do.* First, we can open ourselves to the possibility that God may well want to use us in a large way. History is full of ordinary people who, like Amos, were called to positions of influence far beyond their intentions. Second, we can get the facts. We become global citizens by caring enough to be informed about what happens to our neighbors in Chile and Mozambique. Third, we can become advocates of the powerless and exploited. Our comfortable dinner parties and Sunday School classes need to hear the whimpering cry of the poor. We are strong on love, but soft on justice.

Fourth, we can support relief agencies in their good work. They need our help. Fifth, we can go beyond relief and become involved politically. Life is political; and if we refuse to influence public policy, someone else will. Sixth, we can use our literary skills in the cause of the poor. Letters to the editor, newsletters, magazine articles, good books are all needed. Our hymns and gospel songs need social content. We must write forcefully, honestly, tenderly. Seventh, the ministry of prayer must be taken into the social arena. It is hard work, but necessary to defeat the demonic principalities and powers infesting so many social institutions.

The brief words of this chapter have only touched the edge of the many ways simplicity speaks to the world in which we live. May Jesus Christ, our ever present Teacher, continue to instruct us in how to apply his life-giving Gospel to every institution and structure in human society.

---

* I am indebted to T. Wayne Rieman of Manchester College, Indiana, for several of these practical suggestions.

Epilogue
THE SIMPLICITY
OF SIMPLICITY

At the beginning of this book I underscored the complexity of our task. There simply are no easy answers to the tough questions of how we are to relate with integrity to the modern world. The difficulty of our task is evident enough on the personal level, but the moment we begin to deal with the broader issues of church and state and international relations we are staggered by the immense complexity of simplicity.

It is essential for us to be confronted by this reality if we are to escape superficiality. But there is a danger in understanding the intricacies of these issues. Once we begin to see the complexity of it all, we can become overwhelmed. We despair of ever being able to fit the pieces of the puzzle together. We find ourselves struggling on the personal level with our dishonest speech and obsessive status-seeking and compulsive extravagance—not to mention the complex matters of economics and global hunger and international trade. It is easy to become immobilized by the enormity of our task. Discouragement and then despair can set in all too quickly. Without anyone noticing, we quietly resign ourselves to the status quo: "I can't change the world and I'm not even sure I can (or want) to change my own lifestyle, so I'd better leave things as they are. Nothing ventured, nothing lost!"

But it is exactly at that point that we are tragically mistaken. We have a great deal to lose! Simplicity is part and parcel of our call to be a disciple of Jesus Christ. It is not an "extra" that we can tack onto our Christian experience as we add a tape deck to a new car. It is an essential part of the Classical Disciplines of the Christian life. Simplicity is essential in the way that wheels or brakes or an engine are essential to an automobile; without them there is no functional automobile. Simplicity is essential in the way that prayer and worship or any of the Spiritual Disciplines are essential; without them there is no functional disciple of Christ.

The Spiritual Disciplines (of which simplicity is a vital part) are the conduit through which our obedience flows; they are visible ways by which we express our discipleship. And more importantly, they set us before God in such a way that we can be transformed and conformed to the way of Christ. William Penn said, "To be like Christ, then, is to be a Christian,"[1] which is precisely why simplicity is such an important part of Christian devotion. Nothing is more clear than that Jesus Christ walked in a well-nigh amazing simplicity of life. He was centered in God and had a transparency toward God that ordered everything. Simplicity is part of what it means to be a follower of Christ.

To be sure, the cost of simplicity is great, but the cost of duplicity is greater. Duplicity costs the joyful communion with the divine Center, faith that sees everything in the light of God's governance for good, abiding peace, and the ability to walk cheerfully over the face of the earth in the power of the Lord. In short, it costs the abundant life Jesus said he came to bring. Simplicity may be difficult, but the alternative is immensely more difficult.

The joyful paradox in all this is that while simplicity is complex it is also simple. In the final analysis we are not the ones who have to untangle all the intricacies of our complex world. There are not many things we have to keep in mind—in fact, only one: to be attentive to the voice of the true Shepherd. There are not many decisions we have to make—in fact, only one: to seek first his Kingdom and his righteousness. There are not many tasks we have to do—in fact, only one: to obey him in all things. As Søren Kierkegaard understood so clearly, we are honed down to only one thing, and that is the simplicity of simplicity.

This is why the inward reality of holy obedience to the divine Center is so central to everything about simplicity.

Without that we will become frustrated and stymied by the complexity of it all. With it life is ordered and filled with peace. The only thing we have to do is be, at every moment, attentive to the heavenly Monitor. And as we are, there come welling up whispers of divine guidance and love that make life radiant.

Jesus invited people to share his yoke, adding that his yoke was easy and his burden was light. A horse or ox is trained to work peaceably and well by being yoked or harnessed to one already trained. At first the untrained animal may chafe under the yoke, and try to bolt away. So long as he does, the yoke will be a heavy burden indeed. But as he learns to walk step by step with the trained animal, he learns to walk with ease.

We too are yoked to One who is trained. Our only task is to keep in step with him. He chooses the direction and leads the way. As we walk step by step with him, we soon discover that we have lost the crushing burden of needing to take care of ourselves and get our own way, and we discover that the burden is indeed light. We come into the joyful, simple life of hearing and obeying.

NOTES

Chapter 1. The Complexity of Simplicity

[1] W. Stanley Mooneyham, *What Do You Say to a Hungry World?* (Waco: Word Publishing Co., 1975), p. 32.

[2] Thomas Kelly, *A Testament of Devotion* (New York: Harper & Row Publishers, 1941), p. 124.

[3] Pope John XXIII, *Journal of a Soul,* trans. Dorothy White (New York: McGraw-Hill Book Co., 1965), pp. 278–279.

[4] Dietrich Bonhoeffer, *Ethics,* ed. Eberhard Bethge (New York: The Macmillan Co., 1955), p. 68.

[5] *Celebration of Discipline* (New York: Harper & Row, 1978). The Spiritual Disciplines discussed in that book are meditation, prayer, fasting, study, simplicity, solitude, submission, service, confession, worship, guidance, and celebration. They are described as "classical" not because they are ancient but because they are central to experiential Christianity.

When *Celebration of Discipline* was being prepared for publication many different subtitles had been proposed; hence I was unaware of the final decision. When I received the examination copy of the dustjacket I groaned. The subtitle was, "Paths to Spiritual Growth." That subtitle missed a crucial point. The Disciplines are not independent "paths" as if you can exercise one without the other. Like the fruit of the Spirit they constitute a unity: not "fruits" but "fruit," not "paths" but "path." I wrote an impassioned plea requesting that the plural be changed to a singular, which graciously the house of Harper & Row consented to do.

[6] François Fénelon, *Christian Perfection* (New York: Harper & Brothers, 1947), p. 194.

[7] Ibid.

Chapter 2. The Biblical Roots: The Old Covenant

[1] See the article "The OT Term מִשְׁפָּט in *Theological Dictionary of the New Testament* (Grand Rapids: William B. Eerdmans Publishing Co., 1975). Expanded information on the use of *mishpat* in the Old Testament can be found in this excellent article.

[2] There are many excellent word studies of *shalom* in standard volumes. A very helpful booklet is Howard Macy, *The Shalom of God* (Richmond; Friends United Press, 1973). Two books which deal with *Shalom* in the context of Christian simplicity are John V. Taylor, *Enough Is Enough* (cited below) and Richard K. Taylor, *Economics and the Gospel* (Philadelphia: United Church Press, 1973).

[3] John V. Taylor, *Enough Is Enough* (Minneapolis: Augsburg Publishing House, 1977), p. 42.

Chapter 3. The Biblical Roots: The New Covenant

[1] I am indebted to Dallas Willard of the University of Southern California for the many insights into Matthew 6 that he has given me through both his life and his teaching.

[2] The discussions as to the meaning of ἁπλοῦς are quite involved. An excellent summary of the issue can be found in an unpublished doctoral dissertation by Carol Schaefer, *A Study in the Exegesis of Matt. 6:22 Through an Analysis of Haplous* (Providence: Brown University, 1963). Also of interest is an excellent exegesis of Matt. 6:22–24 by Mark Silliman, *The Dark Amen Versus the Light AMEN* (Wichita: Friends University, 1980). My use of the passage follows the lead of John Wesley, who felt *haplous* referred to a single aim in life, namely God. He used the text to defend the glories of being poor and simple with God, versus rich and godless.

[3] Dallas Willard, in a lecture on the Sermon on the Mount, Spring 1974, Woodlake Avenue Friends Church, Canoga Park, California.

[4] Martin Hengel, *Property and Riches in the Early Church* (Philadelphia: Fortress Press, 1973), p. 27.

Chapter 4. Simplicity Among the Saints

[1] Quoted in D. Elton Trueblood, *The Best of Elton Trueblood: An Anthology*, ed. James R. Newby (Nashville: The Benson Co., 1979), p. 70.

[2] John Woolman, *The Journal of John Woolman* (Secaucus: The Citadel Press, 1972), p. 41.

[3] Quoted in Martin Hengel, *Property and Riches in the Early Church* (Philadelphia: Fortress Press, 1973), p. 45.

[4] Tertullian, "The Apology of Tertullian" in Alexander Roberts and James Donaldson, eds. *The Ante-Nicene Fathers*, 8 vols. (Buffalo: The Christian Literature Publishing Co., 1887), 3:46.

[5] "The Teaching of the Twelve Apostles" in Roberts and Donaldson, *The Ante-Nicene Fathers*, 7:378.

[6] Eusebius, *The Ecclesiastical History*, trans. Christian Frederick Cruse, reprint ed. (Grand Rapids: Baker Book House, 1958), Book IV, Chapter 23, p. 160.

[7] "The First Epistle of Clement to the Corinthians" in Roberts and Donaldson, *The Ante-Nicene Fathers*, 1:15.

[8] "Epistle of Clement to James" in Roberts and Donaldson, *The Ante-Nicene Fathers*, 8:220.

[9] Quoted in *Quotations from Chairman Jesus*, ed. David Kirk (Springfield: Templegate Publishers, 1969), p. 175.

[10] "The First Apology of Justin Martyr" in Roberts and Donaldson, *The Ante-Nicene Fathers*, 1:186.

[11] Ibid., pp. 42–43.

[12] Quoted by Henri Nouwen in "The Desert Counsel to Flee the World," *Sojourners*, 9 (June 1980):15.

[13] Helen Waddell, trans., *The Desert Fathers* (Ann Arbor: The University of Michigan Press, 1957), p. 85.

[14] Quoted by Henri Nouwen, "Silence, The Portable Cell," *Sojourners* 9 (July 1980):22.

[15] Waddell, *The Desert Fathers*, p. 123.

[16] Ibid., p. 112.

[17] Paul Sabatier, *Life of St. Francis of Assisi* (New York: Charles Scribner's Sons, 1894), p. 83.

[18] Ibid., p. 114.

[19] Ibid., p. 307.

[20] Raphael Brown, trans., *The Little Flowers of St. Francis* (Garden City; Doubleday & Company, 1958), p. 68.

[21] Ibid., pp. 81–82.

[22] Ibid., pp. 58–60.

[23] Theodore G. Tappert, ed., *Selected Writings of Martin Luther: 1520–1523* (Philadelphia: Fortress Press, 1967), p. 20.

[24] Ibid., p. 37.

[25] Ibid., p. 43.

[26] Ibid., p. 47.

[27] John Calvin, *Commentaries on the Epistle of Paul the Apostle to the Romans* (Grand Rapids: Wm. B. Eerdmans Publishing Co., 1947), p. 481.

[28] George Fox, *The Journal of George Fox* (London: Cambridge University Press, 1952), p. 11.

[29] Quoted in Lewis Benson, *A Revolutionary Gospel* (Philadelphia: The Tract Association of Friends, 1974), p. 9.

[30] William Penn, *No Cross, No Crown* (London: Richard Barrett, printer, 1857), p. 251.

[31] George Fox, *Works of George Fox,* reprint ed. (Philadelphia: Marcus T. C. Gould, 1831), 4:194.

[32] Hugh Barbour and Arthur Roberts, eds., *Early Quaker Writings* (Grand Rapids: William B. Eerdmans Publishing Co., 1973), p. 115.

[33] Taken from the bulletin of the First Centenary United Methodist Church, Chattanooga, Tennessee, June 29, 1980, p. 1.

[34] John Wesley, *The Journal of John Wesley,* ed. Percy Livingstone Parker (Chicago: Moody Press, 1951), p. 409.

[35] Francis Asbury, *The Journal of Francis Asbury* (London: Epworth Press, 1958), 1:4.

[36] Howard Taylor, *Hudson Taylor's Spiritual Secret* (Chicago: Moody Press, 1932), p. 26.

[37] Kenneth Scott Latourette, *A History of Christianity* (New York: Harper & Brothers, 1953), p. 1186.

[38] J. H. Worcester, *The Life of David Livingstone* (Chicago: Moody Press, n.d.), p. 75.

[39] Ibid., p. 100.

[40] For more information see Dallas Lee, *The Cotton Patch Evidence* (New York: Harper & Row, 1971).

[41] Girolamo Savonarola, *De Simplicitate Christianae Vitae* (Rome: Angelo Belardetti Editore Roma, n.d.,), p. 188. Unfortunately, this book has never been translated into English. I am indebted to Father Lawrence F. Frankovich (O.F.M.) for help in translating crucial sections of this book.

[42] Ibid., pp. 64–65.

[43] Søren Kierkegaard, *Purity of Heart Is to Will One Thing* (New York: Harper & Brothers, 1938), p. 27.

[44] Ibid., p. 29.

[45] Woolman, *The Journal of John Woolman,* p. 41.

[46] Ibid., p. 168.

[47] Ibid., p. 231.

[48] Quoted in Goldian VanderBroeck, ed., *Less Is More* (New York: Harper & Row, 1978), p. 223.

Chapter 5. Inward Simplicity: The Divine Center

[1] J. R. R. Tolkien, *The Silmarillion* (New York: George Allen & Unwin, 1977), p. 8.

[2] Kelly, *A Testament of Devotion,* p. 115.

[3] Ibid.

[4] Ibid., pp. 115–116.

[5] Quoted in Francis Florand, *Stages of Simplicity* (St. Louis: B. Herder Book Co., 1967), p. 147.

[6] I am indebted to Thomas Kelly for the concept of many inward selves. See *A Testament of Devotion*, pp. 114–115.

[7] Frank Laubach, *Learning the Vocabulary of God* (Nashville: The Upper Room, 1956), p. 5.

[8] Ibid., p. 23.

[9] Brother Lawrence (Nicholas Herman of Lorraine), *The Practice of the Presence of God* (Philadelphia: The Judson Press, n.d.), p. 26.

[10] Meister Eckhart, *Meister Eckhart,* trans. C. de B. Evans (London: John M. Watkins, 1956) 1:59.

[11] Quoted in Frank C. Laubach, *Christ Liveth in Me* and *Games with Minutes,* in 1 vol. (Westwood: Fleming H. Revell Co., 1961), p. 61.

[12] Kelly, *A Testament of Devotion*, p. 124.

[13] Blaise Pascal, *Pensees,* trans. W. F. Trotter, The Modern Library (New York: Random House, 1941), p. 74.

[14] Wayne E. Oates, *Nurturing Silence in a Noisy Heart* (Garden City: Doubleday & Co., 1979), p. 3.

[15] Frank C. Laubach, *Open Windows, Swinging Doors* (Glendale: Gospel Light Publications, 1955), pp. 34–35.

[16] Fénelon, *Christian Perfection*, p. 204.

Chapter 6. Inward Simplicity: Holy Obedience

[1] T. S. Eliot, *The Four Quartets* (New York: Harcourt, Brace & World, Inc., 1943), p. 39.

[2] Quoted in Kelly, *A Testament of Devotion*, p. 52.

[3] Fénelon, *Christian Perfection*, p. 196.

[4] Ibid.

[5] Ibid., p. 194.

[6] Ibid.

[7] Brother Lawrence, *The Practice of the Presence of God*, p. 39.

[8] Fénelon, *Christian Perfection*, p. 196.

[9] Ibid., pp. 198–199.

[10] Ibid., p. 201.

[11] Ibid., p. 203.

[12] Ibid., p. 204.

[13] Ibid., p. 197.

[14] Julian of Norwich, *Showings* (New York: Paulist Press, 1978), p. 205.

[15] Blaise Pascal, *Love Aflame: Selections from the Writings of Blaise Pascal* (Wilmore: Asbury Theological Seminary, 1974), p. 3.

[16] Kelly, *A Testament of Devotion*, p. 69.

[17] Søren Kierkegaard, *Christian Discourses,* trans. Walter Lowie (Oxford: Oxford University Press, 1940), p. 322.

[18] In a letter written to U.S. Senator Mark Hatfield as a response to his congratulatory letter to her upon her receipt of the Nobel Peace Prize. Published in *Major Addresses Delivered at the Conference on Faith and Learning* (North Newton: Bethel College, 1980), pp. 85–86.

Chapter 7. Outward Simplicity: Beginning Steps

[1] One especially helpful book is by George Fooshee, *You Can Be Financially Free* (Old Tappan: Fleming H. Revell Co., 1976).

[2] Catherine de Hueck Doherty, *Poustinia: Christian Spirituality of the East for Western Man* (Notre Dame: Ave Maria Press, 1974), p. 216.

[3] Quoted in VanderBroeck, *Less Is More,* p. 26.

[4] Richard E. Byrd, *Alone* (New York: G. P. Putnam's Sons, Inc., 1938), p. 19.

[5] John Wesley, "Nov. 1767," *The Journal of the Reverend John Wesley* (London: The Epworth Press, 1938).

[6] Quoted in VanderBroeck, *Less Is More,* p. 21.

Chapter 8. Outward Simplicity: Longer Strides

[1] Adam Daniel Finnerty, *No More Plastic Jesus* (New York: E. P. Dutton Inc., 1978), p. 17.

[2] John Stott, *Lausanne Occasional Papers, No. 3: The Lausanne Covenant—An Exposition and Commentary* (Wheaton: Lausanne Committee for World Evangelism, 1975), p. 21.

[3] Floyd and Norma Souders, *Friends University: 1898–1973* (North Newton: Mennonite Press, 1974), p. 11.

[4] Quoted in John Mitchell, *Enough Is as Good as a Feast* (An offset from *Third Way Magazine,* London, England, 1979), p. 1.

[5] Elizabeth O'Connor, *Letters to Scattered Pilgrims* (San Francisco: Harper & Row, 1979), p. 5.

[6] Ibid., pp. 6–7.

[7] Mooneyham, *What Do You Say to a Hungry World?* p. 76.

[8] Woolman, *The Journal of John Woolman,* p. 18.

[9] Ibid.

[10] Thomas Merton, *The Sign of Jonas* (New York: Harcourt, Brace and Co., 1953), p. 261.

[11] Jacques Ellul, *Violence: Reflections from a Christian Perspective* (New York: The Seabury Press, 1969), p. 151.

[12] Ibid., p. 155.

[13] Kierkegaard, *Christian Discourses,* p. 344.

[14] Quoted in VanderBroeck, *Less Is More,* p. 70.

[15] Ibid., p. 127.

Chapter 9. Corporate Simplicity: The Church

[1] Quoted in *Post-American* 1 (Summer 1972): 1.

[2] Douglas V. Steere, ed., *Selections from the Writings of Bernard of Clairvaux* (Nashville: The Upper Room, 1961), p. 6.

[3] Quoted by Leland Ryken, in "The Puritan Work Ethic: The Dignity of Life's Labors," in *Christianity Today,* Oct. 19, 1979, p. 17.

[4] Lee, *The Cotton Patch Evidence,* pp. 86–87.

[5] This illustration was suggested to me by Kara Cole in *The Church— Every Person a Minister* (Dublin: Prinit Press, 1980), pp. 11–13.

Chapter 10. Corporate Simplicity: The World

[1] James Scherer, *Global Living Here and Now* (New York: Friendship Press, 1974), p. 6.

[2] Jeremy Rifkin, with Ted Howard, *The Emerging Order* (New York: G. P. Putnam's Sons, 1979), p. 58.

[3] Ibid., p. 60.

[4] Finnerty, *No More Plastic Jesus,* p. 34.

[5] This issue is dealt with in detail in Oscar Cullmann, *The State in the New Testament,* and in Hendrikus Berkhof, *Christ and the Powers.* See also "The Powers of Evil in the New Testament" in the *Evangelical Quarterly* 52, no. 2 (April–June 1980). I have dealt at length with this topic in Chapter 5 of *Quaker Concern in Race Relations: Then and Now,* D.Th.P. diss., Fuller Theological Seminary, 1970).

[6] "The Thailand Statement," *World Evangelization,* Information Bulletin No. 20, a publication of the Lausanne Committee for World Evangelization, September 1980, p. 6.

[7] Ralph D. Winter, *Penetrating the Last Frontiers* (Pasadena: William Carey Library, 1978), pp. 50–52.

[8] Ibid., pp. 49–52. See also Ralph D. Winter, *Six Essential Components of World Evangelization: Goals for 1984* (Pasadena: William Carey Library, 1979), pp. 15–18.

[9] Mooneyham, *What Do You Say to a Hungry World?* pp. 47–48.

[10] The statistics given in the section on world hunger are readily available in most books on the subject. Examples are *The Challenge of World Poverty* by Gunnar Myrdal, *Bread for the World* by Arthur Simon, *The Emerging Order* by Jeremy Rifkin, and *What Do You Say To A Hungry World?* by W. Stanley Mooneyham (publication information for these books is cited elsewhere in these notes).

[11] Bee-Lan Chan Wang, "The Population and Food Dilemma: Christian Perspectives," in *A Reader in Sociology: Christian Perspectives,* ed. Charles De Santo, Calvin Redekop and William Smith-Hinds (Scottdale: Herald Press, 1980), pp. 446–448.

[12] Arthur Simon, *Bread for the World* (Grand Rapids: Wm. B. Eerdmans Publishing Co., 1975), p. 31.

[13] The Presidential Commission on World Hunger, *Overcoming World Hunger: The Challenge Ahead,* 734 Jackson Place, NW, Washington, D.C. 20006, Ambassador Sol M. Linowitz, Chairman, March 1980, p. ix.

[14] *Hunger and Global Security,* flier printed by Bread for the World, 32 Union Square East, New York, New York 10003.

[15] For further information on the subject of world hunger see Gunnar Myrdal, *The Challenge of World Poverty* (New York: Random House, 1971), Jayne Millar, *Focusing on Global Poverty and Development* (Overseas Development Council, 1974), and Freudenberger and Minus, *Christian Responsibility in a Hungry World* (Nashville: Abingdon Press, 1976).

[16] Lewis Carroll, *Alice in Wonderland,* ed. Donald J. Gray (New York: W. W. Norton & Co. Inc., 1971), pp. 88–89.

[17] William Ophuls, *Ecology and the Politics of Scarcity* (San Francisco: W. H. Freeman & Co., 1977), p. 185.

[18] Adam Smith, *The Wealth of Nations,* The Modern Library (New York: Random House, 1937), p. 423.

[19] These four assumptions are taken from the analysis of Smith's economic thought by Jeremy Rifkin, *The Emerging Order,* pp. 35–36.

[20] Quoted in Vance Packard, *The Waste Makers* (New York: McKay, 1960), p. 54.

[21] Ibid., p. 24.

[22] Ibid., p. 99.

[23] Harvey Salgo, "The Obsolescence of Growth: Capitalism and the Environmental Crisis," in *The Review of Radical Political Economics* 5 (Fall 1973): 32.

[24] Ibid., p. 31.

[25] Packard, *The Waste Makers,* p. 228.

[26] Harry Rothman, *Murderous Providence: A Study of Pollution in Industrial Societies* (New York: Bobbs-Merrill Co., 1972), p. 64.

[27] Ed Magnuson, "The Poisoning of America," in *Time* 116 (September 22, 1980): 58.

[28] Ibid.

[29] "Fine Particles in the Atmosphere," *NRDC Newsletter* 7, nos. 2, 3 (March 1978–June 1978), Natural Resources Defense Council, p. 8.

[30] Ward Sinclair, "Studies Warn About Menace of 'Acid Rain,'" *Washington Post,* June 2, 1978, p. A18.

[31] Worldwatch Institute, "The Global Environment and Basic Human Needs," report to the U.S. Council on Environmental Quality, 1978, p. 42.

[32] Preston Cloud, "Mineral Resources in Fact and Fancy," in *Toward a Steady-State Economy,* ed. Herman E. Daly (San Francisco: W. H. Freeman & Co., 1973), p. 74.

[33] Rifkin, *The Emerging Order,* pp. 47–65.

[34] T. Wayne Rieman, "A Christian Response in a Global Community," (paper, Manchester College, September 14, 1976).

[35] Walter Harrelson, "Famine in the Perspective of Biblical Judgments and Promises," in *Lifeboat Ethics: The Moral Dilemmas of World Hunger,* ed. George Lucas and Thomas Ogletree (New York: Harper & Row Publishers, 1976), p. 93.

[36] Kenneth Boulding of the University of Colorado and Donald Hay of Oxford University, England. Though space prohibited my discussion of it, I am particularly indebted to Professor Boulding's *The Economy of Love and Fear,* which is an introductory study in Grants Economics. See also his *Redistribution to the Rich and the Poor* and *Transfers in an Urbanized Economy.* These two gentlemen are in no way responsible for the conclusions I have drawn.

[37] Richard Barnet and Ronald Müller, *Global Reach: The Power of the Multinational Corporations* (New York: Simon & Schuster, 1974), p. 363.

[38] Ibid., p. 13.

[39] Ervin Lastlo et al., *Goals for Mankind* (New York: New American Library, 1978), p. 165.

[40] Barnet & Müller, *Global Reach,* p. 15.

[41] Mark Green and Robert Massie, eds., *The Big Business Reader* (New York: The Pilgrim Press, 1980), p. 381.

[42] Ibid., pp. 399–412.

[43] Barnet and Müller, *Global Reach,* p. 22.

[44] Green and Massie, *The Big Business Reader,* pp. 418–429.

[45] Other specific proposals for bringing accountability to multinational corporations can be found in *Reshaping the International Order:* Report to the Club of Rome (Chapter 15), and Barnet and Müller, *Global Reach* (Chapter 13).

Epilogue: The Simplicity of Simplicity

[1] William Penn, *A Collection of the Works of William Penn,* vol. 1 (London: 1726), p. 840.

Scripture Index

Subject Index